WORLD TRADE LAW AFTER NEOLIBERALISM

World Trade Law after Neoliberalism

Re-imagining the Global Economic Order

ANDREW LANG

OXFORD
UNIVERSITY PRESS

OXFORD
UNIVERSITY PRESS

Great Clarendon Street, Oxford OX2 6DP

Oxford University Press is a department of the University of Oxford.
It furthers the University's objective of excellence in research, scholarship, and education by publishing worldwide in

Oxford New York

Auckland Cape Town Dar es Salaam Hong Kong Karachi
Kuala Lumpur Madrid Melbourne Mexico City Nairobi
New Delhi Shanghai Taipei Toronto

With offices in

Argentina Austria Brazil Chile Czech Republic France Greece
Guatemala Hungary Italy Japan Poland Portugal Singapore
South Korea Switzerland Thailand Turkey Ukraine Vietnam

Oxford is a registered trade mark of Oxford University Press in the UK and in certain other countries

Published in the United States
by Oxford University Press Inc., New York

First published 2011

British Library Cataloguing in Publication Data
Data available

Library of Congress Cataloging in Publication Data
Library of Congress Control Number: 201193732

Typeset by SPI Publisher Services, Pondicherry, India
Printed in Great Britain
on acid-free paper by
CPI Group (UK) Ltd, Croydon, CRO 4YY

ISBN 978–0–19–959264–7

1 3 5 7 9 10 8 6 4 2

For Anouk, and Corin

Acknowledgements

During the preparation of this book, I have been very fortunate to benefit from the generosity and insight of many friends and colleagues, as well as the support of a number of institutions. It was a pleasure to return to my *alma mater*, the University of Sydney, to take up an International Visiting Research Fellowship in the summer of 2010. I am grateful to the entire Faculty, and especially David Kinley, for their generosity and hospitality during my stay there, as well as the intellectual stimulation they provided. In addition, I benefited from kind support from the Oñati International Institute for the Sociology of Law, which enabled me to spend some quiet and delightful time in early 2010 in the north of Spain working on the manuscript. My warm thanks especially to the Institute's Director, Sol Picciotto. The research for Chapter 3 and parts of Chapter 4 were funded by a grant from the British Academy. Some of the interview research for Chapter 9 was conducted in Washington during my time as a Visiting Fellow at the Institute of International Economic Law at Georgetown University. I thank the Institute for the financial support, and especially Jane Bradley and John Jackson for their warm welcome, and their invaluable assistance in the research process itself. My thanks also to the following people for inspiring and informative conversations from which I have learnt a great deal: Rudolf Adlung, Diana Bronson, David Collins, Thomas Cottier, Matt Craven, James Crawford, Jeffrey Dunoff, Geza Feketekuty, James Flett, Mike Gadbaw, James Harrison, Larry Helfer, Paul Hunt, Robert Howse, Sarah Joseph, David Kennedy, Martti Koskenniemi, Miloon Kothari, Genevieve Lessard, Meredith Lewis, Aaditya Mattoo, Federico Ortino, Armin Paasch, Colin Picker, Peter Prove, Don Regan, Kerry Rittich, Robert Rogowski, Caroline Samdup, Krista Schefer, Joanne Scott, Tom Sebastian, Fiona Smith, Gunther Teubner, Dave Trubek, Elisabeth Türk, Bob Vastine, Simon Walker, Robert Wai, Sally-Anne Way, Michael Windfuhr, and Margaret Young.

My two assistants, Aleksandra Bojovic-Stipanovich and Aaron Chickos, worked tirelessly, with great precision, and with wonderful grace throughout the process. Their help was invaluable in the final stages of preparing the manuscript, and I am immensely grateful to them both. Special thanks to Susan Marks, whose work and character has been an important inspiration for me for some time, and who acted as an intellectual sounding board at crucial stages during this project. I am fortunate to have such a mentor and colleague. Love and gratitude above all to my wife, Anouk, who provided an extraordinary combination of intellectual guidance, unwavering encouragement, and, when needed, light relief throughout the project. She read every page, often more than once, and her words provided motivation on innumerable occasions. I am indebted to her in too many ways to list. And to my son Corin, whose birth coincided with the final stages of preparation of the manuscript, I say thank you for providing a welcome diversion from footnote checking with your squeaks and chirrupings.

Preface

The work of international lawyers deeply affects the shape and operation of global economic governance, much more now than it has ever done in the past. Most visibly in the context of world trade—but also in respect of foreign investment, debt, finance, and development—the activity of 'governing' at the global level is increasingly carried out through international legal processes, and by professionals schooled in the techniques, habits of thought, and forms of argument characteristic of international law. The number of international lawyers contributing to the evolution of international economic governance, including through our role as interpreters and evaluators of existing governance practices, continues to grow.

A central theme of this book, then, is an exploration of the role that international legal processes and international lawyers play in the construction and contestation of structures of global economic governance. By 'international lawyers' I am not referring solely to those engaged in the professional practice of international law in and around formal dispute settlement, but much more broadly to the wide range of actors—government officials, NGOs, academics, officials of international organizations, and many others—working in the disciplinary field of international law and engaging in international legal styles of argument. And by 'international legal processes' I am not referring solely to formal processes of judicial dispute settlement, but rather to the huge variety of different activities conducted in an international legal idiom, from writing and thinking about international law all the way through to its concrete operation in specific contexts. This focus on international law does not, it should be said, derive from an exaggerated sense of the importance of international law and legal processes in the conduct of global economic governance. I readily admit that there are often much more powerful forces and actors directly at play, than those associated with international law. Instead I focus on international law in order to highlight the responsibility of international lawyers: the point, in other words, is to emphasize the ways in which the work of international lawyers has important effects on the practice of international economic governance, often in ways we do not realize, in order to encourage a greater sense of moral responsibility for those outcomes.

When the research for this book began in the early 2000s, civil society activism around the Seattle Ministerial of the World Trade Organization was a recent memory, and a series of criticisms of the global trading system and its social consequences had achieved wide notoriety. The public debate which accompanied this activism raised fundamental questions about the social and distributional outcomes of the late twentieth-century global economic order, about the extent to which structures of global economic governance entrench and perpetuate patterns of privilege and disadvantage, power and subjection—and about the ways in which those structures of governance may also open up space for effective contestation in the interests of those who are currently marginalized. Inevitability, and quite rightly, these questions quickly began to be addressed by international lawyers, along broadly two lines of inquiry. On one hand, some began to explore the role that international law and lawyers currently play in producing and entrenching the existing global economic order. How exactly, it was asked, does the work of international lawyers shape the social consequences and normative orientations of international economic governance? What contribution does the professional activity of international lawyers make to the present regime of global economic governance—including its more inequitable and unjust elements? On the other hand, another line of inquiry was also set in train, relating to the emancipatory potential of international law, in the context of global economic governance. What role, if any, should international law and lawyers play in facilitating contestation of the structures of global economic governance in the interests of the presently marginalized? What tools, if any, does international law offer that project?

Answering these questions has rightfully come to be a major professional project for many international lawyers, and I count myself among them. Such questions represent the fundamental normative impulse which provided the initial impetus for this book and has guided it ever since. The imagined audience of the book includes all those who share this impulse.

In the early 2000s, for reasons explained later in this book, one of the key contexts in which international lawyers were turning their minds to these questions was the 'trade and human rights' debate—that is to say, a debate among international lawyers about potential conflicts between international trade law and international human rights law. Claims began to be made that trade liberalization and economic globalization potentially undermined the enjoyment of human rights, particularly social and economic rights. More formally, there were claims that the obligations imposed by international trade law conflict with the obligations imposed on states by international human rights law. Others countered that the norms, rules, and objectives of the trade and human rights regimes were fundamentally mutually compatible, as two halves of a single liberal project of world order.

As a result, this book began life as an intervention into the trade and human rights debate. At one level it continues to serve that purpose: part of the point of this book is to respond to a series of claims made in that debate, and more generally to reflect on its deeper dynamics. For example, I ask what effects, if any, has the trade and human rights debate had on the operation and contestation of the global trade governance? Which kinds of interventions into the debate have been productive, and which have not? Are there any lessons to be learnt from this decade of activity which might inform current attempts by international lawyers to engage in issues around the global governance of trade, investment, and finance? In my view, the time is right for such reflection. In fact, I will be arguing that the trade and human rights debate has in some ways misdirected the energies of international lawyers interested in contributing to the creation of a more just international economic order, and the opening up of productive contestation of its contours.

But while this book is, at one level, a specific intervention into the trade and human rights debate, it also addresses questions of much more general relevance. As will become clear, the political and cultural context for the emergence of the trade and human rights debate was the rise to dominance of 'neoliberalism' as an economic and political ideology over the last three decades of the twentieth century. This major ideological shift deeply transformed the structure, content, and dynamics of international law, and changed what it meant to do international legal work in the area of global economic governance. My broader interest in this book, then, is with the possibilities and limitations of international economic law 'after neoliberalism'. Focusing specifically on the international trade regime, and with the specific normative orientation described above in mind, I begin to explore what shape international legal work should take in the contemporary period. What questions should we equip ourselves to ask? Where should we direct our attention? What projects should we set ourselves, and how are we to contribute most productively to them?

That said, readers who approach this book in the hope of finding specific proposals for the reform of international economic law and institutions will by and large be disappointed. That is not the kind of contribution that my research and reflection have put me in a position to offer—nor do I think it is necessarily the only significant contribution that is needed at this moment. The primary contribution that I seek to make to that project in this book takes the form of a kind of ground-clearing role: my aim is to help to create the ideational conditions of possibility for more open and productive criticism, reflection and re-imagination of structures of global economic governance, by targeting a number of *imaginative* constraints which currently present serious obstacles to such processes. Thus, while this book looks very different from what might be expected from most contributions to the trade and human rights debate, readers will still find in its pages an argument which is practical and pragmatic, and which is I hope of particular utility for participants in that debate, who are motivated by the desire to imagine and pursue the practice of global economic governance in its emancipatory mode.

Andrew Lang

London, England
2011

Contents

List of Abbreviations

AFL-CIO	American Federation of Labor—Congress of Industrial Organizations
AIWN	Asian Indigneous Women's Network
APWLD	Asia-Pacific Forum on Women, Law and Development
APRODEV	Association of Protestant Development Organizations in Europe
ASC	Alianza Social Continental
ASCODE	Association of Central American Peasant Organisations for Cooperation and Development
ATTAC	Association pour la Taxation des Transactions financière et l'Aide aux Citoyens
AWID	Association for Women's Rights in Development
CAFOD	Catholic Overseas Development Agency
CAFTA	Central American Free Trade Agreement
CBD	Convention on Biological Diversity
CDES	Centros de Derechos Economicos y Sociales
CEDHA	Centro de Derechos Humanos y Ambiente
CELS	Centro de Estudios Legales y Sociales
CESCR	Committee on Economic, Social and Cultural Rights
CIIR	Catholic Institute for International Relations
CLADEM	Comité de América Latina y el Caribe para la Defensa de los Derechos de la Mujer
CLOC	Coordinadora Latinoamericana de Organizaciones del Campo (Latin American Coordinating Group of Rural Organisations)
CONACAMI	Confederación Nacional de Comunidades del Perú Afectadas por la Minería
CONAIE	Confederación de Nacionalidades Indigenas del Ecuador
CRC	Committee on the Rights of the Child
CTD	Committee on Trade and Development (GATT/WTO)
CTE	Committee on Trade and Environment (WTO)
CUSFTA	Canada–US Free Trade Agreement
CUT	Central Única dos Trabalhadore
ECOSOC	Economic and Social Council (UN)
EED	Evangelischer Entwicklungsdienst/Church Development Service

EMIT	Working Group on Environmental Measures and International Trade (GATT)
EPZs	export processing zones
ETOs	extraterritorial state obligations
EURO-CIDSE	Coopération Internationale pour le Développement et la Solidarité/ International Cooperation for Development and Solidarity Europe
EUROSTEP	European Solidarity Towards Equal Participation of People
FAO	Food and Agriculture Organization (UN)
FCTC	Framework Convention on Tobacco Control
FIAN	FoodFirst International Action Network
FIDH	Fédération Internationale des ligues des Droits de l'Homme/ International Federation for Human Rights
FTAA	Free trade Area of the Americas
FTAs	free trade agreements
GATS	General Agreement on Trade in Services
GATT	General Agreement on Tariffs and Trade
HIC	Habitat International Coalition
HRW	Human Rights Watch
IATP	Institute for Agriculture and Trade Policy
ICDA	International Coalition for Development Action
ICESCR	International Covenant on Economic, Social and Cultural Rights
ICHRP	International Council on Human Rights Policy
ICLQ	International and Comparative Law Quarterly
IGTN	International Gender and Trade Network
ILO	International Labour Organization
INCHRITI	International NGO Committee on Human Rights and Trade and Investment
IP	intellectual property
ITO	International Trade Organization
ITUC	International Trade Union Confederation
IWLD	Institute for Women, Law and Development
KRRS	Karnatka Rajya Ryota Sangha/Karnatka State Farmers' Association
LDCs	less developed countries
LWF	Lutheran World Federation
MAI	Multilateral Agreement on Investment
MEA	multilateral environmental agreement
MFN	most-favoured nation

MODTLE	Mobilization on Development, Trade, Labour and the Environment
MST	Movimento dos Trabalhadores Rurais Sem Terra (Landless Rural Workers' Movement)
NAFTA	North American Free Trade Agreement
NGLS	Non-Governmental Liaison Service (UN)
NGO	non-governmental organization
NIEO	New International Economic Order
NOVID	Netherlands Organisation for International Development Cooperation
OHCHR	Office of the High Commissioner for Human Rights
PRODH	Centro de Derechos Humanos Miguel Agustin Pro Juárez
PROVEA	Programa Venezolano Educación-Acción en Derechos Humanos
RMALC	Red Mexicana de Acción frente al Libre Comercio
SCM Agreement	Agreement on Subsidies and Countervailing Measures (WTO)
SPS Agreement	Agreement on the Application of Sanitary and Phytosanitary Measures (WTO)
TBT Agreement	Agreement on Technical Barriers to Trade (WTO)
TRIMS	Agreement on Trade-Related Investment Measures (WTO)
TRIPS	Agreement on Trade-Related Aspects of Intellectual Property Rights (WTO)
TWN	Third World Network
UAW	United Auto Workers
UDHR	Universal Declaration of Human Rights
UNCTAD	United Nations Conference on Trade and Development
UNGA	United Nations General Assembly
VCLT	Vienna Convention on the Law of Treaties
WEDO	Women's Environment and Development Organization
WIDE	Women in Development Europe
WiLDAF	Women in Law and Development in Africa
WIPO	World Intellectual Property Organization (UN)
WSF	World Social Forum
WTO	World Trade Organization
WWF	World Wide Fund for Nature

Tables of Treaties and Official Documents of International Organizations

TREATIES

i. GATT/WTO Agreements

ii. Other treaties

OFFICIAL DOCUMENTS OF INTERNATIONAL ORGANIZATIONS

i. GATT/WTO Documents

ii. Official documents of other international organizations, including UN agencies and organs

Tables of Cases

WTO APPELLATE BODY REPORTS

WTO PANEL REPORTS

GATT PANEL REPORTS

1
Introduction

This book is an intervention into a conversation which arose around the turn of the millennium, in the wake of the consolidation of 'neoliberalism' as a dominant theory of the state during the last decades of the twentieth century. While the intellectual roots of neoliberal thinking can be traced back much further, neoliberalism emerged as a salient political force towards the end of the 1970s. In the context of the global economic stagnation and turmoil characteristic of that decade, part of the attraction of neoliberal thought was that it provided a persuasive set of economic ideas about how to resume growth in a faltering world economy, which rejected with equal force the various economic policies associated in the post-war period with socialism, Marxism, Keynesian interventionism, and the mixed economies characteristic of embedded liberalism. Most fundamentally, however—and crucially for the purposes of this book—neoliberal thought represented a turn away from an idea of politics as the creation, mobilization, and realization of the collective purposes of a political community, towards an idea of politics as the facilitation of individuals' pursuit of their own private goals and purposes.[1]

Economically, this redefinition of the meaning of politics was associated with a strong normative preference for 'free markets' and 'free trade'. Neoliberal thought tended to valorize material prosperity as a central human good, and—drawing inspiration from the tradition of neoclassical economics—emphasized free and competitive markets, combined with strong private property rights, as the surest road to wealth creation. The role of the state in economic life, in this way of thinking, was primarily to create the institutional conditions necessary for the establishment of well-functioning markets. While neoliberal thought recognized that market failures exist, their practical significance was minimized by, among other things, the beliefs that they were relatively rare, and that governmental attempts to cure them were likely to make things worse as a result of the susceptibility of public power to special interest capture, and the inadequacy of the structures of knowledge available to governments to guide their regulatory interventions.

Programmatically, as the 'neoliberal state' took concrete institutional form in a variety of countries around the world over the course of the 1980s and 1990s, this general neoliberal preference for free markets came to be imaginatively associated with a recognizable template of concrete policy choices. One common policy preference, for example, has been the withdrawal of the state from a direct role in

[1] R Plant, *The Neo-Liberal State* (OUP, Oxford 2010), 6ff.

economic production through the privatization of state-owned industries, utilities, and sometimes the provision of social services. In addition, the neoliberal state has been active in the creation of new markets, most obviously and significantly in the case of finance, but also in other areas such as telecommunications and transportation. The deregulatory instincts of neoliberal thought have had their most profound impact in spheres such as industrial policy, environmental regulation, labour market regulation, and health and safety regulation. These deregulatory instincts have been accompanied, however, by a strengthening of other forms of state intervention understood as necessary for the creation of markets. Thus, for example, the neoliberal state is highly active in respect of the enforcement of contracts and property rights, the pursuit of anti-inflationary monetary policy, and in the context of security and policing. Neoliberalism is also associated with an adherence to free trade policies, at least in theory—though in practice it has largely only been in the developing world, with the turn away from import substitution, that the neoliberal turn has systematically gone hand in hand with a turn towards unilateral free trade in any doctrinaire sense.

After some early experimentation in Chile in the mid-1970s, it was the United States and United Kingdom which provided the first laboratory for neoliberal ideas during the 1980s. By the middle of the 1990s, these ideas had been adopted—unevenly and partially, but still recognizably—across virtually all areas of the world. The story is well known: debt crises in the early 1980s, combined with the influence of the IMF and World Bank, provided the impetus for structural adjustment across much of the developing world; the end of the Cold War saw the adoption of free market policies across the bulk of the former socialist bloc; while the increased mobility of capital in the wake of financial deregulation in the 1980s created general pressure on governments to restructure their domestic economies in directions more attractive to capital. Just as famously, this spread of neoliberal ideas and policies gave rise to a range of oppositional movements and cultures working against it. One common theme across these movements concerned the redistributive effects of neoliberal reforms, as the privatization of state assets, the erosion of social safety nets, the flexibilization of the labour market, and the marketization of new areas of social life all combined to dramatically redistribute wealth upwards. The neoliberal prioritization of wealth creation and economic efficiency as a primary goal of policy was also criticized as imbalanced and inattentive to alternative social values—and as ineffective in delivering the promised degree of material prosperity. Initially, this opposition was expressed and mobilized in the context of local political struggles around country-specific programmes of neoliberal economic reform. However, as chronicled in Chapter 3, these local political struggles were incrementally transnationalized over the course of the 1990s—just as neoliberalism itself was globalized over roughly the same period—leading to the emergence of the 'global justice movement' at the end of the 1990s, united under the banner of opposition to neoliberal economic globalization.

The political and economic transformations associated with these developments had profound effects on international law. These effects were very obvious in the field of international trade law. While the original trade regime of the General Agreement on Tariffs and Trade (GATT) 1947 was a product of the embedded liberalism of the post-war period, the rise of neoliberalism was associated with an incremental but radical transformation of this GATT regime into the World Trade Organization (WTO) over the course of the Tokyo and Uruguay rounds of trade negotiations. But it was not just trade law which was affected by the global neoliberal turn. As we shall see, international human rights law and international environmental law were also deployed in the context of political struggles around neoliberal economic reforms—both in support of those reforms, and by those seeking to resist what they saw as the erosion of environmental and social protections through the intervention of international economic institutions. As a result of these and other developments, contests over neoliberalism were internalized in the field of international law: that is to say, international lawyers came to be engaged by the questions, challenges, and struggles associated with neoliberal economic globalization, and sought to bring their own disciplinary tools and techniques to bear on them.

At the most general level, then, this book can be understood as a reflection on the enduring implications for international lawyers of the rise of neoliberalism in the late twentieth century. More specifically, the book advances two specific arguments about, first, the impact that global political struggles around neoliberalism have had on international law (and vice versa), and, secondly, the kind of professional projects international lawyers can and should equip themselves to pursue in a world 'after neoliberalism'. Both of these arguments have been inspired by my reading of what I shall refer to as 'the trade and human rights debate'—an international legal debate about the relationship between free trade and the promotion of human rights, which emerged around the turn of the millennium as a direct response to clashes around neoliberal trade policy reforms. As a result, both arguments are framed as responses to claims and perspectives that I first came across within that debate. Despite this particular framing, however, they should also be understood in the broader social and historical context just outlined.

Argument 1: Understanding the neoliberal turn

The first argument I make in this book is a response to a very widespread and influential view of the relationship between neoliberal thought and the international trade regime. This is a view which is most often articulated by progressive critics of the WTO, though many of its elements are also shared more widely. According to this story, the WTO—and the GATT before it—provided a friendly context for the reception of neoliberal ideas as they emerged over the course of the 1970s, 1980s, and 1990s. This was for a number of reasons. For one thing, so this story goes, the GATT regime was always inspired by classical economic thought concerning the mutually beneficial effects of free trade for all countries, and the mutually destructive effects of protectionism. Since neoliberal thought tended to echo classical economic thought very closely in this respect, providing relatively full-throated support for 'free trade' in theory, there seemed to be a natural ideological alignment between neoliberalism and the international trade regime. For another thing, the story continues, the international trade regime seemed to have some kind of normative orientation towards free markets built into its mandate: the trade regime is, after all, about liberalizing trade, which by its nature means removing governmental intervention into trade flows. Nothing would seem to be clearer, therefore, than that the WTO is for free trade and free markets, and against governmental interference—and in that sense is closely aligned with the deregulatory, pro-free market, anti-interventionist impulses of neoliberal economic thought.

As a result, the story continues, the GATT/WTO regime was highly amenable to being harnessed to the neoliberal project of freeing markets and liberalizing trade. The regime, it is said, was in some sense already engaged in that project—at the very least these new neoliberal ideas did not require a radical reorientation of the trade regime, but rather an intensification and logical extension of its existing tendencies and dynamics. Thus, as neoliberal thought increasingly began to influence the trade regime, additional rules were written prohibiting more and more kinds of governmental intervention as illegitimate barriers to trade. These legal rules were also made more effective through the creation of a formalized and compulsory dispute settlement system, backed by the credible threat of retaliatory trade sanctions for non-compliance. In this way, the story concludes, WTO law came to impose something approximating a neoliberal model of economic policy on WTO Members, formally requiring adherence to the many of the programmatic policy choices (privatization, deregulation, liberalization) which tend to be associated with the neoliberal state, as outlined above.

My response to this story begins with three simple observations, all of which are different ways of pointing to the ambiguous, evolving, and internally contested nature of the trade regime. First, I suggest that we must not lose sight of the multiple and often conflicting ideological traditions which have shaped the trade regime over its history, nor overestimate the centrality to it of classical economic liberal thought. To be sure, classical economic thinking about free trade *has* influenced the shape and operation of the trade regime since its inception, but it is historically inaccurate to suggest that this represents the only relevant body of economic thought, or even the most dominant one. In the immediate post-war period, for example, the authority of classical thinking about free trade had been considerably eroded as compared to its heyday in the second half of the nineteenth century. Among post-war planners, the dominant ideological orientation was not classical economic liberalism but embedded liberalism, which combined limited and qualified support for free trade with a commitment to large-scale state interventionism. From the 1960s through to at least the end of the 1970s, another strand of thinking about international trade began to be articulated more forcefully in the trade regime by newly decolonized developing countries, inspired by various strands of socialist and Marxist thought. The influence of neoliberalism over the 1980s and 1990s, then, represented not so much a continuation of the ideological premises of the trade regime, but the next chapter in their evolution. I shall expand upon these claims in Chapter 2—the point I am making here is simply that the story above overestimates the necessity and self-evidence of the connection between the international trade regime and classical economic thought about the benefits of free trade. Furthermore, and as a consequence, it seriously underestimates the degree to which neoliberal thought radically changed the regime. The transformation of international economic law from the 1970s onwards was not, in other words, simply an extension and intensification of the existing dynamics of the trade regime, but a true re-making of the regime, involving the erasure and collective forgetting of prior political commitments, and the marginalization of competing traditions of thought within the regime.

Secondly, the above story also overestimates the extent to which the liberalizing mandate of the trade regime determines its politics. It is true that the trade regime is oriented in some fundamental way towards the pursuit of 'free trade', and that the work of the trade regime involves in large part the limitation and removal of 'illegitimate' governmental interventions into trade flows. On its own, however, this mandate says very little about which specific forms of governmental action are to be disciplined by the trade regime, and which are not. Since every conceivable kind of governmental action has some impact on international trade flows, to make the concept of liberalization meaningful, it is always necessary first of all to distinguish between those forms of governmental action which constitute trade barriers, and those which do not. It turns out that this distinction changes over time, depending entirely on the model of 'normal', 'legitimate', 'non-distorting', or 'optimal' state-market relations which forms the reference point for comparison. In fact, both governmental regulation and *lack of* governmental regulation can be understood as a trade distortion, depending on one's point of view. Both stronger and weaker intellectual property protection—or labour rights protection, or environmental regulation—can be understood to produce a deviation from some imagined pattern of 'undistorted' trade flows. The point, then, is that many of the core concepts of liberal economic thinking about trade—'trade barrier', 'market failure', 'market distortion', and even 'free trade'—are indeterminate, so that the liberalizing mandate of the GATT/WTO regime leaves it fully compatible with a very broad range of different political programmes. The normative orientation of the trade regime, it follows, is determined less by its mandate to remove trade barriers, than by the background processes by which some governmental activities are made visible as trade barriers, while the rest are not. It follows also that there is nothing about the orientation of the GATT/WTO towards 'free trade' which in itself necessarily links the regime to the particular understanding of 'free trade' characteristic of late twentieth-century economic and political throught.

The third observation has to do with the indeterminacy of WTO law. On close inspection, it turns out that much of international trade law consists of ambiguous and generally-worded principles, which contain no unequivocal or determinate prescriptions as to the particular mode of state-market relations which Members must adopt. Its most important regulatory disciplines can be and have been interpreted in very different ways—some of which have the effect of requiring WTO Members to adopt recognizably neoliberal policy orientations, but some of which clearly do not. This is not because the influence of neoliberal thought has so far been only partial and incomplete: in fact, this indeterminacy is particularly characteristic of those new regulatory disciplines introduced in the Uruguay Round, which are typically offered as paradigmatic consequences of the trade regime's neoliberal turn.

I have in mind here the science-based requirements of the SPS Agreement, for example, and the disciplines on actionable subsidies in the SCM Agreement—though in fact the original non-discrimination norms contained in the GATT 1947 are also a perfect illustration. Of course it is true that the evolving jurisprudence under these provisions may serve to turn them durably in a neoliberal direction—but even then, anyone familiar with the jurisprudence of the Appellate Body under these provisions will recognize ambiguity-producing complexity as one of its characteristic features. The result is that it is hard to sustain the view that the creation of the WTO Agreements during the Uruguay Round clearly and unambiguously involved the encoding of a characteristic set of neoliberal policy preferences as formal requirements of WTO law.

The broader claim I seek to make through these observations is that we do not yet have a satisfactory story of the precise ways in which neoliberal thought transformed the trade regime, and that much progressive criticism of the WTO proceeds from an inaccurate account of that transformation. I therefore offer an alternative account in its place which focuses specifically on the *ideational* dimension of this transformation, since it is this dimension which is currently under-appreciated. In my account, the most significant feature of neoliberal thought—at least in terms of its impact on the nature and operation of the WTO—was its re-imagining of the nature of politics. Recall from above that in the neoliberal imagination, politics does not involve the mobilization and pursuit of collective goals and purposes, but rather the creation by government of the conditions in which individuals can effectively pursue their own diverse personal goals and objectives. In the context of the governance of international trade, this idea pointed in two directions.

Applied to the trade regime itself, this idea changed the way that international trade politics were pursued and conducted, by occluding the notion of a 'collective purpose' which animated the regime and provided its normative foundation. No longer was the trade regime imagined as a venue for the pursuit of an international economic order oriented around the collective interests and goals of the small community of Western, liberal nations making up its core. Instead, the trade regime came to be viewed as itself a political marketplace—as little more than a forum for the exchange of trade concessions, and the promotion by each state of their export interests, narrowly defined. As I shall show, this produced a set of important changes in the dynamics of the regime, in the modes of behaviour characteristic of participants, and in the range of actors involved in its decision-making processes. Furthermore, the occlusion of the notion of collective purposes also led directly to changes in the form and style of the regime's legal system. No longer was trade law understood and approached as an expression of the broader, fundamental purposes embodied in the regime. Rather, it existed primarily to serve and facilitate the *political* marketplace of bargained trade concessions, through the strict enforcement of treaty commitments, as well as the global *economic* marketplace, through the protection of traders from the arbitrary exercise of state power. The regime's legal system thus came to be imagined as the embodiment of the rule of law in global trade governance, and was restructured in accordance with such rule of law values as neutrality, predictability, certainty, generality, and objectivity.

Secondly, applied to the domestic politics of WTO Members, the neoliberal idea of politics altered the way in which legitimate governmental intervention was distinguished from illegitimate intervention, for the purposes of GATT/WTO law. The delegitimation of the idea that governments could intervene in the economy in the pursuit of collective social purposes made it more difficult to use the purpose of a measure as a yardstick by which to judge its legitimacy. Instead, the trade regime began to turn more rigorously to technical bodies of knowledge—mainly, though not exclusively, economic styles of policy analysis—to determine whether a particular regulatory measure was legitimate, for example because it was necessary for the efficient functioning of markets, or an optimal solution to a market failure. The neoliberal turn therefore produced a 'technicalization' of international trade law, at the same time as its formalization. Increasingly, claims that certain forms of domestic regulation constituted illegitimate barriers to trade were adjudicated by reference to general legal principles, interpreted in light of particular bodies of technical knowledge concerning appropriate and optimal regulation in particular economic sectors. As long as these bodies of technical knowledge tended to favour 'market-oriented' policies as that term was understood in neoliberal thought, an important tension in the neoliberal transformation of the trade regime could temporarily disappear from view. That is to say, the trade regime could in practice encourage its Members towards the domestic adoption of neoliberal free market policies, while at the same time suppressing any sense that the regime itself was the site of collective politics of any meaningful sort, and without formally imposing a particular vision of state-market relations on its Members.

In short, then, the influence of neoliberal thought on WTO law did not, by and large, take the form of encoding neoliberal policy prescriptions into formal international legal obligations. Instead, it involved first and foremost a discrediting of the idea that economic governance ought to involve the mobilization and pursuit of collective goals and values. The consequence was a new set of ideas about the nature and purpose of the trade regime and trade law, as well a new mode of formal-technical governance, working through general legal principles, interpreted and applied in concert with technical knowledge. An important consequence of this transformation was that it became much more difficult to discuss and debate the possibility or desirability of collective projects of international economic order. This represented, in my view, a significant and enduring impoverishment of discourse around global trade governance, and it is one of the core claims of this book that we need to re-open space for the imagination and contestation of appropriate collective purposes on which to found the practice of international economic governance. But already this anticipates the second argument I make in the book, to which I now turn.

Argument 2: Renewing the politics of collective purpose

This second argument I make also began life as a response to certain ways of criticizing the WTO which are very commonly heard within the trade and human rights debate, and within progressive criticism of the WTO more generally. Two lines of argument in particular have been highly influential. The first has to do with the integrity of domestic democratic processes. It is a sovereign democratic choice, so this argument runs, for a society to determine for itself the form of state-market relations, the kind of regulatory frameworks, and the degree of governmental interventionism that it wishes for its own economy. It is, on this view, an illegitimate intrusion into domestic political processes—an undue erosion of domestic 'regulatory autonomy'—for the WTO to pass judgment on the optimality or appropriateness of regulatory measures passed through legitimate domestic processes, and to effectively determine a single model of state-society relations for WTO Members to pursue. These are matters raising fundamental values choices, which therefore must be decided by each community for itself, through genuinely democratic institutions, not by a supranational body such as the WTO and its judicial organs. Within the trade and human rights debate, this core claim is articulated as a potential for conflict between the kinds of regulatory structures required by trade law and those required by human rights law: human rights law, to put it simply, may require a state to put in place precisely the kinds of interventionist regulatory structures which (it is said) trade law prohibits. Within this line of argument, eliminating incompatibilities between trade law and human rights law requires a relaxation of the WTO's regulatory disciplines, and the adoption of a more deferential approach which accords greater regulatory 'space' to its Members.

The second core criticism has to do with coherence. Outside the trade context, it is a commonplace of progressive criticism of neoliberal economic reforms that they prioritize the value of economic efficiency and the objectives of economic growth and wealth creation above all else, including more important 'social' goals and objectives. In the context of criticism of the WTO, this argument becomes a claim about the institutional myopia of the WTO, and the consequent invisibility of 'social' concerns within it. The WTO, it is said, has a narrow economic mandate to liberalize trade, in order to capture the efficiency gains that such liberalization is thought to bring. In part as a result of its functional specialization, it tends to focus on and prioritize the goal of economic efficiency at the expense of those 'social' goals and objectives which fall outside its mandate. Within the context of the trade and human rights debate, this claim about institutional myopia then goes one step further. Some of goals and objectives which are marginalized within the WTO, it is argued, are those associated with the human rights regime, which for its part tends to focus on and prioritize 'social' values and objectives associated with equality, social protection, the satisfaction of basic needs, and so on. As a result, the typical progressive claim that a better and more just balance ought to be struck between the goal of economic efficiency and other 'social' goals of economic policy, turns in the context of the trade and human rights debate into the claim that there should be greater balance and coherence between the goals of the trade regime, and those of the human rights regime.

In my view, neither of these two lines of criticism represents an adequate response to the trade regime's neoliberal turn. Take, first, the argument concerning 'regulatory autonomy'. Claims that WTO law is too intrusive have led, naturally enough, to a number of efforts to construct a less intrusive form of review, and to the adoption of a series of jurisprudential techniques which are more deferential, modest, and cautious in their orientation. Chastened by criticism of earlier decisions as politically charged, the Appellate Body in particular seems now to be anxious to ensure that the WTO should not be seen to be imposing any particular substantive vision of optimal or legitimate regulation in cases involving sensitive domestic regulatory choices. The most significant and interesting of the techniques it has adopted has been a turn towards procedural review—that is, review of the processes, structures, and institutions through which regulatory decisions are made—understood as a turn away from more intrusive review of the substantive content of domestic regulation. Whatever the benefits of the procedural turn, however, I suggest that it cannot succeed in its aim of producing a substantively neutral, less intrusive form of review, nor even a form of review which preserves substantive regulatory autonomy for WTO Members. There is no conceivable way that WTO review can be neutral as to the substance of domestic regulation in anything but a trivial sense, and there is no way of preserving regulatory 'autonomy', if only because such autonomy is illusory to begin with. It is impossible to design a form of WTO review which is entirely (or even meaningfully) innocent of substantive implications, and to the extent that the architects of WTO law have sought to achieve such goals over the past decade or so, they have set themselves an impossible task. More importantly, to the extent that they seek to do so, then they *repeat* the core failing of neoliberal thought—the divorce of the exercise of public power from the pursuit of legitimate public purposes—rather than rectify it. Thus, I would argue, they run the risk of exacerbating the legitimacy crisis of the WTO, rather than resolving it—after all, in my reading, this legitimacy crisis was not just the result of a more powerful and intrusive WTO, but rather more importantly the result of the separation of the exercise of public power at the international level from the pursuit of collective public purpose, and the exercise of collective moral responsibility.

What about the second line of criticism? The claim that there is insufficient co-ordination between the trade and human rights regimes has focused attention on a variety of institutional strategies for ensuring greater 'coherence' between them. Thus, for example, many progressive voices in the trade and human rights debate advocate the integration of trade and human rights law in WTO dispute settlement, or at least the interpretation of WTO law in the light of human rights law, in order to avoid conflicts between them. Others have argued for procedural and legal mechanisms for taking into account human rights in trade policy-making, for example through the use of routine human rights impact assessments, or raising human rights issues in the WTO's Trade Policy Review Mechanism. Some have argued for the integration of human rights norms and rules into trade agreements, while others still have sought to establish rules and mechanisms for formally hierarchizing the obligations of trade and human rights law.

I offer two related responses to institutional proposals of this kind. First, I suggest that the claim that the decisions taken in and around the trade regime tend to prioritize economic efficiency over other values and objectives—whether as a result of the regime's mandate, or as a result of the influence of neoliberal priorities, or both—is somewhat misleading, at least when stated so baldly. While it is true that the neoliberal turn has in some respects had the effect of diminishing space for the consideration of social objectives and values in global trade governance, this was a *consequence* of the prior and more fundamental redefinition of the nature and purpose of economic governance—as the facilitation of the individual pursuit of life projects, rather than the pursuit of a project directed towards collectively defined goals. Thus, for example, there has been very little direct consideration within the WTO of the distributive, environmental, or social costs of international trade liberalization, not in my view (or at least not directly) because such costs are considered unimportant, but because such matters are not considered appropriate topics of conversation given the limited purpose of international economic governance, as redefined within the neoliberal imagination. These are, in other words, thought to be issues more appropriately addressed at the domestic level, or in other venues and regimes of international governance. The point is an important one, because it suggests that institutional attempts to integrate consideration of 'social' values and objectives into the trade regime are unlikely to bear much fruit unless they are accompanied by a much more fundamental challenge to prevailing understandings of the nature and purpose of the trade regime.

Secondly, I also make the somewhat bolder claim that the story set out above tends to direct critical energies away from their most productive and significant role. As I show in more detail later on, progressive criticisms of neoliberalism were, in the course of their translation and adoption into international law (and more especially into the trade and human rights debate) recast as concerns about a structural problem of a fragmented international legal order. Political contestation around neoliberalism, in other words, was reconstituted as a debate about the appropriate institutional relations between the trade regime and the human rights regime, and the appropriate normative relations between trade law and human rights law. As a direct result, attention began to be focused on potential conflicts between trade and human rights law and objectives, and on institutional and procedural solutions to such conflicts: whether WTO dispute settlement should apply human rights law or otherwise take it into account, whether and how a hierarchy could be established between the obligations imposed by trade law and human rights law, whether and how human rights could be taken into account in the WTO, and so on. The debate proceeded as if it was in the resolution of these questions that the fundamental normative orientation of global economic governance would be decided. It proceeded, that is to say, as if the social outcomes of global economic governance could be made better if only we got the institutional configuration right. All the politics of the international legal order—all the salient normative choices—were 'externalized', in the sense that they seemed to exist primarily in the *relations between* functionally specialized legal regimes, and in the structural architecture which determined those relations.

In my view, this focus on inter-regime relations misses the mark because it is inadvertently complicit in the basic neoliberal move of occluding the question of collective purpose in the conduct of international economic governance. Where critical voices should be generating a debate about the fundamental purposes of global trade governance, instead they have given rise to a discussion of the relative priority to be accorded to the trade project vis-à-vis other projects of international order. What should be a debate about re-opening space for discussing the collective purposes of global trade governance, instead has to a large extent become a debate about the appropriate allocation of authority between the global trade regime and other centres of regulatory and political authority. And what should be an effort to use human rights to re-create a sense of moral community and responsibility within the conduct of trade politics instead has come in significant part to focus on the institutional and procedural structures for the practice of trade governance. It is perhaps the major claim of this book that we need greater attention to the former, even at the expense of less attention to the latter. And it is one of the primary purposes of this book to clear the ground for a discussion of this kind, by removing a number of ideational obstacles to it.

Importantly, the argument I am making here is relevant beyond the confines of the trade and human rights debate. As I will show, the reconstitution of political struggles around neoliberalism as debates about appropriate inter-regime interactions was encouraged in part by the legalization of international economic governance. The legalization of the GATT/WTO system, to simplify somewhat, encouraged its critics to turn to other bodies of international law, such as human rights law and environmental law, as a way of contesting and resisting the perceived impact of WTO obligations on domestic regulatory choices. It is certainly possible, then, that as the legalization of international regimes progresses and entrenches itself, the broad contours of this story will be repeated again and again. In other words, contestation of the institutions and practices of global governance will increasingly be played out as contests between competing international legal regimes, and the competing bodies of technical-legal expertise associated with them. It is one of the claims of this book that, in such a world, the critical and reformative energies of international lawyers should be focused on opening imaginative space for the politics of collective purpose within international legal regimes, at least as much as they are geared towards constructing institutional architectures to structure inter-regime relations. As we shall see, it turns out that a great deal of what we presently do actually makes that objective *more* difficult to achieve.

The structure of the book

It may be useful for readers if, to conclude this introduction, I say something about the content of each chapter, and the precise contribution that each makes to the two arguments set out above. The book is divided into two Parts, of four chapters each, followed by the Conclusion in Chapter 10. Part I, consisting of Chapters 2 to 5, directly addresses the trade and human rights debate, exploring its historical origins, describing what I see as its fundamental dynamics, and assessing its contribution to debates about global economic governance from the perspective of the normative project set out in the Preface.

Chapter 2 sketches the evolving relations between the trade and human rights regimes from the end of the Second World War until the early 1990s. I show that both the trade regime and the human rights regime have historically been more internally contested than is typically portrayed within contemporary trade and human rights literature. I call out and reject the prevalent tendency simply to assume that the trade regime is self-evidently and necessarily associated with classical economic liberalism or radical free-market politics, and that the human rights regime is necessarily associated with the opposite. I show how each regime has been, and continues to be, a venue of struggle between different ideologies, each of which brings with it a different idea of the nature of the human rights project, and the larger purposes which the trade regime should serve. Furthermore, I suggest that major historical shifts in the operation and dynamics of each regime are closely associated with shifts in the nature and dominance of these different traditions within them.

Chapter 2 shows, moreover, that the relationship between the trade and human rights regimes is a function of the relative dominance of these different traditions within each regime at any particular point in time. The mutual isolation of the two regimes in the immediate post-war era, for example, was enabled and produced by a deeper connection between them—that is to say, the dominance in both regimes of the ideology of embedded liberalism, which defined the trade and human rights projects in ways which made them appear perfectly compatible and mutually supportive. Then, as these liberal foundations were challenged and destabilized with the rising power of developing countries and their new ideas about the dynamics of the international economic order, a different relationship between the regimes was imagined. There were attempts to harness the language of human rights in support of the developing countries' project of challenging the contemporary international trading system. Then, from roughly the 1980s onwards, the rise of neoliberalism inaugurated a third phase in the story of the relations between the two regimes, as neoliberal thought found a home of sorts in the trade regime, and as a counter-neoliberal impulse was deeply embedded within the contemporary human rights regime.

While all of this historical material is more or less familiar to careful observers of both regimes, in the context of my argument the point of recalling it is twofold. First, my aim is to *de-reify* the two regimes, and show their internally contested characters—though since it is more important for the purpose of my argument to de-reify the trade regime, that regime is addressed in more detail than the human rights regime. As I explain in subsequent chapters, the reason for doing so is because I think there is a very strong tendency within the trade and human rights debate to reify the trade regime, and that this reifying tendency has directed the debate in some problematic directions. The second point is the corollary: one's view of the relationship between trade and human rights varies depending on which tradition one takes to be representative of or dominant within each regime. Descriptive claims about the relationship between the trade and human rights regimes are therefore always interventions into the internal contests within each regime. They always represent in part a process of positioning both the human rights project and the free trade project within ongoing debates about late twentieth-century neoliberalism. Analysis of the relationship between trade and human rights is therefore never just a process of 'discovery' but always also part of the processes by which the normative orientation of each regime is defined and sustained. One point of exploring the material in Chapter 2, in other words, is to make it crystal clear to participants in the trade and human rights debate that our apparently descriptive claims about the nature of the trade regime and its relationship to human rights are in part *constitutive* of the trade regime—they are part of the broader processes by which a particular understanding of the nature and purposes of the trade regime are produced, consolidated, and disseminated—and that we therefore need to take responsibility for that in our interventions into the debate.

Chapters 3 and 4 then tell the story of the more immediate origins of the trade and human rights debate. Chapter 3 focuses first on the emergence of civil society activism around international trade during the 1980s and 1990s. It shows how local political struggles around the rise of neoliberalism in North America, Western Europe, South America, South Asia, and East Asia gradually coalesced into a loose global network of activist organizations focused on trade issues, as part of a broader civil society movement against neoliberal economic globalization. It then tells the story of the adoption of human rights language by many groups within these activist networks, as a way of articulating their critiques of neoliberal globalization and free trade. It describes the contexts in which human rights language was most readily adopted within the global justice movement, the core individuals and organizations encouraging the use of human rights as a language of resistance to economic globalization, and the motivations, strategies, and logics which propelled them to do so.

Chapter 4 then shifts attention to the official bodies of the international human rights regime, showing how they were then mobilized around trade issues, from about 1998 through to the middle of 2005, in part as a result of the efforts of the civil society networks described in Chapter 3. It traces the growing interest in trade issues of certain parts of the UN human rights machinery during this period, and examines the way in which these bodies began to negotiate their position between the global justice movement on the one hand, and international economic institutions on the other. The final part of Chapter 4 then shows how the deliberate positioning of human rights institutions as a legal counterweight to the international trade regime gave birth to the modern trade and human rights debate. This debate, I argue, is characterized by: a particular way of describing the problem which focuses on legal and normative incoherence between the trade and human rights regime; a diagnosis of the underlying causes of that problem, namely the mutual isolation, self-contained nature, and different functional specializations of each legal regime; and a set of ideas about institutional and procedural solutions to that problem, revolving around ideas of inter-regime co-ordination and integration. Taken together, then, Chapters 3 and 4 illustrate the ways in which domestic political struggles around the rise of neoliberalism were projected into the field of international law in the context of the trade and human rights debate, and were in the process reconfigured as problems of inter-regime coherence.

Two quick points are necessary to forestall confusion over the purposes of these chapters. Since Chapter 3 is in some sense about exposing the political origins of the contemporary trade and human rights debate—describing this debate, in other words, as the result of strategies pursued in the context of particular political struggles—it is possible to read it as an allegation of bad faith, as if participants in the trade and human rights debate are seeking to disguise their underlying political and normative positions through the more neutral language of 'coherence'. This is not my purpose, nor do I think it is an appropriate conclusion to draw from the material I present. Furthermore, since Chapter 4 is about the way in which the debate has been 'reconstituted' as it has been projected into the international legal order, it is possible to understand this chapter as arguing for a reversal of that process, as if we should stop talking about fragmentation and instead talk directly about the 'real' issues underlying the debate, having to do with the desirability of neoliberal economic reforms. I do not think this kind of reversal is possible, nor is it clear to me that it would be self-evidently desirable.

Instead, Chapters 3 and 4 serve to prepare the way for a different kind of question—namely, what are the likely consequences of the reconstitution of political debates in the language of inter-regime coherence? This question can be sharpened somewhat by recalling the argument of Chapter 2, that claims made within the trade and human rights debate represent interventions into the political struggles *internal* to each regime, around the positioning of that regime in relation to (neo)liberal economic thought. Taken together, then, Chapters 2, 3, and 4 serve to pose this question: what impact is the trade and human rights debate likely to have on the processes by which the ideological foundations, values, and normative orientations of the trade regime are contested and defined? More pointedly, has the incorporation of the framework of inter-regime coherence been a useful move, in the sense that it has facilitated productive interventions in debates about global economic governance by international lawyers?

Chapter 5 then attempts to answer these questions. I have already foreshadowed above the basic argument which I make in this chapter, so I only need briefly to recapitulate it here. My view is that debates about global trade governance ought to be oriented towards re-opening space for the re-imagination and productive contestation of the fundamental objectives and purposes which inform the international trade regime. To the extent that the trade and human rights debate has focused our attention on institutional and procedural solutions to the problem of inter-regime coherence, it fails to do that—and to the extent that it reifies the trade regime, it indeed may make that project more difficult. Furthermore, I suggest that *without* a more fundamental debate about the nature and purposes of global trade governance, attempts to integrate the norms and values of human rights into the conduct of global trade governance are unlikely to produce significant change. I illustrate this argument by surveying the relatively limited results of recent attempts to produce greater legal and normative coherence between the trade regime and other international legal regimes, including but not limited to the human rights regime.

The larger purpose of Part I, then, is to make the claim that what is at stake in the trade and human rights debate is not just the allocation of authority between two different legal regimes, nor even the ways in which the values and projects associated with each regime are to be prioritized in relation to one another. What is at stake is also—much more importantly—the ways in which the projects, values, mandates, and normative biases of the trade regime are constituted in the first place. When engaging with the problem of inter-regime conflicts, and proposing solutions to the incoherencies that it throws up, therefore, we must pay close attention to the ways in which the arguments we make and the proposals we advocate will affect such internal processes of regime definition, and either open or close them to productive re-imagination.

As we move from Part I to Part II, the theme of trade and human rights takes a back seat, and a different set of questions are foregrounded which have to do with the politics of regime definition. By what processes is the normative orientation of an international legal regime defined and contested? How does a relatively open-ended legal regime such as that governing international trade come to be associated with a particular vision of state-market relations? Importantly, precisely what role do international law and lawyers play in these processes? In Part II, from Chapter 6 to Chapter 9, I explore these questions in the context of the trade regime's 'neoliberal turn' over the last three decades of the twentieth century. A major purpose of Part II is to provide a better account than we currently have of the precise role that neoliberal thought played in the transformation of the GATT/WTO's legal system over this period.

Chapter 6 performs some necessary theoretical ground-clearing, to prepare the way for this account. One of the reasons for the lack of an adequate narrative of the trade regime's neoliberal turn has been the dominance of objectivist[2] theories of social action in mainstream scholarship on trade law and trade politics since at least the late 1980s. Such theories radically mistake the nature and significance of the ideational dimension of trade politics, sometimes even dismissing it altogether, and, as a result have impoverished our understanding of the historical evolution of the trade regime for about two decades. Since part of my claim in Part II is that neoliberal thought transformed the mental world of professionals involved in the field of international trade governance—that is, the collective symbolic order according to which they interpret the world around them, and understand their professional role within it—it is necessary for me to recall and rehearse some of the basic theoretical moves, first made some decades ago, which justify attention to the ideational dimension of trade politics. For those who are already comfortable with the claim that cognitive frameworks necessarily structure the conduct of trade politics and trade law, Chapter 6 will seem basic. Its inclusion is nevertheless necessary as a result of the continued prevalence of objectivist thinking in the field of international trade law, and the consequent potential for misunderstanding of the arguments that I make in subsequent chapters.

Chapters 7 and 8 provide my account of the trade regime's neoliberal turn. They tell a story of changes to the GATT/WTO's legal system as a function of a changing set of key ideas commonly held by professionals working in the field of international trade law and governance—and also show how those ideational changes were themselves closely associated with underlying structural, institutional, and material

[2] For my use of this term, see Ch 6, pp 172ff.

transformations occurring at the same time. I focus on three closely connected ideas, concerning, first, the nature and purpose of the trade regime, secondly, the role and function of law in the conduct of international trade politics, and thirdly, the image of 'normal, undistorted' trade by reference to which trade barriers are identified and disciplined by trade law. In terms of the impacts of these ideas on GATT/WTO law, I look primarily at the structure and operation of GATT/WTO legal institutions, the practical scope of application of GATT/WTO disciplines in respect of non-tariff barriers, the content of GATT/WTO treaty texts, and the jurisprudential 'style' associated with different periods in the regime's history, consisting primarily of a set of characteristic interpretive techniques, analytical moves, and forms of reasoning. For reasons explained in Chapter 6, I limit myself in this story to illustrations drawn from GATT/WTO jurisprudence on 'domestic regulation'.[3]

Chapter 7 focuses on the first period in the evolution of the GATT's regulatory jurisprudence, the period of embedded liberalism, from 1947 to the early 1970s. During this period, most of the diplomats involved in the professional world of GATT diplomacy—certainly those from the most influential countries—represented government with a more or less shared political commitment in favour of interventionist policies associated with various forms of the democratic welfare state of the time. They shared also a particular understanding of the role of the trade regime and of the specific problem that it was designed to address. One primary purpose of the GATT regime (and the Bretton Woods system more generally) was to help create the international conditions necessary for the flourishing of the welfare state domestically. More specifically the trade regime existed to ensure a stable and relatively open international economic order, and above all to avoid a repeat of the tariff wars seen during the interwar period. This emphasis on stability lent a specific character to the professional world of trade diplomacy, as it encouraged its participants actively to insulate themselves from perceived sources of instability. This meant insularity from both the 'high politics' of other parts of the international institutional order, as well as a degree of insulation from domestic political processes and domestic commercial interests. Trade 'law' within this world, such as it was, was structurally subjected to trade diplomacy: dispute settlement was understood as being largely diplomatic in nature; current and former diplomats made up dispute settlement panels; formal legal training was comparatively rare; and the outcomes of dispute settlement were designed in large part to avoid escalation and satisfy all the parties as far as possible. The legal system of the regime, in other words, operated as an instrument of the collective purposes embodied in the regime as a whole, having to do with the maintenance of stability in international economic relations, as part of a broader liberal political project associated with the global projection of the welfare state.

These ideas about the purpose of the regime, and about the place of law within it, lent a particular character to the approach taken to domestic regulation in the GATT law of the time. For one thing, very few cases were brought concerning what we

[3] For an explanation of the way I use this term, see pp 189–89 below.

might now call domestic regulatory intervention—even though such intervention was quite common and there is every reason to expect that it had significant trade effects. Contracting Parties' shared understanding of the embedded liberal foundation of the post-war GATT meant that vast swathes of trade-distorting domestic policy simply receded from view, since it was understood as part of the 'normal' range of governmental action in the marketplace, undertaken for a clearly legitimate purpose. The absence of many disputes over domestic regulation in this era was also the result of the insularity of the regime and its emphasis on the stability of international economic relations, both of which produced a self-conscious narrowness in its field of view and an unwillingness to venture too far into areas of domestic political sensitivity. Furthermore, the structural subjection of trade law to trade diplomacy lent a particular character to those few cases on domestic regulation which *did* emerge during this period. These cases eschewed rigorous scrutiny of the efficiency of domestic measures in favour of forms of reasoning which drew heavily on informal expectations circulating within the world of trade diplomacy concerning the kinds of governmental action that were considered legitimate, normal, or appropriate. The legitimacy of the intention of the regulating government was generally of greater importance than the pure economic effects of the measure in question. The politics of the trade regime (at least as they related to domestic regulation) were thus defined to a significant extent through the processes by which a particular image of 'normal' domestic regulation was generated, circulated, and contested within an insular community of trade diplomats.

Chapter 8 then turns to the period from roughly 1970 to around 2000—the 'neoliberal turn' itself—when the regime's approach to domestic regulation began to undergo a major transformation. Crucially, a new view emerged at this time concerning the role of the trade regime and the problems it existed to address. International trade was no longer viewed so much as a source of instability to be managed and stabilized by the GATT. Instead, the dynamic growth-creating effects of trade began to be emphasized. The role of the trade regime came to be imagined as the facilitation of deeper and broader economic integration—the creation, even, of a global market—as a key driver of global growth and prosperity. More specifically, a core function of trade law in this new period was to protect private traders against the arbitrary exercise of public power, and to provide the institutions and rules necessary to give certainty and predictability to transnational economic actors. Furthermore, as the number and diversity of its participants increased and any thick sense of collective endeavour thereby became less conceivable, the trade regime itself was re-imagined as a marketplace—a political marketplace, that is, in which states simply came together to promote export interests and exchange trade concessions in their mutual self-interest. The notion that international trade politics constituted in part a collective endeavour, inspired by a substantive vision of international economic order, and was informed by a common set of ideas about the collective purposes for which public power could legitimately be deployed in economic life, was occluded. The GATT/WTO dispute settlement system, then, was no longer understood as serving a collectively defined political project, but primarily as a neutral and objective body for the secure and predictable enforcement of treaty commitments.

This understanding of the function of the trade regime significantly transformed the structure and dynamics of its legal system. For example, the GATT/WTO's legal system developed a degree of formal and practical autonomy from the world of trade diplomacy in which it had previously been so deeply embedded. The function of protecting private interests from arbitrary public power, after all, could not be legitimately and effectively carried out by a legal regime so structurally subjected to trade politics and diplomacy. As an increasing number of cases addressing domestic regulation were brought to GATT/WTO dispute settlement, the principles and processes for evaluating such regulatory measures also changed. The influence of neoliberal thought delegitimated the idea that governments could and should conduct economic policy in the pursuit of collective political projects. As a result, the social purpose of domestic regulation became a less secure yardstick by which to measure its legitimacy, and the GATT/WTO legal system increasingly turned to technical expertise—including economic and scientific expertise—for guidance in its interpretation and application of legal disciplines on domestic regulation. This constituted a significant change in the processes by which the normative orientation of the trade regime was defined. No longer was it about the manufacture and maintenance of a particular image of 'normal government intervention' within the small world of trade diplomacy. Instead, the reference points became those of 'undistorted trade' and 'optimal regulation', as defined through the application of legal-technical knowledge. The politics of the trade regime's approach to domestic regulation were now in some important sense an effect of the creation and deployment of specialized legal-technical knowledge.

Chapter 9 pauses this narrative, to provide an extended case study of the operation of the legal-technical system of governance just described, drawn from the area of trade in services. As is well known, the WTO's General Agreement on Trade in Services (GATS) was negotiated during the Uruguay Round and came into effect in 1995. But this agreement was incomplete, in the specific sense that it consisted essentially of a series of generally-worded regulatory disciplines with little clarity about the precise regulatory reforms these disciplines might require in particular service sectors. Thus the period since 1995 has to a large extent been taken up by a variety of contested efforts to elaborate these general disciplines, and to determine their implications in particular contexts with greater precision. In Chapter 9, I trace these processes of elaboration in a variety of different contexts, and show how they have involved above all the production and deployment of technical knowledge. More precisely, they have involved the linking together of norms and concepts taken from the GATS with specific bodies of technical knowledge about what constitutes optimal and acceptable regulatory practice in different services sectors. At a practical level, this has involved the creation of institutional and interpersonal links between trade professionals and other communities in which regulatory expertise is produced, and the management and facilitation of flows of information between these communities and the WTO.

By using the notion of technical knowledge, I do not mean to evoke an uncontested or apolitical set of processes. On the contrary, these processes have been highly contested, with different countries promoting, resisting, or reshaping the incorporation of different kinds of regulatory knowledge depending on their perceived economic interests. The point is simply that the interpretation, elaboration, and application of GATS disciplines are structured most immediately in and through the deployment, dissemination, and contestation of specialized regulatory and technical knowledge in legal contexts. The dynamics of these processes are a structural effect of the particular networks of relations built between the trade regime and various regulatory communities; of the ways in which different forms of expert regulatory knowledge are incorporated, contested, and reshaped within the professional field of trade governance; and even of the mundane practices of data production through which certain measures are tabulated and made visible as barriers to trade in services. In this world, the role of law and lawyers is complex. Sometimes, law acts as a receptacle for technical knowledge, encoding particular regulatory models into legal obligations. Just as often, general legal norms provide the occasion and impetus for the dissemination of expert knowledge, as well as contestation of it. Law thus helps to sediment and authorize particular forms of knowledge through the production of a kind of legal common sense, and at the same time enables the possibility of contesting and destabilizing such common sense.

The account I offer in Part II, then, describes the normative orientation of the trade regime—its 'politics', perhaps—as in part the emergent product of the activity of a field of professionals whose job it is to put the WTO's legal regime into operation. This field of activity is a terrain of contest, in which familiar political struggles are enacted. But it is also a field of activity with its own internal logic. This logic is a complex product of many factors, but in significant part it is the product of collectively shared ideas among this community of professionals about what the goals of the trade regime are, how international trade law serves those goals, and what the role of such professionals is in facilitating their achievement. More generally, we can think of the normative orientation of the trade regime as in part a product of the constantly evolving professional sensibility, habits of minds, technical knowledge, and routine practices of this community of trade experts—social phenomena which help to structure, give meaning to, and provide the context for, the more visible forms of trade politics which are more commonly described and analysed. I show how this professional sensibility takes shape within particular material conditions, and changes as those underlying material conditions change. I also track how different professional sensibilities produce different interpretive choices, legal styles, and jurisprudential techniques, in the application and elaboration of international trade law.

Chapter 10, the concluding chapter of the book, brings the discussion back to the contemporary world 'after neoliberalism', and revisits the questions with which the project began. For international lawyers interested in global economic governance—and more specifically for those international lawyers engaged in the project of re-imagining the global trade regime in the aftermath of its late twentieth-century legitimacy crisis—what kind of work is likely to be most productive? What questions should we ask, and challenges should we set ourselves in a post-neoliberal era? In this concluding chapter, I examine some of the projects which have sprung up over roughly the last decade in response to precisely these kinds of questions, and in response to the criticisms that have been made of the trade regime since the end of the 1990s. For example, the trade regime's legal-technical turn has attracted a variety of post-positivist critiques, drawing on arguments already rehearsed much earlier in the context of domestic political debates. I show that the WTO is still in the process of gradually working out a response to these critiques, and trace through a number of the different options which have been explored. In some cases, as I will show, we have seen a procedural turn in WTO jurisprudence; in others, a turn towards proportionality analysis as a central jurisprudential technique; in yet others, a turn towards a kind of judicial minimalism. While there are elements in all of these models which are promising, the central argument that I make in Chapter 10 is that none of them represents the pursuit of what for me must be the first aim of work on global trade governance in a post-neoliberal era—namely, the reinvigoration of the notion of a collective purpose to underpin a transformed international economic order, and the re-enlivening of a moral sense in the conduct of international trade politics. I reiterate my call for this kind of work, and offer some suggestions about how international lawyers might more effectively contribute to it.

PART I

REGIME ENCOUNTERS: TRADE AND HUMAN RIGHTS

2

'Trade and Human Rights' in Historical Perspective

Reading the contemporary literature on human rights and international trade, one might be forgiven for assuming that we are living through the first encounter between the international trading system and the human rights regime. A familiar narrative has come to take root in which the UN human rights system and the GATT existed in mutual institutional isolation for five decades after the end of the Second World War, and have only recently been forced to confront one another, as a result of changes in the organization of the global economy, as well as the expansion of each regime's mandate and ambition. There is of course a great deal of truth to this story: in the post-war period and for a long time afterwards, the trade and human rights regimes each developed their own communities, their own preoccupations, vocabularies, and professional sensibilities, and there were few opportunities and even less desire for professional interaction between them. Routine dialogue between the GATT and human rights institutions of the sort which is now discussed was non-existent. But focusing solely or even primarily on this level of institutional isolation obscures some important truths, even as it reveals others.

In the first chapter of this book, then, my aim is to perform some important conceptual ground-clearing by telling a different story of the evolving relationship between the trade and human rights regimes, one which deliberately works against this prevailing narrative of 'isolation' and 'first encounters', and which connects the contemporary trade and human rights debate to earlier political struggles throughout the twentieth century and before. By focusing less on the level of institutional interaction and more on the level of political ideology, I write against the prevailing view that human rights and trade grew up as strangers to one another. I show that there have always been a range of deeply held and well-developed ideas about how international trade relates to the protection and promotion of human rights, and that the nature of this relationship has been a terrain of struggle and political contest for some time. Moreover, periods of profound change and evolution in the nature and orientation of both the human rights and trade regimes in the decades since their birth are intimately connected to the emergence of different narratives about the relationship between the two.

One of the purposes of this chapter, then, is to de-reify our understandings of both the trade and human rights regimes though, given the context of my larger argument, the former will be my main focus. Instead of taking the contemporary form of each regime as my starting point and asking what the relationship between them is, I map (some of) the political struggles which have shaped and reshaped each regime over their history, and show how ideas about the relationship between them have evolved in tandem. In the first part of the chapter, I focus on the first decades of the post-war period, in which the mutual isolation of the two regimes was produced and enabled by their shared commitment to embedded liberalism, which defined their respective mandates in ways which displaced potential conflicts, and which made temporarily plausible the idea that the two could easily be kept separate. In the second part, I look at the erosion of this mutual isolation in the context of the challenges which developing countries mounted within both regimes during the 1960s and 1970s. Finally, in the third section, I begin the story—continued in the next two chapters—of the way in which the neoliberal revolution of the 1980s and 1990s again transformed the relationship between the two regimes, and gave birth to the contemporary trade and human rights debate.

I. The first decades: 'mutual isolation' and its deeper foundations

A. The post-war trade regime

The original blueprint for the post-war international trading system was the Charter of the International Trade Organization (ITO), signed in Havana, Cuba on 24 March 1948 (the 'Havana Charter'). An early draft of this Charter was produced by the US and UK governments in the course of negotiations during and immediately after the Second World War, but this draft was subject to considerable amendment during the course of subsequent multilateral negotiations in London (1946), Geneva (1947), and Havana (1947–8). These negotiations, the last of which involved over fifty nations, brought together countries and negotiators influenced by very different traditions of thinking about the proper organization of international commerce and the social and economic consequences of free trade. The result was a Charter with an ambiguous ideological foundation, a document which tried 'to bridge gaps between different economic systems and different philosophies of economic organization' as well as 'between different concepts of the nature of the economic process'.[1]

Of all the countries involved in the negotiation, the United States brought with it a vision of the post-war international trading system which drew most clearly on the ideas of classical economic liberalism. From early on, the United States, under the leadership of Secretary of State Cordell Hull, advocated strongly for an (almost) complete removal of non-tariff barriers to trade,[2] as well as the progressive reduction of tariffs. The elimination of barriers to trade would lead to a more efficient global

[1] W Diebold, *The End of the ITO* (International Finance Section, Department of Economics and Social Institutions, Princeton University, Princeton, NJ 1952) 21, 37.

[2] KW Dam, *The GATT: Law and International Economic Organization* (University of Chicago Press, Chicago, IL 1970) 12. As will be discussed in Ch 7 below, the meaning of the term 'non-tariff barrier' has changed over time. Here, the removal of non-tariff barriers largely meant the removal of the kind of quantitative restrictions on trade which had emerged during the interwar years.

allocation of productive resources, he argued, laying a strong foundation for the material prosperity necessary for sustained peace among nations. Moreover, Hull believed strongly that 'unhampered trade dovetailed with peace',[3] while high tariffs, trade rivalries, and unfair economic competition between nations was a major contributor to international military conflict. Along with other key figures in the US administration, therefore, he saw a turn away from economic nationalism, and the separation of international commercial relations from destabilizing geopolitical considerations, as central elements in a stable and peaceful post-war international order. Although the more hard-headed mercantilist desire to open foreign markets to US exports was never far from the surface, US foreign trade policy in this period was therefore shaped by liberal economic ideals in a way which had rarely been seen before.

In the United Kingdom, while there was general support for a liberal international economic policy, this was subject to a number of important qualifications.[4] Most importantly, the Depression had entrenched the promotion of full and stable employment as the highest priority of domestic economic policy. While it was recognized that international trade might boost employment in good economic times, the turbulent interwar years had made clear that, in hard times, trade would have the effect of transmitting economic instability globally. The United Kingdom could therefore not agree to an international order based on freedom of trade without some way of protecting the British economy 'from the violent fluctuations that had marked the inter-war period'.[5] This meant two things: the flexibility to restrict international trade where necessary to support the domestic objective of full employment; and the need for assurances from its major trading partners that they would take measures to promote full and stable employment in their own domestic economies, to reduce the potential for international transmission of instability. While the language of 'full employment' meant different things to different people, it certainly connoted a significant departure from classical liberal conceptions of the free market, and was associated across the Atlantic with the kinds of large-scale governmental intervention seen during the New Deal.

That said, the differences between the United States and the United Kingdom on these points should not be overstated. Certain core commitments were shared. For one thing, uppermost in the minds of the architects of the post-war trading system were the disastrous effects of the trade wars of the 1930s, and their determination to ensure that they were never repeated represented one of their core goals. On the other side, but just as importantly, it was equally broadly understood that this goal could not be pursued in the absence of economic stability. Clair Wilcox, who led the US negotiations over the Havana Charter, explicitly recognized that 'there is no hope that a multilateral trading system can be maintained in the face of widespread and protracted unemployment', and that 'where the objectives of domestic stability and

[3] RN Gardner, *Sterling-Dollar Diplomacy* (Clarendon Press, Oxford 1956) 9.
[4] ibid 36–8.
[5] ibid 39.

international freedom come into conflict, the former will be given priority'.[6] Furthermore, the devastating experiences of US farmers in the interwar years had left its own legacy within US domestic politics. Primary commodities were understood to pose special problems of fluctuating prices and uneven production, and a fear of disorder in the market for such commodities led to widespread agreement that the government had a role in providing stability in the sector. As a result, despite important differences of emphasis, the package of proposals which emerged from discussions between the United Kingdom and the United States during the Second World War contained special provisions recognizing the need for government intervention in support of domestic employment and the stabilization of markets in primary commodities, both of which ultimately became chapters of the Havana Charter.[7]

As the Charter was subject to further negotiations from London to Geneva to Havana, it was subject also to the influence of countries with a profoundly different understanding of the role of the state in international commerce from that of either the United States or the United Kingdom. Probably most important was a group of less developed countries, including India, Brazil, and Chile, which argued for the need to use protective trade measures to promote industrial development and diversification, to protect their infant industries, and to stabilize their balance of payments.[8] Their vision of international economic order differed profoundly from that imagined within classical liberal thought, and led to a series of serious clashes particularly with the United States over the circumstances in which less developed countries might be permitted to raise tariffs or impose quantitative restrictions without prior multilateral permission. They managed to secure important concessions reflected primarily in Chapters III and IV of the Charter.[9]

The Havana Charter also bore the imprint of other counter-liberal traditions of thinking about international trade. While different socialist thinkers have taken positions ranging all the way from support for free trade to total closure,[10] one important strand of socialist thinking about international trade has focused on the impact of trade liberalization on labour conditions. Labour movements had long argued, for example, that the opening up of international trade merely intensified dynamics of exploitation already present within capitalism—partly because of the intensification of competitive pressure as new producers gained access to local markets, and in part because increased international commerce was accompanied by an increase in the mobility and concentration of capital. More specifically, they argued that expanded international trade threatened to undermine many of the

[6] C Wilcox, *A Charter for World Trade* (Arno Press, New York 1972) 131.

[7] Havana Charter, United Nations Conference on Trade and Employment, Final Act 'Havana Charter for an International Trade Organization' (21 November 1947–24 March 1948) UN Doc E/CONF.2/78, UN Publications, Sales No 1948.ILD.4, Ch II (Arts 2–7), Ch VI (Arts 55–70).

[8] For a useful summary of these and other objections, as they were repeated and reformulated a decade later, see G Haberler, R de Oliveira Campos, JE Meade, and J Tinbergen, *Trends in International Trade: A report by a panel of experts* (GATT, Geneva 1958) 123–4.

[9] Wilcox (1972) 140–52; Gardner (1966) 364ff.

[10] See generally, BF Hoselitz, 'Socialism, Communism and International Trade' (1949) 57 J of Political Economy 227.

victories the labour movement had won during the preceding century, in terms of legislative protection of working conditions and wages, as a result of competition from products from countries in which wages and the standards of working conditions were significantly lower. Such concerns about the negative effect of international trade on labour protections were voiced within the Charter negotiations by a set of Latin American countries, as well as by international labour unions who attended the meeting as observers.[11] These countries pressed for a series of additional provisions, ranging from a broad exception from liberalization obligations in respect of countries with lower standards of working conditions, to obligations to adopt social security legislation, as well as rights to equal pay for equal work.[12] While most of the proposals were unsuccessful, these countries managed to insert an obligation on parties to 'take whatever action may be appropriate and feasible to eliminate [unfair labour] conditions within [their] territory'.[13]

Furthermore, the Charter was always designed to be agnostic as regards the internal organization of members' economies. The Soviet Union was, after all, one of the nineteen countries invited to the London session of the Preparatory Committee on the Havana Charter—though it did not ultimately take part in those negotiations.[14] More countries with mixed and non-market economies were added to the negotiations as they progressed to Geneva and then Havana, including representatives from the socialist East.[15] It was a premise of the negotiations, then, that the rules would be drafted 'so that they would apply with equal fairness and equal force to the external trade of all nations regardless of whether their internal economies were organized upon the basis of individualism, collectivism, or some combination of the two'.[16] The provisions relating to state trading in Section D of Chapter IV of the Havana Charter were therefore included, to facilitate the application of principles of open trade to economic sectors subject to state control, while other obligations were understood not to require any member to adopt any particular model of state-society relations within its borders.

Thus the Havana Charter represented a complex compromise between different visions of the world economic order, only one of which closely resembled classical

[11] Wilcox (1972) 139; K R Gupta, *A Study of General Agreement on Tariffs and Trade* (S Chand, Delhi 1967) 2.

[12] Wilcox (1972) 138–9.

[13] Havana Charter (1948) Ch II, Art 7. Note also that the Atlantic Charter refers to its signatories' 'desire to bring about the fullest collaboration between all nations in the economic field with the object of securing, for all, *improved labor standards*, economic advancement and social security' (emphasis added): 'The Atlantic Charter, Joint Declaration by the President and The Prime Minister, Declaration of Principles, Known as the Atlantic Charter' (United States United Kingdom) (14 August 1941) 55 Stat app 1603, EAS No 236.

[14] MM Kostecki, *East-West Trade and the GATT System* (Macmillan for the Trade Policy Research Centre, London 1979) 2.

[15] The original 18 parties were the UK, US, USSR (which did not participate), France, Belgium Luxembourg, the Netherlands, Czechoslovakia, Norway, Lebanon, Canada, India, South Africa, New Zealand, Australia, China, Cuba, Brazil, and Chile. Among non market economies, Poland and Hungary joined the negotiations later.

[16] JH Jackson, *World Trade and the Law of the GATT* (Bobbs Merrill, Indianapolis 1969) 54.

economic liberal thought. Indeed it was precisely the compromised nature of the Charter—compromised, that is, from a classical liberal perspective—that ultimately led to its failure. When, in the years between 1947 and 1950, the business community in the United States and then the US Congress itself turned against the Charter, it was largely because the document deviated too far from economic liberal principles, was 'too laden with the ideological paraphernalia of government intervention', and did not bridge the gap between competing ideologies in a way which secured the confidence of US business.[17] As is well known, the Havana Charter was as a result never presented to the US Congress for ratification, and never entered into force.

The failure of the Havana Charter to enter into force left the General Agreement on Tariffs and Trade (GATT) as the only set of treaty rules and principles governing the post-war international trading system. The GATT had been signed in October 1947, during the course of the negotiations over the Charter, by a core group of twenty-three countries which sought to give early impetus to the process of reducing customs duties and did not wish to wait for the conclusion of the more comprehensive negotiations over the Havana Charter.[18] The GATT consisted essentially of Chapter IV of the Charter along with some ancillary provisions, which together set out a legal framework for the elimination of quantitative restrictions on trade and the progressive reduction of customs duties. It was originally intended to serve as an interim agreement only, to be provisionally applied until the coming into force of the Havana Charter. Ultimately, however, it served as the founding constitutional instrument of the post-war international trading system from 1947 through to 1995.

In contrast to the ideological eclecticism and ambiguity of the Havana Charter, the GATT regime reflected at this time a more recognizably liberal vision of world economic order. This was partly because the text of the GATT itself did not contain many of the more obviously 'compromised' parts of the Havana Charter, including the chapters on Employment and Economic Activity, Economic Development and Reconstruction, and Inter-governmental Commodity Agreements. It therefore reflected more closely the original US vision of the broad-based elimination of quantitative restrictions, combined with the progressive reduction of tariffs. But the association of the GATT regime with post-war economic liberalism also had to do with the composition of its Contracting Parties. Although the GATT maintained its formal agnosticism about domestic economic arrangements, all original members of the GATT were market economies, at least to begin with. Those which later instituted fully planned economies were treated as anomalies—the United States, for example, formally renounced its GATT obligations to Czechoslovakia shortly after the latter's new socialist government was installed in 1948, and later political changes in Cuba were met with broadly similar reactions.[19] The GATT regime was thus

[17] Diebold (1952) 13 and generally.

[18] JH Jackson, *Restructuring the GATT System* (Chatham House Papers, London 1990) esp ch 2.

[19] Kostecki (1979) chs 1 and 2.

constituted from early on as a liberal 'club'[20] of nations, and was soon perceived as a forum in which 'like-minded economies could accommodate their need to pursue liberal or open trade policies consistent with market-oriented government'.[21]

At the same time, however, the liberalism of the post-war GATT regime was very far from the classical, laissez-faire liberalism of the nineteenth century. The social backlash and economic instabilities of the late nineteenth century and the interwar period had left their mark on liberal economic thought, and for the moment had tarnished the image of more radical forms of the free market. In contrast with laissez-faire liberalism, the 'embedded liberalism'[22] of the post-war period combined a commitment to free markets with a belief in the responsibility of governments to mitigate the social costs associated with free markets. Above all, it was understood among the key Contracting Parties of the GATT—including most importantly the United States, the United Kingdom and France—that governments had a responsibility to intervene actively to promote full employment, and to protect their populations from economic instability and insecurity. The first decades after the Second World War therefore saw the consolidation and elaboration of policies and institutions associated with the welfare state in all of the major economic players within the GATT regime, each in their own way.[23]

As others have already explained in some detail,[24] and as will be explored further in Chapter 7, this shared commitment to the political ideology of embedded liberalism—at least among the regime's key players—deeply shaped the content and operation of the GATT regime over its first few decades. In these years, the GATT pursued a limited vision of free trade, in which liberalization was subject to numerous qualifications and exceptions where it was thought to conflict with the requirements of economic stability and full employment.[25] The entire agricultural sector was more or less exempt from liberalization commitments under the GATT system, along with the largest and most significant governmental subsidy programmes. Furthermore, liberalization tended to occur gradually, in sectors which promised the least economic disruption. It was accompanied by the possibility of safeguard measures where the consequences of liberalization were great or more sudden than expected. Substantial room was left to Contracting Parties to intervene actively in their

[20] RO Keohane and JS Nye, 'The Club Model of Multilateral Cooperation and Problems of Legitimacy' in RB Porter (ed), *Efficiency, Equity, and Legitimacy: The Multilateral Trading System at the Millennium* (Brookings Institution Press, Washington, DC 2001) 266.

[21] Jackson (1990) 82.

[22] See JG Ruggie, 'International Regimes, Transactions and Change: Embedded Liberalism in the Post-war Economic Order' (1982) 36 Intl Org 379. I will return to this concept in Ch 7 below.

[23] See generally M Blyth, *Great Transformations: Economic Ideas and Institutional Change in the Twentieth Century* (CUP, New York 2002).

[24] Ruggie (1982); See JL Dunoff, '"Trade and": Recent Developments in Trade Policy and Scholarship—And Their Surprising Political Implications' (1997) 17 Northwestern J of Intl L and Bus 759; JL Dunoff, 'Rethinking International Trade' (1998) 19 University of Pennsylvania JIEL 347; JL Dunoff, 'The Death of the Trade Regime' (1999) 10 EJIL 733; Robert Howse, 'From Politics to Technocracy—and Back Again: The Fate of the Multilateral Trading Regime' (2002) 96 AJIL 94.

[25] See ibid, and JA Finlayson and MW Zacher, 'The GATT and the Regulation of Trade Barriers: Regime Dynamics and Functions' (1981) 35 Intl Org 561.

domestic economies: regulatory intervention was disciplined only (or primarily) by the non-discrimination norm—according to which full regulatory powers were preserved, provided only that they were exercised in a non-discriminatory way—rather than being limited or curtailed more substantively. More generally, although the GATT did not ultimately include the Havana Charter's obligation to take action to maintain full employment, it was nevertheless informally predicated on a shared commitment among Contracting Parties to do just that. As a result, a variety of large-scale social programmes associated with the welfare state, which had an important structural effect on the size and content of trade flows between the major economies of the period, were not addressed as distortions of trade but rather came to be viewed as part of the institutional background in which trade flows operated.[26]

The post-war trade regime therefore came to be deeply allied to—indeed in many ways an 'outward projection'[27] of—the Keynesian welfare state in all its varied institutional forms. One of the regime's primary purposes was to maintain the international stability necessary to protect the welfare state from external shocks, and therefore to provide the international conditions for its domestic flourishing. As discussed further in Chapter 7, this emphasis on stability gave an insular character to the regime. Trade diplomats sought to protect trade relations from all manner of destabilizing influences, and to this end developed 'close working relationships with their colleagues from other countries, limiting the disruptive force of parochial concerns emanating from domestic politics'.[28] Cultivating a sense of the technicality of trade relations, they self-consciously held themselves apart from other more 'political' international organizations of the UN system, and in doing so reflected a quintessentially liberal sensibility which sought to insulate economic relations from 'political' interference. It was, in Hudec's words, 'comforting to have one place (one might almost say a club) where likeminded people could get together and do their work in peace'.[29]

B. Economic liberalism and the post-war human rights regime

Like the trade regime, the post-war human rights regime was also born as a complex compromise between different ideological traditions. Henkin, for example, has described the post-war human rights system as a combination of 'eighteenth-century ideas of individual autonomy and freedom' with 'nineteenth- and twentieth-century ideas of socialism and the welfare state'.[30] It is useful to begin, therefore, by briefly

[26] Howse (2002) 95.

[27] A-M Burley, 'Regulating the World: Multilateralism, International Law, and the Projection of the New Deal Regulatory State' in JG Ruggie (ed), *Multilateralism Matters: The Theory and Praxis of an Institutional Form* (Columbia University Press, New York 1993) 125.

[28] Keohane and Nye (2001) 266. See also Ch 7, 197–9.

[29] RE Hudec, *The GATT Legal System and World Trade Diplomacy* (2nd edn, Butterworth Legal Publishers, Salem, NH 1990) 57.

[30] L Henkin, 'Introduction' in L Henkin (ed), *The International Bill of Rights: The Covenant on Civil and Political Rights* (Columbia University Press, New York, NY 1981) 12.

recapitulating some of the key elements of these traditions, in particular their different views on the relationship between human rights and economic liberalism, before looking at how they were combined at the birth of the modern human rights movement. While this is all very familiar terrain, it is nevertheless helpful to traverse it, as it will help to set the stage for later discussion of the evolving relationship between the post-war trade and human rights regimes.

The liberal natural rights tradition of the seventeenth and eighteenth centuries emerged in the context of major political transformations in Western Europe, associated with the gradual construction of the liberal state, and the relocation of ultimate political authority in the individual. In keeping with the focus of political reform movements of the time, the emphasis in this tradition is on what have come to be known as 'liberty rights', or civil and political rights: the right of the individual to life, liberty, and security of the person; the right to be free from arbitrary arrest; the right to a fair trial; freedom of thought, conscience, and religion; freedom of peaceful assembly; the right to participate in government; and so on. Occurring at the same time as these profound political transformations was a similarly radical transformation of economic systems—from feudalism, through the merchant capitalism of the seventeenth and eighteenth centuries, to the industrial capitalism of the late eighteenth and nineteenth centuries. Liberal thinkers were of course also deeply involved in laying the philosophical foundations for these economic transformations, advocating and justifying the new commercial freedoms required for the reorganization of economic life along capitalist lines. The result was a liberal natural rights tradition which strongly combined civic republicanism on the one hand with a commitment to the kinds of economic freedoms associated with a capitalist market economy on the other.

Conceptually, the link between political rights and economic freedoms was made in at least two ways. First, the right to own property and to be free from arbitrary interference with it (one of the more fundamental economic freedoms necessary for the constitution of a market) was understood to derive from the same moral source in natural law as civil and political rights. Locke's justification of the private appropriation of property as a natural and moral consequence of the individual's application of labour and industry is the classic example.[31] Indeed, it is primarily through Locke's writing that the right to property was embedded in the seventeenth- and eighteenth-century natural rights tradition as an immediate and inescapable consequence of the acceptance of moral and political claims based on individual rights. As a result, the right to property was incorporated in a number of the founding documents of the human rights tradition drafted a century later, during the revolutionary period at the end of the eighteenth century. The idea that one of the fundamental purposes of government is to secure individuals' natural rights to property found expression, for example, in Articles I and VI of the 1776 Virginia Declaration of Rights, and

[31] J Locke, *The Second Treatise on Civil Government* [1690] (Prometheus Books, Buffalo, NY 1986).

later, in qualified form, in Articles 2 and 17 of the French Declaration of the Rights of Man.[32]

Secondly, economic freedoms were linked to civil and political rights on utilitarian grounds, as providing the best and most secure foundations for the flourishing of political republicanism. As the moral case for property rights was called into question on account of their regressive distributional consequences, classical liberal thinkers made a case for property rights on the basis of their contribution to mutual prosperity. The beginnings of this argument could already be found in Locke's claim that the acquisition of property by the industrious would tend to increase a nation's productivity, and thus effectively increase the stock of resources available in common for others. But it was Adam Smith, of course, who made this case most powerfully, arguing that an economic system based on extensive property rights, free exchange, and the division of labour helped all—even the poor—to become more prosperous. As the influence of Smith's work spread, it laid the foundation for a new alliance in liberal thinking between republicanism, human rights, and freedom of commerce. This new argument was that freedom of commerce—by fostering general prosperity, but also more generally by encouraging cooperation and mutual dependence within the economic sphere—helped to create the social conditions necessary for the establishment and long-term stability of democratic republican government. Thus Montesquieu famously argued that freedom of commerce can render society more peaceful—'everywhere there is commerce, there are gentle mores'[33]—thoughts echoed later by Mill.[34] Laissez-faire capitalism was therefore understood in this tradition to be central to the spread of liberal republican political ideals.

A similar argument also emerged about international trade itself, to the effect that international trade was conducive to international peace, and therefore helped to counteract external threats to the stability and endurance of new republican governments. Paine, for example, in his *Rights Of Man*, described international commerce generally as a 'pacific system, operating to cordialize nations', and argued that trade between nations promoted international peace, by rendering nations useful to one another.[35] Trade, it was argued, promoted understanding between nations, thereby

[32] Reprinted in MR Ishay (ed), *The Human Rights Reader: Major Political Essays, Speeches and Documents from the Bible to the Present* (Routledge, London 1997) 138–9.

[33] C de S Montesquieu, *The Spirit of Laws* [1750] (Collier Press, New York, NY 1990) 338. For a critical engagement with this traditional liberal reading of Montesquieu, see generally RL Howse, 'Montesquieu on Commerce, Conquest, War and Peace' (2006) 31 Brooklyn J Intl L 693–708.

[34] The doctrine of freedom of commerce 'rests on grounds different from, though equally solid with, the principle of individual liberty... Restrictions on trade, or on production for purposes of trade, are indeed restraints... but the restraints in question affect only that part of conduct which society is competent to restrain, and are wrong solely because they do not really produce the results which it is desired to produce by them': John Stuart Mill, *On Liberty* (Penguin Classics, Harmondsworth 1982) 164. The term 'trade' in the quoted passage refers to commerce generally, not to international trade. But the passage could serve just as well as a summary of the core tenets of liberal economic thinking in this tradition on the relationship between international trade and individual liberty.

[35] Thomas Paine, *Rights of Man* [1791] (Penguin Books, Baltimore, MD 1969) 234.

reducing the misunderstandings that can lead to conflict.[36] Montesquieu extended his views on the effects of commerce generally to those of international trade in particular: 'Peace is the natural effect of trade. Two nations who traffic with each other become reciprocally dependent; for if one has an interest in buying, the other has an interest in selling: and thus their union is founded on their mutual necessities.'[37] Kant, too, saw international commerce as a force for peace, primarily because any outbreak of war would disturb commercial relationships and threaten the continued prosperity of commercial interests.[38]

It is true that, despite this historical connection, there is no necessary logical link between the philosophy of seventeenth- and eighteenth-century natural rights liberalism and the economic freedoms associated with laissez-faire capitalism. As others have noted, there is much in the same tradition—even in Locke's and Smith's writing, as well as that of Montesquieu—that can provide philosophical resources for a very different view of the appropriate relations between the state and the market.[39] For present purposes, however, this is beside the point. What matters for the moment is that the writings of these and other seventeenth- and eighteenth-century liberal thinkers remain an important origin and reference point for an enduring strand of human rights thinking which sees freedom of international commerce and free markets as closely associated with the enjoyment of human rights, and indeed justified and required by human rights principles.

In Vasak's famous terminology, the civil and political rights which emerged during this period of political ferment were the 'first generation' of human rights.[40] A 'second generation' emerged during the nineteenth and early twentieth centuries, with the development of a new human rights tradition, which understood free markets as a potential threat to the enjoyment of human rights. The immediate context was the Industrial Revolution and the 'abuses and misuses of capitalist development'[41] which occurred during the late eighteenth and nineteenth centuries. The growth and spread of industrial capitalism across Europe during this period created a new class of wage labourers, and an economic system which subjected them to new forms of social hardship in the form of degrading and exploitative working conditions, and

[36] ibid; see also TC Walker, 'Two Faces of Liberalism: Kant, Paine, and the Question of Intervention' (2008) 52 Intl Studies Q 449, 458.

[37] Montesquieu [1750] (1990) 316.

[38] For one reading of Kant's view of free trade, see Walker (2008) 458–9.

[39] See generally MCR Craven, *The International Covenant on Economic, Social and Cultural Rights: A Perspective on its Development* (Clarendon Press, New York 1995) 11–12; J Donnelly, *Universal Human Rights in Theory and Practice* (Cornell University Press, Ithaca, NY 2003); J Charvet and EI Kaczynska-Nay, *The Liberal Project and Human Rights: The Theory and Practice of a New World Order* (CUP, New York 2008); J Morsink, 'Inherent Human Rights: The Philosophy of the Universal Declaration' (1984) 6 HRQ 309; RL Siegel, 'Socioeconomic Rights: Past and Future' (1985) 7 HRQ 255; Howse (2006). That said, Locke's work has been and continues to be received and understood as a political philosophy 'fit for the age [of] capitalism' (E Roll, *A History of Economic Thought* (5th edn, Faber, London 1992) 76), premised as it is on the idea of the property-owning self-interested individual so central to the emergence and spread of industrial capitalism.

[40] K Vasak, 'A 30-year Struggle: The Sustained Efforts to Give Force of Law to the Universal Declaration of Human Rights' (1977) 30 UNESCO Courier 28.

[41] BH Weston, 'Human Rights' (1984) 6 HRQ 257, 265.

growing inequalities of wealth and privilege. One result was the emergence of a powerful claim that the state had a responsibility to provide social protection for individuals against the dislocating and degrading forces of the free market. Such protections began to emerge across Europe, in the form of unemployment insurance, factory acts, child labour laws, minimum wages and working conditions, government-provided pensions and social security, and so on. Politically, these programmes were strongly associated with the rise of socialism and the labour movement, though other political and religious traditions also played important roles.[42] Over the course of the twentieth century, they crystallized in the institutionalization of the welfare state, from the New Deal of the United States to the social democracies of Western Europe.

A new and different human rights tradition emerged out of this social and political milieu. The growing social unrest of the working classes during this period reflected their belief that the great political revolutions of the later eighteenth and early nineteenth centuries had been essentially middle class revolutions, leaving untouched the systematic deprivation of a variety of poor and marginalized groups. One response within socialist thought of the period was to reject human rights, by highlighting the intimate connection between the philosophy of natural rights and the growth of capitalist economic structures, and therefore portraying the morality of human rights as itself ultimately an instrument of oppression.[43] But another response was to broaden the human rights agenda. Against what they saw as the *faux* universalism of contemporary liberal conceptions of human rights, some thinkers of this period crafted a human rights sensibility explicitly focused on the poor and marginalized, which sought to apply the techniques and rhetoric of human rights to contemporary problems of social justice and social welfare. Blanc, for example, challenged the tendency of liberal thought to equate freedom with absence of governmental interference, as if the state of nature were the epitome of freedom: 'the freedom of the state of nature was, in fact, only an abominable oppression,

[42] Siegel notes that claims for social protection, in addition to being socialist, are also 'feudal, mercantilist, Methodist, utilitarian, radical, conservative, Roman Catholic—and even liberal. Such diverse perceptions and forces as aristocratic paternalism, fear of social disintegration, utopian musings, belief in "the idea of progress" and political leaders' awareness of the need to integrate additional elements of the population into a solidarity citizenry, cumulatively contributed far more than the various socialist schools to the recent emergence of a broad, if limited, international consensus regarding the social duties of government.' Siegel (1985) 260.

[43] As socialist thinkers watched the entrenchment of middle class power in the aftermath of the French Revolution, they began to associate the ideals of human rights with 'the pretense of a universal liberal and religious morality that camouflaged the particular interests of the bourgeoisie': MR Ishay, *The History of Human Rights: From Ancient Times to the Globalization Era* (University of California Press, Berkeley, CA 2008) 130. Within this story, then, human rights are seen in large part as a product of economic transformation—they begin with 'the requirement on the part of the new economic system to find a way to protect the prerogatives of ownership throughout the ever-lengthening circuits of capital', and provide moral support for the social and economic inequalities which result: see A Woodiwiss, *Human Rights* (Routledge, London 2005) 138.

because it allied itself with inequality of strength'.[44] In a world characterized by profound inequality, it was also argued, true freedom for the vulnerable can only come through collective action to secure that freedom, and by providing the conditions for its enjoyment. Where liberal thinking focused on political institutions as the source of oppression and commerce as an expression of freedom, this new human rights tradition redirected attention to the economic realm as an additional source of oppression, which undermined formal claims to political equality. Moreover, this new tradition focused attention on the material conditions required for the effective enjoyment of human rights. What was the point of the rights to vote, to participate in the political process, it was asked, without the satisfaction of basic needs such as food, shelter, and, above all, work?

The emphasis therefore shifted from civil and political rights to a new corpus of 'social rights'. Ishay has chronicled the ways in which socialist and other movements took the lead in the struggle for human rights during the nineteenth and early twentieth centuries, placing the rights of workers at the centre of human rights activism, campaigning for the abolition of child labour and the improvement of unsanitary, exploitative, and dangerous working conditions generally, as well as explicit claims for a right to work.[45] Since, it was said, the working class could not be free without being educated, they also advocated universal public education, sometimes under the banner of the rights of children, or a right to education itself. Demands for economic equality resulted in the gradual development of rights to social security, social welfare for the poor, and protection against unemployment.[46] Moreover, the same movements were at the forefront of campaigns for universal suffrage. Social rights, in other words, were not pursued at the expense of democratic political rights—on the contrary, the former were understood in this tradition as an important precondition for the effective exercise of the latter. Furthermore, trenchant criticism of property rights during this period went some way towards removing them from the centre of human rights struggles. Formally, these social rights were first given juridical form in the constitutions of socialist states, most prominently in the Soviet Constitution of 1918.[47] But the same ideas were reflected in the politics and institutions of emerging social democratic Western welfare states, even if social rights were not explicitly written into their constitutions. Roosevelt, for example, famously made the connection between New Deal welfarism and social rights in his 1944 State of the Union address, in which he set out a 'new bill of rights' for the United States, which included the rights to 'a useful and

[44] L Blanc, 'On the Material Basis for Rights' (Organization of Labor, 1848 edn) in Micheline R Ishay (ed), *The Human Rights Reader: Major Political Essays, Speeches and Documents from the Bible to the Present* (Routledge, London 1997) 216.

[45] Ishay (2008) ch 3.

[46] RP Claude and BH Weston (eds), *Human Rights in the World Community: Issues and Action* (3rd edn, University of Pennsylvania Press, Philadelphia, PA 2006) 127.

[47] I Szabo, 'Historical Foundations of Human Rights and Subsequent Developments' in K Vasak and P Alston (eds), *The International Dimensions of Human Rights* (Greenwood Press, Westport, CT 1982) 19.

remunerative job', to 'adequate medical care', to 'a good education', and to 'adequate protection from the economic fears of old age, sickness, accident and unemployment'.[48]

This was a period, then, when the language and practice of human rights came to be positioned against laissez-faire capitalism amid widespread scepticism about the ability of unregulated free markets to deliver on their promise of advancing human rights for all. Explicitly challenging the belief that human rights could and would be secured by free markets, human rights movements of the period developed a set of criticisms of liberal economic structures in terms of their detrimental impact on the enjoyment of human rights. With this brief background in mind, then, let us turn to the post-war human rights regime, and in particular its founding constitutive instrument, the Universal Declaration of Human Rights (UDHR). How were these different human rights traditions combined and hierarchized in the process of drafting the UDHR?

Article 68 of the United Nations Charter instructed the new Economic and Social Council of the UN to establish a Commission on Human Rights, on the understanding that it would prepare a draft international bill of rights. The Commission was duly created in February 1946, with Eleanor Roosevelt as chair, and at its first regular meeting in January 1947, the Commission appointed a three-person committee to create a first draft of the bill.[49] As a result of the objections of the Soviet Union, this drafting committee was reconstituted with eight members, now including representatives from Australia, Chile, France, the United Kingdom, and the Soviet Union in addition to the original three. Work continued on the draft both within this drafting committee and in the Commission itself over the course of 1947 and the first half of 1948, until a draft was passed by the Commission in June 1948. This draft was rapidly passed by the Economic and Social Council, and when it reached the General Assembly was given to the Third Committee for further discussion. After eighty-one difficult meetings of the Third Committee,[50] the Universal Declaration was passed as a non-binding resolution of the General Assembly in December 1948, less than nine months after the signing of the Havana Charter of the ITO.

While successive drafts were highly contested, and ultimately the UDHR represented a compromise between the views of at least three different blocs, it is fair to say that the views of Western liberal states and their allies probably had the most profound influence on the character of the UDHR.[51] These states had a majority both on the drafting committee and in the Commission. Key personnel involved in

[48] President Franklin D Roosevelt, State of the Union Message on 6 January 1941, reprinted in (1941) 87 Cong Rec 44, 46.

[49] These were Eleanor Roosevelt (US), PC Chang (China), Charles Malik (Lebanon). See generally JP Humphrey, 'The Universal Declaration of Human Rights: Its History, Impact and Juridical Character' in BG Ramcharan (ed), *Human Rights: Thirty Years after the Universal Declaration* (Martinus Nijhoff, The Hague 1979) 21.

[50] ibid 26.

[51] H Tolley, Jr, *The U.N. Commission on Human Rights* (Westview Press, Boulder, CO 1987) 19–24.

the process—including Eleanor Roosevelt, René Cassin, and Charles Malik, among others—were steeped in Western liberal traditions of human rights,[52] and the texts on which they drew, including drafts requested and submitted from a variety of organizations and senior individuals, were also inspired largely by the same tradition.[53] That said, the views of Western liberal states themselves were not uniform, particularly on the question of the status and inclusion of economic and social rights (the question most relevant for present purposes). Nevertheless, as a whole, Morsink argues that the drafters of the Universal Declaration were 'proud' of the inclusion of social and economic rights, and saw themselves in this regard as correcting an oversight on the part of the great natural rights thinkers of the seventeenth and eighteenth centuries.[54]

This is not to say, however, that social and economic rights were acknowledged by all to be of equal weight to earlier civil and political rights. When the Latin American countries, supported by the socialist bloc, pressed for an amendment to Article 3 of the Declaration, which would have given greater prominence to social and economic rights, making much clearer their formally equal status, representatives from Western liberal countries were successful in resisting the change.[55] The result ultimately, was a document which contained important social and economic rights in Articles 22 to 26, but which devoted considerably more time and prominence to more traditional civil and political rights associated with the seventeenth- and eighteenth-century liberal traditions of human rights. Even the inclusion of these social and economic rights was probably only made possible by the fact that the Declaration was non-binding. In the end, the Soviet Union and other socialist countries abstained from voting for the Declaration, both in the Commission and later in the General Assembly, on account of what they saw as the weakness of its provisions relating to second generation rights.

On this basis, Szabo has criticized the UDHR for being unbalanced, and displaying a bias towards liberal strands of human rights thinking.[56] But it is hardly a classical liberal document. Humphrey, who produced one of the initial drafts for the drafting committee, has described it as an attempt to combine 'humanitarian liberalism with social democracy'.[57] Henkin, too, argued that it is a document

[52] Morsink (1984). See also J Donnelly, 'Human Rights and Western Liberalism' in AA An-Na'im and FM Deng (eds), *Human Rights in Africa: Cross-Cultural Perspectives* (Brookings Institution Press, Washington, DC 1990) 31; VA Leary, 'The Effect of Western Perspectives on International Human Rights' in AA An-Na'im and FM Deng (eds), *Human Rights in Africa: Cross-Cultural Perspectives* (Brookings Institution Press, Washington, DC 1990) 15.

[53] Humphrey (1979) 24.

[54] Morsink (1984) 332, 326.

[55] Morsink (1984) 327ff describes this discussion in some detail. The Latin American support for economic, social and cultural rights more generally is described in Siegel (1985), LJ LeBlanc, 'Economic, Social, and Cultural Rights and the Inter American System' (1977) 19 J of Interamerican Studies and World Affairs 61, and especially MA Glendon, 'The Forgotten Crucible: The Latin American Influence on the Universal Human Rights Idea' (2003) 16 Harvard Human Rights J 27.

[56] Szabo (1982); see also Craven (1995).

[57] J Humphrey, *Human Rights and the United Nations: A Great Adventure* (Transnational Publishers, New York, NY 1984) 39.

'woven of several strands', and that while the rights contained within it do not reflect a single theory of the relation of the individual, the market, and the state, they do 'imply a government that is activist and intervening, that is committed to economic-social planning which would redound as economic-social rights to the individual'.[58] Thus, writing thirty years later, Gros Espiell was able to claim that:

> ... the last 30 years have witnessed the end of the old individualistic conception of human rights in the field of western thought... [States] have stopped adhering merely to civil and political freedoms, and the need has been accepted to recognize and guarantee the effectiveness of economic, social and cultural rights, not only for their own sake, but because without them, civil and political rights have no material basis and are lifeless formulae without reality.[59]

Whatever one makes of the present relevance of such statements, they represent an interesting indication of then-prevailing understandings of the normative foundation of the Declaration.

In the years immediately following the passing of the UDHR, and particularly after the outbreak of war on the Korean Peninsula, the Commission on Human Rights increasingly became a venue for the playing out of the ideological schisms associated with the Cold War.[60] Partisans on both sides sought to use the Commission to embarrass their opponents. The differences of opinion over the status of economic and social rights, already evident during the drafting of the UDHR, widened and were entrenched. On one side, the Soviet Union and its satellites and allies strongly asserted the supremacy of economic and social rights, even to the point of justifying violations of civil and political rights, and sought to focus the attention of the Commission on economic and social issues.[61] On the other side, the United States (particularly after the replacement of Eleanor Roosevelt as its representative in the early 1950s) and its allies hardened their stance against economic and social rights. Such rights, they argued, should not be used to justify state repression, and were positively dangerous to the extent that they seemed to justify large-scale governmental intervention in the economy. Intellectually, this position was buttressed by a series of now-familiar intellectual claims concerning the unenforceable, aspirational, non-binding, and non-justiciable character of social rights—as compared to their fully operational civil and political cousins.[62]

Despite their sense of besiegement and frustration,[63] the Western liberal states probably had the best of this fight in the period from 1948 to 1967.[64] During this

[58] Henkin (1981) 12, 13.

[59] H Gros Espiell, 'The Evolving Concept of Human Rights: Western, Socialist and Third World Approaches' in BG Ramcharan (ed), *Human Rights: Thirty Years after the Universal Declaration* (Martinus Nijhoff, The Hague 1979) 51.

[60] Tolley (1987) 19–24.

[61] For one account of this period, see MB Abram, 'Human Rights and the United Nations: Past as Prologue' (1991) 4 Harvard Human Rights J 69–83.

[62] eg Maurice Cranston, *What are Human Rights?* (Bodley Head, London 1973).

[63] Abram (1991) 69–83, 72.

[64] Tolley (1987) 317.

period, they maintained their numerical dominance in the Commission, no representative of the socialist bloc was appointed Chair of the Commission, and economic and social rights hardly figured in the Commission's work programme.[65] As a result of the pressure from Western liberal voices in the Commission, a decision was taken by the General Assembly—contrary to its initially expressed preference—to draft two human rights treaties, one for civil and political rights and a separate one for social and economic rights. Despite the 'indivisibility' and the formal equality of these two covenants, the latter was considerably undermined as an operational document for decades.

But the relative strength of liberal voices during this period was the result of more than their numerical dominance on the Commission.[66] The presence and influence of the socialist tradition in human rights discourse was also undermined by at least three broader factors. First, the widespread human rights abuses committed by Eastern bloc states undermined the credibility of such nations to speak for and on behalf of human rights.[67] Secondly, the strong commitment of socialist states to the principle of non-intervention in international affairs also limited their ability to contribute to shaping an active human rights agenda. Thirdly, the growth of civil society human rights organizations working within a socialist framework was impeded by that strand of socialist thinking which explicitly dismissed human rights as a language of emancipation and positioned itself against human rights as a situated political project. It was further impeded by the self-conscious desire of human rights groups in the Western world to avoid any association with state socialism. As a result of all of these factors, there was a general disregard for social and economic rights within the human rights movement of the period, particularly among most Western human rights NGOs. To the extent that they were considered, such rights were understood to be fully satisfied by the kinds of regulatory interventions and institutions associated with the post-war welfare state, as the best and most effective instruments for their achievement. Furthermore, intellectual arguments concerning the fundamentally different nature of 'negative' civil and political rights from 'positive' social and economic rights took hold, and it took some decades for the false binaries on which these claims were based to be exposed.[68] The result was a systematic relegation of social and economic rights to a kind of secondary status within the corpus of human rights for a long period.

[65] Tolley (1987) 317.

[66] For one view emphasizing the essentially liberal character of the modern human rights movement, see MW Mutua, 'The Ideology of Human Rights' (1996) 36 Virginia J of Intl L 589; MW Mutua, 'The Transformation of Africa: A Critique of the Rights Discourse' in F Gomez Isa and K De Feyter (eds), *Human Rights and Diversity: International Human Rights Law in a Global Context* (University of Deusto, Bilbao 2009) 899.

[67] T Evans, *The Politics of Human Rights: A Global Perspective* (Pluto Press, London 2001) 14.

[68] See eg H Shue, *Basic Rights: Subsistence, Affluence, and U.S. Foreign Policy* (Princeton University Press, Princeton, NJ 1980).

C. Mutual isolation and embedded liberalism

This brief survey has put us in a position to say something meaningful about the nature of the relationship between the trade and human rights regimes in the first two or three decades of their existence. I noted at the outset that it is customary in the contemporary trade and human rights literature to emphasize the mutual isolation of the two regimes—their existence as separate institutions, and separate professional communities, with little dialogue between them, and little regard for each others' activities. While this picture is largely accurate, what is now clear is that this mutual isolation was *enabled and sustained* by a deeper connection between the two regimes. This connection was the common political commitment, shared by dominant players in both regimes, to embedded liberalism as their foundational political ideology. Put another way, the mutual isolation of both regimes was made possible by the fact that they were two parts of a single liberal project of world order, structured around the international projection of the New Deal welfare state.[69] The post-war international order was one in which the trade and human rights regimes were provisionally unified by the common ideology of embedded liberalism.

The common ideological foundations of the two regimes during this period enabled their isolation in three important ways. First, and probably most importantly, the ideology of embedded liberalism shaped and defined each regime in such a way as to preclude the emergence of major conflicts between the two. As we have seen, on the human rights side this meant emphasizing civil and political rights as the major focus of human rights law and activism, and minimizing the practical effects of social and economic rights by equating them with the establishment of precisely those institutions of social protection associated with the welfare state in the post-war period. On the trade side, it meant a trade regime in which the pursuit of free trade was defined and conducted in ways which minimized and avoided disruption to the kinds of interventions associated with the welfare state. The regime pursued 'multilateral trade' rather than 'free trade' in some classical liberal sense: liberalization was pursued progressively, slowly, and selectively; and the law was drafted and operationalized in ways which permitted—and indeed, presupposed—a high degree of government intervention. The result was that any potential conflicts between the human rights regime and the international trade regime were effectively hidden from view. The projection of embedded liberalism in and through the international political order, shaped the international trade and human rights regimes in such a way as to sublimate conflicts between them, by displacing such conflicts to the domestic realm, and 'resolving' them in the institutions of the liberal democratic welfare state. Embedded liberalism, then, told a story of the mutual compatibility of liberal trade and human rights protection, while simultaneously shaping the trade

[69] E Borgwardt, *A New Deal for the World: America's Vision for Human Rights* (Harvard University Press, Cambridge MA 2005); Burley (1992) 125; MA Glendon, *A World Made New: Eleanor Roosevelt and the Universal Declaration of Human Rights* (1st edn, Random House, New York, NY 2001).

and human rights regimes in such a way as to make such compatibility possible and plausible.

The second way in which the common liberal foundations of the two regimes helped to preclude conflicts and produce isolation between them, has to do with liberal beliefs about the civilizing effects of international commerce. These beliefs, as we saw above, were influential in post-war negotiations over the international economic order. International trade was understood to work as a driver of peaceful coexistence among nations and an instrument of the global spread of civilization, justice, and human rights. Similarly, a secure and predictable open international trading system helped—within this post-war liberal worldview—to provide the stability and growth necessary for the enjoyment of human rights. The deepening of economic ties between similarly-minded nations was thought to reduce the likelihood of military conflict between them, and help to establish a sphere of security and prosperity within the liberal West. Furthermore, the spread of human rights—which in this incarnation put at its core economic liberties and the rule of law—helps to create the conditions for international trade and the opening of new markets. In the imagination of the post-war planners, therefore, a close alliance was built between international commerce and human rights as two halves of a *single* project of world peace. As we shall see, these core claims have proved to be enduring, and still form the basis of the most powerful liberal vision of the relationship between international trade and human rights, in which human rights are knitted together with free markets and free trade as two mutually reinforcing parts of a single vision of international peace and prosperity. This narrative enabled institutional isolation between the two regimes in obvious ways. Safe in the knowledge that they were working towards broadly the same goal, in broadly mutually reinforcing ways, neither community felt threatened by the other, and by and large felt no obvious need to pay close attention to the activities of the other. Subject to the minor exceptions dealt with below, the possibility of a fundamental conflict between the two regimes was implausible to liberal eyes and, as a result, claims of conflict were rarely if ever heard, nor was the possibility easily imagined.

Thirdly, I noted above the way in which the embedded liberal foundations of the GATT regime produced a trade regime focused on maintaining stable international trade relations, and avoiding a repeat of the mutually destructive protectionist war of the 1930s. The result was the constitution of the GATT as an insular community of trade professionals, who consciously sought to isolate themselves and the international trading system from destabilizing political forces. Resistance to the linkage of trade issues with broader geopolitical issues in this world was in this context not just an institutional accident, but a conscious professional project—a way of carrying out the mandate of the GATT. When disputes arose between trading partners, one of the prime objectives of GATT dispute settlement was precisely to ensure that it did not spill over into broader relations between the two countries—and the GATT was proud of its success in doing just that. Thus, the trade regime operated in a mode of technicality and depoliticization, making a clear distinction between the 'low politics' of international trade, and the 'high politics' of matters such as human rights.[70] Indeed, as Alston notes, there was a strong aversion within the trade regime to any linking of trade and human rights issues, for fear of 'politicizing' trade relations,[71] and stepping outside the circumscribed boundaries of their expertise. Where the connection between the two could not be avoided—such as in the case of the imposition of economic sanctions for reasons relating to human rights[72]—the trade regime therefore developed a variety of mechanisms through which the destabilizing influence of this 'politicization' of trade relations could be minimized.[73] For example, from the beginning the GATT contained Article XXI which provided for exceptions to GATT obligations where the UN Security Council imposed economic sanctions on a country and (probably more importantly) where a GATT member considered trade restrictions necessary for the protection of essential security interests. Though there was and remains considerable disagreement about the self-judging character of Article XXI, its practical result was that trade rules could be, and were, flexibly (dis)applied as the circumstances demanded on a case-by-case basis. The point, then, is that the embedded liberal foundations of the two regimes entrenched their mutual isolation in a third way—by imagining the stability of international trade to be predicated on its separation from politics, and therefore creating a community of professionals engaged in actively policing the boundaries between the trade regime and other international regimes. The institutional isolation of the two regimes not only was enabled by their shared liberal premises, but also in practice helped to shield those premises from challenge.

II. The development challenge and the beginnings of regime conflict

From roughly the late 1950s through to at least the late 1970s, a different set of ideas crystallized about the causal dynamics of the international economic order. Unlike the liberalism of the time, which saw an open international economic order as working to advance the prosperity of all nations, the core idea of this new way of thinking was that the international economic order was structured to facilitate the exploitation, and impede the development, of non-industrialized nations—or more pointedly, that it tended to produce the prosperity of the developed North at

[70] RN Cooper, 'Trade Policy is Foreign Policy' (1972) 9 Foreign Policy 18.

[71] P Alston, 'International Trade as an Instrument of Positive Human Rights Policy' (1982) 4 HRQ 155, 168.

[72] There have been a number of instances of such sanctions during the GATT's history—the South African case is one obvious example, but there were others, see generally ibid.

[73] For one account of the way that the GATT dealt with such problems, see O Long, *Law and Its Limitations in the GATT Multilateral Trading System* (Martinus Nijhoff, Dordrecht 1987) 81–3; also Kock (1969) 73; AS Alexandroff and R Sharma 'The National Security Provision—GATT Article XXI' in PFJ Macrory, AE Appleton, and MG Plummer (eds), *The World Trade Organization: Legal, Economic and Political Analysis* (Springer, New York 2005) 1572–9.

the expense of the developing South.[74] In this view, as Rivero explains, underdevelopment was not understood as 'an isolated stage in a country's economic history that is similar to the stages the industrialized countries had to go through', but instead as 'the result of an historical process of economic conditioning imposed on underdeveloped economies by the countries which are now developed'.[75]

It is worth briefly saying something about the causal model which underlay this narrative. Its starting point was the existence of an international division of labour with very specific historical origins. During the eighteenth and nineteenth centuries, so this story goes, as the Industrial Revolution progressed in Western Europe, processes of capital accumulation and scientific and technological advancement in industrializing countries were made possible by the importation and exploitation of natural resources and primary products from the colonial periphery. The first and most basic international division of labour was therefore established: industrialized nations produced and exported manufactured goods as well as technology and capital; non-industrialized nations produced and exported mainly raw materials and primary commodities, and depended on imports of capital and technology from the centre to stimulate their development.

It is this international division of labour which, within this tradition of thinking, structurally subordinated the developing world. The reason for this was the existence of fundamental differences in the markets for manufactures on the one hand, and primary commodities on the other. Over time, it was said, while producers and exporters of manufactures from the industrialized world typically found prices of and demand for their goods to be broadly stable and rising, producers and exporters of raw materials and primary goods encountered the opposite trends of volatility, weak demand, and falling prices. This was for a number of reasons: inelastic demand for primary commodities; the development of synthetic substitutes for natural raw materials; the lower proportion of consumption which is generally taken up by primary commodities as incomes rise; rapidly increasing production volumes as a result of the 'green revolution' in agriculture; and so on. Overall, the result seemed to be a structural imbalance in the global economic order, as peripheral countries were faced with deteriorating terms of trade, resulting in a net transfer of resources from them to the industrialized North. This prevented the accumulation of capital in the nations of the South, further entrenching their dependency on debt, foreign capital, and access to foreign technology to promote their development. For some who subscribed to this line of thought, this structural imbalance was made worse by the fact that the production, pricing, and marketing of much of the developing world's natural resources was to a large extent controlled by foreign private enterprises, some

74 See generally R Prebisch, *Towards a New Trade Policy for Development: Report by the Secretary-General of the United Nation's Conference on Trade and Development* (United Nations, New York 1964); O de Rivero, *New Economic Order and Development Law* (Pergamon Press, New York 1980); FP Reubens (ed), *The Challenge of the New International Economic Order* (Westview Press, Boulder, CO 1981); JA Hart, *The New International Economic Order: Conflict and Cooperation in North South Economic Relations* (Macmillan, London 1983).

75 Rivero (1980) 4.

of which were granted lengthy concessions prior to decolonization. Not only did it appear that much of the profit from the sale of natural resources was repatriated overseas, but the presence of large multinationals also made it more difficult for developing countries to take action to address what they saw as structural deficiencies in markets for natural resources and primary products. Foreign transnational corporations were also accused of providing access to capital, management skills, and technology on unfavourable and exploitative terms.

These ideas gained considerable traction over the course of the late 1950s and 1960s, as the share of world trade enjoyed by developing countries declined, and the difficulties of industrialization in these countries became apparent.[76] Newly decolonized states saw their apparent structural subjugation within the international economic order as the continuation of colonialism in a new guise, and began collectively to press for change. In relation to the trading system, their agenda had a number of aspects. One was to ensure stable—and higher—prices for the exports of developing countries. The main mechanisms advocated to achieve this were international commodity agreements and producer-exporter associations, combined with measures to promote preferential market access for Less Developed Country (LDC) products in industrialized countries. Price indexation was also suggested. Another aspect was the attempt to shift the existing international division of labour, by promoting the production and export of manufactures in developing countries. Again this required measures to ensure preferential market access, but also accelerated industrialization through the transfer of technology and management skills on favourable terms, and unconditional compensatory financial transfers. A third aspect was to limit the cost and improve the quality of transportation and freight services, which acted as serious impediments to developing countries' exports. Furthermore, these measures to change the structural dynamics of the trading system were combined with other demands. Control over the production, pricing, and marketing of natural resources was advocated through the principle of permanent sovereignty over natural resources, as well as new initiatives to regulate large foreign enterprises, including promoting a code of conduct for transnational corporations. There were attempts to secure additional finance for developing countries through debt adjustment, and new concessionary programmes in international financial institutions, as well as exceptions from developed countries' capital outflow restrictions for capital destined for developing countries. A greater voice for developing countries in international economic governance was also advocated through proposed changes to voting rights in the Bretton Woods institutions.

All this, and more, was actively promoted during the 1960s and 1970s by a cohesive G-77, under the rubric of the New International Economic Order (NIEO).[77] This push had an important impact on both the trade and human rights

[76] Haberler (1958).

[77] See eg Declaration on the Establishment of a New International Economic Order, UNGA Res 3201 (S-VI) (1 May 1974) GAOR 6th Special Session UN Doc A/RES/S-6/3201; UNGA, Programme of Action on the Establishment of a New International Economic Order, UNGA Res 3202 (S-VI) (1 May 1974) GAOR 6th Special Session UN Doc A/RES/S-6/3202.

regimes, challenging the centrality of embedded liberalism as the primary ideology of both.

A. Development in the GATT, 1950s–1970s

In the context of the trade regime, many of the ideas and proposals just described had already been raised much earlier by developing countries involved in negotiations over the ITO.[78] Few, however, were addressed in the GATT, and indeed the small number of less developed countries in the group of twenty-three original GATT Contracting Parties has been attributed to the absence in the GATT of provisions on commodities and industrial development.[79] When China, Lebanon, Syria, and Liberia withdrew within a few years, the imbalance was made more pronounced. For the first decade of the GATT's existence, then, through the first three (post-Geneva) rounds of trade negotiations, the special concerns of developing countries were hardly visible.

This changed from the second half of the 1950s. The shift was in part demographic: between 1947 and 1973, membership of the GATT grew from twenty-three to eighty-five, with the bulk of the increase coming from newly indedendent developing country Contracting Parties. In addition, the relative exclusion of developing countries from the post-war trading system—both in terms of their declining share of world trade, and their lack of effective participation in negotiating rounds—was becoming painfully apparent as early as the mid-1950s.[80] Growing agricultural protectionism in the industrialized world over the same period, particularly through the establishment of the European Common Agricultural Policy in 1958, also prompted developing countries to make their voices heard more effectively within the GATT. As a result of their efforts, over the next few years, the GATT left behind its passivity on development-related matters and became, in Dam's words, an 'international body affirmatively, and at times aggressively, attempting to promote the exports of less developed countries'.[81]

After a handful of relatively insignificant early resolutions,[82] the turning point came in 1958 with the publication of a report commissioned by the GATT Contracting Parties, and authored by an eminent panel of four experts, chaired by Gottfried Haberler (the 'Haberler Report').[83] The report clearly laid part of the blame for the difficulties faced by developing countries on policies pursued by the industrialized North, which denied access to its large markets for many of the developing world's most significant exports. The GATT reacted by establishing a committee—the precursor to the present-day Committee on Trade and

[78] R Wilkinson, *The WTO: Crisis and the Governance of Global Trade* (1st edn, Routledge, London 2006) 33ff; Wilcox (1972) 140–52; Gardner (1966) 364ff.
[79] Gupta (1967) 10.
[80] See eg GATT, *International Trade, 1954* (GATT, Geneva 1955); Wilkinson (2006) 53–4.
[81] Dam (1970) 225.
[82] For an account of these, see Wilkinson (2006) 54–5.
[83] Haberler (1958).

Development (CTD)—whose work over the next few years contributed to hastening the removal of some restrictions, including those on tropical products.[84] In the meantime, a core bloc of developing countries sought to shift discussion of these issues to a new venue, which became known as the UN Conference on Trade and Development (UNCTAD). In 1963, in the context of preparations for the first UNCTAD meeting in 1964, a group of twenty-one developing countries put together a 'programme of action', designed to expand the trade of developing countries as a means of furthering their economic development, and were successful in having it adopted as a resolution of the GATT Contracting Parties.[85] In hortatory language, it called for a standstill on new barriers to LDC exports, the rapid elimination of quantitative restrictions on imports from LDCs, and duty-free treatment of tropical products, among other things. Most importantly, however, it set in train a process which led to the amendment of the text of the GATT 1947, in the form of the addition of a new Part IV on Trade and Development.

Most present-day observers of the trade regime are relatively sceptical of the practical impact of Part IV. It contains little by way of precise and binding commitments, and what few principles are contained within it are limited in their effect by language deliberately designed to undermine their bite.[86] Nevertheless, we should not underestimate its significance at the time. Wilkinson describes this as 'the closest the GATT was to come to a critical moment in which existed the potential for a fundamentally distinct shift in [the GATT's] evolutionary trajectory to occur'.[87] Dam, too, notes that the new Part IV 'was of great symbolic importance in expanding the views of all Contracting Parties concerning the new role of the GATT in the thorny problem of development'.[88] More concretely, the new Part IV formally acknowledged that developing countries would not be expected to provide full reciprocity for the concessions they received in multilateral negotiations.[89] In three lengthy Articles, all Contracting Parties clearly acknowledged the need for the expansion and diversification of exports of developing countries, committed to accord high priority to the elimination of barriers to exports of developing countries, and agreed to refrain to the fullest extent possible from introducing new tariffs on imports from LDCs. These Articles also contemplated international cooperation in

[84] Dam (1970) 233–6.

[85] GATT, 'Resolution (Measures for the Expansion of Trade of Developing Countries as a Means of Furthering their Economic Development)' in GATT, *Basic Instruments and Selected Documents, Twelfth Supplement: Decisions, Reports etc. of the Twenty-first Session* (GATT, Geneva 1964) 36ff.

[86] See eg GATT Art XXXVII:1, which imposes obligations on developed Contracting Parties only 'to the fullest extent possible... except when compelling reasons... make it impossible'.

[87] Wilkinson (2006) 63.

[88] Dam (1970) 237.

[89] GATT Art XXXVI:8: 'The developed contracting parties do not expect reciprocity for commitments made by them in trade negotiations to reduce or remove tariffs and other barriers to the trade of less-developed contracting parties'.

respect of the stabilization of commodity prices, a vision which was later at least partially realized outside the auspices of the GATT.[90]

During the Kennedy (1964–67) and Tokyo (1973–79) rounds of trade negotiations, the developing countries obtained at best mixed success in re-orienting the regime towards their interests and goals. Although these countries were successful in their defensive demand to be exempted from the requirement for reciprocity in trade negotiations, this had the effect of further attenuating their engagement with and impact on the positive outcomes of negotiating rounds. In the end, only eleven developing countries exchanged concessions in the Kennedy Round.[91] In the Tokyo Round, developing countries were able to force the inclusion of special and differential treatment provisions in a number of the new Codes, and achieved some success in respect of the reduction of border barriers on tropical products.[92] In addition, 1974 saw the introduction of the Multi-Fibre Arrangement, in place of the 1964 Agreement on International Trade in Cotton Textiles. Although that agreement is now understood to have been a major obstacle to the liberalization of textile trade over the long term, at the time it was designed in part to provide a way to increase the share of developing countries in world textile trade while at the same time providing some stability for producers in the developed world, through the use of detailed and carefully managed country-by-country quotas.[93] Most importantly, however, developing countries were able to achieve a permanent legal waiver for trade preference schemes for LDCs—a major achievement, even if it was undermined by the fact that it contained no positive obligation to provide such preferences. In addition, they secured the adoption of two Declarations, which made it somewhat easier for them to impose safeguards and trade restrictions for balance of payments purposes.[94] Despite these achievements, however, UNCTAD issued a report at the end of the Tokyo Round which harshly, but probably correctly, condemned the round as frustrating and incomplete from the perspective of developing countries.[95] In the end, at the conclusion of the 1970s, with the solidarity of the developing country bloc already being undermined by new economic pressures, debt crises, and changing ideas about appropriate development strategies, the 1960s and early 1970s proved to have been the high point of the development challenge within the GATT.

[90] I refer here to the series of international commodity agreements negotiated from the 1960s onwards, as to which see generally BS Chimni, *International Commodity Agreements* (Croom Helm, New York, NY 1987).

[91] Wilkinson (2006) 72.

[92] See GR Winham, *International Trade and the Tokyo Round Negotiations* (Princeton University Press, Princeton, NJ 1986) 274–80.

[93] Wilkinson (2006) 64–8.

[94] GATT, Declaration on Trade Measures Taken For Balance-of-Payments Purposes, (adopted 28 November 1979) L/4904; GATT, Safeguard Action for Development Purposes, (adopted 28 November 1979) L/4897.

[95] UNCTAD V, *Multilateral Trade Negotiations: Evaluation and Further Recommendations Arising Therefrom* (UNCTAD, Manila 1979).

B. Development in the human rights regime, 1960s–1980s

Just as in the trade regime, developing countries also sought to re-orient the human rights regime towards issues of economic development. At first, when the Commission on Human Rights began to explore the promotion of human rights in the developing world, the development needs of LDCs were used defensively, to deflect international criticism of their authoritarian and illiberal political structures, and to push back against the supposed intrusiveness of international human rights institutions. Authoritarianism was strategically justified in human rights terms on the basis that it could in some circumstances be conducive to development, and therefore to the enjoyment of economic, social, and cultural rights. Since poverty and deprivation caused greater human suffering in developing countries than abuses of civil and political rights, it was argued, the demands of economic development (and economic and social rights) should be given greater priority in such conditions.[96] These arguments gained at least some traction from the mid-1960s: four UN sponsored seminars from 1964 to 1970 explored the special difficulties of achieving adequate human rights protection in developing countries, while the Teheran Declaration of 1968 explicitly observed that 'the achievement of lasting progress in the implementation of human rights is dependent upon sound and effective national and international policies of economic and social development'.[97] They were also articulated more forcefully within the Commission itself once the Third World achieved a majority of votes within that body in 1967.[98] For their part, however, Western liberal nations within the Commission saw this as little more than an attempt by repressive governments to excuse gross violations of human rights, and to avoid human rights obligations. They argued that, far from economic development being a precondition for the enjoyment of human rights, the protection of human rights is an essential precondition of economic development.[99]

Although this antipathy towards human rights scrutiny on the part of many developing countries remained strong, a re-examination of the relationship between development and human rights occurred during the 1970s—at least among some developing countries—at the same time as the G-77 was pushing hard in the General Assembly and throughout the UN system for the inauguration of the NIEO. Instead of just using their development needs defensively to deflect human rights criticisms—though that dynamic certainly continued to be important—some developing country delegations now sought to craft a more positive, offensive human rights agenda around the idea of economic development. I noted above that a core causal claim of the developmental thought of this period was that international economic structures impeded economic development in LDCs, and facilitated their exploitation by the

[96] See eg Tolley (1987) 19–24; Espiell (1979); Charvet and Kaczynska-Nay (2008) 150ff.

[97] International Conference on Human Rights, 'Proclamation of Teheran' Final Act of the International Conference on Human Rights (22 April–13 May 1968) UN Doc A/CONF.32/41 at 3.

[98] See generally Tolley (1987) ch 5.

[99] Tolley (1987) 92–3; Charvet and Kaczynska-Nay (2008) 150ff; Jack Donnelly, 'Human Rights and Development: Complementary or Competing Concerns?' (1984) 36 World Politics 255.

North. On the basis that economic development is a precondition for the enjoyment of economic and social rights, the claim began to be made that these same international economic structures were a major obstacle to the protection and promotion of human rights in the developing world. Against Western claims that human rights violations in the developing world were attributable to immature economic and political systems, these countries began to attribute causal responsibility for human rights violations to existing international economic structures, which produced and sustained the conditions for their economic domination by industrial powers.[100] Human rights could not be realized, it was argued, without the restructuring of the existing international economic order. Thus, over the 1970s, as Rubin notes, the 'terminology of international protection and promotion of economic and human rights [was] increasingly intertwined with that of the new international economic order'.[101] This trend received a significant boost in 1977 when the General Assembly passed Resolution 32/130, stating that 'the realization of the new international economic order is an essential element for the effective promotion of human rights', and directing that economic and development priorities should guide the Commission's and the UN's human rights activities.[102]

One element of the formal link between the NIEO and human rights was the right of self-determination, which had of course served as the core normative foundation for the process of political decolonization. Developing countries now asserted the economic dimension of this right, which they said encompassed freedom from all forms of economic domination.[103] Another link was forged through the creation of a new (and contested) 'right to development'.[104] First floated as an idea in a scholarly article by M'Baye in 1972, the right was first formally recognized in a resolution adopted by the Commission on Human Rights under his chairmanship in 1977.[105] After an influential 1979 report from the UN Secretary General setting out his view of the sources and content of this new right, the General Assembly then explicitly recognized the right in November of the same year.[106] Over the resistance of the Western nations, who saw both the right to development and the NIEO as a

[100] Tolley (1987) 317.

[101] SJ Rubin, 'Economic and Social Human Rights and the New International Economic Order' (1986) 1 American University J of Intl L & Policy 67, 88; UNCHR, 'Report of the Secretary-General on the International Dimensions of the Right to Development as a Human Right' (2 January 1979) UN Doc E/CN.4/1334; see also RJ Vincent, *Human Rights and International Relations* (CUP, Cambridge 2001) 81.

[102] UNGA, 'Alternative Approaches and Ways and Means within the United Nations System for Improving the Effective Enjoyment of Human Rights and Fundamental Freedoms', UNGA Res 32/130 (16 December 1977) 105th Plenary Meeting UN Doc A/RES/32/130.

[103] Vincent (2001) 82; UNGA (UN Doc A/RES/32/130).

[104] For a history of the formal development of this right up to 1985, see Jack Donnelly, 'In Search of the Unicorn: The Jurisprudence and Politics of the Right to Development' (1985) 15 California Western Intl L J 473.

[105] Keba M'Baye, 'Le droit au developpement comme un droit de l'homme' (1972) 5 *Revue des Droits de L'Homme* 505; UN Doc E/CN.4/SR.1389 (1977).

[106] UNCHR (UN Doc E/CN.4/1334); UNGA, Alternative Approaches and Ways and Means within the United Nations System for Improvising the Effective Enjoyment of Human Rights and Fundamental Freedoms UNGA Res 34/46 (23 November 1979) UN Doc A/RES/34/46.

significant threat to their economic interests, the Commission continued to affirm the existence of this right and to commission studies on it. Major human rights NGOs, notably the International Commission of Jurists, also began campaigns on economic justice and the right to development.[107]

The right to development provided a space in which concerns about the social impact of global economic structures could take their place within contemporary human rights practice. This represented something of a resurgence and renewal—even if only a modest one—of the counter-liberal traditions of human rights thinking discussed above, which focused on the threats which free markets and free trade posed to the effective enjoyment of human rights. From 1980, however, the political strength of this line of thinking was significantly diminished. In part, this was to do with an enlargement of the Commission, which reduced the proportionate voting power of the developing countries and resulted in a stronger and more effective caucus of Western liberal nations.[108] These countries were then able to reshape the agenda of the Commission more effectively, so it was more in line with their prioritized interests in civil and political rights. They were also able more strongly to assert their opposition to the international economic demands of the developing countries, which in their view deflected attention from what they saw as the 'root causes' of poverty, namely weak domestic institutions and despotic governments.[109] Nevertheless, work on the right to development continued. On the one hand, this involved some degree of promotional activity, including additional studies from the Secretary General and the Sub-Commission, and a number of seminars, including two examining international structures as a cause of human rights problems in the Third World.[110] More importantly, in 1981 the developing countries were successful in establishing a working group to draft a Declaration specifying the content of the right to development. The group proved unable to reconcile important differences of opinion. It did, however, submit a draft to the General Assembly, which ultimately adopted a Declaration in 1986 over the dissenting vote of the United States and the abstention of others in the Western bloc.[111] It was, in Uvin's words, a 'rhetorical victory' only, which—until its more recent revival of sorts—had little active impact outside the UN bureaucracy.[112]

C. The development challenge and the erosion of mutual isolation

Developmental ideas associated with the NIEO represented a powerful challenge to the embedded liberal bargain which shaped the post-war international economic

[107] HB Tolley, Jr, *The International Commission of Jurists: Global Advocates for Human Rights* (University of Pennsylvania Press, Philadelphia, PA 1994) 144–5.

[108] Tolley (1987) 101.

[109] Abram (1991) 69–83; Donnelly (1985).

[110] Tolley (1987) 152ff.

[111] UNGA, Declaration on the Right to Development, UNGA Res 41/128 (4 December 1986) 97th Plenary Meeting UN Doc A/RES/41/128.

[112] P Uvin, 'From the Right to Development to the Rights-based Approach: How "Human Rights" Entered Development' (2007) 17 Development in Practice 597.

order over its first decades. Since, as I have argued above, the mutual isolation of the trade and human rights regimes in the post-war period depended on their shared commitment to embedded liberalism, the development challenge inevitably led to an erosion of this mutual isolation, and laid the foundation for a different and much more conflictual relationship between the two regimes. This new relationship was predicated on two crucial changes: first, a new understanding of human rights which placed development, and economic and social rights, at the heart of the human rights project; and secondly, a new and coherent body of economic thought which told a plausible story of the causal link between trade and under-development. It was these two elements which made it possible to imagine the international economic order as a structural obstacle to the realization of human rights, and to construct international trade as a 'human rights problem'. The result was that human rights law and language began to be used as a basis for challenging the liberal aspects of international trade law and the operation of the GATT. Thus, for example, the Commission on Human Rights expressed its concern in 1979 that bilateral and multilateral trade policies might negatively affect human rights, to the extent that they established or entrenched an unjust international economic order.[113] One former diplomat also recalls that the right to development was used in meetings in the GATT to 'support compulsory licensing and other forms of intellectual property exploitation'.[114] This was, it should be noted, in the context of a broader push to integrate consideration of human rights into the work of those international institutions and policy-makers dealing with the question of economic development.[115]

That said, this was not 'regime conflict' or 'fragmentation' in the modern sense. There was no suggestion at the time that any conflicts between the outcomes and policies favoured in the GATT and those favoured in the human rights regime had much to do with the different mandates of each regime, their different normative biases, their mutual isolation, or the lack of any institutionalized means of coordinating their functions. This was of course a political struggle between North and South, being played out simultaneously in both regimes, as well as elsewhere in the UN system. The G-77 bloc of developing countries was partially successful, and partially unsuccessful, in reshaping each regime in accordance with its perceived interests and agenda at the time. If there was a conflict between trade and human rights—that is, if the trade regime represented in some sense an obstacle to the realization of human rights—it was understood that this was simply because the developing countries had been somewhat successful in pursuing their NIEO agenda in the human rights regime, and less successful in the trade regime, rather than because each regime had a different built-in 'normative bias'. The two regimes

[113] See the discussion in Alston (1982) 167.
[114] Abram (1991) 78.
[115] See eg P Alston, *Human Rights and the Basic Needs Strategy for Development* (Human Rights and Development Working Papers, Anti-Slavery Society, London 1979), also discussed in JT Gathii, 'Good Governance as a Counter-Insurgency Agenda to Oppositional and Transformative Social Projects in International Law' (1999) 5 Buffalo Human Rights L Rev 107, 135ff, n 49.

simply represented two different venues, offering two different sets of rhetorical and institutional tools, in a single conflict over the ideological foundations and core purposes of the international economic order.

It is worth noting that, in an environment in which each regime was so obviously contested at its foundation—torn between competing ideologies, with fundamentally different conceptions of their proper roles, and the priorities and values that they ought to adopt—it would have been impossible to frame the issue as a problem of regime conflict. To make a claim, for example, that the objectives of the human rights and trade regimes were incompatible in important respects, it would be necessary to take a position on what those objectives were. But whose version of those objectives could be chosen as unproblematically representative of 'the human rights project' or 'the aims of the trade regime' in the hotly contested climate of the 1970s? Any attempt to choose only one would necessarily seem an obviously partial and partisan view, and an unhelpful simplification of a complex social struggle.

So, the mutual isolation between the trade and human rights regimes eroded to some degree over the 1960s and 1970s, as the language of human rights was harnessed to the project to change the international economic order, including GATT rules and procedures. Still, the legacy of mutual professional isolation remained. Writing in 1986, Rubin observed the existence of 'two discrete universes of discourse' in debates about economic and social rights.[116] The first, which contained essentially all of the human rights regime at the time, was the 'theological'[117] universe of 'norm formulation',[118] with its statements of principles, noble concepts, and highly politicized doctrinal disputes. The second, to which the GATT largely belonged, was the operational universe of specialized institutions. He noted that activity in the first universe had helpfully provided an impetus for, and set the ultimate goals for, the work of specialized agencies in the second. At the same time, there were significant difficulties of translation and communication between the normative and operational sides, such that, for example, 'in meeting after meeting at which there is serious discussion of the issues dealt with in the [ICESCR], the Covenant is scarcely mentioned'.[119] In this important sense, then, the two regimes *did* remain disconnected, even in this period. They remained as different professional communities, characterized by different modes of operation, deploying different discourses and different governance techniques.

III. Neoliberal resurgence

The emergence of neoliberal thought in the 1970s, and its rise to prominence in the 1980s and early 1990s, represents the next major stage in the evolving relationship between the trade and human rights regime. This was a period during which the

116 Rubin (1986) 78. 117 ibid 79.
118 ibid 80. 119 ibid 81.

welfare states of the industrialized world were subject to criticism on a number of fronts. The 1973 oil crisis and its attendant economic effects gave rise to concerns about the long-term affordability of the major programmes of social protection associated with welfare liberalism. The same social programmes were also criticized as encouraging dependence, discouraging responsibility, and imposing through their heavy associated tax burden 'an unjustified burden on self-realisation'.[120] Neoliberalism also represented a reversal of the relative faith accorded to governments and markets: market failure was now understood to be exceptional rather than pervasive, and even where market failure existed, the costs and risks of rent-seeking associated with governmental action to correct it were presumed to be greater than the costs of the market failure itself. The result was a transformation of state-market relations, particularly in the industrialized world: the removal of government as a direct producer of goods and services through privatization; the disciplining of government as a consumer of goods and services through new rules and procedures of government procurement; the removal and weakening of those forms of regulation understood as market intervention and burdens on business; and the expansion of those forms of regulation understood as necessary to create and sustain new competitive markets. At the same time, a similar transformation was occurring throughout many parts of the developing world. Faith in inward-looking, state-led development strategies eroded over the course of the 1970s and 1980s, in part because of the success of newly industrializing countries such as Korea and Taiwan, whose rapid growth was attributed to the pursuit of an outward-looking developmental strategy. Structural adjustment policies pursued under the tutelage of the International Monetary Fund (IMF) and World Bank in a series of developing countries in the wake of debt crises during the same period reinforced this trend. The surest path to development, within this new neoliberal framework, involved the freeing of markets, and integration into an emerging globalized economic order.

The 'neoliberal turn' of the 1980s and 1990s also brought with it a new set of ideas about the causal dynamics of the international trading system. Unlike embedded liberalism, the problem of instability did not loom as large in neoliberal thinking about the dynamics of the trading system, and in any case was understood to be best resolved by measures other than trade restrictions. And unlike counter-liberal thinking about development, neoliberal thought did not see the international economic order as exploitative, nor as resulting in a transfer of resources and wealth from the periphery to the centre. Instead, international trade, along with the internationalization of capital flows, was understood as a driver of global growth, an engine of mutual prosperity. This was only in a minor way a revival of the arguments of classical economics about static efficiency gains from the international division of labour—such arguments had after all never really gone away. More importantly, neoliberal thinking about international trade gave pride of place to dynamic efficiencies associated with trade liberalization: the transnational transfer of technology

[120] JE Broadbent, *The Rise and Fall of Economic and Social Rights: Thoughts on Justice and Stability in the North Atlantic Democracies* (Canadian High Commission, London 1997) 25.

and technical skill; the intensification of competitive pressures and therefore innovation; and the opportunities increased trade provided for demonstration effects and 'learning by doing'. Thus, for the first time since the First World War, the dominant case for free trade was linked to the case for free markets, rigorously understood. In contrast to the embedded liberalism, neoliberalism linked free markets, free trade, and economic globalization as inseparable elements of a single package of mutually beneficial global economic reform.

These neoliberal ideas effected a radical transformation of international economic governance. The World Bank and the IMF famously began to press more strongly for domestic free market reforms in developing countries in line with these new ideas. As to the trade regime, the precise nature and extent of the impact of neoliberal ideas remains a subject of considerable contemporary debate. Indeed, the entirety of Chapters 6 to 9 of this book are dedicated to exploring the nature of the impact of neoliberalism, and resistance to neoliberalism, on the dynamics and operation of the trade regime and trade law. For now, it is enough to say that the impact was profound (even if largely misunderstood), and has left a lasting imprint on the trading system. The development challenge was effectively submerged and the traces that it left were hidden from easy visibility, while embedded liberalism, too, was marginalized in the collectively imagined ideological foundations of the trade regime.

What is most relevant for the present chapter is that the rise of neoliberalism also transformed the internal dynamics of the human rights regime, generating a major new faultline between competing traditions within the human rights movement. On one hand, the end of the Cold War further undermined the credibility of socialist voices within the human rights regime,[121] and led to a strengthening and reinvention of classical liberal traditions of human rights thought described earlier, which emphasized civil and political rights and saw economic freedoms and property rights as central parts of the corpus of human rights.[122] Those within this tradition sought to establish a connection between human rights and the neoliberal projects of economic reform described above, on the basis of essentially four core arguments. First, it was argued that the rising prosperity associated with global economic liberalization and market reforms brought its own pressure for democratic political reform, as a newly economically powerful middle class demanded greater influence over political processes.[123] In the 1980s and 1990s, this view gained traction in the popular press, and a number of empirical studies were conducted purporting to show

[121] eg D Beetham, 'What Future for Social and Economic Rights?' (1995) 43 Political Studies 41.

[122] For one view of the neoliberal approach to human rights, see C Scott and P Macklem, 'Constitutional Ropes of Sand or Justiciable Guarantees? Social Rights in a New South African Constitution' (1992) 141 University of Pennsylvania L Rev 1.

[123] eg MC Davis, 'The Price of Rights: Constitutionalism and East Asian Economic Development' (1998) 20 HRQ 303; See also E-U Petersmann, 'Time for a United Nations "Global Compact" for Integrating Human Rights into the Law of Worldwide Organizations: Lessons from European Integration' (2002) 13 EJIL 621, 629.

a connection between economic liberalization and the protection of human rights.[124] Secondly, there was a repackaging of economic reform policies in human rights terms: free market-oriented reforms, it was argued quite simply, led to poverty reduction, and therefore were crucial elements in the promotion of such rights as the rights to food, health, and an adequate standard of living. Thus, for example, from the late 1990s the World Bank began to argue that its existing lending practices had helped to turn rights into reality for many recipients, and that its poverty alleviation efforts had an important human rights role.[125]

Thirdly, in a recapitulation and elaboration of earlier arguments that the protection of democratic rights is conducive to economic development, it has been claimed that the effective enjoyment of some subset of human rights is a necessary precondition to the proper functioning of markets.[126] This claim forms the basis for tying free market economic reform to civil and political reform as a single liberal project of politico-economic transformation.[127] Its impact is most clearly and famously seen in the neo-institutional turn of the World Bank's good governance agenda, which promotes the rule of law, judicial independence, anti-corruption initiatives, and the free flow of market information as the core institutional underpinning of well-functioning markets.[128] The surge of support for political and human rights conditionality in trade and aid policy in the early 1990s is also directly connected to the same line of thinking.[129] Fourthly, and finally, some have drawn a connection between neoliberal market reforms and human rights at the level of principle. Within the field of trade law, Petersmann's claims that economic freedoms rank alongside other 'liberty rights' as an historically under-appreciated element of core human rights protections, is the clearest expression of this point of view.[130] Thus, with this rise of neoliberalism came a re-assertion of the classical liberal vision of the trade and human rights relationship: a vision of fundamental complementarity, of mutual reinforcement of economic and political freedoms coexisting as part of the same political project.

[124] WH Meyer, *Human Rights and International Political Economic in Third World Nations: Multinational Corporations, Foreign Aid, and Repression* (Praeger, Westport, CT 1998); WH Meyer, 'Human Rights and MNC's: Theory Versus Quantitative Analysis' (1996) 18 HRQ 368; See also WT Milner, 'Economic Globalization and Rights: An Empirical Analysis' in A Brysk (ed), *Globalization and Human Rights* (University of California Press, Berkeley, CA 2002) 77.

[125] eg The World Bank, *Development and Human Rights: The Role of the World Bank* (The International Bank for Reconstruction and Development, Washington, DC 1998).

[126] See eg Petersmann (2002) 621, 626.

[127] For an account of this in the Latin American context, see Y Dezalay and BG Garth, *The Internationalization of Palace Wars: Lawyers, Economists, and the Contest to Transform Latin American States* (University of Chicago Press, Chicago, IL 2002) ch 10.

[128] eg The World Bank, *Governance: The World Bank's Experience* (The International Bank for Reconstruction and Development, Washington, DC 1994); For a critical review, see Gatthi (1999); A Orford and J Beard, 'Making the State Safe for the Market: The World Bank's World Development Report 1997' (1998) 22 Melbourne University LR 195; SJ Humphreys, *Theatre of the Rule of Law* (CUP, Cambridge 2010); Kinley (2009) 129ff.

[129] See eg P Uvin, *Human Rights and Development* (Kumarian Press, Bloomfield, CT 2004).

[130] See eg Petersmann (2002) 621, 630.

On the other hand, other strands within the human rights movement have sought to position human rights directly counter to the neoliberal economic project, and use human rights language to contest the market reforms carried out in its name. For those working within these other human rights traditions, the attempt to harness human rights to the neoliberal ideas appears as an illegitimate redefinition of the core values and orientation of the human rights project. Thus, the arguments described above have been variously described as a co-optation of human rights language; as a 'counter-insurgency' against popular criticisms of the neoliberal project;[131] as a 'merger and acquisition' of human rights language;[132] and as the imposition of a 'market friendly' human rights paradigm.[133] They contributed to scepticism about the ability of human rights language to address the issue of economic justice and other human rights violations caused by economic structures rather than individual agents.[134] At the same time, they also led to efforts to renew and revitalize those human rights traditions which understood unregulated free markets as a threat to human rights. Thus, in the second half of the 1990s, a literature began to emerge which drew attention to the negative effects of economic globalization and neoliberal free market reforms on human rights. The range of issues raised in this literature was broad: from the impact of trade liberalization on labour conditions, to the riots and attendant political repression which followed some structural adjustment programmes, to the impact of agricultural import liberalization on food security and availability, to the human rights abuses perpetrated by transnational corporations working in developing countries, to the erosion of the welfare state, among other issues.[135]

This is the context in which the contemporary 'trade and human rights' debate emerged. The core questions animating this debate were basically these: was trade liberalization in conflict with the promotion of human rights, or did they mutually support one another, and in what ways? Were the objectives and values of the trade and human rights regimes compatible, and in what circumstances? Were there conflicts between trade law and human rights law? Broadly speaking, three strands emerged in this debate. The first represented the continuation of classical liberal thinking about the relationship between trade and human rights. Writers in this strand painted a picture of mutual compatibility between the two regimes, based on an understanding of the trade regime as essentially being about the promotion of

[131] Gatthi (1999).

[132] P Alston, 'Resisting the Merger and Acquisition of Human Rights by Trade Law: A Reply to Petersmann' (2002) 13 EJIL 815.

[133] U Baxi, *The Future of Human Rights* (3rd edn, OUP, New Delhi 2008); See also D Schneiderman, 'Habermas, Market-friendly Human Rights, and the Revisibility of Economic Globalization' (2004) 8 Citizenship Studies 419.

[134] See eg MW Mutua, 'Human Rights and Powerlessness: Pathologies of Choice and Substance' (2008) 56 Buffalo L Rev 1027; D Kennedy, 'The International Human Rights Movement: Part of the Problem?' (2002) 15 Harvard Human Rights J 101; T Evans and J Hancock, 'Doing Something Without Doing Anything: International Human Rights Law and the Challenge of Globalisation' (1998) 2 Intl J of Human Rights 1; R Falk, 'Interpreting the Interaction of Global Markets and Human Rights' in A Brysk (ed), *Globalization and Human Rights* (University of California Press, Berkeley, CA 2002) 61.

[135] See generally Chs 3 and 4 below.

economic liberalism, and an understanding of the human rights regime as essentially being about the promotion of political liberalism. The second asserted the existence of conflicts between the two regimes. This was also based on an understanding of the trade regime as founded on classical economic liberalism, but it differed from the first in that it presupposed a vision of human rights influenced by social democratic traditions. Chapters 3 and 4 chronicle in some detail the emergence of this strand of thinking, and chart its impact on the international human rights regime. The third was similar to the first in that it also emphasized the mutual compatibility of the trade and human rights regimes, rather than conflicts between them. However, it did so on a different basis—namely, their shared foundation in the common ideology of embedded liberalism. This third strand was, and remains, significantly less visible than either of the first two. But it has been one of the purposes of this chapter to show that, historically speaking at least, it is well founded.

IV. Conclusion

For most careful observers of the trade and human rights regimes, the bulk of the historical material surveyed in this chapter will come as no surprise. The point of this chapter, then, is not to reveal new historical truths, but rather to call to mind some that are already well known. I do so for the specific reason that these truths are strangely obscured within the contemporary trade and human rights literature, and that our inattentiveness to them tends to lead us down some troubling paths, as described in later chapters. I will conclude, then, with four very simple observations which seem to me to flow directly from the material covered in this chapter. As will become clear, these four observations directly prepare the ground for the arguments that I make in Chapters 3 to 5.

The first observation is that the trade regime and the human rights regimes both have highly contested ideological foundations. In this chapter, I have described each regime as a terrain of conflict on which ideological struggles between various forms of liberalism, socialism, and other traditions of thought have been played out. During any particular historical period, both the trade and human rights regimes represent a contingent compromise between the partisans of each perspective—a compromise which evolves over time as their relative influence changes. Furthermore, each regime is composed of complex and layered social phenomena. While ideas associated with previously dominant ideological traditions may be sidelined and marginalized at any particular point, they leave important traces, which remain available for re-activation in future periods of internal contestation within each regime.[136] One core move which this chapter seeks to make, then, is to de-reify both the trade regime and the human rights regimes. As simple as this move is, it is surprisingly necessary. There is a very strong tendency within the vast bulk of contemporary literature on the trade

[136] See generally ATF Lang, 'Reflecting on Linkage: Cognitive and Institutional Change in the International Trading System' (2007) 70 MLR 523.

regime to treat it as if it were clearly and unproblematically founded upon classical liberal ideas about the beneficial nature of trade liberalization and market freedoms—as if it were self-evidently and necessarily an institution oriented by 'free market' values in the contemporary understanding of that term. In fact, it turns out that classical liberalism represents only one strand in the complex and contested ideological foundations of the trade regime, and one which only relatively recently achieved a degree of dominance. In addition, there is an equally strong tendency within much of the literature on the human rights regime to avoid direct discussion of the nature and implications of ideological contestation of the fundamentals of the human rights project. As Mutua has observed, 'human rights scholars and activists have been reluctant to ask uncomfortable questions about the philosophy and political purposes of the human rights movement', which he attributes to the fact that such questions 'are often taken as a mark of disloyalty to the movement'.[137] Both of these tendencies have, in my view, resulted in very powerful blind spots in our thinking about the role of international law and lawyers in the constitution and transformation of global economic governance, as explained in later chapters.

The second observation is that changes in the relative dominance of different ideological traditions within each regime are associated with major transformations in those regimes' operation and orientation. In other words, the normative orientation of (say) the trade regime—its normative character or 'politics'—is to a significant degree a function of the collective purposes and shared ideologies which animate that regime at any particular point in time. I am well aware, of course, that in making this claim I am taking a particular position within highly contested debates about the nature and dynamics of trade politics.[138] I will have more to say in Chapter 6 about my view of the political dynamics within the trade regime, and how that view relates to other theories of trade politics. For now it is enough to say that my engagement with the historical material set out above has partially aligned my thinking with that of others—such as Ruggie, Gerard and Victoria Curzon, Shonbaum, Winham, Goldstein, and Slaughter—who have emphasized the significant role of ideas, values, and ideologies in shaping the dynamics and operation of the international trade regime since its establishment at the end of the Second World War.[139] An implication of this second observation is that major re-orientations of the trade regime may not be possible without sustained contestation and destabilization of dominant ideas relating to the objectives of the regime, the purposes it serves, and the causal pathways by which it contributes to the achievement of those purposes. As I explain later, I am not suggesting that simply 're-imagining' these dominant ideas is sufficient to achieve transformational change. But I do think, in part on the basis of the historical material surveyed in this chapter,[140] that such a re-imagining will normally be a

[137] Mutua (2009) 906.

[138] eg H Milner, 'The Political Economy of International Trade' (1999) 2 Annual Review of Political Science 91.

[139] See generally Ch 6, pp 177ff.

[140] Though in part also on the basis of the observations in Ch 6 below, and the further historical material reviewed in Chs 7 and 8 below.

necessary condition of change, in the sense that unchallenged dominant ideas can act as an important practical obstacle to it. This is a crucial claim on which much of the remainder of my argument rests.

Thirdly, the relationship between the trade and human rights regimes is in large part a function of the ideological configuration of each at any particular point in time. As noted above, the mutual isolation of the two regimes in their first decades was enabled and produced by the common commitment of the dominant players in each to the politics of welfare liberalism. Then, as these embedded liberal foundations were challenged and destabilized with the rising power of developing countries and their new ideas about the dynamics of the international economic order, a new and more conflictual relationship between the regimes partially emerged. Attempts were made to redefine the human rights project, and to harness it to the project of challenging the international trading system. The rise of neoliberal thought, and resistance to it, then inaugurated a third chapter in the story of the relations between the two regimes, as the trading system became temporarily linked to neoliberal ideas, while various forms of resistance to neoliberalism gradually established a home of sorts in the human rights regime.

This third observation leads directly to the fourth, which is perhaps the most important. The story told in this chapter should sensitize us to the fact that claims about the nature of the relationship between the trade and human rights regimes are necessarily also interventions into the political struggles *internal* to each regime.[141] Claims about the relationship between the trade and human rights regimes, in other words, are never solely empirical claims, as if that relationship is simply there to be 'discovered' or observed. They are also political interventions which—to the extent that they become generally accepted wisdom—have an effect on ongoing struggles to define the constitutive ideological foundations of each system, and they should be understood as such. The claims heard in the 1970s about the obstacles which the international trading system created to the enjoyment of human rights in the developing world were part and parcel of an attempt to reshape the human rights regime in the interests of the developing world. Later claims about the mutual compatibility of trade and human rights were similarly an attempt to re-assert a liberal vision of human rights, in which civil and political rights were combined with economic freedoms as the highest priority of human rights promotion and protection. Contemporary claims about conflicts between economic globalization and human rights can also clearly be understood as an effort to resist this attempt to redefine human rights along neoliberal lines.

While I think this is relatively well recognized—at least implicitly—in relation to the human rights regime, I do not think it is at all well understood that claims about the relationship between trade and human rights *also* have an important effect on struggles to define the normative orientation of the trade regime. More specifically, contemporary claims that there are conflicts between 'free trade' and 'human rights'

[141] This is not just an historical reality but a logical necessity: to describe a relationship between two regimes, after all, necessarily involves taking a position on the contested question of what the values and objectives of each regime are.

tend in my view to reinforce and naturalize the dominance of a particular conception of the nature and purpose of the trade regime. It is incumbent upon participants in the trade and human rights debate to understand, and take responsibility for, these constitutive effects of their interventions. I will return to this observation later. For now, though, it is necessary to continue the historical story by looking in more detail at the period at the end of the twentieth century during which the contemporary trade and human rights debate was born. That is the task of the next chapter.

3

The Global Justice Movement

This chapter, and the next, focus on the immediate background to the contemporary trade and human rights debate, focusing on the years from roughly the mid-1980s to the early 2000s. My aim in these chapters is to illustrate the fundamental transformation that occurred as local political struggles around trade liberalization were first internationalized with the emergence of the global justice movement, and then legalized as they were projected into the spheres and institutions of international politics. In short, debates about the fairness and defensibility of neoliberal programmes of economic reform were transformed in this process into debates about how to achieve coherence in a fragmented international legal order. I show how this transformation has significantly affected the contribution that international law and international lawyers have made to the construction and contestation of global economic governance.

The chapter is structured in two sections. In the first section, I show how the experience of trade liberalization in different countries and regions across the world in the 1980s and 1990s led to a variety of locally specific political struggles around trade across North America, Latin America, Western Europe, and parts of Asia and Africa. I also show how, from the middle of the 1990s to around 2001, these local political struggles came together as part of a broader movement against neoliberal economic globalization (which, following terminology generally preferred within the movement itself, I will call the 'global justice movement'), and began to focus their critical attention on the World Trade Organization. The second section then describes the social construction of trade as a human rights issue. I illustrate the way that some of the NGOs within this movement began to use human rights language as a way of framing and articulating their criticisms of trade liberalization and international trade law. I also ask why it was that human rights seemed to many within the global justice movement to be a useful language of resistance to what they saw as a global neoliberal economic agenda, and why it came to be adopted as such.

I. Mobilization against free trade in the 1980s and 1990s

The civil society protests at the Seattle Ministerial meeting of the WTO in December 1999 are often cited as the birthplace of modern activism around international trade and the WTO. These protests, however, represented the coming together of a number of movements which had been collectively mobilizing around trade since the 1980s. These movements grew up relatively independently in countries from both the developed and developing world, and involved many groups energized by trade issues for the first time.

A. Trade activism in North America and Europe prior to Seattle

One strand of trade activism was born in Canada around the negotiation and domestic implementation of the Canada-US Free Trade Agreement (CUSFTA) in the second half of the 1980s. In 1984, the conservative Mulroney government had come to power on a platform of transforming the Canadian welfare state just as Reagan and Thatcher were doing in the United States and the United Kingdom. Alongside this domestic economic agenda, Mulroney also prioritized the pursuit of a free trade agreement with the United States as a central part of his government's economic and foreign policy platform early in his first term. The result was a strong link in the Canadian political imagination between the pursuit of free trade agreements on the one hand, and the broader neoliberal economic reforms characteristic of the period on the other. National debate around the proposed CUSFTA therefore took on the character of a struggle to maintain the wider social compact on which the Canadian welfare state has historically been founded.[1]

Canadian resistance to the CUSFTA emerged from numerous quarters. First, part of the impetus came from economic nationalists concerned about what they saw as the tendency of economic integration to erode Canada's sovereignty and cultural identity, as well as to undermine its extensive social safety nets.[2] Their immediate agenda was to secure Canadian control over the Canadian economy.[3] Nationalism of this sort had an established pedigree in Canadian politics—the economic nationalist Committee for an Independent Canada (CIC), for example, had been established as early as 1970. A second strand was the Canadian labour movement, which was also heavily involved in organizing opposition to the CUSFTA. With Canadian labour protections significantly stronger than those in the United States, one concern was that free trade across Canada's southern border would lead Canadian firms to relocate to the United States. Furthermore, with the public sector under pressure from the Conservative government's push to downsize government, public sector workers' unions saw in the CUSFTA a dangerous lever to further erode the public provision of essential services and promote privatization. Canadian women's movements also

[1] See generally on the emergence of civil society activism around trade in Canada: JM Ayres, 'Political Process and Popular Protest: The Mobilization against Free Trade in Canada' (1996) 55 American J of Economics and Sociology 473–88; JM Ayres, *Defying Conventional Wisdom: Political Movements and Popular Contention against North American Free Trade* (University of Toronto Press, Toronto 1998); R Bantjes, *Social Movements in a Global Context: Canadian Perspectives* (Canadian Scholars' Press, Toronto 2007) 327ff.

[2] JM Ayres, 'Transnational Political Processes and Contention Against the Global Economy' in J Smith and H Johnston (eds), *Globalization and Resistance: Transnational Dimensions of Social Movements* (Rowman & Littlefield Publishers, Lanham, MD 2002) 195; Bantjes (2007) 327ff.

[3] Ayres (1998) 32.

emerged as a third important strand within the Canadian anti-free trade coalition. As Macdonald observes, there had long been a strong socialist strand within the Canadian feminist movement, which—unlike its liberal counterpart south of the border—proved receptive to activism on economic issues such as trade.[4] Women's groups such as the National Action Committee on the Status of Women concentrated, for example, on the potential negative effects of the CUSFTA on women workers in manufacturing industries, including immigrant workers in the garment industry.

Fourthly, environmental groups such as the Canadian Wildlife Federation and the Canadian Environmental Law Association also joined the movement against the CUSFTA. These groups were keen to protect Canada's relatively strong environmental protection regime from what they saw as US pressure to deregulate, whether through regulatory harmonization directly pursued through the CUSFTA, or through the more general downward pressure on regulation that was thought to arise from the freeing of cross-border trade and investment.[5] Fifthly, these groups were joined and supported by farmers' groups and agriculture lobbies, such as the National Farmers Union. Farmers' groups combined a concern with the impact of open trade on Canadian family farms, with a concern for the preservation of strong environmental regulation.[6] Sixthly, Canadian religious communities were involved in the CUSFTA campaign through such organizations as the Churches' Coalition on Economic Justice.[7] Canadian churches proved to be a significant source of resistance to neoliberal economic policy generally, in part because of their frontline role as charities working with those adversely affected by that policy. But their concern with trade was more internationalist in origin: the Catholic church in particular had deep connections to social movements in the developing world, and through these channels had become sensitized to the destabilizing effects that trade liberalization had had in many developing countries over the 1980s. I will say more about this below. Finally, there were also a large number of smaller and somewhat less significant players in this early trade campaign, including indigenous peoples' networks, and peace activists, as well as Canadian publishers and academics.[8]

The Canadian anti-CUSFTA coalition was therefore strikingly diverse, going well beyond the types of import-competing producer lobbies that are traditionally

[4] L MacDonald, 'Globalization and Social Movements: Comparing Women's Movements' Responses to NAFTA in Mexico, the USA and Canada' (2002) 4 Intl Feminist J of Politics 151–72.

[5] SA Aaronson, *Taking Trade to the Streets: The Lost History of Public Efforts to Shape Globalization* (University of Michigan Press, Ann Arbor, MI 2001) 112.

[6] One chronology of NFU activism around trade and other issues can be found at National Farmers Union, 'The National Farmers Union: Fighting for the family farm over 30 years' (2001) <http://www.nfu.ca/nfuhistory3.pdf> accessed 15 February 2011.

[7] See Episcopal Commission for Social Affairs, 'Ethical Reflections on the Economic Crisis' in EF Sheridan (ed), *Do Justice! The Social Teaching of the Canadian Catholic Bishops* (Jesuit Centre for Social Faith and Justice, Toronto 1987) 399–408; Bantjes (2007) 329.

[8] Ayres (1996) 476; Bantjes (2007) 332; M Atwood, 'Blind Faith and Free Trade' in R Nader, et al (eds), *The Case Against 'Free Trade': GATT, NAFTA, and the Globalization of Corporate Power* (Earth Island Press, San Francisco, CA 1993); M Edelman, 'Transnational Peasant and Farmer Movements and Networks' in H Anheier, M Glasius, and M Kaldor (eds), *Global Civil Society* (OUP, Oxford 2003).

associated with political advocacy against trade. But despite this diversity of substantive agendas, a unified frame for the campaign coalesced over time, which framed the CUSFTA as a threat to the unique progressive Canadian social compact, with its heavy emphasis on social welfare, strong labour protections, generous unemployment insurance, and its commitment to social and environmental regulation. At the same time, the coalition was knit together by a formidable organizational infrastructure. The Council of Canadians, associated most prominently with the names of Maude Barlow and Tony Clarke, was formed in 1985 in part precisely to contest the CUSFTA.[9] In addition, very early on, the Coalition against Free Trade was formed in Ontario, as well as La Coalition Québécoise d'Opposition au Libre-échange.[10] The Pro-Canada Network (a central coalition of coalitions) followed soon after in April 1987, and was the primary locus of opposition to the CUSFTA until the agreement's implementation in 1988, providing a centre for the creation, publication, and dissemination of educational and analytical literature on free trade to activist groups.

Although this coalition of actors ultimately failed in their bid to defeat the CUSFTA, the movement born in this early struggle has proved to be an enduring one. Individuals and organizations initially mobilized on trade issues during this period remain important voices in contemporary debates, and form the nucleus of a strong and growing constellation of Canadian civil society organizations which are among the most engaged in global debates around trade—such as the Council of Canadians, Common Frontiers, Pro-Canada Network, Polaris Institute, Canadian Center for Policy Alternatives, Canadian Council for International Cooperation, Rights and Democracy, Public Service Alliance of Canada, and the Canadian Labour Congress. Their work continues to play an important role in setting the agenda for contemporary trade activism. Furthermore, the substantive issues raised in this initial activism around the CUSFTA—the erosion of social protections and standards of working conditions, threats to environmental and other regulatory standards, the privatization of public services, the impact of trade liberalization on farming communities—have similarly had a lasting influence on the priorities and preoccupations of trade advocacy in subsequent decades.

It was very soon after the end of the CUSFTA campaign that the next stage of North American integration—the negotiation of the North American Free Trade Agreement (NAFTA) between the United States, Canada, and Mexico—drew the attention of this energized and enthusiastic Canadian coalition. Drawing on all the intellectual, organizational, and political work of the previous campaign, Canadian groups began actively seeking to build transnational coalitions with like-minded groups within the United States to contest NAFTA. They discovered an emergent movement against free trade growing within domestic US politics, which in many ways mirrored the basic contours of the Canadian network, albeit with some important additions and modifications. This movement was already energized not

[9] Bantjes (2007) 328. [10] Ayres (2002) 195.

only about NAFTA, but also about the Uruguay Round of GATT negotiations, both of which were being conducted at the same time in the late 1980s and early 1990s.

One very prominent voice in the US movement was Ralph Nader and his consumer advocacy organization, Public Citizen.[11] Public Citizen had been established in 1971, and over time had developed a strong anti-corporate stance in its approach to consumer issues. When that organization came to be interested in trade agreements around the middle of the 1980s, it was on the basis that such agreements 'increased business powers against workers and consumers'.[12] Public Citizen claimed, for example, that the GATT Standards Code—a precursor to new regulatory disciplines negotiated during the WTO's Uruguay Round[13]—opened US consumer and environmental protection legislation to challenge by other countries, acting on behalf of foreign business interests. Nader and his group pointed to a number of regulatory measures concerning the safety of cars, milk, and other foods which had been subject to challenge in some form through the development of international trade law.[14] The GATT's first *Tuna/Dolphin* decision in 1991 (formally initiated in 1990),[15] which explicitly subjected US environmental legislation to foreign challenge, intensified these concerns, and drew the attention of environmental groups such as the Sierra Club, and Friends of the Earth.[16] It was at this point that environmentalists were clearly enjoined in debates around trade in the United States, and environmental groups came to be among the most vocal in the growing coalition against NAFTA. As in Canada, then, one fear about trade agreements in the United States was their potential to undermine national regulatory freedom. Unlike in Canada, however, where trade agreements were framed as a threat to the welfare state, in the United States they were framed as an encroachment on American sovereignty, and as a reflection of the growing political power of 'big business'.

This anti-corporate orientation was shared by another important strand of the growing US coalition against trade, namely farmers' networks. The key mover in this context was the Minnesota-based Institute for Agriculture and Trade Policy (IATP),[17] which had been created in 1986 with Mark Ritchie at the helm. The 1980s had seen a great deal of turmoil in the US agricultural sector, as a combination of market-oriented policy reforms under Reagan and unusual patterns of world production combined to force many small farmers out of business.[18] The result

[11] See generally R Nader et al (eds), *The Case Against 'Free Trade': GATT, NAFTA, and the Globalization of Corporate Power* (Earth Island Press, San Francisco, CA 1993).

[12] Aaronson (2001) 121.

[13] See Ch 8, pp 250–52.

[14] See Nader (1993).

[15] Panel Report, *United States—Restrictions on Imports of Tuna*, (unadopted, 3 September 1991) BISD 39S/155 (DS21/R).

[16] R O'Brien et al, *Contesting Global Governance: Multilateral Economic Institutions and Global Social Movements* (CUP, Cambridge 2000) 146.

[17] Aaronson (2001) 142ff.

[18] See M Ritchie, 'Agricultural Trade Liberalization: Implications for Sustainable Agriculture' in R Nader et al (eds), *The Case Against 'Free Trade': GATT, NAFTA, and the Globalization of Corporate Power* (Earth Island Press, San Francisco, CA 1993).

was a major transformation of agricultural production: the consolidation of smaller farms into larger agribusiness, the further mechanization and intensification of production methods, and the increasing use of chemicals and pesticides. The IATP was created to give a voice to small family farms and farmers, to defend smaller-scale, greener, and healthier farming practices against the emergence of 'factory farms'. It was not opposed in principle to the major tools of agricultural protectionism used at that time in the United States—prominently including large subsidy programmes—but felt that they favoured large agribusinesses over smaller farmers. The focus of this organization was therefore on maintaining high food safety and environmental standards in the agricultural sector, which were understood to be the strengths of small-scale agricultural production, and which were perceived to be under threat in the deregulatory climate of domestic US politics at the time.

Farmers' networks were among the most prominent voices not just on NAFTA, but also on the GATT Uruguay Round. As GATT negotiators in the Uruguay Round began to discuss the reduction of trade barriers in agriculture, small farmers' networks and organizations such as the IATP began to organize GATT protests. Working in concert with other organizations interested in agricultural issues from the United States, Canada, Europe, and globally—such as the American Agricultural Movement, the League of Rural Voters, Community Nutrition Institute, Canadian National Farmers Union, National Family Farm Coalition, and others—farmers' networks managed to organize a protest of around 30,000 people at a Brussels meeting of GATT negotiators in 1990.[19] As public interest began to turn to the NAFTA negotiations in the early 1990s, networks of US-based small farmers began to turn with them, bringing with them a specific preoccupation about the threat which trade agreements posed to domestic health and food safety laws.

Labour groups were also important within the US coalition against NAFTA and the GATT. For organized labour, the substantive concerns were very similar to those described above in relation to the CUSFTA, relating to the loss of jobs through the movement of manufacturing outside the United States, and to the lowering of labour standards as capital became more mobile (and therefore more politically powerful) within North America. Powerful union groups such as the AFL-CIO and UAW voiced early opposition to NAFTA within the domestic US context.[20] Mexico's participation in NAFTA raised additional concerns, relating to the poor treatment of workers in Mexico's *maquiladora* export processing industries. US-based labour groups protested about such treatment on the basis of solidarity. Furthermore,

[19] TG Kidder, 'Networks in Transnational Labor Organizing' in S Khagram, JV Riker, and K Sikkink (eds), *Restructuring World Politics: Transnational Social Movements, Networks and Norms* (University of Minnesota Press, Minneapolis, MN 2002) 278–80; J Brecher, 'The Hierarchs' New World Order—and Ours' in J Brecher, J Brown Childs and J Cutler (eds), *Global Visions: Beyond the New World Order* (South End Press, Boston, MA 1993) 3–16; M Ritchie, 'Cross-border Organizing' in J Mander and E Goldsmith (eds), *The Case Against the Global Economy: And for a Turn Toward the Local* (Sierra Club Books, San Francisco, CA 1996) 494–500; M Edelman, 'Peasant–farmer movements, third world peoples, and the Seattle protests against the World Trade Organization' (2009) 33 *Dialectical Anthropology* 109, 111.

[20] Aaronson (2001) ch 5, esp 136ff.

activism from labour groups around Mexican labour standards also helped to mobilize student activism on US campuses around 'sweatshop' issues, including organizations such as the United Students against Sweatshops and Global Exchange, the latter becoming a central figure in the global justice movement later on.[21]

Finally, another important voice in the anti-NAFTA coalition were US-based development NGOs such as the Development GAP. In part, these groups were concerned with the issues just mentioned, concerning wages and labour conditions in Mexican export industries. But this was part of a more general programme of advocacy to counter the export-oriented, neoliberal model of development which had become entrenched in the developing world over the course of the 1980s, and which Mexican participation in NAFTA seemed to embody. As we shall see in a moment, this agenda reflected a growing wave of activism emerging out of the developing world at the same time, and was strongly connected to the work of a number of Southern-based development NGOs, such as Focus on the Global South and the Third World Network (TWN), which had close ties to the United States.

The US-based network, then, consisted of a shifting coalition of consumer groups, environmental activists, farmers, labour and development groups, and others, each with their own particular concerns about free trade agreements. During the early 1990s, numerous networks began to spring up involving these groups. In 1990, a group of organizations, including Friends of the Earth, the National Farmers Union, Public Citizen, Development GAP, International Ladies Garment Workers Union, the Institute for Policy Studies, and others, came together to study regulatory issues around the GATT.[22] Out of this group grew two other networks: MODTLE (Mobilization on Development, Trade, Labour and the Environment), and the Citizens' Trade Campaign, both founded in 1992. The former worked closely with the Canadian groups mentioned above, and was replaced by the Alliance for Responsible Trade in 1993. As in the earlier fight against the CUSFTA, these groups were ultimately unsuccessful in blocking the coming into effect of NAFTA in 1994. Nevertheless, they continued to gather support and momentum over the course of numerous North American trade-related campaigns during the 1990s, such as the campaigns around the granting of 'fast-track' authority in 1997 and 1998, as well as around the granting of MFN status to China by the US government.

Resistance to NAFTA was not limited to activism in Canada and the United States. Around the same time as these events, a similarly broad coalition was developing in Mexico to mirror those in the United States and Canada—including the Red Mexicana de Acción frente al Libre Comercio (RMALC), a national network of 'labour unions, human rights groups, environmentalists, peasants and

[21] RJS Ross, 'From Anti-Sweatshop, to Global Justice, to Anti-War: Student Participation in Globalization Protests' in B Podobnik and T Reifer (eds), *Transforming Globalization: Challenges and Opportunities in the Post 9/11 Era* (Brill, Boston, MA 2005) 111–21; JS Juris, *Networking Futures: The Movements Against Corporate Globalization* (Duke University Press, Durham, NC 2008) 40.

[22] Aaronson (2001) 122–3

indigenous groups and academics'.[23] This network emerged in somewhat different political circumstances, however, and is best understood in the context of resistance to neoliberal development strategies in other parts of the Americas in the 1980s and late 1990s, discussed below.

Across the Atlantic, a similar European coalition of NGOs and advocacy groups sprang up over the course of the 1990s, during the final years of the Uruguay Round of GATT negotiations. It contained many of the same strands as in the North American movements just described. First, the most visible and vocal actors were farmers' groups, among which the French farmers' union Confédération Paysanne, formed in 1987, is particularly notable as it has remained an influential and at times colourful voice in anti-trade protests since that time.[24] Farmers' groups have been actively engaged in protest against the inclusion of agriculture in the Uruguay Round of GATT negotiations from an early stage, with probably the most famous demonstration occurring in Brussels at a meeting of trade ministers in December 1990.[25] But farmers were also the majority participants in a similar-sized protest in Strasbourg in 1992, as well as a somewhat smaller march in Geneva in December 1993 to mark the conclusion of the Uruguay Round. Secondly, consumer groups were also actively involved in monitoring the Uruguay Round negotiations, primarily through umbrella groups such as the Bureau Européen des Unions de Consommateurs, and the International Organization of Consumers Unions.[26] While these bodies were interested in many aspects of trade negotiations, food safety regulation was of particular concern for them throughout the 1990s, especially in the light of the transatlantic trade dispute over hormone-treated beef ongoing since the 1980s.

Thirdly, some environmental groups were also mobilized around the Uruguay Round negotiations in their final years. The most prominent voice here was the World Wide Fund for Nature (WWF), which published a number of papers on trade issues around this time, and organized a protest against the proposed Agreement on Technical Barriers to Trade in February 1993. Part of the WWF's advocacy was spurred by the GATT's first *Tuna/Dolphin* decision in the early 1990s, and to that extent it mirrored the agenda of North American environmental groups described earlier. But, interestingly, WWF was also concerned with the impact of agricultural liberalization on sustainable farming practices in the South, having heard and taken

[23] RP Korzeniewicz and WC Smith, *Protest and Collaboration: Transnational Civil Society Networks and the Politics of Summitry and Free Trade in the Americas* (North-South Center Press, University of Miami, FL 2001) 13.

[24] Edelman (2009) 109, 115 and generally.

[25] ibid 111; J Croome, *Reshaping the World Trading System: A History of the Uruguay Round* (Kluwer Law International, The Netherlands 1995) 276.

[26] Bureau Européen des Unions de Consommateurs (BEUC) News, No 65 (June 1987); J Murray, 'The GATT negotiations: A statement from BEUC' (Paper presented at the 13th World Congress of the International Organization of Consumer Unions, 8 July 1991); P Mehta and A Davison, *Trading up: The GATT agreement and developing countries* (International Organisation of Consumers Unions, London 1993); P Evans, *Unpacking the GATT: A step by step guide to the Uruguay Round* (International Organisation of Consumers Unions, London 1994).

up some of the issues raised by Southern peasant movements, considered below.[27] It also opposed agricultural protection in the industrialized North, in direct opposition to the farmers' groups above. The WWF remains a leading voice among environmental groups working on trade issues, and has since been joined by others such as Friends of the Earth Europe, and the International Union for Conservation of Nature.

Fourthly, development NGOs have played an important role in European NGO networks around trade—probably more so than in North America. As Wilkinson has chronicled,[28] a number of associations of European development NGOs were mobilized over the course of the Uruguay Round, such as the Association of Protestant Development Organizations in Europe (APRODEV), the International Cooperation for Development and Solidarity Europe (EURO-CIDSE), and European Solidarity Towards Equal Participation of People (EUROSTEP), working primarily through the NGO-GATT Steering Committee established at an UNCTAD NGO conference in 1998. The work of these groups largely reflected and supported the negotiating positions of (some) developing countries in the GATT negotiations themselves, revolving around traditional GATT issues such as the phasing out of the Multifibre Arrangement, the reduction of agricultural subsidies, as well as resistance to the proposed TRIPS and TRIMS agreements. Since the Uruguay Round, development NGOs have been particularly active in Britain. The Trade Justice Movement, for example, prominently included British development NGOs such as the World Development Movement, Christian Aid, Oxfam, Action Aid, and the Catholic Institute for International Relations.[29] I will have more to say about these groups below. Fifthly, and finally, it is necessary to mention ATTAC, a network of socialist, labour, and other left-wing groups and individuals mobilized against neoliberal globalization. Established in France in 1997, it has since taken its place among the leading voices in the European global justice movement.[30]

[27] See eg K Watkins and M Windfuhr, *Agriculture in the Uruguay Round: Implications for Sustainable Development in Developing Countries* (WWF Discussion Paper, Gland, Switzerland 1995); A Clarke, *The GATT, Environmental Protection and Sustainable Development* (WWF Discussion Paper, Gland, Switzerland 1991).

[28] See generally MD Wilkinson, 'Lobbying for Fair Trade: Northern Non-Governmental Development Organisations, the European Community and the GATT Uruguay Round' (1996) 17 Third World Q 251.

[29] See generally C Rootes and C Saunders, 'The Global Justice Movement in Great Britain' in D della Porta (ed), *The Global Justice Movement: Cross-national and Transnational Perspectives* (Paradigm Publishers, Boulder, CO 2007); J Randel, *NGO Campaigning on Trade Issues: Perspectives from Europe* (Development Initiatives for Christian Aid and CIIR, London 1995) 56.

[30] For the origins of ATTAC generally, see B Cassen, 'On the Attack' (2003) 19 New Left Rev 41–60; V Ruggiero, '"Attac": A Global Social Movement?' (2002) 29 Social Justice 48–60; F Kolb, 'The Impact of Transnational Protest on Social Movement Organizations: Mass Media and the Making of ATTAC Germany' in D della Porta and S Tarrow (eds), *Transnational Protest and Global Activism* (Rowman & Littlefield Publishers, Oxford 2005) 95–120; M Ancelovici, 'Organizing against Globalization: The Case of ATTAC in France' (2002) 30 Politics and Society 427–63; D della Porta, M Andretta, L Mosca, and H Reiter (eds), *Globalization from Below: Transnational Activists and Protest Networks* (University of Minnesota Press, Minneapolis, MN 2006) 32.

B. Trade and neoliberal development in Central and South America

At the same time as these developments were occurring in the industrialized world, activism around trade liberalization was also growing in Central and South America, sparked by the debt crises of the first half of the 1980s, and the economic reform programmes which followed in their wake. Faced with unmanageable debt burdens, governments in the region began to cut expenditure in the areas of welfare spending, consumer subsidies, and the provision of social services. The result in some contexts was a major increase in the costs of basic items such as energy, food, and transport, at the same time as reductions in pensions and in the quantity and quality of services such as housing, education, and health care. The privatization of state-owned enterprises was also undertaken in some areas, in part in order to generate liquidity to pay down government debt, and in part to provide an impetus for the development of the private sector. Again, this profoundly affected costs and conditions of living for a large part of the population, as public sector wages and jobs were reduced, and the costs of services provided by these newly privatized entities were marketized. Moreover, these measures to reduce the size and scope of government expenditure were often combined at the same time with attempts to liberalize the economy more generally, as part of a new development strategy focused on private sector development and global economic integration. These liberalizing reforms particularly affected the agricultural sector. On the consumption side, they led to increased penetration of imported foods in domestic markets. In the context of simultaneous currency devaluations and the removal of domestic subsidies for items such as fuel, fertilizer, and transport, this sometimes led to large increases in the costs of basic foodstuffs. On the production side, agricultural production was re-oriented away from the production of basic foods for domestic markets and towards export production, particularly of non-traditional products such as fruit, vegetables, oilseeds, and livestock. This move to export-oriented production tended generally to favour large-scale, capital-intensive production methods, with the result that many peasants and small farmers found themselves removed from their land or otherwise forced out of business.

As these and other policy changes were gradually implemented across the continent during the 1980s and 1990s, they gave rise to new social movements specifically designed to criticize and resist the development model from which they derived their impetus. Part of this resistance consisted of a series of 'austerity protests', first of all during the second half of the 1980s and early 1990s (especially in Peru, Chile, Bolivia, Venezuela, and Argentina), and then again from the late 1990s, with protests in Ecuador in 2000, Argentina in 2001, and Bolivia in 2003 and 2005.[31] While

[31] J Walton, 'Debt, Protest, and the State in Latin America' in S Eckstein (ed), *Power and Popular Protest: Latin American Social Movements* (University of California Press, Los Angeles, CA 1989); J Walton and J Shefner, 'Latin America: Popular Protest and the State' in J Walton and D Seddon (eds), *Free Markets & Food Riots: The Politics of Global Adjustment* (Blackwell, Oxford 1994); World Development Movement (WDM), 'States of Unrest III: Resistance to IMF and World Bank policies in poor countries' (April 2003) <http://www.wdm.org.uk/sites/default/files/statesofunrest319042003.pdf>

many of these protests were focused on issues other than international trade, they did create a political context for the development of resistance to neoliberal globalization generally. In addition, three specific strands of social activism emerged out of this context which have had an important impact on global advocacy specifically around international trade.

The first and probably the most important development was the emergence of peasant networks, or rural social movements, which have rightly been identified as among the most resilient and dynamic actors contesting neoliberal globalization in Latin America.[32] Amongst the most significant of these peasant movements were the Brazilian Landless Rural Workers Movement (MST), the Zapatista rebellion in Mexico, the Confederación de Nacionalidades Indigenas del Ecuador (CONAIE), and the National Confederation of Communities Affected by Mining (CONA-CAMI)—but there are many others.[33] Substantively, these groups originally formed around a wide variety of issues, including protesting at the impact on peasant farmers of large-scale development projects such as dams and mines, as well as advocating agrarian reform and access to productive land for dispossessed farmers and workers. But they have also been very active in championing an alternative model of organized agriculture, based on sustainability, food security, local production, and resistance to modern industrial agriculture.[34] This has placed them in direct opposition to programmes of agricultural liberalization, and to the trade agreements through which such liberalization was seen to be carried out at the international and regional level. These networks have therefore emerged as some of the most engaged civil society groups working in and around international agricultural trade.[35]

The second important context for specifically trade-related activism was the development of export processing zones (EPZs), especially in Central America and the Caribbean basin. The low wages, lack of job security, and working conditions which were prevalent in some of these zones drew the attention of local labour groups in countries such as Nicaragua, Mexico, Honduras, and the Dominican

accessed 15 February 2011; P Almeida and H Johnston, 'Neoliberal Globalization and Popular Movements in Latin America' in H Johnston and P Almeida (eds), *Latin American Social Movements: Globalization, Democratization and Transnational Networks* (Rowman & Littlefield Publishers, Lanham, MD 2006) 3–18; J Shefner, G Pasdirtz, and C Blad, 'Austerity Protests and Immiserating Growth in Mexico and Argentina' in H Johnston and P Almeida (eds), *Latin American Social Movements: Globalization, Democratization and Transnational Networks* (Rowman & Littlefield Publishers, Lanham, MD 2006); ME Keck and K Sikkink, *Activists Beyond Borders: Advocacy Networks in International Politics* (Cornell University Press, Ithaca, NY 1998). Of course these protests did not just take place in Latin America, over 50 'IMF riots' occurred throughout Latin America, the Caribbean, the Middle-East, Africa, and Eastern Europe in the period between 1985 and 1992: see Walton and Seddon (1994).

[32] CD Deere and FS Royce, 'Introduction: The Rise and Impact of National and Transnational Rural Social Movements in Latin America' in CD Deere and FS Royce (eds), *Rural Social Movements in Latin America: Organizing for Sustainable Livelihoods* (University of Florida Press, Gainesville, FL 2009) 1–29, 5; J Seoane and E Taddei, 'From Seattle to Porto Alegre: The Anti-Neoliberal Globalization' (2002) 50 Current Sociology 99–122.

[33] Deere and Royce (2009) 4.

[34] A Starr, *Naming the Enemy: Anti-Corporate Movements Confront Globalization* (Zed Books, London 2000) 59.

[35] See further pp 74ff below

Republic.[36] Importantly, since the labour force in many EPZs was largely feminized, civil society groups focused on gender and women's rights were among the most active on these issues. Women's groups have been particularly adept at transnational organizing around labour rights issues, and in part as a consequence have played a large role in trade activism in the Americas generally.[37]

Finally, the third strand of particular relevance to the present story has to do with trade unions and others opposed to privatization in Latin American countries. In fact, as a number of authors have noted, trade unions and labour movements have—with a number of notable exceptions such as the Brazilian Central Única dos Trabalhadore (CUT)—not generally been the most powerful and dynamic of civil society actors against neoliberalism in the region.[38] These unions emerged from the neoliberal reforms of the early 1980s with greatly reduced powers, and for a variety of reasons have struggled to regain them since.[39] One area in which they have been active, however, has been in organizing protests against the privatization of utilities and other public enterprises, such as in Bolivia in the first half of the 2000s (water utilities), and El Salvador between 1999 and 2003 (health care), as well as Brazil and Argentina. Although this strand of activism was initially quite separate from that relating to trade agreements, this changed when a connection was drawn in these circles in the early 2000s between trends towards privatization on one hand, and the liberalization disciplines in the WTO's General Agreement on Trade in Services (GATS) on the other.[40] At this point, those groups which had previously been primarily mobilized around issues of privatization also came to be part of global networks working on trade liberalization and trade agreements.

Trade issues and trade agreements became the focus of anti-neoliberal activism in the region in the context of the Free Trade Area of the Americas (FTAA), an effort at hemispheric economic integration by thirty American nations. These negotiations

36 J Bandy and J Bickham Mendez, 'A Place of Their Own? Women Organizers in the Maquilas of Nicaragua and Mexico' in H Johnston and P Almeida (eds), *Latin American Social Movements: Globalization, Democratization and Transnational Networks* (Rowman & Littlefield Publishers, Lanham, MD 2006) 131–44; V Carty, 'Transnational Labor Mobilizing in Two Mexican Maquiladoras' in H Johnston and P Almeida (eds), *Latin American Social Movements: Globalization, Democratization and Transnational Networks* (Rowman & Littlefield Publishers, Lanham, MD 2006) 215–29; D Jessup and ME Gordon, 'Organizing in Export Processing Zones: The Bibong Experience in the Dominican Republic' in ME Gordon and L Turner (eds), *Transnational Cooperation amongst Labour Unions* (Cornell University Press, Ithaca, NY 2000) 179–201; EC Brooks, *Unravelling the Garment Industry: transnational organizing and women's work* (University of Minnesota Press, Minneapolis, MN 2007); R Armbruster-Sandoval, 'Globalization and Transnational Labor Organizing: The Honduran Maquiladora Industry and the Kimi Campaign' (2003) 27 Social Science History 551.

37 L Macdonald, 'Gendering Transnational Social Movement Analysis: Women's Groups Contest Free Trade in the Americas' in J Bandy and J Smith (eds), *Coalitions Across Borders: Transnational Protest and Neoliberal Order* (Rowman & Littlefield Publishers, Lanham, MD 2005) 21–42; MacDonald (2002) 151–72; Kidder, 'Networks' in Khagram, Riker, and Sikkink (2002) 281–90.

38 Edelman (2009) 109, 112; Seoane and Taddei (2002) 99–122, 111.

39 See generally C Iranzo and T Patruyo, 'Trade Unionism and Globalization: Thoughts from Latin America' (2002) 50 Current Sociology 57–74.

40 See pp 97–9 below.

were sustained over a period of roughly ten years, from their inception in Miami in 1994, through a series of summits and Ministerial meetings in Santa Cruz (1996), Belo Horizonte (1997), Santiago (1998), San Jose (1999), Toronto (1999), Quebec (2001), and Miami (2003), with the aim of achieving a significant degree of hemispheric economic integration by 2005 (this deadline was ultimately not met). These negotiations rapidly caught the attention of civil society organizations and transnational advocacy networks throughout the Americas, and it was here that the North American trade networks described above joined forces with these Southern groups, as the FTAA became a lightning rod for opposition to neoliberal globalization generally.

The FTAA negotiations provided the impetus for the formation of a number of national and transnational coalitions among different civil society groups with an interest in trade. In Brazil, for example, organizations such as Associação Brasileira de Organizações Não-Governamentais and Federação de Órgãos para Assistência Social e Educacional, provided an early impetus for the formation of transnational coalitions against hemispheric economic integration.[41] Later, the Rede Brasileira pela Integração dos Povos also emerged as an important voice, with the support of these two groups. In Chile, the Alianza Chilena por un Comercio Justo y Responsable was initially formed in opposition to neoliberal reforms under Pinochet, but was involved in the FTAA campaign, and came to focus on the 'negative social, economic and environmental consequences of globalization via trade liberalization'.[42] In Argentina, a number of groups such as Foro de Consulta a la Sociedad Civil sobre el Ajuste Estructural and Dialógo 2000 also helped to generate public opposition to the FTAA. Within Central America, the Latin American Coordinating Group of Rural Organisations (CLOC) and the Association of Central American Peasant Organisations for Cooperation and Development (ASCODE)[43] also joined civil society networks against the FTAA. Many of these groups formally came together in March of 1999 to found the Alianza Social Continental (ASC), one of the key collective forums through which the civil society campaign against the FTAA was formulated. Substantively, the ASC proved to be a heterogenous and evolving mix of moderate reformist and more radically rejectionist voices in FTAA debates. It acted as an important forum for the formulation of alternative models of economic integration, based, for example, on the notion of sustainable development.[44]

Initially, these networks tended not to position themselves against free trade or economic integration in principle. Instead, they sought to integrate social issues into the project of economic integration. One central plank of their platform was the inclusion of labour rights in the FTAA negotiations, reflecting in part the role of labour movements in organizing popular resistance to the FTAA. This went hand in hand, furthermore, with arguments for the inclusion of environmental

[41] Korzeniewicz and Smith (2001) 14.
[42] ibid.
[43] See pp 75–6 below.
[44] S Anderson et al, 'Alternatives for the Americas' <http://www.web.net/comfront/alts4americas/eng/eng.html> accessed 15 February 2011.

norms and principles. In addition, the civil society debate around the FTAA was noteworthy also for its central focus on the question of participation, especially of historically marginalized groups, and its rejection of the 'anti-democratic character of agreements such as the FTAA'.[45] If the substantive issues raised by actors within the network were too diverse to be easily encapsulated within a single frame, all participants could at least agree on the need for greater civil society participation in the process. Enacting these claims, NGOs organized parallel meetings as counterparts to official summits, such as the Peoples' Summit of the Americas in Santiago in 1998.

C. Transnational organizing by rural social movements

Since their influence on the global justice movement has been so profound, especially in relation to trade, it is necessary to say something more about rural social movements from both the developed and developing world. As discussed above, networks of agricultural producers were among the first to mobilize around the Uruguay Round of international trade negotiations in Brussels in 1990. While these protests drew mostly Western European participants, there were also a number of other actors, including Canadian and US farmers' groups who sent about 100 participants across the Atlantic for the occasion.[46] In addition, there was a considerable East Asian presence, with more than 200 representatives of agricultural (mainly rice) producers from Korea and Japan in attendance. Indeed, over the course of the 1990s, East Asian rice producers proved to be very effective in mobilizing against international trade negotiations under the GATT and WTO. In December 1993, for example, Korean acquiescence to the Uruguay Round package of agreements caused major protests throughout that country from farmers, students, and religious and academic groups concerned with the plight of the small family rice producer, historically an important figure in Korean culture.[47] The lead up to the conclusion of the Uruguay Round saw equivalent protests within Japan, where rice has similarly sensitive cultural resonances.[48] Later in the decade, Korean and Japanese farmers continued to be a highly visible presence in the civil society protests at Seattle and subsequent WTO Ministerials, where they formed friendships and common cause with producers of rice, bananas, and other agricultural products from Southeast Asian countries such as Thailand, the Philippines, and Malaysia, who were concerned about agricultural liberalization and large corporate control of global agricultural production.[49]

[45] Alianza Social Continental (ASC), 'Final Declaration of the Summit: Peoples' Summit of the Americas' in R Feinberg and R Rosenberg (eds), *Civil Society and the Summit of the Americas: The 1998 Santiago Summit* (North-South Center Press, Miami, FL 1999).

[46] See p 66 above.

[47] TP Stewart (ed), *The GATT Uruguay Round: Negotiating History (1986–1994)* (Kluwer Law International, The Hague, The Netherlands 1999) 21.

[48] See generally CL Davis, *Food Fights over Free Trade: How International Institutions Promote Agricultural Trade Liberalization* (Princeton University Press, Princeton, NJ 2003) chs 4–6.

[49] Edelman (2009) 109, 120–1; see also P Routledge and A Cumbers, *Global Justice Networks: Geographies of transnational solidarity* (Manchester University Press, Manchester 2009) ch 5.

Agricultural producers and peasants were also organizing in India around the same time. The key organization here is the Karnatka State Farmers Association (or Karnatka Rajya Ryota Sangha (KRRS)), which, starting from 1992, successfully put another issue on the agenda of international trade activism. Their attention was focused on multinational biotechnology companies and seed producers who had begun to develop and claim intellectual property rights over certain seeds and other biological products.[50] An attempt by a US pharmaceutical company to patent products derived from the Indian neem tree caught Indian public attention in particular, and prompted the KRRS to raid the premises of Cargill, a large agribiotech company, in December 1992 and again in November 1993. The same organization successfully staged large-scale protests, including one which drew half a million participants in Bangalore in October 1993.[51] Importantly for the present story, their advocacy efforts were not just directed against multinational corporations, but also against what they saw as the imposition of Western intellectual property regimes on India and the rest of the developing world through the Uruguay Round, in the form of the Agreement on Trade-Related Aspects of Intellectual Property Rights (TRIPs). Leaders of the Indian peasant movement therefore became leading participants in global NGO trade activism around the end of the Uruguay Round, including at the December 1993 Geneva Ministerial at the conclusion of negotiations, and have since become significant players in transnational networks involved in the global justice movement.[52]

But it is the rural social movements of Latin America, introduced above, which have probably provided the greatest impetus for transnational organizing among peasant networks. Most famously, the indigenous Zapatista movement led an uprising in Mexico on New Year's Day 1994, timed to coincide with the coming into force of NAFTA, and in part consciously designed as the first step in building a broad transnational coalition against neoliberalism. News of the uprising was disseminated quickly by civil society organizations, including the North American trade coalitions described above, and directly inspired international 'encounters' in Chiapas (1996) and Barcelona (1997), as well as the creation of People's Global Action in Geneva in 1998. In addition to the Zapatistas, it was primarily the countries of the Central American isthmus (especially Honduras, Costa Rica, Nicaragua, El Salvador, and Panama) which developed as early focal points for transnational peasant organizing and mobilization against neoliberal programmes of adjustment in agriculture. The Food Security Training Program, funded by European donors in 1990, brought together peasant leaders from across Central America, and ultimately led to the formation of ASCODE in 1991, a prominent voice in regional politics over the course of the next several years.[53] But there were

[50] See generally V Shiva, *Protect or plunder?: understanding intellectual property rights* (Zed Books, London 2001).

[51] A Gupta, 'Peasants and Global Environmentalism' in N Haenn and RR Wilk (eds), *The Environment in Anthropology: A Reader in Ecology, Culture, and Sustainable Living* (New York University Press, New York, NY 2006) 302–24, 314

[52] ibid 315.

[53] Edelman (2003) 190

similar organizations emerging across all of the Americas around this time. As noted above, for example, the Brazilian Landless Rural Workers Movement (MST) also built a high profile programme on land reform issues,[54] and it was not long before a wider Latin American network was formed—CLOC, an organization established in 1994 by twenty-one countries, focused on 'food sovereignty, agrarian reform and indigenous rights'.[55]

A crucial development occurred in Mons, Belgium in April 1993, with the establishment of La Vía Campesina, a transnational network of peasant activists from the South and farmers' groups from the North.[56] Initially comprising forty-six member organizations, La Vía Campesina now boasts over 150 member organizations from over fifty countries from the Americas, Asia, Europe, and Africa. It has been a central mobilizing force in the global justice movement, dealing in particular with international trade issues, and played an important role in the Seattle protests against the WTO in 1999, as well as every major global protest since.[57] Later, members of La Vía Campesina took the lead with founders of the European anti-globalization network, ATTAC, in establishing the World Social Forum.[58]

As a result of the efforts of all of these groups, issues of international agricultural trade have taken their place firmly at the centre of progressive criticism of the international trading order. Importantly, however, the historical roots of this movement gave their proposed programme of agricultural reform at least three particular cultural and political inflections. First, the reorganization of agricultural production which this movement supports is understood and pursued broadly, as a means of preserving and protecting the ways of life of indigenous peoples. It is, in other words, part of a political agenda for indigenous rights, and for the protection of indigenous peoples from economic and political domination. Secondly, the claims of peasant groups relating to trade and agriculture are often closely related to activism around environmental and health issues. Thus La Vía Campesina and other farmers' groups have been active in campaigns against unsustainable agricultural practices and genetically modified foods, and in favour of organic and other sustainable farming practices. Thirdly, there is a strong anti-corporate orientation to their advocacy. Transnationalization of agricultural trade is fundamentally linked in this context to the emergence of highly industrialized production techniques, and a high degree of capital concentration in the sector. It is therefore the growing corporate control of agricultural production, just as much as international agricultural trade in itself, which these rural social movements seek to resist.

[54] Starr (2000) 59.
[55] Edelman (2003) 194.
[56] For the origins of La Vía Campesina, see AA Desmarais, 'Globalizing Peasants' in CD Deere and FS Royce, *Rural Social Movements in Latin America: Organizing for Sustainable Livelihoods* (University of Florida Press, Gainesville, FL 2009) 33–54; AA Desmarais, *La Vía Campesina: Globalization and the Power of Peasants* (Pluto Press, London 2007).
[57] Edelman (2009) 109, 114 and generally.
[58] See Cassen (2003) 41–60.

D. Aid and development NGOs

Finally, it is worth saying a few words about aid and development NGOs as another important strand of contemporary global trade activism, as some of the actors in this strand will prove to be influential in the next part of this chapter. At least initially, the bulk of the most important actors within this grouping were aid and charity organizations based in Western Europe, working on alleviating poverty in the Third World. Many of these were religiously affiliated, but not all, and they included Oxfam, Christian Aid, Brot für die Welt, the Church World Service, the World Council of Churches, NOVID, the World Development Movement, Action Aid, and the Catholic Institute for International Relations, among many others. From 1975, the International Coalition for Development Action (ICDA) was formed as an umbrella network, to help these organizations in their lobbying efforts concerning development issues. Almost from its inception, ICDA, along with the UN Non-Governmental Liaison Service (NGLS), was instrumental in organizing civil society participation in, and activity around, the quadrennial UNCTAD conference, starting with UNCTAD IV in Nairobi in 1975. Through this connection, this network of Northern aid and development NGOs was strongly influenced by the NIEO agenda being developed in UNCTAD at the time, discussed in Chapter 2. They began to lobby Northern governments on issues around the NIEO, including the need for greater aid flows, increased market access for developing country products, and commodity price stabilization measures, as well as structural change to the international financial system.[59]

A number of important developments occurred over the course of the 1980s and early 1990s. On one hand, as the momentum behind the NIEO waned, the agenda of these groups shifted somewhat. The debt crisis sweeping many parts of the developing world from the early 1980s led to advocacy on debt relief for poor countries—prefiguring the more recent Jubilee 2000 debt campaign by almost two decades.[60] In addition, at around the same time, a number of these organizations joined forces with environmental groups and nascent peasant movements to protest at the impact of large infrastructure development projects on the environment and the rights of indigenous peoples in the developing world.[61] In addition, with the turn to structural adjustment within the World Bank and the International Monetary Fund over the course of the 1980s, a great deal of attention began to be given

[59] Wilkinson (1996) 251; T Hill, 'UNCTAD and NGOs: A "Loyal Opposition"' <http://www.unsystem.org/ngls/english/factsheets/unctad_and_ngos.htm> accessed 15 February 2011.

[60] On which see A Pettifor, 'The economic bondage of debt—and the birth of a new movement' in L Amoore, *The Global Resistance Reader* (Routledge, New York, NY 2005)

[61] For a history, see R Wade, 'Greening the Bank: The Struggle over the Environment 1970–1995' in D Kapur, JP Lewis, and R Webb (eds), *The World Bank: Its First Half Century* (Volume 2, RR Donnelley and Sons Co, Crawfordsville, IN 1997); also PJ Nelson, 'Agendas, Accountability, and Legitimacy among Transnational Networks Lobbying the World Bank' in S Khagram, JV Riker and K Sikkink (eds), *Restructuring World Politics: Transnational Social Movements, Networks and Norms* (University of Minnesota Press, Minneapolis, MN 2002)

to what they saw as the negative social and development impacts of these policies. Then, in the first few years of the 1990s, development NGOs began activism relating to the Uruguay Round negotiations, as described above.[62]

On the other hand, at the same time as this shift in substantive issues was occurring, Northern-based development NGOs began to build links with other groups, in particular new development NGOs from the South. For example, over the course of the 1980s and early 1990s, NGO networks meeting around UNCTAD quadrennial meetings gradually began to include more and more Southern groups.[63] Prominent among these was the Malaysia-based Third World Network (TWN), established in 1984, which soon emerged as one of the key southern voices on issues of global trade and global economic justice.[64] Similarly, in the context of advocacy around the Uruguay Round, Northern NGOs went to some effort to work together with individuals and organizations from the South, for example through the work of the Brussels-based NGO-GATT Steering Committee.[65] Then, in the early 1990s, these efforts to link with other organizations working on development issues were given a substantial fillip as a result of a number of 'counter-forums' organized in the early 1990s around the UN World Summit for Children (1990), the Rio Earth Summit (1992), and the Beijing Conference (1995).[66] These counter-forums provided the opportunity for Northern and Southern NGOs of many different stripes to discuss, debate, and solidify the intellectual foundations of a relatively comprehensive critique of neoliberal globalization.

Over time, a number of new networks took on particular prominence within this social and intellectual milieu. In 1994, for example, the US-based '50 years is Enough!' campaign was launched—a coalition of 200 organizations seeking to effect significant change on the work of the World Bank and IMF. The International Forum on Globalization was also created in 1994. Although closely tied to the US-based coalitions described earlier, it is focused also on development issues and represents an important forum for bringing together Northern and Southern intellectuals working on international financial institutions, development, and global justice.[67] Walden Bello's Focus on the Global South was created in 1995 in Thailand to generate critical analysis on issues around economic globalization,[68]

[62] See Wilkinson (1996) 254. For example, on 16 and 17 November 1992, ICDA organized, together with EECOD and Germanwatch, an International NGO Conference on the Multilateral Trading Organisation (MTO) in Hamburg.

[63] United Nations Conference on Trade and Development (UNCTAD) <http://www.un-ngls.org/orf/documents/publications.en/ngls.handbook/a14uncta.htm> accessed 15 February 2011.

[64] See generally G Brown, 'Stemming the Tide: Third World Network and Global Governance' (2003/04) Ybk of Intl Co-operation on Environment and Development 73–7; S Denny Anderson (ed), *Views from the South: The Effects of Globalization and the WTO on Third World Countries* (Food First, Oakland, CA 2000).

[65] Wilkinson (1996) 251, 253.

[66] Juris (2008) 41.

[67] G Laxer, 'The Defeat of the Multilateral Agreement on Investment: National Movements Confront Globalization' in G Laxer and S Halperin (eds), *Global Civil Society and Its Limits* (Palgrave Macmillan, Basingstoke 2003) 173.

[68] See generally <http://www.focusweb.org> accessed 15 February 2011.

while the Bretton Woods Project was formed in the same year by a UK-based network of NGOs with the aim of scrutinizing and criticizing the work of the IMF and World Bank, including monitoring their social and environmental impacts.

One result of the formation of these networks has been that the substantive agenda of development NGOs has been influenced by trade issues raised in the context of broader civil society networks against neoliberal globalization. First, development NGOs have been influenced by the work of the women's groups mentioned earlier, concerning the impact of economic globalization on women's rights, particularly in the context of labour conditions in export processing zones. The 1995 Beijing Conference in particular helped to give voice to an emerging feminist critique within development circles, with groups such as the Women in Development Europe network (WIDE) and the Women's Environment and Development Organization (WEDO), who had originally come together around the conference, articulating a critique of neoliberal development as a process which relies on a highly gendered division of labour.[69] Secondly, many development NGOs have adopted the arguments being made by rural social movements, described above, concerning the adverse impacts of agricultural trade liberalization on the rural poor. And thirdly, no doubt in part because of their close connection to some parts of the Geneva trade community through their involvement with UNCTAD, development NGOs have been among the most articulate within the global justice movement in expressing positions in favour of developing countries within GATT/WTO negotiations. Some development NGOs, including Southern NGOs such as TWN under the leadership of Martin Khor, had excellent connections to many developing country representatives, and acted as an important transmission belt for ideas from developing country negotiators within the GATT system out to civil society organizations focusing on the WTO. As these civil society groups educated themselves on the particular technical preoccupations of the trade community, they began articulating claims for greater 'policy space' and 'special and differential treatment' for developing countries within the WTO system, the need to address 'implementation issues' related to the Uruguay Round agreements, the facilitation of technology transfer and diffusion from the North to the South, and greater and more meaningful participation of developing countries in WTO negotiations, as well as stating the dangers of including new issues in the WTO such as investment, government procurement, and competition law. NGOs within this development-oriented community also tended—contrary to the interests of some other NGOs working within the other strands described above—to oppose the inclusion of environmental and labour standards within trade agreements, as they saw in such standards a dangerous invitation to Northern protectionism against products from developing countries.

[69] O'Brien (2000) 36; Juris (2008) 37.

E. Global protest and an emerging global movement around trade

Each of the strands of activism and resistance so far identified has its own unique history and substantive preoccupations. But, as is well known, over the course of roughly six years beginning in the late 1990s, these distinct (if somewhat overlapping) organizational groupings began to knit themselves together in a self-conscious and relatively successful attempt to create a broader civil society movement around the global trading system—itself a part of the wider global justice movement. During this time, these different organizations and individuals came to construct and discover a set of shared orientations and interests, and came to understand themselves as part of a single struggle. New organizational ties and personal networks were created, which themselves helped to create and sustain the conditions for a productive ongoing cross-fertilization of ideas.

The civil society campaign around OECD negotiations on a Multilateral Agreement on Investment (MAI) provided, over a period of roughly eighteen months from 1997 to 1998, one of the first occasions for many of the groups described above to organize collectively around a single issue.[70] This coalition of over 600 organizations[71] included the International Forum on Globalization, ATTAC, Public Citizen, TWN, National Farmers Union, Consumer Nutrition Institute, Women's International League for Peace and Freedom, Catholic Fund for Overseas Development, Council of Canadians—and thus to a significant extent already contained elements from almost all the diverse strands just described.[72] This loose coalition came to attribute the failure of the MAI negotiations in part to their own efforts, and, flushed with their success, looked to organize additional campaigns to continue the momentum. The next large transnational gathering of ministers was in Seattle in December 1999, on the occasion of the third Ministerial Conference of the newly formed WTO. The Seattle protests have been mythologized in the popular imagination as the birthplace of the global justice movement, and a number of histories of the occasion have already been written.[73] Certainly, Seattle helped to crystallize the basic contours and components of progressive resistance to trade liberalization at a time when the substantive critiques of the trading system were still being sharpened and made more concrete. Groups such as the Citizens Trade Campaign, International Forum on Globalization, 50 Years is Enough!, La Vía Campesina, Global Exchange, Friends of the Earth, and many others combined in Seattle to give their individual concerns about the trading system a collective visibility that they had never previously enjoyed. Nevertheless, it was only one step in a longer process. The

[70] See generally Laxer (2003).

[71] C Devereaux, RZ Lawrence, and M Watkins (eds), *Case Studies on US Trade Negotiations: Volume 1, Making the Rules* (Peterson Institute for International Economics, Washington, DC 2006) 140 and ch 4 generally.

[72] Laxer (2003)—though labour was not present at this point.

[73] A Cockburn, J St Clair, and A Sekula, *Five Days that Shook the World: The Battle for Seattle and Beyond* (Verso, London 2000); JC Leite, *The World Social Forum: Strategies of Resistance* (Haymarket Books, Chicago, IL 2005); see also Edelman (2009) 109.

consolidation of this movement continued over the course of regular protests around the meetings of key organizations of global economic governance over the next few years, from Washington to Genoa, from New York to Chiang Mai. With the creation of the World Social Forum in 2001, the movement had a relatively permanent venue of its own for ongoing mobilization, and for the discussion and debate of shared projects.

This rapid creation of new networks and transnational alliances was accompanied by a similarly rapid evolution of ideas. Groups formerly involved in debates on trade at the national and regional level began to change their demands and their language as they came into contact with similar groups in other countries.[74] An over-arching 'master collective action frame'[75] also helped to provide the conditions for collective action—at once highlighting commonalities of interest and shared political priorities among participants, and at the same time helping to make their genuine differences less politically salient. As already foreshadowed, this master frame located the trade debate within a broader common struggle against neoliberalism, understood as a kind of free market fundamentalism. Within this frame, the WTO and the global trading system were, rightly or wrongly, associated with the spread of neoliberalism, and resistance to trade negotiations was conducted on that basis. Another element of the master frame focused on questions of popular sovereignty—since all civil society actors could easily agree on the need for greater transparency and popular participation in trade negotiations, claims about the secretive and anti-democratic nature of trade negotiations became central.

II. Human rights in the global justice movement

Towards the end of the 1990s, at about the same time as the global justice movement was beginning to form in earnest, it became common to hear human rights language associated with criticisms of neoliberal globalization. Claims about the negative impact of economic globalization on small farmers, on women workers, on food safety, and on global patterns of poverty, for example, were articulated as claims about the impact of economic globalization on the enjoyment of the right to food, labour rights, and the rights to health and an adequate standard of living. More generally, the language of human rights was deployed to evoke a different, softer kind of globalization—globalization 'with a human face'. Human rights, that is to say, seemed to provide an attractive normative foundation for a different global economic order, oriented towards economic justice, social welfare, and the reduction of poverty. In the remainder of this chapter, I want to focus on the deployment of human rights language within the global justice movement—the rearticulation of contemporary

[74] M Ritchie, 'A Practitioner's Perspective' in S Khagram, JV Riker and K Sikkink (eds), *Restructuring World Politics: Transnational Social Movements, Networks and Norms* (University of Minnesota Press, Minneapolis, MN 2002) 294–8, 295.

[75] JM Ayres, 'Framing Collective Action Against Neo-Liberalism: The Case of the "Anti-Globalization" Movement' (2004) X(1) J of World-Systems Research 11–34, 20.

concerns about free trade in the language of human rights, the mobilization of human rights actors around trade issues, and the crystallization of a coherent intellectual foundation for a 'human rights critique' of free trade. Which strands of the movement used human rights language? How was human rights language deployed, by whom, and why? I organize this section around four elements: receptive contexts; key actors; crystallizing events; and underlying logics.

A. Receptive contexts

I noted in Chapter 2 that at the beginning of the 1990s there was a resurgence of support in some quarters for making aid and trade flows conditional on a recipient country's human rights record.[76] Advocacy for the increased use of human rights 'conditionality' helped to introduce human rights language into debates on trade as early as the domestic US debates around NAFTA in the early 1990s. Human Rights Watch (HRW), for example, took a position against NAFTA on the basis of the Mexican Salinas government's record in relation to disappearances, press freedoms, the suppression of political dissent, and alleged electoral fraud.[77] HRW was unconvinced that increased economic ties with Mexico would necessarily ameliorate Mexico's human rights record, and in fact were concerned that such ties would send precisely the wrong signal. Over the next five or so years, a preoccupation with the human rights records of trading partners (understood in terms of civil and political rights) continued to animate much human rights activism on trade issues within the United States. Amnesty International opposed negotiations with Chile on its possible accession to NAFTA on the basis of its 'mistreatment of activists and dissidents, as well as execution of political prisoners'.[78] A number of human rights groups were active in campaigns opposing the MFN status of China in the late 1990s on the basis of its human rights record, while a potential WTO challenge to trade and economic sanctions against Cuba and Myanmar energized some human rights actors around the same period.[79]

As these actors began to realize that international trade law—whether the GATT, or NAFTA, or any other free trade agreement—could limit the use of trade power for the purposes of human rights promotion, they began to assert that there was a 'conflict' between trade law and human rights law. They began also to advocate the amendment or modification of international trade law to permit human rights conditionality, at least in some circumstances. As a result, the trade and human rights debate in the United States (such as it was) was for some time associated very

[76] See p 55 above.
[77] Anderson (2000) 119.
[78] K Beerman, 'Moving On: Chile's alternatives to NAFTA' (1996) 18 Harvard Intl Rev 64.
[79] See generally C McCrudden, 'International economic law and the pursuit of human rights: a framework for discussion of the legality of "selective purchasing" laws under the WTO Government Procurement Agreement' (1999) 2 JIEL 3–48; R Howse and M Mutua, *Protecting Human Rights in a Global Economy: Challenges for the World Trade Organisation* (International Centre for Human Rights and Democratic Development, Montreal 2000) <https://www.dd-rd.ca/site/_PDF/publications/globalization/wto/protecting_human_rightsWTO.pdf> accessed 15 February 2011.

closely with familiar debates about the legitimacy of economic ties with countries with poor human rights records, and the importance of conditioning access to US markets on improvements to foreign trading partners' human rights records. 'Linking trade and human rights', in other words, largely meant the use of market power as a tool for the projection of civil and political rights abroad.

As I observed in Chapter 2, this surge of interest in human rights conditionality was by and large associated with a particular kind of liberal tradition within the human rights movement. In my view, there is a clear distinction between this kind of 'linkage' between trade and human rights, and a very different kind of linkage, which uses human rights specifically to contest economic liberalism.[80] This second kind of linkage reflects the kind of counter-liberal traditions within human rights thinking described in Chapter 2. It tends to deploy the social and economic rights contained in the ICESCR, as well as third generation collective rights, to build a challenge to neoliberal economic reforms, and it is the re-emergence of this human rights tradition with which I am most concerned in this chapter.

It was not the major human rights organizations within the developed world which pioneered the use of human rights language to criticize neoliberal globalization. Perhaps this was in part the result of the higher priority these organizations have traditionally accorded to civil and political rights than economic and social rights, and their more general reluctance to engage in advocacy on economic issues. Whatever the reason, the original impetus came from four primary kinds of groups, each of which were perhaps somewhat out of the mainstream of the human rights movement at the time. First, there were groups focused on labour issues. Historically, as Leary has observed, the labour rights and human rights movements have been relatively independent from one another, with labour rights groups rarely using the language of 'human' rights, and human rights organizations focusing on issues other than employment and work.[81] For a variety of reasons this began to change from the second half of the 1990s, as the two movements started to converge.[82] Major unions such as the AFL-CIO as well as the ITUC began to self-consciously deploy human rights language and situate themselves as part of the broader human rights movement. Non-union labour groups, particularly those working on export processing zones such as the Fair Labor Association and the Clean Clothes Campaign, also used human rights in their advocacy work.[83] One consequence of this convergence was the use by labour groups of human rights language when articulating their concerns about economic globalization. As a consequence, many statements and publications on potential conflicts between economic globalization and human rights have foregrounded

[80] P Alston, 'International Trade as an Instrument of Positive Human Rights Policy' (1982) 4 HRQ 155 draws the same distinction.

[81] VA Leary, 'The Paradox of Workers' Rights as Human Rights' in LA Compa and SF Diamond (eds), *Human Rights, Labor Rights, and International Trade* (University of Pennsylvania Press, Philadelphia, PA 2003) 22–47.

[82] See generally K Kolben, 'Labor Rights as Human Rights?' (2010) 50 Virginia J Intl L 449–84.

[83] ibid 458.

labour rights issues.[84] Indeed, in the context of domestic US discussions of the relationship between NAFTA and human rights in the mid-1990s, debates about trade and human rights essentially revolved around the two issues of human rights conditionality and labour rights.[85]

A second important space for the emergence of human rights language within debates about neoliberal globalization arose within the networks of Northern development NGOs described above. For example, perhaps the first book-length treatment of the relationship between economic globalization and human rights was published with the sponsorship of the ICDA, and with the close involvement of the development NGO, Lutheran World Federation (LWF).[86] It had a foreword by a former UN Special Rapporteur on the Realization of Economic, Social and Cultural Rights, and an introduction co-authored by a former Special Rapporteur on the Right to Adequate Housing, both of whom had worked for some time on issues concerning structural adjustment and human rights in development. Since then, groups within the development community—particularly those with religious affiliations such as the Center of Concern, the Ecumenical Advocacy Alliance, Action Aid, Christian Aid, CAFOD, and the LWF—have been among the strongest voices outside the mainstream human rights community to link resistance to trade liberalization with human rights language. The particular receptivity of development NGOs to human rights language will come as no surprise—we saw in the previous chapter that important and enduring links were established between the human rights and development communities during the 1970s, and these continued throughout the 1980s in the context of advocacy around debt, structural adjustment, and so on. The theoretical work of Amartya Sen also provided a significant conceptual framework and intellectual impetus for linking development with human rights, which became particularly influential from the 1990s onwards.

Women's rights organizations provided a third impetus for the use of human rights language in political struggles around neoliberal globalization. While the international women's human rights movement, according to Friedman, became prominent on the international stage only from the late 1970s, it was soon an important part of the present story.[87] This was the result of at least three trends.

[84] eg LA Compa and SF Diamond (eds), *Human Rights, Labor Rights, and International Trade* (University of Pennsylvania Press, Philadelphia, PA 2003); A Taylor and C Thomas (eds), *Global Trade and Global Social Issues* (Routledge Press, New York, NY 1999).

[85] For an example, see JF Smith, 'NAFTA and Human Rights: A Necessary Linkage' (1994) 27 UC Davies L Rev 793.

[86] M Mehra (ed), *Human Rights and Economic Globalisation: Directions for the WTO* (Global Publications Foundation, Uppsala, Sweden 1999).

[87] E Friedman, 'Women's Human Rights: The Emergence of a Movement' in J Peters and A Wolper (eds), *Women's rights, human rights: international feminist perspectives* (Routledge, New York, NY 1995); See also generally AS Fraser, 'Becoming Human: The Origins and Development of Women's Human Rights' (1999) 21 HRQ 853–906, 895ff (which places late 20th century developments in the context of longer historical trends); H Hill, 'From Nairobi to Beijing' in S Mitchell and R Das Pradham (eds), *Back to Basics from Beijing: An Australian Guide to the International Platform for Action* (Australian Council for Overseas Aid 1997) 104, 106; A Orford, 'Contesting Globalization: A Feminist Perspective on the Future of Human Rights' (1998) 8 Transnational L & Contemporary Problems 171–98.

The first was the emergence of networks such as the Institute for Women, Law and Development (IWLD), the Latin American Committee for the Defense of Women's Rights (CLADEM), the Asia-Pacific Forum on Women, Law and Development (APLWD), and Women in Law and Development in Africa (WiLDAF). Then, secondly, during the 1990s, women's groups increasingly began to form alliances with mainstream human rights organizations and to use human rights language to articulate their claims. These efforts were aided considerably by events surrounding the Vienna Conference in 1993 and the Beijing Conference on Women in 1995.[88] Thirdly, a number of these women's human rights groups sharpened their focus on issues of economic and social justice—particularly in Latin America and Canada.[89] Thus, a number of organizations began to focus on issues around the feminization of the labour force in export processing zones in developing counties, as well as the disproportionate impact on women of agricultural liberalization.[90] Again, these contributions were important elements of the early trade and human rights debate in the late 1990s, and were the result in part of an attempt to mainstream women's rights in discussions about human rights and development.[91]

Fourthly, human rights also emerged as an important language of resistance within the networks of peasant groups and rural social movements described above. Recall that the political struggles of these groups around agricultural liberalization and trade agreements were often imagined as, and carried out in the context of, the struggles of indigenous peoples for their political and economic autonomy. As Engle has recently chronicled, the struggles of indigenous movements around the developing world have been couched in the language of human rights (indigenous peoples' rights) since at least the 1970s, first under the rubric of self-determination, and then more recently the right to culture.[92] Furthermore, the use of human rights in the context of indigenous struggles has been actively fostered at the international level through the UN human rights system, from the establishment of what was then the Sub-Commission's Working Group on Indigenous Populations in 1982, through a number of high profile conferences and events, to the Declaration of the

[88] Friedman (1995) 19, 30–2.

[89] MacDonald (2002) 151–72.

[90] eg the Association for Women's Rights in Development (AWID) and International Gender and Trade Network (IGTN); see also generally V Shiva, 'The effects of the WTO on women's rights' <http://www.twnside.org.sg/title/women-ch.htm> accessed 16 February 2011; Orford (1998) 172; and the material cited in the next footnote.

[91] A Espino, 'Globalization, Free Trade and Gender: A Perspective from the Mercosur Countries' in M Mehra (ed), *Human Rights and Economic Globalisation: Directions for the WTO* (Global Publications Foundation, Uppsala, Sweden 1999); L MacDonald, 'Trade with a Female Face: Women and the New International Trade Agenda' in A Taylor and C Thomas (eds), *Global Trade and Global Social Issues* (Routledge Press, New York, NY 1999); and more recently Association for Women's Rights in Development (AWID), 'Achieving Women's Economic and Social Rights: Strategies and lessons from experience' (2006) <http://www.awid.org/eng/content/download/49095/541680/file/ESCR%20Report.pdf> accessed 16 February 2011.

[92] See generally K Engle, *The Elusive Promise of Indigenous Development: Rights, Culture, Strategy* (Duke University Press, London 2010).

Rights of Indigenous Peoples in September 2007. The result was that many individual activists and organizations working in this *milieu* were already familiar with, and personally committed to, international human rights as a language of political struggle. When indigenous rights activists and associated rural social movements turned their attention to trade issues during the 1990s, it was therefore no surprise that they were amenable to the use of human rights to make their claims. Over time a relatively small but vocal body of indigenous groups began to frame their criticisms of trade and investment agreements in the language of the rights of indigenous peoples. A number of Geneva-based indigenous people's groups came together in 1999 in Geneva, at a meeting hosted by the World Council of Churches, and in part as a result, at the Seattle Ministerial later that year, the Indigenous Peoples Caucus—a body of organizations including Tebtebba, AIWN, and the Indigenous Peoples Council—circulated a statement criticizing certain WTO rules as a threat to the 'rights of indigenous peoples', and calling on indigenous peoples to be more actively engaged in WTO issues.[93] At Seattle, these indigenous groups were able not only to disseminate their own concerns, but also to further their links with groups such as the IATP, the TWN and others to develop shared criticisms of the WTO and the TRIPs agreement. By 2003, the Cancún Declaration of Indigenous Peoples was explicitly calling for a 'human rights framework' to 'underpin trade, investment, development and anti-poverty policies and programs'.[94] Furthermore, as explained below, groups such as La Vía Campesina began explicitly to deploy the right to food as part of their normative and rhetorical framework for an alternative vision of agricultural production based on food security and local production.[95]

Finally, it is worth noting that there are a few specific regions and countries in the developing world which have proved to be crucial contexts for the emergence of a human rights critique of neoliberalism. Two of particular significance are India and South Africa. In both countries, the embedding of economic and social rights into national constitutions has been important in establishing and maintaining a strong tradition of human rights activism around issues of economic justice. As the global justice movement grew in popular support in both countries, human rights groups very quickly became involved, and human rights language seemed to have significant resonance with the broader public. But perhaps the most important geographical area has been the Latin American region generally. Dezalay and Garth, for example, have chronicled the ways in which human rights were used as a counter to the

[93] Indigenous Peoples' Organizations, 'Indigenous Peoples' Seattle Declaration' (NGO Position Paper 1999) <http://csdngo.igc.org/Indigenous/indig_seattle.htm> accessed 16 February 2011.

[94] The International Cancun Declaration of Indigenous Peoples (5th WTO Ministerial Conference, Cancun, Mexico, 12 September 2003); International Forum on Globalization, 'Globalization: Effects on Indigenous Peoples' (Map 2003) <http://www.ifg.org/programs/indig/IFGmap.pdf> accessed 16 February 2011; see generally J Mander and V Tauli-Corpuz (eds), *Paradigm Wars: Indigenous Peoples' Resistance to Economic Globalization* (1st edn, Sierra Club Books, San Francisco, CA 2005).

[95] See pp 95–6 below; see also M Pimple, 'Indian Agriculture, Farmers' Rights and the WTO' in M Mehra (ed), *Human Rights and Economic Globalisation: Directions for the WTO* (Global Publications Foundation, Uppsala, Sweden 1999) 80–5; FLS Valente, 'Food for Development and the Human Rights to Food and Nutrition: The Brazilian Experience' in M Mehra (ed), *Human Rights and Economic Globalisation: Directions for the WTO* (Global Publications Foundation, Uppsala, Sweden 1999) 104–12.

economic expertise deployed in the neoliberal transformation of states in the Southern Cone, such as Brazil, Argentina, and Chile.[96] The reasons for this are complex but have to do with a number of historical and institutional factors, including: the historical importance of the human rights movement in the struggle against political oppression in the region; the close linkage between this human rights movement and the Catholic Church, with its liberation theology-inspired focus on social issues; and the institutionalization of human rights in domestic constitutions and legislation.[97] But whatever the reason, it is clear that human rights groups from this region have been at the forefront of the emergence over the 1990s of human rights talk in the global justice movement in the developing world.

These, then, were among the key contexts in which human rights re-emerged in the late 1990s as a language of critique of late twentieth-century economic liberalism. Once again, challenges to claims of a benign relationship between free markets and human rights protection began to be heard, and attention began to be refocused on the obstacles that free markets can pose to the achievement of social rights in particular. However, it was not enough for these receptive contexts merely to exist. The birth of the contemporary trade and human rights debate was also the result of more targeted interventions by a groups of individuals and organizations acting as conduits between the global justice movement on one hand, and the international human rights system on the other. It is to the activity of these actors that I now turn.

B. Key actors

The actors described in this section—whom we might call 'brokers'—have at least two functions. On one hand, they act as representatives (of a sort) of the global justice movement to the human rights system, in the specific sense that they try to convince individuals and bodies in the official UN human rights system to adopt the positions and claims of the global justice movement in their reports, resolutions, and statements, and also encourage human rights NGOs to build work programmes and advocacy campaigns on issues around economic globalization. On the other hand, they act as representatives of the human rights regime to the global justice movement, in the specific sense that they try to convince those working within the global justice movement of the benefits of using human rights language, help to educate them on the meaning and proper use of that language to ensure a degree of consistency with the work of official human rights organs, and bring to their attention the latest reports and recommendations from human rights bodies which may be of assistance to groups within the global justice movement in their advocacy efforts. While the community of brokers which has emerged since the 1990s is not a

[96] See Y Dezalay and BG Garth, *The Internationalization of Palace Wars: Lawyers, Economists, and the Contest to Transform Latin American States* (University of Chicago Press, Chicago, IL 2002) ch 3; see also Keck and Sikkink (1998).

[97] See A Brysk, *The Politics of Human Rights in Argentina: protest, change, and democratization* (Stanford University Press, Stanford, CA 1994); LJ LeBlanc, 'Economic, Social, and Cultural Rights and the Inter American System' (1977) 19 J of Interamerican Studies and World Affairs 64.

large one, it is impossible in this space to chronicle all the efforts of all the groups working within it, and I will focus on only a small handful to give the flavour of the important work they do.

One example is the Canadian NGO International Centre for Human Rights and Democratic Development—also known as 'Rights and Democracy'—which was set up in 1988 by the Canadian Parliament as an independent organization, to 'encourage and support the universal values of human rights and the promotion of democratic institutions and practices around the world'.[98] Its first president was Ed Broadbent, who had been leader of the Canadian National Democratic Party during the 1984 and 1988 Canadian elections, during which the CUSFTA had emerged as a major political issue. Broadbent had both a strong personal interest in the promotion of economic and social rights, which he associated with the preservation of welfare state social protections,[99] and a keen interest in trade agreements, in part as a result of his advocacy around the CUSFTA. Under Broadbent's leadership, Rights and Democracy began to develop an interest in trade liberalization and trade agreements, and their impact on social and economic rights. During the NAFTA campaign, for example, Rights and Democracy—focusing at this point primarily on the potential impact of trade on labour rights—attempted without much success to convince certain members of the Canadian government that human rights ought to be taken into account in governmental decision-making on NAFTA. They also began the process of networking with some Mexican and US human rights organizations at the same time, though at this early stage they did not manage to make social rights a central part of the civil society campaign around NAFTA, nor attract the support of most of the established US-based human rights organizations.

Then, after attending the WTO's Singapore Ministerial in 1996 and the meeting of APEC leaders in Vancouver in 1997 as one of the few human rights organizations present, Rights and Democracy decided to commission a paper, jointly written by a scholar of trade law and a human rights scholar, in an explicit attempt to ground a sustained and well-informed dialogue about the relationship between trade law and human rights law.[100] The paper, inspired in part by the work of Amartya Sen,[101] proved to be highly significant, and remains one of the earliest and most commonly cited articles in the international legal literature in the area. An early draft was prepared in advance of the WTO Ministerial in Singapore in 1999, and was the focus of discussion at a workshop hosted by Rights and Democracy in Seattle, which

[98] International Centre for Human Rights and Democratic Development (Rights and Democracy) <http://www.ichrdd.ca/site/home/index.php?lang=en> accessed 16 February 2011.

[99] See eg JE Broadbent, 'The Challenge to Economic and Social Rights: Thoughts on Citizenship in the Welfare State in the North Atlantic World' (1998) 12 Global Society 15–30; JE Broadbent, 'The Rise and Fall of Economic and Social Rights: What Next?' address to the Congress of the Canadian Federation for the Humanities and Social Sciences (29 May 2000) <http://www.policyalternatives.ca/sites/default/files/uploads/publications/reports/docs/Rise_and_Fall_of_Economic_and_Social_Rights.pdf> accessed 16 February 2011.

[100] Howse and Mutua (2000).

[101] UNHCR (Sub-Commission), 'Mainstreaming the right to development into international trade law and policy at the World Trade Organization: Note by the Secretariat' (9 June 2004) UN Doc E/CN.4/Sub.2/2004/17, para 4.

featured a presentation of the paper by its authors, and was attended by a variety of NGOs and others involved in the protests at that time.[102] In its final form, the paper represented a much broader picture of the relationship between trade and human rights than had previously been articulated. It covered the concerns about transparency of negotiations and labour rights issues which had already been articulated as critiques of trade agreements some years earlier. But it also included a section on 'food safety, technical barriers and services', in which international legal constraints on regulatory autonomy were described as threats to the protection of economic and social rights such as the right to health. Other sections discussed the impact of the TRIPs compulsory licensing provisions on access to drugs and the right to health, and the constraints which WTO obligations may impose on governments seeking to use their procurement power to further their human rights agenda. The latter reflected contemporary debates ignited by a European challenge in the WTO to a Massachusetts law seeking to use state procurement power to ameliorate human rights abuses in Myanmar. Furthermore, and importantly, the paper introduced a new set of systemic proposals, which had to do with the way human rights ought to be taken into account within the WTO. It noted the institutional isolation of the trade and human rights regimes, and argued for greater dialogue between them. It argued for the interpretation of WTO law in the light of human rights law, and identified the Preamble to the WTO Agreement and Article XX of the GATT as important textual bases for the consideration of human rights law. It argued that certain human rights-related objectives should be explicitly considered in the WTO's Trade Policy Review Mechanism, and that *amicus* briefs (including from human rights organizations) should be accepted within WTO dispute settlement proceedings.

Then, in March 2001, members of staff at Rights and Democracy and an academic at the University of Quebec, in partnership and consultation with other organizations, published a lengthy policy paper entitled 'A Human Rights Framework for Trade in the Americas'.[103] The paper represented at that stage one of the most comprehensive formulations of human rights critiques of trade agreements. It contained chapters on the liberalization of essential services and its impact on the rights to health and education, questions of bio-piracy and access to drugs under the TRIPS agreement as a right to health issue, agricultural liberalization and the right to food, and the lack of transparency of trade negotiations, among others. The paper, which was widely circulated, argued for certain forms of systemic integration of human rights into the FTAA: an explicit affirmation of human rights principles in the FTAA; the consideration of human rights jurisprudence in dispute settlement under the FTAA; the inclusion of a trade policy review mechanism within the FTAA to scrutinize the trade agreement's human rights impact; as well as the establishment

[102] The meeting is referred to in the Preface by Warren Allmand to the report, see Howse and Mutua (2000) 3.

[103] D Bronson and L Lamarche, *A Human Rights Framework for Trade in the Americas* (International Centre for Human Rights and Democratic Development, Montreal 2001) <http://www.dd-rd.ca/site/_PDF/publications/globalization/frameworkFinal.pdf> accessed 15 February 2011.

of a committee of experts to address the potential impact of the FTAA on human rights.

According to Korzeniewicz and Smith, this work of Rights and Democracy played a crucial role in bringing a number of human rights groups into the coalition protesting against the FTAA.[104] Until 2001, human rights coalitions in the Americas were hardly organized around the issue of economic integration—their focus was elsewhere. But in part as a result of this paper and the work of Rights and Democracy, a number of human rights NGOs with an interest in the Americas began to mobilize around the FTAA, and some of them established work programmes on trade and investment around this time. A Latin American human rights network on trade began to expand. The Argentina-based Centro de Estudios Legales y Sociales (CELS), for example, participated in discussions on the FTAA, and conducted a joint project with Rights and Democracy on the impact of water privatization on the right to water.[105] Centro de Derechos Humanos Miguel Agustin Pro Juárez (PRODH, Mexico) and Centro de Derechos Humanos y Ambiente (CEDHA, Argentina) were also active in advocating greater transparency of trade negotiations, and monitoring the impact of economic integration on human rights policies.[106] Centros de Derechos Economicos y Sociales (CDES, Ecuador) also emerged as a player in the organization of resistance to regional trade agreements, and in conducting research and advocacy on the impact of FTAs on economic and social rights and the collective rights of indigenous peoples. Others have included Programa Venezolano Educación-Acción en Derechos Humanos (PROVEA, Venezuela), the Colectivo de Abogados (Colombia), and the Latin American and Caribbean Committee for the Defense of Women's Rights (CLADEM), a Latin American human rights network working on gender issues. A number of these organizations were also involved in organizing and participating in a hearing before the Inter-American Commission on Human Rights in October 2004, which specifically addressed the question of the relationship between economic integration, trade, and human rights.[107]

Alongside Rights and Democracy, and quite independent of it, was another network called the International NGO Committee on Human Rights and Trade and Investment (INCHRITI), which played a fundamental role in bringing a human rights focus to civil society activism around trade in the late 1990s. At its inception, INCHRITI was a relatively small group of eight NGOs—some of which, however, were themselves networks and alliances with many affiliated organizations. The most active and significant players in this network were the Geneva-based Lutheran World

[104] Korzeniewicz and Smith (2001) 22.

[105] See Rights and Democracy, *Human Rights Impact Assessments for Foreign Investment Projects* (International Center for Human Rights and Democratic Development, 2007) <http://www.dd-rd.ca/site/_PDF/publications/globalization/hria/full%20report_may_2007.pdf> accessed 30 April 2011.

[106] See generally Center for Human Rights and Environment (CEDHA) <http://www.cedha.org.ar/en/institutional_advocacy/> accessed 16 February 2011.

[107] See *Centro de Derecho Humanos 'Miguel Agustin Pro Juarez' (Centro Pro Juarez)*, 'Los Derechos Humanos en los Procesos de Integracion Economica en las Americas' (Statement for the CIDH, October 2004) <http://www.choike.org/documentos/tlc_cidh_ddhh.pdf> accessed 16 February 2011.

Federation (LWF) and the Habitat International Coalition (HIC)—but it also contained CLADEM, the women's rights network mentioned above, and the Food-First International Action Network (FIAN), among others.[108] Although INCHRITI had been formally created during the course of the civil society mobilization against the MAI in May 1998, members of the network had a longer history of mobilization together around international economic issues, having previously been involved in campaigns around structural adjustment and debt relief. Indeed, key personnel in member organizations of the INCHRITI network had links to the community of development NGOs described earlier, including through ICDA and the NGLS.

INCHRITI did a great deal to lay the groundwork for a critique of neoliberal globalization based firmly on formal legal argument anchored in international human rights law. It had already experimented with rights-based arguments during the MAI campaign, and wasted no time in developing the same arguments in the context of trade. For example, noting that environmental NGOs had previously used international environmental law to argue against the MAI, members of the INCHRITI coalition called on human rights groups to do the same with human rights law—not only against the MAI, but also against global trade agreements.[109] A policy statement released by INCHRITI in 1998 made the claim that human rights law had primacy over all other bodies of international law. It also argued that provisions of the proposed MAI, which restricted the 'regulatory role of the state' and constrained the use of trade policy for development purposes, were potentially incompatible with human rights law. It claimed, furthermore, that trade disputes which dealt with human rights issues should not be adjudicated by trade or investment bodies, but rather by an appropriate human rights forum.[110] This paper therefore contained, in an early form, many of the claims which came to structure the work of many international lawyers on these issues a few short years later.

From 1998 to roughly 2000, INCHRITI's work went in broadly in two directions. On the one hand, Geneva-based members of the coalition were instrumental in mobilizing a number of official human rights bodies on issues around trade and investment.[111] They were remarkably successful, helping to secure a statement of the Committee on Economic, Social and Cultural Rights on 'Globalization and its impact on the enjoyment of economic and social rights' in May 1998, and a resolution of the UN Sub-Commission on the Prevention of Discrimination and Protection of Minorities in August of the same year, asserting human rights to be the primary objective of trade policy.[112] I will say more about this in the next chapter.

[108] The other members included the Center for Equality Rights in Accommodation, the Mazingira Institute, People's Decade for Human Rights Education, and Youth for Unity of Voluntary Action.

[109] M Kothari and T Krause, 'Human Rights or Corporate Rights? The MAI Challenge' (1998) 5 Human Rights Tribune 17.

[110] INCHRITI, 'International NGO Committee on Human Rights in Trade and Investment: Policy Statement' (June 1998).

[111] See also Weissbrodt and Schoff (2003) 26 for further detail on the lobbying efforts of these individuals.

[112] UNHCR (Sub-Commission), 'Human rights as the primary objective of trade, investment and finance policy' (20 August 1998) UN Doc E/CN.4/Sub.2/Res/1998/12.

On the other hand, INCHRITI sought also to convince individuals and organizations within the anti-globalization movement of the benefits of adopting a human rights framework in their advocacy. In the months leading up to the Seattle Ministerial at the end of 1999, for example, individuals closely associated with INCHRITI put together an edited collection entitled *Human Rights and Economic Globalization: Directions for the WTO*, the first book-length treatment of the subject.[113] The book's collection of contributors represented in microcosm many of the strands of the global justice movement discussed in the first half of this chapter. Then, during the Seattle Ministerial itself, INCHRITI hosted a teach-in on the relationship between human rights and the WTO, which included presentations from a number of central intellectual figures in the anti-globalization movement such as Walden Bello, Susan George, Vandana Shiva, and Maude Barlow.[114] For some of the participants, it was their first opportunity to think seriously about the potential benefits that human rights could offer their campaigns.

The ripples from INCHRITI's initial conceptual innovation extended in a number of directions. The idea of a human rights approach to trade caught on relatively quickly, for example, within the Geneva-based human rights and development communities where a number of INCHRITI's most active members were based. A May 2000 strategy meeting jointly held by the CESCR and INCHRITI attracted participants from the International Commission of Jurists, the Peace and Development Centre, and Franciscans International—as well as a number of personnel from the Office of the High Commissioner for Human Rights.[115] Of course, INCHRITI was not the only organization working on human rights and economic globalization in Geneva at this time. Another driving force was FIDH Geneva, which developed a work stream on trade and investment, and began to educate and mobilize its members around WTO issues and events from the late 1990s. In fact, FIDH had established a programme on economic and social rights in 1997, and began publishing on the relationship between the WTO and human rights as early as 1999.[116] It has been among the prominent mainstream human rights organizations working on trade since then.[117] Furthermore, a new organization, 3D→THREE[118] (originally

[113] Mehra (1999).

[114] 'Trading Away Human Rights? The Role of the WTO' (Announcement about a Human Rights Teach-In on 30 November 1999) <http://www.hrea.org/lists/hr-education/markup/msg00062.html> accessed 15 February 2011.

[115] Office of the High Commissioner for Human Rights, 'Record of the Workshop on International Trade, Investment and Finance and Economic, Social and Cultural Rights' (6 May 2000) <http://www.unhchr.ch/tbs/doc.nsf/0/11d06750ac4e7acbc125691f002f01f0?Opendocument> accessed 15 February 2011.

[116] A-C Habbard and M Guiraud, *L'OMC et es droits de l'homme: une équation à résoudre: rapport de position* (FIDH, Paris 1999).

[117] International Federation for Human Rights (FIDH), 'Understanding Global Trade & Human Rights' (Report for National Human Rights NGOs 2005) <http://www.un-ngls.org/orf/FIDH.pdf> accessed 16 February 2011; International Federation for Human Rights (FIDH), 'The WTO and human rights' (Report 2001) <http://www.fidh.org/IMG/pdf/omc320a.pdf> accessed 16 February 2011.

[118] Or, more fully, 3D → Trade-Human Rights-Equitable Economy, see generally <http://www.3Dthree.org> accessed 16 February 2011.

3D Associates), was created in 2001, specifically to work at the nexus of trade and human rights. It is a classic broker organization, seeking to educate human rights organizations on the arcane world of trade and development politics and policy, reformulating trade policy-related research and analysis into a form more digestible by human rights bodies and organizations. Its founder is a legally-trained human rights professional with experience in trade and development policy, who wrote one of the first detailed scholarly treatments of the relationship between human rights law and trade law,[119] and has been active in the area since. One of the main motivations behind the creation of 3D→THREE was the perception that there was a pressing need for an organization which could bridge the increasingly polarized divide between the professional communities associated with the trade and human rights fields of the time—to provide, in other words, a way of communicating the messages of the human rights community in a form that made sense to trade professionals (and vice versa) in the absence of the heated rhetoric which characterized some of the debate at that time. 3D→THREE became a central player within the Geneva community working on trade and human rights, helping to organize events, disseminate publications and information, and importantly to educate civil society organizations interested in trade and economic globalization in relevant aspects of human rights law. It works closely with the other broker organizations described above. In 2002, for example, 3D→THREE organized in collaboration with INCHRITI a workshop for NGOs working on trade issues, to show how human rights mechanisms might be useful in their advocacy. The next year, 3D→THREE collaborated with Rights and Democracy to put together a panel at the WTO Ministerial in Cancún, and worked with FIDH, the IATP, and CEDHA at the Hong Kong Ministerial.[120]

Another important broker organization has been the FoodFirst International Action Network (FIAN), which works in the area of agriculture—and, as it happens, was a founding member of INCHRITI. FIAN was established in 1986 as an organization dedicated to the promotion of the right to food, in part as a response to the relative lack of emphasis which most mainstream human rights organizations gave to social rights at that time. It is based in Germany, but includes members from around the world. FIAN became interested in trade issues towards the middle of the 1990s, as its partner organizations and affiliates in developing countries such as Honduras, Ghana, India, the Philippines, and Brazil began to mobilize around IMF- and World Bank-imposed structural adjustment and agricultural liberalization programmes. In this way, FIAN came to work closely with the peasant movements described in an earlier part of this chapter, and was deeply sensitized to the many issues that those groups had with agricultural liberalization as it had been carried out in the developing world since the 1980s. With its explicit mandate to promote and protect the right to food, FIAN was soon at the forefront of efforts to elaborate and

[119] C Dommen, 'Raising Human Rights Concerns in the World Trade Organization: Actors, Processes and Possible Strategies' (2002) 24 HRQ 1–50.

[120] See eg 3D→THREE, 'Activities 2004–2006: WTO Ministerial Event' <http://www.3dthree.org/en/complement.php?IDcomplement=57&IDpage=53&IDcat=22> accessed 16 February 2011.

determine the connections between agricultural trade liberalization, food insecurity, agrarian reform, and the 'right to food'.

Part of FIAN's work in this area has been case-based—empirically documenting specific abuses of the right to food in various countries around the world, disseminating reports on such cases, and helping to support lobbying efforts to encourage governments to address them. In 1999, FIAN joined forces with La Vía Campesina to create the Global Campaign for Agrarian Reform, an 'emergency human rights network' modelled in part on 'urgent action' campaigns familiar from other areas of human rights activism.[121] This network seeks, among other things, to intervene against violations of the human rights of peasants by disseminating information, to lobby, and to verify reports of specific cases in which the human right to food has been violated.[122] It conducted international research missions to Honduras and Bolivia.[123] More recently, in 2006, FIAN was commissioned alongside a number of other like-minded NGOs to perform studies of the impact of trade liberalization and trade agreements on the right to food of rice farmers in Ghana, Honduras, and Indonesia, milk and maize farmers in Uganda, and milk and honey producers in Zambia.[124] Through these projects, FIAN has helped not only to begin the task of building a necessary body of documentary evidence to support the legal claims of human rights actors, but also to develop a methodology for conducting human rights-based assessments of agricultural policy. Another part of FIAN's work is organizational in nature. It has, for example, helped to develop a relatively close-knit body of NGOs approaching agricultural liberalization issues from a 'right to food' perspective. Thus, for example, it has worked closely with a number of development NGOs, including the Canadian Council for International Cooperation, Brot für die Welt (the sister organization to the British Christian Aid), and Church Development Service (EED, a Protestant Church organization based in Germany working on development issues). In addition, in part through its association with FIAN, the Institute for Agriculture and Trade Policy has begun to incorporate elements of the right to food into their

[121] Edelman (2003) 207.

[122] S Monsalve Suarez, 'Gender and Land' in P Rosset, RC Patel, and M Courville (eds), *Promised Land: Competing Visions of Agrarian Reform* (Food First, Canada 2006) 192–207, 194–5.

[123] ibid 195–6; and see eg FoodFirst Information Action Network (FIAN), 'Agrarian Reform and the Human Right to Food in Honduras' (Report of the FIAN International and Vía Campesina Fact Finding Mission 29 July–2 August 2000) <http://www.fian.org/resources/documents/others/agrarian-reform-and-the-human-right-to-food-in-honduras> accessed 15 February 2011.

[124] A Paasch, F Garbers, and T Hirsch (eds), *Trade Policies and Hunger: The Impact of Trade Liberalisation on the Right to Food of rice farming communities in Ghana, Honduras and Indonesia* (Geneva, EAA 2007); G Falk, *The Right to Food of Milk and Maize Farmers: Report of an investigative mission to Uganda* (Heidelberg, FIAN 2009) <http://www.fian.org/resources/documents/others/the-right-to-food-of-milk-and-maize-farmers/pdf> accessed 15 February 2011; FoodFirst Information Action Network (FIAN), 'Right to Food of Milk and Honey Farmers: Report of an investigative mission to Zambia' <http://www.fian.org/resources/documents/others/right-to-food-of-milk-and-honey-farmers-report-of-an-investigative-mission-to-zambia/pdf> accessed 15 February 2011.

trade policy programmes, and claims to support food as a human right.[125] More generally, FIAN acts as an important node for the generation, growth, and maintenance of this small community of NGOs, and organized a major conference on the global food crisis in late 2008, bringing together many of the key actors working on the right to food.[126]

Moreover, FIAN has acted as a bridge between the human rights community working on the right to food, and the peasant producer networks described above. For example, when the FAO Voluntary Guidelines on the Right to Food were being drafted in the late 1990s, the leadership of FIAN was heavily involved, playing a crucial role in mobilizing and facilitating the input of a network of around 800 groups, including small producers, peasants, and indigenous groups into the FAO negotiations. To some extent, this kind of close collaboration has also helped to promote the adoption of a form of human rights language within the peasant movements connected to the Vía Campesina and other transnational farmer networks, at least on occasion.[127] As noted above, these groups have developed an alternative model of agricultural reform based on the notion of 'food sovereignty'—a model which is opposed to agricultural liberalization, and is instead focused on local production, self sufficiency, and access to land for small farmers.[128] While there has been considerable resistance to the wholesale association of 'food sovereignty' with a 'right to food' approach, in 2002 food sovereignty was collectively defined by representatives of over 400 civil society and farmers organizations to:

> ... include the true right to food and to produce food, which means that all people have the right to safe, nutritious and culturally appropriate food and to food-producing resources and the ability to sustain themselves and their societies.

'Food sovereignty', they went on, 'means the primacy of people's and communities' rights to food and food production over trade concerns'.[129] Later, the Cochabamba

[125] Institute for Agriculture and Trade Policy (IATP), 'Human Rights to Food and Water' <http://www.iatp.org/global/human_rights.cfm> accessed 16 February 2011.

[126] For a report of the conference, see K Geenan, R Künnemann, and Y Tang, *Report of the 2nd conference of the ETO-Consortium Heidelberg, 26–27 September 2008* (Heidelberg, FIAN 2008), <http://www.fian.org/resources/documents/others/report-of-the-2nd-conference-of-the-eto-consortium/pdf> accessed 16 February 2011.

[127] For an example, see FoodFirst Information and Action Network (FIAN), La Vía Campesina, Maastricht Center of Human Rights, 'Agrarian Reform and Human Rights' (Seminar Report 15–17 April 2002) <http://www.fian.org/resources/documents/others/agrarian-reform-and-human-rights> accessed 15 February 2011.

[128] See eg P Rosset, 'Conclusion. Moving Forward: Agrarian Reform as Part of Food Sovereignty' in P Rosset, RC Patel, and M Courville (eds), *Promised Land: Competing Visions of Agrarian Reform* (Food First, Canada 2006) 301–21; P Rosset, 'Agrarian Reform and Food Sovereignty: An Alternative Model for the Rural World' in CD Deere and FS Royce (eds), *Rural Social Movements in Latin America: Organizing for Sustainable Livelihoods* (University of Florida Press, Gainesville, FL 2009) 55–78.

[129] See 'Food Sovereignty: A Right for All—Political Statement of the NGO/CSO forum for Food Sovereignty' (2002) <http://www.foodfirst.org/en/209/> accessed 16 June 2011. See also, for a brief history of the concept of 'food sovereignty' and a formulation which draws on rights language, 'The right to food: Report submitted by the Special Rapporteur on the right to food, Jean Ziegler, in accordance with Commission on Human Rights resolution 2003/25' (9 February 2004) UN Doc E/CN.4/2004/10, paras 26ff.

Declaration acknowledged the 'human right to land and to feed oneself'.[130] In addition, farmers' organizations from the South have at times adopted a loose form of human rights talk, referring to their 'right to food sovereignty' or their 'right to produce locally'.

A third aspect of FIAN's work has been the normative development of human rights law, to make it more directly applicable to international economic relations. One of the difficulties of working with human rights law in the area of agricultural trade liberalization is that the negative effects of trade policy choices in the agricultural sector are often felt overseas, rather than at home. Human rights law, on the other hand, has until recently been almost exclusively focused on the treatment by states of their own populations, within their own territories.[131] FIAN was one of three NGOs—the others being Brot für die Welt and EED—which took the lead in developing a normative framework for the extraterritorial application of human rights standards in the context of the right to food, helping to define a concept of extraterritorial state obligations (ETOs) owed by one state in respect of conditions of hunger and food deprivation in another.[132] They used this concept in a formal context for the first time in 2001 in a parallel report to the Committee on Economic, Social and Cultural Rights, as the Committee was undertaking its periodic review of Germany.[133] FIAN has since published a set of six case studies analysing possible violations of ETOs, three of which relate to ETOs in the context of trade and investment.[134] An 'ETO Consortium'—a group of thirty NGOs, universities, and individuals—has since been established to help to develop the conceptual and legal principles underpinning ETOs across the spectrum of economic, social, and cultural rights.[135]

[130] FoodFirst Information and Action Network (FIAN) and La Vía Campesina, 'Declaración de Cochabamba' (International Seminar 'Agrarian Reform and Gender' 2003) <http://www.fian.org/resources/documents/others/declaration-of-cochabamba/?searchterm=Cochabamba> accessed 15 February 2011.

[131] It is true that Art 11 of the ICESCR, from which the right to adequate food primarily derives, recognizes the 'essential importance of international cooperation', while Art 28 of the non-binding UDHR declares 'everyone is entitled to an international order in which the rights and freedoms set forth in this Declaration can be fully realized'. But these statements are relatively thin and vague, and have only begun to be developed quite recently.

[132] See eg R Kunnemann, 'The Extraterritorial Scope of the International Covenant on Economic, Social and Cultural Rights' (2001) <http://www.fian.org/resources/documents/others/extraterritorial-state-obligations-international-covenant-on-economic-social-and-cultural-rights> accessed 16 February 2011; see also generally on ETOs SI Skogly and M Gibney, 'Transnational Human Rights Obligations' (2002) 24 HRQ 781–98; S Skogly and M Gibney (eds), *Universal Human Rights and Extraterritorial Obligations* (University of Pennsylvania Press, Philadelphia, PA 2010).

[133] M Windfuhr, 'Compliance of Germany with its International Obligations under the International Covenant for Economic, Social and Cultural Rights (ICESCR)' (Parallel Report 2001) <http://www.fao.org/righttofood/kc/downloads/vl/docs/AH194.pdf> accessed 16 February 2011.

[134] eg R Kunnemann and U Hausmann, 'Germany's extraterritorial human rights obligations' (2006) <http://www.fian.org/resources/documents/others/germanys-extraterritorial-human-rights-obligations> accessed 16 February 2011.

[135] See FoodFirst Information Action Network (FIAN), 'ETO Consortium' <http://www.fian.org/programs-and-campaigns/projects/the-eto-consortium> accessed 16 February 2011 and Lancaster University (Law School), 'Universal Human Rights in Practice: States' Extraterritorial Obligations Related to

C. Crystallizing events

For all the important work of these and other groups, human rights language would probably have taken much longer to consolidate and entrench its position in debates around trade were it not for two significant events which developed in the years immediately after Seattle. The first was the rapid emergence of the controversy around the TRIPS agreement and essential pharmaceuticals. As is well known, throughout the late 1980s and 1990s, the US government had developed the practice of responding vigorously whenever governments in key foreign markets took measures which undermined the intellectual property protections enjoyed by US corporations, including US pharmaceutical companies.[136] A dispute arose between the United States and Brazil, for example, in respect of a series of measures enacted between 1996 and 1999 designed to facilitate the production of lower-cost generic versions of anti-retroviral drugs to combat the spread of AIDS in Brazil, alleging violations of the WTO's TRIPS agreement. Between 1997 and 2000, the US government also brought some pressure to bear on the South African government not to pass legislation, which had similar aims to the Brazilian measures. Again, the US government—alongside industry groups—made strong claims alleging the incompatibility of the South African legislation with the TRIPS agreement. Both Brazil and South Africa have strong domestic human rights cultures, as well as a constitutionally enshrined right to health, and as a result in both contexts the domestic political struggle to gain access to affordable anti-retroviral drugs was closely associated with human rights language, and in particular with the right to health. It was natural, then, that in both contexts resistance to US and corporate pressure was articulated in large part as a question of the protection of human rights, and the conflict came to be understood as a clear conflict between WTO rules and (initially domestic) human rights law. This episode did much to gain the attention of global human rights networks, especially around 2000 to 2001, and served as a crystal clear illustration of the potential for conflicts between trade law and international human rights law.

The second event relates to the campaign concerning services privatization which also developed around this time. In many countries, as noted above, one component of the neoliberal turn of the 1980s and 1990s was the disengagement of government from the direct provision of public services. In the developing world, this typically took the form of infrastructure privatization, for example in the water and energy sectors. In some countries—most visibly in various localities across Latin America—the privatization of water infrastructure in particular came to be highly controversial. Within that political culture, the involvement of foreign corporations in newly privatized water infrastructure became emblematic of neoliberal globalization generally, and moreover recalled deep-seated historical concerns in those countries about foreign control of local natural resources. From 2000, a number of major political

Economic, Social and Cultural Rights' <http://www.lancs.ac.uk/fass/projects/humanrights/> accessed 16 February 2011.

[136] See generally p 227 below and surrounding.

protests and uprisings occurred around the issue of water privatization, beginning in Cochabamba, Bolivia but extending also to Brazil, Argentina, and elsewhere.[137] These protests were typically led by a mix of labour unions, indigenous groups, and on occasion environmental organizations. In the developed world, concerns about privatization were primarily focused on 'essential services', especially health and education. Resistance to private sector participation in these sectors was often spearheaded by public services unions, concerned by the potential loss of jobs, reduction of service quality, and the erosion of the broader progressive social compact of which extensive subsidized social services have often been a part.

Services privatization initially had little if anything to do with the WTO, and it was only in the lead-up to the services negotiations in 2000 that the attention of civil society groups interested in contesting privatization turned to trade negotiations. From 2000 to 2003, a diverse group of NGOs came together to protest at what they perceived to be an attempt to extend and 'lock in' the privatization of essential services through WTO GATS commitments. Some international labour unions—most prominently the International Confederation of Free Trade Unions, Public Services International and Education International—played a leading role in this campaign, both at an educational and organizational level. Canadian groups, too, were conspicuous in this area, no doubt in large part due to a combination of their historical sensitivity to trade agreements and the strength of local support for a traditional government role in the supply of governmental services. Groups such as the Alliance for Democracy, the Canadian Center for Policy Alternatives, the Polaris Institute, and the Canadian Environmental Law Association played a part in the campaign.[138] In addition, given the sensitivity and symbolic importance of water privatization throughout some parts of the developing world, the GATS campaign also attracted the support of a variety of development NGOs closely connected to trade activism, such as the IGTN, TWN, ATTAC, WDM, and IFG, as well as environmental groups such as Friends of the Earth.[139]

For a number of reasons, this group of NGOs provided another natural context for the emergence of human rights language. For reasons specific to Canadian legal culture, Canadian NGOs have always been particularly open to human rights perspectives, and it was initially a number of Canadian NGOs who analysed in detail the impact of the GATS on the rights to health, water, and education. The prominence of unions was also important—as noted above, labour groups were among the first to articulate a conflict between trade agreements and human (labour)

[137] See generally M Finger and J Allouche, *Water Privatisation: Trans-national corporations and the re-regulation of the water industry* (Spon Press, London 2002).

[138] See eg M Swenarchuk, *From Global to Local: GATS Impacts on Canadian Municipalities* (Canadian Center for Policy Alternatives, Ottawa 2002); S Sinclair, *GATS: how the World Trade Organization's new 'services' negotiations threaten democracy* (Canadian Centre for Policy Alternatives, Ottawa 2000); S Sinclair, *The GATS Implications for Postal Services* (Canadian Centre for Policy Alternatives, Ottawa 2001); S Sinclair and J Grieshaber-Otto, *Facing the Facts: A Guide to the GATS Debates* (Canadian Center for Policy Alternatives, Ottawa 2002).

[139] One list can be found here: GATS Watch, 'Links to Organisations Critical of GATS' <http://www.gatswatch.org/GATScritics.html> accessed 16 February 2011.

rights, and were by and large comfortable with rights language and keen to introduce it. In this case, it was particularly attractive to have a human rights issue on which labour unions from developed countries could easily agree with their developing country counterparts—this was, after all, one of the major cleavages within the trade and human rights debate. Furthermore, the particular salience of water privatization in Latin America also provided fertile ground for human rights language. Ever since 1980, human rights had been an important language of popular resistance throughout Central and South America, and the legacy of leftist popular resistance movements proved especially amenable to the language of social rights. It is no surprise, then, that in 2004 the Uruguayan people voted in favour of a constitutional amendment defining water as a public good, specifically in opposition to policies of water privatization.[140]

In my view, these two events helped to solidify the place of human rights in debates around trade in the first years of the millennium, after the initial conceptual innovation of the period between roughly 1997 and 2000. In the years since, many of the large established human rights organizations—such as Human Rights Watch, the International Commission of Jurists, and Amnesty International—have developed profiles and programmes in and around trade issues. NGO activism around trade and investment issues has both benefited from and contributed to the resurgence of interest in social and economic rights among some elements of the transnational human rights movement. In addition, many of the groups involved in activism concerning trade, who do not explicitly have a human rights mandate, have begun to deploy human rights arguments to some extent. By the time of the WTO Ministerial in Hong Kong in 2005, it proved possible to put together the NGO Human Rights Caucus, a coalition of over a hundred organizations from virtually all the different strands of the global justice movement described earlier who argued for greater coherence between trade and human rights law.[141] Furthermore, the small coalition of actors who began with INCHRITI in 1998 have continued their work, helping (with others) to form and support the Human Dignity and Human Rights Caucus within the World Social Forum (WSF). Indeed, there has been some degree of mainstreaming of human rights within the WSF itself, and the Charter of the WSF contains reference to human rights.[142] More generally, it is not uncommon to see human rights offered as the normative basis for a different kind of globalization.[143]

[140] MH Mourra, 'Privatization of Water Management in Latin America' in TE Carbonneau and MH Mourra (eds), *Latin American Investment Treaty Arbitration: The Controversies and Conflicts* (Kluwer Law International, The Netherlands 2008) 83–104, 93.

[141] Human Rights Caucus, 'Statement of the Human Rights Caucus On the occasion of the Sixth Ministerial Conference of the World Trade Organization' (10 December 2005) <http://www.dd-rd.ca/site/_PDF/publications/globalization/wto/FINAL_WTO_HR_Caucus_Statement_English.pdf> accessed 16 February 2011.

[142] World Social Forum, 'Charter of Principles' (para 4) <http://www.forumsocialmundial.org.br/main.php?id_menu=4&cd_language=2> accessed 16 February 2011.

[143] eg Amnesty International, as quoted in R Munck, *Globalization and Contestation: The New Great Counter-Movement* (Routledge, New York, NY 2005) 78; M Robinson, 'Shaping Globalization: The Role

Of course, it is important not to overstate the extent to which human rights have been adopted more broadly as the language of the global justice movement. For every NGO which adopts a rights perspective or uses rights language, there are many more which do not, and still more who do so only partially or tangentially. The global justice movement is of course a 'movement of movements', which by its nature probably resists any single framing for the criticisms it brings to bear on contemporary forms of globalization, and the most we can say is that human rights have become one of the many frames which are deployed within that movement.[144] At the same time, however, it is fair to say that human rights have been established by now as one language in which resistance to free trade and free markets has been articulated. According to Munck, human rights 'are now an integral element' of global social movements against neoliberalism and globalization, at least rhetorically.[145]

D. Underlying logics

The story of the constitution of free trade as a human rights issue at the end of the twentieth century is incomplete without a discussion of the ways in which the UN human rights bodies and other official human rights forums took up trade issues from around 1997 onwards. That part of the narrative is continued in the next chapter. But before moving on, I want to conclude this chapter by offering some comments on why human rights have come to be adopted as a language of resistance in civil society advocacy around trade issues. The factors described above—the receptive contexts, the work of the broker organizations, and the crystallizing events—were necessary preconditions for the contemporary trade and human rights debate. But there were also deeper logics at play in this period, having to do with strategies of contestation in a legalized international order.

Part of the story has to do with the internal politics of the human rights movement. I made the point in Chapter 2 that during the late 1980s, and especially the first half of the 1990s, there was a revival and re-centring of ideas associated with the classic liberal human rights tradition within the international human rights movement as a whole. Almost immediately, however, this produced its own reaction and resistance from other traditions within the human rights movement, which are more focused on issues of economic justice, emphasize the importance of social and economic rights, and are profoundly sceptical about the human rights impact of free markets. The use of human rights language to articulate arguments against neoliberal economic globalization—including arguments against trade liberalization—should be understood as part of this reaction. The emergence of human rights criticisms of international trade was, in other words, an important part of a movement to reassert the centrality of economic justice issues within the contemporary human rights movement, and to resist the perceived colonization of human rights values and priorities by (neo)liberal voices. Human rights critiques of trade

of Human Rights' (2003) 97 Proceedings of the Annual Meeting (American Society of International Law) 1–12.

[144] della Porta (2006) 80.
[145] Munck (2005) 75.

liberalization, that is to say, represented one move in the ongoing struggle between various forms of liberal and counter-liberal voices over the heart of the human rights project, the struggle outlined in Chapter 2. In fact, it is worth noting that it has so far been relatively successful. Those who have sought to associate human rights with resistance to neoliberal globalization have to a significant extent succeeded in repositioning human rights in discussions around economic liberalism, so that human rights language is nowadays less often associated with advocacy of free markets, and more often associated with concerns about the social costs of free market and free trade policies.

Another part of the answer to why human rights have been adopted as a language of resistance to neoliberal globalization has to do with the internal politics of the global justice movement. On one level, the use of human rights language within this movement has been the result of highly contingent historical forces—the efforts of key individuals and organizations who happen to have personal commitments to the human rights movement, the development of personal ties between human rights organizations and other groups, and the special historical resonance of human rights language in the particular cultural contexts in which key events in the movement have taken place, and so on. But there are also concrete and well-understood advantages which a human rights framework can bring to the work of political advocacy,[146] of which it is worth mentioning three in the present context. First, and most obviously, invoking the language of human rights seems to give individual political projects a greater degree of legitimacy, elevating them in Alston's words 'above the rank and file of competing [projects]', giving them 'a degree of immunity from challenge and generally endow[ing them], with an aura of timelessness, absoluteness and universal validity'.[147] If, as Henkin has famously suggested, human rights are the 'idea of our time',[148] then there is much to be gained from allying a specific political project to that idea.

Secondly, the adoption of a human rights frame can help in the task of coalition-building. As Bob has noted, when local political struggles are articulated in rights language, they can gain a level of international visibility they may otherwise have lacked.[149] Rights language can help to constitute a sense of common cause with groups in other countries ('we are all engaged in the project of defending human rights') and thus help to build transnational solidarity networks which can mobilize new and additional resources for local political struggles. The material covered in this

[146] On the importance of framing generally within the practice of political advocacy, see JA Noakes and H Johnston, 'Frames of Protest: A Road Map to a Perspective' in H Johnston and JA Noakes (eds), *Frames of Protest: Social Movements and the Framing Perspective* (Rowman & Littlefield Publishers, Lanham, MD 2005) 1–29.

[147] P Alston, 'Making Space for New Human Rights: The Case of the Right to Development' (1988) 1 Harvard Human Rights Ybk 3–40, 3; See also generally N Stammers, 'Social movements and the Social Construction of Human Rights' (1999) 21 HRQ 980–1008.

[148] L Henkin, *The Rights of Man Today* (Stevens and Sons, London 1979) iii.

[149] C Bob, 'Globalization and the Social Construction of Human Rights Campaigns' in A Brysk (ed), *Globalization and Human Rights* (University of California Press, Berkeley, CA 2002) 133–47, 135 and generally; see also generally Keck and Sikkink (1998).

chapter illustrates this dynamic well. Describing the private appropriation of the medicinal qualities of the Indian neem tree as a violation of the rights of indigenous peoples, or the displacement of Brazilian peasant farmers as a violation of the right to food, or the restriction of compulsory licensing in South Africa as a violation of the right to health, are all clear examples of the use of human rights language to internationalize a local cause and thereby build support for it. In each case, local resistance groups have been able to benefit from the ability to create effective transnational coalitions through global human rights networks. Similarly, the FTAA negotiations provide another example where the adoption of a human rights frame resulted in a broadening of civil society networks against trade, as human rights coalitions already engaged with the Inter-American human rights system came to be mobilized around economic integration issues.

Thirdly, human rights were probably useful in that they helped to provide something close to a common normative foundation for a tremendously diverse movement. For the first years of its existence (and to a large extent still) the global justice movement lacked a unifying frame to cohere the disparate threads of its substantive critique of the international economic order. The notion of a common enemy, a common fight against 'neoliberalism' or 'corporate globalization', proved a useful and enduring framework which emerged at that time.[150] But human rights was also important because it offered the promise of a shared *positive* vision, which was sufficiently flexible and general to reflect, contain, and provide a degree of rhetorical unity for, the diverse political projects being pursued within the global justice movement.[151] Human rights, in other words, provided a ready-made, well-accepted framework of principles for a movement sorely in need of a secure normative foundation: 'human rights offer a principle on which to base opposition to the challenges posed by economic globalisation'.[152] Furthermore, not only is human rights a flexible framework, it was also internationalist in orientation. Resistance to international trade is all too easily discredited as nothing more than economic nationalism and parochialism—there is, after all, a long history of such political movements within protectionist coalitions. For many within the global justice movement, this was not a welcome association, partly because association with protectionist coalitions in the traditional sense tended to de-legitimate the movement generally, but also because this association did not fit comfortably with many groups' self-perception as fundamentally internationalist in outlook. Articulating their vision in terms of respect for human rights, then, reaffirmed their internationalist credentials, and helped to make the claims to others within the movement that international law had its positive as well as its negative sides. Particularly for moderates, adopting the human rights frame helped to support

[150] See generally Ayres (2004) 11–34.

[151] Munck (2005) 79 (describing human rights as a 'floating signifier').

[152] See M Kothari, 'Globalisation, Social Action and Human Rights' in M Mehra (ed), *Human Rights and Economic Globalisation: Directions for the WTO* (Global Publications Foundation, Uppsala, Sweden 1999) 37–60, 46, see also 40–1.

claims that the movement was for a different *kind* of globalization, rather than against 'the global' as a blanket proposition.

But there is another reason that human rights came to be adopted as a language of resistance to trade liberalization and economic globalization, which has nothing to do with the internal politics of either the human rights regime or the global justice movement. Instead, it has to do with the legalization of global governance, particularly as it relates to trade. As is well known, the transformation of the GATT into the WTO at the completion of the Uruguay Round involved, among many other things, a legalization of trade politics.[153] One important result of this, for the purposes of the present argument, was that for civil society organizations working in the global justice movement, engaging effectively on international trade issues required personnel with international legal training, who could speak credibly and authoritatively about the impact of WTO law on domestic policy-making processes. Critiquing the GATT/WTO system inevitably involved detailed legal argument and the technical analysis of complex judgments, and therefore over time became increasingly the domain of lawyers and the legally trained, working both within the academy and within civil society. As the field became increasingly populated by those with training in international law, it was almost natural that human rights would emerge as a rhetorical tool for advocacy around international trade. International lawyers are typically familiar with the language of international human rights law, and are very comfortable working with it. Indeed, a number of civil society actors who had been working on trade issues since around the time of the *Tuna/Dolphin* dispute already had some experience of using international environmental law to resist and contest international trade law, and from there it is only a very short step to the use of human rights law for the same purpose.

In addition, international human rights law was useful for the obvious reason that it is itself a body of legal rules binding on states, of the same formal status as international trade law. If one of the main problems of the WTO system, in the view of these civil society actors, was the level of constraint which international trade law imposed on WTO Members, then it was obviously helpful to be able to point to an alternative set of international legal obligations, which make different demands of states, and push in a different direction. Framing critical claims as obligations imposed by international human rights law immediately placed them on a formally equal footing to the obligations imposed by international trade law. Human rights law offered, in other words, the promise of an effective legal shield for states wishing to depart from some of the constraints imposed by trade agreements. In order to make this shield effective and operational, all that was required were credible legal arguments that the measures that these states wished to take in contravention of trade law were required by human rights law—or at least in furtherance of human rights obligations—as well as a willingness on the part of trade dispute settlement bodies to hear legal arguments based on human rights law. As we shall see in the next chapters, there were many who swiftly set about trying to accomplish both of these goals.

153 See generally Ch 8.

4

Inter-Regime Contestation

This chapter begins by chronicling the way that official international human rights bodies began to address international trade issues from about 1998 onwards. During this time, international human rights bodies adopted and re-articulated many of the critiques of trade emanating from the global justice movement—but they did so selectively, incrementally, and usually in a moderated and modified form. The result was that by at least the middle of the 2000s, there was a burgeoning international legal debate concerning the relationship between trade law and human rights law. In the second part of this chapter, I shift gears, and focus on the dominant discursive framework of this debate, which I call the 'coherence framework'. I describe the nature of this discursive framework, and show how it shaped the lines of inquiry and criticism which have so far been characteristic of the trade and human rights debate. The argument I make in this part lays the groundwork for Chapter 5, which explores the way that this discursive framework has decisively oriented the role that international lawyers are currently playing in the construction and contestation of global economic governance.

I. International human rights institutions' engagements with trade

As described in Chapter 2, the first time that the international human rights regime paid close attention to issues around international trade was during the period from the early 1970s to the mid-1980s, when developing countries began to advocate for a 'right to development' as a rhetorical vehicle to support their advocacy for a New International Economic Order (NIEO). From at least the mid-1980s, however, the momentum behind the NIEO had begun to wane. The debt crises which afflicted many developing countries during the early 1980s helped to change the conversation, so that international activism around development issues began to focus most prominently on the issues of debt relief for poor countries, and the social consequences of the structural adjustment programmes which had been implemented in the wake of those crises under the supervision of international financial institutions.[1] This new conversation began to take root in the UN human rights system from about 1989, when the Commission on Human Rights and the Sub-Commission on Prevention of Discrimination and Protection of Minorities began to adopt a series of

[1] See pp 77–8 above.

annual resolutions drawing attention to the social costs of structural adjustment, as well as the pressing problem of foreign debt burdens for developing countries. In 1990, the Sub-Commission requested its Special Rapporteur on Economic, Social and Cultural Rights[2] to submit a report on 'questions of the effects of structural adjustment on economic, social and cultural rights and on the role of the international financial institutions, notably the World Bank and the International Monetary Fund (IMF), in the realization of these rights'.[3] In his two following reports, submitted between 1991 and 1992, the Special Rapporteur reviewed and reinforced a number of the criticisms of structural adjustment programmes contained in reports from organizations such as UNICEF, UNCTAD and UNDP, and echoed their calls for 'adjustment with a human face'.[4] Concerns about structural adjustment also surfaced in other venues within the United Nations over the next few years, for example, in reports of the Special Rapporteur on Extreme Poverty,[5] as well as a 1995 report by the Secretary-General setting out preliminary basic Policy Guidelines on structural adjustment programmes.[6]

Over the course of the 1990s, the conversation shifted again. As the global justice movement gradually coalesced during that decade, concerns about structural adjustment and debt became only one strand of a much larger set of critiques of neoliberal economic globalization, including international trade and investment liberalization.[7] The first human rights institution to take up these critiques, around the middle of the 1990s, was the International Labour Organization, in the context of debate on the impact of globalization on labour rights, and the campaign to include a 'social clause' in the WTO agreements. I will have more to say about this episode in Chapter 5[8]—for now it is sufficient to note that it left a bad taste in the mouths of many developing country delegations in the WTO, who perceived the linkage of trade with labour rights to be primarily motivated by protectionist union lobbies in the North. Indeed, this experience continued to colour the discussion of the relationship between trade and human rights for some time over the course of the second half of the 1990s. In part as a result of this, there was initially considerable resistance to addressing trade issues in UN human right bodies, from representatives of

[2] Danilo Türk, who also sat as chair of the Sub-Commission at the time, and who had previously been Vice-Chairman of the Working Group on the Right to Development from 1981 to 1984.

[3] UNCHR (Sub-Commission), 'The Realization of Economic, Social and Cultural Rights: Second progress report prepared by Mr Danilo Türk, Special Rapporteur' (18 July 1991) UN Doc E/CN.4/Sub.2/1991/17.

[4] ibid; UNCHR (Sub-Commission), 'The Realization of Economic, Social and Cultural Rights: Final report prepared by Mr Danilo Türk, Special Rapporteur' (3 July 1992) UN Doc E/CN.4/Sub.2/1992/16, para 229.

[5] UNCHR (Sub-Commission), 'The Realization of Economic, Social and Cultural Rights: Final report on human rights and extreme poverty, submitted by the Special Rapporteur, Mr Leandro Despouy' (28 June 1996) UN Doc E/CN.4/Sub.2/1996/13, para 89.

[6] UNCHR (Sub-Commission), 'The Realization of Economic, Social and Cultural Rights: Preliminary set of basic policy guidelines on structural adjustment programmes and economic, social and cultural rights' (4 July 1995) UN Doc E/CN.4/Sub.2/1995/10

[7] See generally GM Zagel, 'WTO and Human Rights: Examining Linkages and Suggesting Convergences' (International Development Law Organization Voices of Development Jurists Paper Series 2005) <http://www.worldtradelaw.net/articles/zagelhumanrights.pdf> accessed 15 February 2011.

[8] See pp 137–42 below.

developing countries concerned about the potential use of human rights language to support and legitimate protectionist policies in the North. Another reason for this resistance had to do with the simple problem of unfamiliarity—many working within official UN human rights bodies did not perceive themselves as having the necessary expertise in trade and investment to take the issues on effectively.

However, the resistance from developing countries was largely overcome when it became clear that human rights could be used as a 'shield'—that is, a means to help developing countries to resist pressure from the developed world in the context of trade negotiations and trade policy—rather than as a 'sword' against the interests of developing countries. With this proviso, some developing countries became major sponsors of the push to get the human rights regime to address trade issues. In addition, other developing country governments saw a focus on economic globalization as a welcome chance to reinvigorate work on economic and social rights within the human rights regime—as well as (in the political bodies at least) an opportunity to shift the habitual position of developing countries from accused to accusers in human rights matters. As we shall see, this had an important influence on the kinds of issues which were, and were not, taken up in the human rights regime in subsequent years.[9]

After some initial mobilization over the course of 1998, a major turning point came in April 1999, when the Commission on Human Rights formally requested 'all the treaty bodies, special rapporteurs/representatives, independent experts and working groups of the Commission, within their mandates and where appropriate, to take into consideration the issue of the impact of globalization on the full enjoyment of all human rights in their reports'.[10] From this point, a broad programme on the human rights impact of economic globalization became entrenched as a major focus of attention across a number of international human rights bodies. A particular focus on trade issues emerged within four primary contexts.[11]

[9] Most conspicuously, issues relating to labour conditions and human rights 'conditionality' were hardly addressed within the UN human rights system—though they did continue to receive attention within the broader literature on trade and human rights, and labour rights were of course given considerable attention in the ILO (see Ch 5 below).

[10] UNCHR, 'Globalization and its impact on the full enjoyment of all human rights' (28 April 1999) UN Doc E/CN.4/RES/1999/59. Since then there has been an almost yearly resolution on the issue: UNCHR, 'Globalization and its impact on the full enjoyment of all human rights' (20 April 2001) UN Doc E/CN.4/RES/2001/32; UNCHR, 'Globalization and its impact on the full enjoyment of all human rights' (22 April 2002) UN Doc E/CN.4/RES/2002/28; UNCHR, 'Globalization and its impact on the full enjoyment of all human rights' (22 April 2003) UN Doc E/CN.4/RES/2003/23; UNCHR, 'Globalization and its impact on the full enjoyment of all human rights' (16 April 2004) UN Doc E/CN.4/RES/2004/24; UNCHR, 'Globalization and its impact on the full enjoyment of all human rights' (15 April 2005) UN Doc E/CN.4/RES/2005/17.

[11] For another overview of human rights bodies' work on trade, see W Benedek, 'The World Trade Organization and Human Rights' in W Benedek, K De Feyter, and F Marrella (eds), *Economic Globalisation and Human Rights* (CUP, Cambridge 2007) 137–69, 143ff. For a fascinating account of the forces which led to intellectual property and the TRIPS agreement being included on the agenda of the Sub-Commission, see D Weissbrodt and K Schoff, 'Human Rights Approach to Intellectual Property Protection; The Genesis and Application of Sub-Commission Resolution 2000/7' (2003) 5 Minnesota Intellectual Property Rev 1.

A. The Committee on Economic, Social and Cultural Rights

The mobilization of the Committee on Economic, Social and Cultural Rights (CESCR) around trade issues was in significant part the result of lobbying on behalf of some civil society organizations, prominently including the Geneva-based members of INCHRITI.[12] In April 1998, Kothari and Krause published an article specifically designed as a wake up call to the human rights movement in respect of the (then ongoing) negotiations over a Multilateral Agreement on Investment (MAI).[13] Noting that the human rights community had traditionally been slow to react to violations of economic, social, and cultural rights—referring in particular to its 'sluggish' response to structural adjustment programmes—the authors urged the human rights movement to respond more quickly to what they saw as the threat posed by the MAI to human rights. They observed that environmental groups had 'used the framework of multilateral environmental agreements to marshal international law arguments against the MAI', and argued that the human rights community should do the same with human rights law, particularly economic and social rights. The 'rapidly globalising regime of trade and finance' they suggested, must 'conform to international human rights standards'.[14]

One of the first bodies to respond to this call was the Committee on Economic, Social and Cultural Rights, a body of independent experts originally established by ECOSOC in 1985 to monitor the implementation of the International Covenant on Economic, Social and Cultural Rights (ICESCR). In May 1998, the CESCR held a 'day of general discussion', bringing together a variety of representatives from the Office of the High Commissioner for Human Rights (OHCHR), UN bodies, specialized agencies, NGOs, and individual experts, and addressing a variety of different issues around the theme of the impact of globalization on economic, social, and cultural rights.[15] The statement arising from that day of discussion raised a number of concerns. It noted the global trend towards 'increasing reliance on the free market', a 'diminution in the role of the state', and the privatization and deregulation of a range of activities traditionally associated with state intervention. While acknowledging that these developments 'are not necessarily incompatible' with the ICESCR, it noted specific problems which they could create for the rights to work,

[12] See Weissbrodt and Schoff (2003) 26 for further detail on the lobbying efforts of these individuals.

[13] M Kothari and T Krause, 'Human Rights or Corporate Rights? The MAI Challenge' (1998) 5 Human Rights Tribune 16.

[14] ibid 17.

[15] See eg UNCHR, 'Globalization v. Globalism: Giving Internationalism a Bad Name; Background paper submitted by Mark Ritchie, President, Institute for Agriculture and Trade Policy' (11 May 1998) UN Doc E/C.12/1998/5; UNCHR, 'Globalization and economic and social rights of women: article 2, paragraph 2, and article 7 of the International Covenant on Economic, Social and Cultural Rights; Background paper submitted by Mirta Teitelbaum' (11 May 1998) UN Doc E/C.12/1998/6; UNCHR, 'Globalization and the human rights set forth in articles 6 to 8 of the International Covenant on Economic, Social and Cultural Rights; Background paper submitted by Alejandro Teitelabum' (11 May 1998) UN Doc E/C.12/1998/7, UNCHR, 'Globalization and its impact on the enjoyment of economic and social rights; Background paper submitted by the International Confederation of Free Trade Unions (ICFTU)' (11 May 1998) UN Doc E/C.12/1998/4.

social security, health, and education. The statement called for 'new or complementary approaches' to ensure that these policies were carried out in a manner compatible with economic and social rights. Noting the important role of international organizations in promoting neoliberal policies during the 1980s and 1990s, the CESCR emphasized that these organizations 'should play a positive and constructive role in relation to human rights', and called for the WTO and the Secretary-General to conduct more systematic studies of the impacts of trade and investment policies on human rights—including the MAI.[16]

The following year, in November 1999, the CESCR joined the many civil society voices around the Seattle Ministerial, issuing its own statement to the WTO. This statement urged the WTO 'to undertake a review of... international trade and investment policies and rules' to ensure their consistency with human rights obligations and to ensure that 'human rights principles and obligations are fully integrated in future negotiations in the World Trade Organization' so that 'human rights norms... shape the process of international economic policy formation'.[17] Over the course of the next eight months or so, the CESCR held additional workshops in close collaboration with INCHRITI and other civil society organizations, to develop strategies for ways to take these issues forward.[18]

Having played an important mobilizing role in the early period from 1998 to 2000, the CESCR in the following years incorporated trade issues into its work in two main ways. One way was to introduce a review of certain elements of trade policy in its periodic monitoring and supervision procedure. This was again in large part the result of the activities of NGOs such as 3D→THREE, which did important work educating and informing members of the CESCR on trade issues.[19] As a result, the issues raised in this monitoring procedure corresponded closely with the issues circulating among NGOs involved in the global justice movement, as identified in the previous chapter. For example, the CESCR's Concluding Observations on the Jamaican review of 2001 raised the issue of small farmers' inability to provide for their families 'allegedly owing to trade agreements' which had left them unable to compete with cheaper imported foods.[20] In 2004, the CESCR urged Ecuador 'to conduct an assessment of the effect of international trade rules on the right to health' in the light

[16] CESCR, 'Statement on globalization and its impact on the enjoyment of economic and social rights' (May 1998) <http://www.unhchr.ch/tbs/doc.nsf/0/0fad63/Febf7a89580256738003ee/9a?opendocument> accessed 16 February 2011.

[17] CESCR, 'Statement of the UN Committee on Economic, Social and Cultural Rights to the Third Ministerial Conference of the World Trade Organization (Seattle, 30 November to 3 December 1999)' (26 November 1999) UN Doc E/C.12/1999/9.

[18] See eg CESCR, 'Record of the CESCR and INCHRITI Workshop on International Trade, Investment and Finance and Economic, Social and Cultural Rights: The Role of the Committee on Economic, Social and Cultural Rights' (6 May 2000) <http://www.unhchr.ch/tbs/doc.nsf/0/11d06750ac4e7acbc125691f002f01f0?Opendocument> accessed 15 February 2011.

[19] For a list of Country Briefings published by 3D→THREE in this context see <http://www.3dthree.org/en/page.php?IDpage=23> accessed 16 February 2011, and for an account of that organization's efforts in this respect, see D Ovett, 'Making Trade Policies More Accountable and Human Rights-Consistent: A NGO Perspective of Using Human Rights Instruments in the Case of Access to Medicines' in W Benedek, K De Feyter, and F Marrella (eds), *Economic Globalisation and Human Rights* (CUP, Cambridge 2007) 192–200.

[20] CESCR, 'Concluding observations of the Committee on Economic, Social and Cultural Rights: Jamaica' (30 November 2001) UN Doc E/C.12/1/Add.75, para 15.

of the restrictions placed by trade agreements on the availability and affordability of generic drugs, and to ensure that human rights obligations were taken into account in its conduct of trade negotiations.[21] In a review of Costa Rica, the Committee reflected civil society activism around the Central American Free Trade Agreement (CAFTA), noting its concern about the potential impact of CAFTA on 'traditional agriculture, labour rights, access to health, social security and the intellectual property regimes... access to generic medicines, biodiversity, water and the rights of indigenous communities associated [with] these resources'.[22] The Indian review of 2008 similarly raised the issue of extreme poverty among small farmers 'exacerbated by the introduction of genetically modified seeds by multinational corporations', and recommended that India should review all aspects of negotiations of trade agreements to ensure their conformity with human rights obligations, particularly with reference to the most disadvantaged groups.[23] It is worth noting that since around 2005, the Committee on the Rights of the Child (CRC) has to some extent followed the lead of the CESCR in this respect. Thus, the CRC has noted in its reviews of Botswana, Costa Rica, Ecuador, Nicaragua, and the Philippines that proposed FTAs involving those countries may undermine the provision of essential services and affordable medicines for poor and vulnerable people.[24]

The second way in which the CESCR has incorporated trade issues into its work has been through its General Comments. Over the course of six General Comments—on food, health, water, intellectual property, work, and social security[25]—the CESCR has gradually developed an innovative new set of normative claims designed to give human rights law some practical legal bite in the context of multilateral and bilateral trade negotiations. A variety of formulations have been attempted, all focusing on the need for decisions taken in, through, and by international organizations not to have a negative impact on human rights. In its earliest

[21] CESCR, 'Concluding observations of the Committee on Economic, Social and Cultural Rights: Ecuador' (7 June 2004) UN Doc E/C.12/1/Add.100.

[22] CESCR, 'Consideration of reports submitted by States Parties under Articles 16 and 17 of the Covenant: Costa Rica; Draft concluding observations of the Committee on Economic, Social and Cultural Rights' (4 January 2008) UN Doc E/C.12/CRI/CO/4, para 27.

[23] CESCR, 'Concluding Observations of the Committee on Economic Social and Cultural Rights: India' (8 August 2008) UN Doc E/C.12/IND/CO/5, paras 29, 46.

[24] For a summary of the CRC's (and other treaty monitoring bodies') references to intellectual property and human rights between 2004 and 2006, see 3D→THREE, 'UN Human Rights Treaty Monitoring Bodies Review of State Implementation of International Conventions (ICESCR, ICCPR and CRC): References to Intellectual Property and Human Rights' <http://www.3dthree.org/pdf_3D/Treaty-BodyIPrefs_en.pdf> accessed 15 February 2011; see also Ovett, 'Make Trade Policies More Accountable' in Benedek, De Feyter, and Marrella (2007).

[25] CESCR, 'General Comment 12: The right to adequate food (Art. 11)' (12 May 1999) UN Doc E/C.12/1999/5; CESCR, 'General Comment No. 14 (2000): The right to the highest attainable standard of health' (11 August 2000) UN Doc E/C.12/2000/4; CESCR, 'General Comment No. 15 (2002): The right to water' (20 January 2003) UN Doc E/C.12/2002/11; CESCR, 'General Comment No. 17 (2005): The right of everyone to benefit from the protection of the moral and material interests resulting from any scientific, literary or artistic production of which he or she is the author' (12 January 2006) UN Doc E/C.12/GC/17; CESCR, 'General Comment No. 18: The right to work' (6 February 2006) UN Doc E/C.12/GC/18; CESCR, 'General Comment No. 19: The right to social security' (4 February 2008) UN Doc E/C.12/GC/19.

formulation, for example, the CESCR argued that 'States parties should, in international agreements whenever relevant, ensure that the right to adequate food is given due attention'.[26] A year later, this formulation was expanded somewhat to include the claim that 'States parties should take steps to ensure that these instruments do not adversely impact upon the right to health'.[27] More specifically still, in 2002: 'agreements concerning trade liberalization should not curtail or inhibit a country's capacity to ensure the full realization of the right to water'.[28] The same formulation was adopted in relation to the right to social security.[29] Similarly, 'as members of international organizations such as... the World Trade Organization (WTO), States parties have an obligation to take whatever measures they can to ensure that the policies and decisions of those organizations are in conformity with their obligations under the Covenant'.[30] More positively, in relation to the right to work, 'States parties should endeavour to promote the right to work in other countries as well as in bilateral and multilateral negotiations'.[31] Finally, in addition to these obligations on states themselves to take due account of human rights in trade negotiations, the CESCR has also begun to develop obligations of a sort applying directly to the WTO itself. For example, it has argued that 'international organizations concerned with trade such as the World Trade Organization (WTO), should cooperate effectively with States parties, building on their respective expertise, in relation to the implementation' of human rights.[32]

B. Special Procedures and Special Rapporteurs

The CESCR was not the only human rights body being encouraged to take up trade and investment issues in 1998. Civil society groups were also lobbying the Sub-Commission on Prevention of Discrimination and Protection of Minorities (as it was known until 1999, subsequently the Sub-Commision on the Promotion and Protection of Human Rights) at the same time.[33] Initially, as noted above, these groups encountered a degree of resistance, both from those who saw trade and investment as outside their area of expertise, and from those wary of allying the human rights framework with protectionist interests. But with these concerns overcome, the Sub-Commission's first action came in August 1998 with a resolution, adopted without a vote, entitled 'Human Rights as the primary objective of trade,

[26] CESCR (E/C.12/1999/5) para 36; see also CESCR (UN Doc E/C.12/2000/4) para 39; CESCR (UN Doc E/C.12/GC/19) para 56.
[27] CESCR (UN Doc E/C.12/2000/4) para 39.
[28] CESCR (UN Doc E/C.12/2002/11) para 35.
[29] CESCR (UN Doc E/C.12/GC/19) para 57.
[30] CESCR (UN Doc E/C.12/GC/17) para 56.
[31] CESCR (UN Doc E/C.12/GC/18) para 30.
[32] CESCR (UN Doc E/C.12/2000/4) para 64; CESCR (UN Doc E/C.12/2002/11) para 60; CESCR (UN Doc E/C.12/GC/18) para 53.
[33] See eg M Kothari and P Prove, 'The Sub-Commission and Globalization: Guest Editorial' (1998) 5 (4) Human Rights Tribune 5.

investment and finance policy'.[34] Recalling the CESCR statement a few months earlier, it noted the 'need to re-emphasize the centrality and primacy of human rights obligations . . . including international and regional trade, investment and finance policies, agreements and practices', and called for urgent attention across the human rights system to the human rights impacts of trade and investment agreements, including the Multilateral Agreement on Investment.[35] This was followed the next year by another resolution, which (reflecting a similar shift in attention in civil society from the MAI to the WTO in anticipation of the Seattle Ministerial) focused now on the WTO and trade liberalization.[36]

The first of these Sub-Commission resolutions requested a working paper on the 'ways and means by which the primacy of human rights norms and standards could be better reflected in, and could better inform, international and regional trade, investment and financial policies'.[37] The working paper under this mandate was produced in June 1999.[38] It outlined some key human rights instruments relevant to economic globalization, identified the main international financial institutions to which these human rights ought to be applied, and paid critical attention to the processes by which the (then recently aborted) MAI negotiations had proceeded. While trade and the WTO were addressed only in a minor way, the paper did note the shift of attention that was under way at that time, from the MAI to the WTO. As a result, when the authors were subsequently appointed as Special Rapporteurs on globalization and its impact on the full enjoyment of human rights,[39] their next report dedicated a significant section to the WTO.[40] In keeping with the tone of civil society activism of the period, the report adopted a relatively critical and confrontational attitude to international trade and the GATT/WTO system. The authors expressed their concerns about the impact of WTO rules on food security, the paternalism of rights-based trade sanctions, the non-transparency of WTO negotiations, and the appropriation of the knowledge and biological resources of indigenous peoples. They claimed that WTO agreements are based on economic assumptions

[34] UNCHR (Sub-Commission), Res 1998/12 (20 August 1998) UN Doc E/CN.4/SUB.2/RES/1998/12.

[35] ibid preamble 2.

[36] UNCHR (Sub-Commission), Res 1999/30 (26 August 1999) UN Doc E/CN.4/SUB.2/RES/1999/30. For subsequent years' resolutions, see UNCHR (Sub-Commission) Res 2000/7 (17 August 2000) UN Doc E/CN.4/SUB.2/RES/2000/7; UNCHR (Sub-Commission) Res 2001/4 (15 August 2001) UN Doc E/CN.4/SUB.2/RES/2001/4; UNCHR (Sub-Commission) Res 2001/5 (15 August 2001) UN Doc E/CN.4/SUB.2/RES/2001/5; UNCHR (Sub-Commission) Res 2001/21 (16 August 2001) UN Doc E/CN.4/SUB.2/RES/2001/21; UNCHR (Sub-Commission) Res 2002/11 (14 August 2002) UN Doc E/CN.4/SUB.2/RES/2001/11.

[37] UNCHR (Sub Commission), Res 1998/12 (20 August 1998) UN Doc E/CN.4/SUB.2/RES/1998/12, para 4.

[38] UNCHR (Sub-Commission), 'Human rights as the primary objective of international trade, investment and finance policy and practice: Working paper submitted by J Oloka-Onyango and Deepika Udagama, in accordance with Sub-Commission resolution 1998/12' (17 June 1999) UN Doc E/CN.4/Sub.2/1999/11.

[39] UNCHR (Sub-Commission) Res 1999/8 (25 August 1999) UN Doc E/CN.4/SUB.2/RES/1999/8.

[40] UNCHR (Sub-Commission), 'Preliminary report submitted by J Oloka-Onyango and Deepika Udagama, in accordance with Sub-Commission resolution 1999/8' (15 June 2000) UN Doc E/CN.4/Sub.2/2000/13 paras 13–19.

which are 'grossly unfair and even prejudiced', and 'reflect an agenda that serves only to promote dominant corporate interests'.[41] They described the WTO as a 'practical manifestation of globalization in its trade and commercial aspects' and a 'veritable nightmare' for certain sectors of humanity, particularly the developing countries of the South.[42] Unsurprisingly, this report was received very poorly in the WTO and the Geneva trade community generally, and according to some was one important factor in souring relations between the two regimes in the early years of the emerging dialogue between the trade and human rights communities.[43]

In the following years, these Special Rapporteurs submitted two further papers. The 2001 paper explored some of the 'tensions and complementarities' between international economic law and international human rights.[44] They noted in particular the concerns about the TRIPS agreement and its impact on the right to health and the rights of farmers and indigenous peoples, and the practical accessibility of the WTO's dispute settlement system for developing countries as well as its openness to the public.[45] More generally, they framed the challenge as the need to 'resolv[e] the tensions [between] the two regimes of law . . . [and] to ensure that there is greater coherence between' them.[46] They lamented the fact that 'international economic law has largely not paid much attention to international human rights, and vice versa' and that 'the current system of regulation of the international economy has scant space or time for human rights and other social values'.[47] Their final paper, submitted in 2003, reflected on some of the changes which had occurred in the operation of the WTO since 2001, including the partial resolution of the access to drugs issue in the Doha Declaration.[48] While acknowledging these developments, they noted that:

> While it is quite true that what can be termed human rights considerations do find their way into the negotiations as well as into dispute settlement, this is not necessarily done in a systematic or deliberate manner. Neither are the mechanisms designed in such a way as to ensure that human rights concerns are taken into account as a matter of course.[49]

41 ibid para 14.
42 ibid para 15.
43 C Dommen, 'No Sell-Out on Trade in the Human Rights Commission' (April 2003) <http://198.170.85.29/Trade-Human-Rights-Commission.htm> accessed 15 February 2011; S Singh, 'U.N. Human Rights Commissioner Responds to the WTO' (29 August 2000) <http://www.twnside.org.sg/title/responds.htm> accessed 15 February 2011.
44 UNCHR (Sub-Commission), 'Progress report submitted by J Oloka-Onyango and Deepika Udagama, in accordance with Sub-Commission resolution 1999/8 and Commission on Human Rights decision 2000/102' (2 July 2001) UN Doc E/CN.4/Sub.2/2001/10, paras 14ff.
45 ibid paras 19–53.
46 ibid para 14.
47 ibid para 15.
48 UNCHR (Sub-Commission), 'Final report submitted by J Oloka-Onyango and Deepika Udagama, in accordance with Sub-Commission decision 2000/105' (25 June 2003) UN Doc E/CN.4/Sub.2/2003/14.
49 ibid para 25.

There is, they suggested, 'no guarantee that the imperative of trade concerns does not get superior treatment' to the imperative of protecting human rights.[50]

Other Special Rapporteurs appointed around this time also brought to their roles an interest and expertise in trade issues.[51] For example, the first Special Rapporteur on the right to adequate housing, appointed in 2000 by the Commission on Human Rights,[52] was Miloon Kothari, mentioned in the previous chapter as a key member of the INCHRITI coalition. In his second report in 2002 (and to a lesser extent his third in 2003), he addressed the impact of economic globalization on housing rights, including some reference to the GATS in a section on the privatization of service provision. Drawing on the work of NGOs such as PSIRU and others, the Special Rapporteur adopted particularly strong criticism of water privatization, and specifically warned that 'the . . . GATS . . . in particular, is expected to further deepen the process of privatization of resources and services relevant to housing rights, such as electricity, water, [and] sanitation'.[53] He re-emphasized the 'primacy of human rights' in guiding the activities of states and international institutions which promote privatization.[54]

In 2002, the Commission on Human Rights appointed a Special Rapporteur on the right of everyone to the enjoyment of the highest attainable standard of physical and mental health.[55] Having served as an independent expert on the CESCR from 1999 to 2002, the Special Rapporteur, Paul Hunt, was already focused on trade issues, and issues relating to the WTO were again raised in his consultations with civil society over the initial focus of his mandate.[56] Partly as a result, he took what was at that time the unique step of organizing a 'country mission' to the WTO in 2003. In collaboration with key personnel from the OHCHR, the Special Rapporteur organized a series of meetings with senior staff from the WTO Secretariat, personnel from the Geneva trade delegations of some WTO Members, chairpersons of a number of WTO Committees, and others to discuss the impacts of various

50 ibid para 25.

51 In addition to those discussed below, see UNCHR, 'Adverse effects of the illicit movement and dumping of toxic and dangerous products and wastes on the enjoyment of human rights: Report of the Special Rapporteur, Okechukwu Ibeanu' (14 December 2004) UN Doc E/CN.4/2005/45; UNCHR, 'Question of the realization in all countries of the economic, social and cultural rights contained in the Universal Declaration of Human Rights and in the International Covenant on Economic, Social and Cultural Rights, and study of special problems which the developing countries face in their efforts to achieve these human rights' (17 April 1998) UN Doc E/CN.4/RES/1998/33; and more generally Benedek, 'The World Trade Organization and Human Rights' in Benedek, De Feyter, and Marrella (2007) 147–8.

52 UNCHR, Res 2000/9 (17 April 2000) UN Doc E/CN.4/RES/2000/9.

53 UNCHR, 'Report of the Special Rapporteur on adequate housing as a component of the right to an adequate standard of living, Mr Miloon Kothari' (25 March 2002) UN Doc E/CN.4/2002/59, para 54.

54 ibid para 55.

55 UNCHR, Res 2002/31 (22 April 2002) UN Doc E/CN.4/RES/2002/31.

56 UNCHR, 'The right of everyone to the enjoyment of the highest attainable standard of physical and mental health: Report of the Special Rapporteur, Paul Hunt submitted in accordance with resolution 2002/31' (13 February 2003) UN Doc E/CN.4/2003/58, paras 3, 73–81, 86–9.

WTO agreements on issues related to his mandate.[57] While not all the trade officials understood the relevance of human rights for their work, the Special Rapporteur described the meetings as 'constructive, informative and helpful',[58] and the mission as a whole set an important precedent of constructive dialogue between the two regimes.[59]

The report of this mission set out a number of ways in which human rights norms could and should be brought to bear within the field of trade policy. For example, echoing related work in the CESCR, the Special Rapporteur noted that state 'representatives to international organizations, including the WTO, [should] take due account of the right to health, as well as the obligation of international assistance and cooperation, in all policy-making matters' and that states should 'ensure that no international trade agreement or policy adversely impacts upon the right to health in . . . other countries'.[60] This was, he suggested, particularly important in accession negotiations, where powerful countries should not use their leverage over less powerful acceding countries to require concessions which may undermine the right to health.[61] In addition, the report identified the WTO's Trade Policy Review Mechanism, as well as its technical assistance activities, as spaces in which health and human rights considerations could be more systematically taken into account.[62] Furthermore, it argued that human rights law should be mainstreamed into trade policy-making at the national level, including through the use of human rights impact assessments of proposed trade agreements,[63] as well as more fully participatory modes of decision-making.[64]

The Special Rapporteur's interest in the WTO and trade agreements was also followed up briefly in his 2004 Annual Report,[65] as well as more substantially in a subsequent country mission to Peru.[66] In the latter, the Special Rapporteur raised concerns about the potential inclusion of 'WTO-plus' intellectual property provisions in a proposed US–Peru trade agreement, which could further limit the availability of essential drugs, and urged Peru to take human rights obligations into account as a 'shield' in negotiating free trade agreements. By way of support, a press release of the Special Rapporteur issued around the same time expressed concern about the prospect of the then-ongoing FTA negotiations between the United States

[57] UNCHR, 'The right of everyone to the enjoyment of the highest attainable standard of physical and mental health: Report of the Special Rapporteur, Paul Hunt, Mission to the World Trade Organization' (8 March 2004) UN Doc E/CN.4/2004/49/Add.1, para 4.

[58] ibid para 5.

[59] For one opinion to that effect, see Ovett, 'Making Trade Policies More Accountable' in Benedek, De Feyter, and Marrella (2007) 170–209, 200ff.

[60] UNCHR (E/CN.4/2004/49/Add.1) para 28.

[61] ibid paras 66–9.

[62] ibid paras 64–5.

[63] ibid paras 53–6.

[64] ibid paras 12, 27.

[65] ibid para 80.

[66] UNCHR, 'Report Submitted by the Special Rapporteur on the right of everyone to the highest attainable standard of physical and mental health: Addendum, Mission to Peru' (4 February 2005), UN Doc E/CN.4/2005/51/Add.3, paras 47–51.

and Andean countries including 'TRIPS+' provisions, and noted that 'if the final agreement has the effect of restricting access to essential drugs it will be inconsistent with Peru's national and international human rights obligations'.[67] More recently, in his 2009 Annual Report, the new Special Rapporteur, Anand Grover, returned to the issue of the relationship between the TRIPS agreement and the right to health, in the light of recent developments.[68]

Finally, the two Special Rapporteurs on the right to food—Jean Ziegler from 2000 to 2008 and Olivier de Schutter from 2008 to the present—have contributed greatly to the development of the present human rights agenda on trade issues. From the very beginning of his mandate, the first Special Rapporteur identified contemporary patterns of agricultural trade liberalization as one of the key obstacles to the realization of the right to food globally,[69] and his reports are among the most sustained and detailed treatments of agricultural trading issues in the human rights system.[70] Working closely with civil society organizations working on agricultural liberalization within the global justice movement, including many of those described in Chapter 3, he helped to provide an important institutional space within the human rights system for the airing of their analyses and criticisms. His reports draw heavily for inspiration and support, for example, on the experience and research of

[67] OHCHR, 'US-Peru Trade Negotiations: Special Rapporteur On Right To Health Reminds Parties Of Human Rights Obligations' (5 July 2004) <http://www.ohchr.org/en/NewsEvents/Pages/DisplayNews.aspx?NewsID=1906&LangID=E> accessed 15 February 2011.

[68] UNCHR, 'Report of the Special Rapporteur on the right of everyone to the enjoyment of the highest attainable standard of physical and mental health, Anand Grover' (31 March 2009) UN Doc A/HRC/11/12.

[69] UNCHR, 'The right to food: Report by the Special Rapporteur on the right to food, Mr Jean Ziegler, submitted in accordance with Commission on Human Rights resolution 2000/10' (7 February 2001) UN Doc E/CN.4/2001/53, paras 69–70.

[70] See eg ibid; UNGA, 'Preliminary report of the Special Rapporteur of the Commission on Human Rights on the right to food, Jean Ziegler' (23 July 2001) UN Doc A/56/210; UNCHR, 'The right to food: Report by the Special Rapporteur on the right to food, Mr Jean Ziegler, submitted in accordance with Commission on Human Rights resolution 2001/25' (10 January 2002) UN Doc E/CN.4/2002/58; UNCHR, 'The right to food: Report by the Special Rapporteur on the right to food, Mr Jean Ziegler, submitted in accordance with Commission on Human Rights resolution 2003/25' (9 February 2004) UN Doc E/CN.4/2004/10; UNGA, 'Interim report of the Special Rapporteur of the Commission on Human Rights on the right to food, Jean Ziegler' (27 September 2004) UN Doc A/59/385; UNCHR, 'The right to food: Report by the Special Rapporteur on the right to food, Jean Ziegler' (2005) UN Doc E/CN.4/2005/47; UNGA, 'Interim report of the Special Rapporteur of the Commission on Human Rights on the right to food, Jean Ziegler' (12 September 2005) UN Doc A/60/350; UNCHR, 'Promotion and Protection of all Human Rights, Civil, Political, Economic, Social and Cultural Rights, Including the Right to Development: Report of the Special Rapporteur on the right to food, Jean Ziegler' (10 January 2008) UN Doc A/HRC/7/5; UNCHR, 'The right to food: Report by the Special Rapporteur on the right to food, Mr Jean Ziegler, submitted in accordance with Commission on Human Rights resolution 2000/10: Addendum, Mission to Brazil' (3 January 2003) UN Doc E/CN.4/2003/54/Add.1; UNCHR, 'The right to food: Report by the Special Rapporteur on the right to food, Jean Ziegler: Addendum, Mission to Mongolia' (8 March 2005) UN Doc E/CN.4/2005/47/Add.2; UNCHR, 'Promotion and Protection of all Human Rights, Civil, Political, Economic, Social and Cultural Rights, Including the Right to Development: Report of the Special Rapporteur on the right to food, Jean Ziegler: Addendum, Mission to Bolivia' (30 January 2008) UN Doc A/HRC/7/5/Add.2; UNCHR, 'The right to food: Report by the Special Rapporteur on the right to food, Jean Ziegler: Addendum, Mission to Guatemala' (18 January 2006) UN Doc E/CN.4/2006/44/Add.1.

key civil society organizations in the global justice movement, such as La Vía Campesina, FIAN, MST, Friends of the Earth, Rights and Democracy, ActionAid, the World Wide Fund for Nature, and Oxfam, as well as the publications of figures such as Madeley and Mittal. Their concerns are therefore also his: subsidized imports undermining the livelihoods of small farmers; the growing concentration of land ownership and productive resources in the agricultural sector; price volatility of essential foods; protected agricultural markets in the developed world; international patents held by multinationals depriving poor farmers of access to the means of producing food.[71] His first report to the UN General Assembly constitutes a trenchant critique of the current agricultural trading system as undermining food security and the right to food in fundamental ways.[72]

Aside from these claims about the negative impacts of agricultural trade liberalization and WTO rules on the right to food, the Special Rapporteur's body of work has at least two notable features. The first is its direct and ongoing engagement, in a commentating capacity, with trade negotiations in the WTO and other negotiating arenas. The 2002 report, for example, closely tracked the progress of the Doha negotiations at the time, commenting on the positions taken in those negotiations by different countries, singling out for approval a Norwegian proposal within the WTO calling for rules on agricultural trade which do not conflict with the right to food, as well as a developing country proposal for a 'food security box'.[73] His 2004 report did the same for the Cancún Ministerial. Furthermore, in his country report on Guatemala, the Special Rapporteur warned of the potential dangers of the proposed Central American Free Trade Agreement for Guatemala peasant farmers, and urged Guatemala to adopt a human rights approach in its negotiations.[74] In later years, he expressed similar concerns about European Economic Partnership Agreement (EPA) negotiations between the European Union and certain African and other developing nations.[75] In much the same way as the work of the Special Rapporteur on the right to health, then, this aspect of his work seeks to deploy human rights as a 'shield' to help developing countries resist demands made in a variety of trade negotiating arenas for greater agricultural liberalization.

The second notable feature is the incorporation into these reports of a number of innovative ways of bringing the normative and legal framework of human rights to bear in the context of trade policy-making. While noting with others that human rights must be taken into account in WTO negotiations,[76] and that the WTO

[71] UNCHR (UN Doc E/CN.4/2001/53) eg para 73; UNGA (A/56/210) paras 72–87; See also generally UNHRC, 'Promotion and Protection of all Human Rights, Civil, Political, Economic, Social and Cultural Rights, Including the Right to Development: Report of the Special Rapporteur on the right to food, Olivier De Schutter, Mission to the World Trade Organization' (4 February 2009) UN Doc A/HRC/10/5/Add.2, paras 19ff.

[72] UNGA (UN Doc A/56/210) paras 72–87.

[73] UNCHR (UN Doc E/CN.4/2002/58) paras 109–19.

[74] UNCHR (UN Doc E/CN.4/2006/44/Add.1) para 55.

[75] UNGA, 'Report of the Special Rapporteur on the Right to Food' (2007) UN Doc A/62/289, para 18.

[76] UNGA, 'The right to food: Report of the Special Rapporteur of the Commission on Human Rights on the right to food' (27 August 2002) UN Doc A/57/356, para 47(h).

should advise against the adoption of trade policies that may have an impact on the right to food,[77] the Special Rapporteur at the same time has acknowledged that 'if the right to food is not taken up by the WTO, we must search for other means of integrating human rights and the right to food into the rules of international trade'.[78] In this spirit, in his 2005 report the Special Rapporteur embraced and developed the notion of extraterritorial state obligations, according to which states have an obligation under the ICESCR to refrain from taking decisions that can lead to violations of human rights in other countries.[79] The Special Rapporteur gives the example of subsidies to farmers in developed countries, which 'can have negative impacts on farmers and the right to food in developing countries if food products are "dumped" on developing countries'.[80] As discussed in Chapter 3, the development of the notion of extraterritorial obligations in the context of the right to food was in part the product of the work of organizations such as FIAN, Brot für die Welt, and EED, as well as a number of academic scholars.[81] This represents a potentially significant—if still early—step in asserting the legal and practical relevance of human rights in the context of trade negotiations and trade policy.

This engagement with trade issues has been continued by his successor in the post, Olivier de Schutter. Following the lead of the Special Rapporteur on the right to health, de Schutter organized, in June 2008, a further mission to the WTO, holding meetings with staff of the WTO Secretariat and the Director-General, as well as a number of delegates from WTO Members.[82] In his report, after setting out the challenges which agricultural trade liberalization poses for food security and the right to food, the Special Rapporteur then goes on to call for greater coherence between trade law and human rights obligations.[83] Rule-making in the two regimes, he notes, is uncoordinated, mirroring a similar lack of coordination between policy-makers at the domestic level. Given the hard enforcement mechanisms associated with trade law, he further notes, there is a risk that—contrary to what he sees as the primacy of human rights norms—countries will pay greater attention to trade law where the two conflict. He therefore argues that human rights obligations must be taken into account both in WTO dispute settlement as a guide to interpretation, and in the context of trade negotiations. States should conduct human rights impact assessments, and ensure that trade policy-making is conducted in a participatory and

[77] UNGA (UN Doc A/60/350) para 51.

[78] UNCHR (UN Doc E/CN.4/2002/58) paras 109–19.

[79] UNCHR, 'The right to food: Report of the Special Rapporteur on the right to food, Jean Ziegler' (24 January 2005) UN Doc E/CN.4/2005/47, paras 34–59. See also J B de Mesquita, P Hunt, and R Khosla, 'The Human Rights Responsibility of International Assistance and Cooperation' in S Skogly and M Gibney (eds), *Universal Human Rights and Extraterritorial Obligations* (University of Pennsylvania Press, Philadelphia, PA 2010) 104–29.

[80] ibid para 39.

[81] See p 96 above.

[82] UNHRC, 'Promotion and Protection of all Human Rights, Civil, Political, Economic, Social and Cultural Rights, Including the Right to Development: Report of the Special Rapporteur on the right to food, Olivier de Schutter, Mission to the World Trade Organization' (4 February 2009) UN Doc A/HRC/10/5/Add.2, para 2.

[83] ibid paras 33–49.

transparent manner. Substantively, states should, in his view, limit their dependency on imports of basic foods, and maintain their flexibility to shield their domestic markets from international volatility.

C. The High Commissioner for Human Rights

A third key source of work on trade and investment issues in this period was the Office of the High Commissioner for Human Rights, at the time under the leadership of Mary Robinson. Starting in 2000, the Sub-Commission requested the High Commissioner's office to undertake a series of analyses of the human rights impacts of various aspects of trade and investment agreements.[84] The reports produced under this mandate have proved highly influential in setting a broader human rights agenda on trade issues and providing a sure analytical footing for debate and discussion on trade issues within the human rights movement.

The first report, published in 2001, dealt with the TRIPS agreement and its impact on the right to health.[85] Recall from the previous chapter that 2001 was a time when the progressive activism around trade was squarely focused on the issue of access to essential pharmaceuticals to combat AIDS epidemics in South Africa and Brazil. Both countries had come under pressure from the United States as a result of plans to permit the local production of generics, and the possibility of using human rights law as a form of 'shield' to resist this pressure presented itself as an attractive proposition for Brazil, which was an influential player in the original request.[86] An entire section is devoted to problems relating to the provision of HIV treatments in Brazil.[87] Over the next few years, as the High Commissioner continued consulting civil society groups engaged in trade advocacy, the subject matter of the reports tracked the evolving interests and advocacy of the global justice movement, as set out in the previous chapter. In the second report, published in January 2002, for example, the High Commissioner took the opportunity to explore the criticisms being made of agricultural liberalization by peasant farmers and rural groups in the Third World.[88] This report gave voice to concerns about the displacement of farm labourers, the insecurity of food supply, the consolidation of farmland, and the volatility of global food prices as potential threats to the right to food and (to a lesser

[84] UNCHR (Sub-Commission) Res 2000/7 (UN Doc E/CN.4/SUB.2/RES/2000/7); UNCHR (UN Doc E/CN.4/RES/1999/59).

[85] UNCHR (Sub-Commission), 'The impact of the Agreement on Trade-Related Aspects of Intellectual Property Rights on human rights: Report of the High Commissioner' (27 June 2001) UN Doc E/CN.4/Sub.2/2001/13.

[86] Note Brazil's use of resolutions in the Commission and Sub-Commission from 2001 to this purpose. See, for instance, UNCHR, 'Access to medication in the context of pandemics such as HIV/AIDS, tuberculosis and malaria' (22 April 2003) UN Doc E/CN.4/RES/2003/29; see also generally LR Helfer, 'Regime Shifting: The TRIPs Agreement and New Dynamics of Internationational Intellectual Property Lawmaking' (2004) 29 Yale J of Intl L 1–83, 48–51; Weissbrodt and Schoff (2003) 31ff.

[87] UNCHR (Sub-Commission) (UN Doc E/CN.4/Sub.2/2001/13) paras 51ff.

[88] UNCHR, 'Globalization and its impact on the full enjoyment of human rights: Report of the High Commissioner for Human Rights submitted in accordance with Commission on Human Rights resolution 2001/32' (15 January 2002) UN Doc E/CN.4/2002/54.

extent) the right to development. The third report, six months later, turned to issues concerning trade in services, specifically the potential social costs associated with the commercialization and transnationalization of essential services, such as health, education, and water.[89] This was, it will be recalled, a particular focus of concern and analysis for Canada-based NGOs at this time, while water had become something of a flashpoint for contemporary anti-globalization activism in certain parts of South America at that time as well. This focus on water was continued in the fourth report a year later in 2003, 'Human Rights, Trade and Investment', which dealt with the privatization of essential services and the legal impact of bilateral investment treaties.[90] The fifth report then changed tack somewhat, and looked at the cross-cutting issue of the principle of non-discrimination, examining its different meaning and application in trade law as opposed to human rights law, with special reference to issues around governmental procurement, social labelling, and agricultural trade policy.[91] After a commissioned paper on the right to development (dealt with below), the final report looked at questions surrounding the participation of marginalized individuals and groups in decision-making processes driving globalization.[92]

In addition, in September 2003, the High Commissioner made a submission to the WTO Ministerial Conference in Cancún. Entitled 'Human Rights and Trade', it served as a primer for the trade community, outlining why it is useful to talk about human rights in the trade context, setting out the core of a human rights approach to trade, and providing eight illustrations of the links between human rights and trade.[93]

One striking feature of all these documents is their careful and deliberately moderate tone, very different from the more confrontational tone of some earlier reports,[94] which had proved so off-putting to those within the trade community. This moderate positioning is reflected in the reports in three ways. First, the reports are careful to draw attention to both the positive and negative impacts of trade liberalization on human rights.[95] They consistently refuse to speak in general terms about the relationship between 'trade liberalization' and the protection of human

[89] UNCHR (Sub-Commission), 'Liberalization of trade in services and human rights: Report of the High Commissioner' (25 June 2002) UN Doc E/CN.4/Sub.2/2002/9.

[90] UNCHR (Sub-Commission), 'Human rights, trade and investment: Report of the High Commissioner for Human Rights' (2 July 2003) UN Doc E/CN.4/Sub.2/2003/9.

[91] UNCHR, 'Analytical study of the High Commissioner for Human Rights on the fundamental principle of non-discrimination in the context of globalization' (15 January 2004) UN Doc E/CN.4/2004/40.

[92] UNCHR, 'Analytical study of the High Commissioner for Human Rights on the fundamental principle of participation and its application in the context of globalization: Report of the High Commissioner' (23 October 2004) UN Doc E/CN.4/2005/41.

[93] OHCHR, 'Human Rights and Trade' (5th WTO Ministerial Conference, 2003) <http://www2.ohchr.org/english/issues/globalization/trade/docs/5WTOMinisterialCancun.pdf> accessed 15 February 2011.

[94] See p 112 above.

[95] See eg UNCHR (Sub-Commission) (UN Doc E/CN.4/Sub.2/2001/13) para 37; UNCHR (UN Doc E/CN.4/2002/54) para 33; UNCHR (Sub-Commission) (UN Doc E/CN.4/Sub.2/2002/9) paras 39, 41, 42, 43, 47; UNCHR (Sub-Commission) (UN Doc E/CN.4/Sub.2/2003/9) paras 6, 56.

rights, preferring instead to focus on specific examples and issue areas.[96] And they repeatedly emphasize that there is no per se incompatibility between trade or investment liberalization and the protection of human rights—what matters is the way that liberalization is carried out, and the effects that it has in concrete contexts.[97] Thus, in the statement to the WTO's Cancún Ministerial, the High Commissioner notes that:

> Human rights law is neutral with regard to trade liberalization or trade protectionism . . . a human rights approach to trade focuses on processes and outcomes—how trade affects the enjoyment of human rights—and places the promotion and protection of human rights among the objectives of trade reform.[98]

Secondly, the reports are equally careful to limit their claims as to the degree of incompatibility between the rules and objectives of trade law, and those of human rights law. For example, the report on the TRIPS agreement points to some commonalities of approach between that agreement and Article 15 of the UDHR—both, it notes, seek to strike a balance between the interests of producers and consumers of technological knowledge, with the objective of promoting social and economic welfare[99]—and argues that the 'flexibility inherent in the TRIPS agreement' can be used to ensure that intellectual property systems are adjusted to be in compliance with human rights obligations.[100] The report on the GATS similarly notes ambiguities in the application of the disciplines of that agreement, and argues that interpretation of its disciplines should take into account states' obligations under human rights law to avoid inconsistencies.[101]

Thirdly, the recommendations made in these reports are also very carefully framed. Recognizing the problems associated with proposing substantive trade policies, one strategy that the High Commissioner has adopted has been to encourage states to pay greater attention to human rights in decision-making processes around trade issues. Thus, states should 'implement' trade obligations 'bearing in mind . . . their human rights obligations'.[102] They should monitor the human rights outcomes of trade policies, and conduct systematic human rights impact assessments of trade agreements.[103] There should be increased dialogue between trade policy and human rights-related communities at both the national and international level,

[96] eg UNCHR (Sub-Commission) (UN Doc E/CN.4/Sub.2/2003/9) paras 6ff; UNCHR (UN Doc E/CN.4/2002/54) para 32.

[97] eg UNCHR (Sub-Commission) (UN Doc E/CN.4/Sub.2/2002/9) para 50: 'The key question from a human rights perspective is not whether liberalization does or does not promote human rights; rather, it is how to determine the right form and pace of liberalization to ensure the protection of human rights and how to reverse policies that are unsuccessful'; see also UNCHR (Sub-Commission) (UN Doc E/CN.4/Sub.2/2003/9) para 56.

[98] OHCHR, 'Human Rights and Trade' 4.

[99] UNCHR (Sub-Commission) (UN Doc E/CN.4/Sub.2/2001/13) para 16.

[100] ibid para 29.

[101] UNCHR (Sub-Commission) (UN Doc E/CN.4/Sub.2/2002/9) paras 51ff.

[102] UNCHR (Sub-Commission) (UN Doc E/CN.4/Sub.2/2001/13) para 60.

[103] ibid para 61; UNCHR (UN Doc E/CN.4/2002/54) para 46; UNCHR (Sub-Commission) (UN Doc E/CN.4/Sub.2/2002/9) para 72; UNCHR (Sub-Commission) (UN Doc E/CN.4/Sub.2/2003/9) para 63; UNCHR (UN Doc E/CN.4/2004/40) para 55; UNCHR (UN Doc E/CN.4/2005/41) para 50.

including increased cooperation between the trade and human rights regime.[104] Similarly, human rights obligations should be taken into account in the interpretation of international trade obligations.[105] To that end, explicit reference to human rights should be incorporated into amended texts of trade law, perhaps as an objective of trade and investment liberalization.[106] Finally, and more generally, attention to human rights in decision-making processes around trade should include making those processes more transparent, participatory, and accountable. Thus, decisions on trade both at the national level and in international organizations should ensure effective participation by civil society and currently under-represented groups.[107] States should also establish mechanisms for transparency, accountability, and public participation in domestic programmes of services liberalization.[108]

That said, the High Commissioner did lend support in these reports to a number of more specific policy or legal changes which were being advocated at the same time by developing countries within the trading system. For example, in the 2001 report on TRIPS, the High Commissioner specifically encourages WTO Members to grant compulsory licences and permit parallel importation where to do so might promote the enjoyment of the right to health.[109] In addition, the report on agriculture argues for: greater flexibility in terms of allowing developing countries to raise tariffs and grant domestic support in respect of agricultural products; the establishment of enforcement measures for the WTO's Marrakesh Declaration; and 'allowing food-insecure States to enjoy a higher *de minimus* limit for trade-distorting domestic support for basic foodstuffs compared to non-food crops or non-food-security crops'.[110] Moreover, also in relation to the agricultural sector, the High Commissioner advocates specific national level measures to protect poor and small farmers from the adverse effects of trade liberalization, including poverty alleviation strategies,[111] 'promoting assistance to raise productivity and production for small farmers; targeting support for food security crops; increasing investment in the sector; and establishing social safety nets for vulnerable individuals and groups to promote food security'.[112] These proposals closely reflect the ideas circulating among civil society networks of small farmers described in the previous chapter, and should be seen in part as a way of lending the support of the human rights regime to them. They also reflect the emphasis placed by the High Commissioner and others in the human rights community on the role of the state as the primary guarantor of human rights, even in the context of economic globalization.

[104] UNCHR (Sub-Commission) (UN Doc E/CN.4/Sub.2/2002/9) para 74; UNCHR (Sub-Commission) (UN Doc E/CN.4/Sub.2/2003/9) para 62; UNCHR (UN Doc E/CN.4/2004/40) para 54

[105] eg UNCHR (Sub-Commission) (UN Doc E/CN.4/Sub.2/2002/9) para 71.

[106] UNCHR (Sub-Commission) (UN Doc E/CN.4/Sub.2/2001/13) para 68; UNCHR (UN Doc E/CN.4/2002/54) para 45; UNCHR (UN Doc E/CN.4/Sub.2/2003/9) para 57.

[107] See generally UNCHR (Sub-Commission) (UN Doc E/CN.4/2005/41).

[108] UNCHR (Sub-Commission) (UN Doc E/CN.4/Sub.2/2003/9) para 61.

[109] UNCHR (Sub-Commission) (UN Doc E/CN.4/Sub.2/2001/13) para 66.

[110] UNCHR (UN Doc E/CN.4/2002/54) paras 47ff.

[111] ibid para 47.

[112] UNCHR (UN Doc E/CN.4/2004/40) para 53.

D. The right to development

While concerns about trade and economic globalization have primarily been articulated in the context of work on 'second generation' economic and social rights, there has also been some work to operationalize the right to development in debates around trade. The Working Group on the Right to Development was established in 1998 to monitor progress in the implementation of the right to development. From 1998 to 2004, the Working Group was supported and informed by the annual reports of the Independent Expert on the Right to Development, and from 2005 the Independent Expert was replaced by a High-Level Task Force on the Implementation of the Right to Development, comprising five independent experts, to provide the necessary knowledge and analysis to assist the Working Group. In his final report in 2004, the Independent Expert began to give voice to criticisms of the contemporary international trading order from the perspective of economic development—outlining differences of opinion among development economists about the centrality of trade to development, expressing concern about the impacts of the TRIPS agreement on technology transfer and economic growth in developing countries, and noting imbalances in WTO rules in relation to the market access they achieve for developing as opposed to developed country exports.[113] The High-Level Task Force has to some extent continued and expanded this work, relatively consistently noting the concerns of country delegates, NGO participants and others with regard to the impact of the TRIPS agreement on access to drugs, the problems posed by non-tariff barriers to developing country exports, and the importance of trade capacity-building.[114]

More important, in terms of its visibility and intellectual influence, has been a paper commissioned by the High Commissioner in 2004, authored by Howse and entitled 'Mainstreaming the right to development into trade law and policy at the WTO'.[115] Under the rubric of the right to development, and drawing on the work of Sen, Rodrik, and others, the paper articulates an alternative normative framework for the conduct of trade and development policy, composed of six core elements, or claims. First, it notes, development cannot be pursued at the expense of human rights, even temporarily—instead, policy choices must be guided by the aim of ensuring mutual reinforcement between human rights and economic growth. Secondly, the goals and outcomes of development policy must be assessed in terms of the full range of human rights, not merely a subsection of them. Thirdly, states and state officials are responsible for their policy choices in all venues, including international

[113] UNCHR, 'Review of progress and obstacles in the promotion, implementation, operationalization, and enjoyment of the right to development: Consideration of the sixth report of the independent expert on the right to development, Implementing the right to development in the current global context' (17 February 2004) UN Doc E/CN.4/2004/WG.18/2, paras 11, 21, 34.

[114] See eg Report of the High-Level Task Force on the Implementation of the Right to Development on its Sixth Session (24 February 2010) UN Doc A/HRC/15/WG.2/TF/2.

[115] UNCHR (Sub-Commission), 'Mainstreaming the right to development into international trade law and policy at the World Trade Organization: Note by the Secretariat' (9 June 2004) UN Doc E/CN.4/Sub.2/2004/17.

organizations, and must be guided by this normative framework in all of them. Fourthly, development policy-making must be open and participatory. Fifthly, the right to development encourages inter-institutional cooperation, and rejects the view that 'development is best achieved through different institutions sticking to one aspect of the matter that purportedly corresponds to their respective expertise and authority, and operating in an autonomous and largely uncoordinated fashion'.[116] Finally, the right to development rejects the view that development is a deterministic or mechanical process. On the basis of this core normative framework—different, it is claimed, from that which prevails within the WTO—the report suggests a number of concrete institutional changes to the practice and structure of the WTO. For example, it suggests that there must be routine assessment of the human rights impact of trade policies, including in and through the WTO's Trade Policy Review Mechanism; that technical assistance activities conducted in and through the WTO must be altered to include greater attention to public education and to ensure the participation of other UN agencies in the delivery of assistance; that mechanisms must be established to more easily change and adapt particular WTO rules as the need arises; that a greater diversity of expertise must be included within the WTO Secretariat and the WTO's dispute settlement organs; and that the right to development must be used in the interpretation of WTO law.[117]

II. The discursive framework of 'coherence'

The result of all of this was the rapid emergence of the contemporary 'trade and human rights' debate over the first five or so years of the twenty-first century.[118] This debate quickly came to include a relatively broad array of different actors, including scholars of international law (from both the trade and human rights sides, as well as others), professionals working in both the trade and human rights regimes, and civil society groups of many types, including the original NGOs involved in the global justice movement.[119] During these years, the trade and human rights debate became

[116] ibid para 19.

[117] ibid paras 25–49.

[118] In fact, there were a handful of key scholars working at the vanguard of the human rights field who began this debate as early as the late 1990s. See eg P Alston, 'The Universal Declaration in an Era of Globalisation' in B Van der Heijden et al, *Reflections on the Universal Declaration of Human Rights: A Fiftieth Anniversary Anthology* (Kluwer, The Hague, 1998) 28–32; P Alston, 'The Myopia of the Handmaidens: International Lawyers and Globalization' (1997) 3 EJIL 435–48; R Fairbrother and R McCorquodale, 'Globalization and Human Rights' (1999) 21(3) HRQ 735–76; Howse and Mutua (2000); A Orford, 'Contesting Globalization: A Feminist Perspective on the Future of Human Rights' (1998) 8 Transnational Law and Contemporary Problems 171–98; as well as the contributions to the symposium entitled 'The Universal Declaration at 50 and the Challenge of Global Markets' (1999) 25 Brooklyn J of Intl L.

[119] See eg the two books produced as a result of a number of important conferences on the issue in 2001, 2003, and 2004: T Cottier, E Bürgi, and J Pauwelyn (eds), *Human Rights and International Trade* (OUP, Oxford 2005) and F Abbott, C Breining-Kaufman, and T Cottier (eds), *International Trade and Human Rights: Foundations and Conceptual Issues* (University of Michigan Press, Ann Arbor 2006), as well as the work of the Trade Committee of the International Law Association at its conferences in London (2000), New Delhi (2002), and Berlin (2004).

one of the more visible and important venues through which the social and political struggles outlined in the previous chapters came to affect the work and thought of those working in the field of international law.

The impetus for this new conversation was clear: suddenly, there was a wide range of authoritative and well-respected international human rights institutions suggesting the possibility of conflicts between the objectives of the trade and human rights regimes, in a way which could not fail to catch the attention, particularly of international lawyers interested in global economic governance. Such claims of conflict were especially arresting for those, including many working in the field of international economic law including the present author, whose thinking about the relationship between trade and human rights had previously been influenced primarily by the liberal traditions discussed in Chapter 2. Such liberal traditions emphasized the mutual compatibility of free trade and human rights, and therefore suggested a vision quite the opposite of the claims that were emerging from these human rights bodies. A series of important questions were therefore posed and discussed: what *was* the nature of the relationship between the trade regime and the human rights regime? In what ways were they in conflict, and in what ways were they compatible? There was, in Cottier's famous phrase, 'a relationship to discover'[120] between trade and human rights—a complex and perhaps even contradictory set of causal and normative relations, which needed to be mapped in order to work out how the two regimes might more productively relate to one another.

A large part of this debate was therefore oriented towards the exploration of conflicts and compatibilities between the objectives, values, and rules of the two regimes. This involved, for example, identifying the values of each regime, comparing them, and characterizing their similarities and differences. It involved investigating the consequences of trade liberalization on human rights outcomes—were they positive or negative, on balance? And it involved legal argument about the precise meaning of trade law and human rights law, to determine whether they imposed obligations which conflicted with one another. Although this was carried out in the language of description and empirical investigation, the arguments made in this context reflected existing divisions between different strands of thinking about the relationship between economic freedoms and the enjoyment of human rights described in Chapter 2. The classical liberal tradition made its influence felt through arguments that trade liberalization and the promotion of human rights were essentially compatible goals. Trade liberalization, it was argued for example, increases prosperity, and is the best way to produce a higher standard of living for the world's poor.[121] Studies were conducted and cited which purported to show a significant correlation between a country's degree of economic openness, and its standards of human rights protection. Conversely, some forms of human rights protection were also said to be essential to the proper functioning of markets:

[120] T Cottier, 'Trade and Human Rights: A Relationship to Discover' (2002) 5 JIEL 111–32.

[121] See, for a thoughtful example, M Warner, 'Globalization and Human Rights: An Economic Model' (1999) 25 Brooklyn J of Intl L 99–112.

freedom of speech and expression, for example, is an important tool to ensure the free circulation of information on which markets rely.[122] At the level of each regime's underlying philosophy, some based their claims for compatibility between the two regimes on perceptions of their shared liberal moral foundations. The trade regime, for example, was said to be complementary to the human rights regime, in the sense of protecting economic freedoms, which were said to have been historically under-emphasized by the human rights movement, but of equal moral significance to the civil and political freedoms more commonly associated with human rights.[123] Indeed, it was argued, the 'right to trade' could productively be added to the human rights corpus.[124]

On the other hand, progressive critics of the WTO were focused primarily on identifying potential *in*compatibilities between trade liberalization and human rights protection. Many of these contributions echoed and elaborated the kinds of issues already discussed above: the impact of agricultural trade liberalization on food security;[125] the impact of the TRIPS agreement on the access of farmers to seeds and other productive resources; the problem of human rights-based trade sanctions;[126] and the question of access to essential pharmaceuticals.[127] Others identified more and different issues—for example, the relationship between trade in tobacco products and the right to health,[128] the central role of trade in conflict diamonds in sustaining human rights abuses in Sub-Saharan Africa,[129] or the particular problems raised by the then-recent *EC—Hormones* and *EC—Asbestos* decisions of the WTO's Appellate Body.[130] Thus, during the first few years of the trade and human rights debate, we saw a proliferation of claims of potential conflict between trade law and human rights law: the TRIPS agreement may conflict with the right to health if it unduly restricts the granting of compulsory licences,[131]

[122] See eg T Cottier, 'Freedom of Expression: Linkages between Freedom of Expression and Competition Rules in International Trade—The Hertel Case and Beyond' in T Cottier, J Pauwelyn, and E Bürgi (eds), *Human Rights and International Trade* (OUP, Oxford 2005).

[123] See eg EU Petersmann, 'Time for a "Global Compact" for Integrating Human Rights into the Law of Worldwide Organizations: Lessons from European Integration' (2002) 13 EJIL 621–50; AH Lim, 'Trade and Human Rights: What's at Issue?' (2001) 35 J of World Trade 275–300, 277–8, 282.

[124] eg EU Petersmann, 'The WTO Constitution and Human Rights' (2000) 3 JIEL 19–25.

[125] eg C Breining-Kaufman, 'The Right to Food and Trade in Agriculture' in T Cottier, E Bürgi, and J Pauwelyn (eds), *Human Rights and International Trade* (OUP, Oxford 2005).

[126] eg SH Cleveland, 'Human Rights Sanctions and International Trade: A Theory of Compatibility' (2002) 5 JIEL 133–89.

[127] For an early example, see F Abbott, 'The "Rule of Reason" and the Right to Health: Integrating Human Rights and Competition Principles in the context of TRIPS' in T Cottier, E Bürgi, and J Pauwelyn (eds), *Human Rights and International Trade* (OUP, Oxford 2005) 279.

[128] AL Taylor, 'Trade, Human Rights, and the WHO Framework Convention on Tobacco Control: Just what the Doctor Ordered?' in T Cottier, E Bürgi, and J Pauwelyn (eds), *Human Rights and International Trade* (OUP, Oxford 2005).

[129] KN Schefer, 'Stopping Trade in Conflict Diamonds: Exploring the Trade and Human Rights Interface with the WTO Waiver for the Kimberley Process' in T Cottier, E Bürgi and J Pauwelyn (eds), *Human Rights and International Trade* (OUP, Oxford 2005).

[130] C Dommen, 'Raising Human Rights Concerns in the World Trade Organization: Actors, Processes and Possible Strategies' (2002) 24 HRQ 1–50.

[131] Ibid.

the Agreement on Agriculture may undermine the right to food where it mandates agricultural liberalization with negative effects on food security,[132] the Agreement on the Application of Sanitary and Phytosanitary Measures may undermine the rights to food and health if it is interpreted to restrict recourse to precautionary food safety regulation,[133] the GATT and and Agreement on Technical Barriers to Trade may conflict with the right to health if they restrict the ability of states to implement adequate product safety standards,[134] the GATS may undermine the rights to health, education, or water if it leads to the liberalization of essential services without adequate safeguards to protect the poor, and so on.

Importantly, this focus on potential conflicts was accompanied by an emphasis on *coherence* as a normative goal. If the problem was legal conflict—or incoherence—then it went without saying that the solution was a greater degree of inter-regime coherence. Broadly speaking, 'coherence' between the goals of the trade regime and the human rights regime broke down into two claims, both of which reflected the kinds of arguments being made more broadly in the context of public discussion of the WTO at the time. On one hand, achieving coherence meant limiting the intrusiveness of WTO obligations, particularly as regards domestic regulation. In simple terms, it was argued that the human rights obligations which states have undertaken may require them to adopt certain forms of regulation and adopt certain kinds of interventionist policies, which are prohibited under WTO law. For example, respecting the right to health may require a country to grant compulsory licences for the production of generic copies of patented pharmaceuticals, even where such grant may be prohibited by the TRIPS agreement. The rights to water and health may require states to limit and regulate the private provision of certain essential services, even where that is prohibited by the GATS. The right to food may require the protection of small local agricultural producers in developing countries, even where such protection violates liberalization commitments undertaken by those countries in the WTO. From this perspective, then, a large part of what it means to ensure 'coherence' between the trade regime and the human rights regime involves limiting the constraining impact of WTO law, and ensuring that a greater degree of market intervention is permitted by WTO disciplines, where such intervention is or may be required by human rights law. Human rights law, to recall the phrase used above, is being used in this line of argument as a legal 'shield' against the potentially constraining impact of WTO law. As a result, this line of argument is also associated with efforts to ensure that human rights law can be taken into account during WTO dispute settlement—at least as a guide to its interpretation, but even better as a substantive defence against a claim of violation of WTO law—and with efforts

[132] eg Breining-Kaufman, 'The Right to Food and Trade in Agirculture' in Cottier, Bürgi, and Pauwelyn (2005).

[133] Dommen (2002).

[134] ibid; A Orford, 'Contesting Globalization: A Feminist Perspective on the Future of Human Rights' (1998) 8 Transnational L & Contemporary Problems 172.

to ensure that human rights obligations are raised in the context of trade negotiations as a way of resisting certain demands which might be made in them. The call for 'coherence', in this argument, then, was another way of expressing the view that the scope and intrusiveness of WTO disciplines should be limited, and WTO Members' 'regulatory autonomy' should be expanded.

The other meaning of coherence had to do with inter-regime coordination. Within debates about economic globalization generally, it is a commonplace progressive claim that neoliberal economic reforms prioritize the value of economic efficiency, and the objectives of economic growth and wealth creation above all else, including more important 'social' goals and objectives. In the context of criticism of the WTO at the turn of the millennium, this claim was recapitulated, but with an institutional gloss. The prioritization of 'economic' over 'social' policy goals became a claim about the institutional myopia of the WTO. The WTO, it was said, has a narrow economic mandate to liberalize trade, in order to capture the efficiency gains that such liberalization is thought to bring. In part as a result of its functional specialization, it was said, it tends to focus on and prioritize the goal of economic efficiency, at the expense of goals and objectives which fall outside its mandate. In other words, by its nature, the WTO tended to privilege 'trade values', 'trade objectives' over other legitimate projects of the international community. Some of these other, marginalized projects were those associated with the human rights regime: the claim became then, that because of its institutional mandate, the WTO tended to pursue trade liberalization in a single-minded manner, at the expense of the kinds of social projects valorized and pursued by the same nations in the context of the human rights regime.

Note how the adoption of the coherence framework here redefines the problem at issue. As was made clear in Chapter 2, early civil society activism around trade had its own definition of the problem towards which their advocacy was directed: in short, it was the problem of the adverse social consequences of neoliberal economic reforms, particularly as they were reflected in the global trading system. Within the language of coherence, the definition of the problem has changed: while concern about neoliberal economic policies and their social consequences still animated the debate in important ways, attention was more directly focused on the problem of inter-regime conflict. That is to say, political struggles and debates about the social consequences of the global trading system came to be reconstituted as debates about the incoherence of the international legal order, and about the relationship between the trade and human rights regimes. This was a structural problem of the international order: a consequence of its division into separate, specialized regimes, without any mechanism for systematically ensuring compatibility between the activities, objectives, and norms of each. The structural incoherence of the international order, on this view, was the underlying cause of the social consequences associated with economic globalization—or at least one important cause. For those critical of the trade regime, then, the adverse social consequences of trade liberalization as carried out in the WTO came to be treated as the result of a deeper problem, namely the lack of attention to social concerns and social values within the international trade regime. Is it not a problem, asks Fox, that the WTO 'has no eyes or ears to see or hear of liberalization's [social] impacts'?[135] This lack of attention to social concerns in the trade regime was itself, in this view, the result of its functional specialization (which produced a particular normative bias), as well as its 'splendid isolation' from other regimes such as the human rights regime, which precluded the kinds of dialogue which might reconcile these differences of approach. Conflicts between trade law and human rights law were presented as the outcome of functional specialization and the structural disaggregation of the international order:

> The human rights obligations of WTO members and the commitments they make through the conclusion of agreements under the WTO framework remain uncoordinated. At the international level, this lack of coordination is one example among others of the problem of fragmentation of international law into a number of self-contained regimes, each with their own norms and dispute-settlement mechanisms, and relatively autonomous vis-à-vis both each other and general international law.[136]

Others similarly blamed 'policy incoherence'[137] at the national level, or the 'artificial separation' between the trade and human rights regime leading to 'lack of co-ordinated global governance'.[138] At heart, then, if the trade regime produced laws which undermined human rights protections, this was seen to be a problem of institutional design: a result of the functional specialization of the trade regime, which produced a partiality of vision or bias in the way that it operated; and the lack of adequate mechanisms to coordinate its work with that of other international bodies.

The result was that progressive activism in this mode tended to emphasize 'architectural' questions of institutional design as a solution to the problems that they perceived in the governance of global trade. If the underlying problem was the decentralization of international governance, then it follows that remedial efforts must be to devise appropriate rules and procedures for the allocation of authority between different institutions, and for coordination between them. Thus, many working in this area have focused on the structural relations between the trade regime and the human rights regime, looking for ways to integrate and develop mechanisms of coordination between the two. As we saw above, this has meant, for example: helping to develop and discuss normative and institutional hierarchies to resolve legal conflicts between them; calling for systematic consideration of human rights law in the interpretation and application of WTO obligations; arguing for greater policy space for states *vis-à-vis* the international trade regime, where that is required

[135] EM Fox, 'Globalization and Human Rights: Looking out for the Welfare of the Worst Off' (2002) 35 NYU J of Intl L and Policy 201–20.

[136] UNHRC, 'Promotion and Protection of all Human Rights, Civil, Political, Economic, Social and Cultural Rights, Including the Right to Development: Report of the Special Rapporteur on the right to food, Olivier De Schutter, Mission to the World Trade Organization' (4 February 2009) UN Doc A/HRC/10/5/Add.2 para 33; see also International Council on Human Rights Policy (ICHRP), 'Human Rights in the Global Economy: Report From a Colloquium' (2010) <http://www.ichrp.org/files/documents/185/210_human_rights_global_economy_colloquium_report.pdf> accessed 15 February 2011, at 9.

[137] ICHRP, ibid.

[138] Benedek, 'The World Trade Organization and Human Rights' in Benedek, De Feyter, and Marrella (2007) 138; A Aaronson and JM Zimmerman, *Trade Imbalance: The Struggle to Weigh Human Rights Concerns in Policymaking* (CUP, Cambridge 2008) 5.

by human rights norms; advocating a more deferential attitude on the part of the WTO towards the expertise of other international regimes and structurally linking the consideration of trade issues and social (human rights) issues in the same institutional space, including through the use of human rights impact assessments.[139]

For the critics of the WTO, then, 'coherence' primarily implied two kinds of changes to the WTO and WTO law. First, coherence seemed to require a more modest, less intrusive WTO, which allowed its Members greater regulatory space—space they may require to fulfil their human rights obligations adequately. Secondly, it seemed also to require a new institutional and legal architecture governing the relationship between the trade and human rights regimes, and their associated bodies of law. This new architecture would both help to ensure that conflicts between regimes were less likely to arise—by ensuring that the norms and principles associated with one were taken into account in the operation of the other—and provide clearer guidance on how conflicts ought to be resolved where they did occur. While both of these lines of inquiry represent equally important impulses in contemporary debate about global trade, in the next chapter I want temporarily to set aside the first of these two lines of inquiry (returning to it later in the book, most obviously in Chapter 10), and instead concentrate attention on the second.

III. Conclusion

What emerges, then, from this account of the historical evolution of the contemporary trade and human rights debate, told over the last two chapters? We have seen that its most immediate origins lie in the range of local political struggles around trade liberalization and neoliberal economic reforms which emerged during the 1980s and 1990s across the world. As these local political struggles were internationalized with the emergence of the global justice movement, these instances of trade activism came to be understood as merely one strand of a broader political project of contesting neoliberal economic globalization. Then, as the attention of the global justice movement focused on the law of the WTO in the late 1990s, and as globalization activists simultaneously began to turn to human rights law to articulate their arguments, a further decisive reframing occurred. Claims that contemporary forms of economic globalization were socially regressive were strongly tied to claims that global economic governance was structurally deficient, fragmented, and incoherent. In the same way, the project to imagine a new and different kind of economic globalization was in significant part reframed as a project to achieve coherence in global economic governance through architectural reform of

[139] A good example is K De Feyter, *Human Rights: Social Justice in the Age of the Market* (Zed Books, London 2005) 176: his list of 'the practical implications of a human rights approach' contains four items, two of which are that 'human rights law prevails over trade law' and that 'WTO disputes should be settled in conformity with international human rights law'. The other two relate to the need for domestic legislative bodies to take human rights law into account, and the human rights accountability of TNCs.

the legal and institutional structures that relate different international regimes to one another.

By summarizing the story in this way, I am not suggesting that such architectural questions are the only questions which have been addressed, nor that all participants in the trade and human rights debate have uncritically adopted this discursive framework of coherence. I do claim, however, that the language of coherence has had an important and enduring impact on debates about global economic governance and its reform. This is particularly true within the field of international law. It goes without saying that the major political struggles around economic globalization at the end of the 1990s were of intense interest to many within the college of international lawyers. However, as long as these debates remained conversations about the social and economic outcomes of international trade, and about the proper role of the state in regulating and directing economic activity, the questions they threw up did not appear amenable to the application of professional legal expertise. It was not at all clear what international lawyers could offer in the context of these highly 'politicized' debates. The coherence framework helped to resolve that problem, however, by helping to provide international lawyers with a way of contributing meaningfully to the conversation while at the same time avoiding partisan argumentation. It did this in a number of ways. First, international lawyers were well placed to identify conflicts between international legal regimes—this is, after all, a quintessentially legal task. Conversely, the application of legal expertise to the question of conflicts between international regimes also had the practical effect—even if not the intention—of obscuring the political dynamics which produced these conflicts in the first place, and in so doing helped to reproduce the reifying effects of the coherence framework. Formal occlusion of the political stakes of the debate, and its transformation into a discussion between representatives of two bodies of technical legal and policy expertise, suited lawyers and legal styles of argument ill-suited to direct engagement in political debates.[140]

Secondly, the discursive framework of coherence offered the possibility of being on the side of the internal coherence of international law—a suitably neutral and systemic norm which appealed to lawyers needing to maintain a degree of distance from more overtly political debates. Thirdly, and perhaps most importantly, as I have shown, the coherence framework shifted the debate to questions of institutional design, and the constitutional structure of the international order. While the resolution of inter-regime legal conflicts clearly in many cases required making choices between different substantive values, and was therefore beyond the professional competence of international lawyers, international lawyers *could* legitimately offer their expertise on the question of how such conflicts would currently be resolved as a matter of general international law, as well as the question of what

[140] In conversation, the point has rightly been made to me that 'coherence-talk' can in principle have the opposite effect, of exposing fundamental tensions and political contradictions, rather than obscuring them, and thereby provoking systemic change precisely by showing the impossibility of coherence in contemporary structures of governance as they are currently constituted. Without denying this possibility, my argument is that in practice, at least, the effect has so far been in the opposite direction.

institutional and legal structures might be most appropriate and legitimate for their resolution.

It is fair to say, then, that the work of international lawyers has been an important factor involved in entrenching coherence as a framework for debate about global trade governance. At the same time, this framework has itself shaped the work of international lawyers working in this area. I turn in the next chapter to the question of how exactly it has done so, how exactly it has oriented the contributions that international lawyers have offered to the construction and contestation of global economic governance, in the context of the trade and human rights debate. Has reconstituting the debate as one about the 'coherence' of the international legal order made that debate more or less likely to result in transformational change to the governance of international trade? Has it opened up or closed off space for productive debate? Has it enhanced—or dissipated—the critical potential of human rights discourse as a tool for contesting existing practices of global economic governance? Though (as I hope is clear) I do not by any means deny the significance and value of the interventions and events described in this and the previous chapter, I will argue in Chapter 5 that the framework of coherence has oriented the work of international lawyers involved in this debate in some troubling and perhaps even counterproductive ways.

5

The Limits of Coherence

It will be my argument in this chapter that the critical potential of human rights as a tool for transforming global economic governance has so far been partially but significantly undermined by the tendency of many participants on all sides of the trade and human rights debate to adopt the essentializing, or reifying, discursive mode characteristic of the language of coherence. In the first section, I set out the basic reasons why I believe that founding a vision of reformed global trade governance on the idea of 'coherence' can miss the mark, and perhaps even make a genuine re-imagining of contemporary forms of trade governance more difficult to achieve. In the second, I offer three illustrations of reformative projects inspired by this normative vision, and suggest that their limited success so far can be traced in part to the underlying logics identified in the first section.

I. Coherence and its consequences

I concluded Chapter 4 by noting that one of the core criticisms made of the trade regime within the context of the trade and human rights debate has to do with what its critics perceive as its single-minded focus on its trade mandate, and the relative invisibility of 'non-trade'—social, environmental, distributional—objectives and concerns within the regime. There is, it is said, insufficient attention paid to the social and environmental impacts of trade policy decisions within the community of international trade professionals, and, as a result, a structural bias has emerged in the operation of the regime in favour of the economic objectives of trade policy over conflicting social and environmental objectives. Since the reason for the invisibility of 'non-trade' concerns is usually said to be the functional specialization and structurally limited mandate of the trade regime, along with the structurally fragmented nature of international law and governance, this line of argument has led to a series of 'architectural' projects of institutional or procedural reform designed to better integrate the trade and human rights regimes, as described in the previous chapter. I will be showing, in a later chapter of this book, that this line of reasoning is based on a misdiagnosis of the problems of contemporary global trade governance, such as they are. In this chapter, however, my claim is that the architectural projects which are the end result of this line of inquiry are not likely to be as effective as their proponents seem to believe, even taken on their own terms.

Let me begin by drawing attention to one of the most common and most obvious obstacles which is faced by those who seek to ensure that human rights influence the work of the WTO. This obstacle is ideational in nature, and we might for the moment call it the 'thin' view of the role of the WTO. According to this view, the WTO is nothing more than a venue for the exchange of trade concessions between consenting States, a marketplace of sorts in which States negotiate trade bargains in accordance with their own economic priorities and objectives. According to this view, the WTO simply does not have the competence, mandate, expertise or institutional infrastructure necessary to do much else, including considering the environmental, social, or distributional aspects of the global trading system. The WTO is, in this view, not an institution of general competence, but merely one of a much broader constellation of institutions engaged in the governance of world trade, and the professionals who work within it have a very specific contribution to make to the operation of that system of governance. According to this prevalent view, and to simplify somewhat: it is the role of governmental officials working through the WTO to increase global aggregate wealth by negotiating the mutual reduction of trade barriers, but it is a matter for other (usually domestic) sites of governance to ensure, for example, that this wealth is distributed in ways they understand to be fair, to compensate the losers if and as they see fit, or to ensure that the increase in economic activity which results occurs in a sustainable way. It is quite simply beyond the competence of the WTO to address human rights issues.

This is what Howse has described as the 'watertight compartments' view of the WTO.[1] He illustrates its character in this way:

> One former GATT Director-General . . . wrote in the *Financial Times*, after the failure of the Fifth WTO Ministerial Conference, held in 2003 in Cancun, Mexico (as if lecturing to developing countries who thought otherwise), 'the WTO is not an aid agency'. Or, as the WTO Singapore Ministerial Declaration of 1996 suggested, the ILO is the competent body for labour issues. Human rights impacts of trade laws and policies are something to be addressed outside the WTO—'we' do the 'trade', they do the 'human rights'. Interpretations of trade rules are owned by the trade people; so whatever might be done to deal with the human rights impacts of trade law and policies doesn't mean changing or affecting those policies, but instead a different unconnected set of policies, which in any case must not threaten the meanings of trade law and policy developed by the trade people . . .[2]

For those who adhere to the 'watertight compartments' view of the nature and purpose of the WTO, therefore, the claims of critics that the WTO should take (say) human rights into account seem misguided because the human rights consequences of trade liberalization are by definition the responsibility of other sites of governance. Of course, such arguments only make sense if, and to the extent that, the purpose and institutional competence of the trade regime is taken as given. It is

[1] UNCHR (Sub-Commission), 'Mainstreaming the right to development into international trade law and policy at the World Trade Organization: Note by the Secretariat' (9 June 2004) UN Doc E/CN.4/Sub.2/2004/17, para 19.
[2] ibid para 20.

only then that it seems appropriate to turn a discussion about which problems the trade regime *should* equip itself to address into a discussion about which problems the trade regime is *already* equipped to address. The point remains, however, that this 'thin' view of the role and competence of the WTO represents a crucial part of the ideational infrastructure which divorces the exercise of decision-making power in and around the trade regime from responsibility for the social and environmental consequences of those decisions. The incoherence of international law and governance, we might say, has both an ideational as well as an institutional reality.

The simple point I wish to make is that the 'thin' view of the role and purpose of the trade regime acts as an ideational obstacle to attempts to render 'non-trade' social concerns more visible within the WTO, because it allocates responsibility for the social consequences of trade liberalization to other institutions of governance. It is, in other words, this view of the limited nature and purpose of the WTO which makes it seem unnecessary, inappropriate, and even illegitimate to consider the social, environmental, or distributional consequences of trade policy choices made in the course of decision-making within the WTO itself.

It follows that projects to transform global trade governance through greater institutional coherence between the trade and human rights regimes are unlikely to make much headway without simultaneously challenging and destabilizing this ideational infrastructure. That is to say, putting in place procedural and institutional mechanisms to ensure that human rights concerns are taken into account is unlikely to yield substantial change without a simultaneous rethinking and destabilization of underlying ideas about the nature, purpose, and institutional mandate of the trade regime. It turns out that those working in and around the trade regime already have a well-developed and sophisticated set of ideas about the ways their work can (and can't) legitimately contribute to the global enjoyment of human rights. If change is to occur, therefore, it cannot be simply through ensuring that 'human rights are taken into account', but rather through a re-imagination of the role that the trading system can legitimately and appropriately play in the pursuit of the human rights project, as well as a destabilization of existing causal ideas about how trade liberalization does and does not contribute to the promotion and protection of human rights.

This is a crucial point: too often, institutional or procedural innovations designed to achieve integration between the trade and human rights regimes are treated in the literature as if they are in themselves likely to have a beneficial impact—taking human rights law into account in WTO dispute settlement, promoting forms of consultation and cooperation between the trade and human rights regimes, undertaking human rights impact assessments, and so on. However, if I am right, such institutional and procedural mechanisms can perfectly easily be implemented, without any significant change to the outcomes or operation of international trade negotiations, if there is no simultaneous destabilization of the frameworks of knowledge used to determine, understand, and analyse the causal impact of international trade, or prevalent ideas about the institutional purpose and competence of the trade regime. One danger, then, is that in such circumstances 'coherence' between the trade and human rights regimes at the legal or institutional level may in fact provide an appearance of genuine change which masks a less promising reality. At the very least, projects of this kind may divert critical resources and attention from contestation at the ideational level and therefore close off space for a more productive and open discussion about the proper role and function of the trade regime in contemporary circumstances.[3]

The first point, then, is that architectural projects may not be successful without more debate about the fundamental purposes and goals of the international trade regime. The next point I want to make is slightly different. There are, it seems to me, a number of ways in which progressive criticism of the WTO within the context of the trade and human rights debate may actually make it *more* difficult to have these kinds of debates. The best example of this, which I have written about elsewhere,[4] has to do with the way that the language of coherence directs our attention towards the appropriate *balance* to be struck between the goals and objectives of the trade regime on the one hand, and the human rights regime on the other. The progressive claim, of course, is that the present system of fragmented governance has resulted in an imbalance in favour of the former, and that a more coherent system is necessary if we are to achieve a better integration of the two sets of goals. My difficulty with this line of argument will be immediately clear, namely, that it takes a particular understanding of the goals and objectives of each regime for granted. It takes for granted, in other words, a particular way of conceiving the function and institutional mandate of the trade and human rights regime which are both contestable and in fact of relatively recent historical provenance.[5] Instead of asking what the meaning and purpose of the liberal trade project should be in contemporary conditions, this argument suggests that we should balance the competing demands of the human rights project and the liberal trade project—*now taken as given*. In other words, questions about the fundamental purpose of the trade regime are put to one side, and instead we have discussions about how to deal with situations in which the trade project (now taken as given) comes into conflict with other legitimate social projects associated with the human rights regime. In this crucial sense, the processes by which the mandate and purposes of the trade regime are produced and contested are hidden from view—their outcome is the starting point of discussion, rather than itself the subject of debate—and therefore shielded from contestation, and naturalized. Indeed, it is also possible (though my argument does not require it) that the contrast which is

[3] Though it is framed somewhat differently, the argument I am making here is very close to the argument David Kennedy makes in 'The Politics of the Invisible College: International Governance and the Politics of Expertise' (2001) European Human Rights L Rev 463, 467ff. Institutional projects of coherence in the context of progressive criticism of the trade regime, in other words, can be thought of as one illustration of progressives' tendency to 'blame the structure' of governance for its regressive outcomes. See also D Kennedy, *The Dark Sides of Virtue: Reassessing International Humanitarianism* (Princeton University Press, Princeton, NJ 2004) ch 1.

[4] See eg ATF Lang, 'Reflecting on Linkage: Cognitive and Institutional Change in the International Trading System' (2007) 70 MLR 523.

[5] See generally Ch 8.

often drawn between 'trade objectives' and 'human rights objectives' within the trade and human rights debate can be unhappily constitutive—helping, in other words, to define human rights objectives as different from, and constitutively outside, those associated with the trade regime. In what universe is it acceptable for any decision-maker not to explicitly take into account the consequences of her decisions for working conditions, for food security, or for distributional equity? Only in the universe in which those consequences are understood as part of a conceptually distinct domain of policy expertise: as 'human rights issues', and therefore not as 'trade issues'. As Gathii has noted, the language of coherence may thus help actually to exclude the consideration of the 'social' within the trade regime, by presenting it as *already* outside—that is, as beyond its domain of expertise, and its institutional competence.[6]

Another example of this dynamic has to do with the commonly heard claim that the domain of operation of the WTO is now too broad, that it should focus more narrowly on a traditional trade agenda, and that it should limit its activity in respect of 'non-trade' domestic regulatory measures, as that term has traditionally been understood. Crucially, for the purposes of the present argument, this claim is typically premised on, and justified by reference to, the limited institutional competence of the trade regime: the WTO is and always has been about trade policy, not environmental or social policy; its dispute settlement bodies do not have the expertise or competence to assess the desirability or appropriateness of 'non-trade' regulatory measures; the WTO should focus on addressing the remaining issues in its core competence rather than stretching itself to cover more and more issues which go beyond that core competence, and so on. It may well be that limiting the scope of the application or 'intrusiveness' of WTO disciplines is desirable, in some contexts and in some respects—I will return to that point in Chapter 10. My point at this stage is different: it is that this argument relies on a set of ideas about the limited competence and expertise of the WTO, which are precisely those ideas which act as a barrier to the meaningful consideration by trade professionals working within the trade regime of the social, environmental, or human rights consequences of their decisions. If I am right, then it is more important to challenge prevailing ideas about the role and purpose of the trade regime, than it is to change the formal scope of application of its legal disciplines. In an unexpected way, then, progressive criticism of the narrow mandate of the trade regime can become part of the processes through which inattention to social outcomes within the WTO is naturalized, and made more difficult to disrupt.

Both of these examples are in fact illustrations of the more general claim that the language of coherence, which is characteristic of the trade and human rights debate, tends to reify the trade regime (and, for that matter, the human rights regime, though that is not my focus here). For example, by treating the relationship between the objectives and values of the two regimes as something to be 'discovered' (rather than made), the debate proceeds as if those objectives and values are readily identifiable, and perhaps even self-evident. Similarly, by describing the activities, operations, and

[6] JT Gathii, 'Re-Characterizing the Social in the Constitutionalization of the WTO: A Preliminary Analysis' (2001) 7 Widener L Symposium J 137–73.

normative orientation of each regime as a consequence of their functional specialization, the terms of the debate tend to naturalize particular interpretations of those functions. Furthermore, by identifying potential legal conflicts between the two bodies of law, the debate inevitably tends to de-emphasize the indeterminacy and plasticity of both legal systems. And, finally, by proceeding as if the problem were about achieving coherence between the respective projects of two regimes, the debate does not readily allow for discussion of the possibility that these projects are both heavily contested. More generally, by treating a particular vision of the objectives, values, and function of both regimes as given and self-evident, the essentializing language of the coherence framework therefore makes it more difficult to contest and re-imagine them.

Importantly, my claim that the trade and human rights debate is reifying is not a claim about the beliefs of participants in the debate, but a claim about the consequences of the particular ways of speaking and writing which are characteristic of the debate. If pressed, I suspect that most who write and think in this area would readily acknowledge the internally contested and indeterminate nature of both regimes. The point is that the terms of the debate—the questions asked, and the argumentative positions which are open—do not leave much room for de-reifying interventions. As a result, participants in the debate tend to produce a style of argument which proceeds *as if* the two regimes and their objectives, values, and rules were readily identifiable 'things', open to positivistic exploration.

The thrust and animating impulse of my objections to projects of institutional coherence should now be clear. I do not deny that some degree of institutional or legal integration between the trade and human rights regimes may be desirable and beneficial in some respects. Nor is it my intention to work against the underlying normative orientation of claims that the two regimes ought to be better integrated. Instead, my argument is that such projects risk turning our attention away from other kinds of debates and discussions which are an important precondition for productive re-imagining of global trade governance in response to contemporary challenges. These are, put simply, debates about the proper purpose and role of the trade regime and the collective normative vision in which its activity ought to be grounded. Furthermore, the pursuit of institutional and legal 'coherence' in the absence of such debates makes the success of such projects, measured on their own terms, significantly less likely. In the remainder of this chapter, I give three illustrations of these dynamics at work.

II. Strategies of inter-regime integration

A. Integration as aggregation

It is useful to begin with perhaps the most famous attempt to integrate human rights-related concerns into the WTO, namely the debate in the mid-1990s around the inclusion of a 'social clause' in the GATT. As noted in Chapter 3, it has been well understood for more than a century that trade liberalization can in some circumstances undermine wages, employment, and working conditions in domestic industries subject to increased competitive pressure from foreign producers. Over the course of the fifty-year history of the GATT, there were periodic attempts to address labour rights and employment issues within the international trade regime. The 1950s, for example, saw proposals for new GATT provisions on these issues from the United States, New Zealand, and Britain—the latter specifically contemplating the use of trade sanctions against countries which did not eradicate 'unfair labour standards'.[7] After some tentative discussions during the Tokyo Round,[8] the US delegation (at the explicit direction of the US Congress) sought the establishment of a working party on the relationship between international trade and labour standards at the beginning of the Uruguay Round, and then again at its conclusion.[9] Both were unsuccessful. But the debate over the inclusion of a 'social clause' within the WTO agreements took on a much higher profile in the years immediately following the creation of the WTO, partly as a result of the rise of transnational labour activism around international trade at the time. While the exact content and operation of a 'social clause' differed from proposal to proposal, the core idea was that such a clause would 'require exporting countries to recognize and uphold a set of core labour standards and allow sanctions to be taken against those who fail to do so'.[10] For its supporters, such a clause would go some way towards integrating a 'social dimension' into the work of the WTO, and would constitute an explicit and legally enforceable acknowledgement that the project of liberalizing trade should give way to the normative claims of internationally agreed labour standards where the two seemed to be in tension.

In the lead-up to the 1996 WTO Ministerial in Singapore, both the United States and Norway put forward another proposal for the creation of a WTO working group. They were supported in this by a number of other WTO delegations, as well as a large network of civil society actors from both North and South, including the International Confederation of Free Trade Unions.[11] There was entrenched opposition, however, from both developed and developing country governments, led by India and Malaysia, and also supported by a range of civil society actors. This opposition was based on a number of concerns, the most important of which was the long-standing concern that such a social clause could be abused by developed countries to justify and legitimate protectionist policies, and undermine the comparative advantage of developing countries in labour-intensive industries. Other concerns were that the inclusion of labour issues on the WTO's agenda would

[7] See F Weiss, 'Internationally recognized labour standards and trade' in F Weiss, E Denters, and P de Waart (eds), *International Economic Law with a Human Face* (Kluwer Law International, The Hague, The Netherlands 1998) 92–3; see also A Blackett, 'Whither Social Clause? Human Rights, Trade Theory and Treaty Interpretation' (1999) 31 Columbia Human Rights L Rev 1, 7–8; for a broader history up to the 1970s, see G Hansson, *Social clauses and international trade: an economic analysis of labour standards in trade policy* (Croom Helm, London 1983) 22.

[8] R Wilkinson and S Hughes, 'International Labour Standards and World Trade: No Role for the World Trade Organisation?' (1998) 3 New Political Economy 375, 375.

[9] Weiss, 'Internationally Recognized labour standards' in Weiss, Denters, and de Waart (1998) 93ff.

[10] I take this succinct summary from Wilkinson and Hughes (1998) n 1.

[11] On the range of NGO coalitions in support of this campaign, see R Broad (ed), *Global Backlash: Citizen Initiatives for a Just World Economy* (Rowman and Littlefield Publishers, Lanham, MD 2002) 123ff; see also generally G van Roozendaal, *Trade Unions & Global Governance: The Debate on a Social Clause* (Continuum, London 2002).

dissipate and undermine its core project of reducing barriers to trade, and that it was outside the mandate of the WTO to consider 'non-trade' issues such as labour standards.[12] Ultimately, the Ministerial Declaration which emerged from the Singapore Meeting contained a compromise in which Ministers 'renew[ed their] commitment to the observance of internationally recognized core labour standards', noted firmly that the 'International Labour Organisation is the competent body to set out and deal with those standards', rejected 'the use of labour standards for protectionist purposes', and noted the continuing cooperation of the ILO and WTO Secretariats around the issue.[13] While the precise meaning of this text is unclear and disputed,[14] the practical result has been to relegate explicit discussion of labour issues in the WTO to more marginal venues such as the Trade Policy Review Mechanism—and even there the discussion of labour issues is politically sensitive.[15] More generally, labour issues have been in practice excluded from explicit consideration in the WTO, and in the years immediately following the Singapore Ministerial, the ILO took the initiative in respect of the trade–labour linkage.[16]

To this point, the story is a classic illustration of the way in which attempts to integrate consideration of social concerns into trade policy-making can be short-circuited by arguments based on a particular understanding of the role and institutional competence of the WTO. One response, of course, would have been to contest this understanding, to show how the WTO was already and necessarily implicated in the governance of labour standards, and thereby to provoke a much broader debate about what the appropriate role and competence of the WTO should be in the light of contemporary conditions and challenges relating to work and employment. Instead, since then, the momentum has shifted to a different kind of linkage between trade liberalization and labour standards, through the incorporation of provisions on labour issues in bilateral and regional trade agreements. The United States, in particular, has quite a long and developed practice of incorporating labour rights in some form into its regional trade agreements, and currently has at least thirteen such agreements experimenting with a variety of models of linkage.[17] One model is the labour side agreement to NAFTA, the North American Agreement on Labor Cooperation. Agreed at the conclusion of NAFTA in 1993, this well-known

[12] See also S Charnovitz, 'Triangulating the World Trade Organization' (2002) 96 AJIL 28, 28.

[13] WTO, Singapore Ministerial Declaration (13 December 1996) WTO Doc WT/MIN(96)/DEC, para 4.

[14] Some commentators suggest that the Declaration has in some sense incorporated labour issues into the mandate of the WTO, others argue that the intention of the delegates was clearly to put the issue to one side. See VA Leary, 'The WTO and the Social Clause: Post-Singapore' (1997) 1 EJIL 118.

[15] See SA Aaronson and JM Zimmerman, *Trade Imbalance: The Struggle to Weigh Human Rights Concerns in Trade Policymaking* (CUP, Cambridge 2008) 52ff.

[16] Wilkinson and Hughes (1998) 379.

[17] These include free trade agreements with Jordan, Singapore, Chile, Australia, Morocco, Bahrain, Oman, Dominican Republic, Peru, Colombia, Panama, and Korea, as well as the North American Agreement on Labor Cooperation 32 ILM 1499 (NAALC (1994)). See generally ILO, 'The Social Clause: Issues and Challenges' <http://actrav.itcilo.org/actrav-english/telearn/global/ilo/guide/hodlim2.htm#5.1.1.%20Labour%20Standards%20in%20US%20Trade%20and%20Investment%20Legislation> accessed 17 February 2011; see also Aaronson and Zimmerman (2008) ch 6.

agreement contains provisions requiring signatories to enforce their own labour laws, promoting transnational cooperation between domestic labour ministries, and establishing a soft monitoring and complaints procedure.[18] It does not, however, condition market access on respect for defined labour standards. Since then, labour rights issues have migrated into the main body of some US trade agreements, and labour provisions have been made subject to the dispute settlement mechanisms in others. Some other countries have begun to follow suit. Canadian free trade agreements with Chile and Costa Rica, for example, both largely followed the NAFTA model. In addition to these bilateral agreements, the United States has incorporated references to labour rights in its preferential market access schemes, sometimes including some form of hard conditionality. The US GSP scheme, for example, has since its inception required a determination that a developing country 'has taken or is taking steps' to ensure 'internationally recognized rights' within its territory, both before preferences are extended, and as a condition of their maintenance.[19] Similar provisions were included in the 1991 Andean Trade Promotion Act, the Caribbean Basin Initiative, and the African Growth and Opportunity Act in 2000.[20]

The European Union also has a history of incorporating clauses relating to human rights in its international economic agreements with developing countries, starting from the conclusion of the Lomé IV Convention in 1989, and including well over a hundred agreements of various sorts since then.[21] Importantly, however, EC practice in this area goes well beyond labour right issues, and includes in principle the entire gamut of human rights norms. The relevant clauses in its agreements are very broad, referring to 'human rights' or 'fundamental human rights', 'good governance', 'respect for the rule of law', and in some cases adherence to the 'principles of market economy'. Since 1993, most of these agreements have provided for their suspension in the case of serious human rights abuses by one party. It is also worth noting that the EC's 2006 GSP+ scheme also included human and labour rights as part of its eligibility conditions: an applicant must have ratified and implemented sixteen specified human and labour rights conventions,[22] as well as accepting regular

[18] NAALC (1994); For a summary of earlier US efforts to include labour rights issues in trade instruments on a unilateral basis, see L Compa, 'Labor Rights and Labor Standards in International Trade' (1993) 25 J of L and Policy in Intl Business 165.

[19] 19 USC §§ 2461–6; Caribbean Basin Recovery Act, 19 USC §§ 2701–6 (1988).

[20] See generally W Clatanoff, 'Labor Standards in Recent U.S. Trade Agreements' (2005) 5 Richmond J of Global L and Business 109, 110.

[21] For a thorough review of these agreements, see L Bartels, *Human Rights Conditionality in the EU's International Agreements* (OUP, Oxford 2005).

[22] International Covenant on Civil and Political Rights; International Covenant on Economic Social and Cultural Rights; International Convention on the Elimination of All Forms of Racial Discrimination; Convention on the Elimination of All Forms of Discrimination Against Women; Convention Against Torture and other Cruel, Inhuman or Degrading Treatment or Punishment; Convention on the Rights of the Child; Convention on the Prevention and Punishment of the Crime of Genocide; Convention concerning Minimum Age for Admission to Employment (No 138); Convention concerning the Prohibition and Immediate Action for the Elimination of the Worst Forms of Child Labour (No 182); Convention concerning the Abolition of Forced Labour (No 105); Convention concerning Forced or Compulsory Labour (No 29); Convention concerning Equal Remuneration of Men and Women Workers for Work of Equal Value (No 100); Convention concerning Discrimination in Respect of Employment

monitoring and review of implementation, in order to be eligible for the preference schemes.[23] In addition, the EC's Economic Partnership Agreements, at least in their draft form, also contain commitments to a variety of ILO conventions on core labour standards.[24]

While all of this has been lauded as creating linkage between trade and human rights,[25] the argument I wish to make is that it represents a particularly weak form of integration, which works solely in an 'aggregative' mode. What I mean by that is simply that in this form of linkage, human rights become merely an accompaniment to trade liberalization, an additional set of policies which must be carried out at the same time as the forms of economic integration also encouraged by these agreements. Human rights law no longer connotes a different way of doing trade policy, 'but instead a different unconnected set of policies, which [do] not threaten the meanings of trade law and policy developed by the trade people'.[26] They contain neither a clear mechanism nor even an incentive for economic policy-makers to ensure that human rights norms influence the nature, degree, and form of trade liberalization carried out pursuant to international agreements. They do little to promote a new way of making decisions about trade policy, which places social objectives at the core of their design and architecture. The examples of integration just described therefore constitute a 'weak' form of integration, in the important sense that they do little if anything to activate the critical potential of human rights as a new normative framework for economic globalization. Indeed, they may even serve as instruments for the promotion of a human rights agenda which is very different from that which animates human rights-based criticisms of international trade at the international level. For example, while the EC's human rights conditionality covers economic and social rights in principle, the pre-eminent focus in practice has been on democratic rights and issues around good governance, violations of which have been at issue in virtually all instances in which the consultation and suspension mechanisms have been activated.[27] Thus, while it is true that the European Union is linking trade with 'human rights', in doing so, it has shifted the focus of its trade-related human rights activity from international economic structures to domestic institutions of governance, and from economic and social rights to their civil and political counterparts.[28]

and Occupation (No 111); Convention concerning Freedom of Association and Protection of the Right to Organise (No 87); Convention concerning the Application of the Principles of the Right to Organise and to Bargain Collectively (No 98); International Convention on the Suppression and Punishment of the Crime of Apartheid.

23 Bartels (2005); Council Regulation 980/2005 of 27 June 2005 [2005] OJ L169/1, § 2.

24 G Marceau, 'Trade and Labour' in D Bethlehem et al (eds), *The Oxford Handbook of International Trade Law* (OUP, Oxford 2009) 562.

25 See eg Aaronson and Zimmerman (2008) 51ff, 133–5, 163ff.

26 UNCHR (Sub Commission) (UN Doc E/CN.4/Sub.2/2004/17) para 20.

27 Bartels (2005); L Bartels, 'Human Rights and Democracy Clauses in the EU's International Agreements' (2005) Note Prepared for the European Parliament's Subcommittee on Human Rights, vii <http://www.law.ed.ac.uk/file_download/publications/3_568_humanrightsanddemocracyclausesintheeu-sin.pdf> accessed 17 February 2011; see also Aaronson and Zimmerman (2008) 142.

28 For a similar argument in a different context, see M Goodwin and K Rose-Sender, 'Linking Corruption and Human Rights: an Unwelcome Addition to the Development Discourse' in M Boersma

To my eyes, therefore, the story is to a large extent illustrative of the ways in which a failure to contest existing understandings of the competence, mandate, and role of the trade regime and of trade professionals, has meant that the existing dynamics of trade policy-making have remained largely unchanged by efforts to integrate trade and human rights—except that now they are sometimes accompanied by other projects as well.

B. Legislative hierarchization through formal conflicts rules

The prospect of real or potential conflicts between trade and human rights law raises questions about the proper horizontal allocation of authority between the two regimes, and about the possibility of hierarchizing the two bodies of law relative to one another. In the early stages of the trade and human rights debate, as we have seen, the claim was made that human rights law had 'primacy' over most other bodies of international law, including international trade law, either on the basis of Article 103 of the UN Charter, or more generally based on the *jus cogens* nature of human rights protections.[29] As a general legal proposition, however, this concept of the 'primacy' of human rights law is contestable at best, and is not broadly accepted.[30] Generally speaking, it appears that states assume that there is 'a horizontal relationship between . . . different international legal regimes, including international human rights law'.[31] More generally, as the ILC's Study Group on the problem of fragmentation has observed, there is no presently available 'homogenous, hierarchical meta-system', whether in international law or anywhere else, to which we can turn to resolve such inter-regime conflicts in a simple, final, or unambiguous way.[32] A number of efforts have therefore been undertaken to construct such a system of meta-rules, in the sense of defining the hierarchical relations between trade law and other bodies of international law in specific contexts. Work on such meta-rules has explored a number of possible forms, including waivers of WTO obligations; authoritative interpretations which clarify WTO obligations or explicitly subject them to other rules; or the incorporation of 'conflicts clauses' in subsequent

and H Nelen (eds), *Corruption & Human Rights: Interdisciplinary Perspectives* (Intersentia, Belgium 2010) 221–40.

[29] See W Allmand, 'Trading in Human Rights—The Primacy of Human Rights in International Law' (1999) *Technical Annex to the Brief to the Standing Committee on Foreign Affairs and International Trade* <http://www.dd-rd.ca/site/publications/index.php?subsection=catalogue&lang=en&id=1297> accessed 17 February 2011; INCHRITI Fédération Internationale des Ligues des Droits de l'Homme, 'Rapport l'OMC et les droits de l'homme' No 320 (2001).

[30] eg G Marceau, 'WTO Dispute Settlement and Human Rights' (2002) 13 EJIL 753, 798, n 140; JE Alvarez, 'How Not to Link: Institutional Conundrums of an Expanded Trade Regime' (2001) 7 Widener L Symposium J 1, 6; LR Helfer, 'Constitutional Analogies in the International Legal System' (2003) 37 Loyola of Los Angeles L Rev 193, 214–15.

[31] International Council on Human Rights Policy, 'Human Rights in the Global Economy: Report From a Colloquium' (2010) <http://www.ichrp.org/files/documents/185/210_human_rights_global_economy_colloquium_report.pdf> accessed 17 February 2011.

[32] International Law Commission, 'Fragmentation of International Law: Difficulties Arising from the Diversification and Expansion of International Law', (13 April 2006) UN Doc A/CN.4/L.682 para 493.

multilateral agreements, which purport to define the hierarchical relationship between these agreements and WTO law.

There have been a number of attempts to use other treaty regimes to resist and contest WTO law, by no means limited to the human rights context. None of them has been particularly successful, at least not in any direct way. One example occurred in the context of negotiations on the Framework Convention on Tobacco Control (FCTC), an initiative of the World Health Organization with its origins in the first half of the 1990s.[33] Part of the impetus for the FCTC derived from the rapid growth of global trade in tobacco products which had occurred over the course of the 1980s and 1990s, and which had increased the market penetration of tobacco products in a wide range of developing and transitional economies during the period.[34] According to some within the health policy community, this growth had been facilitated by 'the expansion and entrenchment of a liberal trading regime under the auspices of GATT and WTO' which in their view represented 'an opportunity that [transnational tobacco companies had] been quick to exploit'.[35] The FCTC process therefore quite explicitly represented an attempt by some groups to counter these efforts of tobacco companies and to provide a counterweight to the liberalizing effects of trade law.[36] The FCTC negotiations, involving a broad range of stakeholders, including extensive participation from civil society, were therefore designed to strengthen effective tobacco control policies at all levels of governance.[37] During the negotiations, it was explicitly recognized that the tobacco control measures favoured in the FCTC were likely to be subject to scrutiny and challenge under the law of the WTO. In part as a result, the Secretariat of the WTO was involved in an Ad Hoc Inter-Agency Task Force on Tobacco Control, established in 1999, working to highlight potential areas of conflict between the FCTC and international trade disciplines, and to advise on how conflicts might be avoided.[38] In addition, during the course of negotiations, a number of civil society groups proposed language to be included in the FCTC to ensure that it took primacy over prior international trade obligations for the purposes of international law.[39] The issue of the relative primacy of the FCTC and the WTO agreements was a contentious one in the negotiations,

[33] For an account of these origins, see R Roemer, A Taylor, and J Lariviere, 'Origins of the WHO Framework Convention on Tobacco Control' (2005) 95 American J of Public Health 936.

[34] AL Taylor and DW Bettcher, 'WHO Framework Convention on Tobacco Control: A Global "Good" for Public Health' (2000) 78 Bulletin of the World Health Organization 920, 924; see also J Collin, K Lee, and K Bissell 'Global health governance? The Framework Convention on Tobacco Control' (2002) 23 Third World Q 265–82, 266.

[35] Collin, Lee, and Bissell (2002) 272–3; see also JN Eckhardt, 'Balancing Interests in Free Trade and Health: How the WHO's Framework Convention on Tobacco Control Can Withstand WTO Scrutiny' (2002) 12 Duke J of Comparative & Intl Law 197, Taylor and Bettcher (2000).

[36] Collin, Lee, and Bissell (2002) 278.

[37] ibid.

[38] ibid 275–6; Eckhardt (2002) 214ff; see also WHO and WTO Secretariat, 'WTO Agreements & Public Health' (2002) <http://www.wto.org/english/res_e/booksp_e/who_wto_e.pdf> accessed 17 February 2011.

[39] See Campaign for Tobacco-Free Kids, 'Public Health, International Trade and the Framework Convention on Tobacco Control' (2001) 21 <http://www.tobaccofreekids.org/campaign/global/framework/docs/Policy.pdf> accessed 17 February 2011; Physicians for a Smoke-Free Canada, 'Trade

however, and agreement was not possible on the inclusion of a conflicts clause which clearly hierarchized one body of law or the other. Article 2 of the Framework Convention, entitled 'Relationship between this Convention and other agreements and legal instruments', essentially avoids resolving the issue, even as the Preamble notes in ambiguous language that parties are 'determined to give priority to their right to protect public health'.[40] There is still significant uncertainty as to which set of international legal obligations will take precedence in the event of a conflict, for the purposes of international law.[41]

A similar story emerges from other negotiations. Another example is the 2005 UNESCO Convention on the Protection and Promotion of the Diversity of Cultural Expression, which was the initiative of a group of states, led by Canada and France, who were concerned about the impact of trade liberalization on cultural diversity, particularly in the context of trade in audiovisual products.[42] After having failed in their bid to include a 'cultural exception' in key WTO texts during the Uruguay Round, as well as an attempt to include a similar provision in the proposed Multilateral Agreement on Investment,[43] these countries sought to create a 'counterbalance' to WTO rules,[44] through the promulgation of new rules and principles on cultural diversity in an institutional context less focused on the promotion and protection of trade flows.[45] The Convention, adopted in 2005 after some years of negotiation, reaffirms the right of signatories to adopt measures to protect and promote cultural diversity, and explicitly permits the subsidization of domestic producers, as well as the maintenance of local content thresholds and quotas.[46] It was, according to Hahn, designed in significant part to create a 'safe haven' from WTO obligations for protectionist measures designed to ensure cultural diversity.[47] However, its formal utility in that respect is undermined by the inclusion of Article

Agreements and Tobacco Use' (Submission to the WHO, 2000) 4 <http://www.smoke-free.ca/pdf_1/pscsubmission.pdf> accessed 17 February 2011.

[40] WHO Framework Convention on Tobacco Control (FCTC) <http://whqlibdoc.who.int/publications/2003/9241591013.pdf> accessed February 2011; see also ER Shaffer, JE Brenner, and TP Houston, 'International trade agreements: a threat to tobacco control policy' (2005) 14 (Supplement 2) Tobacco Control ii19.

[41] See DW Zeigler, 'International trade agreements challenge tobacco and alcohol control policies' (2006) 25 Drug and Alcohol Review 567, 576.

[42] For a history of the events leading to this Convention, see I Bernier, 'A UNESCO International Convention on Cultural Diversity' (2003) <http://www.diversite-culturelle.qc.ca/fileadmin/documents/pdf/update0303.pdf> accessed 17 February 2011; M Hahn, 'A Clash of Cultures? The UNESCO Diversity Convention and International Trade Law' (2006) 9 JIEL 515.

[43] Bernier (2003) 3ff.

[44] CB Graber, 'The New UNESCO Convention on Cultural Diversity: A Counterbalance to the WTO?' (2006) 9 JIEL 553; CB Graber, 'Substantive Rights and Obligations under the UNESCO Convention on Cultural Diversity' (NCCR Trade Working Paper 2008) 1 <http://phase1.nccr-trade.org/images/stories/publications/Graber_maastricht_18.9.07.pdf> accessed 17 February 2011.

[45] T Voon, 'UNESCO and the WTO: A Clash of Cultures?' (2006) 55 ICLQ 635, 636.

[46] UNESCO Convention on the Protection and Promotion of the Diversity of Cultural Expressions, Art 6; see Hahn (2006); M Footer and CB Graber, 'Trade Liberalization and Cultural Policy' (2000) 3 JIEL 115; Graber (2006).

[47] Hahn (2006) 533.

20, as a result of efforts of the United States and its allies, which perceived the Convention primarily as a commercial instrument of protection for foreign cultural industries.[48] That Article, while complex in its structure and overall effect, protects the integrity of existing WTO obligations.[49]

The negotiations over the Biosafety Protocol in the late 1990s are a famous illustration of the same dynamic.[50] The possibility of a conflict between the Protocol and relevant WTO agreements—and the intention to use the former to modify the latter—was denied by all sides throughout the negotiation of the Protocol.[51] However, it was at the same time recognized that the Protocol's use of strong precautionary language (different from that adopted in the relevant WTO agreements) 'might create ambiguities that would give a country determined to avoid its WTO obligations' the cover to do so.[52] The release of Panel and Appellate Body decisions in the *EC—Hormones* case during the course of the negotiations only exacerbated these concerns. Major agricultural exporting nations, led by the United States, therefore pressed for the inclusion of a savings clause in the Protocol, which would make clear that it did not alter existing international obligations, including those in the WTO agreements. Other countries resisted, preferring either silence in the text of the Protocol, or some middle position.[53] In the context of civil society activism around trade issues occurring at the same time, the issue was invested with particular significance, as it appeared to implicate constitutional questions of how to balance trade and environmental goals.[54] The ultimate solution was again an ambiguous one, but one which by most accounts did little if anything to change the legal status quo in respect of existing WTO commitments.[55] The Preamble to the Protocol emphasizes

[48] Bernier (2003) 3; Hahn (2006) 517.

[49] By virtue of Art 20, Parties agree to 'foster mutual supportiveness between this Convention and the other treaties to which they are parties' and 'when interpreting and applying the other treaties to which they are parties or when entering into other international obligations' to 'take into account the relevant provisions of this Convention', but at the same time they agree that 'Nothing in this Convention shall be interpreted as modifying rights and obligations of the Parties under any other treaties to which they are parties'; see the detailed analysis in Hahn (2006) 539–46; see also H Ruiz Fabri, 'Reflections on Possible Future Legal Implications of the Convention' in N Obuljen and J Smiers (eds), *UNESCO's Convention on the Protection and Promotion of the Diversity of Cultural Expressions: Making it Work* (Institute for International Relations, Zagreb 2006) 73–87.

[50] See generally, R Falkner, 'Regulating Biotech Trade: The Cartagena Protocol on Biosafety' (2000) 76 International Affairs (Royal Institute of International Affairs 1944) 299; S Saffrin, 'Treaties in Collision? The Biosafety Protocol and the World Trade Organization Agreements' (2002) 96 AJIL 606.

[51] But see N Krisch, 'Pluralism in Postnational Risk Regulation: The Dispute over GMOs and Trade' (2010) 1 Transnational Legal Theory 1, 6 and surrounding.

[52] Saffrin (2002) 611.

[53] ibid 614ff; see also PG Gayathri and RR Kurup, 'Reconciling the Bio Safety Protocol and the WTO Regime: Problems, Perspectives and Possibilities' (2009) 1 American J of Economics and Business Administration 236.

[54] Falkner (2000) 299 and generally.

[55] Saffrin (2002); S Charnovitz, 'The Supervision of Health and Biosafety Regulation by World Trade Rules' (2000) 13 Tulane Environmental L J 271, 300, stating that the Biosafety Protocol appears compatible with the SPS Agreement; GL Gaston and RS Abate, 'The Biosafety Protocol and the World Trade Organization: Can the Two Coexist?' (2000) 12 Pace Intl L Rev 107, 109, concluding that trade measures contained in the Biosafety Protocol are compatible with WTO principles; AH Qureshi, 'The Cartagena Protocol on Biosafety and the WTO—Co-Existence or Incoherence?' (2000) 49 ICLQ 835,

that it 'shall not be interpreted as implying a change in the rights and obligations of a Party under any existing international agreements', while also clarifying in another paragraph that this preambular statement 'is not intended to subordinate this Protocol to other international agreements'. The Preamble further states that 'trade and environment agreements should be mutually supportive with a view to achieving sustainable development'.[56]

Within the WTO itself, the problem of the hierarchical relationship between WTO agreements and multilateral environmental agreements (MEAs) has been discussed in the context of the Committee on Trade and Environment (CTE), a body established in 1995 as the successor to the GATT's Working Group on Environmental Measures and International Trade.[57] Negotiations on the WTO–MEA relationship, occurring within the CTE between 1995 and the Singapore Ministerial in 1996, saw states adopt a range of positions, depending primarily on their perceptions of their trade interests (understood in modern mercantilist terms as the promotion of exports and limitation of disruptive or politically sensitive imports).[58] Some favoured 'strong' integration, in the form of a formal amendment to or an authoritative interpretation of Article XX to explicitly permit trade measures taken pursuant to MEAs in defined conditions. Others, not convinced that potential conflicts were a major problem, thought that a form of 'weak integration', consisting primarily of ad hoc waivers for specific MEAs, would be sufficient. A number of intermediate positions were also proposed.[59] In the end, the approach adopted by the CTE and endorsed at the Singapore Ministerial[60] was relatively weak, proposing no changes to WTO rules, reaffirming the right of Members to challenge MEAs under WTO law, and expressing confidence that potential problems could be resolved through greater cooperation and the proper design of environmental trade measures.[61] A number of explanations of this result have been offered: the lack of the institutional and social conditions necessary for complex learning and the production of a 'common lifeworld' amongst negotiators;[62] a lack of consensus between

854; GR Winham, 'International regime conflict in trade and environment: the Biosafety Protocol and the WTO' (2003) 2 World Trade Rev 131, 143ff; O Rivera-Torres, 'The Biosafety Protocol and the WTO' (2003) 26 Boston College Intl and Comparative L Rev 263, 287ff.

[56] Cartagena Protocol on Biosafety, Preamble.

[57] See generally G Shaffer, 'The Nexus of Law and Politics: The WTO's Committee on Trade and Environment' in RH Steinberg (ed), *The Greening of Trade Law: International Trade Organizations and Environmental Issues* (Rowman and Littlefield Publishers, Lanham, MD 2002) 81–114; M Gabler, 'Norms, Institutions and Social Learning: An Explanation for Weak Policy Integration' (2010) 10 Global Environmental Politics 80–117; R Tarasofsky and A Palmer, 'The WTO in crisis: lessons learned from the Doha negotiations on the environment' (2006) 82 Intl Affairs 899–915.

[58] Shaffer (2002) 92, 104, and generally.

[59] Gabler (2010) 101ff; see also R Tarasofsky, 'The WTO Committee on Trade and Environment: Is it making a Difference?' (1999) 3 Max Planck Ybk of United Nations L 471.

[60] Subject to the condition that the Chairman read a statement prior to the report's adoption that indicated that nothing in the report affected the balance of rights and obligations of members under WTO rules.

[61] WTO, Committee on Trade and Environment, *Report (1996) of the Committee on Trade and Environment* (12 November 1996) WTO Doc WT/CTE/1.

[62] Gabler (2010) 106, 113.

delegations and among competing constituencies within states;[63] and the compatibility of weak forms of integration with the existing trade frame.[64] Then, in 2001, the CTE was given a negotiating mandate for the first time on 'the relationship between existing WTO rules and specific trade obligations set out in multilateral environmental agreements'.[65] This mandate, however, was significantly constrained by the carve-out of environmental trade measures applied to non-parties, as well as by the qualification that negotiations 'must not add to, diminish or alter the balance of the rights and obligations of Members under existing WTO Agreements'.[66] Even within this limited mandate, however, the negotiations have been seen as 'divisive and aimless'.[67] They have been sidetracked largely onto preliminary definitional issues, and show few signs of overcoming the underlying normative deadlock between those countries which seek clear exemptions from trade rules for MEAs and those which oppose such exemptions.[68]

All of these attempts to construct a system of 'constitutional' rules governing the relative priority to be accorded to different bodies of international law, then, have faltered at an early stage. None has been clearly successful, either in the sense of producing clear conflicts rules, or in the sense of producing an institutional and social space for the productive discussion of the values questions which underlie inter-regime conflicts. On the contrary, the consistent pattern is of negotiators actively avoiding the resolution of constitutional questions, obfuscating or denying the reality of normative conflicts, and steering clear of any principled attempt at the hierarchization of values—except in order to maintain the legal status quo as far as possible. There are of course many reasons for this, many of which are specific to the particular dynamics of each negotiation. But what is common to all of these contexts, of course, is that negotiators are being asked to address questions which are to some extent outside their domain of professional competence, which implicate fundamental values choices on which governments profoundly disagree, and which often raise sensitive issues of democratic legitimacy. All of these features make serious discussion more difficult, and induce a tendency towards avoidance on the part of cautious and pragmatic negotiators, particularly in the context of negotiations within an institution of limited functional competence. The point, in short, is that this is a strategy which demands political decision-making of a quasi-constitutional form, but is carried out in the absence of an appropriate constitutional 'mindset'.[69] The examples offered above represent, in other words, attempts to construct architectural solutions to the problem of international legal conflict and incoherence, in the absence of efforts to construct an appropriate *ideational* infrastructure which might support,

[63] Shaffer (2002) 92–3.
[64] Gabler (2010) 102.
[65] WTO, Doha Ministerial Declaration of 14 November 2001, WT/MIN(01)/DEC/1, para 31(i).
[66] ibid para 32.
[67] Tarasofsky and Palmer (2006) 905.
[68] Gabler (2010) 109–10; see also R Eckersley, 'The Big Chill: The WTO and MEAs' (2004) 4 Global Environmental Politics 24, 33.
[69] M Koskenniemi, 'Constitutionalism as Mindset: Reflection on Kantian Themes About International Law and Globalization' (2007) 8 Theoretical Inquiries in L 9.

sustain, and give meaning to such solutions. Their relative inefficacy derives most fundamentally, in my view, from that disjunction.

C. Human rights law in WTO dispute settlement

Since at least the late 1990s there has been an ongoing discussion about the extent to which WTO Panels and the Appellate Body should take into account rules of general public international law in their resolution of trade disputes. This is a well-known discussion, and needs little recapitulation here. In brief: those in favour see the use of public international law by WTO dispute settlement bodies as a way of embedding WTO law within a broader international legal and normative order, and correcting what they see as the narrowness of normative vision which accompanies the trade regime's specialized mandate.[70] It is seen as one mechanism by which the WTO legal system might be made more sensitive to a broader array of normative concerns than simply the pursuit of free trade:

> Reference to interpretative norms of general public international law enhances the legitimacy of the dispute-settlement organs in adjudicating competing values, as they are not specific to a regime that has traditionally privileged a single value—that of free trade.[71]

Thus, some would prefer public international law rules to be broadly applicable in WTO proceedings, including as a defence to a violation of WTO law. Others favour softer forms of integration, arguing primarily for the use of public international law to help guide the interpretation of ambiguous WTO norms, so as to shape their content and application in a more subtle way. Within the trade and human rights debate, it has been a consistent claim of those sympathetic to a progressive human rights project to argue for the interpretation of WTO law in the light of human rights obligations.[72] On the other side, there are those who argue that public international law should not be used in WTO proceedings, at least not in any way which materially alters the substance of WTO law, or undermines the bargain which

[70] See generally J Pauwelyn, *Conflict of Norms in Public International Law: How WTO Law Relates to Other Rules of International Law* (CUP, Cambridge 2004); J Pauwelyn, 'The Role of Public International Law in the WTO: How Far Can We Go?' (2001) 95 AJIL 535; G Marceau, 'A Call for Coherence in International Law: Praise for prohibition against "Clinical Isolation" in WTO Dispute Settlement' (1999) 33 J of World Trade L 87; L Bartels, 'Applicable Law in WTO Dispute Settlement Proceedings' (2001) 35 J of World Trade 499; P Mavroïdis, 'Das GATT als self-contained Regime' (1991) 6 Recht der International Wirtschaft 497; J Cameron and KR Gray, 'Principles of International Law in the WTO Dispute Settlement Body' (2001) 50 ICLQ 248.

[71] R Howse and K Nicolaïdis, 'Enhancing WTO Legitimacy: Constitutionalization or Global Subsidiarity?' (2003) 16 Governance 73.

[72] See eg R Howse and M Mutua, *Protecting Human Rights in a Global Economy: Challenges for the World Trade Organization* (International Centre for Human Rights and Democratic Development, Montreal, Quebec 2000); Marceau (2002) 753; C Dommen, 'Raising Human Rights Concerns in the World Trade Organization: Actors, Processes and Possible Strategies' (2002) 24 HRQ 1; J Harrison, *The Human Rights Impact of the World Trade Organization* (Hart Publishing, Portland, OR 2007) as well as the reports of the High Commissioner for Human Rights referred to in Ch 4 above. However, see also C Dommen, *The WTO, international trade, and human rights* (2004) <http://www.3dthree.org/pdf_3D/WTOmainstreamingHR> accessed 17 February 2011; Kinley (2009) 76.

negotiators thought they were getting at the end of the Uruguay Round.[73] Although those who hold this view do so for a number of reasons, in significant part it is based on a perception of the limited function, vocation, and competence of WTO dispute settlement bodies: WTO Panels and the Appellate Body have neither the mandate nor the competence to interpret and apply bodies of law other than the covered agreements, and for them to do so would be to assume illegitimately an authority that they simply do not have.

At first, there were signs that the WTO's Appellate Body might be receptive to an integrative approach to the interpretation of WTO agreements. In its very first case in 1996, for example, the Appellate Body noted that Article 3(2) of the Dispute Settlement Understanding, which refers to the need to interpret WTO law in accordance with the customary international law rules of treaty interpretation, 'reflects a measure of recognition that the [GATT] is not to be read in clinical isolation from public international law'.[74] While this statement is in fact quite a modest one, it was read by many observers as a strong indication that the Appellate Body did not see international trade law as a self-contained regime, but as part of a larger normative system. It was followed just over two years later by the Appellate Body's decision in *US—Shrimp*, which went much further in its use of public international law as an aid to the interpretation of Article XX(g) of the GATT. While the particular interpretive point at issue was not particularly controversial in the context of the case—namely, whether the term 'exhaustible natural resources' in Article XX(g) included living creatures—the importance of the decision lay in its liberal reference to a wide range of hard and soft instruments of international law, including international environmental law. These included: a report of the World Commission on Environment and Development; two seminal ICJ cases; *Oppenheim's International Law*; the UN Convention on the Law of the Sea; the Convention on Biological Diversity; Agenda 21; and the Convention on International Trade in Endangered Species, among many others.[75] All of this material, and much more besides, was marshalled in broad support of the notion that the international community places great emphasis on the conservation of living natural resources, that it has in recent decades come to use the term exhaustible natural resources to include living resources, and that Article XX(g) of the GATT ought therefore to be interpreted to include reference to living creatures such as turtles.[76] In the same case, the Appellate Body expressed the view that the *chapeau* of Article XX was an application of the general principle of law known as *abus de droit*, and should be interpreted in the light of that general principle as appropriate.[77] On the procedural side, it also determined that it had the authority to receive and consider *amicus curiae*

[73] JP Trachtman, 'Transcending "Trade and ..."—an Institutional Perspective' (2002) 96 AJIL 77.

[74] Appellate Body Report, *United States—Standards for Reformulated and Conventional Gasoline* (adopted 20 May 1996) WT/DS2/AB/R at 17.

[75] Appellate Body Report, *United States—Import Prohibition of Certain Shrimp and Shrimp Products* (adopted 6 November 1998) WT/DS58/AB/R para 128ff.

[76] ibid para 131.

[77] ibid para 158.

briefs, including a number submitted from NGOs working in the field of international environmental law.[78] All three of these decisions arguably demonstrated an openness to normative influences outside those traditionally considered central to international trade law. Then, in early 2000, the Panel in *Korea—Government Procurement* went significantly further. In a decision which has since been roundly criticized, the Panel suggested that rules of customary international law apply 'generally to the economic relations between the WTO Members', at least to the extent that they do not contract out of it through the WTO agreements. Specifically, they suggested that the rules of international law relevant to treaty negotiation (here, those relating to good faith and error) 'apply to the WTO treaties and to the process of treaty formation under the WTO'.[79]

However, in part as a result of resistance on the part of WTO Members themselves, these tentative steps towards systemic and normative openness were soon replaced by a much more cautious and inward-looking approach. One element of this new approach has been a real reluctance on the part of the Appellate Body to venture outside its own circumscribed domain of competence and expertise, in the sense of making pronouncements about the substantive content of rules of international law beyond the WTO. The first example of this came in 1999 (not coincidentally, during negotiations around the Biosafety Protocol, described above), with the Appellate Body's decision in *EC—Hormones*. In that case, the European Communities had sought unsuccessfully before the Panel to use the precautionary principle as a rule or general principle of customary international law, to support their ban on imports of hormone-treated beef. When the case came before the Appellate Body, the first issue was whether the precautionary principle was indeed part of customary international law. On this point, it did not feel competent to decide:

> The status of the precautionary principle in international law continues to be the subject of debate among academics, law practitioners, regulators and judges. The precautionary principle is regarded by some as having crystallized into a general principle of customary international *environmental* law. Whether it has been widely accepted by Members as a principle of *general* or *customary international law* appears less than clear. We consider, however, that it is unnecessary, and probably imprudent, for the Appellate Body in this appeal to take a position on this important, but abstract, question.[80]

The Appellate Body also went on to say that, even if the precautionary principle were part of customary international law, it would not 'override' the provisions of the SPS agreement—not a controversial proposition in itself, but significant as a signal that the Appellate Body would not look kindly on attempts to use 'non-WTO' law to

[78] ibid paras 79–91.

[79] Panel Report, *Korea—Measures Affecting Government Procurement* (adopted 19 June 2000) WT/DS163/R, para 7.96, also n 753.

[80] Appellate Body Report, *EC—Measures Concerning Meat and Meat Products* (adopted 13 February 1998) WT/DS26/AB/R and WT/DS48/AB/R, para 123, footnote omitted.

significantly re-orient the content of the WTO's normative order, narrowly conceived.[81] This approach was precisely echoed seven years later by the Panel in *EC—Biotech*, when it was confronted with the same question.[82] Another example comes from the Appellate Body's 2006 decision in *Mexico—Soft Drinks*.[83] In that case, brought by the United States, one of Mexico's arguments was that the Appellate Body should decline to hear the case, on the basis that the United States had violated its NAFTA obligations towards Mexico, and should not be able to profit from that illegal act in the context of WTO proceedings.[84] The Appellate Body rejected the argument on the specific basis that accepting it would 'entail a determination whether the United States has acted consistently or inconsistently with its NAFTA obligations', a determination which, it found, was outside the Appellate Body's mandate and competence.[85]

A second, closely related, element of this new approach has been a strong tendency to avoid, whenever possible, definitively addressing 'constitutional' questions from a systemic perspective. The Appellate Body has, for example, resolutely avoided the problem of potential conflicts between WTO law and other bodies of international law, shied away from resolving the problems caused by multiple forums for the resolution of trade disputes, and resisted any temptation to take on the task of integrating WTO law into its broader normative environment. Thus in *Argentina—Footwear*, the Appellate Body was able to avoid the problem of a potential conflict between Argentina's commitments to the IMF and its obligations under the IMF agreement, by noting that Argentina had failed to show the existence of a legally binding commitment owed to the IMF.[86] It also suggested that in the absence of any effort on the part of WTO Members themselves to address the question of potential conflicts, it would also be reluctant to do so on its own initiative.[87] In the *Mexico—Soft Drinks* case referred to above, a case which could have been brought before either the WTO or a NAFTA panel, the Appellate Body was explicitly faced with questions relating to the fragmentation of the international legal order. Its decision that it had no discretion to decline jurisdiction can usefully be understood as a way of returning the problem of institutional fragmentation back to the non-judicial actors to resolve. The Appellate Body, in other words, chose not to do what it could have done, namely to begin the judicial elaboration of doctrines and procedures which might systematically allocate adjudicative authority between different trade tribunals, more

[81] ibid para 125.

[82] Panel Report, *European Communities—Measures Affecting the Approval and Marketing of Biotech Products* (21 November 2006) WT/DS291–3/R, paras 7.88–7.89.

[83] Appellate Body Report, *Mexico—Tax Measures on Soft Drinks and other Beverages* (adopted 24 March 2006) WT/DS308/AB/R.

[84] See ibid para 55ff.

[85] ibid para 56. One case in which both the Panel and the Appellate Body have interpreted 'non-WTO' law was *European Communities—Regime for the Importation, Sale and Distribution of Bananas* WT/DS27. In that case, however, the law in question was the Lomé IV Convention, which was explicitly incorporated into WTO law by the waiver which was itself being interpreted.

[86] Appellate Body Report, *Argentina—Safeguard Measures on Imports of Footwear* (adopted 12 January 2000) WT/DS121/AB/R, para 69.

[87] ibid para 72.

modestly leaving that task for others to pursue. Its decision in *Brazil—Retreaded Tyres* can be understood similarly. In that case, the Appellate Body was faced with a choice between imposing obligations on Brazil which apparently conflicted with its obligations under the MERCOSUR agreements, or attempting the task of crafting a solution to that conflict. In the end, it again cautiously left the latter task for others to accomplish, simply applying WTO law and paying essentially no attention to how the ensuing conflict between Brazil's WTO and MERCOSUR obligations might be resolved.[88]

Most dramatically, the (unappealed) 2006 Panel decision in *EC—Biotech* appears to have significantly closed off space for the use of public international law in the interpretation of WTO obligations. As is well known, one of the issues before the Panel in that case was whether the relevant WTO agreements should be interpreted in the light of the Convention on Biological Diversity and the Biosafety Protocol, both of which contained some form of the precautionary principle. Recall from above that the issue of the relative priority as between the Biosafety Protocol and WTO obligations had been hotly contested during negotiations over the Protocol itself, and had been only partially resolved through the inclusion of an ambiguous combination of preambular clauses. In addition, the Convention on Biological Diversity (CBD) itself contained a conflicts clause, which was less ambiguous but still open to conflicting interpretation and application.[89] Deciding, perhaps, that it would not do by interpretation what the Members had found it impossible to do through negotiation, the Panel refused the EC's invitation to engage in a form of 'soft' constitutionalization, by refusing to take either of these instruments into account in its interpretation of the relevant WTO agreements under Article 31(3)(c) of the Vienna Convention on the Law of Treaties (VCLT). This was on the basis that Article 31(3)(c) only required the Panel to take into account those rules of international law which are applicable in the relations between all parties to the WTO agreements—that is, those rules which have been agreed to by all WTO Members.[90] While the Panel acknowledged that it was permitted take the CBD and the Biosafety Protocol into account under other provisions (including Article 31(1)) of the VCLT, it was not *required* to under Article 31(3)(c)—and in this case decided that it was neither 'necessary' nor 'appropriate' to do so.[91]

[88] See *Mexico—Soft Drinks (AB)* paras 44–54; Appellate Body Report, *Brazil—Measures Affecting Imports of Retreaded Tyres* (adopted 17 December 2007) WT/DS332/AB/R, para 213ff.

[89] Art 22, 'Relationship with Other International Conventions' states: '1. The provisions of this Convention shall not affect the rights and obligations of any Contracting Party deriving from any existing international agreement, except where the exercise of those rights and obligations would cause a serious damage or threat to biological diversity. 2. Contracting Parties shall implement this Convention with respect to the marine environment consistently with the rights and obligations of States under the law of the sea.'

[90] *EC—Biotech (Panel)* para 7.70 and surrounding.

[91] ibid para 7.95; see also Panel Report, *United States—Definitive Anti-Dumping and Countervailing Duties on Certain Products from China* (adopted 25 March 2011) WT/DS379/R, para 8.87 for a similarly cautious approach as regards the ILC Articles on State Responsibility.

This line of cases since 1999 represents—at least for the time being—a relatively unequivocal rejection of a constitutional approach to the interpretation and application of WTO law. It is based, in my opinion, largely on the view of the Appellate Body that it has neither the mandate nor the legitimacy to engage in a process of even soft and incremental constitutionalization on behalf, as it were, of the international community. My interpretation of this line of cases is fortified by the fact that both Panels and the Appellate Body have proved themselves perfectly willing to take into account 'non-WTO' material, when to do so does *not* seem to raise fundamental issues of a constitutional kind, but instead appears merely to involve the transmission of specialized expertise. Thus, for example, as Young has shown, even the Panel in the *EC—Biotech* case flexibly (though not always coherently) referred to a wide range of non-WTO material in its decision.[92] This was primarily to help with the meaning of phrases such as 'pest', 'disease', 'toxin', or 'contaminant', which have particular meanings within specialized technical discourses.[93] While the interpretation of these phrases is vitally important in the sense that they help to define the scope of application of SPS disciplines, it is clear that the Panel saw their interpretation as raising technical questions of textual signification rather than constitutional questions of normative hierarchy. Similarly, in other cases, Panels have readily consulted with WIPO and the IMF on technical questions considered to be within their specialized domain of expertise.[94]

So far, then, it has been an uphill battle to instil even a 'soft' constitutional mindset in the judicial bodies of the WTO,[95] and it is possible that proponents of constitutionalization have underestimated the structurally embedded nature of the functionalist frame in WTO dispute settlement. Panels and the Appellate Body are acutely aware of their fragile legitimacy—and of the need to maintain the support of WTO Members. It is no coincidence that the Appellate Body began to take a much more cautious approach to WTO interpretation after some significant criticisms of its decision by members, and as more and more instances of apparently 'strategic' conflicts between WTO law and non-WTO law arose over time.[96] As a judicial body, the Appellate Body does not appear to be ready to take on the role of addressing the difficult and fundamental issues that such potential conflicts raise, and its turn away from a fuller use of international law can very often be understood as a way of enacting and enforcing its distance from 'political' questions not appropriate for resolution by a judicial body. While the dispute settlement system is much more formally autonomous than it once was, it is not entirely so,[97] and there

[92] MA Young, 'The WTO's Use of Relevant Rules of International Law: An Analysis of the Biotech Case' (2007) 56 ICLQ 907.

[93] See Young (2007) 922ff.

[94] Panel Report, *India—Quantitative Restrictions of Imports of Agricultural, Textile and Industrial Products* (adopted 22 September 1999) WT/DS90/R (IMF, on BOP measures); Panel Report, *United States—Section 110(5) of the US Copyright Act* (adopted 27 July 2000) WT/DS160/R (WIPO).

[95] For an alternative view, see Krisch (2010).

[96] Of the kind discussed above pp 143ff.

[97] See generally on this point, T Broude, *International Governance in the WTO: Judicial Boundaries and Political Capitulation* (Cameron May, London 2004).

are important limits to the extent to which it can take the lead in the project of systemic normative integration. This is particularly the case where states themselves have time and again shown themselves unable to resolve their differences over such questions. Whatever the reason, however, this evolving story of the relationship between WTO law and 'non-WTO' law in trade dispute settlement is illustrative of precisely the dynamic identified at the beginning of this chapter—namely, the impossibility of producing normative integration and change solely through institutional and procedural mechanisms, without an accompanying movement towards a new and different mindset within the professional communities operating within international regimes.

III. Conclusion to Part I

It may be useful if I conclude this chapter by drawing out what I see as three key points which emerge from the material presented over the course of the entirety of Part I of the book. Each of them is in some way a response to criticisms of the WTO and of WTO law—and the projects for reform or transformation of the trade regime associated with those criticisms—which have been voiced in the context of the trade and human rights debate.

My first point has to do with the institutional-architectural orientation of many contemporary projects for the reform of global trade governance. We can usefully imagine the politics of a structurally fragmented international order to be defined and carried out in two complementary ways. On one hand, the politics and ethical orientation of global governance is determined in part by the structural relationships between centres of power—the legal and practical allocation of authority between them, the boundaries between their different domains of operation, and the rules and structures which determine resolution of conflicts between them. On the other hand, the politics of global governance is *also* defined by the processes and structures internal to each regime, through which each regime's normative orientation and mission is defined, defended, and contested. The transformation of global economic governance, therefore, can take the form either of a realignment of the relative power of the regimes and their values, or a reconstitution of the values and structural biases of each regime. I have suggested in this chapter that the success of the former depends on the latter. More than that, the burden of this chapter—and indeed of this Part of the book—is that the trade and human rights debate, in its present form, tends to direct the attention of international lawyers primarily to the former, even when it could more productively be directed primarily to the latter. 'Less than an architectural project', to borrow Koskenniemi's language, we should imagine the reform of global trade governance as 'a programme of moral and political regeneration'.[98] My argument, therefore, can in part be understood as a call to focus greater attention on the internal politics of regime definition, on the re-imagination of the collective

[98] Koskenniemi (2007) 18.

purposes which ought to be pursued by the trade regime in contemporary conditions.

My second point is that the language of 'coherence' which has so far structured so deeply the interaction between the trade and human rights communities, may in practice make this kind of re-imagination more difficult. This is because the language of coherence in the context of the trade and human rights debate has tended to reify the international trade regime, in part by treating the mission, values, and objectives of the trade regime as given for the purposes of discussion, and thereby making them more difficult to contest.[99] One of the reasons I have spent so much time retelling the history of the trade and human rights debate over these last chapters will now be clear—precisely as a way to de-reify and re-historicize our understanding of both regimes, as a direct counter to the reifying tendencies of the coherence framework. Thus, against the idea that a regime's function and mandate determine its normative orientation, I have shown that such mandates are continually reinterpreted and contested over time. And against the idea that conflicts between regimes are largely the result of their functional specialization or mutual isolation, I have shown that they derive from specific political struggles and strategies conducted in the context of an historically specific ideological context. We would do well to understand that while the politics of the trade regime are in some sense the product of its functional specialization, in fact the reverse is also true: the meaning of the trade regime's specialized function is itself the product of ongoing political struggle.

It may be objected that this second point misses the mark, that the call to create a trade regime which is consistent with human rights principles should be understood as a de-reifying call to re-imagine the fundamental contours of the liberal trade project as it is presently understood. It is true that, at their best, human rights critiques of the trade regime do precisely that. My point, however, is that this project could be much more successful, and human rights engagement with the WTO could be much more productive, if it was conducted with a more explicit recognition and acknowledgement of the trade regime's internally contested nature, and its historical association with precisely the kind of political projects which many progressive human rights advocates favour. Understanding and emphasizing these aspects of the trade regime will, in my view, help to create new spaces and strategies for contestation, and increase the persuasiveness and salience of the claims that they make within the field of international trade law and governance. It may require, however, the jettisoning—or at least serious reconstruction—of coherence as a framework of debate.

The third point has to do with what I called at the outset of this chapter the 'thin' view of the nature and role of the WTO, as little more than the forum for the exchange of trade concessions. I suggested that this view represents a significant ideational obstacle to the kind of fundamental debate about the purposes of the regime that I am advocating, and that it needs to be disturbed and destabilized—in

[99] For a similar argument, see SA Dillon, 'A Farewell to Linkage: International Trade Law and Global Sustainability Indicators' (2002) 55 Rutgers L Rev 87.

the sense of being made visible and subject to scrutiny and reflection—if that debate is to occur. This third point, then, acts as a prelude to Part II of the book, since in many ways, it is precisely that kind of destabilizing, ground-clearing effect that I seek to achieve in the next four chapters. In those chapters, I show how this 'thin' view of the nature and purpose of the WTO is of relatively recent origin, I show how its emergence was part of a much broader transformation of the trade regime and trade law during the last three decades of the twentieth century, and I explore the effects its emergence has had on the way that international trade law has evolved and been applied. As we move from Part I to Part II, then, the theme of coherence between the trade and human rights regimes takes a back seat, and a different set of questions is brought to the fore instead. By what processes is the normative orientation of the international trade regime defined and sustained in any particular historical period? What role do 'ideas' play in such processes? How does a relatively open-ended—and highly contested—legal regime such as that governing international trade come to be associated with a particular vision of state–market relations? Precisely what role do international law and lawyers play in these processes? And what does the example of the trade regime tell us about the way that the normative biases of international legal regimes more generally are constructed, contested, sustained, and transformed in the contemporary international order?

PART II

THE TRADE REGIME AND THE NEOLIBERAL TURN

6

Against Objectivism

Between the beginning of the Tokyo Round of trade negotiations in 1973 and the end of the twentieth century, the international trade regime underwent a fundamental transformation. The most dramatic and visible effects of this transformation were seen in the regime's legal order, which was radically altered along at least four axes. Most famously, the GATT's diplomatic form of dispute resolution was transformed into the WTO's judicialized dispute settlement system, which enjoyed a significant degree of formal autonomy from the processes of trade diplomacy.[1] Dispute settlement was made compulsory, its procedures and operation were substantially formalized, and it was supported by a stronger set of enforcement mechanisms based on the quasi automatic authorization of retaliatory trade sanctions. Furthermore, the scope of application of this legal order was significantly expanded—both formally and as a practical matter—as the regime added intellectual property and services to its mandate, shifted its focus of attention away from trade barriers imposed at the border, and increasingly began to impose disciplines on 'behind the border' barriers. As the law's scope of application expanded, so too did its normative content. The norms of non-discrimination and transparency were supplemented by new disciplines on domestic regulation, based on norms of necessity, scientific rationality, procedural legitimacy, and consistency. Thousands of pages of new law were created, as negotiators sought to elaborate the content and meaning of liberalization commitments in the areas of agriculture, services, textiles, subsidies, and trade remedies, among others. Finally, the interpretive jurisprudence produced by GATT/WTO dispute settlement bodies also underwent a profound modification, as existing GATT disciplines were reinterpreted, and new jurisprudential styles, with their own particular interpretive techniques, were adopted and developed.

At about the same time as this transformation was occurring, there was a resurgence of economic liberalism in both the developed and developing world, as part of a global 'neoliberal turn' over the two decades spanning the end of the Cold War. While it is clear that there is some connection between this ideological turn and the changes to the GATT/WTO system just described, the nature of that connection is

[1] See generally A Reich, 'From Diplomacy to Law: The Juridicization of International Trade Relations' (1997) 17 Northwestern J Intl L and Business 775; D Palmeter and PC Mavroidis, *Dispute Settlement in the World Trade Organization: Practice and Procedure* (2nd edn, CUP, Cambridge 2004); JHH Weiler, 'The Rule of Lawyers and the Ethos of Diplomats. Reflections on the Internal and External Legitimacy of WTO' (2001) 35 J of World Trade 191; J Pauwelyn, 'The Transformation of World Trade' (2005) 104 Michigan L Rev 1.

in my view not well understood, and too often caricatured. It is one of the purposes of the next four chapters to provide an account of the way in which the gradual rise to dominance of economic liberalism over the 1970s, 1980s, and 1990s reshaped the GATT/WTO's legal system—and to do so in a way which avoids what I see as the simplifications and distortions of existing explanations. I do not think, for example, that neoliberal free market-oriented policy prescriptions were encoded into WTO law during the Uruguay Round, in the sense that WTO law became something of a blueprint for neoliberal economic policy prescriptions as they related to trade. Moreover, I do not consider that the changes to the GATT/WTO during the Tokyo and Uruguay Rounds represented merely an extension and intensification of existing dynamics within the trade regime. Nor, finally, do I find it sufficient to explain the outcomes of Tokyo and Uruguay Rounds as simply mechanical or fortuitous outcomes reflecting the preferences of powerful states in trade negotiations, without paying attention to the way that neoliberal thought structured and reconfigured the way that governments understood and went about the task of pursuing their interests in the context of those negotiations.

The story that I wish to tell about this period of the GATT/WTO's history is set out in Chapters 7, 8, and 9. Chapter 7 addresses the first period of the GATT's history, from 1947 to roughly the end of the 1960s, as necessary background in order to understand the novelty of what came after. Chapter 8 provides an account of the transformation of the trade regime over the last three decades of the twentieth century. It describes this as a transformation of the trade regime's 'legal imagination'—a transformation, in other words, at the level of intersubjective frameworks of meaning operating in and around the international trade regime, including the emergence of what I referred to in Chapter 5 as the 'thin' view of the role and purpose of the GATT/WTO system—which had institutional, textual, jurisprudential, and normative manifestations at the level of WTO law itself. These ideational changes, I suggest, are themselves closely associated with underlying structural, institutional, and material transformations occurring at the same time. Chapter 9 supports and further extends the claims made in Chapter 8, through a detailed case study of the elaboration of an international legal framework governing trade in services.

Since the story that I tell focuses on the interpretive dimension of trade politics, and because the dominance of objectivist explanations of trade politics in the contemporary literature can lead to serious misunderstandings of my argument, it is necessary that I spend some time anticipating those misunderstandings, and clarifying the theoretical premises of the following chapters. That is the purpose of the present chapter. In particular, my aim is to explain why emphasizing the role of 'ideas' of trade professionals as an explanatory factor need not necessarily entail a departure from an understanding of trade politics in which states are engaged in simple 'bargaining' in the pursuit of their 'material interests'.[2] There will be many

[2] For one example of this misunderstanding, forcefully articulated, see RH Steinberg, 'The Hidden World of WTO Governance: A Reply to Andrew Lang and Joanne Scott' (2009) 20 EJIL 1063.

readers for whom this proposition is self-evident, and who can probably safely skip directly to Chapter 7.

There is also a more general purpose to these next four chapters, which needs to be clearly stated at the outset. The core questions which animate the following chapters all have to do with the way that international legal regimes are contingently but durably tied to particular, situated projects of political reform, and to particular visions of international economic order. Is it useful to talk about a particular model of state–market relations being 'encoded' into international law, and propagated by it? If so, what are the precise mechanisms by which these connections are made? By whom and in what contexts are they made? How, in other words, are the 'politics' and 'normative orientations' of international legal regimes defined, and how are they contested, or shielded from contestation? Are law and lawyers active participants in these processes, and, if so, what roles do they play? It is my hope that the answers that I offer to these questions in the context of the international trade regime can be developed in relation to other regimes of international governance.

I. The objectivist fallacy

A. The traditional state-centric, interest group model of trade politics

In their 2006 book entitled *The Evolution of the Trade Regime: Politics, Law and Economics of the GATT and the WTO*, Barton, Goldstein, Gosling, and Steinberg set out very crisply the model of trade politics which currently dominates literature on the trade regime:

> . . . states are still the primary actors in the international system . . . International institutions are voluntary organizations; states adhere to their mandates out of self-interest. Given a world of sovereign nation-states, we would expect that decision-making processes will either formally reflect the interests of powerful states, or will be supplemented by informal action that allows their expression of power.[3]

In the GATT/WTO regime, in this basic model, states bargain with one another in pursuit of their own self-interest, typically seeking the greatest possible market access for their exports while at the same time avoiding, as far as possible, making market access commitments of their own, at least where such commitments have domestic political costs. The outcomes of these negotiations, as reflected in the texts of the WTO agreements, fundamentally reflect the distribution of power between these state actors, so that the most powerful states are typically able to demand more market access for their exports than less powerful states.

Even in its simplest form, this model requires some elaboration of the concepts of 'power' and 'interest'. On the concept of 'power', Barton et al note that:

[3] JH Barton, JL Goldstein, TE Josling, and RH Steinberg, *The Evolution of the Trade Regime: Politics, Law, and Economics of the GATT and the WTO* (Princeton University Press, Princeton, NJ 2006) 10.

> . . . in analyzing trade relationships, market size—the capacity to open or close a market—may offer the best first approximation of bargaining power . . . Market opening and closure have been treated as the currency of trade negotiations in the postwar era . . . By this measure the United States must be considered the dominant state in shaping GATT and WTO institutions over their history.[4]

Power, therefore, is defined as the 'ability to get others to do what they otherwise would not do',[5] and is measured primarily in economic terms. On the question of state 'interest', Barton et al adopt a domestic interest group model of the formation of national trade policy preferences. 'Classic political analyses of international trade policy in the twentieth century', they note, 'were often stories about how powerful domestic actors . . . —business organizations and trade associations—shaped national trade policy'.[6] Trade policy preferences of states, on this view, are the outcome of struggles between different domestic groups seeking to have their trade policy preferences adopted by the official organs of the state. Policy is determined in part by the distribution of power between these groups, where 'power' is again measured in economic terms, so that an industry body is more powerful the more it contributes to domestic employment, economic growth, exports, and so on.[7]

This simple model has of course been elaborated, challenged, and developed in numerous ways. Some, for example, have argued that domestic institutional structures are an important independent causal influence on the trade policy preferences of states, since different institutional structures aggregate the preferences of different political actors in different ways, giving some a more effective voice within policy-making processes than others.[8] Others have begun to explore the independent causal impact of negotiating processes within the WTO on the outcomes of trade negotiations,[9] as well as the role played by such non-state actors as the GATT/WTO Secretariat in them.[10] An important strand of research has also focused on the role of 'ideas' in trade policy-making processes, about which I will say more below.[11] The authors of the above volume go on to incorporate some of the insights of this

[4] Barton et al (2006) 10–11 (references omitted).

[5] Barton et al (2006), citing RO Keohane and JS Nye, *Power and Interdependence: World Politics in Transition* (Little, Brown and Company, Boston, MA 1977).

[6] Barton et al (2006) 14 (references omitted).

[7] ibid 10ff.

[8] See eg HV Milner, 'The Political Economy of International Trade' (1999) 2 Annual Rev of Political Science 91; J Goldstein, *Ideas, Interests, and American Trade Policy* (Cornell University Press, Ithaca, NY 1993); PA Hall and RCR Taylor, 'Political Science and the Three New Institutionalisms' (1996) 44 *Political Studies* 936.

[9] See eg JS Odell (ed), *Negotiating Trade: Developing Countries in the WTO and NAFTA* (CUP, Cambridge 2006).

[10] See eg Y Xu and P Weller, *The Governance of World Trade: International Civil Servants and the GATT/WTO* (Edward Elgar Publishing, Cheltenham, UK 2004); GC Shaffer, 'The Nexus of Law and Politics: The WTO's Committee of Trade and Environment' in RH Steinberg (ed), *The Greening of Trade Law: International Trade Organizations and Environmental Issues* (Rowman and Littlefield, Oxford 2002) 81.

[11] Goldstein (1993); J Goldstein, 'Ideas, Institutions and American Trade Policy' (1988) Intl Org 179; D Tussie (ed), *The Politics of Trade: The Role of Research in Trade Policy and Negotiation* (Brill Academic Publishers, Boston, MA 2009); WJ Drake and K Nicolaïdis, 'Ideas, Interests, and Institutionalization: "Trade in Services" and the Uruguay Round' (1992) 46 Intl Org 37; JG Ruggie, 'International Regimes,

literature in their model. Nevertheless, it is fair to say that many—perhaps most—contemporary accounts of trade politics in the GATT/WTO system rest fundamentally on the basic model set out above, including many by sophisticated authors. It is necessary to pause at this point, then, to assess some of its strengths and weaknesses as an explanatory model for the trade regime's late twentieth-century transformation.

There are many aspects of this transformation that would seem at first sight to be explained even by this very simple model. The expansion of the scope of international trade law to cover services and intellectual property, for example, has been explained as the outcome of the efforts of well-organized corporate interests from the financial services, telecommunications, transport, and pharmaceutical sectors in the United States. Seeking more secure access to foreign markets for their products, these interests were instrumental in having these issues placed on the agenda of the Uruguay Round.[12] Similarly, the trade regime's shift of attention from tariff barriers to 'behind the border' barriers seems to be explicable in the same terms: as tariff barriers decreased in commercial significance over the course of the 1950s and 1960s, non-tariff regulatory measures became, in this story, the most commercially significant impediments for firms seeking to access foreign markets, and the inclusion of non-tariff barriers on the negotiating agenda in both the Tokyo and Uruguay Rounds is therefore best understood as a response to pressure from these firms. Furthermore, the story of the formalization and judicialization of dispute settlement during the Uruguay Round can usefully be understood as the product of self-interested inter-state bargaining.[13] As discussed in more detail in Chapter 8, by the time of the Uruguay Round, the United States had long been keen to strengthen GATT dispute settlement as part of an effective response to the proliferation of non-tariff barriers during the 1970s. While the EC and other countries steadfastly resisted this pressure for some time, they were forced to concede the point when the United States demonstrated its willingness to use unilateral section 301 sanctioning procedures in the late 1980s—with the *quid pro quo* being the United States' renunciation of its ability to use such procedures in the future. Similar stories have been told about virtually all aspects of the Uruguay Round negotiations, resting on essentially the same theoretical premises of self-interested bargaining between states, in accordance with narrowly defined material interests.

As intuitive as this explanatory model seems to be at first glance, it has serious inadequacies. I will explain these inadequacies by first outlining two specific explanatory failings, relating to the changing interpretation of WTO law, and its expanding scope. I will then show how these specific problems are both products of a more general underlying problem of all objectivist explanations of social action. My use of the term 'objectivist' reflects its usage by Bourdieu, who deployed the term to refer to explanations of the social world which treat it as 'an objective structure, grasped from

Transactions and Change: Embedded Liberalism in the Postwar Economic Order' (1982) 36 Intl Org 379.

[12] For an account of these forces in the services context, see Ch 9 below.

[13] Xu and Weller (2004) 197–229.

the outside, whose articulations can be materially observed, measured, and mapped out independently of the representations of those who live in it'.[14] Indeed, it will quickly become apparent that a number of the basic analytical moves I make, and some of the concepts I use, in this chapter draw inspiration from Bourdieu's writing.

B. Formalism and legal interpretation

Probably the most obvious problem with the explanatory model just described is that it lacks a theory of legal interpretation. Interpretation is ignored because WTO rules are treated as if they had a relatively clear and determinate content. Indeed the relative determinacy of WTO law is a premise on which the model rests: the claim that the treaty texts produced out of negotiations reflect the underlying material interests of states and the distribution of power between them, for example, presupposes that the content, meaning, and implications of those treaty texts are readily identifiable.

The problem is, of course, that GATT/WTO obligations are vastly more ambiguous in their meaning than is typically acknowledged in contemporary literature, particularly by non-lawyers. Both Hudec and Jackson, the two preeminent writers on the first few decades of the law of the GATT, consistently emphasize the ambiguity of the law, and of the decisions of Panels and Working Parties applying the law in the context of particular disputes.[15] Despite what is often said about the Uruguay Round texts providing greater precision and clarity to GATT/WTO law, tremendous ambiguity remained even after the creation of the WTO—particularly as regards the important new disciplines on domestic regulation negotiated during that round. In virtually every area of domestic regulation, negotiators have chosen to proceed largely by way of generally worded principles. Such principles are highly indeterminate in their meaning, and their impact on regulatory choices at the national level is governed to a very large extent by the way they are interpreted and reinterpreted over time. For example, we shall see over the next few chapters that both the national treatment and most-favoured nation treatment obligations have been interpreted in very different ways at different points during the history of the trade regime, with very different implications for domestic regulation. The same can be said of Article XX of the GATT, which sets out general exceptions to GATT obligations. Similarly, we shall also see that the requirement

[14] I take this useful summary of Bourdieu's use of the term from LJD Wacquant, 'Toward a Social Praxeology: The Structure and Logic of Bourdieu's Sociology' in P Bourdieu and LJD Wacquant, *An Invitation to Reflexive Sociology* (Polity Press, Cambridge 1992) 1–60, 7–8. See also P Bourdieu, *In Other Words: Essays Towards a Reflexive Sociology* (Matthew Adamson (trs), Polity Press, Cambridge 1990) 124ff.

[15] eg JH Jackson, *World Trade and the Law of GATT: A Legal Analysis of the General Agreement on Tariffs and Trade* (Bobbs-Merrill, Indianapolis, IN 1969) 755, 761. While there are some statements in Hudec's work which suggest that the original GATT 1947 was drafted in very precise and specific language (see eg RE Hudec, 'The GATT Legal System: A Diplomat's Jurisprudence' (1970) J World Trade L 615), it is very clear from Hudec's work as a whole that he profoundly understood the centrality and functionality of ambiguity in the early GATT system, and his work hardly proceeded from a naïve view of law as clear and determinate. See generally Ch 7 below.

that sanitary and phytosanitary measures be 'based on scientific principles and . . . not maintained with sufficient scientific evidence'[16] has already been shown to be amenable to different interpretive approaches, which place very different degrees of constraint on WTO Members' food safety regulation. Even those obligations which are apparently more concrete and specific turn out, upon closer inspection, not to be as clearly constraining as is often presumed. The scope and impact of the prohibition of export subsidies contained in Article 3 of the Agreement on Subsidies and Countervailing Measures, to take just one example, changes significantly depending on interpretation of the phrase 'contingent . . . upon export performance'.[17] Even the unambiguous requirement in the Agreement on Trade-Related Aspects of Intellectual Property Rights to provide patent protection for a term of twenty years to 'any inventions . . . in all fields of technology', is subject to qualifications and exceptions which are themselves highly ambiguous in their scope.[18] In WTO law, just as in any other area of law, then, it is untenable to cling to a naïve view of legal interpretation as an automatic or mechanical task.

Thus, it is an obvious point, but one which needs making, that the interpretation of WTO disciplines matters a great deal. The corollary is that the content and effect of WTO law is determined not just by the processes through which texts are negotiated, but also by the manner of their interpretation and application: it is through these processes of interpretation and application that the ambiguous and indeterminate general disciplines of international trade law are tied to concrete projects of political and economic reform. It follows that any account of the trade regime's neoliberal turn must include an account of the particular interpretive techniques and choices characteristic of the period, and an explanation of how and why they are different from earlier and later periods. How and why was the non-discrimination norm interpreted differently in the last two decades of the twentieth century, as compared to the first few decades of the GATT's existence? Why were certain interpretations of the science provisions of the SPS agreement chosen in the late 1990s, and why have they changed since? These changes are a fundamental part of any story of the trade regime's neoliberal turn, but are entirely missed by the simple explanatory model set out above. Because they are not accompanied by an explanation of legal interpretation, then, simple objectivist explanatory models of the trade regime's neoliberal turn are at best seriously incomplete, and at worst misleading.[19]

[16] Agreement on the Application of Sanitary and Phytosanitary Measures (15 April 1994) LT/UR/A-1A/12, art 2.2.

[17] Agreement on Subsidies and Countervailing Measures (15 April 1994) LT/UR/A-1A/9, art 3.1.

[18] Agreement on Trade-Related Aspects of Intellectual Property Rights (15 April 1994) LT/UR/A-1C/IP/1, arts 27(2), 30, 31.

[19] This explanatory gap is not remedied, it should be said, by work which seeks to describe 'constraints' on interpretation. What is needed is an account of the forces and factors which *produce* particular interpretive dispositions, rather than solely an account of the constraints on interpretive freedoms (RH Steinberg, 'Judicial Lawmaking at the WTO: Discursive, Constitutional, and Political Constraints' (2004) 98 AJIL 247).

It is worth pausing to note that one implication of this line of thinking is that we must reject the simple notion—in many ways implausible, yet strangely tenacious—that the result of the rise of neoliberalism during the 1980s and 1990s was to write into WTO law new norms which required its Members to adopt particular policy choices, which clearly prohibited interventionist policies, or which formally required adherence to a particular neoliberal model of state–market relations. At the very least, the idea that WTO law is legally enforcing a particular configuration of state–market relations through its rules, if it is to be credible, must be accompanied by a theory of interpretation which accounts in some detail for the influence of neoliberal thought on the processes of interpretation of WTO law. More generally, what is needed is a theory of the relationship between political projects such as neoliberalism and WTO law, which accounts for the large degree of indeterminacy of most if not all of the WTO's legal norms.

There are three responses to my claim that WTO obligations are highly ambiguous, which need to be briefly anticipated. The first and most common response is to acknowledge the indeterminacy of WTO law, but to argue in response that it is the function of WTO jurisprudence gradually to eliminate this indeterminacy through formal processes of quasi-judicial interpretation. It will quickly be seen that this is no answer at all. For one thing, it fails to recognize the indeterminacy of that jurisprudence itself. Much more importantly, it begs the question of what generates and structures the interpretive approach of Panels and the Appellate Body, and why their interpretive approaches evolve in different directions at different points in the regime's history. The point I am making is that we need a theory to explain these questions, as the formal processes of legal interpretation do not contain within themselves the principles of their own dynamic.

A second response to the claim of indeterminacy may be to argue that the dynamics of legal interpretation are more or less the same as those governing the making of the law in the context of trade negotiations. In other words, the material distribution of power between state actors also structures the interpretation of international trade law, so that legal norms are over time interpreted broadly in line with the economic interests of the most powerful states. If this were true, the simple state-centric, pressure group model described above could be resurrected as an accurate description of the structural dynamics of the international trade regime and its legal order. There is something to this claim. It is true that the distribution of material economic power between states and other actors is highly relevant to understanding the dynamics of struggles over the interpretation of WTO law. Material economic power can be and often is converted into the 'symbolic power'[20] to make interpretive legal claims which command respect. But it would

[20] The term is of course take from Bourdieu's work, see eg P Bourdieu, *Language and Symbolic Power* (Raymond and Adamson (trs), Polity Press, Cambridge 1991); P Bourdieu, 'Symbolic Power' in Denis Gleeson (ed), *Identity and Structure: Issues in the Sociology of Education* (Nafferton Books, Driffield 1977). I use the term here to refer specifically to a power to state authoritatively and persuasively what the texts of WTO law mean, but this is of course only one species of symbolic power, which more generally consists of the power to define socially authoritative and legitimate systems of meaning and categories of thought for

be a mistake to conclude that the distribution of the power to determine the content of WTO law corresponds precisely to the distribution of material power between states in the context of negotiations.[21] It is in all cases necessary to look in detail at the precise mechanisms by which one is converted into the other, the 'rate of exchange' between the two, and the other means by which symbolic power can be accumulated and exercised. Furthermore, one would have to take account of the fact that an actor's power authoritatively to shape the content of WTO law can in fact be increased through strategies which explicitly negate and deny the structuring influence of material interests on legal interpretation. Everything depends on the precise social conditions in question. In most cases it will be too simplistic to understand the internal logic of a legal field as nothing more than a 'direct reflection of existing social power relations' outside it.[22]

A third common response is to resist the characterization of international trade law as fundamentally indeterminate. Interpreters of WTO law, this argument runs, are not free agents—they do not have an unconstrained set of interpretive choices from which they can choose according to their own personal preferences. But this response involves a serious misunderstanding. Arguments about the indeterminacy of legal norms are too often misheard as claims that the interpreters of law are unconstrained, or that what 'really' drives legal interpretation are the personal preferences or ideologies of those interpreters. In fact, the opposite is true: the implicit theory of legal interpretation which underlies my account starts from the premise that though interpretive choices are not determined by the textual content of the norms and rules being interpreted, legal interpretation is still a deeply structured social process. Within any field of law, durable patterns and styles of interpretation regularly emerge and over time are consolidated, contested, and reproduced. These habits of interpretation express particular legal 'styles' or 'sensibilities'[23]—mindsets, common to the relevant community of professional interpreters, composed of categories of perception, habits of evaluation, and principles of action which together constitute a collectively shared framework of meaning which structures the interpretive process.[24] In the context of GATT/WTO dispute settlement, Hudec has described this the most eloquently:

those subjected to it. For a fascinating application of the concept in the context of the study of the WTO, see M Eagleton-Pierce, *Uncovering Symbolic Power: Power Analysis, Southern Countries, and the World Trade Organization* (D Phil dissertation, University of Oxford, 2008), a work which proceeds from precisely the premises I advocate in this chapter.

[21] For an interesting interrogation of the relationship between 'legal capacity' and other traditional measures of the power and influence of a state within the WTO system, see ML Busch, E Reinhardt, and G Shaffer, 'Does Legal Capacity Matter? A Survey of WTO Members' (2009) 8 World Trade Rev 559.

[22] P Bourdieu, 'The Force of Law: Toward a Sociology of the Juridical Field' (1987) 38 Hastings LJ 805, 814

[23] D Kennedy, 'The International Style in Postwar Law and Policy' (1994) 1 Utah L Rev 7; D Kennedy, 'The Disciplines of International Law and Policy' (1999) 12 Leiden J Intl L 9.

[24] For a similar view, see I Johnstone, 'Treaty Interpretation: The Authority of Interpretive Communities' (1990) 12 Michigan J Intl L 371.

> Anyone who has studied judicial opinions closely must have shared the suspicion that judges are not always the conscious master of the devices they use. Value judgments insinuate themselves in diabolical ways, so do less-than-fully conscious attitudes about the nature of the audience, the institution, and the functions being performed. To explain what the judge really does, one must be prepared to recognize the influence of factors the judge himself may not be aware of... It is submitted that the same phenomena exist in decisions such as the one presently being examined. A diplomat steeped in the atmosphere of the GATT cannot help but acquire working habits and instincts which reflect his situation. He acquires a 'feel' for things, a smell for trouble... In looking at his work, therefore, as with the work of a judge, one ought to be willing to go beyond the surface explanations and to try to make sense of the feels and smells which are the mainspring of his work.[25]

I will be arguing that the trade regime's neoliberal turn involved changes to precisely these 'working habits', 'instincts', 'feels and smells', and 'less-than-fully-conscious attitudes' which constitute the mental world which interpreters of GATT/WTO law inhabit. Put differently, the neoliberal turn involved a transformation of the collective symbolic order—the shared frameworks of meaning—through which interpreters of GATT/WTO law make sense of indeterminate principles and come to appreciate certain interpretations as more persuasive, appropriate, accurate, or more objective than others. Understanding the neoliberal turn necessitates not only an account of the content of that symbolic order, but also the social and material conditions of its production, reproduction, and contestation.

To be clear, when I refer to the interpretation of GATT/WTO law, I am not referring solely to the activity of bodies granted formal interpretive authority, such as WTO Panels, the Appellate Body, or WTO Members acting collectively pursuant to Article IX:2 of the WTO Agreement. Interpretive claims about the proper meaning of WTO obligations are also made, authorized, and contested by a much larger interpretive community, which includes WTO delegates in a variety of formal and semi-formal arenas, legal advisers to governments, scholars and students of trade law, commercial actors and business associations, environmental and human rights NGOs, even some members of the US Congress and other domestic political actors, all of whom are consciously or unconsciously engaged in a symbolic struggle to define the meaning of WTO law in particular contexts and for particular purposes. Each of these actors engages in the field with specific dispositions and interests, and makes interpretive claims on the basis of them.[26] Furthermore, different categories of actors enter the field with different degrees of practical interpretive authority, translating into different abilities to influence the acceptance and consolidation of those interpretive claims which they prefer. The actions of all these actors within this broad domain of interpretive activity are at one and the same time structured by the legal 'mindsets' and 'sensibilities' mentioned above and can

[25] Hudec (1970) 650–1.

[26] See Johnstone (1990) 373–80 for a useful summary of some of the key literature from which this claim draws. See also generally J Nedelsky, 'Communities of Judgment and Human Rights' (2000) 1(2) Theoretical Enquiries in Law 245.

also represent strategic actions designed to change those symbolic structures, or to resist change to them.

C. Functionalism and the expanding scope of GATT/WTO disciplines

A second difficulty with the simple explanatory model of international trade politics set out above is its inadequate account of the expanding scope of international trade law. Why was it that from at least the 1970s, the international trade regime increasingly turned its attention from 'border barriers' to 'behind the border' trade barriers, and became increasingly involved in the oversight of different forms of domestic regulation? One very simple answer runs as follows. Exporting firms face a number of obstacles and barriers to seeking to gain access to foreign markets for their products and services, which change in their nature and commercial significance over time. When particular barriers become commercially significant for those exporting firms with influence over the formation of their country's negotiating positions in the GATT/WTO, they will place pressure on their governments to raise these barriers as issues in the next round of trade negotiations. If a government is sufficiently powerful in the GATT context, these barriers will be placed on the agenda and subject to negotiation and possible international legal discipline. The exact nature of those disciplines will depend on the material interests of different states involved in these negotiations, and the distribution of material power between them. Why, then, did 'behind the border' barriers get onto the GATT agenda during the late 1960s and early 1970s? Simply because these kinds of trade barriers became commercially significant to major commercial exporters at this time. Thus Long accounts for the turn to domestic regulation as follows:

> At the time when the General Agreement entered into effect... international trade was being stifled by quantitative restrictions and very high customs duties. Attention was therefore first concentrated on these particular trade barriers... As time passed and the progressive reduction of customs duties and quantitative restrictions continued, a new phenomenon emerged. Non-tariff measures became more clearly seen and felt as an important obstacle to international trade. Governments have had increasing recourse to these measures.[27]

Precisely the same explanation is repeated throughout the bulk of the literature.[28]

One obvious problem with this explanation is that it fails to provide any account of the content of the general disciplines which were developed to address these new non-tariff barriers. But a deeper and more fundamental problem is its failure to recognize that the identification of a barrier or impediment to trade is in part an interpretive act, resulting from the application of particular forms and categories of knowledge to the social world. Since virtually every conceivable form of

[27] O Long, *Law and Its Limitations in the GATT Multilateral Trade System* (M Nijhoff, Boston, MA 1985) 25.

[28] EH Preeg, *Traders and Diplomats: An Analysis of the Kennedy Round of Negotiations under the General Agreement on Tariffs and Trade* (Brookings Institution, Washington, DC 1970) 12, 24; Reich (1997) 830–9; Jackson (1969) 518; RE Hudec, *The GATT Legal System and World Trade Diplomacy* (2nd edn, Butterworth Legal Publishers, Salem, NH 1990) 232.

governmental action has some direct or indirect impact on trade, the selection of a particular set of measures as 'barriers to trade' involves the application of principles of selection and categorization.[29] For example, although domestic systems of property law clearly affect patterns of trade in profound ways, we tend to think of such systems as forming the background institutional context in which trade operates. Restrictions on economic freedoms deriving from competition law also, depending on their content, tend to be thought of as government action to support the integrity of a market, rather than a distortion of economic activity. Similarly, we draw distinctions between government actions which constitute trade 'distortions' on the one hand, and other kinds of government actions which correct pre-existing market distortions on the other. Needless to say, the choice of how to characterize a particular governmental action is not self-evident. Is a tax on heavy cars a distortion of the market or the correction of a market failure? Are export incentives provided to businesses in EPZs unfair trade-distorting subsidies, or beneficial measures to facilitate the insertion of developing countries into the trading system on fair terms? Is a particular currency policy a trade distortion, or simply part of the background context within which traders work? Where foreign countries establish lower standards of intellectual property or labour rights protection, is that a trade distortion, or are attempts to restrict 'unfair competition' from products from those countries themselves the trade distortions? The answers to these questions are not self-evident, and obviously involve acts of interpretation. The domain of application of international trade law, therefore, depends in part on the collective habits of interpretation and principles of evaluation which participants in the field of trade governance characteristically use to determine what constitutes a trade barrier.

This insight, it should be noted, has been around almost since the time that the trade regime began to turn its attention to domestic regulation in the late 1960s. In his 1971 commentary on the Kennedy Round negotiations, Evans noted that the notion of 'non-tariff barrier', if taken literally, would be almost limitless in its application, and that it is only the commonly shared understandings among negotiators about what it could and should mean that give it concrete meaning in the field of international trade negotiations.[30] Then, in the mid-1980s, Tarullo sharpened the observation somewhat, noting that in order to classify a governmental measure as a 'distortion' of trade, it is necessary to compare it to an inevitably contingent image of normal, 'undistorted' trade. More concretely, he suggested that an image of 'normal' market relations derived from Western industrial states structured the operation of US trade remedies laws,[31] as well as the content and scope of application of the

[29] For an interesting example of a WTO Panel explicitly grappling with this (often implicit) interpretive process, see *United States—Definitive Anti-Dumping and Countervailing Duties on Certain Products from China*, Panel Report, WT/DS379/R (adopted 25 March 2011) paras 10.105–10.148.

[30] JW Evans, *The Kennedy Round in American Trade Policy: The Twilight of the GATT?* (Harvard University Press, Cambridge, MA 1971) 87–8.

[31] DK Tarullo, 'Beyond Normalcy in the Regulation of International Trade' (1987) 100 Harvard L Rev 546, 552ff.

disciplines of GATT law.[32] At around the same time, Goldstein also noted the way that domestic US trade remedies laws use 'the relationship between the American state and private industry [as] the model . . . to evaluate actions taken by other nations'.[33] Kennedy, too, has consistently demonstrated the indeterminacy of the notion of 'trade barrier', and has argued that the project of creating an open international trading order does not in itself define or dictate, as a matter of logic, the forms of governmental regulation which must or must not be removed to further that project in particular contexts. With Tarullo, he suggests that such judgments are made contextually, and are guided by prevalent images of normal and abnormal trade.[34] Then, most recently, Howse has recalled the problem in these terms:

> . . . liberalization entails selecting a set of trade barriers or restrictions and legally prohibiting them. However, there will always be a rather huge number of possible nontrade or not explicitly trade-based policies that individual members can implement, which will undermine the value of negotiated legal disciplines to their trading partners . . . Which of these is legitimate and acceptable domestic policy, and which is 'cheating' or reneging on my trade liberalization commitments . . . ? *There is no natural or self-evident baseline or rule that can solve this basic dilemma.*[35]

In practice, Howse argues, this baseline is defined in significant part by the 'intuitive understanding[s]' of professionals working inside the trade regime about what constitutes normal governmental regulation, and what should and should not be made visible as a barrier to trade.[36]

It is my claim that we must understand the expansion of the domain of the trade regime during the last decades of the twentieth century as, in part, the product of a transformation in these 'intuitive understandings', or 'principles of vision and division' which the trade community uses to distinguish legitimate domestic regulation from illegitimate trade distortions.[37] At any particular point in time, there exist within the field of international trade governance a range of commonly accepted categories, as well as habitual ways of applying those categories, which structure the way that certain kinds of governmental actions are collectively made visible as trade barriers, and others not. They form a kind of 'established code'[38] by reference to which existing and new trade problems are identified, evaluated, and addressed. During the trade regime's neoliberal turn, these principles of vision underwent a profound change, which was

[32] DK Tarullo, 'Logic, Myth and the International Economic Order' (1985) 26 Harvard Intl LJ 553.

[33] Goldstein (1993) 198.

[34] D Kennedy, 'Turning to Market Democracy: A Tale of Two Architectures' (1991) 32 Harvard Intl LJ 373, 379ff; Kennedy (1999) 50ff.

[35] R Howse, 'From Politics to Technocracy—and Back Again: The Fate of the Multilateral Trading Regime' (2002) 96 AJIL 94, 95–6.

[36] Howse (2002) 104.

[37] The terminology of 'principles of vision and division' is again Bourdieu's, who uses it to capture generally the classificatory schemes by which actors construct the social world in a given field of social action. See eg Bourdieu (1990) 132; P Bourdieu, *Practical Reason: on the Theory of Action* (Stanford University Press, Stanford, CA 1998) 8, 53.

[38] See G Curzon, *Multilateral Commercial Diplomacy: The General Agreement on Tariffs and Trade and its Impact on National Commercial Policies and Techniques* (Michael Joseph, London 1965) 335.

reflected not only in the way that new kinds of governmental measures were made visible as 'trade barriers', but also in the content of the new regulatory disciplines which were developed to address these measures. An adequate account of this transformation, therefore, must provide an explanation of how these principles of vision were changed, as well as of the effects that these changes had on the politics and dynamics of the trade regime's approach to domestic regulation. Moreover, since these principles of vision are themselves the object and product of ongoing political struggle, our explanation of the trade regime's neoliberal turn must also include an account of the actors, processes, contests, and strategies involved in producing and contesting them. Our account of this period in the trade regime's history, in other words, must seek to understand the actors and processes involved in the construction of legitimate and authorized forms of knowledge about what does and does not count as an illegitimate 'trade barrier'. Ultimately, then, the simple objectivist model described above is inadequate because it provides no such account—it treats trade barriers as objective properties of the social world, and the expansion of the trade regime simply as the progressive 'recognition' of more and more trade barriers. By failing even to recognize the exercise of symbolic or interpretive power as a central part of this story, it provides us with no way of understanding the causes and consequences of the deployment of such power.

D. Objectivism and the interpretive dimension of social action

It would be possible to multiply the explanatory failings of this simple model of trade politics. But it will already be clear that the two criticisms made so far are in fact merely specific instances of a more fundamental problem. Put simply, that problem is that this model of trade politics entirely ignores the interpretive dimension of social action. It falls into the category of 'objectivist' forms of social explanation, in that it seeks to uncover the objective relations which structure the operation of the trade regime, independently of the subjective perceptions of social actors working within it. This objectivist form of explanation *is* useful and powerful in some contexts, and represents a crucial first step in building a full theory of social action. As a practical matter, it can be an important initial analytical move to isolate the non-perceptual elements of the social world in order to construct a model of the objective structures which shape it. However, it is a serious mistake to stop at this point. A full account of social action—whether in the field of international trade governance or anywhere else—must reintroduce the phenomenological dimension into its model of social action. A story of the evolution and operation of the international trade regime, in other words, must include not only the structural constraints which the social world places on actors in that regime, but also the ways in which those actors perceive, interpret, and represent the world to themselves. It must include the mental structures which inhabit the minds of social actors in the trade regime, that is to say, the symbolic structures and frameworks of meaning through which these actors make sense of the world and which orient their actions in it. In order to understand the dynamics and drivers of the field of international trade governance, then, it is necessary to analyse *both* the objective relations which structure the field independently of people's minds, *and* the perceptions and interpretive habits of those who inhabit the field and work within it, as well as the relationship between them.

Careful observers of the trade regime have developed a number of words to describe the particular forms of consciousness of those who inhabit the field of international trade governance. Some talk of a 'GATT philosophy'[39] or 'ideology'[40] and of the 'spirit permeating' the regime,[41] others refer to a shared sense of social purpose,[42] while others still identify a particular 'feel',[43] 'ethos'[44], set of 'mantras',[45] or 'sensibility'[46] characteristic of participants in the field. Some of these terms are no doubt too nebulous, and some will have connotations for some readers which are liable to mislead. Some appear to come close to Bourdieu's concept of the 'habitus'.[47] What matters for the present argument, though, is simply that all of these observers share the basic insight that the characteristic mindsets and ways of thinking of participants in the field of trade politics have an important effect on the choices that are made. Specifically, they have a significant effect on the choices which are involved in the creation, elaboration, application, and interpretation of international trade law. These observers also all recognize that the production, contestation, naturalization, and legitimation of these mindsets and ways of thinking is a very significant aspect of the work which goes on in and around the trade regime. Any account of the politics of the trade regime which fails to take into account this 'symbolic work' is therefore seriously inadequate.

In a recent article, Steinberg invokes the image of a hypothetical US representative to the WTO, and asks what explanatory model best accounts for the choices she makes as she engages in discussions and negotiations in the trade regime. He argues that she is best imagined as an agent of the US government, and that the positions she takes in discussions and negotiations will be 'driven by [her] position as [a] government representative[] and by material forces within [her] country'.[48] There is, he argues, very little need for this explanatory model to include any notion of the mindset of this US representative, as this mindset exercises little if any independent causal impact on her behaviour—she is a constrained agent, acting in accordance with her country's material interests and the instructions of her superiors. As will be clear by now, the problem with Steinberg's model is not that it is wrong. Nor is the real problem even that this model is 'incomplete', if incomplete means only that

39 Curzon (1965) 53.

40 G Curzon and V Curzon, 'GATT: Traders' Club' in RW Cox and HK Jacobson (eds), *The Anatomy of Influence: Decision Making in International Organizations* (Yale University Press, New Haven, CT 1973) 320.

41 Curzon (1965) 332.

42 Ruggie (1982).

43 Hudec (1970) 651.

44 Weiler (2001).

45 JH Jackson, 'The WTO "constitution" and proposed reforms: seven "mantras" revisited' (2001) 4 (1) JIEL 67.

46 Kennedy (1994) eg 17.

47 Defined, for example, as 'a set of… relations "deposited" within individual bodies in the form of mental and corporeal schemata of perception, appreciation and action': (Wacquant, 1992) 16.

48 Steinberg (2009) 1071.

it is missing crucial additional causal variables which if added to the model will better account for this hypothetical representative's behaviour. Rather, Steinberg's model is inadequate in part because it fails to explain the conditions for the emergence of this logic of action—that is, the emergence of a system of trade policy-making in which trade policy choices become the aggregation of interest group preferences. This logic of action is instead presented as an unerring and universal law of nature, rather than a property of a specific, historically situated social system. Furthermore, and crucially, Steinberg's model is inadequate because it is radically indeterminate, and in fact tells us virtually nothing about the choices that this representative and her superiors might actually make in any concrete context. This is the most important point, and needs some further explanation.

Take, for example, the process of negotiating a definition of the prudential regulation provision in the GATS Annex on Financial Services. Clearly, our imagined representative will seek to safeguard the material interests of her country's major financial services exporters, as well as those of her domestic regulators. But what are those interests? Do financial services exporters prefer as limited as possible a prudential carve-out, to limit foreign regulators' capacity to interfere with their foreign operations? Surely financial firms, too, have an interest in ensuring that foreign financial markets are well-regulated and stable? Where do these firms draw the line between over-regulation and sensible regulation which ought to be permitted? What if they draw the line differently from domestic regulators—how should the competing interests of domestic regulators and exporting firms be arbitrated? Should some degree of flexibility be included in the text, in case ideas about appropriate regulation change, or would that permit too much flexibility for other countries to 'cheat'? Does the WTO even have a legitimate role to play in supervising financial regulation? It is no answer, of course, to say that these are questions for the firms and regulators themselves—the point is that at some stage, whether by the firms or government officials or anyone else, these interpretive choices are being made, and Steinberg's model tells us nothing about how they are made.

Then, in the context of negotiations themselves, another series of questions arises. It is accepted, of course, that all delegates are representatives acting in the interests of their states. But it is also recognized that trade negotiations are also governed by a norm of reciprocity, and by a desire to achieve a meaningful result. When is it appropriate to make a concession in your bargaining position to maintain a sense of equal exchange among bargaining partners—a sense which might be crucial for the success of negotiations? Furthermore, when is it appropriate to sacrifice short-term goals for long-term objectives? How should one balance one's commitment to advancing the interests of domestic businesses with one's commitment to the integrity and stability of the trading system generally, not to mention a broader principled commitment to 'free trade'? When is a demand of a particular domestic constituency simply inappropriate or unrealistic, so that it becomes the task of the negotiator to lower the expectations of that constituency? Again, it is no answer to say that these questions are to be answered by instructions from the capital—they will need to be answered somewhere, and the answers to them cannot be deduced from some abstract notion of 'material interest'. There is, necessarily, interpretation at every stage.[49]

It turns out, then, that in order actually to make meaningful the idea that participants in the trade regime act in the material interests of their sending states, it is necessary to import a thick framework of meaning to help us (and the hypothetical representative) to answer these questions, and thereby to derive concrete principles of action, evaluation, and choice in concrete contexts.[50] Like all objectivist models of social action, Steinberg's model imagines trade delegates as mere automatons or machines, as if their choices and actions were fully determined by objective social structures. But just as it is wrong to see the interpretation of law as a quasi-automatic process of rule application, so too it is wrong to see the behaviour of actors in the field of international trade governance as mechanically determined by rules and logics established by the distribution of economic power among states. In fact, they are active participants in their world, constantly and actively interpreting the social world around them. Through those interpretive processes, they formulate principles of action, and link abstract understandings of their 'interests' to concrete choices and strategies in response to real-world problems. This does not mean that they are 'free', for in doing so, they draw on and deploy pre-existing collective frameworks of interpretation and forms of knowledge which are already available, and which are in some sense normal, authorized, and legitimate in the field of international trade governance. Over time, they develop a 'feel for the game',[51] a durable sensibility or mindset from which they derive habits of action, underlying logics of behaviour, and basic principles of judgment and evaluation. It is this sensibility that we must understand, then, if we are to genuinely grasp the direct wellsprings of action for participants in the trade regime, as well as the regime itself. And we must understand the patterned changes to this sensibility over time if we are to comprehend the nature of regime transformation. Importantly, by 'understanding' this sensibility, I mean not only that we must describe its content and the way it impacts behaviour, but also the way it is constructed, contested, and reproduced, and the material forces which provide its conditions of possibility. Even if it is less visible than other forms of social action, this is a crucial aspect of trade politics.[52]

To many participants within the field, and indeed some observers of it, these kinds of interpretive acts disappear from view, or seem insignificant, because they feel natural and self-evident. It is not really open to interpretation, it might be said, that it was in the material interests of the United States to press for the TRIPS agreement during the Uruguay Round—after all, US companies obviously stood to gain

[49] See eg A Das, 'Research Uptake in an Institutionalized Setting: The Case of Trade Facilitation in India' in Tussie (2009) 181, for a similar view in the trade context.

[50] E Adler and PM Haas, 'Conclusion: Epistemic Communities, World Order, and the Creation of a Reflective Research Program' (1992) 46 Intl Org 367, 368.

[51] eg P Bourdieu and LJD Wacquant, *An Invitation to Reflexive Sociology* (Chicago University Press, Chicago, IL 1992) 128.

[52] '[A]gents in the political field are continuously engaged in a labour of representation by which they seek to construct and impose a particular vision of the social world, while at the same time seeking to mobilize the support of those upon whom their power ultimately depends': Bourdieu (1991) 26.

billions of dollars from strengthened global IP protection. Perhaps, this argument continues, there were some difficult decisions to be made in relation to the details of the agreement, but the United States' basic orientation could hardly have been different. But it is part of the point of the next three chapters to show that *all* strategies and choices made by participants in the trade regime rest on particular, contestable frameworks of meaning and symbolic structures, just as these symbolic structures take shape in particular material conditions of possibility. From this perspective, that some ways of knowing and acting in the world assume a 'taken for granted' character is itself a fact which needs explanation. Indeed, it is more than a fact which needs explanation, it is an *effect of power*. Understanding the processes, projects, actors, and strategies through which those forms of knowledge and action appear natural, self-evident, and authoritative is the first stage in opening them to contestation, and understanding how other possibilities might be realized.

It is worth pointing out that, with some qualifications, objectivist explanations are perfectly adequate for some limited explanatory tasks. The reason that I have stressed their limitations here is that they are clearly inadequate to explain periods of profound regime change, such as that which occurred to the trade regime during the last three decades of the twentieth century. We cannot understand the nature and extent of the trade regime's neoliberal turn, I contend, without attending to the perceptual dimension of social action within that regime, for the simple reason that this turn worked in some fundamental way at the level of a perceptual transformation—that is, through a change to the symbolic structures and interpretive habits characteristic of the field of international trade governance.

This, in my view, is probably the most important lesson to be drawn from Ruggie's 1982 reflections on the 'embedded liberalism' of the post-war GATT regime.[53] One of the aims of that article was to reflect on the question of the nature and extent of change to the international trade regime in the context of the 'new protectionism' of the 1970s and early 1980s. Ruggie argued that objectivist theoretical models—and here he had in mind primarily hegemonic stability theory, which is now no longer the important theoretical force it once was—could not adequately comprehend the nature of these changes, precisely because they do not 'encompass the phenomenological dimension of international regimes'.[54] As a result, he observed, such models may be able to predict the 'form' of international regimes, but not their 'content'.[55] Ruggie's way of reintroducing this phenomenological dimension was through the notion of 'legitimate social purpose'—the nature and operation of international regimes, he argued, is not just a function of the distribution of power, but also the legitimate social purposes for which that power is deployed:

> ... to say anything sensible about the *content* of international economic orders and about the regimes which serve them, it is necessary to look at how power and legitimate social purpose become fused to project political authority into the international system.[56]

[53] Ruggie (1982) 36. [54] ibid 382. [55] ibid. [56] ibid.

Once the element of social purpose is taken into account, he argued, the changes to the trade regime can be understood entirely differently. While the 'new protectionism' of the 1970s was associated with new and different institutional forms in the GATT, and therefore seemed to represent an example of regime change, in fact these new institutional forms represented the continuation of the *same* social purpose (captured by the notion of 'embedded liberalism') in changed economic conditions. In fact, he suggested it was the 'resurgent ethos of liberal capitalism'—not the spread of new forms of protectionism—which at that time constituted the most important potential driver of change to the trade regime.[57]

With Ruggie, I shall also be arguing that the trade regime's neoliberal turn was in part a redefinition of prevalent ideas about the 'legitimate social purposes' in pursuit of which states should intervene in their economies, and which the practice global economic order governance serves. More generally, however, I will argue that this neoliberal turn is best understood as a fundamental transformation of the symbolic order associated with the field of international trade governance.

II. Avoiding subjectivism and idealism

There are a number of well-known bodies of existing literature on the role of interpretation—or 'ideas'—in the making of trade policy. While it would take another book to explain in full how my own thinking relates to them, it is worth making a few basic comments to forestall and correct misunderstandings of my argument.

A. Subjective policy preferences versus intersubjective interpretive dispositions

There has always been a strand of thinking about the trade regime which emphasizes the influence of the subjective policy preferences of negotiators, policy-makers, and their governments on the operation of the GATT/WTO system.[58] From this perspective, the 'values' of key decision-makers—that is to say, whether or not they are 'free traders', and to what extent—significantly shape the decisions they make. Historians of the trade regime have commonly stressed 'values' as one important explanatory factor accounting for the longevity and success of the trade regime. Gerard and Victoria Curzon, for example, have suggested that:

> ... historically speaking it is a fact that European governments pursued freer trade policies after the war because they genuinely believed that, on the whole, their economies would benefit thereby. This is confirmed, as far as the United Kingdom is concerned, by officials

[57] ibid 413.
[58] See generally Milner (1999) 98ff.

involved in the execution of British post-war trade policy. Trade liberalization was supported by both parties and there was enough acceptance of the principle by exporters for ministers to stand out against all but the most vociferous pressure groups.[59]

Slaughter, too, has argued that the shape of the post-war trade regime largely reflected the preferences and ideas of a group of 'American policymakers who projected the philosophy, substance and form of the New Deal regulatory state onto the world'.[60] It has also been argued that post-war US trade policy in the GATT was governed in part by an 'ideological factor', consisting of a particular mix of economic and political liberalism characteristic of US politics of the period.[61] Winham states quite unequivocally that:

> ...the most important factor in explaining the liberal results of the Tokyo Round was the environment of liberal values within which the negotiation was conducted... Governments and individual negotiators at the Tokyo Round were motivated by the fundamental belief that life could be better through a policy of liberalism and international cooperation.[62]

In a different but related vein, Mably, Narlikar, and Tussie have more recently sought to understand the precise nature and extent of the impact which academic and other policy-oriented research has on the negotiating positions and strategies of developing countries in the WTO.[63] At the domestic level, Krueger has argued that the turn from import substitution policies to trade liberalization in the developing world during the 1980s and 1990s is best explained by the evolution and adoption of new ideas about appropriate trade and development policies which occurred in influential sectors of the economics profession during this period.[64]

Perhaps most famously, Goldstein engaged in a series of studies which sought to uncover and characterize the precise impact of ideas on US trade policy from the nineteenth century to the middle of the 1990s.[65] Her work explicitly does not seek to contest the claim that trade policy is structured by the material interests of powerful actors, but instead looks at the ideas which structure the ways in which those interests are conceived at both the actor level and the national level, as well as the strategies

[59] G Curzon and V Curzon, 'The Management of Trade Relations in the GATT' in A Shonfield (ed), *International Economic Relations of the Western World, 1959–1971* (OUP, Oxford 1976) 143, 195.

[60] A-M Burley (as she then was), 'Regulating the World: Multilateralism, International Law, and the Projection of the New Deal Regulatory State' in JG Ruggie (ed), *Multilateralism Matters: The Theory and Praxis of an Institutional Form* (Columbia University Press, New York, NY 1993) 125. See also JG Ikenberry, 'A World Economy Restored: Expert Consensus and the Anglo-American Postwar Settlement' (1992) 46 Intl Org 289, eg 304 and generally.

[61] Curzon and Curzon (1976) 95.

[62] GR Winham, *International Trade and the Tokyo Round Negotiation* (Princeton University Press, Princeton, NJ 1986) 400. For a similar view, see H Yoshimatsu, 'The Influence of Liberal Ideas on the GATT Regimes: The Case of the Tokyo Round' (1998) ICSEAD Working Paper Series Vol 98–04.

[63] A Narlikar and D Tussie, 'Multiple Access Points: Knowledge Generation for the Group of Twenty' and P Mably, 'Centralized Production: The Group of 33' both in Tussie (2009) 213, 239.

[64] AO Krueger, 'Trade Policy and Economic Development: How We Learn' (1997) 87 American Econ Rev 1. See also D Tussie, 'The Politics of Trade: The Role of Research in Trade Policy and Negotiations' in Tussie (2009) 1ff.

[65] Goldstein (1988); Goldstein (1993).

which are adopted to pursue them.[66] She shows, for example, how the institutions associated with the formulation and application of different aspects of US trade policy were deeply shaped by the prevailing ideas about appropriate and desirable trade policy at the time of their creation, and that these institutional structures continue to give these ideas an enduring hold over trade policy-making, even in the context of changes in underlying economic interests and distributions of power. At a more general level, she argues also that 'in the US, liberal beliefs about trade policy-making have dominated the debate and thinking of those involved with policy-making', to the extent that liberal ideas were 'elevated... into a realm untouchable by interest group politics'.[67]

The line of argument that I am evoking here has a few characteristic features.[68] First, it focuses primarily on normative policy ideas—that is to say, ideas about what kinds of trade policies are most desirable, most effective, or most appropriate in a particular context. These ideas might be nothing more than very general policy orientations, they might take the form of more concrete economic models, or they may be very specific, consisting of beliefs about the likely outcomes of specific trade policy choices in particular sectors, based on concrete analytical research. Secondly, these ideas are treated as subjective in nature. They exist and have their influence inside the heads of decision-makers, they are transmitted via subjective processes of persuasion and argumentation, and they matter to the extent that policy-makers are 'convinced' by them, and therefore look to them for guidance in the choices they make. Thirdly, the questions that characteristically arise in the context of research in this vein have to do with the nature and extent of, and the preconditions for, the *independent* causal influence of policy ideas on policy choices, as compared to the influence of other factors. What precise role do normative policy ideas play in particular policy-making contexts? Do they determine the content of policy choices, act as focal points for cooperative solutions, or do they legitimate pre-existing choices? In what conditions are ideas of this sort likely to have a significant impact on policy choices? Do they need an influential 'champion' within governmental circles?[69] Is their influence greater in conditions of uncertainty, or where they 'fit' with pre-existing worldviews and disposition in government?[70] Most importantly, how significant are policy ideas as compared to other sources of influence on policy-making? One of the aims of research in this mode, then, is to isolate the independent causal impact, if any, of 'ideas', as compared to other influences on policy-making.

[66] See eg Goldstein (1993) 9.

[67] Goldstein (1988) 182–3. See also generally on the impact of free trade as an idea on US and European trade policy, RE Baldwin, *The Political Economy of U.S. Import Policy* (MIT Press, Cambridge, MA 1986); CP Kindleberger, 'The Rise of Free Trade in Western Europe' (1975) 35 J of Econ History 20.

[68] This line of inquiry corresponds loosely with what Hasenclever et al, refer to as 'weak cognitivism', see A Hasenclever, P Mayer, and V Rittberger, *Theories of International Regimes* (Cambridge Studies in International Relations: 55, CUP, New York, NY 1997); A Hasenclever, P Mayer, and V Rittberger, 'Integrating Theories of International Regimes' (2000) 26 Rev of Intl Studies 3.

[69] See eg R Gomez and M Gunderson, 'Creation of Values and Principles: Canada's Experience with the CUSFTA and NAFTA' in Tussie (2009) 42.

[70] PM Haas, 'Introduction: Epistemic Communities and International Policy Coordination' (1992) 46 Intl Org 1; Tussie (2009) 122, 202ff.

The most significant piece of evidence in this line of inquiry would be a situation in which policy ideas are able to direct decision-makers away from the choices which would seem to be dictated by other sources of influence, such as interest group pressure.

It is perfectly possible to construct an account of the trade regime's neoliberal turn along these lines. The 1980s and 1990s saw the re-emergence of a fairly rigorous form of free market economic liberalism as the dominant economic ideology throughout many parts of the world. A core tenet of economic liberalism is the mutually beneficial nature of free trade between nations. It is intuitively appealing, then, to hypothesize a reasonably direct causal link between the spread of beliefs about the benefits of free trade throughout policy-making communities globally on the one hand, and the expansion and transformation of the WTO on the other. Since WTO Member governments began to believe more strongly in the benefits of free trade, this argument might run, they were more likely to accept international trade liberalization commitments.

This is not my argument. One reason for not pursuing this line of inquiry is that I think it has less explanatory value than is often assumed. As a number of observers have noted, the rise of economic liberalism in the industrialized world did not result in a turn towards 'free trade', at least not as that term is normally understood.[71] And while there *was* a much more pronounced turn towards free trade in the developing world, this did little if anything to transform the mercantilist approach of developing countries in multilateral trade negotiations.[72] Nor is there any evidence to suggest that policy-makers generally became less susceptible to interest group pressure during this period, and were therefore more likely to base their choices on subjective policy preferences—indeed, what evidence we have points in precisely the opposite direction.[73] Moreover, it is contrary to experience to suppose that either the community of trade negotiators in Geneva, or their capital-based networks of policy-makers, are largely made up of doctrinaire free traders in a classical liberal mould.[74] Thus, while there *is* no doubt an interesting story to be told about the precise nature and extent of the influence of doctrinaire free trade convictions on trade policy choices in and around the trade regime during the 1980s and 1990s, my interest and attention will primarily be directed elsewhere.

One of the biggest differences between the argument that I am making, and the line of argument just described, is in the nature of the 'ideas' that are the primary focus of attention as well as the nature of the influence they have. Actors in the field of international trade governance are influenced not just by principled or normative beliefs about what constitutes desirable and beneficial trade policy. Like all of us, they inhabit an entire mental world made up of

[71] See eg RE Baldwin, *The Multilateral Trade Negotiations: Toward Greater Liberalization?* (American Enterprise Institute for Public Policy Research, Washington, DC 1979) ch 8.

[72] AO Krueger, 'Trends in the Trade Policies of Developing Countries' in CS Pearson, J Riedel, and I Frank, *The Direction of Trade Policy: Papers in Honor of Isaiah Frank* (Basil Blackwell, Oxford 1990) 104.

[73] See generally Ch 8 below.

[74] For a contrary view, see PJ Arnold, 'Disciplining Domestic Regulation: The World Trade Organization and the Market for Professional Services' (2005) 30 Accounting, Organizations and Society 299, 303, which sets out a view of the WTO as a site in which neoliberal political preferences are dominant.

a huge array of different kinds of ideas, including all the principles of comprehension, classification, and evaluation that help them to make the world around them meaningful. They include, for example: concepts and categories for interpreting the world, causal beliefs about how the world economy works, and about the causal dynamics of trade politics; professional norms about the nature and purpose of the trade regime and the particular role that they play in it; and legal ideas about the nature of law and the way it works. Most of these ideas exist in the background, as part of the taken-for-granted context which must simply be understood and adopted as part of the process of becoming a competent, professional, and effective actor in the field. Most of these ideas, furthermore, are intersubjective rather than subjective in nature: that is to say, key elements of this mental world are not the free product of each subjective mind, but rather a social product, collectively produced. Furthermore, their influence on the behaviour of actors in the field of international trade governance tends to be constitutive, rather than causal.

These, then, are the key differences between the argument that I am making, and the 'subjectivist' line of argument described above. My focus is not so much on principled beliefs of trade actors, but on their interpretive dispositions. It is less on the direct causal impact of subject policy ideas, and more on the constitutive impact of collectively authorized frameworks of meaning which exist in the background of trade politics. My argument, as I have said, will be that the trade regime's neoliberal turn was in significant part a transformation of these intersubjective frameworks of meaning—more specifically, a transformation of collective ideas about the nature and purpose of the trade regime, collective ideas about the function of law in trade politics, and collective principles and techniques for evaluating the legitimacy of governmental action—and my purpose will be to show how this transformation of the GATT/WTO's 'legal imagination' radically reshaped the form, structure, content, and interpretation of international trade law.

None of this is particularly complicated, and the distinctions that I have just drawn are well-rehearsed in the literature on the role of ideas in international politics. I repeat them only to avoid confusion. One of the reasons that misunderstandings may arise is because at certain points my argument traverses similar ground to that which is commonly covered in purer subjectivist accounts. For example, in both Chapters 8 and 9, the story I tell *does* include a prominent place for the kinds of technical, policy-oriented knowledge that I have just said I am less interested in: for example, technical expertise relating to optimal regulatory policy in different sectors; data on the nature and incidence of barriers to trade in services; and scientific knowledge about the nature and extent of the health effects of various traded products. What I wish to make clear here, then, is that I make reference to such technical expertise and policy-relevant knowledge in the service of a different kind of argument. For example, in Chapter 8, my main purpose is to show how the increasing use of technical knowledge in the formulation, application, and interpretation of international trade law was the *result* of a broader change at the level of the regime's 'legal imagination'. More specifically, I claim that the technicalization of disciplines on domestic regulation was a way of constituting the objectivity and neutrality of the GATT/WTO legal system, and of instantiating its separation from the world of trade diplomacy. In Chapter 9, my main aim is to show how the production and circulation of technical expert knowledge in and around the trade regime is involved in the creation and contestation of broader intersubjective frameworks of meaning circulating among participants in the trade regime—affecting their interpretive dispositions, not (or not necessarily) their normative beliefs. It is one thing to argue that this kind of technical knowledge shapes the categories, concepts, and principles they use to interpret the world, but it is quite another to argue that trade professionals look to technical policy proposals for substantive guidance in determining the choices they make.[75] It is perfectly possible for technical knowledge to have little direct effect on actors' choices, while still profoundly shaping their background habits of perception, analytical turns of mind, and cognitive maps.

It follows that while I am interested in the processes by which actors draw on research and policy ideas in the trade context, I analyse particular practices of knowledge production as instances of the production (and contestation) of the broader symbolic order at work within the field of international trade governance. I approach them with the aim of excavating lessons about the content of that order, and the manner in which it is produced, rather than lessons about the impact of ideas on policy choices. In neither Chapter 8 nor Chapter 9 is my discussion of the influence of technical expertise framed as a claim about the impact of 'ideas' on the behaviour of actors in the trade regime, as compared to other causal factors. My argument starts from the position that ideas and interpretation are a necessary component of all social action, and that the trade regime is a field saturated with 'ideas' of all sorts—including 'partial information, anecdotes, and accumulated experiences and practices'[76] as well as other sorts of local knowledge—before technical knowledge even enters it. My argument, in other words, is not an argument about the salience of ideas as compared to other causal factors, but an argument about the changing nature of the ideational environment characteristic of the mental world that trade professionals inhabit.

It will be immediately clear that the argument I am making shares much in common with the epistemic communities literature.[77] Most fundamentally, I clearly share the basic conviction of that literature that interpretation is an inescapable part of all social action, and that in that sense reality is socially constructed.[78] Furthermore, I share its primary focus on the intersubjective element of international legal and political processes. I am likewise interested in the ways in which meanings,

[75] Botto and Bianculli, for example, argue that knowledge can have an 'indirect' impact on trade policy by contributing to a 'gradual shift in concepts and paradigms', and by 'clarifying, accelerating and legitimising changes in conceptual thinking and, therefore, in policies': M Botto and AC Bianculli, 'The Case of Argentine Research in Building Regional Integration' in Tussie (2009) 83, 85–6. See also C Weiss, 'The Many Meanings of Research Utilization' (1979) 39(5) Public Administration Review 426 and K Ajayi and P Osafo-Kwaako, 'The Adoption of the Common External Tariff in Nigeria' in Tussie (2009) 121, 144.

[76] Botto and Bianculli, ibid 86.

[77] See generally Vol 46(1) of International Organization (Winter 1992).

[78] Haas (1992) 21ff.

concepts, and interpretations become valid or 'taken-for-granted' descriptions of the world-as-it-is, in a given area of international relations.[79] The aim of both my work and the epistemic communities literature is, broadly speaking, to illuminate the processes by which legitimate and authoritative principles of vision are objectified and made available for deployment in particular international contexts. I share an interest, in other words, in the exercise of symbolic power, or the 'labour of representation' at work within international regimes, by which actors 'seek to construct and impose a particular vision of the social world'.[80] Moreover, I share the aim of overcoming the continuing divide between structural and interpretivist explanations of international legal and political phenomena.

That said, it is worth making clear that I do not view the trade regime as an 'epistemic community' itself, either in its present incarnation, or in its earlier forms, at least as that term is defined by Haas.[81] One reason, as Ikenberry has noted, is that the shared commitments and beliefs that exist within the trade regime are more in the nature of a 'common professional orientation... not a set of causal scientific tenets or a common economic doctrine' in a strict sense.[82] More importantly, participants in the trade regime do not exhibit the same normative cohesion as epistemic communities at the level of 'principled beliefs'. This is clearly the case in the present trade regime, which is better characterized as a terrain of contestation, normatively speaking—while it is perhaps true that participants tend to share a commitment to 'freer trade' in a very general sense, this is more in the nature of a professional commitment, and in any case is far too general to translate into a shared political project and programme of action of the kind associated with epistemic communities. What they *do* share, in my view, however, is a common vocabulary and frame of reference for the airing of their disagreements: a common set of concepts, causal assumptions, interpretive habits, and so on, which form the basis of shared expectations about each others' behaviours. In that sense, they share an 'imagination'. The trade regime, then, is perhaps better characterized as a 'profession' or 'discipline' in the taxonomy proposed by Haas,[83] or as an 'epistemic community' conforming to Ruggie's original definition.[84] I have also found it useful to think of it as a 'field' in Bourdieu's sense—as a social arena of struggle between actors with regular and patterned dispositions, structured and organized by shared fundamental principles of vision and significance.[85]

[79] See eg E Adler, 'The Emergence of Cooperation: National Epistemic Communities and the International Evolution of the Idea of Nuclear Arms Control' (1992) 46 Intl Org 101, 105–6.

[80] Bourdieu (1991) 26.

[81] Haas (1992) 3.

[82] Ikenberry (1992) 293.

[83] Haas (1992) 16–20. See also Kennedy (1999).

[84] 'I have borrowed this term [*episteme*] from Michel Foucault to refer to a dominant way of looking at social reality, a set of shared symbols and references, mutual expectations and a mutual predictability of intention. Epistemic communities may be said to consist of interrelated roles which grow up around an *episteme*; they delimit, for their members, *the* proper construction of social reality'. JG Ruggie, 'International Responses to Technology' (1975) 29 Intl Org 557, 569–70.

[85] Bourdieu and Wacquant (1992).

Epistemic communities do enter into my story, however, in the context of my attempts to interrogate the way in which these shared principles of vision are produced and contested. Epistemic communities are certainly among the most relevant and influential actors in those processes.[86] But it is worth noting that my focus is deliberately broader than that of the epistemic communities literature, in at least two respects. First, I am interested in other forms of knowledge involved in the production of the trade regime's characteristic 'imagination', not just the kind of technical knowledge produced by epistemic communities. The work of being a professional in the field of international trade governance, as Feketekuty reminds us, requires a judicious mixture of 'economic theory, political pragmatism, and commercial savvy'.[87] Secondly, even in respect of technical expertise, the actors involved in the production and dissemination of this form of knowledge are not always best understood as part of epistemic communities. For one thing, they are most often not part of a pre-existing scientific community, but a loose network of organizations and individuals coming together around trade negotiations for a limited time and purpose.[88] For another, as we shall see, they are often more self-consciously involved in the production of technical knowledge as part of a political or commercial project than seems to be the case with epistemic communities, at least in their ideal definition.

B. Interpretive dispositions are structured as well as structuring

One of the difficulties of advancing theoretical claims which emphasize the significance of the interpretive dimension of social life—particularly in the context of theorizing about international trade politics—is that they are often misunderstood as necessarily idealist theoretical claims. That is to say, as soon as one suggests that 'ideas' and 'interpretation' are important in structuring trade politics, one tends to be misperceived as suggesting that actors in the field of international trade politics are free agents, governed by their subjective beliefs, interpretive habits, and personal worldviews, and unconstrained by the interests of actors with material power. Claims about the significance of 'ideas' in trade policy-making are often interpreted as a challenge to, and move away from, structural explanations based on underlying material interests and economic logics. For some, there seems to be a belief that in order to acknowledge the significance of ideas one has simultaneously to downgrade the significance of states' and other actors' material interests.

It will be clear by now, I hope, that I think this is wrong, and it would be a fundamental error to read the argument I make in that way. 'Ideas' and interpretive frameworks enter my explanatory model not as an alternative to interest-based explanation, but as a way of making them meaningful. Furthermore, material logics

[86] See generally Ch 9 below.
[87] G Feketekuty, *International Trade in Services: An Overview and Blueprint for Negotiations* (AEI and Ballinger, Cambridge, MA 1988) 149.
[88] Ikenberry (1992) 293.

re-enter my analysis not as determining causal factors in the mode of objectivist analysis, but rather as the structuring conditions of possibility for the production and reproduction of symbolic structures.

That said, it is equally true that interpretivist explanations—including in fact my own previous work—can falsely create the impression that 'ideas' are the fundamental and primary drivers of social action and social change. To the extent that such explanations seek to expose and explain the *structuring* impact of ideational frameworks on social action, they can inadvertently obscure their simultaneously *structured* nature. That is to say, while it is true that the interpretive side of social action is in an important sense active and creative—in other words, it is the active mobilization of a particular vision of social reality—it is also a highly structured or governed activity. As I have said, the symbolic structures which agents deploy in their active interpretation and appreciation of social reality are collectively produced and legitimated, and internalized within the minds of actors. Moreover, these symbolic structures are themselves the objects and products of social struggle between actors with interests, pursuing specific political projects, and wielding specific forms and amounts of power. The result is that the symbolic structures which govern actors' perceptual and behavioural dispositions are themselves shaped by the objective relations and material distributions of power which exist within the field of international trade law and governance. Behavioural and decisional logics within this field are produced and sustained by specific ideational configurations, but these ideational configurations in turn reflect the material conditions of their production and reproduction.

For this reason, although my focus in the following chapters is on the structuring power of interpretive frames on the operation and evolution of international trade law, I also self-consciously seek to give some indication of the objective material conditions in which these interpretive frames are produced and by which they are structured. Thus, for example, I ground the emergence of a new 'legal imagination' in the GATT/WTO from the 1970s in the context of the declining commercial hegemony of the United States from the late 1960s onwards, the economic tumult of the 1970s, and the increasing number and institutional diversity of countries belonging to the GATT/WTO system, as well as the distribution of symbolic power between different actors within the field of international trade governance. Given the nature of the argument that I am making, and the literature to which I am responding, there is, I acknowledge, still a risk that my argument will under-emphasize—or at least under-explore—the nature of the structuring power that objective material logics exert on the legal imagination. If so, that effect is an inadvertent product of the corrective emphasis of my argument, rather than the deliberate product of an underlying theoretical disposition.

III. Conclusion

It may be helpful if I conclude this chapter by briefly recapitulating the core elements of the explanatory model which emerges from the above reflections. As already noted, this explanatory model is offered as a corrective to what I perceive as the weaknesses of existing accounts of the transformation of the GATT/WTO legal system over the last three decades of the twentieth century.

My account suggests that the trade regime's neoliberal turn was, in significant part, a transformation of the symbolic order which structures and orients the field of international trade governance—the 'ways of thinking' and interpretive dispositions of participants in the field. I describe this as the emergence of a new 'legal imagination', which was both reflected in, and sustained by, specific changes in the institutions, texts, jurisprudence, and scope of application of WTO law.

If this is true, then a full account of this neoliberal turn would therefore necessarily include at least three elements. First, it must include a description of the *nature and content* of changes to that symbolic order. What changes occurred in the sensibilities of trade professionals, their worldviews, and the ideational frameworks which shape their actions, during this period? Similarly, what changes occurred during this period in the configuration of actors and processes through which symbolic power was exercised? How widespread were these changes? Secondly, an account of the regime's neoliberal period must explain the *impacts* of this new symbolic order. It must explain, that is, the nature of the relationship between, on the one hand, changes to this symbolic order, and on the other, contemporaneous changes to the institutions and structure of GATT/WTO law, its political orientations and normative biases, its domain of operation, and the range of actors involved in the field and the logics which govern their behaviours, and so on. Thirdly, this account must also provide an explanation of the underlying causal dynamics which *produced* this new symbolic order. This includes a description of its material and structural conditions of possibility, as well as the actors, processes, and forms of power involved in its construction and legitimation. While I do not pretend to provide a full and complete account of the trade regime's neoliberal turn over the following chapters, I will address aspects of all of these three elements.

Two key terms of my analysis are therefore the 'field of international trade governance' and the 'symbolic order' which is associated with that field. I use the term 'symbolic order' to refer in a generic way to the collective structures of meaning and interpretive frameworks operative within the field at any particular time. I spell out three of its more concrete elements below. As for the 'field of international trade governance', following Bourdieu, I define this as a structured arena of social struggle over the rules, institutions, norms, and practices of the international trade regime.[89] It is impossible to define in advance the boundaries of this field, primarily because those boundaries change through time, and are in themselves an object of contestation within the field itself. Nevertheless, we may identify key participants in the field, including diplomats and other state officials in WTO delegations, officials in domestic trade (and other) ministries and their legal advisers working on international trade negotiations and related matters, businesses and commercial associations closely connected to trade negotiators and negotiations, NGOs working on issues around the WTO and governance of trade, the WTO Secretariat and personnel in

[89] See p 183 above.

other international organizations with a professional interest in trade issues, and academics working on international economic law, among others.[90] It goes without saying that this field overlaps with others. Thus, many of the actors described above will also be participants in the organizational fields associated with, say, domestic political parties, or the field of human rights activism, or the field associated with the regulation and transnational governance of the telecommunications sector. While the existence of overlapping fields may make it somewhat more difficult to isolate the particular structural logics and mindsets characteristic of the field of international trade governance, the nature and existence of those logics nevertheless remains a central social fact to be determined in this form of analysis.

As far as the content of this symbolic order is concerned, my research has suggested that three specific elements are among the most significant, and I will therefore focus on those. The first element is made up of a cluster of ideas about what we might call the 'collective purpose' of the international trade regime. While it is common now to talk of the mission of the trade regime in parsimonious and abstract terms—such as the 'liberalization of trade' or the 'reduction and removal of trade barriers'—the reality is that the project of trade liberalization carried out through the GATT/WTO regime has historically been shaped by a much denser and more concrete sense of purpose, which changes from period to period in its history.[91] This sense of purpose is itself produced and sustained by a complex ideational infrastructure, which includes: causal economic ideas about the precise contribution that international trade makes to the improvement of global welfare, as well as the specific causal mechanisms by which that contribution occurs; economic ideas about the costs and risks of international trade liberalization, both generally and in particular sectors; political ideas about the institutions best placed to address these costs; institutional ideas about the nature and content of the trade regime's mandate, the particular problems it is designed to resolve, and the specific contribution that it can (and cannot) make to the resolution of those problems.

The second, related, element consists of ideas about law—specifically, beliefs about the nature of GATT/WTO law and the precise contribution that law can and cannot make to the achievement of the regime's goals. Together with the background beliefs about collective purpose, this complex constellation of ideas helps to produce a body of collectively held beliefs about the mission and purpose of the GATT/WTO legal system, which orients the way that certain social phenomena are constructed as 'problems' for the law to address, as well as the approach that different actors within the regime adopt in addressing those problems through law. It helps to produce a particular sensibility and sense of professional role among participants in the trade regime carrying out legal activities.

The third element of the symbolic order that I will address consists of the 'principles of vision and division' according to which actors in the field of international trade governance identify illegitimate trade barriers and distortions of trade,

[90] For an account of key actors in early decades, see Curzon and Curzon (1973) 313ff.

[91] See also Curzon and Curzon (1973) 321.

and distinguish them from other forms of governmental action. Again, this is a complex set of ideas. It includes the different categories to which specific forms of governmental action can be interpretively assigned, as well as habitual ways of applying those categories to specific forms of governmental action. It also includes a set of beliefs about the different purposes for which governments can legitimately intervene in particular economic sectors, as well as argumentative techniques and evaluative principles for determining the appropriateness of specific ways of achieving these purposes. I will be arguing that the content of these categories, interpretive habits, beliefs, argumentative techniques, and evaluative principles changed over the course of the trade regime's turn from embedded liberalism to neoliberalism. In addition, I will suggest that this change at the level of content was itself the result of a more fundamental change in their mode of production—that is, the actors, processes, and institutional structures through which such categories, beliefs, and principles are produced and made authoritative.

In relation to the *impact* of the changed symbolic structures associated with the neoliberal turn, my focus will be on the GATT/WTO's legal order. Specifically, my aim is to track changes to the symbolic order of the trade regime against changes in four core elements of its legal order on the other. The first element is the structure of the WTO's legal order, in the sense of its degree of formalization and structural separation from trade politics and trade diplomacy. The second is its practical scope of application, by which I am referring not just to changes in the range of governmental measures which are formally within the scope of WTO legal disciplines, but more significantly, changes to the range of measures which as a practical matter are brought to the attention of trade officials and raised before the WTO dispute settlement system. The third is the textual content of WTO law, as well as to some extent the processes of negotiation by which this textual content is determined. Fourthly and finally, I will focus in some detail on the interpretation of WTO law. My aim here will be to identify the particular legal sensibilities, jurisprudential styles, and interpretive techniques characteristic of the case law produced during the trade regime's neoliberal period, and trace their connection with the underlying transformation of the regime's larger symbolic order which occurred at the same time.

My particular focus will be on the GATT/WTO's approach to 'domestic regulation'. While I acknowledge that this to some extent limits the generality of my argument,[92] the fact is that the turn to domestic regulation—to 'behind the border' barriers to trade—is one of the most important features of the regime's neoliberal turn, and it is here that one sees most clearly its new dynamics at play. While it is

[92] More specifically, I acknowledge that the logics which govern the negotiation and application of disciplines on border barriers, especially tariffs, may differ in significant ways from the logics I describe in respect of domestic regulation in the following chapters, and I deliberately make no claims about that aspect of the trade regime's work. However, I am confident that the core conclusions of my argument are equally applicable across essentially all other areas of domestic regulation which have so far fallen within the domain of the WTO.

again impossible to define the notion of 'domestic regulation' conclusively in advance of the investigation—precisely because the content of this category is one of the objects of contemporary symbolic contestation within the field, and part of what is at stake in the interpretation of WTO law—for the purposes of analysis, I will adopt a broad definition reflecting common usage in the field, which refers to all forms of governmental intervention other than traditional tariffs and other border barriers, and which includes measures relating to health and consumer protection, product and food safety, prudential and financial regulation, industrial policy, regional development, environmental protection, and so on.[93]

As regards the question of the *production* of the symbolic order structuring the field of international trade governance during its neoliberal period, I offer two specific contributions. First, in Chapter 9, I provide a detailed account of the symbolic construction of the 'principles of vision and division' operative in the services context. That is to say, I look at the ways in which 'trade barriers' are defined and identified in the services context, and I set out in detail the way that specific actors, with a variety of interests and agendas, are engaged in a struggle to entrench and objectify their particular vision of the distinction between trade barriers and legitimate regulation in that context. The case studies provided in that chapter offer a window onto the dynamics of symbolic production operating generally within the contemporary trade regime. Secondly, I focus specifically on the role that law plays in the construction and entrenchment of the regime's symbolic order. Law thus appears twice in my account: first, changes to the workings of the GATT/WTO's legal order are described as the product of transformations of the broader symbolic framework at work within the trade regime; secondly, legal processes figure as an important part of the mechanisms through which that symbolic framework is produced and reproduced over time. I argue here that lawyers play an active role in selecting particular forms of knowledge to guide the elaboration and interpretation of international trade law, and that this process of incorporation represents a kind of consecration, in the sense that law and lawyers thus endow these forms of knowledge—and groups of knowledge producers—with symbolic authority to define the legitimate, and collectively held, principles of vision to be deployed in the field of international trade governance.

[93] Some, but not all, would also include trade remedy legislation such as anti-dumping duty and countervailing duty regimes within the notion of 'domestic regulation'.

7

Embedded Liberalism and Purposive Law

This chapter examines the GATT during its first two decades, with particular attention to the operation of its legal regime, and its approach to 'domestic regulation'. In the first section, I draw on a range of existing histories of the trade regime to recall the way that the regime's purpose was collectively imagined during this period, and the role which law was understood to play in the achievement of these purposes. In the second section, I show how this ideational framework, and the institutional processes which reflected and embodied it, produced a peculiarly limited and modest approach to the oversight of domestic regulation during this period.

I. The nature and purpose of the post-war trade regime

A. Two philosophies and the embedded liberal compromise

The planners of the post-war international economic order were guided in large part by a common desire to avoid a repetition of what had occurred during the interwar years.[1] International trade relations had been severely disrupted during the First World War, as participants sought to encourage domestic production of products essential to war, and to limit imports from and exports to their enemies.[2] In the immediate aftermath of the First World War, a number of factors combined to entrench this trend towards protection. Given widespread perceptions of the fragility of the international peace established in Versailles, former belligerents continued to prioritize self-sufficiency as an economic policy, particularly in respect of products considered essential. The same was true also of the numerous smaller European states formed in the aftermath of the First World War after the break-up of the major European empires, with the result that 'Eastern and South Eastern Europe were transformed into an area bristling with frontiers and barriers to trade'.[3] In addition, on the periphery of the international economic system, those countries which had

[1] G Curzon and V Curzon, 'The Management of Trade Relations in the GATT' in A Shonfield (ed), *International Economic Relations of the Western World, 1959–1971, Volume 1: Politics and Trade* (OUP, London 1976) 143, 144; RE Hudec, *The GATT Legal System and World Trade Diplomacy* (2nd edn, Butterworths, Salem, NH 1990) 5.

[2] See generally G Curzon, *Multilateral commercial diplomacy: the General Agreement on Tariffs and Trade and its impact on national commercial policies and techniques* (Michael Joseph, London 1965) 20ff.

[3] ibid 21.

developed industrial capacity for the first time during the war were reluctant to permit the rapid disappearance of these industries as patterns of trade returned to normal, and resorted to trade measures as a means of protection.

Between 1920 and 1929, at a series of conferences in Brussels (1920), Genoa (1922), and Geneva (twice in 1927), members of the League of Nations attempted to address these developments in commercial policy. Though they neither endorsed nor pursued full liberalization, they reiterated their formal commitment to a series of principles, including the undesirability of exchange controls as limits on international trade, the 'removal of obstacles created by instability in administrative and legal measures', the 'progressive suppression of import and export prohibitions', and the transparency and stability of tariff restrictions on trade.[4] In part as a result, non-tariff barriers to trade—which at that time essentially meant prohibitions, exchange controls, and quantitative restrictions—were largely removed by the mid-1920s, with the process continuing even as late as 1930. Tariffs, on the other hand, were not reduced, and indeed in most countries continued to rise, sometimes spectacularly.[5] France, Germany, the United Kingdom and the United States all markedly increased their applied duties during this period, as a way of easing the domestic impacts of the profound economic instability of the period.

The onset of the Depression from 1929 brought these efforts to re-establish a more liberal international economic order, such as they were, to a rapid halt. For primary producing countries, the rapid fall in global agricultural prices, combined with the withdrawal of US capital after the stock market crash of 1929, led to falling incomes at the producer level and severe balance of payments problems at the country level. Economic instability in one country rapidly spread internationally, both because of falling global demand for world exports, and as a result of surges of cut-price imports from countries seeking sources of foreign exchange. In the face of very high levels of domestic unemployment, countries reluctantly sought to insulate themselves from global economic instability through renewed resort to barriers to trade. Most famously, the United States introduced the Smoot-Hawley Tariff Act of 1930, substantially increasing its already high tariff levels, which prompted retaliatory measures from other countries around the world which saw no other option than to follow suit. These higher tariffs were accompanied by myriad new or resurrected forms of more exotic trade barriers, including not only import prohibitions, but also quotas, exchange controls, local content and local mixing requirements, and—especially after the collapse of the Gold Standard in 1931—competitive currency devaluations.[6] Over the next few years, three more specific trends emerged: the development of far-reaching government intervention in the agricultural sector, including state trading and price stabilization regimes, requiring

[4] See generally WA Brown, *The United States and the restoration of world trade: an analysis and appraisal of the ITO charter and the General Agreement on Tariffs and Trade* (Brookings Institution, Washington, DC 1950) 29–37.

[5] Curzon (1965) 22.

[6] G Kenwood and A Lougheed, *Growth of the International Economy 1820–2000* (Routledge, London 1999) 198–205.

virtually complete insulation of the sector from international trade; the establishment of closer economic relations among small groups of countries, providing mutual preferences for one another's products on a discriminatory basis, including the British Imperial Preferences; and the growth of international cartels in Europe as a means of fostering greater economic stability in certain industrial sectors.[7] The effect of all these developments was dramatic, with the value of world trade falling by about a third in the two years after 1929, and the persistence of trade barriers dampening global demand and hampering economic recovery throughout the 1930s.

There were efforts to reverse this catastrophic failure of commercial policy from the mid 1930s, most prominently through the United States' Reciprocal Trade Agreements Act of 1934, and the network of twenty bilateral trade agreements which the United States signed between 1934 and 1939 under the leadership of US Secretary of State Cordell Hull. But these were undermined by the political instability of the period, and it was not until the final years of the Second World War that efforts to reconstruct a multilateral trading order began seriously to take shape. While the post-war planners—initially, officials in the United Kingdom and United States—were united by a common desire not to return to the trading system of the 1930s, there was no clear agreement on the appropriate lessons to be learnt from the experience of the interwar period. There were, broadly speaking, two 'philosophies'[8] which emerged at this time, with somewhat different interpretations of the causes and consequences of commercial policy during the 1930s, and different prescriptions for the post-war trading order. As outlined in Chapter 2, both of these philosophies had an important influence on the post-war GATT regime.

The first philosophy, which tends to be better remembered today within legal scholarship on the trade regime, is represented in the figure of Cordell Hull, who was a major influence on post-war economic planning on the American side, and brought a clear set of views about the importance of a broadly liberal international trading order to world peace and prosperity.[9] The proliferation of barriers to international trade during the interwar years, within this philosophy, had caused or at the very least intensified and prolonged the Depression of the 1930s by suppressing world demand. More than that, the trade wars of the period led in a straight line to the outbreak of the Second World War, by inflaming political hostilities and resentment in foreign countries:

> Nations have more often than not . . . raised up trade barriers with complete disregard for the damaging effects on the trade and livelihood of other peoples . . . The resultant misery, bewilderment and resentment, together with other equally pernicious contributory causes,

[7] Brown (1950) 38–42.

[8] Curzon and Curzon (1976) 149.

[9] RN Gardner, *Sterling-dollar diplomacy: Anglo-American collaboration in the reconstruction of multilateral trade* (Clarendon Press, Oxford 1956) 102. For a more detailed account see WR Allen, 'The International Trade Philosophy of Cordell Hull, 1907–1933' (1953) 43 American Economic Rev 101, 116.

paved the way for the rise of those very dictatorships which have plunged almost the entire world into war.[10]

Specifically, the practice of *discriminatory* trade—the formation of trading blocs, and the use of commercial policy to reward friends and punish enemies—was seen to be particularly problematic, and undermining of international peace. Discrimination, it was argued, is 'invariably resented by the countries which are discriminated against, and three centuries of experience demonstrates that under all circumstances [it] operate[s] to poison international relations and to make more difficult the task of maintaining international harmony'.[11] Though also shared by many British economists,[12] this preference for a more open, non-discriminatory, and liberal trading order was particularly prominent in the United States, which emerged from the war as the world's industrial engine, confident of its capacity to compete in virtually all industrial sectors around the world.[13] It entered negotiations over the post-war economic order with a goal of eliminating all non-tariff barriers to trade—at least as that term was understood at the time—with an exception only for balance of payments measures.[14]

Although this represents the more recognizably liberal strand of post-war thinking about the international economic order, writers of the period have, as noted in Chapter 2, consistently stressed that it was far from a doctrinaire classical position on free trade, certainly outside a few individuals in the State Department.[15] As Viner famously asserted, in a 1947 article in support of the compromised Havana Charter:

> . . . there are few free traders in the present-day world, no one pays any attention to their views, and no person in authority anywhere advocates free trade. The practical issue turns on whether existing trade barriers should be reduced, and if so, how much . . .[16]

While Viner may be somewhat overstating the case here for emphasis, the point is an important one. As Kock has noted, while domestic debate in the United States focused on the reinstitution of 'free trade' as part of the maintenance of the American 'free enterprise' system, both of those terms remained somewhat nebulous in their meaning.[17] Certainly, it is clear that 'free trade' usually meant the removal of quantitative restrictions, exchange controls, and the other administrative controls of trade which had proliferated during the 1930s, rather than the total elimination of

[10] US Secretary of State Sumner Wells, 1941, cited in JH Jackson, *World trade and the law of GATT: a legal analysis of the General Agreement on Tariffs and Trade* (Bobbs-Merill, Indianapolis, IN 1969) 38. For a clear expression of this general philosophy see C Wilcox, *A Charter for World Trade* (Macmillan Co, New York, NY 1949) 5.

[11] J Viner, 'Conflicts of Principle in Drafting a Trade Charter' (1947) 25 *Foreign Affairs* 612, 616.

[12] Curzon and Curzon (1976) 148.

[13] JK Galbraith, *Economics in Perspective: A Critical History* (Houghton Mifflin, Boston, MA 1987) 160.

[14] Hudec (1990) 15.

[15] GJ Ikenberry, 'A world economy restored: expert consensus and the Anglo-American postwar settlement' (1992) 46 Intl Org 289, eg 305 and generally.

[16] Viner (1947) 613.

[17] K Kock, *International trade policy and the GATT: 1947–1967* (Almqvist & Wiksell, Stockholm 1969) 7.

tariffs.[18] Moreover, 'free trade' meant non-discriminatory trade above all—that is, the re-establishment of the norm of unconditional MFN treatment in the post-war trading order, and the elimination of regional blocs and preference regimes as far as possible. The post-war planners in the liberal mould, then, were far from ideologues. They were careful to avoid taking a doctrinaire position on trade matters, and sought also to avoid the impression during the Havana Charter negotiations of seeking to impose a particular vision of liberal capitalism on the rest of the world.[19]

The second philosophy, more prominent in the United Kingdom than in the United States in part as a result of the influence of Keynes on economic thinking in that country, proceeded from a somewhat different starting point. This philosophy remembered the Depression primarily as an experience of unemployment and economic instability. From this perspective, it was the instability of free markets, combined with the prolonged and regular periods of unemployment that accompanied such instability, which had led to the political revolutions of the first half of the twentieth century, and ultimately the descent into a second world war.[20] The fundamental problem facing post-war planners, on this view, was the problem of unemployment, and the first and over-riding goal of economic policy must be the attainment of full and stable employment. This prioritization of full employment policies governed the attitude towards international trade of those who shared this way of thinking. On one hand, it was fully acknowledged that international trade would support employment growth, by opening foreign markets to domestic exports and boosting global demand. At the same time, there were at least two serious difficulties with a policy of free trade. First, pursuing a free trade policy opened up domestic economies to sources of instability caused by economic fluctuations in major trading partners. The experience of the Depression taught policy-makers to expect and plan for 'bleak times',[21] and they knew that they needed to maintain some ability to insulate themselves from international sources of instability. Many countries were particularly unwilling to expose themselves again to the 'notorious instability of the American economy',[22] which had proved so disastrous in the interwar years. Secondly, the pursuit of a full employment policy through the kinds of inflationary demand management policies developed by Keynes could lead to serious balance of payments difficulties, particularly if other countries did not follow suit.[23] The United Kingdom in particular sought to ensure that it was able to impose major trade restrictions in such cases, without triggering another trade war of the kind that was seen during the early 1930s.

This second philosophy, then, by no means jettisoned freer trade as an important goal of the post-war trading system. It was, however, based on a causal account of the dynamics of the international economy which stressed economic integration as a

[18] ibid 8; Viner (1947) 617.
[19] Viner (1947) 614, 627.
[20] See generally K Polanyí, *Origins of our time: the great transformation* (V Gollancz, London 1945).
[21] Curzon and Curzon (1976) 148.
[22] Viner (1947) 622.
[23] ibid 621; Kock (1969) 10.

cause of instability, and gave lesser weight to trade as a driver of prosperity. In Hansen's words:

> We have learned that the removal of trade obstacles undertaken by itself alone is not a feasible program. A liberal trade policy must be undertaken side by side with a program of development, expansion and full employment throughout the world...[24]

More than that, there were important circumstances in which the goal of liberalizing trade must, in this view, give way to the higher priority of maintaining full and stable employment.

As noted in Chapter 2, both of these two philosophies influenced negotiations over the shape of the post-war trading order, and both were reflected in the text of Chapter IV of the Havana Charter, and therefore ultimately the GATT 1947.[25] In some respects, the evolution of the GATT over the following two decades can be understood as a 'tug of war' between the two.[26] But there was enough overlap between the two to form a compromise—the compromise of 'embedded liberalism', discussed in Chapter 2.[27] Key players in the negotiations shared a common view of the legitimacy of state intervention to secure domestic stability, even if they disagreed on the precise form and depth that that intervention should take in particular circumstances.[28] The post-war international trading order was therefore designed in a way which safeguarded the ability of states to pursue policies of domestic stability, while at the same time moving away from the bilateralism and discrimination of interwar commercial policy towards a more open and multilateral international trading system.

It is therefore common among historians of the trade regime to talk of the initial GATT as being built upon, and sustained by, a shared normative commitment to interventionist domestic policies of a broadly Keynesian kind—that is, a broadly shared understanding of what constituted the 'normal' and legitimate purposes for which governments might intervene in economic life. Of course, it is important to be clear about precisely what was shared, and to what extent. Ikenberry, for example, argues that the negotiation of post-war monetary and trade order was enabled by the existence of a community of policy specialists who articulated a 'more or less coherent governing philosophy of postwar economic order', and that this shared basic vision among specialists defined a middle ground in negotiations, enabling the possibility of bridging political divisions.[29] Hudec argues that the international conferences of the interwar period had given trade policy officials a chance to wrestle with the meaning of the typical provisions in trade treaties of the time, and 'in the

[24] AH Hansen, *America's Role in the World Economy* (WW Norton & Co, New York, NY 1945) 92; see also Kock (1969) 10.

[25] Kock (1969) 270, 273–4.

[26] Curzon and Curzon (1976) 149.

[27] JG Ruggie, 'International Regimes, Transactions, and Change: Embedded Liberalism in the Postwar Economic Order' (1982) 36 Intl Org 379. See pp 29–30 above.

[28] ibid 394.

[29] Ikenberry (1992) 292ff.

process, to clarify among themselves what those generalities meant'.[30] 'For the most part', he said, they 'found themselves in complete agreement about particular issues of substantive policy', even where there might be underlying differences of broader political vision.[31] Furthermore, it should be stressed that this shared substantive policy consensus as regards specific trade instruments was primarily 'shared' among the three or four key countries in the negotiations, and in particular the United States and the United Kingdom, rather than all Contracting Parties to the GATT. The maintenance of a 'consensus' for the following two decades had much to do with the continuing authority of these countries in the GATT during this time, and was enabled by the fact that 'outsiders [to this group of key countries] had accepted the GATT from the beginning with the knowledge that it was meant to be the proprietary instrument of the inner group'.[32]

We should not forget, too, that the consensus underlying the post-war GATT regime was the product of a particular political and material context. As we saw in Chapter 2, for example, the sustainability of the embedded liberal compromise over the first decades of the GATT's existence depended in part on the marginalization of the interests of developing countries within the regime—in particular, the effective exclusion of agriculture and textiles from liberalizing commitments under the GATT. The delicate compromise between international liberalization and domestic stability could not have survived politically if the industrialized West had opened its borders fully to imports of agricultural products and light manufactured goods from the developing world. Indeed, as we shall see, it was in significant part the rise of the newly industrializing countries over the course of the 1960s and 1970s which led to the erosion of embedded liberalism around that time. Moreover, the GATT 'consensus' was made possible precisely because GATT membership was limited almost exclusively to a small number of countries, all of which had domestic market economies[33]—and, importantly, because the GATT was in part understood as a way of maintaining Western unity during the Cold War, by placing it on a firm and stable economic footing.[34] The Cold War too, then, provided part of the material and political basis for the continuation and acceptance of a particular collective political commitment in the post-war GATT.

That said, the fact remains that a fairly strong set of shared understandings existed about what the purpose and objectives of the regime were, and what its legal provisions did and did not mean. The fundamental and primary purpose of the post-war regime was *international stability*, in the specific sense of preventing a repeat

[30] Hudec (1990) 8.

[31] ibid 9.

[32] ibid 131.

[33] EH Preeg, *Traders and diplomats: an analysis of the Kennedy round of negotiations under the General Agreement on Tariffs and Trade* (Brookings Institution, Washington, DC 1970) 24.

[34] Curzon and Curzon (1976) 177; Preeg (1970) 5 (the GATT was 'a pillar of solidarity among non-communist countries'); TB Curtis and JR Vastine, *The Kennedy Round and the future of American trade* (Praeger, New York, NY 1971) 3 ('the solidarity and prosperity that would be promoted by the Kennedy Round promised to strengthen the West's ability to oppose communism and soviet imperialism'); IM Destler, *American Trade Politics* (Institute for International Economics, Washington, DC 2005) 7.

of the disastrous trade wars of the early 1930s.[35] Such stability, it was understood, was a necessary precondition of the flourishing of the social democratic welfare state. This, broadly understood, was the historically situated collective project that participants understood themselves to be engaging in. Thus, although the removal of trade barriers was of course an important intermediate purpose of the regime, liberalization was in fact a less important norm during the first two decades of the trade regime's history than is often assumed.[36] Liberalization was pursued not through the application of a rigid principle, but only as far as states were practically able, and only as far as was consistent with the broader norm of economic stability. This emphasis on stability, moreover, meant that measures taken to maintain domestic economic stability and full employment took precedence over international commitments wherever they came into serious conflict. Thus, Article XII:3(d) recognized that 'as a result of domestic policies directed towards the achievement and maintenance of full and productive employment . . . a contracting party may experience a high level of demand for imports involving a threat to its monetary reserves', and permitted the use of quantitative trade restrictions in such circumstances. This was highly significant, as such domestic policies could have major, if indirect, impacts on trade.[37] Similar exceptions were inserted for domestic price stabilization programmes for agricultural products and other commodities, as well as for the use of safeguard measures in situations of destabilizing and unforeseen import surges.[38] More generally, there were provisions for the waiver or renegotiation of tariff and other commitments contained in the GATT, available to be activated when necessary.[39] More important than the norm of liberalization, then, at least in these early years, were the norms of non-discrimination and reciprocity. Non-discrimination, especially MFN treatment, helped to prevent further balkanization of international trade and the subjugation of commercial policy to the destabilizing influences of broader geopolitical priorities. Reciprocity helped to ensure that the priority of the trade regime during this period was to maintain the balance of concessions between Contracting Parties, such that 'when unforeseen disturbances occur[red] to upset this balance . . . the organization's energies [were] devoted to restoring the original balance as quickly as possible'.[40]

This normative emphasis on stability was also reflected in the institutional form of the GATT in the post-war period, in three primary ways. The first was through the creation of a system for the management of trade disputes which focused on the goals of containment and non-escalation, rather than the rigid enforcement of legal rules. I will say more about this in a moment. The second was the self-conscious policing of the boundary between the 'low politics' of international trade and the 'high politics'

[35] DA Irwin, 'The GATT in Historical Perspective' (1995) 85 American Economic Rev 323, 326.

[36] JA Finlayson and MW Zacher, 'The GATT and the regulation of trade barrier: regime dynamics and functions' (1981) 35 International Organization 561, 570.

[37] Viner (1947) 619.

[38] See eg GATT, Arts XI, XIX.

[39] GATT, Arts XXV, XXVIII.

[40] G Curzon and V Curzon, 'GATT: Trader's Club' in RW Cox and HK Jacobson (eds), *Anatomy of Influence: Decision Making in International Organization* (Yale University Press, New Haven, CT 1973) 298, 321.

of foreign policy more generally.[41] In the light of what were seen as the destabilizing and destructive influences that geopolitical concerns could have on the conduct of commercial policy, the GATT and its participants cultivated an apolitical ethos. They sought to insulate themselves from the broader world of international politics, and resisted any attempts to connect trade issues with what were understood as matters of high politics.[42] 'Trade negotiations', wrote Gerard and Victoria Curzon in the 1970s, 'tend to be self-contained... [and] attempts to use totally unconnected political or economic levers with which to extract trade concessions are rare and deeply resented when they do in fact occur'.[43] In disputes involving 'political' elements, the Contracting Parties made 'every effort to avoid involvement in the political substance of the matter, leaving the responsibility for this to the competent organizations'.[44] On those relatively rare occasions where, for example, East-West tensions unavoidably spilled over into the GATT—such as the breakdown of trade relations between the United States and Czechoslovakia in the late 1940s—the GATT contracting parties adopted, as far as possible, an avoidance strategy, pragmatically accepting the facts as they were, on the basis that it was 'not their role to mediate in a political issue arising out of the cold war'.[45]

Thirdly, this self-consciously insular sensibility was reflected also in the more general social autonomy of the community making up the field of international trade governance at the time. The early GATT has often been compared 'more... to a club than an international organization or an international commercial parliament':

> The discussions within four walls, the attempts at reconciliation rather than head-on conflicts by affirmation of rights, the private meetings 'to talk things over' are all features of this club-like atmosphere.[46]

Hudec, too, described the early GATT as a 'club'—a 'place where like-minded officials could communicate without having to spell things out in confrontation-producing clarity'.[47] More recently, Weiler has described this atmosphere in these terms:

> A very dominant feature of the GATT was its self-referential and even communitarian ethos explicable in constructivist terms. The GATT successfully managed a relative insulation from the 'outside' world of international relations and established among its practitioners a closely knit environment revolving round a certain set of shared normative values (of free trade) and

[41] RN Cooper, 'Trade Policy is Foreign Policy' (1972) 9 *Foreign Policy* 18.

[42] Curzon and Curzon (1975) 328; Kock (1969) 273.

[43] Curzon and Curzon (1976) 163, 199.

[44] O Long, *Law and its limitations in the GATT multilateral trade system* (M Nijhoff, Boston, MA 1985) 81–3, giving some examples from a somewhat later period.

[45] Curzon (1965). For one list of where geopolitical issues did influence GATT practice, see Long (1985) 81–3; see also Curzon and Curzon (1973) 328.

[46] Curzon (1965) 52–3.

[47] RE Hudec, 'The GATT Legal System: A Diplomat's Jurisprudence' (1970) 4 J of World Trade L 615, 635.

shared institutional (and personal) ambitions situated in a matrix of long-term first-name contacts and friendly personal relationships.[48]

The Curzons note that, while delegates were of course subject to pressures from protectionist interest groups in their capitals, there was an 'absence of protectionist lobbies in Geneva', and the 'comings and goings of their country's delegates to and from Geneva seemed to have escaped their influence'.[49] The point is not that this social separation—the relatively small size and club-like feel of the GATT regime—meant that decision-makers within the regime were insulated from the influence of protectionist lobbies, or directions from their capitals back home, and were free agents in any simple way. There is ample evidence, if any is needed, that trade negotiators consulted with domestic industries, even if not to the same extent as they do today.[50] The point, rather, is that this structurally insular aspect of the field is the direct institutional and social analogue of the characteristic mindset of trade professionals of the time—a mindset which was oriented towards the maintenance of stable international commercial relations as a primary objective of the regime, and which actively maintained a self-consciously apolitical posture as a way of managing and containing the potentially destabilizing influence of domestic and international political forces. It is this shared ethos and collective sense of purpose, I will argue, that deeply structured the nature, operation, and evolution of the GATT's legal disciplines on domestic regulation during that time.

B. The role of law: purposive law and embedded legal forms

Before I turn to explain that impact, however, there is another important part of the ideational context of the post-war GATT that needs to be addressed. In addition to ideas about the precise role and function of the GATT in the post-war international order, there was also another set of ideas about the role that *law* could and could not play in the achievement of the GATT's objectives. Hudec has explained that during the negotiations over the Havana Charter—which, as explained in Chapter 2, were ongoing during the drafting of the GATT—there were two currents of thinking about the place of law and legal obligations in establishing the post-war international economic order.[51] On one hand, there were those who were determined to create a 'harder' legal infrastructure than the 'ineffective multilateral conventions promulgated by the international economic conferences' of the interwar period.[52] They

[48] JHH Weiler, 'The Rule of Lawyers and the Ethos of Diplomats: Reflections on the Internal and External Legitimacy of WTO' (2001) 35 J of World Trade 191, 192; see also RO Keohane and JS Nye, Jr, 'The Club Model of Multilateral Cooperation and the World Trade Organization: Problems of Democratic Legitimacy' in R Porter et al (eds), *Efficiency, Equity and Legitimacy: The Multilateral Trading System at the Millennium* (Brookings Institution Press, Washington, DC 2001); R Howse, 'From Politics to Technocracy—and Back Again: The Fate of the Multilateral Trading Regime' (2002) 96 AJIL 94; Finlayson and Zacher (1981) 600.

[49] Curzon (1965) 53; Curzon and Curzon (1976) 175; Curzon and Curzon (1973) 317.

[50] Curzon and Curzon (1976) 159, 175, 184, Preeg (1970) 78; Curzon (1965) 129.

[51] Hudec (1970) 619ff.

[52] ibid 619; Hudec (1990) 7, 22, 26, 289.

therefore sought, at least in some respects, to spell out legal obligations with some precision in the Havana Charter, and in early drafts made these obligations enforceable through a formal complaints procedure, and justiciable in the International Court of Justice.[53] As Jackson has also noted, one of the oft-cited advantages of the Charter (and subsequently the GATT), at least from this perspective, was that 'the rights and obligations embodied in [the] agreement are contractual in nature and legally binding'.[54] This view of law was similar to that which has recently been resurrected in some recent accounts of the trade regime[55]—a view in which law is seen primarily as a way of producing predictability and certainty by ensuring that the trade policy behaviour of a state conforms to the prior expectations of its trading partners. There was even a proposal in 1947 to establish a procedure for direct citizen complaint in cases of violation of international trade law, though it did not receive much support.[56] The United States was always the strongest champion of this view of law, and, as we shall see in the next chapter, was in large part responsible for its rise to dominance from the mid-1970s onwards.

On the other hand, there was an alternative view of the role of law, which placed much less emphasis on formally binding obligations, and which saw legal ambiguity as a potentially constructive force. This view was based in part on a particular understanding of the kind of judgment which was required in the context of economic disputes, reflected in this passage in a memorandum submitted by the United Kingdom during Charter negotiations:

> ... there are numerous provisions in the Charter which require the discretion and economic judgment rather than precise interpretation of the terms of the Charter ... In almost every conceivable case arising under the Charter the issues will of their nature involve the element of economic appraisal and assessment and will not be purely legal in character, and it will be impossible to say where economic judgment ends and legal judgment begins.[57]

As Hudec notes, the issue was not just to ensure that dispute settlement was guided by economic (not just legal) forms of expertise, and controlled by 'pragmatic economic experts whose judgment was not cluttered by legalistic ritual'.[58] The point was also to ensure that dispute settlement was animated by a spirit of political compromise and discretion, which a more formalized legal machinery might discourage.[59] More generally, law was primarily seen in purposive terms as an instrument of the broader purposes underlying the regime as a whole, rather than just as a

[53] N Weinrichter, 'Perspectives on the changing spirit of GATT' (1999) 3 *European Integration Online Papers* <http://eiop.or.at/eiop/pdf/1999-010.pdf> accessed 15 February 2011, rightly describes the ITO as a highly legalized international organization; see also Hudec (1990) 26ff.

[54] Jackson (1969) 755.

[55] See below pp 241ff.

[56] Jackson (1969) 187.

[57] UN Economic and Social Council, 'Article 86: Summary of Points Made by Mr Shackle Regarding Interpretation and Settlement of Disputes' (14 February 1947) UN Doc E/PC/T/C.6/W.77, cited in Hudec (1970) 622–3.

[58] Hudec (1970) 618; Hudec (1990) 25.

[59] Hudec (1970) 619, 623.

mechanism for producing clear rules and therefore predictable behaviour.[60] This meant that the drafters had to ensure a certain degree of ambiguity and flexibility in the texts, forms, and procedures of the law, to allow for the mobilization and deployment of appropriately sensitive discretion and judgment in particular cases. Thus, the softness of the GATT's ultimate dispute settlement procedures, and the indeterminate language of much of its texts, was not—or not only—a pragmatic concession to the reality that governments would not accept more binding commitments. It also reflected a view that these legal forms would produce a more effective and operational dispute settlement machinery than more formal alternatives.

Both of these views of the appropriate role of law in international trade politics—and variants of them—have been in play within the trade regime from its very beginning. Accounts differ as to the precise ebbs and flows between them over the course of its first few decades. Hudec describes the flexible legal style as more or less dominant in the GATT from the very beginning, through to the Tokyo Round.[61] While it is true that there was a distinct change in the operation of the dispute settlement in the 1960s, as Contracting Parties came to see formal legal proceedings as overly aggressive,[62] in Hudec's account this did not represent so much a change in ideas about the nature of law's role in international trade politics, as an erosion of a belief in law's efficacy in general. In any case, whatever the precise turns and twists, to most contemporary eyes it seems clear that the GATT's early approach to law leaned much more towards the flexible and diplomatic than the formal and juridified.[63]

It is useful to remind ourselves that this tendency was not just a product of the internal politics of the trade regime itself, but of broader political and legal transformations characteristic of the period running from roughly the 1930s to the 1970s. The emergence of the welfare state during that period was associated with a broader transformation in the characteristic form of law, from 'formal rational legal systems' towards 'purposive . . . [or] substantively rational law, law used as an instrument of purposive, goal-oriented intervention', particularly in the context of the collective regulation of economic activity.[64] This transformation in the nature and function of law, from formal rational law towards 'purposive law', was also felt at the

[60] An interesting illustration of this view is Jackson (1969) 5: 'law . . . should be subservient to goals that essentially come from outside the limits' of law itself. Cf this statement with the view of the nature and function of law in JH Jackson, 'The Birth of the GATT-MTN System: A Constitutional Appraisal' (1980) 12 Law and Policy in International Business 21.

[61] See generally Hudec (1970); see also Viner (1947) 615.

[62] Jackson (1969) 759.

[63] For a number of accounts using this or a similar concept, see A Reich, 'From Diplomacy to Law: The Juridicization of International Trade Relations' (1997) 17 Northwestern J of Intl L and Business 775; D Palmeter and PC Mavroïdis, *Dispute Settlement in the World Trade Organization: Practice and Procedure* (2nd edn, CUP, Cambridge 2004); J Pauwelyn, 'The Transformation of World Trade' (2005) 104 Michigan Law Rev 1.

[64] G Teubner, 'Substantive and Reflexive Elements in Modern Law' (1983) 17 Law & Society Rev 239, 240, 253ff, 268; see also D Kennedy, 'The "Rule of Law," Political Choices, and Development Common Sense' in DM Trubek and A Santos (eds), *The New Law and Economic Development: A Critical Appraisal* (CUP, Cambridge 2006) 98–110; D Kennedy, 'Three Globalizations of Law and Legal Thought: 1850–2000' in Trubek and Santos (2006) 19.

international level, including in the GATT. Slaughter, following Mitrany and Maier, has persuasively argued that the post-war international order, including the GATT, represented in important respects the international projection of the organizing principles of political power characteristic of the welfare state of the time. This, in her account, did not just mean a projection of its substantive commitment to government intervention to protect the welfare of citizens. It also meant the projection and proliferation of the particular institutional forms characteristic of the welfare state—namely, specialized administrative agencies with functional mandates exercising independent expertise over a specific field of social life.[65] It also meant, most relevantly, the emergence of 'purposive' legal forms, in precisely the mode described above. The point, then, is that the 'embedded liberalism' of the post-war period should be understood not just as a set of substantive political commitments to interventionism, and a set of shared ideas about the regime's collective purpose, but also a commitment to a particular style and mode of deploying law in international governance.

These ideas about law's proper role and function produced a GATT legal system within the trade regime with at least five noteworthy structural features.[66] First, it was structurally subordinated to (or embedded in) the field of trade diplomacy. As is well known, the earliest disputes within the GATT system were resolved by trade delegations themselves, in a plenary meeting of the Contracting Parties, or in working parties staffed by governmental representatives. Members of dispute settlement panels and working parties were drawn almost exclusively from the community of trade diplomats. These panel members, 'although ostensibly acting in an individual capacity, nevertheless [were] representing a country in the GATT'.[67] Virtually all significant stages of the dispute settlement process required the consent of all delegates of GATT Contracting Parties to proceed. The result was that dispute settlement was an extension of diplomatic processes, and the internal logic and dynamics of the law more or less followed those of trade diplomacy. In addition, panels and working parties did not feel that they could substantively address questions brought before them on which there was strong and ongoing disagreement among the Contracting Parties. There was a consistent practice of pushing such disputes back to more regular processes of diplomacy and negotiation.[68]

Secondly, the text of the GATT itself represented only a very partial and even misleading window onto the normative universe of the GATT's legal system during this period. While this is no doubt true of all legal systems to some extent, it was

[65] A-M Burley [Slaughter], 'Regulating the World: Multilateralism, International Law, and the Projection of the New Deal Regulatory State' in J Ruggie (ed), *From Multilateralism Matters* (Columbia University Press, New York, NY 1993) 125; D Mitrany, *A Working Peace System* (Quadrangle Books, Chicago, IL 1966).

[66] See generally Hudec (1990) ch 17; see also T Broude, *International Governance in the World Trade Organization: Judicial Boundaries and Political Capitulation* (Cameron and May, London 2004) for a useful account.

[67] Jackson (1980) 42; Reich (1997) 796.

[68] See eg *Uruguay—Recourse to Article XXIII*, GATT Panel Report, L/1923, adopted 16 November 1962, BISD 11S/95.

particularly striking in the GATT context, and frequently commented upon by writers of the period. There was a large body of informal norms which sprang up in and around the formal texts, which exercised a powerful pull on Contracting Parties, and which structured the interpretation and application of the law:

> Slowly 'rules of the game' have evolved which are as important as the Articles of Agreement. While the latter may sometimes be ignored, the former seldom are. They have never been codified but have come to be recognized by participating countries when statesmen speak of the 'GATT philosophy'.[69]

These rules of the game can be thought of as 'customary norms',[70] which reflect the 'GATT consensus existing at the time'[71]—or at least that which passed for consensus given the dynamics of the trade diplomacy. Sometimes, these customary norms included the tacit acceptance of the violation of legal norms.[72] To a large extent, the GATT's legal system relied on the existence of this underlying and evolving substratum of informal norms, without which it simply could not function effectively.[73]

Thirdly, GATT dispute settlement also functioned as a venue and mechanism for the production and mobilization of community opinion in the world of trade diplomacy. Dispute resolution involved, in part, an intricate process of producing and reflecting the prevailing 'commonsense', and applying it to the dispute at issue. Hudec's careful account, written in 1970, of the 1952 *Belgian Family Allowances* Panel Report, remains the best and subtlest description of this process in action.[74] I will say more about this decision below, but for now it is enough to note Hudec's revealing general descriptions of the function of the Panel Report in that case:

> The Panel could not simply state the law... directly. What it could do, however, was to suggest... a conclusion in terms vague enough to avoid being pinned down and yet clear enough in the context to add some authority to the idea. These suggestions... could invite a community reaction somewhat stronger than the document itself... Rather than being a final resolution of the legal issue, the Panel decision is simply the first stage in a larger decision-making process that involves the whole community. The decision seeks to energize and influence community opinion, but it does so in a way which requires the community, as it were, to vote on the answer proposed.[75]

One lesson from Hudec's analysis is that GATT law, and GATT dispute settlement, was profoundly shaped by the 'community consensus' underlying the texts, and that this informal community consensus informed the text's interpretation and application in fundamental ways. Another lesson, however, is that legal processes in the

69 Curzon (1965) 53.
70 Jackson (1969) 757.
71 Hudec (1970) 665.
72 RE Hudec, *Adjudication of International Trade Disputes* (Trade Policy Research Centre, London 1978) ch 2; JH Jackson, 'The Crumbling Institutions of the Liberal Trade System' (1978) 12 J of World Trade L 93; Jackson (1969) 757; Long (1985) 19.
73 See generally Hudec (1978), Hudec (1990) 202–3; Finlayson and Zacher (1981) 588.
74 Hudec (1970).
75 ibid 657.

GATT had a *creative* function. They were an important part of the processes by which this community consensus developed, and helped to provide the formal basis for 'absorbing such developments into a regular legal framework'.[76] This process recalls Dam's description of GATT law as a set of 'procedures and [a] process [which] serves to identify the common interest in complex situations'.[77] Law, in other words, was closely tied to the processes by which particular perceptions and ways of interpreting the world were produced within the community of trade diplomats, and commonsense interpretive frameworks were generated and mobilized among them.

Crucially, a corollary of this is that the operation of GATT law during this time—its politics and normative orientation as expressed in actual legal practices, rather than texts—was determined in part by the specific political and social processes by which 'consensus' was formed within this diplomatic world. It was here, in these background processes through which a particular commonsense was constructed, that the structural biases and normative orientation of the legal system were contested and reproduced. The power to direct the operation of the law derived in part from the power to legitimately define a particular version of commonsense for the community.

Fourthly, the characteristic legal forms associated with this legal order were ambiguous and flexible, not only in panel reports, but also in treaty texts. Hudec describes the legal style of the period as displaying a 'sophisticated and often artistic use of ambiguity', which often seemed to 'represent a deliberate policy to avoid stating even the simplest of ideas clearly and without qualification'.[78] Ambiguity was important as a way of ensuring sufficient flexibility in the law to permit it to express whatever informal community consensus existed at any particular point in time, modulating according to circumstances. Furthermore:

> ... the ability to express ideas in this vague and cloudy manner allows the community to bring to bear whatever degree of consensus does exist. A suggestive statement, however ambiguous, provides something formal and official on which the community can focus its attitudes. The statement itself will point to the preferred result, and support expressed for that statement can create some pressure of consensus toward that end. Part of that pressure lies in the possibility that, faced with a specific case, the community may find itself willing to take a more positive stand than it has taken before. The ambiguous gesture invites such a development, and furnishes a vehicle through which it may come about.[79]

In many early GATT panel reports, then, one searches in vain for a clear statement of the law, or indeed a clear statement of the outcome of the dispute.[80] Precisely because of its structural subjection to the logics and dynamics of trade diplomacy, the GATT 'developed [legal] forms and techniques which work[ed] to suppress the

[76] ibid 630.
[77] KW Dam, *The GATT: Law and International Economic Organization* (University of Chicago Press, Chicago, IL 1970) 4, 5.
[78] Hudec (1970) 630.
[79] ibid.
[80] ibid 650.

law's natural instinct for final decisions'.[81] The intentional and functional nature of this is often under-appreciated. What has come to appear to contemporary eyes as an inadequate legal framework of imprecise and to some extent contradictory rules without clear and predictable consequences, was in fact well suited to the legal consciousness of the period. Relatively vague legal forms couched in the language of general principles gave interpreters the needed flexibility to interpret and apply the law in accordance with the spirit of the collective project which animated the regime. Indeed, it is no exaggeration to say that the legal forms contained in the GATT can only be made to make sense as a coherent whole, and can only be made operable and workable, to the extent that they are imagined and interpreted by reference to a clear understanding of the nature and purpose of the GATT, such as that provided by the ideology of embedded liberalism in the immediate post-war decades.

Finally, the overall purpose of dispute settlement in the GATT during this period was to contain trade disputes—to rebalance expectations, and to avoid escalation. This is a consistent theme of all observers of the period. Long, for example, suggests that 'the development of an understanding between the parties—or a mutually acceptable solution—is the main objective of the dispute settlement procedure'.[82] The Curzons saw the GATT as founded upon an 'unwritten credo' of maintaining a 'balance' across imports and exports between trading partners, and dispute settlement as all about the rapid restoration of that balance when it was upset.[83] This way of imagining the purpose of dispute settlement was again clearly the product of a characteristically 'embedded liberal' legal sensibility. For one thing, an instrumental or purposive view of the law meant that legal processes of dispute settlement were understood as serving the broader aims of trade diplomacy, and therefore were in large part governed by the same powerful norm of reciprocity as was the diplomatic process of the time. For another thing, if the substantive purpose of the trade regime at the time was the maintenance of international stability, and the avoidance of another protectionist trade war, then it is only natural that dispute settlement should be understood as a pragmatic process of de-escalation and mutual resolution, rather than the rigid application of juridical rules.

II. Approaches to domestic regulation in the GATT's early decades

We have seen, then, that when the post-war GATT regime was born, there existed a small GATT community whose key players shared a set of ideas about the kinds of trade policies which were and were not considered broadly acceptable, about the role that the GATT could and should play in the maintenance of the international trading system, and about the role of GATT law in the resolution of trade disputes. These shared ideas were reflected in a set of characteristic institutional forms, social

81 ibid 665.
82 Long (1985) 76.
83 Curzon and Curzon (1973) 321, see also Weinrichter (1999); Weiler (2001).

practices, and legal structures which more or less endured over the first two decades of the GATT's existence. This section examines the GATT's approach during this period to the broad issue of 'non-tariff barriers', and demonstrates that this approach was informed and structured by the shared ideas and institutional forms just described.

For the architects of the post-war international trading order, the term 'non-tariff barrier' connoted a much narrower range of governmental measures than it does today. Their immediate priority was to remove whatever remained of the more restrictive, exotic commercial policy instruments which had been put in place during the interwar period, including quotas, foreign exchange restrictions, licensing requirements, and so on.[84] As a result, Article XI of the GATT outlawed, in broadly worded terms, all 'prohibitions or restrictions other than duties, taxes or other charges, whether made effective through quotas, import or export licences or other measures'. While this provision was subject to some important exceptions—primarily those required for the purpose of maintaining domestic economic stability, as described above—it covered the bulk of these very distorting instruments, most of which were eliminated quite quickly.[85] Another set of non-tariff barriers which were of concern to post-war negotiators related to the administrative treatment of foreign products at the border, for example in respect of customs formalities and customs valuation, as well as the imposition of foreign marks of origin. These were addressed in Articles VII, VIII, and IX of the GATT.

While the focus was therefore squarely on border barriers, it was not possible entirely to ignore other forms of government action, which might be characterized as 'domestic', 'internal', or 'behind the border' in nature. The reason for this is familiar to trade lawyers, and simple enough to state: the benefits of any reduction in border barriers to trade might be entirely nullified were a country to impose internal measures which disadvantaged the ability of foreign products to compete fairly on domestic markets once they had entered the country. One category of 'internal measures' which was of particular concern for some countries during the negotiations was internal taxes and charges.[86] As a result, Article III:2 of the GATT contained an obligation not to use internal taxes and charges to discriminate against imported products:

> The products of the territory of any contracting party imported into the territory of any other contracting party shall not be subject, directly or indirectly, to internal taxes or other internal charges of any kind in excess of those applied, directly or indirectly, to like domestic products. Moreover, no contracting party shall otherwise apply internal taxes or other internal charges to imported or domestic products in a manner contrary to the principles set forth in paragraph 1.[87]

[84] See above p193 and surrounding; also Preeg (1970) 24.

[85] Currency exchange restrictions were addressed in the Articles of Agreement of the IMF rather than in the GATT.

[86] Hudec (1990) 126.

[87] For a drafting history of the text, see DA Irwin, PC Mavroïdis and AO Sykes, *The Genesis of the GATT* (CUP, Cambridge 2008) 138ff.

This was supported by Article I, which extended the MFN non-discrimination norm to measures covered by Article III:2. A second specific category of internal measures of interest to some negotiators was local mixing and local content requirements. Although a prohibition of these measures was strongly resisted by developing countries in negotiations over the Havana Charter,[88] a provision to that effect was included in both the Charter, and in Article III:5 of the GATT.[89] Negotiations over two other kinds of internal measures did not result in clear disciplines, even though both could affect trade very significantly: anti-dumping duties and domestic subsidies. As Jackson has noted, disciplines on subsidies posed specific problems, in part because there was no clear consensus among the Contracting Parties on where the line should be drawn between 'justifiable government policies on the one hand, and policies that constitute a dangerous and improper attempt to export one's own problems' on the other, and in part because it was recognized that subsidies were a preferable policy as compared to tariffs and quotas.[90] In the end, the 1947 text placed very few, if any, substantive restrictions on the ability of states to put in place domestic subsidies.[91]

But the negotiators also knew that these specific categories of internal measures did not exhaust the range of possible measures that governments could put in place to undermine their obligations under the GATT. Indeed, as noted in Chapter 6, since virtually all actions of a government in and around its domestic market have some direct or indirect impact on trade, this range of possible measures is limitless, and it is impossible to specify in advance what they might be.[92] Drawing on similar efforts during the interwar years,[93] the drafters of the GATT therefore developed a three-pronged strategy to address trade-restrictive internal measures as they arose. The first prong was to apply the two non-discrimination norms to *all* internal law and regulations which had an impact on trade. Thus, the national treatment norm was given general application to internal measures in Article III:4:

> The products of the territory of any contracting party imported into the territory of any other contracting party shall be accorded treatment no less favourable than that accorded to like products of national origin in respect of all laws, regulations and requirements affecting their internal sale, offering for sale, purchase, transportation, distribution or use.

The MFN norm was extended to the same category of measures by Article I:1. Secondly, these norms were then subject to the provisions of Articles III:8(a), XX, and XXI, which provided for exceptions for governmental procurement, as well as

[88] Brown (1950) 108–9.

[89] Art III:5 states: 'No contracting party shall establish or maintain any internal quantitative regulation relating to the mixture, processing or use of products in specified amounts or proportions which requires, directly or indirectly, that any specified amount or proportion of any product which is the subject of the regulation must be supplied from domestic sources. Moreover, no contracting party shall otherwise apply internal quantitative regulations in a manner contrary to the principles set forth in paragraph 1.'

[90] See generally Jackson (1969) 367.

[91] GATT, Arts XVI and III:8(b); Curzon and Curzon (1976) 195.

[92] Hudec (1990) 24.

[93] ibid, Hudec (1970) 617.

for governmental measures for a range of legitimate purposes, including the protection of national security, the protection of animal and human health, the conservation of exhaustible natural resources, and so on. Then, thirdly, in apparent recognition of the fact that even this flexible legal framework might not have been adaptable enough to respond adequately to all future challenges, a mechanism was created through which any Contracting Party could complain if it 'should consider that any benefit accruing to it directly or indirectly under [the GATT] is being nullified or impaired' as the result of 'the application by another contracting party of any measure, *whether or not it conflicts with the provisions of this Agreement*'.[94] This clause had come to be included as a standard part of trade agreements during the years leading up to the Second World War,[95] and it was included in the GATT on the basis that it would permit the Contracting Parties to respond flexibly to any new situation which might upset the careful balance set out in the agreement.[96]

It takes only a moment's reflection to see how broad and intrusive these disciplines had the potential to be. Putting to one side for a moment the limited carve-outs and exceptions described above, there is little in these provisions which a priori excludes any kind of domestic governmental actions from GATT oversight, even those which apparently have nothing directly to do with trade policy.[97] The non-discrimination norms apply to all 'laws, regulations or requirements' which affect the 'internal sale, offering for sale, purchase, transportation, distribution or use' of foreign goods. There is nothing in the text which limits this to direct or significant effects, and certainly nothing which limits it to measures explicitly targeted at imports.[98] There are few aspects of fiscal and monetary policy, employment policy, industrial policy, controls on capital flow, even labour regulation and immigration controls which could not be brought within this definition with a minimum of creative thinking. Moreover, as we shall see in the next chapter, these non-discrimination norms can in principle have significant substantive bite, particularly where they are interpreted as prohibiting *de facto*, indirect or even merely accidental and fortuitous discrimination between products in the marketplace. Furthermore, for its part, the nullification and impairment clause had perhaps an even greater scope of potential application. As the South African delegate noted in the negotiations over the equivalent provision in the Havana Charter, it had the effect, at least in practice, of giving an international institution the power to declare new obligations where none existed before:[99]

It appears to me that what it says is this: In this wide world of sin there are certain sins which we have not yet discovered and which after long examination we cannot define; but there being such sins, we will provide some sort of punishment for them *if* we find out what they are and

[94] Art XXIII:1(b) (emphasis added).

[95] Hudec (1990) 24; Hudec (1970) 617 and surrounding.

[96] Hudec (1990) 40.

[97] For another view of the tremendous formal breadth of these provisions see JW Evans, *The Kennedy Round in American trade policy: the twilight of the GATT?* (Harvard University Press, Cambridge, MA 1971) 87; see also Hudec (1990) 121 (who describes them as 'virtually unlimited in scope').

[98] See Panel Report, *Italian Discrimination Against Imported Agricultural Machinery* (adopted 23 October 1958) BISD 7S/60 (L/833) paras 12–15.

[99] See Hudec (1990) 39.

> if we find anybody committing them . . . seeing that there are such sins, and in spite of the fact that we do not know what they are, and in spite of the fact that we do not know under what circumstances we are going to apply any punishment to them, we shall still provide a sort of vague and general 'sword of Damocles', if such a thing is possible, to hang over the heads of all the people who may possibly commit this sin.[100]

As a matter of purely textual interpretation, it is hard to argue with this characterization.

Why, then, did the Contracting Parties find themselves able to agree to these provisions, despite their potentially serious limitations on sovereignty? The answer, in short, was that the Contracting Parties themselves could be trusted not to abuse this power—'it would be a very great pity if we could not trust an international organization formed out of our own membership to interpret this clause intelligently and with sufficient discretion'[101]—and that in any case the dispute settlement mechanism ultimately rested on soft enforcement mechanisms. The workability and acceptability of these potentially intrusive mechanisms, in other words, was founded on the existence of a broadly shared informal consensus as to the 'meaning and purpose of the GATT',[102] as well as a set of institutions which ensured that this consensus could practically shape the interpretation and application of GATT law. This gave negotiators comfort that the virtually limitless formal application of GATT disciplines to domestic regulation would in practice be kept within strictly limited and reasonable boundaries.[103]

This expectation proved, more or less, to be well founded. This shared consensus as to the meaning and purpose of the GATT—itself deeply informed by the normative framework of embedded liberalism, as described above—helped to ensure that, of all the different internal governmental actions which influenced trade flows during the first two decades of the GATT's existence, only a few very specific categories were made visible as barriers to trade, and brought before dispute settlement. The remainder were implicitly understood to be normal or background regulation, never intended to be subject to GATT oversight. Thus, of the sixty-two formal GATT disputes which Hudec lists as occurring during the first two decades of the GATT's existence,[104] twenty-four involved traditional border barriers (quantitative restrictions and tariff charges and one case involving export fee). While 'internal' measures therefore constituted over half of the disputes, virtually all of these cases were brought in relation to internal measures of the kind which were specifically raised in the context of negotiations over the GATT 1947, and which were therefore already clearly acknowledged by these negotiators as trade barriers,

[100] UN Economic and Social Council, 'Verbatim Report of the Preparatory Committee of the UN Conference on Trade and Employment' (26 June 1947) UN Doc E/PC/T/B/PV/33, cited in Hudec (1990) 42.

[101] Cited in Hudec (1990) 41. The reference to an 'international organization' is explained by the fact that this statement was made in the context of Havana Charter negotiations.

[102] ibid 297; Howse (2002) 97.

[103] See Hudec (1990) 41ff.

[104] ibid 302ff; see also RE Hudec, *Enforcing International Trade Law: The Evolution of the Modern GATT Legal System* (Butterworth Legal Publishers, Salem, NH 1993) 375ff.

and made visible as such. Thus, of these thirty-eight disputes about internal measures, fifteen were brought in respect of internal tax measures, eleven involved export subsidies, three related to trade remedies actions, and five to domestic subsidies. Only three related to domestic measures of a miscellaneous kind, none of which produced a panel report: the first being a dispute about a Hawaiian law requiring all vendors of foreign eggs to display a sign to that effect; the second involving Greek credit facilities; and the third relating to pricing practices of a British government-owned steel industry.[105] Although it is true that some of the disputes about internal taxes and domestic subsidies raised real questions about whether the specific measure in dispute was of the kind which was intended to be covered by the GATT, it is nevertheless significant that the vast bulk of all disputes were brought in respect of categories of measures which were already understood as serious trade barriers at the time that the GATT was negotiated, and legitimately within its purview. In this respect, Hudec also finds it noteworthy that the application of GATT disciplines in the regime's early years focused on practices which were 'major target[s] of postwar commercial policy reforms, so that transgressions in . . . these areas might have appeared to be of greater than normal significance'.[106]

There are, to be sure, other reasons why the practical scope of application of GATT disciplines was kept in relatively limited bounds during these years, and was not extended to the kinds of measures which are now routinely brought before WTO dispute settlement. It has been argued, for example, that other kinds of 'behind the border' barriers were not in existence during that time, or at least were commercially insignificant, so there was simply no pressing need to bring such cases. It has also been suggested that claims were not brought in respect of certain measures because they were not subject to effective GATT discipline, so that a claim against them was less likely to succeed and therefore to be brought. Nevertheless, while these reasons are part of the explanation, they do not provide an adequate account on their own. It is clear that many 'behind the border' barriers which have only recently become subject to more frequent dispute resolution—such as labelling requirements, or food safety restrictions—already existed at this time in many countries.[107] On the question of commercial significance, Hudec notes that a significant proportion of GATT disputes were brought in respect of measures which had only minor commercial significance.[108] Moreover, it is not clear on the evidence that non-tariff barriers actually *were* commercially insignificant during this period, even as compared to two decades later.[109] As to their amenability to effective GATT discipline, this explanation must deal with the problem of the broad formal scope of GATT disciplines

[105] See Hudec (1990) 312 (No 37), 314 (No 48), 318 (No 62). The one dispute not counted in this breakdown (of the 38) is Panel Report, *Uruguay—Recourse to Article XXIII* (adopted 16 November 1962) BISD 11S/95 (L/1923).

[106] Hudec (1990) 106.

[107] See Brown (1950) 35; Curtis and Vastine (1971) 4, 202; Evans (1971) 87ff.

[108] Hudec (1990) 103–5.

[109] Evans (1971) 307–9.

described above, as well as the fact that eleven disputes were brought in respect of export subsidies, notwithstanding the lack of effective discipline on such measures.

One of my claims, then, is that the limited practical scope of application of the GATT during these years was in significant part the result of informal understandings among those in the GATT community about its limited legitimate scope of scrutiny.[110] These understandings were in turn the product of a number of features of the field described above: generally shared views that many different kinds of highly interventionist domestic policies were 'normal'; an orientation towards stability and the containment of disputes which left GATT diplomats disinclined to test the boundaries of the non-discrimination provisions if to do so risked destabilizing trade relations and trespassing on jealously guarded domestic policy priorities; the structural embedding of the GATT's legal system within the world of trade diplomacy and the separation of the world of trade diplomacy from that of 'high politics'; and a prevailing view that the law ought properly to be interpreted and applied in accordance with the norms and expectations of that world. These orientations produced a field of trade law and policy which was narrowly defined (relative to the present day), focused on tariffs and other kinds of trade measures understood at the time as quantitative restrictions, and unwilling to scrutinize 'internal' measures except in the clearest circumstances of circumvention of liberalization commitments. Even if it was recognized that internal regulation could pose problems for traders, that fact alone did not make all such regulation a proper subject of strict oversight within the international trade regime. I shall return to this claim when I address the unsuccessful turn to internal non-tariff barriers in the Kennedy Round, below.

My second claim is that these informal norms and expectations circulating among trade diplomats and others in the trade regime also deeply shaped the *interpretation* of GATT disciplines in those disputes involving internal regulations.[111] When GATT panels were asked to judge and declare the permissibility of domestic regulations which were the subject of dispute, they did so by reference to a variety of overlapping standards, including backgrounds norms concerning reasonable or normal domestic regulation, particularly among its most powerful actors,[112] as well as informal understandings of what the drafters 'meant to say'.[113] The interpretation of these norms therefore came to reflect a broader inclination of the Contracting Parties to limit the potentially constraining impact of GATT disciplines on their domestic regulation, especially where such constraint would work against their shared substantive political commitment to domestic interventionism to safeguard to economic stability and the welfare of their populations.[114] Thus, they developed an approach to the non-discrimination norm which focused primarily on *de jure*

[110] For similar arguments, see Howse (2002); R Wai, 'Countering, Branding, Dealing: Using Economic and Social Rights in and around the International Trade Regime' (2003) 14 EJIL 35, 46.

[111] With this claim, I am following Hudec (1990); Hudec (1970); Howse (2002).

[112] Hudec (1990) 131–2.

[113] See also Curzon (1965) 322: 'the "philosophy" of an agreement provides a measure by which an individual country's action is judged to be "good" or "bad"'.

[114] JL Dunoff, '"Trade and": Recent Developments in Trade Policy and Scholarship—And Their Surprising Political Implications' (1997) 17 Northwestern J of Intl L and Business 759; JL Dunoff,

discrimination and discriminatory intent as the primary criterion of illegality. And they developed an approach to 'nullification and impairment' which focused on the reasonable expectations of the parties to negotiations.

A number of the early cases on internal tax and subsidy measures can serve as illustrations of these basic dynamics.[115] In August 1948, during the meeting of the Second Session of the GATT Contracting Parties, the Chairman was asked by Pakistan's delegate to make a ruling concerning the application of Article I to an Indian measure, according to which an excise tax on domestic products was rebated to the producer if the goods were exported to any country other than Pakistan. The Chairman was quick to rule that Article I was indeed applicable to the measure, and had a strong textual basis for doing so. Article I by its terms applied to all measures covered by 'paragraphs 2 and 4 of Article III', and it was certainly arguable that this was an internal taxation measure covered by Article III:2, even though it related to exports. To the extent that some textual ambiguity existed, this was easily disregarded. In Hudec's words:

> The Chairman was, after all, one of the authors of the text in question. And so, for that matter, were most of the Secretariat officials and the other delegates in the room. No matter how hard they might try to look at the bare text alone in this situation, it was inevitable that everyone's interpretation would be dominated by their own highly authoritative recollection of what they 'had meant to say'.[116]

This is hardly surprising, nor perhaps is it particularly noteworthy that an international legal text is being interpreted in the light of the clear intentions of its authors. What is more interesting, though, is that subsequent discussion of this matter, including in the context of the drafting of a clarifying amendment to Article I, proceeded on the basis that while paragraph 2 language applied to exports as well as imports, paragraph 4 language did not.[117] This is a perfectly understandable premise, as to have decided otherwise 'would have been to impose (or recognize) an obligation of enormous reach, with little practical utility'.[118] But it had no textual basis. In the end, as Hudec has argued, what was guiding the Contracting Parties in this context was not so much their recollection of what they meant to say—'it is unlikely that they had ever really considered the question of exports at all'[119]—but rather a 'fairly clear, coherent and authoritative consensus about the policy and purposes of the General Agreement'.[120] Here, that consensus proved strong enough to override the clear terms of the text, with the effect of limiting its constraining effect.

'Rethinking International Trade' (1998) 19 University of Pennsylvania J of Intl Economic L 347; JL Dunoff, 'The Death of the Trade Regime' (1999) 10 EJIL 733.

[115] The following pages draw heavily on Hudec (1990) and Hudec (1970).
[116] Hudec (1990) 116.
[117] Hudec (1990) 120.
[118] ibid 121.
[119] ibid.
[120] ibid.

The following year, the French delegate complained about a Brazilian internal taxation measure which imposed taxes on certain imported luxury products at a rate double that imposed on like domestic products. Since this measure was already in place when the GATT was signed, it was permitted. But was it permitted for Brazil to raise the underlying tax rate, such that the absolute tax differential between imported and domestic products was massively increased, even though the former were still taxed at double the rate of the latter? The text was not clear. A Working Party was formed, which included Brazil, France, the United Kingdom, and the United States among its seven members. The latter three countries—at that stage clearly the first among equals within the GATT regime—were evidently of the view that Brazil's actions were prohibited, but Brazil would not concede the legal point. Although this stalemate was not formally resolved by the report of the Working Party, the reality was clear:

> Brazil's legal position was unlikely to be accepted by the Contracting Parties, and Brazil must have known this. The line-up on the other side was simply too overpowering. The Big Three were quite sure of their position, and, having virtually written the General Agreement and the Protocol themselves, their views would carry the greatest weight. The Secretariat was equally convinced of the same view.[121]

When the matter was raised again the following year, the Working Party report was treated as if it had definitively found that Brazil's measure violated the GATT—'it is not impossible that the delegates . . . simply confused their own well-settled views on the legal issues with a not-too-well-remembered document in which those views had been expressed'[122]—and Brazil did not object. No reference was made in subsequent documentation to Brazil's legal arguments. The 'inner-group consensus seemed to be taken for granted as the authoritative word'.[123]

The *Belgian Family Allowances* case, which began with a complaint by Norway and Denmark against Belgium in 1951, concerned a tax imposed by Belgium on imported goods which were purchased by local government bodies. The purpose of the tax was to help to pay for Belgium's generous system of family allowances, by supplementing the revenue raised by a domestic payroll tax. It was levied only on those goods which came from countries which did not have a programme of family allowances equivalent to that of Belgium itself—in other words, products would be exempt from the tax if they came from a country which did have a roughly equivalent programme. The tax was therefore arguably designed (in principle at least) to help to equalize the competitive disadvantage that certain producers faced as a result of the creation of this social welfare programme. Norway and Denmark brought the complaint when, in September 1950, products from Sweden were granted an exemption while their products were not. What is interesting was that Norway and Denmark did *not* argue that the entire tax was in violation of Article I of the GATT—though that argument was certainly textually open, as the tax clearly treated identical imports from different countries differently. Instead, they accepted the

[121] ibid 126. [122] ibid. [123] ibid 131.

basic tax regime, but argued that their family allowance programmes were at least as generous as Sweden's, and that it was therefore discriminatory to grant an exemption for Swedish products, and not theirs. According to Hudec, both the complainants and the members of the Panel which was subsequently convened 'shared . . . a hunch that the real reason for the Swedish exemption had been that Sweden paid for the exemption as part of the trade agreement concessions'[124] negotiated in September 1950. When, later, the Belgian government granted a further exemption, this time to Switzerland, 'the suspicion that exemptions were being sold for commercial advantages was, rightly or wrongly, confirmed' within the GATT.[125]

It is not clear why Denmark and Norway argued their case on the narrower ground, rather than simply arguing that the measure as a whole was discriminatory.[126] It may have been that they simply wished to have access to the benefit of the exemption, as a commercial matter. It may have been that the justice of the situation was clearer on the narrower ground. Outlawing a tax genuinely designed to financially and politically support an important domestic programme of social welfare may just have been a step too far, particularly if other countries might have wished to keep open that policy themselves. Where a discriminatory *intention* existed, however, a finding of a violation of Article I was clear. In the end, the Panel produced a report which could be read as endorsing either the broader or the narrower proposition.[127]

But what is clear is that the broad perception that a discriminatory intent was behind the Belgian measure was crucial to mobilizing community opinion within the GATT against the Belgian measure. In this respect, the case is reflective of a broader tendency in the GATT's early years to treat intention as, in practice, the critical element of a claim of discrimination.[128] The few disputes arising under Articles I and III at this time overwhelmingly concerned direct and explicit discrimination. In practice, then, and despite its somewhat ambiguous and indeterminate formal face, the non-discrimination norm seems to have been understood to be there to prohibit directly discriminatory regulation—rather than other forms of regulation which incidentally or indirectly undermined the commercial opportunities available to foreign products, which as we shall see became much more commonly the subject of dispute settlement later on.

Finally, it is worth referring briefly to a brace of decisions which illustrate the importance which panels tended to attach to norms and expectations internal to the community of GATT diplomats in reaching their conclusions, and the easy

124 ibid 141.

125 Hudec (1970) 661.

126 This may also have been because the Belgian law was from 1939, and mandatory pre-GATT legislation which would otherwise be inconsistent with the GATT was grandfathered by the Protocol of Provisional Application. For a careful and considered review of Hudec's analysis of this case, see S Charnovitz, 'Belgian Family Allowances and the challenge of origin-based discrimination' (2005) 4 World Trade Rev 7.

127 Hudec (1970) 650ff.

128 Hudec (1978) 61, n 113 notes this tendency in respect of subsidy claims. It is worth noting that no examples exist of a finding of *de facto* discrimination in early GATT cases, in the absence of a fairly clear indication of discriminatory intent.

familiarity with which they evoked such norms. *Australia—Ammonium Sulfate* concerned an Australian decision to remove a subsidy on particular kinds of fertilizer, which were predominantly imported, while maintaining it for others, which were predominantly locally produced. In discussing whether the two products were 'like' one another for the purposes of Article I of the GATT, the Working Party noted that the two products were given different tariff classifications not only by Australia but also by many other countries around the world, and on that basis considered the products unlike one another.[129] Tariff classifications here represented the best evidence available to the Working Party of the beliefs and expectations of those within the field of trade policy and diplomacy about whether these two products could legitimately be treated differently.[130] The same case also involved a nullification and impairment claim, and the Working Party took the opportunity to limit such claims to measures which 'could not reasonably have been anticipated by' the relevant parties at the time of the negotiations. The fact that the Working Party felt confident in evoking the notion of reasonable anticipation 'is just one more indication of the closely knit consensus on which the early GATT system rested'.[131] Then, in *Germany—Sardines*, the Panel again looked to expectations within the diplomatic community for guidance on the question of the 'likeness' of different species of sardine, noting that:

> ... it would be sufficient to consider whether in the conduct of the negotiations at Torquay the two parties agreed expressly or tacitly to treat these preparations as if they were 'like products'.[132]

Although this tendency to look for guidance to norms circulating within the field of trade policy and diplomacy became less overt over time, it was a pervasive and to some extent enduring characteristic of GATT legal interpretation on the issue of 'likeness' during this period.

Overall, then, what we see during the first decades of the GATT's existence is a modest and limited approach to the disciplining of 'internal' barriers to trade, or what we now call 'domestic regulation'. The kinds of measures which were the subject of complaint were by and large limited to those which had a direct and immediate impact on trade. They were also confined primarily to those kinds of measures which the negotiators of the GATT had clearly and explicitly understood to be potential targets of discipline. Moreover, the non-discrimination norm tended to be applied in practice only in cases of *de jure* discrimination against imports, or in those cases where a clear protectionist or discriminatory intent was either manifest or

[129] Working Party Report, *The Australian Subsidy on Ammonium Sulphate* (3 April 1950) BISD II/188 (GATT/CP.4/39) para 8.

[130] For a similar interpretation of the reason for drawing on tariff classifications in the context of Art I, see generally RE Hudec, '"Like Products": The Differences in Meaning in GATT Articles I and III' in T Cottier and P Mavroïdis (eds), *Regulatory Barriers and the Principle of Non-Discrimination in World Trade Law* (University of Michigan Press, Ann Arbor, MI 2000) 101.

[131] Hudec (1990) 167.

[132] Panel Report, *Treatment by Germany of Imports of Sardines* (31 October 1952) BISD IS/53 (G/26) para 12.

strongly suspected. Although this modest approach excluded from oversight a great deal of government intervention and policy which affected trade flows in very significant (if indirect) ways, it was very much in keeping with the 'spirit' of embedded liberalism described in the first part of this chapter. Recall that the purpose of the trade regime at that time was commonly understood in relatively limited terms: to avoid a repeat of the trade wars of the early 1930s and to reverse the proliferation of the kinds of restrictive non-tariff measures which were instituted during that period, and more generally to provide stability in international commercial relations, as a precondition for the achievement of domestic economic stability and full employment. The general disciplines which the GATT imposed on internal measures were understood to play a supportive role only. They were there to ensure that the careful bargain which was struck in relation to traditional trade restrictions could be resurrected and restabilized if it was undermined by an internal measure which the GATT Contracting Parties saw as illegitimate. To use the non-discrimination norms to reshape domestic state–market relations more actively, by challenging all forms of internal governmental intervention which indirectly affected conditions of competition on the domestic market, went well beyond what was understood to be the purpose of the GATT. More than that, too intrusive an application of GATT disciplines on internal regulation would *undermine* that purpose, as it would run the risk of itself upsetting the delicate balance of concessions embodied in the original agreement, and undermining support for the trading system as a whole. Moreover, extending the GATT's scope of application to matters of domestic political sensitivity would risk undermining the clear mutual separation which the trade community was so careful to maintain during this period, between 'technical' issues of trade policy on the one hand, and issues relating to 'high politics' on the other. As noted above, the institutional and social insulation of the trade field was itself a functional expression of the priority given to international stability in the context of embedded liberalism.

Thus, while the substantive spirit of embedded liberalism produced a limited understanding of the meaning and purpose of the GATT's disciplines on internal measures, the flexible institutional and legal forms associated with embedded liberalism ensured that this limited vision governed the operation of those disciplines in practice. The flexibility and ambiguity of the text, the structural embeddedness of the dispute settlement system in the world of trade diplomacy, and the emergence of an interpretive style which placed greatest weight on the shared norms and expectations of the diplomatic community, all ensured that the limiting informal norms of the trade community itself counted more than the formal breadth of the text. This was tolerable to the GATT's commercial constituencies—primarily domestic exporting firms seeking greater access to foreign markets—because the work that the GATT was doing in reducing tariffs and other border barriers was still commercially highly significant for these firms, even if it was less so than some might have liked. As trade and economic activity rapidly expanded in the post-war decades, the shared prosperity it produced temporarily muted any concerns that some of these actors might have had about the GATT's self-consciously limited vision.

Already by the middle of the 1960s, however, the material and political basis for this shared vision was beginning to erode.[133] The formation of the European Economic Community in the late 1950s provided a substantial counterweight to the political and economic dominance of the United States, and represented a 'new and more powerful force in GATT affairs, with goals and objectives that had not been anticipated in the original GATT blueprint'.[134] During the 1960s, intense import competition from low-cost products, especially from an emerging Japan which was gaining dominance in sectors such as textiles and clothing, placed pressure on the ability of industrialized states to maintain their commitment to the substantive bargain embodied in the GATT. Recessions in the United States and elsewhere at the beginning and end of the 1960s, intensified this pressure to some degree. The emergence of more and more developing countries as members of the GATT also put significant pressure on the regime, as described in Chapter 2. At the same time, the immediate fear of a repeat of the trade wars of the 1930s was waning.[135]

As a result of all these developments, the substantive policy consensus underlying the GATT 1947 itself began to erode. More and more legal obligations contained in the GATT appeared unsuitable for contemporary economic problems and priorities, and increasingly countries turned to measures which violated at least the letter of the original agreement. The emergence of the EEC and other regional trade agreements, for example, seriously undermined Article XXIV as a meaningful source of constraint and oversight of preferential arrangements. Developing countries as a whole were exempted from many of the most significant GATT disciplines, and both agricultural trade and trade in textiles and clothing were essentially removed from normal GATT discipline.

Ruggie has rightly argued that many of these measures, and those which followed during the economic turmoil of the 1970s, represented attempts to resurrect the spirit of embedded liberalism—that is, to find new tools and techniques to maintain the same basic compromise between domestic and international stability in transformed economic conditions.[136] But at the same time, it is also true that this period saw the beginning of the erosion of embedded liberalism, and the start of a shift in the relative dominance of the different philosophies which had always been present and in tension within the GATT system. Certainly, by the 1970s, it was possible to talk of a 'schism in [the] sense of common purpose' underlying the regime.[137]

It will come as no surprise that, just as the shared political commitment to embedded liberalism began to erode, there were significant efforts to shift the focus of the GATT's attention to domestic regulation, and to describe more areas of governmental activity as potential obstacles to international trade. Non-tariff

[133] D Harvey, *A Brief History of Neoliberalism* (OUP, Oxford 2007) 12ff.
[134] Hudec (1990) 211.
[135] ibid.
[136] Ruggie (1982); JG Ruggie, 'Embedded Liberalism Revisited: Institutions and Progress in International Economic Relations' in E Adler and B Crawford (eds), *Progress in Postwar International Relations* (Columbia University Press, New York, NY 1991) 202.
[137] Hudec (1990) 297.

barriers had become increasingly visible to exporters as barriers to access to foreign markets, and some began to agitate for their inclusion on the GATT agenda. These efforts were most powerful within the United States. As that country found its economic dominance increasingly challenged, and as its trade balance deteriorated towards the second half of the 1960s, the claim became increasingly common that US exports were unfairly and disproportionately hindered by foreign non-tariff barriers that had not been subject to removal through the GATT.[138] As a result, numerous publications began to emerge which identified and categorized a range of non-tariff barriers which had either never been 'recognized' before, or had received very little attention in practice within post-war trade policy circles.[139] These included: labelling requirements; safety standards for farm machinery; inspection requirements for imported seeds and livestock; sanitation and health standards; testing requirements for drugs; consumer and environmental protection standards; government subsidy of research and development; border tax adjustments; government procurement practices; differential application of domestic regulations; and even the mere fact of disparate standards in different foreign markets.[140] By the late 1960s, these efforts had gained some traction within the United States, where the above measures were all regularly included in standard lists of non-tariff barriers produced at the time—a term which had by now taken on an entirely different meaning from that understood just two decades earlier.[141] In addition, it had become received wisdom, especially in Washington political circles and more broadly within the US trade policy community, that these non-tariff barriers had become the most commercially significant barriers to US exports, and that sooner or later it was imperative that the GATT should address them if it was to continue to have American support.[142] The proliferation of such barriers, it was said, had upset the balance of concessions which formed the heart of the post-war agreement.

But incorporating internal non-tariff barriers of this sort on the GATT agenda proved to be difficult. In significant part as a result of US action on the issue, the GATT Ministerial Declarations in 1963—the year before the commencement of the Kennedy Round—asked the GATT's Trade Negotiations Committee to set 'rules to govern and methods to be employed in the treatment of non-tariff barriers'.[143] However, the concept of 'non-tariff barrier' was not defined, and in the end the

[138] See Evans (1971) 304ff.

[139] 'Administrative and Technical Regulations: The Lesser Known Obstacles to Trade', *The OECD Observer*, No 4, June 1963; MS Massel, *Non-tariff barriers as an obstacle to world trade* (Brookings Institution, Washington, DC 1965); WB Kelly, Jr, 'Non-Tariff Barriers' in BA Balassa and ME Kreinin (eds), *Studies in International Trade Liberalization: Problems and Prospects for the Industrial Countries* (Johns Hopkins Press, Baltimore, MA 1967) 265–314; R Baldwin, *Non-Tariff Distortions of International Trade* (George Allen & Unwin, Sydney 1970); Curtis and Vastine (1971) 202ff; Evans (1971) 86ff. Much significant work was done in the OECD, see Curzon and Curzon (1975) 312.

[140] These examples are taken from the material cited in n 139 above.

[141] See below pp 223ff.

[142] Though it is clear that their commercial significance was increasing, Evans (1971) 307–9 disputes the factual basis for this strong claim.

[143] Cited in Curtis and Vastine (1971) 204. There had been an earlier attempt to include non-tariff barriers in the Dillon Round which had been resoundingly rejected by the EEC, see Kock (1969) 101.

Kennedy Round only dealt with a limited number of specific internal measures. Perhaps most significantly, this round of negotiations produced the International Anti-Dumping Code, which was effectively an embryonic international standard for the drafting of domestic anti-dumping laws, and provided something of a model for the subsequent codes negotiated during the Tokyo Round.[144] Apart from that, however, there were only piecemeal negotiations on isolated individual measures. The United States agreed to remove its 'American Selling Price' regulation, whereby customs duties on a small range of goods were levied on a base determined by the price of domestic competitor goods.[145] In return, a number of European countries agreed to modify their systems of road tax, which imposed a higher tax burden on large vehicles of the kind used and sold by American companies.[146] But even these agreements did not survive scrutiny by the US Congress, which vetoed the two non-tariff barrier agreements which imposed restrictions on US trade legislation and policy. A number of major non-tariff issues raised during the course of negotiations were hardly addressed at all, perhaps the most prominent being the problem of how border tax adjustments should be dealt with appropriately under the GATT, in the light of a recent rethinking of the theory underpinning the original GATT compromise on the issue.[147] All in all, the results of the Kennedy Round in respect of non-tariff barriers are generally agreed to have been meagre.

A number of different reasons have been offered to explain the reluctance of GATT negotiators to take up internal non-tariff barriers at this time. Gerard and Victoria Curzon argue that incorporating negotiations on non-tariff barriers did not fit comfortably with the self-consciously 'self-contained' nature of trade negotiations, and was initially resented by some as an illegitimate linkage of trade issues with issues outside the traditional field of trade.[148] They also suggest that the inclusion of non-tariff barriers was made more difficult by the strength of the norm of reciprocity: rules on non-tariff barriers made it more difficult for negotiators to assess the degree of reciprocity in a negotiated package, as it was not clear who would benefit from the inclusion of a new general discipline on a particular kind of domestic regulation, and by how much.[149] This was particularly the case since the incidence of non-tariff barriers was not equally distributed among participants in the Kennedy Round, making reciprocity an even trickier issue to assess and manage. But perhaps most importantly, it mattered a great deal that there was simply no substantive agreement at the level of policy about what counted as an illegitimate obstacle to trade, and what was a legitimate domestic regulation.[150] Since these measures had not been part of the original bargain struck by the post-war architects, and since it had never been the purpose of the GATT to subject them to strict oversight, GATT participants had no

144 Preeg (1970) 166ff; Curtis and Vastine (1971) 205ff.
145 Evans (1971) 90ff.
146 Curtis and Vastine (1971) 204; Curzon and Curzon (1976) 191–2.
147 Preeg (1970) 135–6; Curtis and Vastine (1971) 235; Hudec (1990) 231–2; Evans (1971) 95ff.
148 Curzon and Curzon (1976) 163.
149 ibid 164; Evans (1971) 256–7; Finlayson and Zacher (1981) 575; Weinrichter (1999) 3.
150 Evans (1971) 256, 260.

shared view as to the nature of normal or appropriate regulation in these new areas, nor any collectively authorized forms of knowledge or principles of evaluation by which to create and legitimate such a shared view.

Precisely the same problems made GATT dispute settlement ill-suited to address disputes over non-tariff barriers. Hudec argues that the erosion of the substantive policy consensus underlying the post-war GATT regime was one of the most significant reasons that GATT dispute settlement was hardly used at all from 1963 to the end of that decade.[151] Since, as described above, dispute settlement worked precisely by mobilizing and reflecting that community consensus among trade diplomats, it was not equipped for situations in which such underlying consensus did not exist or could not be subtly manufactured. This was paradigmatically the case with respect to non-tariff barriers. Precisely because the dispute settlement system had been imagined in purposive terms as an instrument of collective purpose, and had as a result been deeply embedded within the diplomatic world, it was singularly poorly equipped to play the role of objective and neutral arbiter in difficult disputes about internal non-tariff barriers.

What the experience of non-tariff barrier negotiations in the Kennedy Round makes clear, then, is that the trade regime's turn to 'behind the border' barriers during the late 1960s and 1970s was not simply the continuation of its old agenda in new areas—as if dealing with the problems caused by internal regulations was simply the next stage of a single process of trade liberalization which had begun in the post-war era with tariff and non-tariff border barriers. The collective ideas, norms, social structures, and institutions which had been created during the embedded liberal period acted as an obstacle to the scrutiny of internal measures, not as a prelude to such scrutiny. Thus, if the trade regime were to address internal non-tariff barriers in a serious and rigorous way, it would require a root-and-branch transformation of the regime—a re-imagining of the economic and political purposes for which it existed, a new definition of the problems it was designed to address, a new understanding of the proper role and function of law in the achievement of those purposes, and a new set of institutions and social practices to reflect this new collective project. In the end, this transformation was at least two decades in the making, and came to fruition only with the Uruguay Round of negotiations. The story of this transformation is taken up in the next chapter.

[151] Hudec (1990) 287ff; Hudec (1978) 43; Long (1985) 88; see also Jackson (1969) 759.

8

Neoliberalism and the Formal-Technical Turn

Launched in 1973 and finally concluding in 1979, the Tokyo Round of trade negotiations was conducted against the backdrop of significant global economic turmoil. Inflation had begun to emerge as a major domestic concern in many Western nations as early as the second half of the 1960s, in part as the result of rising governmental expenditure without a concomitant rise in taxation.[1] Inflation in turn had affected the value of currencies, putting pressure on the post-war international monetary system of pegged exchange rates, and ultimately prompting the United States in 1971 to suspend the convertibility of the dollar into gold other than at open market rates. The first oil shock of 1973, as well as the instability of international commodity markets more generally, helped to usher in a period of slow or negative growth, high inflation, and levels of unemployment not seen for decades.[2] The seemingly inexorable march of economic progress and prosperity, which by and large had characterized the two decades after the end of the Second World War, was replaced by widespread concern about the ability of the international economic system to produce sustained growth.

One response of some governments to this new and disturbing international economic environment was to re-assert their commitment to embedded liberalism, and buttress it with new policy measures. In this spirit, a range of new protective instruments was established and elaborated to shield domestic economies from the destabilizing influence of international trade. The most notorious of these new measures were so-called 'voluntary export restraints', which were informal intergovernmental agreements according to which exporting states and their firms agreed voluntarily to limit their exports to foreign markets. But these measures were also accompanied by orderly marketing arrangements of all kinds, a much more expansive use of safeguards and restrictions for balance of payments purposes, minimum price agreements, import surcharges, prior import deposits, and many other measures of dubious legality under the GATT, but operating in practice outside its

[1] GR Winham, *International Trade and the Tokyo Round Negotiations* (Princeton University Press, Princeton, NJ 1986) 5.

[2] S Golt, *The GATT Negotiations, 1973–79. The Closing Stage and A Policy Statement by the British North American Committee—The GATT Negotiations, 1973–79: The Closing Stage* (The British–North American Committee, London 1978) 4.

purview.[3] As a number of observers have persuasively argued, the rise of this 'New Protectionism' did not by any means reflect a wholesale rejection of the ideal of an open international trading order, but rather an attempt to maintain the core political and economic priorities associated with the embedded liberal compromise in the face of a transformed international economic environment.[4] These new trade restrictions, in other words, were largely pursued and imagined as useful and temporary instruments 'for orderly adaptation to economic change', to 'minimize disruption and facilitate adjustment in industries that [were] being severely affected by imports'.[5] They were attempts to protect and continue domestic full employment policies in the face of international economic forces which were undermining them, while still maintaining a real commitment to open trade where possible, at least in the long term.

Another response, however, was to turn away from embedded liberalism. Without question, the economic turmoil of the 1970s helped to erode political support for the normative priorities of embedded liberalism, both within the trade regime and more broadly in the domestic politics of its Contracting Parties. It helped to provide the conditions for the re-emergence and re-strengthening of a purer form of economic liberalism—neoliberalism—which emphasized the freeing of markets as the primary strategy for growth and prosperity. On this view, the most important priorities of government in response to economic disruption and stagnation should be to deal effectively with the problem of inflation, to allow the market system to function effectively, and to foster wealth- and job-creating private investment. Neither economic stability nor full employment figured prominently as priorities of domestic economic policy in this view, and the new wave of protectionist measures designed to support those objectives were seen as misguided and counterproductive.

In the end, the results of the Tokyo Round were a compromise between those seeking to reshape the regime in accordance with the newly invigorated ideas of economic liberalism, and those who sought to maintain its normative foundations closer to its original post-war form. But this was also a turning point in the relative dominance of these two traditions in the trade regime, inaugurating a period of at least three decades during which a purer form of economic liberalism became the more dominant ideology in international trade governance. The purpose of this chapter is to trace the impact that the rise of neoliberalism had on the institutions and practices of the international trade regime from the 1970s through to the end of the 1990s. My focus

[3] JG Ruggie, 'International Regimes, Transactions and Change: Embedded Liberalism in the Post-war Economic Order' (1982) 36 Intl Org 379 410ff; O Long, *Law and Its Limitations in the GATT Multilateral Trading System* (Martinus Nijhoff, Dordrecht 1985) 83; Winham (1986) 70ff; Golt (1978) 8.

[4] Ruggie (1982); JG Ruggie, 'Embedded Liberalism Revisited: Institutions and Progress in International Economic Relations' in E Adler and B Crawford (eds), *Progress in Postwar International Relations* (Columbia University Press, New York 1991) 201; Golt (1978) 6; G Curzon and V Curzon, 'The Management of Trade Relations in the GATT' in Andrew Shonfield (ed), *International Economic Relations of the Western World, 1959–1971, Volume 1: Politics and Trade* (OUP, Oxford 1976) 253ff, in relation to early versions of this in the 1960s.

[5] Golt (1978) vi (reprint of A Policy Statement on the GATT Negotiations by the British North American Committee).

will be on the ideational dimension of this transformation period in the regime's history, rather than its material underpinnings, since the latter is much better understood and described in the existing literature than the former. I suggest that at some fundamental level this transformation included in its ideational dimension a reconstitution of the way that trade professionals made sense of the world in which they worked and imagined their role within it. I also chart the re-constitution of the GATT/WTO's legal system from a mechanism working through the mobilization and application of diplomatic consensus through flexible norms, to one operating through the constitution, authorization, and projection of technical knowledge through formalized law. I show how this was associated with new ideas about the purpose of the trade regime and the role of law within it. Of course, this change was neither complete nor clean—the WTO's legal system remains to some extent still subject to diplomatic control,[6] and there are many aspects of the GATT's early legal system which still endure. Nevertheless, my aim in this chapter is to highlight the discontinuities rather than the continuities, as I think this helps us to see more clearly the fundamental ideational elements of the trade regime's 'neoliberal turn' over the last three decades of the twentieth century.

I. The expanding scope of application of GATT/WTO disciplines on domestic regulation

As chronicled in Chapter 7, by the beginning of the 1970s, the GATT had been used to challenge only a highly restricted range of internal regulatory measures which affected international trade in a direct and obviously discriminatory way. By the end of the 1990s, however, as informal norms limiting the scope of application of the GATT regulatory disciplines were gradually reconstituted, the range of measures subject to challenge under Articles I and III of the GATT had broadened considerably. Cases had been brought against an extraordinarily diverse range of domestic regulations and institutions, many of which apparently had very little to do with trade, and affected it only incidentally or inadvertently. Famously, GATT/WTO cases were brought against measures to promote the sustainable harvesting of tuna and shrimp, a ban on the import and sale of asbestos products, the establishment of fuel economy standards for automobiles in the United States, the internal structure of the Japanese retail market for photographic film, food safety measures relating to the use of growth-promoting hormones in agriculture, and intellectual property (IP) regulation among many others. Such cases are now commonplace. Virtually all aspects of WTO Members' domestic policies are now potentially open to re description as trade barriers, and are thereby potentially subject to discipline under WTO law. This radical expansion in the scope of application of GATT/WTO law was not simply the inexorable result of the progressive liberalization of international trade—as if the turn to 'behind the border' barriers to trade

[6] See generally T Broude, *International Governance in the World Trade Organization: Judicial Boundaries and Political Capitulation* (Cameron and May, London 2004).

occurred in the 1970s solely because border barriers had by then been largely eliminated, so that domestic regulation was the obvious next step. It was in part the result of a twofold imaginative change consisting of, first, a redefinition of the commonsense concept of 'trade barrier', and second, a rethinking of the nature and purpose of the trade regime itself. This was in turn associated with the emergence of neoliberal styles of thinking, and since the United States was the most prominent and powerful voice of the new economic liberalism in the trade regime at this time, it is necessary to turn first to the domestic US trade politics of the period.

A. The United States and the turn to 'unfair trade'

The most significant background to US trade politics of the late 1960s and 1970s was the widespread perception of a decline of American competitive supremacy in many important areas of commerce. The creation of the European Community in the late 1950s, and especially its expansion to include the United Kingdom, Denmark, Ireland, and Norway during the 1960s, had firmly established a European challenge to the economic hegemony of the United States. When the Tokyo Round began, the EC accounted for a significantly higher percentage of world trade than the United States.[7] In addition, Japan emerged from the 1960s with a reputation for significant competitive prowess, initially in the cotton textile industry, but very quickly also in a much broader array of industrial sectors. It was widely apprehended that other newly industrializing countries were not far behind.[8] Significantly, the United States recorded its first trade deficit for over a decade in 1971, a structural development which caused increasing concern over the first half of the 1970s as it persisted.

The declining competitiveness of US industry gave rise to the perception, initially among private businesses and commentators, that US producers were subject to unfair competition. There were two halves to this claim. The first was that access to foreign markets for US products was impeded by a range of non-tariff barriers, many of which were less visible and less transparent than traditional trade barriers, but (it was claimed) at least as significant in terms of their effects on market access.[9] Thus some suggested that the EC's tariff concessions given during the GATT were 'meaningless in trade terms' as a result of the EC's heavy reliance on non-tariff measures which were not disciplined by the GATT.[10] The United States' trade deficit with Japan also gave rise to significant consternation within the US business community, including concerns that the institutional structure of the Japanese domestic economy as a whole created important market access obstacles for foreign goods. The second half of the claim was that 'foreign governments

[7] Winham (1986) 28.

[8] Golt (1978) 5.

[9] See Winham (1986) 72.

[10] Winham (1986) 34, citing G Curzon, 'Crisis in the International Trading System' in H Corbet and R Jackson (eds), *In Search of a New World Economic Order* (John Wiley and Sons, New York, NY 1974) 33, 37.

systematically, purposefully, and pervasively intervene in their economies to gain international commercial advantage'.[11] The primary target here again was Japan, where close collaboration between government and export industries gave rise to widespread perceptions of large-scale governmental assistance.[12] More generally, the use of subsidies as a tool of industrial and employment policy—once understood as a desirable alternative to tariff protection—underwent a major re-evaluation, so that the increasing involvement of foreign governments in the productive side of the economy came to be seen, particularly within the United States, as a major distortion of competition between imports and domestic producers in both markets.[13]

As a number of commentators have noted, it is not at all clear that these perceptions were well supported by facts. There was little concrete data available on the trade-restrictive effects of non-tariff barriers in foreign countries, and little evidence that foreign countries restricted imports more than the United States itself.[14] Furthermore, there was little indication that these non-tariff barriers explained the growing US trade deficit—there were other more obvious reasons for that.[15] Nevertheless, it was apart from anything else a 'convenient excuse'[16] in Pearson's words for a government under pressure to blame unfair practices of foreign governments for the growing trade deficit, and the business community found a receptive ear in the US government.[17] Evans cites Congressman Peter Rodino as a typical example of the prevailing sentiment of the period:

> It has come to my attention and to the attention of many other Members of the Congress that many of our trading partners abroad have already increased their border taxes to levels that more than offset the current reductions which they agreed to make at Geneva, so that the net effect, once again, is all give on our part and all take on their part. Their cost of entering the US market is substantially reduced, but our cost of entering their market remains approximately the same.[18]

This relatively new emphasis on 'unfair trade' was reflected in the Trade Act of 1974, which among other things contained the grant to the Executive of negotiating authority for the Tokyo Round. Section 102(b) made it clear that a major priority for US trade policy would be to seek 'to harmonize, reduce, or eliminate' non-tariff trade barriers so as to assure 'substantially equivalent competitive opportunities for

[11] CS Pearson, 'Free Trade, Fair Trade? The Reagan Accord' in CS Pearson and J Riedel (eds), *The Direction of Trade Policy: Papers in Honor of Isaiah Frank* (Basil Blackwell, Oxford 1990) 53; also RE Baldwin, 'U.S. Trade Policy, 1945–1988: From Foreign to Domestic Policy' in Pearson and Riedel (1990) 9, 14.

[12] Pearson (1990) 53.

[13] S Golt, *Trade Issues in the Mid 1980's* (The British–North American Committee, London 1982) 23–4, R Baldwin, *The Multilateral Trade Negotiations: Toward Greater Liberalization?* (American Enterprise Institute for Public Policy Research, Washington, DC 1979) 9–10; Golt (1978) 8–9; Winham (1986) 116–20.

[14] JW Evans, *The Kennedy Round in American trade policy: the twilight of the GATT?* (Harvard University Press, Cambridge, MA 1971) 307ff.

[15] Baldwin (1990) 16; Pearson (1990) 53.

[16] Pearson (1990) 53.

[17] Evans (1971) 305, Baldwin (1990) 16, GC Shaffer, *Defending Interests: Public-Private Partnerships in WTO Litigation* (The Brookings Institution, Washington, DC 2003) 20.

[18] Cited in Evans (1971) 304–5.

the commerce of the United States', and to seek further disciplines on unfair trading practices.[19] The failure of the GATT effectively to address such measures was by now seen in the United States as one of its major failings and a serious cause of 'imbalance' in the underlying GATT bargain, so that prioritization of non-tariff barriers was seen as necessary to 'establish fairness and equity in international trading relations'.[20] As Baldwin has argued, this turn to 'fair trade' (understood in the sense just described, rather than its more modern sense) constituted perhaps the most profound and enduring re-orientation of US trade policy of this period and the subsequent decades.[21] More specifically, US trade policy at this time has been described (perhaps with some overstatement) as animated by 'the conviction that foreigners are fundamentally unfair and it is the right and responsibility of the US government to make over foreign economic policies to give [US producers] some commercial advantage, and to do this on a unilateral basis using the threat of trade retaliation'.[22]

In the previous chapter, I suggested that the mindset of the participants working in the post-war trade regime consisted partly of a broadly shared set of categories and evaluative principles which made some forms of governmental action visible as barriers to trade, and others not. By and large, the notion of a 'barrier to trade' at that time primarily referred to the kinds of tariff and non-tariff barriers which had been the staple of trade policy during the interwar years, and which had been explicitly addressed during GATT and ITO negotiations. While it was recognized that other, internal measures could in principle constitute trade barriers where they affected international trade, in practice this residual category only seemed to capture internal measures which impacted imports in a direct, obvious, and intentional way. Generally speaking, all other internal measures merely constituted the background institutional context in which trade occurred. Then, when it came to evaluating the legitimacy of any particular disputed measure, I suggested—following Hudec—that this process was guided primarily by reference to background informal norms circulating among the community of trade diplomats about normal and appropriate governmental action, about the purpose of the GATT, and about the nature and legitimacy of the intention behind the measure in question. Together, these categories and evaluative principles constituted the conceptual apparatus according to which illegitimate barriers to trade were made visible and subject to international discipline through the GATT.

The US emphasis on 'unfair trade practices' during the 1970s represented the beginnings of a fundamental change to this conceptual apparatus. The key move was to redefine a barrier to trade primarily in terms of its economic effects, rather than its form or intention. In this approach, a governmental action constituted a barrier to trade if—and to the extent that—it 'distorted' the conditions of competition between foreign and domestic products, as compared to the conditions of competition which would exist in an imagined 'free' market. Provided this effect could be

[19] Trade Act of 1974, Pub L 93–618, 88 Stat 1978, 19 USC § 102(b) (now § 2102(2)).
[20] 19 USC § 102(c) (now § 2102(3)).
[21] Baldwin (1990) 9ff; also Pearson (1990) 55; Winham (1986) 72.
[22] Pearson (1990) 55.

shown, no distinction in principle could be made (for the purposes of classification) between different kinds of governmental action on the basis, say, of the form or underlying intention of the measure. The increasing use of the term 'trade distortion' in preference to 'trade barrier' from the 1970s onwards signalled this refocusing of attention away from the form or intention of a measure, towards its economic effects as the primary principle of visibility.

In this view, the notion of the free market acts as the primary reference point for the interpretation and evaluation of governmental action: in simple terms, forms of governmental action are imagined primarily as either constraints on market freedoms, or as preconditions for the enjoyment of those freedoms. In the context of international trade, forms of foreign governmental action are similarly interpreted and evaluated as trade barriers (or not) by reference to an imagined ideal of a market which is free and undistorted, characterized by fair competition between foreign and domestic products. It follows that the exact nature of the imagined 'free market' that is used as a comparator in this framework of interpretation plays an important role in determining what kinds of foreign governmental measures are made visible as 'trade distortions'.

In practice, when one country alleges that another country's measure is an unfair trade practice (or trade distortion), it will implicitly use the institutional form of its own domestic market as the primary reference point against which fairness and distortions are measured.[23] This is in part because governments will generally not choose to challenge abroad the kinds of actions that they may wish to use themselves, and in part because of the parochial tendency to imagine and define the nature of a 'free market' in the terms with which one is most familiar. The result is that the notion of a 'trade distortion' comes to be equated in practice with the existence of a commercially significant institutional or regulatory difference between countries.

Thus, as a direct result of the resurgence of liberal economic thought and the turn to 'unfair trade', US trade policy began to operate according to a new logic, according to which more and more institutional and regulatory *differences* between foreign markets and the domestic US market were gradually made visible as barriers to US exports—as 'distortions' of conditions of competition between foreign products and their domestic US counterparts. These institutional and regulatory differences could consist not only of 'over-regulation' by foreign markets, but also 'under-regulation'. For example, differences between US and foreign IP regimes came to be viewed within the US as a major 'distortion' of international trade, since competition with foreign products produced contrary to high US IP standards was seen as 'unfair'. Similarly, relatively low foreign standards of labour and environmental protection were also described as distortions of competition between domestic and foreign goods. On the other side, the fact that food safety regulators in the European Union tended to adopt different and stricter approaches as compared to their US counterparts—that different regulatory 'cultures' developed on different sides of the Atlantic—led to intensified claims that European food safety regimes amounted to trade barriers. As noted above, the particular institutional relations between Japanese

[23] See pp 170–1 above.

firms and the Japanese government—very unfamiliar to American eyes—were also increasingly described as barriers to American exports.

Although it was established in the 1970s, this expansionist logic was significantly intensified during the 1980s, and then even more so after the end of the Cold War. The pursuit of more rigorous free market policies in the United States, the United Kingdom, and other industrialized countries during these decades multiplied claims of unfair trade practices on the part of other countries which had not followed the same path. As domestic institutions in the United States (and other countries which followed this path) came to resemble a more radical form of the free market in the context of neoliberal structural reforms, more and more forms of foreign governmental intervention came to appear to domestic commercial actors as an unfair interference in free competition. With the spread of neoliberal thought, many previously acceptable forms of intervention were also delegitimated as outdated or misguided policy choices, with the same result. This was, it should be said, also assisted by the emergence of the concept of the 'global market' around the same time, a concept which also blurred the distinction between the notion of a 'trade distortion' and other forms of domestic governmental intervention in the market. During this period, opening up a country's borders to international trade was seen in many contexts as just one part of a broader process of removing constraints on free markets—and conversely, domestic internal constraints on free markets were seen as just another kind of distortion of transnational economic flows. Thus an inherently expansionist dynamic was newly instilled into the trade regime, according to which it constantly expanded its scope of application by redescribing more institutional and regulatory differences between countries as trade distortions.

B. The GATT as political marketplace

I have described so far some of the changes that led to the emergence of a new 'commonsense' in US trade policy circles, according to which foreign internal institutional and regulatory arrangements came to appear self-evidently as distorting barriers to US exports. But it remains to be explained how and why this commonsense was adopted more broadly within the GATT, so that it came to be accepted as normal and appropriate that the GATT develop and apply rules to constrain domestic regulation—which, after all, was and remains a jealously guarded aspect of sovereign economic authority. Part of the answer to this, of course, has to do with the economic importance of the United States, which in practice tends to be associated with a substantial degree of symbolic power to constitute and impose a particular interpretation of the world on others, including the power authoritatively to define new categories of 'trade barrier'. I will describe some of the symbolic processes through which this power was exercised later in the chapter. But another part of the answer has to do with the re-imagining of the nature and purpose of the GATT itself, which had the result of removing informal, intersubjective constraints on the regime's domain of application, and making it amenable for the first time to an almost unlimited expansion (in principle at least) of its own scope of application. In order to explore this change, it is useful to return to the US Trade Act of 1974.

The Trade Act's emphasis on unfair trade and on foreign non-tariff barriers was accompanied by a significant change in the institutional structure according to which US foreign trade policy was conducted. For example, the legislation famously included section 301, a provision which was the centrepiece of a legal mechanism through which US businesses could formally petition for action to be taken by the Executive against unfair foreign trade practices. Under this provision, the President was required to 'take all appropriate and feasible steps within his power'—including unilateral retaliatory action—to remove foreign trade practices determined to be 'unreasonable, justifiable or discriminatory' and injurious to US industry. This included foreign trade practices which were not illegal under the GATT at the time. Section 301 was later amended numerous times to expand its coverage, to restrict the discretion of the President in his handling of complaints, and to tighten procedural timelines. It was also supplemented by a procedure requiring the United States Trade Representative (USTR) to examine the trade practices of countries which maintained an 'excessive [trade] surplus' with the United States, to determine if there was a pattern of unfair trade practices, and mandating measures to remove them.[24] Although the use of the section 301 procedure was only sporadic until the second half of the 1980s, it was deployed effectively on some occasions during the Tokyo Round,[25] and clearly signalled a newly aggressive US policy of trade reciprocity. In addition to section 301, the Trade Act of 1974 also revived and reinvigorated an older provision of US trade legislation, which empowered domestic industries to bring complaints in domestic judicial fora against unfair foreign trade practices resulting in over-competitive imports, and which provided a range of potential remedies against these imports, including exclusion from the US domestic market.[26]

Furthermore, the Act also created a large network of private sector advisory committees to provide information and input to trade negotiators. At the highest level was the Advisory Committee for Trade Negotiations, comprising forty-five appointed members from 'labor, industry, agriculture, small business, service industries, retailers, consumer interests and the general public'.[27] Beneath this committee were three policy advisory committees representing labour, industry, and agriculture,

[24] Baldwin (1990) 16; see now 19 USC §§ 2411–2419.

[25] RE Hudec, 'GATT Dispute Settlement after the Tokyo Round: An Unfinished Business' (1980) 13 Cornell Intl LJ 145, 156 n 26 gives examples of the use of the section 301 procedure, including in the context of the following disputes: Panel Report, *Japanese Measures on Imports of Leather* (adopted 6 November 1979) BISD 26S/320 (L/4789); Panel Report, *Japan Measures on Imports of Thrown Silk Yarn* (adopted 17 May 1978) BISD 25S/107 (L/4637), Panel Report, *EEC—Measures on Animal Feed Proteins* (adopted 14 March 1978) BISD 25S/49 (L/4599); Panel Report, *EEC—Programme of Minimum Import Prices, Licences and Surety Deposits for Certain Processed Fruits and Vegetables* (adopted 18 October 1978) BISD 25S/68 (L/4687); Working Party Report, *Canadian Import Quotas on Eggs* (adopted 17 February 1976) BISD 23S/91 (L/4279).

[26] See eg NC Knight, 'Section 337 and the GATT: A Necessary Protection or an Unfair Trade Practice?' (1988) Georgia J of Intl and Comp L 47; KW Abbott, 'United States—Section 337 Of The Tariff Act Of 1930' (1990) 84 AJIL 274; JS Neeley and H Ishida, 'Section 337 and National Treatment under GATT: A Proposal for Legislative Reform' (1989) 13 Fordham Intl LJ 276; MC Modak-Truran, Comment, 'Section 337 and GATT in the Akzo Controversy' (1988) 9 Northwestern J of Intl L and Business 382.

[27] Winham (1986) 135.

which themselves sat above an array of specialized committees. Beneath the Industrial Policy Advisory Committee, for example, worked twenty-seven sector-specific industry sector advisory committees. The committees would have access to the relevant information to provide advice to negotiators during the course of the Round, and also had a right to advise Congress on the desirability of the final negotiated package when it came back to that body for approval and implementing legislation.[28]

Winham's account of the Tokyo Round negotiations remains the subtlest analysis of the impact of this newly established structure of committees on the internal dynamics of US trade policy. On the one hand, he notes that the existence of these committees clearly increased the level of influence which certain industries had over the positions taken by the United States in negotiations.[29] While business interests have of course always been very active in lobbying around trade negotiations, the bureaucratization and institutionalization of their input was a new development with a new dynamic. Over the course of the negotiations, USTR officials conducted hundreds of meetings with these committees, often initiating communications with relevant actors to solicit their input, and reporting back to them on the conduct of negotiations. Even in Geneva itself, the insulation which characterized trade negotiations in Geneva during the GATT's first decades was decisively eroded, at least as far as the United States was concerned, even to the extent that negotiators conducted 'a series of briefing tours in Geneva with on-site negotiating teams'.[30]

On the other hand, the committee system did not just represent a mechanism for the institutionalization of interest group control over negotiators. It also, conversely, provided opportunities for negotiators to manage and control the efforts of special interest groups, and to resist the influence of those seeking protectionism. Communication with constituency groups occurred 'in an environment defined by trade officials', which helped to give the trade officials 'some capacity to help shape the kinds of demands that would be made on the government'.[31] The wealth of information available to negotiators through these committees helped to provide them with the tools to evaluate proposals made by certain groups, and some capacity to resist them where they considered that appropriate.[32] Most importantly, they were able to balance the demands of protectionist interest groups against those of export-oriented industries, and in so doing resist what they saw as some of the more extreme demands for protection arising from domestic constituencies.[33] While this balancing strategy had been harnessed by trade negotiators in previous rounds, the formalized committee system made it available in a much more routine way for the control of

[28] See Winham (1986) 134–6; IM Destler, *American Trade Politics* (4th edn, Institute for International Economics, Washington, DC 2005) 8.

[29] Winham (1986) 315.

[30] ibid 309.

[31] ibid 316.

[32] ibid 316.

[33] ibid 316, 345.

domestic special interest groups oriented towards protection.[34] Internally, the role of the public trade official became much more explicitly and centrally oriented towards the management and control of domestic constituencies—both responding to their preferences and at the same time actively shaping the expression of those preferences, as well as the way in which they were aggregated.[35]

The newly aggressive unilateral enforcement mechanisms under sections 301 and 337, described above, were also used as a way to control and resist the influence of commercial actors seeking greater protection. When a domestic industry petitioned the US government for relief from over-competitive or unfair imports, these mechanisms gave the government the option of aggressively seeking to change foreign governments' practices on behalf of the complaining industry, rather than giving in to the domestic industry's demand for greater import protection. A good example is the herring and salmon dispute between Canada and the United States in the mid-1980s, which started as a request by domestic US fishing interests for retaliatory trade restrictions under section 301, but ended up as a successful GATT (and FTA) claim against Canada's original export restriction.[36]

As well as inaugurating a reorientation of the internal role of the USTR, this new institutional environment also seemed to have an effect on its *external* role and approach. A number of historians of the Tokyo Round describe a change in the nature of the leadership role that the US took in that round as compared to earlier rounds. Winham, for example, records 'a common perception among US negotiators . . . that where previously the United States might occasionally have sacrificed specific objective interests to keep intact the institutional values of the GATT, at the Tokyo Round it was less willing to forego the tangible benefits for its conception of wider institutional values'.[37] It seems that other delegates involved in the negotiations noticed the same thing, and initially did not see this new aggressiveness as in keeping with the prior practice of the GATT. They were proud of their own relative distance from naked commercial interest.[38] Pearson, too, saw a new willingness (during the Tokyo Round but also in the decade after) on the part of the United States to 'use its remaining economic power to push its immediate interests without great regard for preserving the traditional principles of liberal trade'—adherence to which principles had always been understood as being in the United States' interest in a broader and more diffuse sense.[39] This 'elevation of [immediate] US commercial

[34] ibid 345ff and see also 299 for an excellent example in the context of negotiations over the Wine Gallon issue.

[35] ibid 343–4; P Sutherland, 'The Politics of Trade Policy Development—The New Complexity' in PFJ Macrory, AE Appleton, and MG Plummer (eds), *The World Trade Organization: Legal, Economic and Political Analysis, Volume 1* (Springer Science+Business Media, New York, NY 2005) 27, 28.

[36] See TL McDorman, 'International Trade Law Meets International Fisheries Law: The Canada-U.S. Salmon and Herring Dispute' (1990) 7 Intl Arbitration 107; RE Hudec, *Enforcing International Trade Law: The Evolution of the Modern GATT Legal System* (Butterworth Legal Publishers, Salem, NH 1993) 543.

[37] Winham (1986) 387.

[38] ibid 339–40; Shaffer (2003) 23, citing a former Canadian ambassador to the WTO.

[39] Pearson (1990) 54.

interest', he suggests, was 'new in postwar US policy'.[40] Preeg also noticed a tendency on the part of the US government to play a more active role in the support of US export industries in the years after the Tokyo Round.[41]

As the quotation from Pearson suggests, a number of commentators saw this turn to aggressive reciprocity on the part of the United States as a turn *away* from a more doctrinaire adherence to economic liberalism, particularly as it was accompanied in some cases by an equivalently aggressive defence of domestic protectionist interests. Importantly, however, it is better seen as a new reconciliation of the demands of economic and political liberalism—or more specifically, the apparently conflicting demands of pursuing a free trade policy while still responding to domestic interest groups. As should by now be clear, the idea was that if *all* countries aggressively pursued their commercial interests within the GATT, the collective effect would be to make it *less* likely that domestic protectionist interests could exercise undue influence over the formulation of trade policy, since the combined pressure from foreign countries and from domestic export interests would counteract that influence. The beauty of the GATT's system of reciprocal bargaining, on this view, was that each country's responsiveness to the demands of domestic commercial interests would in itself create the political conditions for the removal of trade barriers in accordance with the principles of economic liberalism. Imagined in this way, in fact, the trade regime required and presupposed the kind of relatively aggressive behaviour which the United States had begun to adopt, if it was to function most effectively.

The broader point that all of this material leads us to is that the specific *institutional* changes which the Trade Act of 1974 made as regards the conduct and operation of US trade policy both reflected and helped to produce a much broader *imaginative* change concerning the nature and purpose of the international trade regime, and the appropriate professional role of trade policy officials. This imaginative change was rapidly entrenched in theoretical writing on the trade regime over the course of the 1980s, and reached the level of self-evident commonsense within the community of trade policy professionals over the same period. This needs to be explained in some detail.

The architects of the post-war trade regime, as I have shown, saw themselves as engaged in a collective political project of rebuilding an international economic order conducive to enduring peace and prosperity for the world, or at least for that part of it represented by its members. This sense of collective endeavour was sustained by their shared commitment to embedded liberalism, and to the social purposes broadly associated with the post-war welfare state. Over the 1960s and 1970s, as the number and diversity of participants in the GATT expanded, and the regime became increasingly multipolar, this shared consensus deteriorated. As a result, the idea of the trade regime as a collective political endeavour also began to deteriorate, to be replaced by a new idea more suited to the emerging late twentieth-century international trading order. In short, the trade regime was re-imagined as itself a *marketplace*. The GATT, in other words,

[40] ibid 54.

[41] EH Preeg, *Traders in a Brave New World: The Uruguay Round and the Future of the International Trading System* (University of Chicago Press, Chicago, IL 1995) 22.

came to be understood primarily as a forum for negotiations—not just as an aspect of its operation, which of course had always been the case, but as its essential and primary raison d'être. It was a venue in which states came together to bargain and exchange trade concessions, in a way roughly analogous to the transactions entered into by participants in a marketplace. Within this imagined marketplace, the basic coin was market access: each participant sought to gain market access for its traders, and transactions proceeded by way of mutual exchange of market access concessions. The purpose of the trade regime was simply to facilitate such transactions, in the interests of increasing global economic efficiency and providing opportunities for greater wealth creation and welfare enhancement. This is the 'thin' view of the nature and purpose of the WTO, which I introduced in Chapter 5.

Like the idea of the market more generally, this core idea was both descriptive and normative. It was descriptive in the sense that it purported to describe the basic motivations and objectives of states in the trade regime, as well as the nature of the transactions into which they entered. And it was normative in the sense that it rested on the idea that this bargained exchange of concessions was mutually beneficial: not only were exchanged concessions presumptively beneficial because states entered into these transactions voluntarily, but also more substantively beneficial in that they had the effect of fostering welfare-enhancing economic growth through global economic integration. In this sense, the idea of the trade regime as a marketplace was the key concept through which a new reconciliation between the demands of political and economic liberalism was struck in the context of international trade politics.

As these ideas gained greater and greater traction, theoretical inquiry into the GATT came to focus more and more on the image of the trade regime as a marketplace.[42] Under the influence of neoliberal institutionalism, for example, game theoretic explanations of the GATT became influential through the 1980s.[43] The conduct of trade policy was imagined as a Prisoners' Dilemma, in which the uncoordinated action of states acting in pursuit of their commercial and political interests would tend towards a sub-optimal equilibrium. Trade agreements such as the GATT were necessary, on this view, to provide the basis for mutually beneficial cooperative action, leading to optimal outcomes.[44] The mainstreaming of public choice explanations of trade policy during the same period was another important development.[45] Public choice theory had for some time been used to explain the

[42] For a similar account, see N Weinrichter, 'Perspectives on the changing spirit of GATT' (1999) 3 *European Integration Online Papers* <http://eiop.or.at/eiop/pdf/1999-010.pdf> accessed 15 February 2011.

[43] See generally RO Keohane and JS Nye, *Power and Interdependence: World Politics in Transition* (Little, Brown and Company, Boston, MA 1977) on neoliberal institutionalism. Also RO Keohane, *After Hegemony: Cooperation and Discord in the World Political Economy* (Princeton University Press, Princeton, NJ 1984).

[44] See eg KW Abbott, 'The Trading Nation's Dilemma: The Functions of the Law of International Trade' (1985) 26 Harvard Intl LJ 501, 503–7, 522. See also S Charnovitz, 'Triangulating the World Trade Organization' (2002) 96 AJIL 28, 36–7; J Goldstein and LL Martin, 'Legalization, Trade Liberalization, and Domestic Politics: A Cautionary Note' (2000) 54 Intl Org 603, 620.

[45] D Zang, 'Divided by Common Language: "Capture" Theories in GATT/WTO and the Communicative Impasse' (2009) 32 Hastings Intl and Comparative L Rev 423. In fact, this claim goes at least as far

prevalence of protectionist policy in the face of clear economic evidence that it undermined national welfare. The core claim, to simplify somewhat, was that the few special interests in favour of protection could exercise disproportionate influence over policy-making because they were better organized, more active, and more alert than the bulk of individuals whose interests were only indirectly or less intensely affected by trade. As regards the trade regime itself, public choice theory supported the view that aggressive championing of export interests through trade negotiations was generally beneficial, as it provided a counterweight to the inherent tendency of protectionist special interests to capture domestic trade policy-making processes. During the 1980s, this theory 'gained influence among trade economists and international lawyers associated with the GATT', and became part of the lingua franca of the professional world of trade politics.[46] Other theoretical accounts of international trade politics—such as Winham's interesting explanation of the formation of negotiating coalitions through the use of Coasian economics[47]—also proceeded on the basis of a marketplace metaphor of international trade politics.

One of the first observers to write about the reconceptualization of the trade regime as a marketplace—or something very close to it—was Kenneth Abbott, in a brace of articles published in the early 1990s. Drawing on the work of Damaska, Abbott distinguished between two ideal types, which he called a 'private interests community' and a 'public interests community'. A community organized on the private interests model, in this taxonomy:

> ...has no independent community interests or goals; the satisfaction of its individual members is the community's only concern. The only social role for community institutions is to provide a framework within which its members can pursue their private interests.[48]

A public interest community, on the other hand 'has its own independent vision of the good, its own common goals and interests, and it uses all the tools at its disposal to implement that vision'.[49] The distinction is a suggestive one in the context of the present argument, as it is clear that the idea of the trade regime as a forum for negotiation or a marketplace is analogous to the idea of the GATT as a 'private interest community'. Interestingly, Abbott's claim was that the GATT was and had always been 'structured along the lines of a private interests community', but that it 'actually possesses the central characteristic of a public interest community'. He argued, therefore, for strengthening of the 'public' aspect of the GATT's institutions

back as EE Schattschneider, *Politics, Pressures and the Tariff: A Study of Free Private Enterprise in Pressure Politics, As Shown in the 1929–1930 Revision of the Tariff* (Prentice-Hall, New York, NY 1935), and was understood as a relevant dynamic of trade negotiations from early on (see eg Curzon and Curzon (1976)). However, it was only later that it was mainstreamed and centralized as a dominant explanatory claim.

[46] Zang (2009) 438.

[47] GR Winham, 'An Institutional Theory of WTO Decision-Making: Why Negotiation in the WTO Resembles Law-Making in the US Congress' (2006) Munk Centre for International Studies Occasional Paper No 11.

[48] KW Abbott, 'The Uruguay Round and Dispute Resolution: Building a Private-Interests System of Justice' (1992) Columbia Business L Rev 111.

[49] Abbott 'The Uruguay Round and Dispute Resolution' (1992) 114.

and practices.[50] The historical claim that I am making, however, is that both ways of imagining the GATT have been present and in tension with one another from its inception, but that the decisive re-imagining and restructuring of the GATT along the lines of a purely private interest community is a relatively recent phenomenon, and was the result of the considerable strengthening of liberal thought in the trade regime from the 1970s onwards.

We might describe this process of reconceptualization as a redefinition of the 'collective purpose' which animated and oriented the trade regime. But it is probably more accurately described as a reconceptualization of the nature of the trade regime which left no clear room for the notion of 'collective' purpose at all. In a marketplace, or a forum for negotiations, there are only actors with their own purposes. A transaction, or a negotiated exchange of concessions, is not really a manifestation of a 'collective purpose', but simply a situation in which the individual purposes and objectives of parties to the exchange coincide. To put the same point differently, the trade regime came to imagine itself as a collective endeavour in the absence of a collective purpose or collective political commitment. As will become clear in later chapters, I view this as a decisive conceptual move, because it effectively entrenched and legitimated a separation between the exercise of power in the governance of international trade on the one hand, and on the other hand the pursuit of legitimate public purposes, collectively defined. I will be suggesting that this separation lay at the heart of the WTO's legitimacy crisis at the end of the twentieth century.

As this way of thinking became more influential, it became more and more common to describe the 'purpose' of the trade regime in functional terms by reference to the regime's effects, or by reference to the individual purposes of each Contracting Party, rather than by reference to collectively shared ideas actually circulating among a community of individuals. Thus, the purpose of the GATT was to reduce obstacles to world trade, 'to roll back trade barriers',[51] its 'over-riding goal . . . [was] an open world trading system free of governmental restriction',[52] or the 'total elimination of barriers to free trade through successive reduction'.[53] Observers of the trade regime in the early 1970s might have been surprised that this was in fact the 'over-riding goal' of the trade regime, given its limited scope and its apparent tolerance of many forms of restriction and intervention. But in a kind of historical revisionism, many observers of the period explained this tolerance purely as the result of political resistance by special interests, or the incremental nature of trade liberalization. The GATT regime, on this view, had *always* been fundamentally oriented towards the kind of entirely free trade favoured by rigorous economic liberalism, but had simply not yet been fully successful in achieving that aim.

[50] Abbott, 'The Uruguay Round and Dispute Resolution' (1992) 115–16. See also KW Abbott, 'GATT as a Public Institution: The Uruguay Round and Beyond' (1992) 18 Brooklyn J of Intl L 31.

[51] DA Irwin, 'The GATT in Historical Perspective' (1995) 85 American Economic Rev 323, 324.

[52] Winham (1986) 404.

[53] TN Srinivasan, 'Nondiscrimination in GATT/WTO: Was there Anything to Begin with and is there Anything Left?' (2005) 4 World Trade Rev 69, 76.

I said above that the influence of neoliberal thought redefined not only commonsense understandings of the nature and purpose of the trade regime, but also commonsense understandings of the professional role of trade officials working in and around the trade regime in both domestic and international institutional settings. As regards the appropriate role of trade policy-makers, this had two aspects. Internally, as described above, their role was to respond to, but also manage, the diversity of special interests seeking influence over trade policy, in ways which tended to divert pressure for protectionism and foster support for the eradication of foreign trade barriers.[54] This role was supported and legitimated by public choice theory, described above, which saw domestic pressures for protectionism as the result of a structural failure of domestic political institutions. Externally, the role of trade officials was to represent and promote domestic commercial interests aggressively, both offensively and defensively. The claim is not, of course, that this external role was new—the promotion of export interests is as old as mercantilism itself—but rather that it was embedded in a new narrative which gave it a particular character, intensity, and legitimacy, and liberated it from some of the moderating influences of the post-war embedded liberal period. Thus, one of the effects of the proliferation of theories of the GATT based on the metaphor of the marketplace was to normalize and legitimate this very particular understanding of the motivations and behaviours of participants in the trade regime, and the specific notion of commercial interest on which it rested. By presupposing a model of behaviour in which states primarily acted on behalf of their export interests (understood as a rough proxy for the national interest in this context), these theories helped to naturalize this behavioural role, so that over time it came to be understood as a self-evident starting point of trade politics.[55] Furthermore, by showing how this model of behaviour led to mutually beneficial outcomes, they also legitimated it.

I have shown above how the institutional arrangements associated with the US Trade Act of 1974 reflected this understanding of the proper conduct and purpose of trade policy. Shaffer has described this institutional transformation as a form of 'public-private partnership', the basic function of which 'is to facilitate the formation of ad hoc public-private networks to develop and exploit public international economic law in order to advance US national and commercial interests'.[56] He connects this development to a broader trend towards the privatization of governance functions with the emergence of the neoliberal state.[57] He has, furthermore, tracked the diffusion of these institutional forms across many of the major players within the trade regime. The EC, for example, instituted its own counterpart to section 301 proceedings—the New Commercial Policy Instrument—in 1984, permitting

[54] See eg Winham (1986) 343 and surrounding; C Lipson, 'The Transformation of Trade: The Sources and Effects of Regime Change' (1982) 36 Intl Org 417, 454.

[55] The point is similar to that made by Adler (1992).

[56] Shaffer (2003) 20 and generally.

[57] Shaffer (2003) ch 2.

private industry to petition the Commission to initiate a GATT complaint in some circumstances.[58] It was later replaced with a much broader instrument, the Trade Barrier Regulation, just before the formal creation of the WTO. Though few see the Trade Barrier Regulation as equal in effectiveness to its US counterpart, the European Commission has also more generally been much more proactive in fostering partnerships with export-oriented commercial actors since the middle of the 1990s, as part of its own more aggressive approach to international trade policy.[59] Shaffer and his co-authors have also described the emergence of analogous institutional structures in Brazil, attributing that country's relative recent success in WTO dispute settlement to the creation of similar kinds of public–private partnerships.[60] China also established its own equivalent to section 301—the Foreign Trade Barrier Investigation mechanism—in 2002.[61] Similar stories about the increasingly close and more institutionalized links between trade negotiators and an array of private interests can also be told about any number of other countries active in WTO negotiations.[62] After the conclusion of the Uruguay Round, for example, the WTO's Director-General commented on the unprecedented profusion of interest groups and lobbies in and around the negotiations, on a scale which had not been seen in earlier periods of the GATT's history.[63]

In Chapter 7, I described the way that the 'embedded liberal' mindset which characterized the post-war trade regime had its institutional counterpart in the *insularity* of the trade regime, and in a series of practices in which this insularity was carefully and deliberately policed. What is clear, then, is that the erosion of the embedded liberal mindset was associated with a similar erosion of this self-conscious tendency towards insularity, and the creation of much closer and more institutionalized links between the GATT community and a wider variety of domestic interest groups. This dynamic was given a considerable boost, as the increasing transnationalization of economic activity over the course of the 1980s and 1990s gave birth to a new and rapidly expanding group of transnational businesses, actively oriented towards foreign markets as their primary strategy of expansion and growth.[64] This provided the opportunity and impetus for the further development of alliances between trade officials and domestic export-oriented firms, through the public–private partnerships just described. The proliferation of these new firms, and their substantial economic clout, helped to ensure the success of that strategy, and thus its broader adoption across different countries. But these (and many other) material

[58] See eg Shaffer (2003) 85 and surrounding.

[59] Shaffer (2003) ch 4 and generally.

[60] See eg Gregory C Shaffer, M Ratton, S Badin, and B Rosenberg, 'The Trials of Winning at the WTO: What Lies Behind Brazil's Success' (2008) 41 Cornell Intl LJ 383.

[61] See H Gao, 'Taking Justice into your Own Hand: The TBI Mechanism in China' (2010) 44 J of World Trade 633.

[62] eg in relation to Canada and Japan in the Tokyo Round itself, see Winham (1986) ch 8.

[63] Sutherland, 'The Politics of Trade Policy Development' in Macrory, Appleton, and Plummer (2005) 28. See also Winham (1986) 343.

[64] GR Winham, 'An Interpretative History of the Uruguay Round Negotiation' in Macrory, Appleton, and Plummer (2005) 3, 22–3. See also Preeg (1995).

economic changes underpinning the late twentieth-century transformation of the trade regime are already well understood and have been well described elsewhere, so I will not dwell on them—the point of this section (and this chapter more generally) is that these material changes could not have had the effect that they did without an accompanying change at the level of ideas.

C. The consequence: the expanding scope of application of international trade law

We are now in a position to say something meaningful about the underlying causes of the radical change in the scope of application of GATT/WTO law over the last three decades of the twentieth century. There was, as I have just said, a material and institutional basis for this change, involving the increasing multipolarity and diversity of the membership of the trade regime, the growing transnationalization of the economy and of economic actors, emerging challenges to US economic hegemony, the increasing commercial significance of domestic regulation as impediments to exports, among many other factors commonly referenced in histories of this period. But this change also had an indispensable ideational basis, and it is this which is my primary focus of attention. On one hand, the elision between the idea of a trade barrier and that of a trade distortion—with the effects of a measure, rather than its form or intention, becoming a primary principle of classification—laid the foundation for this expansion by providing a conceptual framework within which virtually any form of foreign governmental action could with sufficient effort be symbolically constructed as a distortion of trade. On the other hand, the re-description of the trade regime as being solely a marketplace—nothing more than a forum for negotiations among individual states, rather than the venue for the pursuit of a collective project of international economic order—facilitated the expansion of the trade regime's scope of vision in three other ways. First, the intensification and institutionalization of alliances between trade officials and domestic export-oriented commercial interests helped to provide an environment in which trade officials were professionally more amenable to claims by business that foreign governmental measures amounted to trade barriers. Secondly, by imagining the purpose of the trade regime as simply being the reduction of trade barriers, a presumption was established that, once a trade barrier was collectively identified, there was no principled reason why the trade regime should not address it. This aggregative dynamic was in turn intensified by the tendency towards 'logrolling' in large multilateral negotiations of the type seen in the Uruguay Round. Thirdly, by eroding and delegitimating the very idea that there was such a thing as a 'collective project' of GATT contracting parties, it also removed the limiting effect that this idea had had on the GATT's scope of operation during the post-war period. The limited scope of vision of the post-war GATT, in other words, was a product of a collectively shared understanding of its limited purpose and mandate. Once that shared understanding eroded, and the GATT was imagined as little more than a venue for bargaining, the stage was set for a dramatic expansion of its domain of operation.

At the same time, a change was taking place with respect to the image of 'normal trade' and 'normal regulation' which implicitly structures the characterization of certain kinds of government action. The high degree of domestic interventionism and institutional diversity characteristic of the embedded liberal period provided one view of the 'normal' against which few domestic interventions could unambiguously be described as impediments to trade, and in the context of which the principle of free trade was understood as compatible with many different institutional configurations of the market. This view of 'normal' government intervention was increasingly challenged, as noted above, over the 1970s and 1980s as the welfare state came under attack. Governmental activity in the marketplace as a direct buyer and seller of goods and services was criticized for crowding out private investment. Industrial policy fell out of favour as ineffective and counterproductive. Regulatory structures were exposed by public choice theory as subject to capture, and the prospect of government failure came to be perceived as a greater and more widespread problem than that of market failure. It may be an overstatement to say that the image of state-market relations contained in neoliberal thought became the 'new normal' against which the notion of a trade distortion was measured within the field of international trade governance; but it is certainly the case that the criticisms of governmental interventionism associated with the rise to prominence of neoliberal thought were influential in trade law and policy circles and helped to institutionalize a frame of mind receptive to the construction of new forms of domestic regulation as trade distortions.

The result was the inauguration of a new dynamic within international trade politics, according to which the scope of the trade regime was incrementally expanded, as more and more institutional and regulatory differences between nations were re-described as 'trade barriers', as a result of the efforts of powerful actors working through the 'public–private partnerships' described above. Entire categories of domestic governmental action which had once been relegated to the background as self-evidently outside the domain of trade policy were now foregrounded, reconstructed as potential impediments to trade, and therefore made objects of legitimate international scrutiny and discipline. In addition, and alongside this, alternative ways of describing the problems posed by domestic regulation became dominant. It was no longer just that domestic regulation could be used by protectionist governments to undermine the liberalization of border barriers—though that was still emphasized. It was also that the sheer diversity of regulatory regimes facing exporters was an impediment to trade in itself, and that even non-protectionist regulation could unnecessarily impede trade flows if it were sub-optimally or inefficiently designed.

It is worth re-emphasizing that this process involved the application of symbolic power—that is, the attempt to create a particular interpretation of the world as authoritative within the world of international trade governance, including a particular image of the 'free market' against which to assess governmental measures as 'distortions' of free trade. This was, naturally, a highly contested process, as countries often had diametrically opposed views of what constitutes a trade distortion in any particular context. If it was now accepted that the trade regime had to turn its attention to 'domestic regulation', it was by no means clear precisely what domestic regulations constituted a trade distortion, and how one was to distinguish between legitimate and illegitimate, necessary and unnecessary, domestic regulation. Thus, for example, when lower foreign IP protection began to be seen as a trade distortion within US trade policy circles, and section 337 of the Trade Act of 1974 began to be used as a way of remedying that problem, other countries asserted that section 337 itself constituted a distortion of free trade, and its application soon became a subject of complaint.[65] The problem is a general one: one person's remedy for a pre-existing trade distortion is another person's trade distortion. Without collectively shared habits of interpretation—shared meanings for the concepts of 'distortion' or 'market failure', or authorized principles and techniques of evaluation in specific cases—it would remain fundamentally unclear how the trade regime should approach any specific case. My account of the ideational dimension of the trade regime's neoliberal turn is incomplete, therefore, without considering how this dilemma was resolved.

II. The formalization and technicalization of GATT/WTO disciplines on domestic regulation

We saw in the previous chapter that some attempts to address certain domestic non-tariff barriers had been made in the Kennedy Round, but with few significant results. As just noted, it is one thing to raise a trading partner's 'unfair' or distorting internal measure as a problem in the course of negotiations, but it is quite another to convince a critical mass of governments that the measure is in fact unfair, that it is sufficiently significant to require international discipline, and that it is part of the legitimate role of the GATT to discipline it. At the end of the 1960s, there was simply no consensus view among trade negotiators and their governments about how and where to draw the line between an unfair trade distortion and a legitimate form of governmental intervention.[66] At the insistence of the United States, however, the GATT Contracting Parties agreed immediately after the conclusion of the Kennedy Round to initiate a programme of conceptual work on non-tariff barriers. The first substantive task was to compile a list of non-tariff barriers in preparation for the next negotiating round. Over the next year, an initial list was compiled by the GATT Secretariat on the basis of submissions made by Contracting Parties about the non-tariff barriers present in other countries, produced in consultation with domestic industry.[67] The task was carried out diligently, and the list was updated regularly, so that by the early 1970s, it contained over 900 items, covering matters as varied as subsidies, technical standards, labelling requirements, food safety and quarantine measures, and customs

[65] See below pp 267–8.

[66] See eg RE Hudec, *Adjudication of International Trade Disputes* (Trade Policy Research Centre, London 1978) 15ff, 18; Hudec (1990) 202ff.

[67] Winham (1986) 86ff.

procedures, as well as many others. These were organized into five groups, and some preliminary work was carried out to determine which were amenable to negotiation in the GATT, and what form those negotiations might take.[68] While this process by no means solved the problem of a lack of substantive consensus, it performed the crucial function of making certain kinds of governmental action collectively visible as trade barriers within the community of trade negotiators in Geneva:

> Negotiating [non-tariff barriers] was problematic in that they were largely undefinable... often concealed, and incomparable, and that their effects were unknown precisely but generally thought to be pernicious. Negotiators had to achieve an intellectual understanding of these measures before they could negotiate their removal. In general terms, the task was to gather data about [non-tariff barriers]; to list, categorize, and structure that data into workable groups and subgroups; to relate the new data to existing GATT trade rules and obligations; and finally to create a negotiating structure that was congruent to the structure that was found in the data. From this process, negotiable definitions of [non-tariff barriers] emerged... Essentially this was a bureaucratic act, [and] it was a creative act as well.[69]

The process of compiling and organizing the list of non-tariff barriers, in other words, was a process in which collective ways of appreciating and understanding certain forms of governmental activity were gradually constituted and organized. It provided a 'common stock of ideas' on the basis of which negotiations could proceed.[70] The compilation had an 'educative' function in the sense that its negotiators came to adopt and accept the categories and evaluative principles on the basis of which it had been put together—a function which, it appears, did not stop once the negotiations themselves started.[71] The problem still remained, of course, of building a thicker and more substantive consensus about how these different measures should be treated, and how to distinguish between legitimate and illegitimate instances of non-tariff measures which affected international trade. In the end, negotiators sought to resolve this difficulty through two very closely connected changes to the GATT's legal system. The first was the formalization of the GATT's dispute settlement provisions, to provide a more effective mechanism for the resolution of disputes of this kind. The second was the emergence of a new mode of legal reasoning and legal norm production which mixed the operation and elaboration of law with the application of expert technical knowledge. Both of these developments, I suggest, were inspired at some fundamental level by the emergence of different ways of thinking about the nature and purpose of law in economic governance.

A. From purposive to formal legal structures

I said in the previous chapter that there were two different approaches to law and dispute settlement at play during the negotiations over the GATT and the Havana

68 See generally Winham (1986) 86ff; Golt (1978) 20ff; Evans (1971) 259 and surrounding.
69 Winham (1986) 88.
70 Golt (1978) 20.
71 Winham (1986) 105.

Charter. Ultimately, the dominant approach (captured in the phrase 'purposive law') saw law primarily as an instrument for the achievement and expression of collective social and political purposes. The result was a legal system with four core features: the frequent use of ambiguous, flexible, and adaptable legal norms; the social and structural embeddedness of the dispute settlement process in the world of trade diplomacy; an interpretive style which relied heavily and relatively explicitly on informal norms and expectations circulating among the community of trade diplomats; and a soft system of enforcement relying primarily on the constitution and mobilization of community consensus for or against a particular challenged measure.

The United States has historically tended towards a more 'legalist' approach to dispute settlement within the GATT,[72] and it returned to this theme in the 1970s. In addition to new disciplines on non-tariff barriers, reform of GATT dispute settlement was also explicitly listed as an objective of US trade policy going into the Tokyo Round in the Trade Act of 1974.[73] This objective was closely tied to the turn to unfair trade: what was needed to deal with the problem of unfair trade practices, it seemed to US officials, was a clear set of rules, strictly enforced, by a formal and effective dispute settlement system. In this way of thinking, the legal system of the GATT existed, quite simply, to ensure that Contracting Parties to the GATT were held to the negotiated commitments they made. The treaty texts recorded those commitments, and the dispute settlement mechanism existed to ensure as far as possible that they were adhered to. International trade law existed to provide certainty and predictability for Contracting Parties and their traders, and to protect them against interference by the arbitrary and illegitimate exercise of public power by foreign governments.

Though there was considerable resistance from other countries during the Tokyo Round, especially from the EC, this strand of thinking about the function of law in trade politics gradually became more dominant within the field. This was in part the result of a variety of factors internal to the trade regime.[74] The proliferation of new forms of protectionism during the 1970s, for example, helped to entrench the perception that the GATT needed a harder and more effective mechanism for enforcing its disciplines. This perception was intensified as a result of the increasing level of obstruction, delay, and hostility which characterized GATT dispute settlement during the 1960s and 1970s.[75] However, these new ideas about the role of law also reflected broader developments occurring outside the trade regime. I suggested in the previous chapter that the post-war regime's adoption of a purposive and instrumental approach to law represented in significant part a projection of approaches to law and modes of governance characteristic of the domestic welfare state. As the welfare state gradually transitioned into the neoliberal state from the

[72] Winham (1986) 32–3; Golt (1978) 12.

[73] Hudec (1980) 156, citing 19 USC §§ 2131, 2121(a)(1), (9).

[74] These factors are described, for example, in Hudec (1993); Hudec (1978); and the publications by Jackson cited in n 83 below.

[75] Hudec (1978) 11–13.

1970s, it brought with it a different set of ideas about the role of law in governing economic life.[76]

As Kennedy describes it, within neoliberal thought, law 'emerged as a limit on the state',[77] as the guarantor of the private rights of economic actors against interference by state action. The operation of law came to be less about the fulfilment of collective economic projects and more about protecting the pursuit of individual economic projects against arbitrary and unjustified interference by public power. In addition, law helped to establish the institutional underpinning for the pursuit of individual economic projects in the market, by providing a mechanism for the enforcement of contractual bargains between market participants. Law, in other words, existed in significant part to respond to economic actors' needs for certainty and predictability. This is a crucial point: as we shall see below, the idea that international trade law existed to limit the arbitrary exercise of public power, and to provide certainty and predictability to traders, had a fundamental impact on the interpretive choices made in difficult cases during this period.

It is worth noting that there is a clear connection between this way of understanding the function of international trade law, and the re-description of the trade regime as a 'marketplace' or 'private interest community', elaborated above. As Abbott notes, a public interest community 'uses all tools at its disposal, including its legal system, to implement... [its] communal vision of the public good'. Legal institutions 'function actively to elaborate and implement community policy'.[78] In a private interest community, on the other hand, legal institutions exist primarily 'to provide a framework for the pursuit of private interests'. As far as possible, the rules governing behaviour are those contractually consented to by parties, and legal institutions 'function only to maintain order and to provide a forum for resolving disputes' in a neutral manner.[79]

There is ample evidence of the spread of this way of thinking about the role of law within the field of international trade governance from at least the late 1970s. In the aftermath of the Tokyo Round, observers of the trade regime celebrated the 'reduction in the scope for arbitrary government constraints' on international trade, and the concomitant increase in predictability and certainty for traders.[80] New agreements covering non-tariff barriers and strengthened dispute settlement were said to have 'restor[ed] a greater degree of order in international commerce'.[81] They were seen by some as a first step in the 'battle to restore and reinvigorate the international

[76] See generally A Aman, 'Law, Markets and Democracy: A Role for Law in the Neo Liberal State' (2007) 51 New York Law School L Rev 801; D Kennedy, 'The "Rule of Law," Political Choices, and Development Common Sense' in DM Trubek and A Santos (eds), *The New Law and Economic Development: A Critical Appraisal* (CUP, Cambridge 2006) 95–173, D Kennedy, 'Three Globalizations of Law and Legal Thought: 1850–2000' in Trubek and Santos (2006) 19–73.

[77] David Kennedy (2006) 138.

[78] Abbott 'GATT as a Public Institution' (1992) 35.

[79] ibid 34 5. See also Abbott 'The Uruguay Round and Dispute Resolution' (1992) 118.

[80] Winham (1986) 362.

[81] Baldwin (1979) 4.

rule of law'.[82] Over the course of the 1980s, these ideas were most famously and most elaborately developed by Jackson, who argued for a more rule-oriented framework for the conduct of international trade politics.[83] Arguing that inadequate legal and institutional frameworks were among the reasons for the near breakdown of the system in the 1970s,[84] he made a series of influential arguments in favour of a more formal, more judicial, and more professional dispute settlement mechanism.[85] These arguments were explicitly based on the idea that international trade law existed in part to provide predictability and stability for both governments and private business persons, to allow them to engage in mutually beneficial coordinated activities and transactions.[86] Petersmann, too, developed a theory of the 'constitutional' functions of international trade law in a series of articles published from the mid-1980s and throughout the 1990s. Basing his argument in part on the public choice accounts of domestic trade politics referred to above, he suggested that international trade law helped to correct for the disproportionate influence of special interests by providing a quasi-constitutional restriction on the conduct of trade policy.[87] He championed the view that international trade law existed to protect the economic freedoms and rights of traders against unjustified interference by public power.[88] It existed, in his view, as an external constitutional constraint on state power, to rectify an internal constitutional failure. Others explored the extent to which WTO agreements could or should be seen to grant individual rights to private traders, or should be given direct effect in domestic jurisdictions.[89] A version of this constitutionalist view of WTO law even began to appear in WTO Panel decisions (albeit only sporadically and in a significantly moderated form). Thus, for example, both *Tuna/Dolphin* panels in the 1980s appeared to give great weight in their decisions to the fact that permitting the US measures at issue would in their view radically

[82] Golt (1982) 28.

[83] JH Jackson, *Restructuring the GATT System* (Chatham House Papers, London 1990); JH Jackson, 'Strengthening the International Legal Framework of the GATT MTN System: Reform Proposals for the New GATT Round' in E-U Petersmann and M Hilf (eds), *The New GATT Round of Multilateral Trade Negotiations: Legal and Economic Problems* (Kluwer, Dordrecht 1988); JH Jackson, 'Governmental Disputes in International Trade Relations: A Proposal in the Context of GATT' (1979) 13 J of World Trade L 1; JH Jackson, 'The Crumbling Institutions of the Liberal Trade System' (1978) 12 J of World Trade L 93; JH Jackson, 'The Birth of the GATT-MTN System: A Constitutional Appraisal' (1980) 12 L and Policy in Intl Business 21.

[84] Jackson 'Crumbling Institutions' (1978).

[85] See eg Jackson (1980).

[86] eg Jackson (1980) 25–6.

[87] See eg E-U Petersmann, 'Trade Policy as a Constitutional Problem: On the "Domestic Policy Functions" of International Trade Rules' (1986) 41 Swiss Rev Intl Econ Rel 405; E-U Petersmann, 'International and European Foreign Trade Law: GATT Dispute Settlement Proceedings Against the EEC' (1985) 22 CMLR 441.

[88] ibid. See also W Roepke, 'Economic Order and International Law' (1954) 86 Recueil des Cours 203, for an early example.

[89] S Charnovitz, 'The WTO and the Rights of the Individual' (2001) 36 Intereconomics 98. See also JH Jackson, *Implementing the Tokyo Round: National Constitutions and International Economic Rules* (University of Michigan Press, Ann Arbor, MI 1984); A Reich, 'From Diplomacy to Law: The Juridicization of International Trade Relations' (1997) 17 Northwestern J of Intl L and Business 775.

undermine 'legal security' for traders and trading nations.[90] The Panel in *US—Section 301*, in the course of a lengthy passage noteworthy for its direct attention to individual traders as stakeholders in the WTO system, described the 'objects and purposes of the DSU, and the WTO more generally' as having to do with 'the creation of market conditions conducive to individual economic activity in national and global markets and to the provision of a secure and predictable multilateral trading system.'[91]

But the best evidence of the influence of this way of thinking about law is the increasing dissatisfaction which GATT Contracting Parties felt with regard to the existing dispute resolution system, and the institutional transformations to GATT/WTO dispute settlement which occurred, albeit unevenly,[92] over the course of the 1980s and 1990s. These institutional transformations had the effect of bringing the GATT's legal system much more into line with the values associated with this new way of thinking about law: namely, the values of neutrality and objectivity, precision, effectiveness and strict enforceability, rapidity, expertise, and professionalism. The story of this institutional transformation has been extensively chronicled elsewhere, and there is no need for me to do more than briefly recapitulate some of its highlights. The decisive move was probably the incremental abolition of the requirement for consensus at all stages of the dispute settlement process, from the establishment of a panel, the selection of panellists, and the adoption of the report, to the authorization of retaliation. The final replacement of this requirement with the reverse consensus rule at the conclusion of the Uruguay Round went a long way towards creating a truly compulsory and automatic system of dispute settlement, backed by meaningful sanctions. As regards the quality and coherence of the legal reasoning, this was incrementally enhanced through the emergence of legal textbooks and the GATT Analytical Index from the late 1960s onwards;[93] the creation of the GATT's legal office in 1981[94] and the gradual expansion of legal expertise in the GATT Secretariat from that time;[95] the increasing use of panellists with legal expertise; and ultimately the creation of a system of appellate review during the Uruguay Round. The new Secretariat serving the Appellate Body cultivated a self-conscious detachment from many of the other aspects of the WTO's operation in its early years, which was reflected also in the highly formalized, precise, and textualist modes of legal reasoning characteristic of early Appellate Body reports. The

[90] Panel Report, *United States—Restrictions on Imports of Tuna* (unadopted, 3 September 1991) BISD 39S/155 (DS21/R) ('*Tuna/Dolphin I*') paras 5.27–5.32; Panel Report, *United States—Restrictions on Imports of Tuna* (unadopted, 16 June 1994) (DS29/R) ('*Tuna/Dolphin II*') paras 5.26–5.27.

[91] Panel Report, *United States—Sections 301–310 of the Trade Act of 1974* (adopted 27 Jaunary 2000) WT/DS152/R, para 7.71.

[92] See eg Hudec (1980) and Jackson 'Crumbling Institutions' (1978) in relation to the 'management' of trade relations during the 1980s and concerns about the erosion of legalization at the time.

[93] Thiébaut Flory, *Le G.A.T.T., droit international et commerce mondial* (Librairie générale de droit et de jurisprudence, Paris 1968); Jackson (1969); Kulwant Rai Gupta, *A Study of General Agreement on Tariffs and Trade* (S Chand, Delhi 1967).

[94] Hudec (1993) 137–8.

[95] Pauwelyn (2005).

Secretariat has developed into a major repository and source of professional legal expertise in the field of international trade governance.

Importantly, widespread concerns about the objectivity and neutrality of the GATT procedure also provoked the gradual disembedding of the dispute settlement system from the processes of trade diplomacy. While the structural embedding of dispute settlement in the diplomatic process was perfectly well suited to a purposive approach to law, from the new perspective it appeared as a considerable threat to the impartiality and rigour of the dispute settlement process. It was no longer so legitimate to distinguish acceptable from unacceptable regulation by referring back to the prevailing norms and expectations within the tight-knit community of trade diplomats making up the GATT. The new ideas about the role of the GATT/WTO system and its legal framework placed a premium on the separation between the 'law' and 'politics' of international trade, and logically necessitated a normative framework to judge the acceptability of public action which was in some meaningful sense external to trade politics. Nor was it a question of interpreting the law purposively in the sense of channelling the 'spirit' of the law—perhaps the spirit of 'embedded liberalism'—to guide the development and application of flexible rules. Again, the new ideas about law had assumed away any collective social purpose or collective political project animating the law. Law was now imagined as protecting the pursuit of individual projects, arbitrating between different individual projects, and providing an institutional space for the fulfilment of those projects.

The re-imagination of law as a bulwark against public interference with private rights necessitated a self-conscious distancing of trade law from 'trade politics' or trade diplomacy, as well as a new formal structure and set of professional practices to institute a clearer boundary between them. The gradual constitution of 'trade law' as a legal field in its own right implied the development of a professional mindset within trade law which to a significant extent resisted explicit and excessive deference to the ethos of the diplomat's world—precisely as a way of asserting the autonomy of the law. Thus, while government officials still remained the preferred choice as panel members, it was made clearer that they acted in their own independent capacity, and could not take instructions from their home government. There were increasing calls for—and use of—outside non-governmental experts as panel members, albeit with a preference for those with some intimate knowledge of the workings of the GATT.[96] The nullification and impairment provision moved from being a minor but important mechanism to ensure the flexible and purposive operation of the GATT's legal system in accordance with the expectations of trade diplomats, to an essentially inactive provision in the present regime. While it is true that the autonomization of law within the governance of international trade is still incomplete,[97] and that we continue to see a significant degree of soft control exerted by the community of trade diplomats over the evolution and interpretation of trade law, there has therefore been a clear trend in the direction of formal independence.

[96] Hudec (1978); GATT, *Trade Policies for a Better Future* (GATT, Geneva 1985) 55 (known as the 'Leutwiler Report'); Baldwin (1979) 8.

[97] See generally Broude (2004).

B. Outside technical expertise

If the search for objectivity and neutrality in GATT dispute settlement led to its formalization and autonomization, it also led in another direction as well. As more and more disputes arose regarding complex aspects of domestic regulation which related to trade policy only indirectly, GATT Contracting Parties began increasingly turning to various forms of specialized technical expertise both to frame their arguments, and to help to resolve their disputes. As a strategy to rebuild a substantive consensus on legitimate and appropriate domestic regulation, this had mixed success at best, but over time this turn to technical expertise became a characteristic element of the operation, elaboration, and interpretation of GATT disciplines on domestic regulation. A few examples will help to provide the flavour.

The first example concerns the issue of border tax adjustments, which became a major cause of friction in the final years of the 1960s, particularly between the United States and the EC.[98] When a country imposes a new tax on domestic products or their producers, it will often wish to counteract the competitive disadvantage which these domestic products or producers face *vis-à-vis* foreign products as a result of the new tax. It may do this by imposing a tax on imported products at the border equivalent to the new internal tax, and by remitting the tax on domestic products if they are exported to foreign markets. It was quite clear that the GATT permitted such 'border tax adjustments'—but it did so only in respect of 'indirect taxes' (including taxes on products themselves, levied on the producer but borne by the consumer), and not 'direct taxes' (such as income tax). This distinction represented a codification of the practice of Contracting Parties at the time of the drafting of the initial GATT, which in turn reflected classical theory of tax shifting, prevalent at the time, according to which in a perfectly competitive market indirect taxes are always passed on to the price of the product, while direct taxes are not. If this assumption were not correct, then producers in those countries which relied mostly on direct taxes—such as the United States at the time—would be at a competitive disadvantage as compared to producers in countries which relied mostly on indirect taxes.

When, in 1968, the EC and other countries moved to a system of taxation based on indirect taxes, they instituted a new package of border tax adjustments at the same time.[99] Faced with new taxes on their exports to the EC, many in the United States 'concluded that Europeans were flaunting their tariff-cutting commitments and providing substitute protection in the form of border tax adjustments'.[100] The

[98] See generally JC Phillips, 'Border Tax Adjustments in International Trade' (1976) 9 University of Queensland LJ 151; OECD, 'Border Tax Adjustments and Tax Structures in OECD Member Countries—Report on Tax Adjustments Applied to Exports and Imports in OECD Member Countries' cited in Phillips (1976) n 2; Evans (1971); GATT, *Border Tax Adjustments: Report of the Working Party Adopted on 2 December 1970* (adopted 2 December 1970) BISD 18S/99 (L/3464), and material cited in n 101 below.

[99] See TB Curtis and JR Vastine, Jr, *The Kennedy Round and the Future of American Trade* (Praeger, New York, NY 1971) 235.

[100] Ibid.

issue became a sore one for the United States in its relationship with the EC. One significant part of the effort by the United States (and other interested states) to address the question was undertaken at the level of technical argumentation. Academic research and the work of government economists already provided the basis for a sound theoretical argument against the classical distinction between direct and indirect taxes, which 'supported and intensified the businessman's reaction'.[101] The OECD had also conducted a technical study of border tax adjustments, which revisited the fundamental economic assumptions of underlying GATT rules.[102] The United States and others therefore marshalled this material to make 'the theoretical case . . . with increasing frequency during and after the Kennedy Round' that a new approach should be adopted.[103] A GATT Working Party was created in April 1968 to study and discuss the issue, meeting twelve times over the course of the next thirty months, and the report of the Working Party makes clear that in this forum the United States and its allies again pressed their claims in part in a technical idiom.[104] Unsurprisingly, however, those countries relying primarily on direct taxes countered with their own technical arguments. In the end, neither side was able to have their preferred view generally accepted, and the report is largely confined to recording the differing arguments made. A new notification and consultation procedure was recommended, but it lacked substance. In the face of implacable resistance, and in the absence of a more effective dispute settlement system, there was little more that the United States could immediately do. The issue was taken up again during negotiations over the Standards Code during the Tokyo Round.[105]

The second example concerns the dispute over the US Domestic International Sales Corporation (DISC).[106] The dispute began in 1971 with the passing of a US law which provided certain tax benefits to US exporters, passed at the same time as Nixon suspended the gold convertibility of the US dollar. The impetus for the law was the conviction that foreign tax regimes provided an unfair advantage to their producers, by permitting those producers to route their exports through shelf corporations established in third country tax havens. Since these tax havens imposed little or no income tax, and since the producers were in practice able to sell to their shelf companies at below market rates, they were able to escape considerable income tax liability. By way of response, the US law provided a complicated structure for the

[101] Evans (1971) 96. For some of the literature, see OECD, 'Border Tax Adjustments' cited in Phillips (1976) n 2; HB Malmgren, 'The Border Tax Problem: Tax Harmonization in Europe and U.S. Business' (1969) XVII Canadian Tax J 34; HB Junz, 'Issues and Objectives of US Foreign Trade Policy' in *Issues and Objectives of U.S. Foreign Trade Policy* (Joint Economic Committee of Congress, Government Printing Office, Washington, DC 1967) 31–40; S Weintraub, 'Border Tax Adjustments and the GATT' (1965) 17 Tax Executive 304.

[102] OECD, 'Border Tax Adjustments' cited in Phillips (1976) n 2.

[103] Evans (1971) 96.

[104] GATT, *Border Tax Adjustments* (1970).

[105] See Subsidies Code, Agreement on Interpretation and Application of Articles VI, XVI and XXIII of the General Agreement on Tariffs and Trade (1 January 1980) BISD 26S/56 Annex, paras (e) and (g).

[106] See generally Panel Report, *United States Tax Legislation (DISC)* (adopted 7 December 1981) BISD 23S/98 (L/4422), see also BISD 28S/114 (L/5271); Hudec (1993) ch 5; Hudec (1978) 60ff; JH Jackson, 'The Jurisprudence of International Trade: The DISC Case in GATT' (1978) 72 AJIL 747.

indefinite deferral of income tax on 50 per cent of the profits which US producers make from export sales. The EC almost immediately requested consultations on the measure, alleging a violation of Article XVI:4 of the GATT, which prohibited the grant of certain export subsidies. According to Hudec, relevant US officials felt strongly that they were in the right as a matter of policy:

> According to US tax experts, the European laws permitted exporters to shift an unjustifiably large share of their export income to tax-haven entities because they permitted under-pricing of the goods 'sold' to those entities. United States tax practice, by comparison, was to apply fairly rigorous 'arm's length pricing' standards. The US tax officials found it particularly irritating, therefore, to be accused of subsidization by European tax officials who, they believed, were actively promoting even greater subsidies at home.[107]

As a result, the United States decided to bring a counterclaim against the tax policies of three different European countries, which, they argued, had essentially the same economic effect as the US DISC legislation. It seems that, as a matter of technical economic analysis, the US claim 'was difficult to refute', and was commonly accepted among taxation experts.[108] Convinced that it was right on the merits of the case, the United States insisted that a single panel be tasked with hearing the claim against the DISC legislation as well as the United States' counterclaims—and that the panel contain at least one tax expert. They succeeded, and in the end the panel of five members contained two European tax experts, one from the London School of Economics and one from the University of Turin.[109] In the end, the Panel was convinced by the United States' argument that the European and US measures were functionally equivalent in terms of their economic effects, and found all the measures to be in violation of Article XVI:4 of the GATT.[110] It is not clear whether this decision was affected by the presence of tax experts who were familiar with, and receptive to, the United States' technical arguments—but who were relatively unfamiliar with the world of trade diplomacy. What is clear is that the decision against the European tax measures was fundamentally unpalatable in political terms: it would have required a 'revolution in world tax practice'; and it went against the clear understanding of all trade negotiators about what was and was not the intended effect of Article XVI:4.[111] The reports were not adopted until a compromise was found five years later.

While this experience reinforced the need for expert adjudicators to have intimate knowledge of GATT affairs,[112] it did not halt the turn to the objectivity of technical knowledge in the operation and elaboration of GATT regulatory disciplines. As is well known, the Tokyo Round ultimately produced a number of plurilateral 'Codes' putting in place new or more elaborate disciplines for various categories of non-tariff

107 Hudec (1993) 68.
108 ibid 83.
109 ibid 70.
110 See Jackson (1978) 762–3, *US–DISC* (1981).
111 Hudec (1993) 84.
112 Hudec (1978).

barriers, the most important of which were the Subsidies Code, the Standards Code, the Code on Government Procurement, and an updated Anti-Dumping Code to replace the Kennedy Round agreement.[113] To a significant extent, these negotiations were carried out in close consultation with specialists in the areas under negotiation.[114] That said, by and large these negotiations did not seek to set out substantive rules about the content of appropriate and inappropriate regulation, at least not at a very specific level. Instead, the primary model adopted was to draft general regulatory principles applicable to entire areas of regulation, combined with mechanisms for the judicious application where appropriate of specialized technical knowledge relating to the specific regulatory field at issue in the context of interpretation and dispute settlement.

The Standards Code is the clearest example of this strategy. It laid down the general principle that technical regulations and standards must not be 'prepared, adopted or applied with a view to creating obstacles to international trade', nor have 'the effect of creating unnecessary obstacles to international trade'. It applied the national treatment obligation to technical standards, adopting the terminology of Article III:4 of the GATT almost unchanged. It required parties to use international standards as a basis for their technical regulations and standards—at least where such standards were not 'inappropriate for the Parties concerned'. And it obliged parties, where appropriate, to specify technical regulations and standards in terms of performance rather than design or descriptive characteristics.[115] The Code did not address the substantive legitimacy of specific technical measures, nor were specific measures ever seriously discussed during negotiations.[116] These (and other) general obligations were then supplemented by an enhanced dispute settlement mechanism, available by right to a complaining party. Disputes were to be handled in the first instance by a newly established Committee on Technical Barriers to Trade, composed of representatives of each of the Parties. The Committee had the power to consult 'competent bodies and experts in matters under consideration' for information and assistance, and to invite such bodies to attend its meetings.[117] If the Committee was not initially able to facilitate a satisfactory resolution, a party could request the establishment of a 'technical expert group', which was empowered to make statements concerning the relevant facts, as well as to make findings concerning, for example, 'the detailed scientific judgments

[113] Subsidies Code (1980); Standards Code, Agreement on Technical Barriers to Trade (1 January 1980) BISD 26S/8; Agreement on Government Procurement (1 January 1981) BISD 26S/33; Anti-Dumping Code, Agreement on Implementation of Article VI of the General Agreement on Tariffs and Trade (1 January 1980) BISD 26S/171.

[114] See eg Winham (1986) ch 6. The same is true of the SPS Agreement in the Uruguay Round: see DW Drezner, *All Politics Is Global: Explaining International Regulatory Regimes* (Princeton University Press, Princeton, NJ 2007) 161–3; D Prévost and P Van den Bossche, 'The Agreement on the Application of Sanitary and Phytosanitary Measures' in Macrory, Appleton, and Plummer (2005) 231.

[115] Standards Code (1980) arts 2.1, 2.2, and 2.4.

[116] Winham (1986), eg 101–4.

[117] Standards Code (1980) art 14.8.

involved, whether the measure was necessary for the protection of human, animal or plant life or health, and whether a legitimate scientific judgment is involved'.[118] If the dispute was still not resolved through this procedure, either party could by right request the establishment of a panel, which was required to use the report of the technical expert group as the basis for its assessment of questions of a technical nature. Neither technical expert groups nor panels could contain citizens of countries which were parties to the dispute, and they served strictly in their individual capacities, without instructions from government.[119] Reports of both kinds of bodies were submitted to the Committee for consideration and action, including making recommendations to one or more parties, and taking a decision (by consensus) to authorize retaliation if the circumstances were serious enough.

This approach was further entrenched during the Uruguay Round, during which the Standards Code was replaced by the SPS and TBT agreements.[120] The primary innovation of the SPS Agreement was a turn to scientific expertise as an arbiter of the boundary between legitimate and illegitimate domestic regulation. Article 2.2 of that agreement, for example, requires that SPS measures be 'based on scientific principles', and that they not be 'maintained without sufficient scientific evidence', while Article 5.1 requires that they be based on a scientific risk assessment.[121] The result of these provisions is that WTO dispute settlement panels now routinely scrutinize the scientific basis of its domestic food safety regulation, and that argument over such measures is to a large extent carried out as a contest between different forms of scientific expertise.[122] Another similar innovation was the incorporation of new and different harmonization obligations in the SPS and TBT agreements. This was probably the most direct response of negotiators to the problems caused for the trading system by the mere fact of regulatory diversity, as described above. Both agreements try to limit this diversity, and encourage a degree of convergence, by encouraging WTO Members, in certain circumstances, to base their regulatory measures on relevant international standards.[123] In the SPS area, such international standards are promulgated by technical international bodies such as the Codex Alimentarius Commission, the World Organisation for Animal Health (OIE), and the Secretariat of the International Plant Protection Convention.[124] In addition, both the SPS and TBT agreements—and indeed the Dispute Settlement Understanding more generally—follow the lead of the Standards Code in providing specifically for the incorporation of the views of technical experts in dispute settlement, through such means as Technical Expert Groups and Expert Review

[118] ibid art 14.9.

[119] ibid Annex 2 and Annex 3.

[120] For an account of the negotiation of the SPS Agreement, see Prévost and Van den Bossche, 'The Agreement on the Application of Sanitary and Phytosanitary Measures' in Macrory, Appleton, and Plummer (2005) 231.

[121] See WTO, Agreement of the Application of Sanitary and Phytosanitary Measures (15 April 1994) LT/UR/A-1A/12, arts 2.2, 5.

[122] See eg J Pauwelyn, 'Expert Advice in WTO Dispute Settlement' in GA Bermann and PC Mavroidis (eds), *Trade and Human Health and Safety* (CUP, Cambridge 2006) 235, 251–2.

[124] SPS Agreement (1994) Annex A, para 3.

[123] SPS Agreement (1994) art 3; WTO, Agreement on Technical Barriers to Trade (15 April 1994) LT/UR/A-1A/10 ('TBT Agreement'), art 2.4.

[124] SPS Agreement (1994) Annex A, para 3.

Groups.[125] Expert bodies were also created by other WTO agreements, including the Permanent Group of Experts established under Article 24 of the SCM Agreement, and the Technical Committee on Customs Valuation created by the Agreement on Customs Valuation.[126] Quite apart from these mechanisms, there has been increasing use of expert evidence in GATT/WTO dispute settlement since the end of the Uruguay Round in a variety of ways, including the use of panel-appointed experts, consultation with international organizations, and the submission of detailed expert evidence by parties themselves.[127]

C. Formal law and technical expertise

I have argued so far that over the course of the last few decades of the twentieth century, the GATT/WTO legal system changed its character, becoming both more formalized, and more 'technicalized'. In an immediate sense, this occurred as a result of the need for effective dispute resolution in respect of newly identified, 'behind the border' barriers to trade. More fundamentally, however, it was the result of the resurgence of a particular view of the role of law in international trade politics, which stressed the need for objective and neutral enforcement of inter-state bargains and the constraint of arbitrary public power. On one side, this new emphasis on the neutrality and objectivity of law necessitated a turn away from the 'internal' shared norms and expectations of the diplomatic community as the primary source of normative guidance in the interpretation and elaboration of trade law. This led to the formalization of the GATT/WTO's legal system, and its increasing autonomization from the world of trade diplomacy. On the other side, the need for law to act as an objective external constraint on arbitrary public power provided an impetus for the increasing technicalization of the legal system, which was *experienced as a depoliticization* of law and legal reasoning, and which was a constitutive sign of law's objectivity. This turn to technical expertise is best understood, in other words, as part of the disembedding of trade law from trade diplomacy, as it helped to constitute the boundary between the two, and to ensure the objectivity and neutrality of legal procedures.[128] Formalization and technicalization went hand in hand, as two sides of a single basic transformation.

It is important that I be clear precisely what I mean when I talk about the incorporation of technical expertise into the processes of interpreting and elaborating

[125] ibid art 11; TBT Agreement (1994) art 14; WTO, Understanding on Rules and Procedures Governing the Settlement of Disputes (15 April 1994) LT/UR/A-2/DS/U/1 ('DSU'), art 13 and Appendix 4.

[126] WTO, Agreement on Subsidies and Countervailing Measures (15 April 1994) LT/UR/A-1A/9 ('SCM Agreement'), art 24.3; WTO, Agreement on Implementation of Article VII of the General Agreement on Tariffs and Trade 1994 (15 April 1994) LT/UR/A-1A/4, art 18.2 and Annex II.

[127] Pauwelyn (2006).

[128] GR Winham, 'The World Trade Organization: Institution-building in the Multilateral Trade System' (1998) 21 The World Economy 349, 362, also notes the emphasis that negotiators placed on the technical nature of panel procedure.

disciplines on domestic regulation. Part of this has to do with formal consultation with experts and the explicit evaluation of scientific and technical expertise, as just described. But the phenomenon I am describing is much broader than that. I am interested in the emergence of a form of legal reasoning within the field of international trade law which combined an intensely formalist style with a propensity to draw normative inspiration and analytical turns of mind from the rational discourses of the policy sciences.[129] This sometimes takes the form of explicit borrowing from technical discourses—one example would be the attempt to incorporate the technical distinction between 'risk assessment' and 'risk management' into jurisprudence under the SPS Agreement.[130] More often, however, it will take a softer form, involving the adoption of characteristic habits of thought or conceptual distinctions from economics or other policy disciplines in a much looser way. For experts in the fields from which the interpreters of trade law are seeking guidance, this form of borrowing can be frustrating, and can lead to the perception that trade tribunals are insufficiently rigorous in the application of technical knowledge.[131] Borrowing will typically be a creative act rather than an automatic one: the process of legal interpretation, in other words, comes to be in part a creative process of selecting and arbitrating between different forms of technical expertise, reinterpreting or even misunderstanding concepts and ideas drawn from policy discourses, and actively creating a new unique body of mixed technical-legal expertise to guide the interpretation of the general regulatory disciplines of WTO law. The next section illustrates these processes in the context of the evolution of the jurisprudence under Articles I, III, and XX of the GATT over the course of the 1980s and 1990s.

III. The changing jurisprudence on domestic regulation, 1980–2000

Over the last two decades of the twentieth century, partly in response to the political, economic, and conceptual developments just outlined, a number GATT/WTO disputes were brought over domestic regulatory measures which were not designed as trade policy measures, but which nevertheless had an indirect or incidental trade-restricting effect. As set out in the Chapter 7, prior to the Uruguay Round the primary legal framework for addressing these kinds of measures consisted of the non-discrimination norms contained in Articles I and III of the GATT, the general exceptions provisions contained in Article XX, and the possibility of 'non-violation' complaints under Article XXIII:1(b). As the GATT/WTO's legal system became more formal and judicialized, the third limb of this framework—non-violation complaints—came to be seen as something of an historical oddity, and it fell into

[129] See for a similar argument in a different context David Kennedy (2006).

[130] See the discussion of the *EC—Hormones* dispute, below p 338 and surrounding.

[131] See eg A Mattoo and A Subramanian, 'Regulatory Autonomy and Multilateral Disciplines: The Dilemma and a Possible Resolution' (1998) 1 JIEL 303. See also H Horn and PC Mavroidis, 'Still Hazy after All These Years: The Interpretation of National Treatment in the GATT/WTO Case-law on Tax Discrimination' (2004) 15 EJIL 39.

desuetude, as noted above. As a result, many of the most significant cases during this period were brought under Articles I, III, and XX of the GATT.[132]

In this section, I describe the way in which these GATT provisions were reinterpreted over the course of the late 1980s and 1990s. On one hand, the notion of discrimination underlying Articles I and III was reinterpreted to mean something very close to the economic concept of a market distortion. On the other, in the context of interpreting Article XX, panels began to turn to specialized technical knowledge for guidance as to when particular regulatory interventions were objectively justified and optimally designed.

A. Discrimination as market distortion

It is by now very well understood that the notion of 'non-discrimination' in international trade law is susceptible to a number of different interpretations, ranging from the very narrow to the very broad. At the narrower end, prohibiting 'discrimination' against foreign products may be understood simply as outlawing measures which intentionally single out foreign products for adverse treatment based solely on their origin—whether this occurs explicitly or in a disguised way. From this perspective, the non-discrimination norm contained in Article III of the GATT is essentially an 'anti-protectionism' norm and ought to be applied solely to those internal measures which are expressly or implicitly motivated by a protectionist intent. I have shown in Chapter 7 that, during the first few decades of its existence, the application of this provisions was, in practice, indeed limited to precisely those kinds of internal measures. For that reason, it is fair to say that the GATT 1947 originally afforded its Contracting Parties a considerable degree of regulatory freedom. At the broader end of the spectrum of possible interpretations, however, the prohibition of discriminatory internal measures may be understood also to catch measures that distinguish between products based on criteria other than their origin, which are not protectionist in their purpose and intent, but which nevertheless have an incidental or accidental negative impact on some foreign products. Interpreted in this way, the principle of non-discrimination may, at its extreme, effectively require substantively equal treatment of all similar products, regardless of the basis on which they might be treated differently.

One of the key distinctions between these two approaches is that the broader interpretation focuses on the detrimental *effects* of a measure on foreign products, while the narrower interpretation focuses primarily on its discriminatory *intent*. The characteristic feature of the jurisprudence under, and the commentary on, the GATT non-discrimination norms from at least the late 1980s onwards has been the existence of an ongoing struggle between approaches to discrimination which emphasize the protectionist intent of a measure, and those which emphasize its

[132] In addition, after 1995, significant cases on domestic regulation have also been brought under new agreements negotiated in the Uruguay Round, such as the GATS, the SCM Agreement, the TBT Agreement and the SPS Agreement. The latter is dealt with in more detail in Ch 10 below.

effects. Over the course of the 1990s, the clear trend was incrementally but decisively to eliminate virtually any explicit consideration of intent in the interpretation of GATT non-discrimination norms. This section charts this trend through a series of interpretive developments during that period.[133]

In my view, virtually all of the interpretive developments described in this section are closely connected to, and driven by, an implicit association which began to be made between the notion of discrimination under Articles I and III and the notion of a 'market distortion' from economic analysis. That is to say, the underlying conceptual move which drove this new jurisprudence (even if it was never quite fully realized) was to equate a discriminatory regulation with any regulation which shifted patterns of domestic consumption away from foreign products and towards their domestic counterparts. The development of an effects- rather than intent-based approach to discrimination, in other words, was the consequence of treating the legal concept of discrimination as more or less synonymous with the effects-based economic concept of a market distortion.

The object and purpose of Articles I and III

There have always been at least two strands of thinking about the objects and purposes of the non-discrimination norm in GATT law, as it relates to internal regulatory measures. While they are by no means incompatible, there is a distinct difference of emphasis between them.

On one hand, there is the view that the non-discrimination norms primarily exist to support the broader project of removing border barriers, and to ensure that internal regulations are not used as a means of undermining or reneging on commitments to reduce border barriers. To that end, they are directed towards the elimination of indirect or hidden protectionism once goods enter into a domestic market, and the basic task of applying the non-discrimination norm primarily involves distinguishing legitimate domestic regulation from regulation with protectionist motives. It is certainly arguable that this understanding of the object and purpose of the non-discrimination norms was dominant in the minds of the post-war drafters of the GATT. Srinivasan, for example, argues that:

> ... it is clear that the signatories viewed discriminatory treatment in international commerce, not as being unfair in some relevant sense ... but as subverting the broad objectives that signatories sought to promote through GATT.[134]

[133] For similar histories, see generally L Ehring, 'De Facto Discrimination in WTO Law: National and Most Favored-Nation Treatment—or Equal Treatment?' (2002) 36 J of World Trade 921; G Verhoosel, *National Treatment and WTO Dispute Settlement: Adjudicating the Boundaries of Regulatory Autonomy* (Hart Publishing, Oxford 2002); RE Hudec, 'GATT/WTO Constraints on National Regulation: Requiem for an "Aim and Effects" Test' (1998) 32 Intl L 619; Mattoo and Subramanian (1998); Srinivasan (2005); Horn and Mavroïdis (2004), H Horn and PC Mavroïdis, 'Economic and Legal Aspects of the Most Favoured Nation Clause' (2001) 17 European J of Political Economy 223.

[134] Srinivasan (2005) 74–5.

This view is reflected in other literature, as well as in the drafting history of the provision.[135] It is, arguably at least, also reflected in paragraph 1 of Article III, which refers to the use of domestic regulation 'so as to afford protection to domestic production',[136] and was probably reflected in one of the earliest reasoned decisions on Article III in *Italy—Agricultural Machinery*, which referred to the objective of eliminating 'indirect protection'.[137]

On the other hand, another view of the non-discrimination norms sees them as having the primary purpose of ensuring the competitive neutrality of internal regulations—that is, of maintaining perfect competitive equality between imported and domestic products once imported products have entered the domestic market. While this way of thinking and talking about the purpose of the non-discrimination norms has been around since very early on,[138] it became much more common during the late 1980s and 1990s. Thus, for example, in the 1987 *US—Superfund* report, the Panel emphasized that one of the purposes of GATT Article III was to 'protect[] expectations of the competitive relationship between imported and domestic products'.[139] That Article exists, the Panel went on, not only to protect current trade 'but also the predictability needed to plan future trade'.[140] Thus the provision 'obliges contracting parties to establish certain competitive conditions for imported products', such that any 'change in the competitive relationship' would seem to be contrary to it.[141] Later, the Panel in *Korea—Alcohol* also noted that Article III 'serves to protect the expectations of competitive opportunities', and that it 'focuses on the promotion of economic opportunities for importers through the elimination of discriminatory governmental measures which impair fair international trade'.[142] This was also reflected in commentary on Article III, particularly from the late 1990s. In one paper, for example, Hudec argued that 'the basic policy of Article III is the economic policy to eliminate market distortions caused by internal measures'.[143]

[135] Panel Report, *Japan—Customs Duties, Taxes and Labelling Practices on Imported Wines and Alcoholic Beverages* (adopted 10 November 1987) BISD 34S/83 (L/6216) para 5.5: 'The drafting history confirms that Article III:2 was designed with "the intention that internal taxes on goods should not be used as a means of protection"'. Cf *Japan—Alcohol (AB)* 17 and n 39.

[136] GATT, Art III:1.

[137] Panel Report, *Italian Discrimination Against Imported Agricultural Machinery* (adopted 23 October 1958) BISD 7S/60 (L/833) para 11; Japan–Alcchol (AS) (1996), n 39.

[138] As stated in the 1970 Working Party Report on Border Tax Adjustments in respect of the various GATT provisions on taxation, 'the philosophy behind these provisions was the ensuring of a certain trade neutrality'. GATT, *Border Tax Adjustments* (1970). This accords with the broader objective of Article III 'to provide equal conditions of competition once goods had been cleared through customs' and to protect thereby the benefits accruing from tariff concessions: *Japan—Alcoholic Beverages I* (1987) para 5.5; *Japan—Alcohol (AB)* (1996) n 39.

[139] Panel Report, *United States—Taxes on Petroleum and Certain Imported Substances* (adopted 17 June 1987) BISD 34S/136 (L/6175)('*US—Superfund*') para 5.1.9.

[140] *US—Superfund* (1987) para 5.2.2.

[141] ibid para 5.1.9.

[142] Panel Report, *Korea—Taxes on Alcoholic Beverages* (adopted 17 Feburary 1999), WT/DS75/R and WT/DS84/R, paras 10.92, 10.81.

[143] RE Hudec, '"Like Product": The Differences in Meaning in GATT Articles I and III' in T Cottier and PC Mavroïdis (eds), *Regulatory Barriers and the Principle of Non-Discrimination in World Trade Law* (University of Michigan Press, Ann Arbor, MI 1998) 101–24, 108.

Jackson, too, has suggested that non-discrimination norms have the 'salutary effect of minimizing distortions of the "market" principles that motivate many arguments in favour of liberal trade'.[144] Others, reflecting on recent trends in the jurisprudence, characterize the purpose of Article III as requiring 'regulatory neutrality'.[145] In all of these formulations, the emphasis on the maintenance of strict competitive equality marked something of a departure from the prior emphasis on the goal of avoiding 'indirect protection' once goods had cleared customs. The shift was subtle, but clear—away from an emphasis on protective intent as the focus of attention, towards detrimental economic impact and the elimination of market 'distortions'. This shift had important consequential impacts on the interpretation of key elements of Articles I and III.

'Like products' and related concepts

One of the most important steps in the formal application of GATT non-discrimination norms involves a comparison between the foreign product at issue and another product, which is allegedly being treated more favourably. In order for the non-discrimination norm to apply, it must first be shown that these products are sufficiently similar to one another that they ought to be treated in a non-discriminatory way. The phrase used to describe the degree of similarity required varies between different provisions: in Article I, as well as in the first sentence of paragraph 2 and paragraph 4 of Article III, the term used is 'like product'; in the second sentence of Article III:2 the relevant term is 'directly competitive or substitutable products'. Another way in which the non-discrimination norms were influenced by the economic concept of trade distortion was through the reinterpretation of these phrases.

During the 1980s, there were two decided cases on the notion of 'like products' under Article I:1, which illustrate nicely the two different approaches which stood in competition with one another at the time.[146] *Spain—Unroasted Coffee* was a 1981 complaint brought by Brazil against Spain, and concerned Spain's differential tariff treatment of different unroasted coffee beans, depending on the type of coffee bean in question (Robusta, unwashed Arabica, mild, Columbia mild, and so on). One of the issues in question was whether different kinds of coffee bean were 'like products' within the meaning of Article I:1. In making its determination, the Panel adopted a market-based approach, based on competition between the products in the domestic market.[147] While it considered a number of different factors, the most important criterion seems to have been the way that these products were perceived by consumers in the marketplace:

[144] JH Jackson, *The World Trading System: Law and Policy of International Economic Relations* (2nd edn, MIT Press, Cambridge, MA 1997) 159.

[145] Horn and Mavroïdis (2004) 50.

[146] Readers will note that neither dispute concerns a 'domestic regulation' as that term has been defined for the purposes of this book. Nevertheless, these two cases are commonly understood to represent useful illustrative milestones in the evolution of the meaning of like products in GATT jurisprudence, and for that reason I include them in my story.

[147] See Hudec, 'Differences in Meaning' (1998) 13, for a similar interpretation.

> ... unroasted coffee was mainly, if not exclusively, sold in the form of blends, combining various types of coffee, and ... coffee in its end-use, was universally regarded as a well-defined and single product intended for drinking.[148]

In the light of this, evidence of organoleptic differences between the products (relating to their taste, colour, odour, and feel) were not particularly significant.[149]

A different approach, however, was adopted in a case that Canada brought against Japan in respect of alleged discriminatory treatment of Canadian exports of lumber to Japan, as compared to exports of lumber to Japan from other countries.[150] Japan afforded preferential tariff treatment to lumber made from tree species which were generally found in the United States, as compared to lumber made from tree species which were generally found in Canada. Canada argued that the two were 'like products', as required by Article I, and on a market-oriented approach it would seem to have had a very strong argument: consumers clearly did not purchase lumber on the basis of the species of tree from which it came, and there was no difference at all between the different end uses towards which the two different types of lumber were put. Indeed, it was very difficult physically to tell the difference between the two. Japan argued, however, that the adoption of an objective, market-based test would be inappropriate, in part because it would cause confusion in the context of tariff negotiations. The background to the case was a bargained exchange of market access concessions between Japan and the United States, in an agreement in which Canada did not participate.[151] Japan's tariff distinction represented a way of ensuring that Canada did not benefit from this agreement, when it had not offered anything in return—a common and accepted way of addressing the 'free rider' problem caused by the MFN principle, provided it was not abused.[152] The Panel deferred to this perception of the legitimacy of this practice, and was convinced by the practical need to ensure that negotiators had the freedom to continue this practice as necessary. Noting that 'tariff differentiation [was] basically a legitimate means of trade policy', a tariff distinction of this sort:

> ... is a legitimate means of adapting the tariff scheme to each contracting party's trade policy interests, comprising both its protection needs and its requirements for the purposes of tariff- and trade negotiations.[153]

Instead of relying on market-oriented criteria of 'likeness', then, it gave greater weight to the practices and expectations of the Contracting Parties.

These two cases, then, represent two distinct ways of interpreting the concept of 'like products'. *Japan—Lumber* looked primarily to the norms and expectations of the internal world of trade diplomacy for an indication of the legitimacy of

[148] Panel Report, *Spain—Tariff Treatment of Unroasted Coffee* (adopted 11 June 1981) BISD 28S/102 (L/5135) para 4.7.

[149] ibid para 4.6.

[150] Panel Report, *Canada/Japan—Tariff on Imports of Spruce, Pine, Fir (SPF) Dimension Lumber* (adopted 19 July 1989) BISD 36S/167 (L/6470) ('*Japan—Lumber*').

[151] Hudec 'Differences in Meaning' (1998) 114.

[152] ibid, 109.

[153] *Japan—Lumber*, paras 5.9, 5.10.

distinguishing between the products in question. This is an approach very much in keeping with the interpretive approach described in the previous chapter, which I linked with 'embedded liberalism' and its associated legal mindset. It was adopted in at least two other cases dealing with the concept.[154] *Spain—Unroasted Coffee*, however, looked primarily to the market for guidance as to what constituted 'like products'. It focused on consumers' tastes and habits, and the products' end uses in the marketplace, as the determinative criteria for an assessment of the relevant degree of similarity between products. As we shall see, it was this latter approach that became the dominant one in the application of the non-discrimination norms to internal measures under Article III, though not without some controversy and resistance.

The tone was set in 1987 with the *US—Superfund* Panel Report. One significant aspect of this report was its adoption of a relatively rigorous (albeit brief and uncontested) market-based approach to 'like products' under Article III:2:

> The domestic products subject to the tax are: crude oil, crude oil condensates, and natural gasoline. The imported products subject to the tax are: crude oil, crude oil condensates, natural gasoline, refined and residual oil, and certain other liquid hydrocarbon products. The imported and domestic products are thus either identical or, in the case of imported liquid hydrocarbon products, serve substantially identical end-uses. The imported and domestic products subject to the tax on petroleum are therefore in the view of the Panel 'like products' within the meaning of Article III:2.[155]

The primary emphasis on end-uses in the marketplace—and, just as significantly, the absence of any explicit consideration of the expectations of negotiators, or the normal treatment of such products within trade policy circles—situates this decision much closer to *Spain—Unroasted Coffee* than to *Japan—Lumber*.

However, in a brace of cases in the first half of the 1990s,[156] a contrary line of jurisprudence briefly emerged. In the first case, *US—Malt Beverages*, the Panel recognized that Article III had at least two objectives, exactly as noted above: first, supporting and ensuring the effectiveness of market access commitments under Articles I and II; and secondly, the 'additional function . . . to enhance non-discriminatory conditions of competition between imported and domestic products'.[157] Crucially, however, the Panel relied on the wording of Article III:1 to conclude that:

> . . . the purpose of Article III is thus not to prevent contracting parties from using their fiscal and regulatory powers for purposes other than to afford protection to domestic production. Specifically, the purpose of Article III is not to prevent contracting parties from differentiating

[154] Working Party Report, *The Australian Subsidy on Ammonium Sulfate* (adopted 3 April 1950) BISD II/188 (GATT/CP.4/39), *EEC—Animal Feed Proteins* (1978). See Hudec, 'Differences in Meaning' (1998) Section II.

[155] *US—Superfund* (1987) para 5.1.1.

[156] Panel Report, *United States—Measures Affecting Alcoholic and Malt Beverages* (adopted 19 June 1992) BISD 39S/206 (DS23/R)('*US—Malt Beverages*'); Panel Report, *United States—Taxes on Automobiles* (unadopted, 11 October 1994) DS31/R ('*US—Taxes on Automobiles*').

[157] *US—Malt Beverages* (1992) para 5.9.

between different product categories for policy purposes unrelated to the protection of domestic production.[158]

On the basis of this understanding of the purpose of Article III, the Panel developed a new interpretation of 'like products' which was quite different from the market-based test. 'Like products', it said, was to be interpreted in the light of the aims and effects of the regulatory measure. That is to say, the question of whether two products were 'like' one another was, according to this approach, to depend in significant part on whether the regulating state had a legitimate reason for distinguishing between the products, in addition to whether the distinction inherently had the effect of protecting local producers from foreign competition. Thus, for example, the Panel concluded that a Mississippi tax on wine based solely on the variety of grape used treated 'like products' differently because there was no legitimate reason to distinguish between grape varieties in this way. It was merely a way of subsidizing local wine producers.[159] On the other hand, point of sale restrictions on beer, which varied as between beers with different alcohol content, were found not to be discriminatory. The relevant beers were not 'like products', in part because there were good regulatory reasons to treat them differently.[160] The same approach was followed two years later in *US—Taxes on Automobiles.*[161]

Clearly, this is an interpretation which places great weight on the legitimacy of the objectives of a regulatory measure, and corresponds relatively closely to the narrow interpretation of Article III described above, according to which only origin-based discrimination with explicit or implicit protectionist intent is prohibited. And, although it admittedly relies on a fairly strained reading of the text of Article III, it has the distinct advantage of explicitly acknowledging the reality that the 'likeness' of products can only ever be evaluated from a particular perspective and for a particular purpose. However, this interpretation turned out to be both controversial and short-lived.[162] The *US—Taxes on Automobiles* report was vigorously contested by the EC, and ultimately was not adopted.[163] Shortly after the creation of the WTO, in only its second ruling, the Appellate Body rejected the proposition that 'like products' should be interpreted in the light of the aims and effects of the measure at issue.[164] In that case, *Japan—Alcohol*, the United States, the EC, and Canada joined to challenge a Japanese tax measure which taxed *shochu* (a primarily locally produced beverage) at a lower rate than many imported alcoholic beverages, including vodka, whisky, rum, genever, brandy, and liqueurs. Claims were made under both the first and second sentence of Article III:2, so the Appellate Body was required to comment on the

[158] ibid para 5.25.

[159] ibid para 5.26.

[160] ibid paras 5.74–5.75.

[161] See eg *US—Taxes on Automobiles* (1994) (unadopted) para 5.10.

[162] Hudec 'Requiem' (1998); Appellate Body Report, *Japan—Taxes on Alcoholic Beverages* (adopted 1 November 1996) WT/DS8/AB/R, WT/DS10/AB/R and WT/DS11/AB/R ('*Japan—Alcohol*'); Appellate Body Report, *European Communities—Regime for the Importation, Sale and Distribution of Bananas* (adopted 25 September 1997) WT/DS27/AB/R ('*EC—Bananas*').

[163] Hudec 'Requiem' (1998) 16.

[164] *Japan—Alcohol (AB)*, 18ff.

interpretation of both the term 'like product' and the term 'directly competitive or substitutable' product. Recalling in part the terms of an earlier Working Party Report, the Appellate Body affirmed the Panel's approach, deciding that the same criteria were relevant to the interpretation of both terms:

> . . . the product's end-uses in a given market; consumers' tastes and habits, which change from country to country; the product's properties, nature and quality [as well as the tariff classification practices of WTO Members].[165]

In the context of interpreting the term 'directly competitive or substitutable', however, it said that 'greater emphasis should be placed on elasticity of substitution'—indeed common end-uses are 'the decisive criterion' in this respect.[166]

This test for 'directly competitive or substitutable products' is an exclusively market-based approach, and in this and subsequent cases, the issue has been determined by consideration of evidence such as technical studies of cross-price elasticity of demand, extensive surveys of consumers on their consumption choices, and the marketing strategies of producers.[167] As regards the interpretation of 'like products', the turn to a market-based approach was not so obvious, since the physical properties of the products at issue have been considered to be more salient.[168] Even here, however, it was made clear in *Japan—Alcohol* that 'like products' under Article III:2 is a subset of 'directly competitive and substitutable' products, with the result that economic evidence of potential market competition between products has in practice become a *sine qua non* of complainants' cases under Article III:2. To be clear—and to repeat a point I made earlier—I am not suggesting that the interpretation of 'likeness' has become 'economic' in the sense of precisely reflecting a rigorous technical econometric analysis of competitiveness. As others have noted, if that were the model, the rigour of the analysis would leave a great deal to be desired.[169] I am suggesting, however, that this reinterpretation of 'likeness' has been fundamentally inspired by economic concepts and economic styles of analysis.

A few years later, in its *EC—Asbestos* decision, a majority of the Appellate Body[170] made it clear that a market-based approach should also be adopted for the purposes of interpreting 'likeness' in Article III:4:

> . . . a determination of 'likeness' under Article III:4 is, fundamentally, a determination about the *nature and extent of a competitive relationship between and among products.* In saying this, we

[165] *Japan—Alcohol (AB)* (1996) 20. See also Appellate Body Report, *European Communities—Regime for the Importation, Sale and Distribution of Bananas* (adopted 25 September 1997) ('*EC—Bananas*') WT/DS27/AB/R, paras 215–16.

[166] *Japan—Alcohol (Panel)* (1996) paras 6.22, 6.28, affirmed by *Japan—Alcohol (AB)* (1996) 25.

[167] *Japan—Alcohol (Panel)* (1996) paras 6.28ff; *Korea—Alcohol (Panel)* (1998) paras 10.44ff; Panel Report, *Chile—Taxes on Alcoholic Beverages* (adopted 12 January 2000) WT/DS87/R and WT/DS110/R, paras 7.12–7.88.

[168] *Japan—Alcohol (Panel)* (1996) eg 139.

[169] Mattoo and Subramanian (1998); Horn and Mavroidis (2004).

[170] cf Appellate Body Report, *European Communities—Measures Affecting Asbestos and Asbestos-Containing Products* (adopted 5 April 2001) WT/DS135/AB/R, paras 149–54 (the concurring opinion).

are mindful that there is a spectrum of degrees of 'competitiveness' or 'substitutability' of products in the marketplace, and that it is difficult, if not impossible, in the abstract, to indicate precisely where on this spectrum the word 'like' in Article III:4 of the GATT 1994 falls. We are not saying that all products which are in some competitive relationship are 'like products' under Article III:4 . . . However, we recognize that the relationship between these two provisions is important, because there is no sharp distinction between fiscal regulation, covered by Article III:2, and non-fiscal regulation, covered by Article III:4. [171]

Here, then, we have an approach to the interpretation of likeness which has no room for explicit and direct consideration of the purpose or objective of a regulatory measure, and instead looks primarily to the consumer and to the market to determine whether or not it is legitimate and appropriate to make distinctions between particular products. In their ideal form, it seems, these criteria for likeness and related concepts 'should . . . be seen as "technical" descriptions of the functioning of the market, and should not be influenced by value judgments concerning the legitimacy of the regulation'.[172] The move from looking to the illegitimacy of intent as defined by the norms and expectations of trade negotiators, to reliance on objective economic evidence and survey data, as an indication of the applicability of the non-discrimination norm, illustrates nicely the new jurisprudential style which accompanied the disembedding of the GATT/WTO's legal system from the world of trade diplomacy.

Other interpretive developments

This focus on economic effects in the context of likeness analysis was complemented by other interpretive developments, which had the effect of significantly expanding the prohibitive effect of Article III of the GATT, so that it seemed to outlaw all kinds of governmental intervention, provided only that they had some trade-distortive effect. First, the standards of differential treatment contained in Article III continued to be interpreted in ways which did not appear to permit consideration of intention. In order to show a violation under paragraph 2, for example, it is only necessary to show that foreign products are taxed 'in excess of' domestic products (under the first sentence), or that foreign products are 'not similarly taxed' as compared to their domestic counterparts (under the second sentence). It is abundantly clear from the case law that these only require proof of differential taxation, regardless of the purpose of the measure.[173] Under Article III:4, the relevant standard is captured in the phrase 'less favourable treatment', and again—at least until the end of the 1990s[174]—this has been interpreted without regard to the purpose of the regulatory

[171] *EC—Asbestos (AB)* (2001) para 99 (emphasis added).
[172] Horn and Mavroïdis (2004) 60.
[173] See eg *Japan—Alcohol (AB)* (1996) 23, 26–7.
[174] See pp 317–18 below.

measure. Thus, any regulatory measure which 'modifies the conditions of competition'[175] to the detriment of a foreign product, or which imposes an additional burden on foreign products, or which upsets the effective equality of opportunities[176] between foreign and domestic products, has been treated as a violation of the 'less favourable treatment' standard, without any explicit consideration of any justification for the differential treatment.

Secondly, what little textual basis there is in Article III for an explicit consideration of regulatory purpose began to be minimized. Paragraph 1 of Article III expresses the general principle that domestic regulatory measures ought not to be applied 'so as to afford protection to domestic production', and it had been suggested by some that this wording effectively imported into the remainder of Article III an explicit consideration of regulatory purpose. However, in *Japan—Alcohol*, both the Panel and the Appellate Body rejected this position. It was, they said, only where paragraph 1 was directly referenced by a later paragraph—that is, only in the second sentence of paragraph 2—that an explicit consideration of regulatory purpose was permitted.[177] Even there, it was emphasized that the question of whether a regulatory measure was applied 'so as to afford protection to domestic production' was less about the subjective intention behind a measure than its objective application and effect:

> [This] is not an issue of intent. It is not necessary for a panel to sort through the many reasons legislators and regulators have for what they do and weigh the relative significance of those reasons to establish legislative or regulatory intent. If the measure is applied to imported or domestic products so as to afford protection to domestic production, then it does not matter that there may not have been any desire to engage in protectionism in the minds of the legislators or the regulators who imposed the measure.[178]

The judgment seemed at the time a clear indication from the Appellate Body of a reticence to take regulatory purpose into account, at least not explicitly, and to rely instead on an 'objective analysis of the structure and application of the measure in question on domestic as compared to imported products'.[179] Although the Appellate Body clarified its position in subsequent cases, the reticence to adopt an explicitly intent-based interpretation remained.[180]

Thirdly, this shift away from scrutinizing the intention of a measure was coupled in some cases with significantly stricter scrutiny of the discriminatory effects of a

[175] Panel Report, *Italy—Agricultural Machinery* (1958) para 12; or which could reasonably expected to do so (Panel Report, *China—Measures Affecting Trading Rights and Distribution Services for Certain Publications and Audiovisual Entertainment Products* (adopted 19 January 2010) WT/DS363/R, para 7.1471).

[176] Panel Report, *United States—Section 337 of the Tariff Act of 1930* (adopted 7 November 1989) BISD 36S/345 (L/6439) para 5.11.

[177] *Japan—Alcohol (AB)* (1996) 23.

[178] ibid 27–8.

[179] ibid 29. For one interpretation, see Verhoosel (2002). cf Hudec, 'Requiem' (1998) n 25 and accompanying text.

[180] Appellate Body Report, *Chile—Taxes on Alcoholic Beverages* (adopted 12 January 2000) WT/DS87/AB/R and WT/DS110/AB/R, paras 62–72, Appellate Body Report, *Korea—Taxes on Alcoholic Beverages* (adopted 17 February 1999) WT/DS75/AB/R and WT/DS84/AB/R, para 150. See Horn and Mavroïdis (2004) for a useful discussion of this material.

measure. Quite incredibly, there were some indications in a handful of early cases during this period that the less favourable treatment of even *some* foreign products could constitute a violation of Article III, even if the bulk of foreign products were treated more favourably under the regulatory measure at issue.[181] This approach—what Ehring has called the application of the 'diagonal test'[182]—would have been truly revolutionary had it properly taken hold, as it is hard to imagine any regulatory measure which does not treat at least *some* foreign products more harshly than *some* domestic products. To the extent that the Article III non-discrimination norm is entirely an effects-based standard, applied on a product-by-product basis, and without consideration of the purpose of the measure, then even inadvertent or inevitable 'discrimination' of this kind could in principle violate it. On this approach, the prohibition of discrimination would therefore come to be in practice a requirement to treat foreign products and domestic products identically in all respects, whether or not there may be legitimate regulatory reasons for doing so.

As a result of these trends in the jurisprudence, the non-discrimination norm became a much more powerful tool to wield against domestic regulation, even that which was apparently 'non-discriminatory' in the sense that that term had been traditionally understood. 'Discrimination' began to look very much like 'trade-distorting market intervention'. Probably the apotheosis of this approach was the Panel decision in *EC—Asbestos* which concerned a regulatory measure banning the sale (and importation, marketing, and so forth) of asbestos and certain products containing asbestos.[183] In a move which concerned a number of observers, the Panel found this regulatory measure to be a violation of Article III:4, since it treated asbestos products less favourably than other kinds of insulating fibres by banning the former and not the latter—notwithstanding the clear differences between the products in terms of their effects on human health. Many would find the decision that a perfectly legitimate regulatory measure banning the sale of unsafe products is 'discriminatory' to be intuitively unappealing. But it makes perfect sense when the notion of discrimination is understood in the thin economic sense as a distortion of pre-existing consumption patterns away from imported product towards domestic counterparts.

The Panel went on, of course, to find that the measure was nevertheless justified under Article XX. Importantly, then, what this decision makes clear is that this broadening of the non-discrimination obligation usually occurred not so much as a means of prohibiting more and more forms of regulation, as if that were an end in itself, but rather for the much more specific purpose of ensuring that domestic regulation came to be subject to the additional disciplines contained in Article XX.

[181] For a comprehensive discussion of the relevant cases, see Ehring (2002).

[182] ibid 921.

[183] Panel Report, *European Communities—Measures Affecting Asbestos and Asbestos-Containing Products* (adopted 5 April 2001) WT/DS135/R.

Recall that Article XX acts as a general exception to Article III (and other GATT disciplines)—that is to say, it permits discrimination against foreign products provided it is 'necessary'[184] to do so to fulfil one of the legitimate objectives listed, and provided it does not constitute a 'disguised restriction' on trade or 'arbitrary or unjustifiable discrimination'. The necessity test is a particularly useful and important juridical tool when dealing with domestic regulation, as it permits WTO panels to distinguish regulation which has an inadvertent but unavoidable impact on trade (permitted) from regulation which has an inadvertent and *avoidable* impact on trade (not permitted). In other words, it is through the application of the necessity test—and not through the application of the non-discrimination standard—that the WTO can encourage its Members to design their regulatory standards optimally, that is to say, in a way which minimizes their trade impact while still achieving their regulatory objectives. Since WTO panels began to see it as their task during this period to encourage optimal, non-arbitrary regulatory design on the part of WTO Members, there was therefore a strong impetus for them to find a violation of Article III—for in the absence of such a finding, they would not get to the necessity test, which was the next stage of the legal analysis. Part of the purpose and the effect of the reinterpretation of Article III, in other words, was to shift the centre of gravity of the legal discipline of domestic regulation under the GATT from the non-discrimination test in Article III to the necessity test in Article XX.

B. Article XX

The identification of a 'distortion' of international trade is only the first step of analysis, as not all distortions of trade flows are illegitimate or undesirable. Thus, as Article III was broadened, the task of determining the legitimacy or illegitimacy of particular distorting regulations fell primarily to Article XX. As is well known, one of the most significant consequences of this development was the importation of a means–end rationality test into certain paragraphs of Article XX, which required, broadly speaking, that the regulatory measure in question be the least trade-restrictive (or least GATT-inconsistent) means of achieving the regulatory objective in question.[185] The attraction of this approach is clear. On one hand, it permitted a way for the GATT/WTO legal system to deliver on its new promise of disciplining arbitrary public power, and ensuring strict oversight of apparently proliferating non-tariff barriers. On the other, the focus on *means* and not ends meant that legal interpretation could—for a time at least—credibly appear as a neutral, technical and objective process, rather than just another means for making contested political choices about the desirability of different kinds of regulatory regimes.

As a direct result of the turn to means–ends rationality, dispute settlement panels found themselves turning with increasing frequency to different forms of technical

[184] The necessity test is, of course, only relevant under paragraphs (a), (b), and (d) of that article.

[185] See eg Panel Report, *United States—Section 337 of the Tariff Act of 1930* (adopted 7 November 1989) BISD 36S/345 (L/6439) para 5.26; Panel Report, *Thailand—Restrictions on Importation of Internal Taxes on Cigarettes* (adopted 7 November 1990) BISD 37S/200 (DS10/R) para 75.

expertise for guidance. That is to say, technical expertise became one important way of defining an objective range of acceptable and appropriate regulatory methods, against which to judge the acceptability of the trade-restrictive regulation in question. A characteristic turn of the jurisprudence during this period, then, was its tendency to mix 'legal' reasoning concerning the interpretation of Article XX with 'technical' reasoning about the optimal or sub-optimal design of the measure in question relative to its purposes.

I can illustrate what I mean by this mixing of legal and technical analysis by reference to an article published in 1998 by two influential commentators on the WTO's approach to domestic regulation.[186] In this article, Mattoo and Subramanian propose an interpretation of Articles III and XX of the GATT based on economic analysis of the design of the regulatory measure in question. The first step of their analysis would be an analysis of the similarity of the products in question based exclusively on their economic competitiveness, as described above. Where the competitiveness of imported goods is detrimentally impacted by a regulatory measure, the next step in their analysis is to 'distinguish between situations in which protectionist effect is an incidental consequence of a domestic measure and those in which it is not'.[187] Here, they argue, 'it would seem to be important to consider whether the measure in question was the economically optimal means of achieving the particular objective'.[188] More specifically:

> There [should] be a presumption in favour of the choice of the economically optimal policy to achieve a legitimate objective. A Member choosing to pursue an objective by a measure other than the economically optimal would need to justify this choice.[189]

The authors rightly observe that their proposal goes significantly beyond what has been accepted in GATT jurisprudence, at least in the sense that they suggest a much more rigorous incorporation of the economic theory of instrument choice into WTO legal interpretation than has been seen in the cases so far. At the same time, their proposal represents in many respects merely an extension or purification of an existing tendency in GATT/WTO jurisprudence, which has developed since the 1980s. It is true that GATT and WTO panels have tended to look during this period to technical expertise to *guide* their interpretation of GATT/WTO law, rather than determine it so strictly. And it is also true that panels have looked to a variety of forms of technical expertise, rather than just economic analysis of instrument choice. Nevertheless, they have had increasing recourse to technical knowledge in the context of legal decision-making, such that legal interpretation has come in part to include the mobilization and application of technical knowledge. The result is that outcomes in cases involving internal regulations with an indirect impact on international trade have been influenced in significant part by the ways in which different kinds of technical knowledge are understood, received, contested, applied, rejected, or balanced

186 Mattoo and Subramanian (1998).
187 ibid 315.
188 ibid 316.
189 ibid 315.

by interpreters in the process of legal interpretation. A handful of brief examples from Article XX should make this point clearer.

In 1983 and then again in 1989, two cases were brought against the United States on the basis of section 337 of the US Tariff Act of 1930, a provision which declared unlawful under US law 'unfair methods of competition and unfair trade acts in the importation of articles into the United States'[190] in certain circumstances. Although this provision had existed in some form in US legislation since 1922, it had been revitalized first by the Trade Act of 1974 described above, and then again in 1988.[191] As a result, it had become the preferred route for claims by US producers in respect of the importation of goods into the United States which allegedly infringed US IP law. This procedure became highly controversial over the course of the 1980s. The United States had come to see differing standards of IP protection around the world as a trade issue, and was determined to enforce its own high standards of protection against imported products as a way of ensuring 'fair competition' in US markets. Other countries, however, saw this procedure as a discriminatory non-tariff barrier in itself, a way of protecting the US market from competitive goods in an unfair manner. In particular, they argued that the option which domestic producers had of bringing section 337 proceedings before the International Trade Commission (rather than just in the US domestic courts) created significant disadvantages for imported products as compared to their domestic counterparts. In the first GATT challenge to proceedings under section 337, the Panel report cautiously found that a US exclusion order granted against certain automotive spring assemblies, preventing their importation, was 'necessary to secure compliance' with US patent law under Article XX(d) primarily because the alternative—domestic court proceedings—would have only bound parties to that proceeding, and would therefore have been ineffective against automotive springs produced or purchased by other businesses.[192] In addition, however, it did nebulously indicate that there was a 'strong possibility' that the grant of an exclusion order in section 337 proceedings could violate the GATT in other circumstances.[193]

By the time of the second case, this ambiguous and substantively quite loose approach to oversight—reminiscent in some ways of the diplomatic style of earlier GATT jurisprudence—was replaced by a much more rigorous and detailed discussion of the precise design of the section 337 process. At the beginning of its analysis of Article XX(d), the second Panel explicitly noted that its decision did not trespass onto the obviously political question of the appropriate level of IP protection that the United States and other countries could provide, but instead focused entirely on the 'technical' question of the appropriate means used to achieve those objectives:

> The Panel wished to make it clear that [its decision] does not mean that a contracting party could be asked to change its substantive patent law or its desired level of enforcement of that law . . . However, it does mean that if a contracting party could reasonably secure that level of

[190] Tariff Act of 1930, ch 479 § 337.

[191] Knight (1988).

[192] See Panel Report, *United States—Imports of Certain Automotive Spring Assemblies* (adopted 26 May 1983) BISD 30S/107 (L/5333).

[193] ibid para 66.

enforcement in a manner that is not inconsistent with other GATT provisions, it would be required to do so.[194]

The Panel then proceeded to pick apart and criticize certain aspects of the section 337 process, assessing the objective rationality of each of its individual elements. It rejected the US claim that separate section 337 proceedings were 'necessary' because domestic US courts did not have jurisdiction over process patents—on the basis that other countries had granted domestic courts jurisdiction over process patents, and there was no reason why the United States could not follow suit. It also rejected the US argument that special proceedings were necessary because of the difficulties of service of process on foreign manufacturers. However, it acknowledged that there may well be an 'objective need' to provide limited *in rem* remedies uniquely against foreign products, because 'it is seldom feasible to secure enforcement of the rulings of a court of the country of importation by local courts in the country of production' and because *in personam* orders against importers could be easily circumvented.[195] However, it then went on also to reject the idea that *in rem* remedies should be applied to products produced by non-parties to the proceedings.

Just one year later, this approach was taken a step further in the report of the Panel in *Thailand—Cigarettes*, concerning import restrictions and internal taxes on imported cigarettes imposed by that country. Thailand argued that these restrictions were justified under Article XX(b) as necessary to pursue its public health policy of reducing the consumption of tobacco. The Panel adopted the means–end rationality approach of the Panel in the *US—Section 337* decision, affirming that:

> ... the import restrictions imposed by Thailand could be considered to be 'necessary' in terms of Article XX(b) only if there were no alternative measure consistent with the General Agreement, or less inconsistent with it, which Thailand could reasonably be expected to employ to achieve its health policy objectives.[196]

In order to help it to assess the effectiveness of alternative measures, and at the request of Thailand, the Panel asked the World Health Organization (WHO) to 'present its conclusions on technical aspects of the case, such as the health effects of cigarette use and consumption, and on related issues for which the WHO was competent'.[197] Representatives of the WHO made submissions, not only concerning the health effects of smoking, but also about WHO recommended smoking control policies as developed by a WHO Expert Committee in the early 1980s, the advertising practices of large tobacco multinationals, and the experience of tobacco import liberalization in developing countries. These submissions were largely in support of the Thai restrictions. For its part, the United States questioned the competence of the WHO to provide expert guidance on some of the questions it had addressed, and

[194] *United States—Section 337* (1989) para 5.26.
[195] ibid para 5.31.
[196] *Thailand—Cigarettes* (1990) para 75.
[197] *Thailand—Cigarettes* (1990) para 50.

referred to research from other independent scientific and expert bodies to counter some of the WHO claims.[198] In the end, the Panel's decision that the Thai measures were not justified under Article XX(b) was explicitly justified by reference to the array of expertise that had been put before it. It decided, for example, that bans on advertising could effectively reduce demand, in part on the basis of a resolution of the WHO encouraging the use of such measures. It decided that pricing strategies were a reasonable alternative, again in part on the basis of the same resolution.[199] It also found support for its conclusion in the Report of the WHO Expert Committee on Smoking Strategies in Developing Countries.[200]

An even clearer example is the Panel decision in *EC—Asbestos*, mentioned earlier, involving a Canadian challenge to a French ban on products containing asbestos for public health reasons. Having found that this ban was discriminatory, the Panel went on to consider whether it was justified under Article XX(b) as necessary to protect human life and health. Canada argued that the particular products of export interest to it posed no detectable risk to human health, that the dangerous forms of chrysotile asbestos products had long since ceased to be marketed, and that certain 'controlled use' procedures would achieve the same level of protection as a total ban. The EC disagreed. Both parties submitted extensive scientific evidence in support of their positions, and the Panel consulted also with independent scientific experts. It pointed out that its role was not 'to settle a scientific debate' but rather to 'determine whether there is sufficient scientific evidence to conclude that there exists a risk for human life or health and that the measures taken by France are necessary in relation to the objectives pursued'.[201] On the basis of the expert evidence it had heard, as well as publications of the WHO and other international bodies, the Panel agreed that the EC had made a prima facie case for the existence of a health risk.[202] It noted, as confirmed by a number of studies, that the efficacy of the 'controlled use' as a less trade restrictive alternative had yet to be proven.[203]

This technicalization of the Article XX jurisprudence has continued in many of the decided cases during and since the 1990s, though as we shall see in Chapter 10 there has been something of a change in some cases since roughly 2000.[204] That said, I am not suggesting it has been an even or uniform process. In some cases, it seems not to have been necessary to have recourse to large amounts of technical evidence to conclude that a measure was not justified by Article XX. *US—Taxes on Automobiles* and *US—Gasoline* are good examples of this—though even in those cases, it is still true that means–end rationality still remained the focus of analysis, and the decisions were based on assessments of the technical feasibility and optimality of alternative measures.[205] The main exceptions to this technicalizing trend during the 1990s,

[198] ibid paras 58ff. [199] ibid para 79. [200] ibid para 80.
[201] *EC—Asbestos* (Panel) (2000) paras 8.181–8.182. [202] ibid para 8.194 and surrounding.
[203] ibid para 8.209. [204] See below pp 320ff.
[205] In *US—Taxes on Automobiles* (1994) (unadopted), described earlier, the Panel was willing to require the US to substantially redesign its CAFE fuel economy standards on the basis that the particular methods of accounting that it used had an unnecessarily detrimental impact on imported cars, notwithstanding the clearly legitimate environmental objectives of those standards overall. In *US—Gasoline*, both the Panel Report, *United States—Standards for Reformulated and Conventional Gasoline* (adopted 20 May

then, are the two famous *Tuna/Dolphin* decisions, as well as the Panel decision in *Shrimp/Turtle*, which adopted the same approach. The reason for this difference, however, was arguably that the measures in these cases were, rightly or wrongly, perceived to be of a fundamentally different kind: not domestic public policy measures which incidentally or indirectly necessitated some form of trade restriction, but rather measures which sought to effectively impose US environmental policy preferences on countries which exported products to US markets. Whereas close technical parsing seemed appropriate in the case of the first kind of measure, the second kind of measure appeared to pose a much more significant threat to the multilateral trading system, and required a different response:

> . . . if an interpretation of the chapeau of Article XX were to be followed which would allow a Member to adopt measures conditioning access to its market for a given product upon the adoption by the exporting Members of certain policies, including conservation policies, GATT 1994 and the WTO Agreement could no longer serve as a multilateral framework for trade among Members as security and predictability of trade relations under those agreements would be threatened. This follows because, if one WTO Member were allowed to adopt such measures, then other Members would also have the right to adopt similar measures on the same subject but with differing, or even conflicting, requirements. If that happened, it would be impossible for exporting Members to comply at the same time with multiple conflicting policy requirements. Indeed, as each of these requirements would necessitate the adoption of a policy applicable not only to export production (such as specific standards applicable only to goods exported to the country requiring them) but also to domestic production, it would be impossible for a country to adopt one of those policies without running the risk of breaching other Members' conflicting policy requirements for the same product and being refused access to these other markets. We note that, in the present case, there would not even be the possibility of adapting one's export production to the respective requirements of the different Members. Market access for goods could become subject to an increasing number of conflicting policy requirements for the same product and this would rapidly lead to the end of the WTO multilateral trading system.[206]

Thus, it was primarily on the basis of the existential threat that these measures apparently posed to the multilateral trading system as a whole, that they were found not to be justified under Article XX. This is not then a decision based on technical expertise—but, importantly, it is still clearly a decision which is closely associated with the legal imagination described earlier in this chapter. The difference here is simply that the concerns of certainty, order, and predictability—such over-riding concerns in the legal imagination of the WTO during this period—seemed in this instance to require a turn away from close technical parsing, and a clear policy

1996) WT/DS2/R and the Appellate Body Report, *United States—Standards for Reformulated and Conventional Gasoline* (adopted 20 May 1996) WT/DS2/AB/R at 27 disagreed, for example, with the US's claim that permitting individual baselines for foreign suppliers of gasoline was not technically feasible, noting that there are 'established techniques for checking, verification, assessment and enforcement of data relating to imported goods' which were in fact routinely used for other trade policy purposes.

[206] Panel Report, *United States—Import Prohibition of Certain Shrimp and Shrimp Products* (adopted 16 November 1998) WT/DS58/R, para 7.45. See also Panel Report, *United States—Restrictions of Imports of Tuna* (unadopted, 16 June 1994) DS29/R, para 5.26.

decision to disallow measures of this type. As is well known, a new and more subtle approach to such measures was adopted in the Appellate Body's decision in *Shrimp/Turtle*, a point to which I shall return in Chapter 10.

IV. Conclusion: a new legal imagination

The investigation conducted over the last two chapters has revealed that the neoliberal turn of the trade regime during the last two to three decades of the twentieth century was associated with the development of a different kind of legal sensibility, and a new vernacular of legal argument. This new style of legal thought was one which loosely and creatively integrated a variety of forms of technical expertise into the vocabulary of law, so that the forms of knowledge characteristic of economics and other sciences became an important part of the framework in which law was interpreted and applied.

When I say that technical ideas of optimal regulatory design provided important evaluative guidance for the trade regime as it turned to internal measures, I am not suggesting that the trade regime became a 'regulatory institution', in the sense of seeking to impose a particular vision of ideal regulation in any particular sector. Instead, as we have seen, the GATT/WTO played an oversight role: encouraging harmonization and convergence where it was possible and desirable, monitoring and minimizing the adverse trade effects of regulatory measures where it was not, and continuing to identify and attempt to eliminate forms of regulatory protectionism. What I am suggesting, however, is that all of these tasks were deeply informed by technical and expert ways of discussing and evaluating what does and does not constitute an appropriate use of regulatory power. The law became in part a venue for the circulation of these forms of knowledge, and legal interpretation became in part a process of drawing on, arbitrating between, and evaluating the relevance of, selected forms of expertise as a way of giving meaning to indeterminate legal norms. As a corollary, the operation of WTO law came in significant part to be determined by the particular way in which different forms of technical knowledge were knitted together—adopted, rejected, parsed, reconfigured—during the legal processes of interpretation and elaboration.

I illustrated this process through the evolving jurisprudence on Articles I, III, and XX of the GATT—in part because this is one of the only areas of jurisprudence in which clear comparison with earlier decades of GATT legal history are possible. One way of exploring this argument further would be to examine other areas of the jurisprudence on domestic regulation in which this tendency towards technicalization is also observable. In this respect, the jurisprudence on subsidies under first the Subsidies Code, and then the SCM Agreement is an excellent example—as is of course the jurisprudence under the SPS Agreement, to which I will return in Chapter 10. In the next chapter, however, instead of taking this path, I want to push my argument in a somewhat different direction. As a consequence of this technicalization of GATT/WTO jurisprudence on domestic regulation, part of the politics of the trade regime came to be a contest to define particular forms of expertise and knowledge as the most suitable or appropriate for use in the elaboration and interpretation of WTO law. In other words, the struggles characteristic of trade politics—between states acting in their commercial interests—were increasingly played out on the terrain of technical knowledge. The technicalization of WTO law, in other words, was not a turn away from trade politics, but a (partial) redirection of it. The purpose of the next chapter, then, is to begin to understand the dynamics of this turn, by investigating one particular context in which it has most visibly taken place.

9

Trade in Services

In this chapter I pause the historical narrative that I have been telling up to this point, and instead provide a case study of the processes I described in a general way in the previous chapter. My purpose here is to illustrate and explore in greater depth the operation of the technicalized legal imagination, the genesis of which I described in Chapter 8. More specifically, it is to describe and understand the processes by which particular forms of technical knowledge come to guide the elaboration, application, and interpretation of international trade law, and come to be sedimented within the background commonsense that sustains and informs the operation of the WTO's legal system.

The case study that I use is that of trade in services. One of the major innovations of the Uruguay Round of trade negotiations was the creation of the General Agreement on Trade in Services (GATS). This agreement, which establishes a legal framework for the progressive liberalization of international trade in services, is in many respects an exemplary product of the formal-technical legal order I described in Chapter 8. Since there are few if any 'border barriers' to trade in services, the provisions of the GATS apply almost exclusively to domestic regulation. Its disciplines are predominantly in the form of vaguely worded general obligations, and the text of the agreement therefore contains very little specific guidance as regards the particular regulatory measures which are likely to be prohibited or permitted by it. Consequently, in accordance with the logics I identified in Chapter 8, the practical operation of the GATS is likely to be governed in part by the principles and forms of knowledge which are deployed to distinguish the legitimate domestic regulation of service sectors from illegitimate 'distortion' of them—and by the contested processes through which those principles are defined. These forms of knowledge are, it should be said, still very much under construction in the services context—in most service sectors, there simply is no clear consensus view among negotiators and other relevant actors within the field about what kinds of regulatory changes might legitimately and reasonably be required by GATS disciplines, nor even about the ways in which one might distinguish legitimate from illegitimate regulation. For present purposes, however, this is an advantage, since it means that we are able to observe very clearly the symbolic processes by which these forms of knowledge are being constructed and contested as the GATS is gradually operationalized.

I. An open-ended agreement

It is sometimes said that the issue of trade in services has been around since the earliest days of the post-war international trade regime, on the basis that the Havana Charter contained references to services such as telecommunications, transport, and insurance as 'substantial elements of international trade'.[1] In reality, however, services at that time were primarily understood as facilitators of trade in goods, rather than as 'traded' themselves, and it was not until the Tokyo Round that the issue of 'trade in services' in the modern sense was brought before the GATT. The impetus for this came from the United States. From the early 1970s, in the context of the broader transformation of US trade policy described in Chapter 8, a handful of US services firms had begun a campaign to persuade US law-makers that the service sector was among the most important sources of export growth and job creation in the US economy, and that access to foreign markets for US services firms should be prioritized in trade negotiations. Financial services firms were prominent in this group—early leaders were Ronald Shelp and Hank Greenberg from the American International Group—but it also included others from the air transport, construction, and marine underwriting industries.[2] The efforts of these firms reaped an early return with the passing of the US Trade Act of 1974, which among other things instructed the President to begin international negotiations on trade in services in the Tokyo Round.[3] But it was during the second half of the 1970s that services issues rapidly grew in significance, at least in the domestic US context. An increasing number of powerful commercial actors began to mobilize around services issues, with American Express joining the effort in 1978, Citicorp a year later, and the US Chamber of Commerce establishing a special committee for services industries around the same time.[4] In addition, as discussed in the previous chapter, a close collaboration developed around this time between the private sector and relevant parts of the US government through such bodies as the Advisory Committee for Trade Negotiations, as well as the recently created White House Interagency Task Force on Services and Multilateral Trade Negotiations, Industry Sector Advisory Committees, and the Services Policy Advisory Committee.[5]

[1] United Nations Conference on Trade and Employment, Final Act 'Havana Charter for an International Trade Organization' (21 November 1947–24 March 1948) UN Doc E/CONF.2/78, UN Publications, Sales No 1948 ILD 4, art 53.

[2] See generally HL Freeman, 'A Pioneer's View of Financial Services Negotiations in the GATT and in the World Trade Organization: 17 Years of Work for Something or Nothing?' (1997) 22 The Geneva Papers on Risk and Insurance 392; JD Aronson, *Negotiating to Launch Negotiations: Getting Trade in Services onto the GATT Agenda* (Pew Case Studies in International Affairs: Case 125, Washington, DC 1992) 4; G Feketekuty, *International Trade in Services: An Overview and Blueprint for Negotiations* (AEI and Ballinger, Cambridge, MA 1988) 299; RJ Krommenacker, 'Trade Related Services and GATT' (1979) 13 J of World Trade L 510; RK Shelp, *Beyond Industrialization: Ascendancy of the Global Service Economy* (Praeger, New York, NY 1981).

[3] Aronson (1992) 4.

[4] Freeman (1997) 392–3; Aronson (1992) 4.

[5] Krommenacker (1979) 519–21; Aronson (1992) 10.

As a consequence of this work, the United States began to raise the issue of services in the context of GATT negotiations. But by the conclusion of the Tokyo Round in 1979, their efforts had yielded only minor results: the extension of some aspects of the Government Procurement Code to cover incidental services, certain provisions dealing with the international testing services in the Standards Code, and a prohibition on subsidies to services used to export goods in the Subsidies Code.[6] Apart from those provisions, the only significant concession the United States was able to secure from its major trading partners was a commitment to undertake a study of trade in services through the Trade Committee of the OECD.[7] By and large, the issue was far too new—and it was raised too late in the negotiations, after the negotiating mandate had been established—for rules governing 'trade in services' per se ever to seriously be considered at that stage.

Nevertheless, the experience of the Tokyo Round left an important legacy, in the form of a small but significant group of individuals and organizations within US trade circles energized about services issues, and keen to continue to press this new agenda on the international stage.[8] One of the places to which they turned in the aftermath of the Tokyo Round was the OECD's Trade Committee. The US representative to this Committee was Geza Feketekuty, an assistant US trade representative, who brought considerable energy and personal conviction to the job, and in the years to come became a central figure in the project of advancing the liberalization of international trade in services.[9] Initially, Feketekuty encountered some resistance from the other industrialized countries represented on the Trade Committee, who suspected US firms to be the primary and perhaps only beneficiaries of services liberalization, and were reluctant to take action without further knowledge of their national interests in the matter. Over the course of the early 1980s, however, US officials and private sector groups organized a 'bombardment of studies'[10] showing the importance of the services sector—and services exports—to a range of developed countries, not just the United States. According to Aronson, as other countries' representatives began to engage with the services issue in the Trade Committee, largely in response to US submissions, they too concluded with some surprise that they would benefit from freer trade in services.[11] As a result, work in the OECD gathered momentum. At this stage, the most important work done in the Trade Committee was 'conceptual': defining services trade; drawing a distinction between services trade and services investment; identifying the principal

[6] Agreement on Government Procurement (1 January 1981) BISD 26S/33, Art I; Standards Code, Agreement on Technical Barriers to Trade (1 January 1980) BISD 26S/8, eg Art 5; Subsidies Code, Agreement on Interpretation and Application of Articles VI, XVI and XXIII of the General Agreement on Tariffs and Trade (1 January 1980) BISD 26S/56, Annex.

[7] Aronson (1992) 4–5.

[8] This was particularly the case after the appointment of William Brock as USTR in 1979: Feketekuty (1988) 305.

[9] See generally Aronson (1992).

[10] Y Xu and P Weller, *The Governance of World Trade: International Civil Servants and the GATT/WTO* (Edward Elgar Publishing, Cheltenham, UK 2004) 139.

[11] Aronson (1992) 14.

impediments to trade; and tackling the issue of 'determining when regulation meets a legitimate public need and when it simply distorts market forces'.[12] In due course, the Trade Committee lent its support for multilateral negotiations on trade in services,[13] and worked for some years on a model framework agreement of trade principles.[14]

With the support of a now much larger, better organized, and more internationalized network of services industry representatives,[15] the United States again began to press in the GATT for negotiations on services in the build-up to what was to become the Uruguay Round of trade negotiations.[16] Just as in the OECD, it first encountered stiff resistance from virtually all quarters—from wary industrialized countries, to developing countries, who perceived themselves to have no comparative advantage in major service sectors, and saw liberalization as a threat to their ability to develop it.[17] At the GATT Ministerial in 1982, the United States was only able to secure an agreement that interested nations would undertake studies of their own services sectors and report back. Two years later, for the reasons just noted, OECD countries had largely dropped their concerns. On the other hand, over the same two years developing countries had initiated a work programme on services in UNCTAD to help them formulate positions, and on the basis of this research hardened their resistance. In the end they agreed only to the formation of a 'group' (not a working party) to look into services issues.[18] Then, in 1986, the issue came to a head in Punta del Este, as the Uruguay Round was launched and a final decision had to be made whether or not to include services within the negotiating mandate. Although the result was formally a compromise, substantively the resistance of the developing countries had by this stage been overcome. There were many reasons for this, ranging from successful tactics to divide developing country coalitions,[19] the emergence of new research from UNCTAD and other respected sources to the effect that some

[12] Shelp, 'Trade in Services' (1986–7) 65 Foreign Policy 64, 72.

[13] WJ Drake and K Nicolaïdis, 'Ideas, Interests, and Institutionalization: "Trade in Services" and the Uruguay Round' (1992) Intl Org 37, 51; Feketekuty (1988) 319. See also JV Reyna, 'Services' in TP Stewart (ed), *The GATT Uruguay Round: A Negotiating History Vol II: Commentary* (Kluwer, The Hague 1999) 2354, n 73.

[14] Aronson (1992) 14; Drake and Nicolaïdis (1992) 60.

[15] eg the Coalition of Service Industries (CSI) and the Liberalisation of Trade in Services Committee (LOTIS) were both created in the early 1980s.

[16] At the same time, it is worth noting, the US was also successful in including services in its free trade agreement with Israel, signed in 1985.

[17] See eg J Croome, *Reshaping the World Trading System: A History of the Uruguay Round* (Diane Publishing Co, Geneva 1995) 16; Aronson (1992) 15; Xu and Weller (2004) 142 and surrounding. A useful summary of the emergence of services as a trade issue in the US context and then in the GATT/WTO context is in JS Jarreau, 'Interpreting the General Agreement on Trade in Services and the WTO Instruments Relevant to the International Trade of Financial Services' (1999) North Carolina J of Intl L and Commercial Reg 1, 10–24.

[18] Note Shelp (1986–7) 74.

[19] Aronson (1992) 36; Drake and Nicolaïdis (1992) 66–7. See also JB Richardson, 'What Really Happened at Punta del Este: Understanding the Framework of the Uruguay Round' in D Riddle (ed), *Toward an International Service and Information Economy* (Friedrich Ebert Foundation, Bonn 1987) 202; PS Randhawa, 'Punta del Este and After: Negotiations on Trade in Services and the Uruguay Round' (1987) 21 J of World Trade L 163.

developing countries might have a comparative advantage in some service sectors,[20] and the perception that it was a necessary concession for developing countries to make, in order to gain greater access to developed country goods markets.[21] Whatever the reason, services were now on the negotiating agenda of the Uruguay Round.

Over the course of the Uruguay Round, from 1986 through to the end of 1993, the services negotiations had broadly three aspects. The Punta del Este Ministerial Declaration itself had foreshadowed two of them, calling first of all for a 'multilateral framework of principles and rules for trade in services' as well as for 'an elaboration of possible disciplines for individual sectors'.[22] Following the same logic as the Declaration, negotiations therefore over time came to include both the drafting of a framework agreement, which contained the core general principles to be applied to barriers to trade in services, as well as sector-specific negotiations on how these general principles should be applied, or augmented, in respect of particular service sectors. Then—though there was initially some difference of opinion as to whether it was permitted by the Punta del Este Declaration—a third aspect of negotiations emerged in the final years of the Uruguay Round, which involved the reciprocal exchange of bargained concessions in particular service sectors.

In respect of the first aspect of the negotiations, the drafting of a framework agreement, a number of early challenges arose. Some countries lamented the paucity of data on international trade flows in services, and questioned whether substantive negotiations could continue in their absence. While these concerns gave rise to considerable efforts to augment existing data, it was recognized that such efforts would not bear fruit for some time, and ultimately there was a tacit if reluctant agreement that discussions on the framework agreement could not wait.[23] Then, the drafting of the framework agreement itself gave rise to a number of issues and disagreements, of which four are worthy of special mention. The first was the definition of trade in services. What, precisely, should count as 'trade' in services? Should 'trade in services' be distinguished from foreign investment in the services sector, and if so how? Should it include the movement of labour, as individuals moved from one country to another to provide services? A second issue concerned the coverage of the agreement. Should it apply to all service sectors, or only some? How should different service sectors be categorized and defined? Thirdly, there was the issue of what broad rules and principles should be included in the agreement. Should the GATT principles of transparency, national treatment, unconditional MFN, market access, and progressive liberalization simply be transposed to the services context? What modifications or additions ought to be made to them to take into account the specificity of the services context? A fourth issue, related to the third, concerned domestic regulation. Since it was recognized from very early on that

[20] Drake and Nicolaïdis (1992) 66–7.
[21] Reyna (1999) 235ff.
[22] GATT, Ministerial Declaration on the Uruguay Round (20 September 1986) BISD 33S/19. See also generally Feketekuty (1988) chs 10, 11, which sets out clearly the vision of a framework agreement combined with sectoral elaborations of the general principles contained in the framework agreement.
[23] Croome (1995) 123, 127–8.

many service sectors were highly regulated, and that most impediments to trade in services were regulatory in nature, there was a question as to how the framework agreement might formally distinguish legitimate regulation from illegitimate barriers to trade.[24]

As has been well chronicled elsewhere, negotiations on all of these issues were hard fought.[25] Interestingly, on the conceptual aspects of these broader issues, negotiators not infrequently turned for guidance to a variety of different actors with specialist knowledge for ideas which might help them to formulate their interests, and which might help to bridge political differences between negotiating parties. For example, the GATT Secretariat itself sometimes played an important mediating role as an 'honest broker' to break deadlocks between Contracting Parties.[26] According to Xu and Weller, the handful of individuals working in the Service Division from 1987 were on a number of occasions called upon by the Chair of the negotiating group on services to offer their expertise to help craft a framework agreement which was both feasible in the context of the negotiations, as well as intellectually coherent and defensible.[27] The GATT Secretariat was supported in this task by their counterparts in UNCTAD and the OECD, who also had considerable expertise and experience in the services area. In turn, these three institutions acted as nodal points for the reception and dissemination of papers, books, and other material produced by a much larger community of think-tanks, business lobby groups, academics, government officials, and others. This is Drake and Nicolaïdis' 'epistemic community' of services experts,[28] which had emerged over the course of the 1970s and rapidly grown and diversified over the course of the Uruguay Round, as the negotiations produced demand for the kind of knowledge they could supply. From the early 1980s, this community had been heavily engaged in elaborating the conceptual aspects of international trade in services, developing definitions of trade in services, examining the meaning of trade liberalization in different service sectors, and so on. All this background conceptual work proved crucial during the Uruguay Round negotiations, heavily informing the papers which the Secretariat circulated among negotiators in the initial stages of discussions, and providing the 'basic ideas, concepts, rules and principles' which would be incorporated in some form into successive drafts of the GATS.[29] One reason for the significance of this expertise no doubt came from the nature of the negotiations themselves. Since negotiations over general rules and principles (as compared to, say, the exchange of concessions, which was only to come later) put a premium on objectivity and generalizability, compromise solutions stood a better chance of success if they came not from a negotiating party itself, but from a structurally impartial body, drawing on the accepted ideas of a larger community of specialists.

[24] Croome (1995) 122ff; Drake and Nicolaïdis (1992) 78.
[25] See generally Reyna (1999); Croome (1995); Drake and Nicolaïdis (1992).
[26] Xu and Weller (2004) 147ff. See also Drake and Nicolaïdis (1992) 84 and generally.
[27] Xu and Weller (2004) 151–2 and generally.
[28] See generally Drake and Nicolaïdis (1992).
[29] Xu and Weller (2004) 148 and generally. See also Drake and Nicolaïdis (1992) 78 and generally.

By the end of 1993, a compromise had finally taken shape on all the issues mentioned above, which was reflected in the new General Agreement on Trade in Services. The question of the definition of trade in services was resolved by Article I:2, which defined trade in services to include the supply of a service:

(a) from the territory of one Member into the territory of any other Member;
(b) in the territory of one Member to the service consumer of any other Member;
(c) by a service supplier of one Member, through commercial presence in the territory of any other Member;
(d) by a service supplier of one Member, through presence of natural persons of a Member in the territory of any other Member.

In a classic North–South compromise, then, 'services trade' includes—in its GATS definition at least—most aspects of foreign investment in service sectors (of most interest to the developed world), as well as some aspects of temporary transnational labour movements (of most interest to the developing world). On the question of coverage, another compromise emerged between those who wished to ensure universal coverage and those who wished to exempt particular service sectors. On one hand, no service sector was excluded a priori: the agreement applies to all 'measures affecting trade in services' (Article I:1), and services are defined inclusively as 'any service in any sector except services supplied in the exercise of governmental authority' (Article I:3(b)). On the other hand, it was agreed that the most important disciplines contained in the GATS,[30] would only apply to those service sectors which each country specifically agreed to inscribe in a document known as its Schedule of Commitments. If a WTO Member inscribed no sectors in its Schedule, then these 'specific obligations' could not be invoked against it. To give greater clarity to these Schedules, a document was prepared by the Secretariat setting out a draft classification table for the entire range of services which were the subject of negotiations. Titled the Services Sectoral Classification List, but also referred to as the 'W/120', it was based on a statistical classification standard promulgated by the UN Statistics Division called the Central Product Classification, as it stood in 1991.[31]

As to the substantive rules and principles ultimately included in the GATS, most were taken from the GATT. Article II sets out the MFN obligation, while Article XVII contains the national treatment norm. Article XVI, entitled 'Market Access' singles out six different categories of measure for prohibition—such as limitations on the number of services suppliers operating in a sector, limitations on the total value of service transactions, measures which restrict or require particular types of legal entity, and so on. Article III contains transparency obligations very similar to those found in the GATT, while Article VIII imposes certain requirements on Members to

[30] The main exception to this statement is the most-favoured nation treatment obligation contained in Art II, which is a general obligation not a specific commitment. However, as is well known, even this general obligation was ultimately subject to 'temporary' exceptions.

[31] See WTO, *Services Sectoral Classification List* (10 July 1991) MTN.GNS/W/120. At the time, the CPC was in a provisional form (CPCProv)—it has since had numerous updates, but there is no mechanism for these updates to be automatically reflected in the GATS.

ensure that monopolies and other businesses within their jurisdiction with exclusive market power do not engage in anti-competitive practices. All of these disciplines are subject to a variety of exceptions, contained, for example, in Articles XIV and XIV*bis*, which to a large extent mirror the content of Articles XX and XXI of the GATT. Other exceptions cover government procurement, and economic integration agreements, as well as measures taken to safeguard a country's balance of payments position.[32] In addition, there were four distinct areas in which GATS negotiators had not been able to agree general rules and disciplines in time for the end of the Uruguay Round: safeguards, subsidies, government procurement, and so-called 'domestic regulation'. As a result, the GATS mandated ongoing negotiations to produce new general rules in those areas.[33]

On the more specific issue of distinguishing regulatory trade distortions from legitimate regulation, the GATS is not particularly informative. During negotiations, there had been differences of opinion between those countries which, in Drake and Nicolaïdis' words, began 'from the baseline of labelling as potential [trade barriers] anything that restricted competition',[34] and those which were not ready to 'equate trade liberalization with rapid, across-the-board deregulation'.[35] All countries could readily agree in principle on the sovereign right to regulate of all Members, but it quickly proved impossible to frame a general rule setting the boundary between legitimate and illegitimate regulation.[36] Interestingly, the EC proposed the creation of a standing expert 'Regulation Committee' to perform that function, but the proposal did not attract support.[37] Efforts to identify commonly agreed barriers to trade did not progress far.[38] The result was a preambular reference in the GATS recognizing 'the right of Members to regulate', combined with Article VI, which among others things requires Members to administer their domestic regulations 'in a reasonable, objective and impartial manner', and envisages negotiations on future disciplines. Other than the indicative list contained in Article XVI, then, the GATS does not identify a set of specific 'trade barriers' which are the subject of its disciplines. Instead, it was left largely to the sectoral negotiations to discuss more specifically the kinds of regulatory measures which could and could not be maintained in each service sector subject to liberalization commitments.

I said above that there were three broad aspects to the GATS negotiations: drafting a framework agreement containing broad rules and principles; elaborating the concrete implications of those general principles in specific sectoral negotiations;

[32] GATS, Arts VIII (Government Procurement), V (Economic Integration), XII (Restrictions to Safeguard the Balance of Payments).

[33] GATS, Arts XV (Subsidies), X (Emergency Safeguard Measures), XIII (Government Procurement), VI (Domestic Regulation).

[34] Drake and Nicolaïdis (1992) 70, 78.

[35] ibid 78. As Sauvé notes, this remained a major fault line in the Doha Round: P Sauvé, 'Completing the GATS Framework: Addressing Uruguay Round Leftovers' (2002) 57 Aussenwirtschaft 301.

[36] Reyna (1999) 2381.

[37] M Marconini, 'The Uruguay Round Negotiations on Services' in PA Messerlin and K Sauvant (eds), *The Uruguay Round: Services in the World Economy* (The World Bank, Washington, DC 1990) 19, 22, and 25, n 12. See also Drake and Nicolaïdis (1992) 78.

[38] Croome (1995) 127.

and the exchange of concessions. In the end, work on the latter two aspects progressed to a far lesser extent than on the first. In respect of the exchange of concessions, it is clear that the initial expectations and ambitions of those countries pressing for significant liberalization were not met. As has been often noted, there were few commitments made in the Uruguay Round, and the vast majority of commitments that were made did no more than lock in existing levels of liberalization.[39] This was in part because the inherent uncertainties of the new framework made negotiators reluctant to risk serious concessions.[40] It was also no doubt in part because negotiations on the exchange of concessions did not even begin until 1991, and even then were hampered by uncertainty as to the US position on the MFN principle.[41] Moreover, in the tight final months of negotiations during the Uruguay Round, it proved impossible to reach agreement on the exchange of concessions in a number of crucial service sectors, including financial services and telecommunications.[42] As a result, negotiators continued to work on these issues even after the formal completion of the round, intending initially to complete negotiations on these sectors within approximately six months.

More importantly for the purposes of the present chapter, work on the concrete sectoral implications of services liberalization also remained largely at a preliminary stage, even at the end of the Uruguay Round. As noted above, it was recognized from very early on that differences between service sectors—in terms of their market structure, regulatory objectives, and historical and institutional development—would require special attention, and the Punta del Este Ministerial Declaration of 1986 had for this reason called for the 'elaboration of possible disciplines for individual sectors' to address such issues. By the time of the Montreal Mid-term Review in December 1988, little if anything had been done. Throughout 1989, however, some movement occurred: for example, discussions during the six formal meetings of the negotiating group on services were conducted around a series of papers drafted and circulated by the Secretariat on telecommunications, transport,

[39] B Hoekman, 'Assessing the General Agreement on Trade in Services' in W Martin and LA Winters (eds), *The Uruguay Round and Developing Countries* (CUP, Cambridge 1996) 88; R Adlung, 'Services Negotiations in the Doha Round: Lost in Flexibility?' (2006) 9 JIEL 865, 874; R Adlung and M Roy, 'Turning Hills into Mountains? Current Commitments Under the General Agreement on Trade in Services and Prospects for Change' (2005) 39 J of World Trade 1161.

[40] A Mattoo, 'Services in a Development Round: Three Goals and Three Proposals' (2005) 39 J of World Trade 1223, 1231.

[41] See eg Croome (1995) 313.

[42] In addition, negotiations continued on the movement of Natural Persons. See 'Decision on Negotiations on Movement of Natural Persons adopted by Ministers in Marrakesh on 15 April 1994' in Final Act Embodying the Results of the Uruguay Round of Multilateral Trade Negotiations (15 April 1994) MTN/FA; WTO, Council for Trade in Services, *Draft Decision on movement of Natural Persons Commitments* (21 July 1995) S/C/W/8; WTO, Council for Trade in Services, *Report of the Meeting held on 21 July 1995: Note by the Secretariat* (29 August 1995) S/C/M/5; WTO, *Third Protocol to the General Agreement on Trade in Services* (24 July 1995) S/L/12). They also continued on Maritime Transport Services, see 'Decision on Negotiations on Maritime Transport Services' in Final Act Embodying the Results of the Uruguay Round of Multilateral Trade Negotiations (15 April 1994) MTN/FA; WTO, Council for Trade in Services, *Report of the Meeting held on 28 June 1996: Note by the Secretariat* (8 August 1996) S/C/M/11.

tourism, professional, and financial services.[43] These papers again drew on prior work carried out within the OECD and UNCTAD, as well as more broadly within the services epistemic community.[44] To some extent, they were important in shaping negotiators' expectations as to what counted as trade in services in each sector, and what kinds of barriers might be subject to negotiation in the years ahead.[45] Some important conceptual issues were also identified in these discussions, at least at a high level of generality. It became clear, for example, in the telecommunications context that negotiators would need to distinguish between 'basic' and 'enhanced' telecommunications services. In other sectors, the sheer scale of regulatory changes which might be needed also became apparent for the first time.[46]

As a result, working groups were created to discuss individual sectors, and work began in these groups on how the general principles contained in the emerging framework agreement might be interpreted and augmented in each sector.[47] These groups were somewhat different from 'normal' trade negotiations in that sector specialists from national ministries were heavily involved in discussions, and were indeed the dominant players according to some accounts.[48] This lent a different dynamic to the negotiations, as these sector specialists tended to be convinced of the special character of their sectors, keen to maintain regulatory freedom, and resistant to the imposition of new rules by an institution of which they knew little.[49] To some extent, therefore, the sectoral discussions at this stage concentrated more on crafting exceptional and special sectoral rules, rather than interpreting and elaborating the general disciplines contained in the GATS.[50] Ultimately, while a number of sectoral annexes were attached to the draft agreement prepared for the Brussels Ministerial, all of the operative language remained up for discussion, and some of the annexes frankly amounted merely to derogations from GATS principles rather than elaborations of them.[51]

Then, once a decision was taken that GATS principles would by and large only apply to those sectors to which each contracting party specifically committed, and only to the extent agreed by that party, the need for special sectoral rules became less urgent. Nevertheless, sectoral discussions continued throughout 1991,[52] and the draft text released by Director-General Dunkel in December 1992 ultimately had four sectoral annexes on labour mobility, transport services, financial services, and telecommunications—though the first two were still little more than general limitations on and exceptions to the scope of GATS disciplines. By the conclusion of the

43 See eg Reyna (1999) 2372–3.
44 Drake and Nicolaïdis (1992) 81.
45 Xu and Weller (2004) 152.
46 ibid 152; Croome (1995) 243–4.
47 Reyna (1999) 2389ff.
48 Croome (1995) 247.
49 Croome (1995) 247; Drake and Nicolaïdis (1992) 83; see also H Gao, 'Evaluating Alternative Approaches to GATS Negotiations: Sectoral, Formulae and Other Alternatives' in P Sauvé, M Panizzon, and N Pohl (eds), *GATS and the Regulation of International Trade in Services* (CUP, Cambridge 2007) 183, 201.
50 Drake and Nicolaïdis (1992) 90–1; Croome (1995) 250.
51 Reyna (1999) 2395.
52 Reyna (1999) 2408–9; Croome (1995) 314ff.

Uruguay Round, the number of annexes had expanded somewhat, but their content had not fundamentally changed. Furthermore, as discussed above, negotiations on telecommunications and financial services remained unfinished.

Thus, what ultimately emerged from the Uruguay Round, was a relatively complete framework agreement containing familiar general principles such as non-discrimination and market access, but very little clarity on what those principles might mean in terms of the concrete projects of regulatory reform that they implied in particular sectors. This ambiguity caused significant problems at the very end of negotiations in 1993, as officials from different parts of the US administration raised concerns about the potential unintended impact of GATS principles on social security entitlements, and on certain obscure taxation issues.[53] While there was enough unanimity on these points to resolve them relatively quickly and informally, the ambiguity they reflected no doubt contributed to the unwillingness of negotiators to schedule a significant level of commitments. The legal uncertainty was simply too great.

What is clear from this story is that the GATS did not simply inscribe particular projects of regulatory reform into concrete regulatory disciplines and legally oblige WTO Members to follow them. It did not, in other words, encode particular prescriptions about optimal regulation into determinate legal obligations. Instead, it was an open-ended agreement, creating many more questions than answers about what its effects were likely to be, and even about what the core concepts on which it was founded actually meant. For example, is the online delivery of an electronic book the supply of a service or a good? Does the outsourcing of a manufacturing process turn the provision of that process into a service, rather than an aspect of goods production? Furthermore, indeterminate GATT principles require elaboration and conceptual clarification if their meaning in particular sectors is to be made clear. Are zoning restrictions on the location of hotels properly described as limitations on the supply of tourism services? Might censorship restrictions on the sale of DVDs be understood as a limitation on the supply of entertainment services—and if so, how should one distinguish legitimate from illegitimate censorship restrictions?[54]

In order for the GATS to be put into operation, questions such as these had to be answered. Relevant aspects of the world had to be re-described and reclassified in the language of trade in services—and particular ways of doing so had to be sufficiently commonly accepted among the trade community to provide a secure foundation and guide for the process of interpreting and elaborating the GATS. As a result, over the course of the Uruguay Round, and since then, we have seen the emergence and flourishing of a community of professionals who have taken on the task of operationalizing the GATS: classifying different kinds of economic activity as 'trade in services'; cataloguing and typologizing barriers to that trade; exploring the potential applications of GATS disciplines to particular regulatory measures; and so on. This is a field of knowledge in itself, and part of its role is to help to construct the underlying

[53] Croome (1995) 356, 358.

[54] For a general discussion of the conceptual difficulties inherent in distinguishing 'barriers to services trade' from other kinds of regulations, see Feketekuty (1998) ch 7.

'principles of vision'—the concepts, causal models, evaluative principles, and interpretive frameworks—which, as I said in Chapter 6, structure the interpretation of the texts of international trade law. Its key actors include all those partisan actors we usually associate with trade negotiations: states, state officials, commercial firms, and so on. But they also include professionals with specialized expertise in the services area working in institutions such as the GATT Secretariat, UNCTAD, the OECD, and other knowledge-producing bodies with symbolic authority in the field. It is through the work of all of these actors, then, that shared ideas about what constitutes trade in services, and a barrier to services trade, are produced, disseminated, and contested. In the remainder of this chapter, my task is to explore these processes in a number of contexts, and to draw some conclusions about their underlying dynamics. I begin first with the telecommunications negotiations, which continued in the years immediately following the end of the Uruguay Round.

II. Telecommunications

As noted above, by the end of the Uruguay Round the telecommunications negotiations had not reached a conclusion which was satisfactory to the major players. An Annex on Telecommunications had been agreed and attached to the GATS, but this Annex was focused on ensuring that foreign service suppliers had access to local public telecommunications services on reasonable terms. It therefore addressed issues quite different from the opening up of domestic telecommunications services markets to foreign private telecommunications companies.[55] On this latter issue, the number of countries willing to undertake market access and national treatment commitments in the telecommunications sector was very low.[56] As a result, negotiators agreed to continue the negotiations after the conclusion of the broader round, under the auspices of a newly created Negotiating Group on Basic Telecommunications (NGBT).

One of the most significant activities of this group was the drafting between 1994 and 1996 of what came to be known as the 'Reference Paper'—essentially a set of core principles of pro-competitive regulation for the telecommunications sector. While establishing regulatory standards was (and remains) highly unusual in the context of international trade negotiations, there were at least two reasons why it was thought necessary in the telecommunications context. First, it was generally agreed that the particular structure of the telecommunications sector (where competitors often rely on the incumbent for access to infrastructure) meant that market access commitments in that sector could easily be undermined by the exploitative behaviour of dominant local firms. It therefore seemed clear to negotiators that market access commitments had to be accompanied by some kind of pro-competitive

[55] GATS, Annex on Telecommunications, para 2(c).

[56] See eg LB Sherman, '"Wildly Enthusiastic" About the First Multilateral Agreement on Trade in Telecommunications Services' (1999) 51 Federal Communications LJ 61, 66.

regulatory reform if they were to be meaningful.[57] Secondly, and just as importantly, it was thought that a document was needed to help negotiators to understand what kinds of regulatory reform might generally be expected to follow from taking market access commitments in the telecommunications sector.[58] This would give some comfort to negotiators offering commitments, and also help to ensure a common set of expectations. The process of creating the Reference Paper was therefore understood as 'an opportunity to create a firm set of common understandings' about how the telecommunications sector ought to be governed where market access commitments were undertaken, and how the transition to liberalization was to be managed.[59]

Negotiators did not have to look far for guidance on regulatory principles, as by the mid-1990s there was already a well-established body of specialized technical knowledge on the creation of modern, competitive telecommunications markets, as well as a community seeking to spread this expertise globally. The experience of telecommunications liberalization in a handful of industrialized countries during the late 1980s and early 1990s had given rise to what Cowhey and Aronson call an 'international reform coalition' which actively promoted the benefits of competition in telecommunications markets across most industrialized countries.[60] One structural reason for this advocacy effort was because the prevailing international transfer payment system tended to disadvantage those countries with competitive telecommunications markets as compared to those still in the hands of a public monopoly.[61] But it was also because domestic liberalization—particularly in the United States and Europe—had created powerful new private operators and equipment manufacturers who now sought to establish footholds in existing and emerging foreign markets. The existing international regime governing telecommunications, the International Telecommunications Union (ITU), had proved resistant to the new ideas coming from this reform coalition. The services negotiations provided an opportunity to bypass the ITU,[62] and as a result some advocates of telecommunications liberalization were keen to find a home in the GATS for their regulatory expertise. After some

[57] ibid 71.

[58] ibid 73; WTO, Negotiating Group on Basic Telecommunications, *Report on the Meeting of 15 December 1995* (22 December 1995) S/NGBT/11, para 5; WTO, *Negotiating Group on Basic Telecommunications, Report on the Meeting of 26 January 1996* (14 February 1996) S/NGBT/12, para 6.

[59] PF Cowhey and MM Klimenko, 'The WTO Agreement and Telecommunications Policy Reforms' (2001) World Bank Policy Research Paper No 2601, at 5.

[60] PF Cowhey and JD Aronson, *Transforming Global Information and Communication Markets: The Political Economy of Innovation* (The MIT Press, Cambridge, MA 2009) 151. It has also been called an epistemic community itself: PF Cowhey, 'The International Telecommunications Regime: The Political Roots of Regimes for High Technology' (1990) 44 Intl Org 169.

[61] See PF Cowhey, 'TCC Benchmarks and the Reform of the International Telecommunications Market' (1998) 11 Telecommunications Policy 911.

[62] Cowhey and Aronson (2009) 151, 154, 169. It should be acknowledged, however, that from about 2000 onwards the ITU embraced this new agenda and there are now good links between that organization and the WTO.

'substantial coaching',[63] major commercial players in the sector also became convinced that the GATT/WTO was the right venue for this effort.

It was to this body of specialized knowledge that services negotiators turned for guidance and active input in drafting the Reference Paper. It was drafted by a select group of delegates called the 'Room A Group', which consisted initially of representatives from five industrialized countries which had experience in liberalizing their own domestic telecommunications markets.[64] In close collaboration with their domestic regulators, this group developed a set of general regulatory principles which they then circulated to all members of the NGBT—merely as a 'tool' to help negotiators to understand what regulatory commitments might be on the table for negotiation.[65] This was not an entirely straightforward process, as the regulatory regimes in each of the countries represented were not identical, and the representatives were naturally concerned to ensure that their countries would not need to undertake major changes to their existing regulatory structures. But at that time there was a sufficiently uniform and coherent body of expertise about how competition in the telecommunication sector ought to be introduced and managed that these difficulties proved surmountable. Ultimately, then, the Reference Paper was in many respects a codification of the knowledge which had been gained from the first decade of experimentation with liberalization of telecommunications markets in a handful of developed countries, representing what was at the time considered to be 'best practice'.[66] In the words of one commentator close to the negotiations, the Reference Paper was understood as 'a transfer of know-how to other countries, [a document] that offer[ed] the opportunity to avoid years of trial and error.'[67]

That said, the principles set out in the Reference Paper were still at a fairly broad level of generality. One lesson which negotiators had learnt during their sectoral discussions was the importance of permitting flexibility in the implementation of regulatory obligations.[68] The drafters therefore understood their task to be to identify the core objectives and principles of an appropriate regulatory regime, and to leave it to each Member to determine their preferred means of implementation.[69] Thus, the Reference Paper provides generally that 'appropriate measures shall be maintained for . . . preventing suppliers . . . from engaging in or continuing anti-competitive practices', and supplements this general framework with three

[63] Cowhey and Aronson (2009) 307, n 14.

[64] These countries were the US, Australia, New Zealand, Japan, Korea, and the EU (counted for these purposes as a single negotiating unit): Sherman (1999) 71.

[65] WTO, Negotiating Group on Basic Telecommunications, *Report on the Meeting of 26 January 1996* (14 February 1996) S/NGBT/12, para 6.

[66] L Tuthill, 'The GATS and New Rules for Regulators' (1997) 21 Telecommunications Policy 783, 784.

[67] D Roseman, 'Domestic Regulation and Trade in Telecommunications Services: Experience and Prospects under the GATS' in A Matoo and P Sauvé (eds), *Domestic Regulation & Service Trade Liberalization* (The World Bank and OUP, Oxford 2003) 83, 90.

[68] Roseman (2003) 103.

[69] Sherman (1999) 73; Cowhey and Aronson (2009) 170; JH Rohlfs and JG Sidak, 'Exporting Telecommunications Regulation: The U.S.-Japan Negotiations on Interconnection Pricing' (2002) 43 Harvard Intl LJ 317, 327.

illustrations of the kinds of anti-competitive practices to be prevented. It requires that universal service obligations be administered in a 'transparent, non-discriminatory and competitively neutral manner' and that they be 'not more burdensome than necessary'. It requires the independence of regulatory authorities in equally general terms, expressing no preference as between a general, sector-specific, or other kind of regulator. It requires that the allocation of scarce resources (such as frequencies) be carried out in an 'objective, timely, transparent and non-discriminatory manner'.[70] The generality of these principles would permit their content to evolve as ideas about best practice evolved, and the lack of specificity was acceptable in the light of the existence of an established and relatively authoritative body of shared expertise on these matters.

Although the Reference Paper was not originally drafted as a set of binding obligations, in the end it became precisely that. At the formal conclusion of the telecommunications negotiations, sixty-nine countries had scheduled commitments in the telecommunications sector, of which fifty-three had signed on to the Reference Paper as a set of additional commitments they were prepared to accept—a number which has since risen to above eighty.[71] However, for the purposes of the present story, the significance is not (just) that the Reference Paper became binding—it is that the process of drafting and negotiating the Reference Paper helped to create within, and disseminate among, the relevant community of trade delegates and negotiators a particular body of knowledge about what the liberalization of trade in telecommunications services would and would not mean. As Cowhey and Aronson have observed, the telecommunications negotiations in the WTO 'changed the expertise' and 'altered the competition of the expert community' which until then had structured the international governance of international telecommunications.[72] This new expertise not only found a home in the new WTO, it also began to circulate among trade professionals themselves, and to become part of the vocabulary of that part of the trade profession with a particular interest in telecommunications services. As telecoms specialists and trade negotiators worked closely together during the Uruguay Round[73]—the close partnership between the US Federal Communications Commission under Reed Hundt and the USTR under Charlene Barshefksy during the Uruguay Round being the paradigmatic example—trade professionals began to look to this regulatory expertise to make the general GATS framework meaningful and commercially significant in the telecommunications sector.

[70] WTO, *Reference Paper: Fourth Protocol to the General Agreement on Trade in Services* (1997) 36 ILM 354 paras 1.1, 1.2, 3, 5, and 6.

[71] Sherman (1999) 63; WTO, Services: Sector by Sector, Telecommunications Services <http://www.wto.org/english/tratop_e/serv_e/telecom_e/telecom_e.htm> last visited 14 February 2011.

[72] Cowhey and Aronson (2009) 149.

[73] By all accounts, regulators and trade professionals worked closely together in these negotiations: Sherman (1999) 95; Cowhey and Aronson (2009) 166; Rolhfs and Sidak (2002) 356; JD Aronson, 'Telecom Agreement Tops Expectations' in GC Hufbauer and E Wada (eds), *Unfinished Business: Telecommunications after the Uruguay Round* (Institute for International Economics, Washington, DC 1997) 17, 19.

What we have here, then, is one model of the close relations created between law and expert knowledge in the shadow of the GATS. Negotiations on the elaboration of general GATS principles provided a space and mechanism for the mobilization of a particular body of regulatory expertise, which in turn circulated within legal discourse and helped to give meaning to general legal principles contained in the GATS. An alliance between indeterminate legal principles and determinate programmes of regulatory reform was created in part through the elaboration of further more detailed legal disciplines (the Reference Paper), but probably more importantly through the close relations established between regulatory experts and legal professionals, and the creation of a tightly-knit social system for the ongoing circulation of knowledge between them. Of course, a process like this does not simply happen. In the telecommunications context, it required the directed efforts of the international reform coalition referred to above, who were seeking an international home for their ideas outside the ITU, and were supported by powerful commercial interests. Even then, it required the acquiescence of other countries in the negotiations, and in that respect was aided by the broad sense prevalent at the time that recent revolutions in digital technology meant that 'a profound globalization of the information industry was both inevitable and a driving force for national economic growth'.[74] In some respects, this confluence of factors was unique.

Moreover, the close relations thus forged between legal knowledge and specialist regulatory knowledge are not static, but rather dynamic and contested. The project of linking general GATS principles to particular regulatory choices in the telecommunications sector, in other words, is an ongoing project, carried out and contested in a variety of venues in and around the trade regime. It is worth briefly mentioning two simple illustrations. The first is the controversy which arose in 1996 around the issue of spectrum management measures—that is, the ways that governments divide and allocate spectrum between a limited number of telecommunications service suppliers. On one hand, the issues at stake were technical. Strictly speaking, spectrum management measures limited the number of service suppliers which could operate in a particular telecommunications market, even if those limitations were often more to do with technological constraints than policy preferences. Did that mean that such measures were prohibited as a market access constraint under Article XVI(2)(a) of the GATS? Surely this would not be a reasonable result, as it was of course understood by all that some form of spectrum management was unavoidable. On the other hand, there was also a genuine dilemma concerning how to discipline spectrum allocation as a matter of policy. It was recognized that the spectrum allocation could be manipulated in ways which seriously 'distort[ed] competition' and disadvantaged foreign entrants.[75] It was also recognized that regulators had to balance a series of complex interests in their decisions around spectrum allocation, and that the trade regime was not well positioned to second-guess their decisions. The issue was discussed at some length within the NGBT, and was noted also in the

[74] Cowhey and Klimenko (2001) 3.
[75] Cowhey and Aronson (2009) 173.

WTO's Council for Trade in Services.[76] Ultimately, in the words of one member of the US delegation, a decision was taken that '[spectrum allocation] decisions obviously made to favour a national champion will be subject to dispute settlement, while decisions based strictly on technical issues... will not be challengeable'.[77] More specifically, an agreement was reached, and quasi-formalized in a 'Chairman's Note',[78] that spectrum management measures would not be per se prohibited under Article XVI of the GATS, as might be thought from the wording of that provision, but rather be subject to the more general and loosely worded requirements of Article VI of the GATS and paragraph 6 of the Reference Paper concerning transparency, objective administration, non-discrimination, and so on.

In this case, it seems agreement was possible in part because of the presence of a number of individuals who had been actively involved throughout the Uruguay Round, and who could speak authoritatively about what was or was not implicitly understood through the negotiations. In addition, it was possible precisely because of the existence of a recognized and authoritative body of expertise about telecommunications regulation. It was tolerably clear, in other words, that specialists in the field would know the difference between 'decisions obviously made to favour a national champion' and purely '"technical" decisions' when they saw it.

This episode is interesting for a number of reasons. For one thing, it nicely illustrates the way that broadly shared ideas about the concrete implications of general GATS disciplines can and are generated in and through a variety of background discursive processes at work within the trade regime—as well as the conditions in which this is possible. (Such discussions, it should be noted, may just as easily end in disagreement, not consensus, and in practice that tends to happen more often.) For another thing, the episode is also interesting for the way in which it illustrates the particular legal forms which seem to be characteristically produced by such processes. Here the formal solution is a messy combination of ambiguously drafted norms (Article VI of the GATS and paragraph 6 of the Reference Paper), and a Chairman's Note of unclear formal authority, though apparently decisive practical significance. Other similar issues have given rise to similar legal forms: minuted but formally non-binding gentlemen's agreements not to bring dispute settlement in respect of particular measures; similarly soft 'truces' in respect of other measures; temporary waivers of WTO obligations; and so on.[79] These are perhaps the characteristic forms of a legal regime which works through the mobilization, accretion, and projection of technical regulatory expertise around general legal principles—forms which allow for both for the evolving nature of technical expertise, and the indeterminate character of legal rules.

[76] WTO. Council for Trade in Services, *Report of the Meeting held on 11 and 15 April 1997* (2 May 1997) S/C/M/18; WTO: Group on Basic Telecommunications, *Chairman's Note: Market Access Limitations on Spectrum Availability* (3 February 1997) S/GBT/W/3. See also Sherman (1999) 91ff.

[77] Sherman (1999) 93.

[78] WTO Doc S/GBT/W/3 (1997) 372.

[79] See eg WTO: Group on Basic Telecommunications, *Report of the Meeting of 15 February 1997* (10 March 1997) S/GBT/M/9.

The second example is closely related, in that it illustrates the use of these kinds of documents in formal dispute settlement. Around 2000, a dispute emerged between the United States and Mexico concerning the termination in Mexico of voice, fax, and data transmissions which originated in the United States. The US authorities objected to the prices which were charged for termination of these transmissions in Mexico, which they viewed as unreasonable and not cost-oriented, as well as to the legislative framework which gave Mexico's largest telecommunications provider, Telmex, the exclusive right to set interconnection rates for all incoming traffic for the entire market. After almost two years of consultations, a Panel was established in 2002. One of its three members was a specialist from the World Bank in the area of telecommunications reform in developing countries, including Mexico in particular.

For the purposes of the present argument, the Panel's decision is noteworthy for the extent to which it draws on a broader body of technical expertise concerning the experience of telecommunications liberalization worldwide to support and guide its legal conclusions. For example, in determining that the Mexican interconnection rates were not 'cost-oriented', it looked at an ITU recommendation concerning the different cost elements which should be taken into account,[80] and noted the general trend in a variety of national jurisdictions towards incremental cost methodologies as a 'de facto standard' and the policy reasons behind that trend.[81] Similarly, its interpretation of the term 'anti-competitive' in the Reference Paper was 'informed by the use of this term in Members' own competition legislation', as summarized in a 2001 note by the Secretariat.[82] In addition, its somewhat surprising treatment of the accounting rate issue raised by Mexico displays a keen awareness of the surrounding historical and political context, and is consistent with the tenor of the work of the 'international reform coalition' of telecommunications specialists, referred to above, to limit and erode the old accounting rate system in favour of a more market-oriented interconnection regime.[83] The decision therefore arguably represents an example of the way in which forms of regulatory expertise circulating within the trade regime come to be incorporated into formal processes of interpretation of the GATS, sometimes even taking on what appears to be decisive interpretive significance.

III. Financial services

In addition to the telecommunications sector, the financial services sector was among the most important and most hotly contested issues during the Uruguay Round. I noted above that a coalition of large US financial firms, most prominently AIG,

[80] Panel Report, *Mexico—Measures Affecting Telecommunications Services* (adopted 1 June 2004) WT/DS204/R, para 7.170.

[81] ibid para 7.175.

[82] ibid para 7.234 and n 982.

[83] See, eg, ibid para 7.130ff.

American Express, and Citicorp, had from the beginning been among the most important and vocal advocates for the incorporation of services into the GATT mandate.[84] Over time, the initial enthusiasm and vision of these firms developed into a strong transatlantic alliance involving many of the major players in the financial sector, deeply committed to pursuing market opening through the international trade regime.[85] In part as a result, the United States—and later, the European Union—became firm advocates of a meaningful agreement on financial services liberalization during the Uruguay Round. On the other hand, developing countries as a whole were opposed to the idea, and were not at all convinced that financial liberalization was fully consistent with their economic development priorities, nor with domestic economic stability. This disagreement between advocates of liberalization from the North and sceptics from the South dominated much of the financial services negotiations during and after the Uruguay Round, as major *demandeur* countries sought to generate a critical mass of commitments to make an agreement worthwhile. This took some time: as is well known, the original financial services negotiations continued after the end of the Uruguay Round, since the level of commitments agreed to by the formal close of negotiations was thought to be insufficient by the major players in the negotiations, particularly the United States. Ultimately, it was not until December 1997 that agreement was finally reached on a package of rules and commitments among negotiating countries. The substance of this agreement is contained in a number of separate documents: the GATS itself, associated country Schedules, the Annex on Financial Services, and the Understanding on Commitments in Financial Services.[86]

Alongside this North–South negotiation, however, another set of issues had to be addressed, even among those countries willing to consider liberalization commitments in the sector. As Key explains, 'the process of [financial sector] liberalization involves . . . reaching a consensus on where to draw the line between regulations that are simply anticompetitive barriers to trade—and should therefore be eliminated—and regulations that serve legitimate purposes'.[87] In addition, since liberalization

[84] Freeman (1997) 392–3; W Dobson and P Jacquet, *Financial Services Liberalization in the WTO* (Institute for International Economics, Washington, DC 1998) 71.

[85] P Sauvé and K Steinfatt, 'Financial Services and the WTO: What Next?' in RE Litan, P Masson, and M Pomerleano (eds), *Open Doors: Foreign Participation in Financial Systems in Developing Countries* (The World Bank Group, the International Monetary Fund and the Brookings Institution Press, Washington, DC 2001) 351, 353.

[86] For a discussion of these agreements and the processes leading up to their adoption, see generally Jarreau (1999); EH Leroux, 'Eleven Years of GATS Case Law: What Have We Learned?' (2007) 10 JIEL 749; A Gkoutzinis, 'International Trade in Banking Services and the Role of the WTO: Discussing the Legal Framework and Policy Objectives of the General Agreement on Trade in Services and the Current State of Play in the Doha Round of Trade Negotiations' (2005) 39 The Intl Lawyer 877; LE Panourgias, *Banking Regulation and World Trade Law. GATS, EU and Prudential Institution-Building* (Hart Publishing, Oxford 2006); D Snyder, 'Free Trade in Insurance and Domestic Regulation: In Harmony or in Conflict?' (2007) 26 J of Insurance Regulation 115.

[87] SJ Key, *The Doha Round and Financial Services Negotiations* (American Enterprise Institute Press, Washington, DC 2003) 11. See also S Claessens, 'Regulatory Reform and Trade Liberalization in Financial Services' in A Mattoo and P Sauvé (eds), *Domestic Regulation and Service Trade Liberalization* (OUP and The World Bank, Washington, DC 2003) 129, 129–31.

introduces new risks and regulatory challenges in the financial sector, it is generally agreed that liberalization must often be accompanied by strengthened regulatory frameworks to ensure the integrity and stability of the sector. For both of these reasons, at least some discussion of regulatory standards was a necessary accompaniment to more traditional negotiations over the extent of liberalization commitments which each country was prepared to offer.

It was obvious to negotiators that these questions were best addressed by those having some familiarity and professional expertise with financial regulation—indeed, finance officials insisted that the trade negotiations should include players with such expertise.[88] As a result, while trade officials were responsible for the overall outcome of the negotiations, finance ministries did most of the actual negotiating from the very beginning—or at least this was the case for those from the major developed countries who were the primary drivers of the negotiations.[89] As a result, in the same way as described above in relation to telecommunications, the sectoral regulatory expertise that these specialists brought with them came to shape the elaboration of the law in important ways. That said, the relationship of these finance officials with the trade regime was somewhat different from that of the international reform coalition of telecommunications experts described above. For one thing, the financial community already had an elaborate international apparatus for the discussion and development of international standards on regulatory disciplines in the areas of banking (the Basel Committee), insurance (the International Association of Insurance Supervisors), and securities (the International Organization of Securities Commissions). There was neither a need nor a desire to use the trade regime to circumvent these bodies, nor to pursue a different policy agenda within the trade regime. On the contrary, the financial community was keen not to have the trade regime replicate or interfere with the work of these other international bodies, through (say) the incorporation of core regulatory principles for the financial sector into WTO law.[90] Similarly, the financial sector specialists involved in WTO negotiations were also eager to ensure that any potential WTO disciplines did not interfere with their ability to pursue their own regulatory objectives domestically. Financial regulators expressed concern, for example, that international trade disciplines might constrain their ability to establish and maintain strong prudential regulation. This concern was particularly acute given that trade disciplines would in the normal course of events be interpreted and administered by tribunals with trade, rather than financial, expertise. Thus, while these financial experts were committed to the liberalization of global financial markets, and saw the GATT/WTO as an important venue in which this agenda could be advanced, they were cautious about involving the GATT/WTO on the regulatory side, which they saw as potentially 'ceding power' to the trade regime.[91]

[88] SJ Key, 'Financial Services in the Uruguay Round and the WTO' (1997) Group of Thirty Occasional Paper No 54, at 13; Dobson and Jacquet (1998) 72.

[89] Dobson and Jacquet (1998) 97; Freeman (1997) 396.

[90] See eg Dobson and Jacquet (1998) 72.

[91] Freeman (1997) 396.

The result of this was that while the regulatory expertise of financial sector specialists shaped the elaborated legal framework which ultimately emerged from the Uruguay Round, it did so primarily by restricting the scope and limiting the impact of GATS disciplines. This was accomplished primarily in two ways. First, and most obviously, an Annex on Financial Services was negotiated, which limited the application of the disciplines contained in the GATS in a number of respects. For example, it clarified that central banking activities, and financial activities by public entities using public funds, are not covered by GATS disciplines.[92] More importantly, the Annex contains paragraph 2(a), which excludes the application of GATS disciplines to 'measures taken for prudential reasons', including measures taken 'for the protection of investors, depositors, policy holders or persons to whom a fiduciary duty is owed by a financial service supplier, or to ensure the integrity and stability of the financial system'.[93] Although the wording is somewhat ambiguous, when the entirety of the provision is taken into account this exception is probably subject only to the qualification that such measures not be used as a means of avoiding GATS obligations. Despite its vagueness, this provision provided some comfort to financial regulators that GATS disciplines would not unduly interfere with their regulatory prerogatives.

The second method of limiting the impact of GATS disciplines is more subtle, and requires some additional explanation by way of background. Within the literature on financial sector liberalization, a distinction is commonly drawn between three broad types of liberalization, which—adopting Key's terminology—can be referred to as 'first pillar', 'second pillar', and 'third pillar' liberalization.[94] First pillar liberalization, in Key's framework, involves the establishment or operation of foreign financial institutions in the domestic market, providing financial products in competition with domestic business. This involves the removal of measures which more or less explicitly discriminate against foreign service suppliers in favour of their domestic counterparts. Examples might include restrictions on foreign ownership of banks, restrictions on the rights of foreign banks to establish local branches, or prohibitions on the supply of particular services by foreign financial firms. First pillar liberalization also involves the removal of structural limitations on the competitiveness of domestic markets which have the effect of excluding foreign firms, such as limitations on the number of banks which can operate in the domestic market. Second pillar liberalization is quite different, in that it involves the removal of non-discriminatory, structural impediments to trade in financial services, which apply in principle to all businesses operating in the domestic market. Examples of these kinds of barriers which are given in the literature include prohibitions on affiliation

[92] WTO, Annex on Financial Services (15 April 1994) MTN/FA, para 1(b).

[93] Annex on Financial Services, para 2(a).

[94] Key (2003) 12ff. See also Sauvé and Steinfatt (2001) 355–6 (using different terminology to capture a closely related idea).

between banks and insurance companies, interest rate controls, rules prohibiting certain funds from investing in foreign entities, failure to maintain or apply effective competition policy, or strict asset allocation requirements for pension funds, or unduly restrictive capital adequacy ratios, lending limits, and other prudential requirements.[95] Third pillar liberalization is full capital account liberalization. This implies the complete elimination of all limitations on the freedom of capital to enter or exit a country—in whatever form, context, and quantity.

While these technical distinctions are never explicitly spelt out either in the text of the GATS or the Annex on Financial Services, there is some evidence that they have shaped the expectations of negotiators and others within the financial services field about what the impact of GATS commitments is likely to be, as well as strong evidence that they have a continuing role in influencing ongoing legal debates about the content and meaning of GATS disciplines on financial regulation.

For example, it is a consistent claim within that literature that 'trade liberalization' in the financial services sector is conceptually different from full capital account liberalization (third pillar), and that GATS rules therefore cannot and do not require full opening of the capital account (only partial). This claim has been made, for example, in papers circulated by the Secretariat to WTO delegations.[96] It is made also in explanatory literature on the GATS published by WTO Members, and by officials close to the negotiations.[97] In the present Doha Round of negotiations, some delegates have explicitly referred back to this implicit understanding, as a way of taking objection to what they perceive as attempts to blur the boundaries between trade liberalization and capital account liberalization in the present round.[98] The claim is also made in academic literature on the GATS.[99] Indeed, there have been many attempts to show how WTO obligations have the effect of stopping short of full capital account liberalization, through a careful parsing of the ambiguous terms of the GATS—or at least to argue for interpretations of the GATS which reflect and entrench the distinction between trade liberalization and capital account liberalization.[100]

95 These examples are taken from Key (2003) 16. The difference between Key's first and second pillar liberalization is similar to the distinction drawn by other writers between 'positive integration' and 'negative integration'.

96 See eg M Kono and L Schuknecht, 'Financial Services Trade, Capital Flows, and Financial Stability' (1998) WTO Staff Working Paper ERAD-98-12.

97 European Commission, *GATS—The General Agreement on Trade in Services: A Guide for Business* (Office for Official Publications of The European Communities, Luxembourg 1995); Key (2003).

98 WTO: Committee on Trade in Financial Services, *Report of the Meeting held on 2 December 2002: Note by the Secretariat* (11 February 2003) S/FIN/M/38; WTO: Committee on Trade in Financial Services, *Report of the Meeting held on 26 February 2003: Note by Secretariat* (7 April 2003) S/FIN/M/39; WTO: Committee on Trade in Financial Services, *Report of the Meeting held on 16 May 2003: Note by the Secretariat* (30 June 2003) S/FIN/M/40.

99 eg Sauvé and Steinfatt (2001).

100 See eg Kono and Schuknecht (1998); P Sorsa, 'The GATS Agreement on Financial Services: A Modest Start to Multilateral Liberalization' (1997) IMF Working Paper No 97/55, for two of many examples.

The distinction between first and second pillar liberalization also seems to be helping to structure and inform debates about the meaning and implication of GATS principles in the context of the financial services sector. Key, for example, has written that the primary aim of negotiators in the financial services negotiations was first pillar liberalization. There was a broad 'consensus' among negotiators, she argues, that first pillar measures could not in principle be 'legitimate prudential measure[s]', and that Articles XVI and XVII of the GATS operated to prohibit such measures, unaffected by the prudential carve-out.[101] She claims, moreover, that measures which come under the category of second pillar liberalization are more ambiguous in terms of their desirability: it is understood to be a matter of expert judgment in a particular context whether such measures are necessary and optimally designed for a legitimate purpose. As a result, she suggests, they are not prohibited per se, but subject to much softer disciplines: primarily the transparency obligations, requiring their publication (Article III); the requirement that they be administered in a reasonable, objective, and impartial manner (Article VI:1); and, in due course, a necessity test (Article VI:4). To this list we may add the 'best endeavours' obligations contained in the Understanding on Commitments in Financial Services, for those countries which have agreed to it.[102] Similar views as to the application of GATS disciplines circulate elsewhere in the literature on financial services regulation. Gkoutzinis, for example, evokes the related distinction between 'negative integration' which addresses 'direct' barriers to trade (similar to first pillar liberalization) and 'positive integration' which addresses 'indirect' barriers to trade (similar to second pillar liberalization), and argues that GATS principles do little to deal with the latter.[103] Sauvé and Steinfatt propose the continued pursuit of a 'traditional contestability agenda' through the GATS, which they understand as focusing on the elimination of discriminatory barriers to effective market entry (first pillar), and only invoking transparency and harmonization norms to discipline non-discriminatory regulations which apply post-establishment (second pillar).[104]

Of course, it is one thing for the distinctions drawn within specialist literature on financial services to shape informally the expectations of negotiators, commentators, scholars, and others working in the field concerning the impact of GATS disciplines—it is quite another for these expectations to have a shaping influence on formal and authoritative processes of legal interpretation within WTO dispute settlement. After all, it is not at all clear from the text of the GATS that the legal framework created during the financial services negotiations actually *does* correspond

[101] Key (2003) 35.
[102] WTO, *Understanding on Commitments in Financial Services* (15 April 1994) LT/UR/U/1, paras 10–11.
[103] Gkoutzinis (2005) 902, 908 and generally.
[104] See eg Sauvé and Steinfatt (2001) 355–6.

to the relatively limited image of liberalization which, according to the literature at least, the negotiators seem to have had in mind. As should be clear from Chapter 8, the national treatment norm is clearly ambiguous enough to cover much more than 'first pillar' barriers as described above, and to be potentially more deregulatory in nature than it may initially appear. For another, the provision on prudential measures is of very unclear scope, given that little if any guidance is given in the text of the GATS as to precisely how an interpreter is to make the crucial judgment as to whether a measure is truly 'prudential' or not, and given that it is subject to the proviso that prudential measures shall not be used as a means of avoiding the Member's commitments under the GATS.

It was partly for these reasons, then, that finance officials insisted on including a provision in the Annex on Financial Services, requiring that 'panels for disputes on prudential issues and other financial matters shall have the necessary expertise relevant to the specific financial service under dispute'.[105] Reminiscent of the approach taken in the *DISC* dispute described in Chapter 8, we can understand this as an attempt by financial sector specialists to maintain a significant degree of input into the formal interpretive process—to institutionalize the free flow of information and expertise from finance sector specialists to lawyers involved in processes of formal legal interpretation. Indeed, this provision represents the compromise ultimately reached between finance officials who originally sought an entirely separate dispute settlement mechanism for financial disputes, and trade officials for whom that was unacceptable.[106] For precisely the same reason, one sees throughout the literature the extremely common claim that GATS principles should be interpreted in the light of international regulatory standards set in other international bodies such as the Basel Committee, the International Organization of Securities Commissions (IOSCO), and the International Association of Insurance Supervisors (IAIS).[107] While this is a contestable proposition as a matter of both law and policy, if it is accepted within WTO dispute settlement, it will represent another mechanism through which the interpretation of GATS principles comes to be systematically shaped and informed by particular kinds of financial sector expertise.[108]

So far, then, we have a broadly similar story to that of the telecommunications negotiations set out above: a story of the elaboration and interpretation of a body of international legal disciplines by reference to a field of technical regulatory expertise. I have said that in the financial services context, this field of technical expertise

[105] GATS, Annex on Financial Services, para 4.

[106] Key (1997) 21.

[107] See eg K Alexander, 'The GATS and Financial Services: The Role of Regulatory Transparency' (2007) 20 Cambridge Rev of Intl Affairs 111, 127; R Bismuth, 'Financial Sector Regulation and Financial Services Liberalization at the Crossroads: The Relevance of International Financial Standards in WTO Law' (2010) 44 J of World Trade 489, 500 n 71; Gkoutinis (2005) 908; MJ Hahn, 'WTO Rules on Trade in Financial Services: A Victory of Greed over Reason?' in R Grote and T Marauhn (eds), *The Regulation of International Financial Markets: Perspective for Reform* (CUP, Cambridge 2006) 176–205, 202; Panourgias (2006) 107; Sauvé and Steinfatt (2001) 366; Snyder (2007) 120.

[108] Leroux also notes that the interpretation of the prudential carve-out 'will evolve based in large part on the practices of States and their financial regulators and what is, at a particular point in time, considered to be prudential': EH Leroux, 'Trade in Financial Services Under the World Trade Organization' (2002) 36 J of World Trade 413, 430.

tended to limit and constrain the potential impact of GATS norms—though it is also the case that in some important instances financial regulatory expertise was mobilized in the pursuit of deregulatory purposes.[109] When we turn to the period after the completion of the financial services negotiations in the late 1990s, however, we see a somewhat different dynamic emerging, in which the tendency to turn to this financial sector expertise in the elaboration of GATS norms has been hotly contested—and successfully blocked—primarily by developing country delegations.

The first post-Uruguay Round of services negotiations was due to begin in 2000. In the years leading up to their commencement, it became clear to many that if this round of negotiations was to result in substantially broader and deeper liberalization commitments—perhaps even extending further into second pillar liberalization—it would need to be built on the foundation of a clearer and more extensive set of shared ideas about what did and did not constitute legitimate and acceptable forms of regulation of the financial sector. These ideas would have to be 'shared' in two senses: first, shared as between the financial and trade communities so as to ensure that financial regulators and officials felt more comfortable giving the WTO more authority in this area; and secondly, shared within the financial community itself, which even at that time was sharply divided, particularly in the wake of a series of severe financial crises across a number of developing countries during the 1990s. Thus, for example, in an article published just as the GATS 2000 negotiations were beginning, Sauvé and Steinfatt argued that 'the most pressing challenge in the area of rulemaking will be that of fostering acceptance and cooperation . . . on the part of financial regulators' and called for 'continued, deeper dialogue between the trade policy and financial regulation communities' to achieve that aim.[110] Furthermore, they argued, 'promoting regulatory dialogue' should be a core objective of the GATS negotiations.[111] In a stronger vein, others have made proposals for the negotiation of a set of core principles of precompetitive regulation in the financial sector, similar to the Reference Paper in the telecommunications context.[112]

One way of trying to build such shared ideas was to encourage information flow between officials working on financial services in the WTO context and those working in international regulatory standard-setting bodies such as the Bank for International Settlements (BIS), IOSCO, and IAIS. The home states of major international financial firms have advocated this most vigorously, for example in the

[109] eg the US agreed to use its 'best efforts' to remove certain restrictions contained in the Glass-Steagall Act, while Japan agreed to remove certain restrictions on asset management services, as well as other measures. Thus, while negotiators were not comfortable with imposing substantive prohibitions of non-discriminatory, structural regulations, they were more comfortable with negotiating on these measures on a case-by-case basis. As Key explains, in these contexts, the negotiations involved marshalling a 'critical mass' of regulators and experts who believed that such measures were inappropriate or unnecessary to achieve their stated prudential purposes and persuading the implementing country to accept that view: Key (2003) in, 48.

[110] Sauvé and Steinfatt (2001) 362–3.

[111] Sauvé and Steinfatt (2001) 363. See also Gkoutzinis (2005) 909.

[112] Claessens, 'Regulatory Reform and Trade Liberalization in Financial Services' in Mattoo and Sauvé (2003) 144 n 12.

Council for Trade in Services and its subsidiary bodies.[113] For instance, in early 2000, the WTO's Committee on Trade in Financial Services considered a request that the IAIS be granted observer status in the Committee. Representatives from the European Union, Canada, the United States, and Japan spoke in support of the request, in part on the basis that proper supervision of insurance markets was a precondition to liberalization, and that the work of the IAIS on developing standards for such supervision would be of use to ongoing liberalization efforts within the WTO.[114] Around the same time, the Japanese delegation, along with others, made a proposal that the IAIS, Basel Committee, and IOSCO be asked to submit written documents and make oral presentations on their work to the Committee, for the purpose of informing the delegates about relevant regulatory issues in preparation for the negotiations.[115] Australia also proposed clarifying the meaning of the prudential measures provision through recourse to international standards promulgated by the Basel Committee.[116]

These efforts have, however, been strongly contested, primarily by developing countries, which are concerned about their lack of voice in these standard-setting bodies, and are reluctant to give special interpretive weight to principles drafted in their view essentially by representatives of the industrialized North.[117] Thus, a number of developing countries, most prominently Malaysia—historically one of the developing countries most strongly opposed to financial services liberalization—objected to the presence of the IAIS in the Committee, and no consensus on the matter was achieved after nine months. Australia's proposal was also fiercely resisted. Indeed, any and all attempts to build a common informal understanding of the meaning of the prudential measures provision through discussion in the Committee have been equally forcefully resisted: it is not just the acceptability of existing international standards which is at stake, it is also that many developing countries object to any activity which approximates regulatory standard-setting of any kind within the WTO.[118] As a result, apart from the circulation of technical documents and some presentations by the World Bank and the IMF,[119] there has been

[113] Bismuth (2010) 504ff; WTO, Council for Trade in Services, *Communication from the European Communities and their Member States, GATS 2000: Financial Services* (22 December 2000) S/CSS/W/39, para 20.

[114] WTO, Committee on Trade in Financial Services, *Report of the Meeting held on 13 April 2000: Note by the Secretariat* (8 May 2000) S/FIN/M/25, para 8; WTO, Committee on Trade in Financial Services, *Report of the Meeting held on 25 May 2000: Note by the Secretariat* (29 June 2000) S/FIN/M/26; WTO, Committee on Trade in Financial Services, *Report of the Meeting held on 13 July 2000: Note by the Secretariat* (23 August 2000) S/FIN/M/27; WTO, Committee on Trade in Financial Services, *Report of the Meeting held on 9 October 2000: Note by the Secretariat* (20 November 2000) S/FIN/M/28.

[115] See eg WTO Doc S/FIN/M/26, para 22.

[116] WTO Doc S/FIN/M/25.

[117] See eg WTO, Committee on Trade in Financial Services, *Report of the Meeting held on 6 October 2003: Note by the Secretariat* (12 November 2003) S/FIN/M/42. See also R Grynberg and S Silva, 'Harmonization without Representation: Small States, the Basel Committee, and the WTO' (2006) 34 World Development 1123.

[118] See eg WTO Doc S/FIN/M/28, para 23.

[119] Such presentations are referred to in WTO, Committee on Trade in Financial Services, *Report of the Meeting held on 4 June 2002: Note by the Secretariat* (8 July 2002) S/FIN/M/35, paras 36–7; WTO,

considerable resistance to the circulation of knowledge and expertise between the WTO and the international standard-setting bodies relevant to financial services. This is, in part, precisely because delegates recognize that the circulation of such expertise is potentially significant and politically charged, in the sense that it can affect the background ideas and frameworks of knowledge which are drawn on to shape the evolution, application, and interpretation of the disciplines of the GATS.[120]

Alongside these efforts to promote dialogue with international regulatory bodies, there have been attempts to foster peer-to-peer dialogue among WTO Members, in the hope of initiating a process of mutual learning, and even building a body of shared knowledge and expertise around financial regulation within the relevant trade community. Thus, the Committee on Trade in Financial Services was host to an information exchange programme, in which Members were encouraged to make presentations to the Committee on their recent experience with liberalization and regulatory reform in the financial services sector.[121] These presentations, often accompanied by a written submission from the Member's representative, typically focused on the substance of recent legislative changes, as well as the challenges and difficulties that the country faced in the process of liberalization, and the tools it used to deal with such challenges. Other delegates commented on the presentation, asked clarifying questions, and at times offered their own views on the appropriate lessons to be drawn from the experiences related. Written responses to the questions raised in the Committee were circulated in the weeks after a meeting, and the discussion sometimes continued for a number of future meetings afterwards. Those Members who made presentations did so on a voluntary basis.

This routine was designed in part to help to build, within the relevant sections of the trade community, a broadly shared set of ideas about the particular challenges which are commonly faced in the financial sector, and how regulators normally and legitimately deal with such challenges. To some extent, perhaps, they achieved that

Committee on Trade in Financial Services, *Report of the Meeting held on 2 December 2002: Note by the Secretariat* (11 February 2003) WTO Doc S/FIN/M/38.

[120] On the political consequences of information exchange in earlier stages of the GATT's history, see Winham (1986) 85–90. It is worth noting that precisely the same dynamic—the turn to international standard-setting agencies to guide norm development under the GATS and the contestation of that turn—has occurred to some extent in the Working Party on Professional Services, in the context of discussing disciplines in the accountancy sector. C Trolliet and J Hegarty, 'Regulatory Reform and Trade Liberalization in Accountancy Services' in Mattoo and Sauvé (2003) 150ff.

[121] See eg WTO Doc S/FIN/M/38; WTO, Committee on Trade in Financial Services, *Communication from Hong Kong, China* (3 December 2002) S/FIN/W/25; WTO Doc S/FIN/M/40; WTO, Committee on Trade in Financial Services, *Communication from Switzerland: E-banking in Switzerland* (30 April 2003) S/FIN/W/26; WTO Doc S/FIN/M/27, para 45; WTO, Committee on Trade in Financial Services, *Communication from Japan. The Establishment of the Financial Services Agency* (13 July 2000) S/FIN/W/15; WTO, Committee on Trade in Financial Services, *Report of the Meeting held on 19 September 2005: Note by the Secretariat* (23 September 2005) S/FIN/M/50; WTO, Committee on Trade in Financial Services, *Report of the Meeting held on 11 October 2001: Note by the Secretariat* (9 November 2001) S/FIN/M/32; WTO, Committee on Trade in Financial Services, *Report of the Meeting held on 7 July 2003: Note by the Secretariat* (13 August 2003) S/FIN/M/41; WTO, Committee on Trade in Financial Services, *Report of the Meeting held on 28 September 2004. Note by the Secretariat* (29 October 2004) S/FIN/M/46.

aim, at least within some small sub-groupings within the range of delegates attending the meetings of the Committee. More obviously, however, these discussions were also a domain of contestation. Delegates in the Committee disagreed about the appropriate lessons to be learnt from particular experiences of liberalization. Some—most often developing countries with a keen defensive interest in financial services—seemed to be quite vigilant, ensuring that no easy consensus in favour of the benefits of financial liberalization emerged from the discussions. Presentations broadly in favour of financial liberalization were countered by presentations of the considerable dangers and challenges posed by the opening of the financial sector. Faultlines emerged in these discussions which broadly corresponded with the perceived interests that those countries have in future negotiations. Countries coalesced around different bodies of expert knowledge about the costs and benefits of financial liberalization and regulation, so that conflicting interests and political disagreements were expressed as competing claims about the desirability of different ways of organizing the sector. Attempts to build shared ideas about 'best regulatory practice', or to secure general adherence to a common and uniform core of basic regulatory principles, were therefore largely unsuccessful.

IV. Catalogues

The previous two sections were concerned with the incorporation, circulation, and contestation of regulatory norms within the trade regime. This section shifts focus somewhat to look at the generation of information on the nature, extent, and impact of barriers to trade in services. Recall from Chapter 8 that a similar process of data gathering occurred prior to the Tokyo Round, as a prelude to the imposition of new disciplines on domestic regulation affecting trade in goods.[122] In that case, as Winham has argued, the collection of data represented an important process by which shared ideas were gradually formed, and negotiators were educated into a collectively shared way of interpreting and classifying different governmental measures as a prelude to negotiations over them.[123] It has begun to perform a similar function in the context of services negotiations.

The first catalogue of barriers to trade in services, or at least the first to aim at comprehensiveness, was produced in the context of the US efforts, described earlier, to raise services issues in the context of the OECD's Trade Committee.[124] In the early stages of discussions within the Trade Committee about how to approach the services issue, the US representative (Feketekuty) came to the view that the best initial step would be for the OECD to conduct a study on existing barriers to trade in services. Such a study, the United States argued, could help to assess the scope and nature of the problem, identify priority issue areas, and provide guidance as to the next steps. In order to demonstrate the feasibility of this option, the United States

[122] See above pp 240–1.
[123] Winham (1986) 88, 105.
[124] This account draws primarily on Aronson (1992) and Feketekuty (1998).

rapidly put together an incomplete but indicative report which set out what it saw as the main kinds of existing barriers, and obtained agreement to conduct a more comprehensive study.[125] This comprehensive study was put together over the course of 1979 by the USTR, working closely with the US Chamber of Commerce. It was based on data gathered from a questionnaire sent by the Chamber of Commerce to its relevant members, asking them about the barriers that they faced in gaining access to export markets of interest to them. This information was collected and processed, and the report was submitted to the OECD at the end of 1979. It was entitled the USTR Inventory of Barriers to Trade in Services, and it organized the barriers by country, sector, and barrier type. As Feketekuty himself has acknowledged, this initial report had its flaws, sometimes citing outdated foreign legislation or misinterpreting its meaning.[126] However, it went through a number of different editions, and remained probably the most comprehensive and influential reference document on the nature of trade barriers in services sectors for at least a decade.

Over the course of the 1980s and into the 1990s, data gathering by the US government on the barriers that its services industries faced overseas gradually became more routine and more comprehensive. In 1983, and then again in 1985, Price Waterhouse contributed to this project by conducting further surveys of services firms. Then, from 1986, the USTR was mandated to produce an annual survey of barriers to US exports by country, covering barriers to trade in both goods and services.[127] This annual report is based on information collectively compiled by the USTR and the US Departments of Commerce and Agriculture, supplemented with information provided by members of the private sector trade advisory committees, as well as US embassies.[128] It is designed as part of a comprehensive package of measures aiming to bring pressure to bear on foreign countries to open their markets to US exports. In addition, other US agencies provide regular reports on trade restrictions in specific sectors, such as the Treasury Department's quadrennial National Treatment Study, which addresses the treatment of US financial firms in foreign markets.[129]

Other countries, which for the same reasons also accumulate data on foreign trade barriers as a routine part of their trade policy, began to turn their minds to services barriers at around the same time. In 1986, the European Commission requested an accounting firm to compile as exhaustive as possible a list of 'all the available

[125] This report drew heavily on four chapters from B Griffiths, *Invisible Barriers to Invisible Trade* (Macmillan, London 1975), two of which sketched the main types of relevant barriers.

[126] Feketekuty (1988) 316 and surrounding.

[127] In accordance with § 181 of the Trade Act of 1974 (Pub L No 93 618, 88 Stat 1978) as amended.

[128] See eg United States Trade Representative, *2009 National Trade Estimate Report on Foreign Trade Barriers* (Office of the United States Trade Representative 2009) 1.

[129] See eg United States Department of the Treasury, *National Treatment Study* (Treasury Department, Washington, DC 1998).

information on barriers to trade in services'.[130] The EC now maintains a searchable online database of barriers to EC exports, compiles an annual survey of barriers to trade and investment for European firms seeking to do business in the United States, and consistently solicits the views of business on the nature and extent of barriers through surveys, informal contacts, and an online complaint mechanism. Japan has also published its Report on the WTO Consistency of Trade Policies by Major Trading Partners since 1992.[131]

Regardless of the rigour with which these reports are produced, their claim to comprehensiveness and impartiality is undermined by the context in which they are made. In these contexts the focus is on capturing and responding to the on-the-ground concerns of domestic businesses, and, as a result, the information produced at the national level tends broadly to reflect and codify the perceptions of domestic commercial actors as to what does and does not constitute a barrier to trade. A measure will not be made visible as a trade barrier through these processes unless there is some indication from private firms that it is of commercial significance to them. Moreover, given the motivations and experiences of the actors surveyed, and the institutional context in which the catalogues are produced, the process is likely to produce a list of trade barriers which is broader than most. Within the context of multilateral trade negotiations on services, therefore, the demand has arisen for data on existing barriers which has some greater claim to objectivity.

To the extent that this demand has been met—and it should be recalled that this is still a project very much in its infancy—it has been primarily academic and international institutions which have done so. The World Bank, for example, was active in the area initially. The first post-GATS attempt at a more rigorous and comprehensive mapping of global trade barriers in services was conducted by Hoekman, a senior economist working at the World Bank, in 1995.[132] Since then, figures on services barriers have been incorporated into the World Bank's annual World Trade Indicators publication.[133] In addition, the Trade Committee of the OECD has probably done the most to advance this work conceptually, in a programme which has been active for some time. It has, for example, compiled lists of indicative trade barriers in at least seven different service sectors,[134] leading to a consolidated inventory of barriers to services trade.[135] It has progressed several steps down the path of producing a standardized Sectoral Trade Restrictiveness Index to help in the

[130] Peat, Marwick, Mitchell, *A Typology of Trade Barriers to International Services Industries* (EC Commission, Brussels 1986).

[131] See Japan, Ministry of Economy, Trade and Industry (METI), Reports <http://www.meti.go.jp/english/report/index_report.html> last visited 14 February 2011.

[132] B Hoekman, 'Tentative First Steps: An Assessment of the Uruguay Round Agreement on Services' (1995) World Bank Policy Research Working Paper No 1455. See also Hoekman (1996) 88.

[133] See eg G Zanini and R Islam, *World Trade Indicators 2008: Benchmarking Policy and Performance* (The World Bank, 2008) 20ff.

[134] See OECD: Trade and Agriculture Directorate, Trade Committee, 'Towards a Services Trade Restrictiveness Index (STRI): A Proposal for a Road Map for Future Trade Committee Work on Services' (27 June 2007) TAD/TC(2007) 4.

[135] See eg OECD: Trade Directorate, Trade Committee, 'Assessing Barriers to Trade in Services: Revised Consolidated List of Cross-Sectoral Barriers' (28 February 2001) TD/TC/WP(99)58/FINAL.

quantification of the restrictive impact of domestic regulations.[136] OECD staff have begun to collect and publish information on barriers to trade in particular service sectors in non-OECD countries—for example, in banking and telecommunications services in certain transition economies,[137] as well as the banking, telecommunications, and transport sectors in particular countries.[138] Some of this work has also been undertaken in collaboration with UNCTAD. Joint OECD–UNCTAD sectoral checklists were prepared for GATS negotiators for six different service sectors, for example, covering such issues as the sector's economic importance, common trade barriers in the sector, risks and benefits of liberalization, and policy goals of liberalization.[139] At a general level, UNCTAD has been working more broadly to 'develop methodologies to identify, classify and quantify NTBs [non-tariff barriers]', to 'analyse the impact of NTBs on international trade', and to 'build analytical and statistical capacities to assess how NTBs affect developing country exports'.[140] It has produced and commissioned a variety of analyses of the barriers to developing country services exports, and has conducted over thirty assessments of trade in services in particular countries.[141] In addition, even before the end of the Uruguay Round, UNCTAD had begun to investigate the possibility of compiling a global searchable database of NTBs in services, to complement its existing database on similar measures in the goods context ('TRAINS'). It has since done exactly that, creating its Measures Affecting Trade in Services (MAST) database, which—as sources of data become more sophisticated and comprehensive—is intended to act as a statistical and policy tool in the area.

[136] OECD (2007).

[137] N Dihel and B Kalinova, 'Services Barriers and their Economic Impact: Examples of Banking and Telecommunications Services in Selected Transition Economies' (2004) OECD Trade Policy Working Paper No 7.

[138] MA Marouani and L Munro, 'Assessing Barriers to Trade in Services in the MENA Region' (2009) OECD Trade Policy Working Paper No 84.

[139] OECD, 'Managing Request-Offer Negotiations under the GATS: The Case of Construction Services' (2005) TD/TC/WP(2005)10/FINAL; M Geloso Grosso, 'Managing Request-Offer Negotiations Under the GATS: The Case of Environmental Services' (15 February 2005) OECD Trade Policy Working Paper No 11 (TD/TC/WP(2004)8/FINAL); M Geloso Grosso, 'Managing Request-Offer Negotiations under the GATS: The Case of Legal Services' (14 June 2004) OECD Trade Policy Working Paper No 2 (TD/TC/WP(2003)40/FINAL); S Zarrilli, 'Managing Request-Offer Negotiations under the GATS: The Case of Energy Services' (5 November 2003) TD/TC/WP(2003)24/FINAL; J Kazeki, 'Managing Request-Offer Negotiations under the GATS: The Case of Insurance Services' (4 November 2003) TD/TC/WP(2003)17/FINAL; HK Nordås, E Pinali, and M Geloso Grosso, 'Logistics and Time as a Trade Barrier' (30 May 2006) OECD Trade Policy Working Paper No 35 (TD/TC/WP(2006)3/FINAL).

[140] See United Nations Conference on Trade and Development, Trade in Services and Non-tariff Barriers <http://www.unctad.org/Templates/Page.asp?intItemID=3848&lang=1> last visited 14 February 2011. For a useful review of the literature on services liberalization and developing countries, see J Whalley, 'Assessing the Benefits to Developing Countries of Liberalisation in Services Trade' (2004) 27 The World Economy 1223.

[141] See eg UNCTAD. Commission on Trade in Goods and Services, and Commodities, *Trade in Services and Development Implications: Note by the UNCTAD Secretariat* (16 January 2006) TD/B/COM.1/77 and (2 February 2007) TD/B/COM.1/85.

How are choices made within this literature about what to count (and what not to count) as a 'barrier' to services trade? One of the techniques deployed, particularly in the early studies, was to look to the WTO itself, both as a source of data on its Members' trade policies, but also for a general indication of what is collectively considered to be a 'trade barrier' by those working within the regime. The work of the WTO incidentally produces a number of documents which are useful for this purpose. For example, during both the Uruguay Round and the subsequent services negotiations, it was a common technique for a questionnaire or survey to be circulated among Members in the very early stages of negotiations, asking them specific questions about the structure of particular domestic service sectors, and the scope of governmental action within them. Thus, the Negotiating Group on Maritime Transport Services distributed a questionnaire requesting information from Members on the different kinds of measures they had in place in the sector.[142] So too did the Negotiating Group on Basic Telecommunications.[143] After the Uruguay Round, the Working Party on Professional Services also distributed a questionnaire in respect of domestic regulation in the accountancy sector, which was useful in producing a rough list of trade restrictions in that sector for the purposes of negotiation.[144] In addition, the Council for Trade in Services itself receives and compiles information on certain trade barriers imposed by WTO Members pursuant to a number of transparency disciplines contained in the GATS. For example, Article III:3 of the GATS requires Members to inform the Council promptly of any new measures they establish which significantly affect trade in services covered by its liberalization commitments. Even the schedules of commitments entered into by each participant in the Uruguay Round negotiations produced a database of sorts—albeit a very rough one—containing information about existing barriers to trade in services. Furthermore, the Trade Policy Review Mechanism provides a venue in which particular kinds of governmental regulation are systematically and collectively made visible as trade barriers.

This WTO material has been used in the research on barriers to trade described above. For example, Hoekman's ground-breaking study used GATS schedules as its primary data source, calculating the incidence of trade barriers sector by sector and country by country, according to the level of liberalization commitments made in each WTO Member's GATS schedule.[145] A number of studies since then have reproduced precisely this methodology, sometimes updated to reflect changes in the

[142] WTO: Negotiating Group on Maritime Transport Services, *Questionnaire on Maritime Transport Services: Note by the Secretariat* (21 October 1994) WTO Doc S/NGMTS/W/2.

[143] WTO: Negotiating Group on Basic Telecommunications, *Questionnaire on Basic Telecommunications: Note by Secretariat* (15 July 1994) WTO Doc TS/NGBT/W/3.

[144] WTO: Working Party on Professional Services, *Questionnaire on the Accountancy Sector: Note by the Secretariat* (3 April 1996) WTO Doc S/WPPS/W/7. This followed on from previous questionnaires conducted by the OECD, ISAR, and IFAC.

[145] Hoekman (1995).

content of schedules.[146] McGuire and his co-authors, in their review of barriers to trade in maritime transport services, drew on information derived from responses to the questionnaire distributed by the WTO's Negotiating Group on Maritime Transport Services, as well as from Trade Policy Reviews conducted by the WTO.[147] Kalirajan and Nguyen-Hong also draw on Trade Policy Reviews, and WTO-compiled lists of MFN exemptions, as well as the WTO questionnaire on the accountancy sector.[148]

However, given the obvious limitations of these data sources, new and more sophisticated methodologies for measuring barriers to trade have been developed. Aside from quantitative methodologies, which are less relevant in the present context and in any case not the preferred option,[149] the most common solution appears to be to turn to sectoral experts. This methodology, as pioneered by the Australian Productivity Commission in the lead-up to the initiation of the GATS 2000 negotiations, is divided into two stages.[150]

The first stage is the *qualitative identification* of trade barriers, sector by sector, on the basis of 'the judgment of sectoral experts'.[151] This typically involves sending out questionnaires to sectoral experts in different countries, as well as mining existing sectoral databases and information provided by other specialized sectoral agencies. One of the attractions of using case-by-case expert judgment is that it permits subtle distinctions to be drawn between 'trade enhancing' and 'trade restricting' regulatory measures, or between measures which are 'trade restricting' and those which are necessary in order to achieve a particular domestic policy objective. It is recognized within the literature that this is one of the most difficult elements of the exercise, involving a high degree of judgment. McGuire, for example, notes that the standard definition of a trade barrier—that is, 'any measure that distorts the efficient

[146] See eg A Mattoo, 'Financial Services and the WTO: Liberalization in the Developing and Transition Economies' (1998) WTO Staff Working Paper TISD9803.WPF (preliminary draft); M Marko, 'An Evaluation of the Basic Telecommunications Service Agreement' (1998) Centre for Intl Econ Studies Discussion Paper No 98/09; Pacific Economic and Cooperation Council, *Survey of Impediments to Trade and Investment in the APEC Region: A Report by the Pacific Economic Cooperation Council for APEC* (PECC, Singapore 1995); S Kemp, 'Trade in Education Services and the Impacts of Barriers to Trade' in C Findlay and T Warren (eds), *Impediments to Trade in Services: Measurement and Policy Implications* (Routledge, London 2000) 231–44.

[147] G McGuire, M Schuele, and T Smith, 'Restrictiveness of international trade in maritime services' in Findlay and Warren (2000) 172–88.

[148] D Nguyen-Hong, 'Restrictions on Trade in Professional Services' (2000) Productivity Commission Staff Research Paper, AusInfo, Canberra, August; K Kalirajan, 'Restrictions on Trade in Distribution Services' (2000) Productivity Commission Staff Research Paper No 1638.

[149] Interestingly, despite their relative lack of sophistication as compared to price and quantity impact studies, Chen and Schembri conclude that frequency-type studies still provide the most reliable data by many measures: Z Chen and L Schembri, 'Measuring the Barriers to Trade in Services: Literature and Methodologies' in JM Curtis and D Ciuriak (eds), *Trade Policy Research 2002* (Department of Foreign Affairs and International Trade, Ottawa 2002) 219–85, 250. See also RM Stern, 'Quantifying Barriers to Trade in Services' in BM Hoekman, P English, and A Mattoo (eds), *Development, Trade and the WTO: A Handbook* (The World Bank, Washington, DC 2002) 247–58; N Diehl and B Shepherd, 'Modal Estimates of Services Barriers' (2007) OECD Trade Policy Working Paper No 51.

[150] Diehl and Shepherd (2007).

[151] Marouani and Munro (2009) 6.

allocation of resources in the services sector'[152]—involves a degree of normative judgment, both about the existence of a market failure, and about the nature of optimal regulation.[153] One response to this problem, within the literature, has been to propose a series of 'expert workshops' to help to define the distinction.[154] For example, since 1999, the OECD has held numerous meetings of services experts—on occasion bringing together trade negotiators with industry experts and economic modellers—to share information on recent work mapping services barriers and their effects, to discuss the appropriate treatment and classification of specific regulatory measures, and so on.[155] Other solutions suggested include the use of international standards as a regulatory benchmark.

The second stage is the *quantification* of the 'trade restrictiveness' of each type of regulatory measure identified in the first stage. This involves an assessment of the commercial significance and economic impact of each kind of measure. While there are a number of methods for assessing this, again the most frequent method is based on expert judgment, using a priori judgments about the relative restrictiveness of different barriers.[156]

It needs to be acknowledged again that this body of work is still very young, that so far it has mostly raised questions rather than constructed clear, shared understandings of what does and does not constitute a barrier to trade in the services context, and that the literature that has been produced has had relatively little circulation among the community of trade professionals. Nevertheless, the processes I have just described are useful illustrations—in an embryonic but still paradigmatic way—of the core function that technical knowledge production can play in defining the terrain of trade politics. I have made the point repeatedly throughout this book that the question of what constitutes a 'trade barrier' is not amenable to an entirely objective answer, but instead is always a contested matter. The work of data

[152] This orthodox definition is taken from M Bosworth, C Findlay, R Trewin, and T Warren, 'Price-impact Measures of Impediments to Services Trade' in Findlay and Warren (2000) 42. See also A Hardin and L Holmes, *Services Trade and Foreign Direct Investment* (Australian Government Publication Service, Canberra 1997) 31–2.

[153] See G McGuire, 'Methodologies for Measuring Restrictions on Trade in Services' in OECD, *Quantifying the Benefits of Liberalising Trade in Services* (OECD, Paris 2003) 36–7; G McGuire, 'Australia's Restrictions on Trade in Financial Services' (1998) Staff Research Paper, Australian Productivity Commission. See also Hardin and Holmes (1997) 30; F Kimura, M Ando, and T Fujii, 'Estimating the Ad Valorem Equivalent of Barriers to Foreign Direct Investment in the Telecommunication Services Sectors in Russia' (2004) World Bank Policy Paper at 7. OECD (2007) para 17 highlights the difficult issue of distinguishing trade barriers from 'regulations that address market imperfections . . . [or] public policy including distributional objectives'.

[154] OECD (2007) para 15. For a similar approach, see A Colecchia, 'Measuring Barriers to Market Access for Services: A Pilot Study on Accountancy Services' in Findlay and Warren (2000) 262, para 17.

[155] OECD Services Experts Meetings have occurred, for example, in June 1999, May 2000, March 2002, November 2003, February 2005, and February 2007, and, in addition to the reports of the meetings themselves, have led to three publications: OECD (2003); Mattoo and Sauvé (2003); World Bank, International Organisation for Migration (IOM) and OECD, *Trade and Migration: Building Bridges for Global Labour Mobility* (OECD Publishing, Paris 2004). There was also a joint OECD–UNCTAD Workshop on Trade in Services in June 2006.

[156] OECD (2003); Marouani and Munro (2009); Diehl and Shepherd (2007).

collection I have just described can be understood as a way of attempting to produce a relatively authoritative view of what constitutes a trade barrier, and transforming that view into an apparently objective description of the world as it is, or at least as a shared starting point of negotiation. This objectification is made effective primarily through a logic of repetition, or accretion, the underlying dynamics of which are clear from the material just cited—even if the process is still very far from complete in the specific contexts described. As we saw, some of the first catalogues of barriers to trade were produced by countries with strong export interests in particular service sectors. These interests were reflected in (and of course mediated by) the Uruguay Round negotiations, and the GATS Schedules which those negotiations produced. Those GATS Schedules—and other documents, surveys, and questionnaires produced as by-products of the negotiations—formed the key data sources for the first global surveys of barriers to trade in services conducted by the World Bank and academic institutions. These initial surveys in turn represented the starting point for subsequent work, which supplemented them with additional surveys, recourse to databases provided by other specialized agencies, and the input of experts familiar with services negotiations within the trade regime. More generally, this work evolves according to an aggregative dynamic, through which subsequent compilations have tended to draw on, and cumulatively supplement, prior work. In principle, there is ideally a relatively constant circulation of the products of this technical work among the research community which is producing it, as well as within the relevant parts of the trade regime itself. As happened in the years before the Tokyo Round, at some point—perhaps after a certain period of time, or perhaps when negotiations move to the more difficult phase of bargaining over what disciplines ought to be applied and what commitments ought to be made—the time for challenging the content and basic assumptions of these documents passes. Documents which are initially produced as purely informative guides for negotiators tend to harden, and are treated as if they were more or less authoritative and exhaustive lists of trade barriers in the service sectors under consideration.

V. Conclusion to Part II

Over the last four chapters, I have sought to provide an explanation of the relationship between the transformation of the trade regime during the period from 1970 to 2000, and the rise of neoliberalism as a dominant political and economic ideology over roughly the same period. It will be clear by now that my account is very different from other accounts which implicitly or explicitly structure much writing in this area. For example, I do not believe that the kinds of free market principles associated with late twentieth-century neoliberal thought were written into international trade law, in the sense that GATT/WTO disciplines came clearly and unambiguously to require the pursuit of neoliberal free market economic policies. It turns out that the encoding of such principles into the legal rules of the trade regime was more ambiguous, less complete, and more reversible than is usually claimed. Most of the new disciplines on domestic regulation incorporated into GATT/WTO law during this period—with only a few exceptions—took the form of general regulatory principles, rather than substantive (de)regulatory mandates, and are therefore highly open-ended in their potential effects. In addition, I resist the claim that there is an inherent connection between the free market orientation associated with neoliberal thought and the mandate of the trade regime to liberalize trade. I have shown that the mandate of the trade regime is both evolving and compatible with a wide variety of different forms and levels of regulation—both 'over-regulation' and 'under-regulation' can be and have been understood as 'barriers' to international trade.

Instead, I have focused on the ideational dimension of regime change, and argued that the last three decades of the twentieth century saw a transformation of the 'legal imagination' of the GATT/WTO. During its first two decades, the GATT's legal system was structurally embedded in the insular world of trade diplomacy, and its operation was deeply shaped by a dense body of informal norms and expectations which circulated throughout the community of trade diplomats. Its broad and ambiguous disciplines on internal regulation were limited and guided in practice by the perceptions of that community as to what constituted normal, appropriate, or legitimate forms of governmental intervention, and what on the other hand constituted illegitimate cheating on the carefully negotiated bargain they had struck during the early rounds of trade negotiations. These perceptions were in turn the product of a broader 'spirit' of embedded liberalism, made up of shared ideas about the legitimate purposes of governmental intervention in the market, the concrete purposes and objectives of the GATT in the maintenance of international stability, and the proper role of law in the achievement of those purposes. These informal ideas were produced and contested in a variety of ways, but by and large reflected the domestic institutional arrangements of a handful of the most economically significant GATT Contracting Parties, as well as the specific social dynamics of a tight knit community of trade diplomats.

By the end of the century, this legal system had changed in virtually all its fundamental elements. Most obviously, its scope of operation had massively expanded, interpretive trends had made its disciplines on domestic regulation more 'intrusive', and its dispute settlement system had become radically judicialized. It is common to explain these and other changes to the regime by reference to the power and interests of actors who materially benefited from them. But it has been the point of this Part to suggest that such explanations are inadequate on their own, and that these transformations to the GATT/WTO legal system would not have been possible without a simultaneous re-definition of prevailing ideas about the nature and purpose of the trade regime, and the role of law in the fulfilment of its purposes. The late twentieth-century transformation of the GATT/WTO system, in other words, had an indispensable ideational dimension, which is rarely recognized.

One feature of this new legal system is its powerful expansionist tendency. I chronicled in Chapter 8 the way that more and more forms of domestic regulation were described as 'trade barriers' over the course of the 1980s and 1990s, and brought within the domain of vision of the GATT/WTO legal system. In the years since, this trend has continued more or less unabated, and in my view is likely to continue to do so at least in the medium term. The informal norms which limited the practical scope of operation of GATT disciplines in the GATT's early decades have been substantially eroded. Moreover, as the malleability and plasticity of the concept of trade barrier has been made increasingly apparent, it has only become more likely that its boundaries will be stretched further by creative legal and economic argumentation in disputes over a broader and broader range of domestic institutional and regulatory structures. The transformation of the trade regime in the final three decades of the twentieth century, in other words, has produced a dynamic in which its horizon of vision is constantly expanding, at a greater or lesser rate, according to the commercial priorities of its Members.

Another feature of the system is its tendency to produce a greater degree of institutional and regulatory convergence across trading partners, if only because it is precisely institutional and regulatory *di*vergence which triggers the application of GATT/WTO regulatory disciplines. That said, the *content* of this tendency towards convergence—that is, the specific institutional form of 'free trade' or the 'free market' towards which WTO law pushes WTO Members—is not clear, in the sense that it is not determined by the texts of the law itself. It depends, in part, on the forms of specialized regulatory knowledge which happen to be implicitly accepted as most persuasive, authoritative, objective, or appropriate to interpreters and decision-makers in any particular context, and therefore come to structure their thinking, and their interpretation of the law. This in turns depends on the symbolic politics at work within the trade regime—that is, the actors and processes involved in the construction and contestation of collectively authorized ways of seeing the world, which become part of the mindset of professionals working in the field of international trade governance.

Part of the point of the present chapter was to illustrate the degree to which those processes are open, in the sense that the content of the structures of knowledge that they produce is open to contestation, and constantly subject to change. Interested parties in trade negotiations—states, governments, companies, other private interests—seek to link the indeterminate texts of international trade law to their preferred projects of regulatory reform, or to resist linkages pursued by others. The substantive bias of the trade regime—its 'politics'—is therefore in part the product of the distribution of symbolic power among participants in the field of international trade governance, the content and relative dominance of different bodies of technical knowledge circulating in and around that field, and the institutional form of the markets within those countries most willing to use international trade law against foreign domestic regulation, among many other factors. As just noted, the confluence of these and many other structuring factors may have contingently and temporarily produced a substantive orientation in the application of WTO law towards the kinds of free market policies associated with late twentieth-century economic liberalism, but this should not be misunderstood as an inherent or necessary consequence of the WTO's neoliberal turn. In the medium term, the outcomes of the system I am describing are vastly more open than is usually suggested.

A third feature of the system is the particular formal-technical character of the legal work that it produces. It is a distinctive feature of much legal interpretation in this system that it mixes careful parsing of textual provisions in the manner of formalist legal expertise with a rich knowledge of relevant policy debates in the sector under consideration. It is a form of legal work in which law and technical expertise are tightly bound together. Crucially, however, we should not imagine this solely as a passive process, according to which the law is simply shaped and determined by existing structures of technical knowledge. One of the most important implications of the material covered in this chapter is that these formal-technical processes of legal interpretation are also always interventions into a domain of symbolic struggle. That it to say, legal interpretation involves the implicit selection and incorporation of particular forms of technical expertise to guide the interpretation and elaboration of indeterminate legal norms. In this sense, it is one role of law to act as a kind of gatekeeper: to objectify particular forms of technical expertise, to knit them together with the law itself, and to help to sanctify them as commonsense. It is in the process of legal interpretation and elaboration that contests between forms of expert knowledge are played out, that some kinds of knowledge come to circulate more pervasively than others and are thereby sedimented within the background commonsense that sustains and informs the application of the law. Law and lawyers, in other words, are necessarily part of the symbolic contests played out within the trade regime, whether or not we realize it, and it is part of our professional responsibility to understand the role that we play in it, to ensure that it is a productive one.

PART III

CONCLUSION

10

Conclusion: After Neoliberalism?

The late twentieth-century transformation of the international trade regime came under sustained criticism almost as soon as it took recognizable shape, and by the turn of the millennium was commonly acknowledged to be in the midst of a legitimacy crisis. This concluding chapter assesses the ways in which the WTO's legal system has responded to this crisis. Section I briefly recapitulates the events which led to the WTO's legitimacy crisis at the end of the 1990s, many of which have already been described in some detail in Chapters 2 and 3. Sections II and III describe what I see as the most significant jurisprudential trends which have arisen by way of response since the turn of the millennium, focusing primarily on a growing movement towards greater deference and the 'proceduralization' of WTO jurisprudence involving politically sensitive domestic regulation. In section IV, I reflect on these jurisprudential developments, and in the light of the material covered in the previous eight chapters, attempt to assess whether they reflect an attractive, defensible, and sustainable normative foundation for global economic governance in a world 'after neoliberalism'.

I. Crisis of legitimacy in a post-neoliberal era

At the end of the twentieth century, the WTO's dispute settlement system found itself under pressure from at least two sides. On one side were a variety of 'external' constituencies—NGOs and other civil society organizations newly energized around trade issues but lacking 'insider' experience of trade law and diplomacy—who had come to see the WTO as something of a threat to their cherished political causes. Some of these organizations were those associated with the global justice movement, already described in some detail in Chapter 3, which saw the WTO largely as a champion of neoliberal ideology at the international level. In Chapters 4 and 5, I identified and addressed one of the core criticisms that this movement levelled at the WTO, having to do with its institutional and normative isolation vis-à-vis other international regimes. I suggested that this criticism to some extent missed the mark, and that the architectural projects of governance reform that it inspired were, in their present form, unlikely to lead to the kinds of transformative change that their advocates imagined. But I also identified a second core criticism that was made of the WTO at this time, namely that in its turn to 'behind the border' trade barriers, it had expanded unduly beyond its core 'trade' mandate, and had become too intrusive of domestic regulatory autonomy. It is the subject of this second criticism—and the important effects it has had on the development of WTO law since around 2000—to which I want to turn now, and which forms the primary subject of this final chapter.

Broad public concern about the excessive 'intrusiveness' of the WTO law was fed by the series of cases described in Chapter 8, in which GATT and WTO panels found themselves having to determine the legality of a variety of different regulatory measures having to do with public health, consumer protection, and environmental protection, among other matters of considerable political sensitivity. The results of these cases, as well as the mere fact that they were being brought at all, created a great deal of public anxiety about the potential of WTO law to undermine the ability of states to regulate their economies as they saw fit. The *Thailand—Cigarettes* dispute, for example, created an impression among some observers that GATT disciplines could and would be used to challenge tobacco control regulation, with the real risk that the commercial interests of multinational tobacco companies would be favoured over the public health objectives of developing country governments. Similarly, *Tuna/Dolphin I* seemed to the casual observer to raise the prospect that the objective of trade liberalization would, at least in some circumstances, trump that of environmental protection. Then, after the WTO was formed, and more and more disputes arose involving the kinds of domestic regulatory measures favoured by progressives (from pollution control measures in *US—Gasoline*, to food safety regimes in *EC—Hormones*, environmental regulation in *US—Shrimp*, and product safety measures in *EC—Asbestos*), constituencies in favour of such regulation began to protest at what they saw as an unjustified intrusion into the domestic regulatory space of WTO Members.[1]

These newly energized groups did not accept the reassurances of many within the regime that international trade law, properly interpreted, maintained considerable regulatory flexibility for Members. Nor did they accept the idea that the imposition and application of GATT regulatory disciplines was a purely technical matter, which primarily addressed the means which states used to address regulatory problems, rather than limiting the substantive regulatory priorities they were permitted to pursue. The rigid distinction between the 'ends' of regulation (the domain of politics) and regulatory 'means' (a technical question) was called into question. It became a common criticism of WTO cases addressing domestic regulation that WTO judicial bodies were in these cases necessarily engaging in substantive value choices—balancing the objective of free trade against other regulatory objectives, and second-guessing the regulatory priorities and objectives of sovereign states. This claim was typically accompanied by the argument that value choices of this kind should more properly be made at the domestic level, through political structures which have greater democratic legitimacy than international judicial tribunals. The WTO, it was said, should adopt a more deferential approach to the review of domestic regulation involving significant public values. Although there were of course many

[1] These developments are described in R Howse, 'From Politics to Technocracy—and Back Again: The Fate of the Multilateral Trading Regime' (2002) 96 AJIL 94,102ff.

other kinds of responses as well, it is fair to say that the primary goal of these constituencies was to resist what they saw as the over-intrusiveness of WTO law, and to limit the power and reach of WTO disciplines in order to maintain a greater degree of 'regulatory autonomy' for WTO Members.

On the other side were a set of 'internal' constituencies exerting their own pressures on the WTO's dispute settlement bodies.[2] The new dispute settlement system was still young, and the Appellate Body was keenly aware of the need to build its legitimacy vis-à-vis the community of trade professionals who had created it, and who as the sole consumers of its services had the power to determine its immediate future. Already by the late 1990s, for example in relation to the use of *amicus curiae* briefs from civil society groups, a series of warning shots had been fired which put the Appellate Body on notice of the consequences which might follow if it strayed too far from the views and wishes of the states which made up the WTO membership. While the Appellate Body clearly needed to assert its authority and its independence from diplomatic control—and did so effectively—nevertheless the watchful eye of WTO Member states exerted its own pressure on the Appellate Body. This was particularly true in cases involving sensitive domestic regulation, where there was a danger of the Appellate Body being seen as over-reaching its limited authority and undermining the expectations of Members as to their remaining scope of regulatory autonomy. In this respect at least, the pressures of internal and external legitimacy both pointed broadly in the same direction.

How, then, was the dispute settlement system to respond to these pressures? One response, favoured in general terms by many of the civil society organizations referred to above, could have been to re-inscribe limits—whether formally or informally—on the practical scope of application of WTO law, so as to ensure that fewer forms of domestic regulation were subject to scrutiny under WTO law. But this was quickly understood to be impossible. In the *lingua franca* of trade professionals, 'the toothpaste was out of the tube', and it was simply not possible to return to a trade regime which was narrowly focused on (say) border barriers, and only a small subset of domestic regulations which had direct and immediate impacts on trade flows. It is not hard to see why this might be so: as a greater variety and diversity of domestic regulations were challenged before WTO dispute settlement, any practical limits which shared expectations had at one time placed on the scope of operation of WTO law were eroded. Moreover, a variety of new structural forces favoured its ongoing expansion: more and more businesses became active in trade politics and sought to engage the WTO's dispute settlement system to further their commercial interests, private law firms employing bright and incentivized lawyers were given greater control over the conduct and argumentation of some cases, and scholars of international trade law themselves explored the limits of WTO disciplines, speculating on their potential impact. Even the arguments of the 'outsider' critics of the

[2] I take the concept of 'internal' and 'external' legitimacy constituencies for the WTO from JHH Weiler, 'The Rule of Lawyers and the Ethos of Diplomats: Reflections on the Internal and External Legitimacy of WTO' (2001) 35 J of World Trade 191.

WTO inadvertently entrenched this tendency, to the extent that they conducted and disseminated analyses of WTO disciplines demonstrating their potential application to a wide variety of forms of social regulation. One consequence of such forces was that they made it abundantly clear that, precisely because there was no uncontested or self-evident way of defining what was or was not a trade barrier, there was equally no uncontested or self-evident principle on the basis of which to assert clear *outer* limits to the domain of the WTO. It turned out that a great deal of regulation could credibly be described as a trade barrier—as recent disputes over Chinese currency and censorship policies, US regulation on flavoured cigarettes, and EC regulation of seal products vividly illustrate—and, with the WTO's new dispute settlement mechanism, there was often a strong incentive to do so. The end result, then, was that the newly expansionist tendency of the WTO system—that is, its tendency to re-describe more and more forms of inter-institutional differences as trade barriers, and subject them to international legal scrutiny—was very difficult, if not impossible, to reverse.

If the scope of application of WTO disciplines on domestic regulation could not be meaningfully limited, what was needed was a new way of reviewing such legislation which blunted some of the criticisms made of earlier cases, as well as a new set of ideas on which the normative legitimacy of WTO disciplines could be re-founded. Howse has described the emergence of a number of attempts to do just that, from the re-assertion of a kind of naïve textualist formalism ('we are only implementing what the Members themselves have agreed') to more ambitious attempts to constitutionalize the WTO.[3] Neither proved, frankly, to be particularly successful as responses to the WTO's legitimacy crisis: the former was never likely to persuade anyone familiar with the nature and content of WTO law, while the latter was too ambitious for either the insider or outsider constituencies to fully endorse. Instead, the Appellate Body took for itself the task of crafting a new approach to the review of domestic regulation, one which would seek to avoid the intrusiveness of the technicalized jurisprudence of the neoliberal era, which would be modest and limited in its ambitions, and which would credibly resurrect the impression that the WTO does not interfere with genuinely 'political' issues more appropriately dealt with at the domestic level. Chastened by criticism of earlier decisions, the Appellate Body in particular was now anxious to ensure that the WTO should not be seen to be imposing any particular vision of optimal or legitimate regulation in cases involving sensitive domestic regulatory choices.

In this task, the Appellate Body could turn for inspiration to a variety of developments which had occurred in domestic legal systems over the previous three or so decades. The WTO was, after all, in a predicament which had become commonplace in legal regimes of economic governance in many contemporary post-industrial states, of finding an appropriate form of law in response to post-positivist critiques of the modern rationalist project. In the next two sections, I explore a number of

[3] Howse (2002) 105. See also generally R Howse and K Nicolaïdis, 'Enhancing WTO Legitimacy: Constitutionalization or Global Subsidiarity?' (2003) 16 Governance 73.

attempts by the Appellate Body to re-craft its own jurisprudence in the light of the same challenge.

II. New developments in GATT disciplines on domestic regulation

A. The revival of non-discrimination as an 'anti-protectionism' norm

In Chapter 8, I showed how the interpretation of the GATT non-discrimination norms during the 1980s and 1990s drew inspiration from the economic concept of a 'market distortion', with the effect that virtually all explicit consideration of regulatory purpose was removed from the application of GATT non-discrimination norms. The apotheosis of this approach, I suggested, was the Panel decision in *EC—Asbestos*, which found that the clear public health justification for a ban on the importation and sale of products containing asbestos was essentially irrelevant to the question of whether the ban was discriminatory for the purposes of Article III of the GATT.[4]

This reinterpretation of the non-discrimination norm was, as I have said above, subject to criticism as an offensive over-reach on the part of GATT/WTO dispute settlement, which unjustifiably interfered with domestic regulatory prerogatives. In the light of this criticism—and also in the light of the fact that, if pressed to its logical limit, this new interpretation expanded the non-discrimination norm almost indefinitely—it was perhaps only a matter of time before it was modified. Thus, from around the end of the 1990s—indeed, from the Appellate Body's decision in *EC—Asbestos* itself—there were a series of further developments in the jurisprudence under Articles I and III of the GATT, which had the combined effect of returning them somewhat closer to their original, and more limited, 'anti-protectionist' orientation. Thus, consideration of regulatory purpose has been reintroduced, albeit in a somewhat modified form, by refocusing these provisions on preventing and prohibiting 'origin-based' discrimination, rather than eliminating all distortions of competition, whatever their basis.

As far as Article III is concerned, the reintroduction of purpose has occurred in at least two ways. First, and most importantly, in relation to Article III:4, the Appellate Body has reinterpreted the term 'less favourable treatment' in ways reminiscent of the old 'aims and effects' approach to 'likeness'. I noted in Chapter 8 that the orthodox interpretation of 'less favourable treatment' during the 1990s—which, it should be acknowledged, is still the starting point of contemporary interpretation—captures any measure which adversely modifies the conditions of competition as between foreign and domestic products, and which denies foreign products effective equality of commercial opportunity in the domestic marketplace. In *EC—Asbestos*, however, the Appellate Body hinted that something more than a mere adverse economic effect might be required:

[4] See above pp 254ff.

The term 'less favourable treatment' expresses the general principle, in Article III:1, that internal regulations 'should not be applied . . . so as to afford protection to domestic production'. If there is 'less favourable treatment' of the group of 'like' imported products, there is, conversely, 'protection' of the group of 'like' domestic products . . . A Member may draw distinctions between products which have been found to be 'like', without, for this reason alone, according to the group of 'like' imported products 'less favourable treatment' than that accorded to the group of 'like' domestic products.[5]

While this statement was strictly obiter, and somewhat cryptic, it certainly appeared to be a signal that the national treatment norm in Article III would be interpreted so as to prohibit only 'protectionist' regulations, rather than all regulations which drew a distinction between products and therefore modified the conditions of competition between them. The Appellate Body subsequently clarified its position with a similar observation in *Dominican Republic—Cigarettes*:

. . . the existence of a detrimental effect on a given imported product resulting from a measure does not necessarily imply that this measure accords less favourable treatment to imports, *if the detrimental effect is explained by factors or circumstances unrelated to the foreign origin of the product*, such as the market share of the importer in this case.[6]

Article III, the Appellate Body seems to be suggesting here, is not engaged in all circumstances in which a regulation has a detrimental or disproportionate impact on foreign products, but only where that impact is 'explained by . . . the foreign origin of the product[s] in question'. Similarly, in *EC—Biotech*, the Panel expressly referred to the above jurisprudence of the Appellate Body, and rejected the complainants' claims of discrimination primarily on the basis that the differential treatment in question had not been proven to be on the basis of the foreign origin of the products in question, but rather on the basis of the EC's perceptions of their safety.[7] While this line of interpretation still needs some further clarification, it seems to be roughly equivalent in its function as the 'aims and effects' test was in its day: that is to say, it limits the prohibitive effect of the national treatment obligation to regulatory measures which are 'protectionist' in the sense that they implicitly or explicitly single out foreign products specifically on the basis of their foreign origin. This takes us very far from the approach of the Panel in *EC—Asbestos*, in the sense that it has now become clear that in order to show a violation of the national treatment norm, it is necessary to show something more than a mere distortion of competition in economic terms.

Secondly, early indications of movement towards a 'diagonal test' for discrimination have not been picked up with any enthusiasm in more recent cases, and in fact

[5] Appellate Body Report, *European Communities—Measures Affecting Asbestos and Asbestos-Containing Products* (adopted 5 April 2001) WT/DS135/AB/R, para 100.

[6] Appellate Body Report, *Dominican Republic—Measures Affecting the Importation and Internal Sale of Cigarettes* (adopted 19 May 2005) WT/DS302/AB/R, para 96, emphasis added.

[7] Panel Report, *European Communities—Measures Affecting the Approval and Marketing of Biotech Products* (adopted 21 November 2006) WT/DS291-3/R, paras 7.2499–7.2517 (in relation to Art III:4), and paras 7.2398–7.2419 (in relation to the non-discrimination norm contained in Annex C(1)(a) of the SPS Agreement).

the trend seems to be going in the other direction, towards an entrenchment of an 'asymmetric impact test'.[8] In order to show discrimination under Article III, in other words, it seems necessary to show—at least in practice, if not formally—that domestic products *as a whole* are treated more favourably than imported like products *as a whole*.[9] This is significant in the present context because asymmetric impact can logically only be relevant under the non-discrimination provisions if the purpose of those provisions is understood to be limited to the prohibition of origin-based discrimination.

In respect of Article I, the MFN norm, the same basic move towards origin-based discrimination has been made in the context of the interpretation of the word 'unconditionally'. Article I, it will be recalled, requires that any advantage offered by a WTO Member to the products of one country be offered 'unconditionally' to the like products of all other WTO members. In *Indonesia—Autos*, the term 'unconditionally' had been interpreted strictly to mean that the imposition of any conditions unrelated to the product itself—whatever their motivation or intended effect, whether protectionist or not—were prohibited by Article I.[10] This interpretation is paradigmatic of the approach described in Chapter 8, since it tends towards prohibiting any measure which upsets or distorts the competitive relationship between substitutable products in the marketplace. However, in a later case, the Panel in *Canada—Autos* took a different approach, arguing that the non-discrimination norm in Article I prohibited the imposition of only those conditions which amounted to origin-based discrimination:

> An advantage can be granted subject to conditions without necessarily implying that it is not accorded 'unconditionally' to the like product of other Members. More specifically, the fact that conditions attached to such an advantage are not related to the imported product itself does not necessarily imply that such conditions are discriminatory with respect to the origin of imported products.[11]

This second approach has since become the dominant one, being adopted in the *Colombia—Ports of Entry* Panel, and then in the Panel decision in *US—Poultry*.[12] Here again, then, we see a shift in the non-discrimination norm, away from a strict equation of the concept with that of a competitive distortion, and towards an approach which focuses more attention on the aims of the measure in question.

[8] See above p 264. The terms are taken from L Ehring, 'De Facto Discrimination in WTO Law: National and Most-Favored-Nation Treatment—or Equal Treatment?' (2002) 36 J of World Trade 921.

[9] See Ehring (2002), and Panel Report, *Mexico—Tax Measures on Soft Drinks and other Beverages* (adopted 24 March 2006) WT/DS308/R, para 8.54 (in respect of Article III:2, first sentence).

[10] Panel Report, *Indonesia—Certain Measures Affecting the Automobile Industry* (adopted 23 July 1998) WT/DS54/R, WT/DS55/R, WT/DS59/R, WT/DS64/R, paras 14.143ff. See also Panel Report, *European Communities—Conditions for the Granting of Tariff Preferences to Developing Countries* (adopted 20 April 2004) WT/DS246/R, paras 7.55–7.60.

[11] Panel Report, *Canada—Certain Measures Affecting the Automotive Industry* (adopted 19 June 2000) WT/DS139/R, WT/DS142/R, para 10.24.

[12] Panel Report, *Colombia—Indicative Prices and Restrictions on Ports of Entry* (adopted 20 May 2009) WT/DS366/R, paras 7.361–7.362; Panel Report, *United States—Certain Measures Affecting Imports of Poultry from China* (adopted 25 October 2010) WT/DS392/R, paras 7.436ff.

The result is a less intrusive form of regulatory oversight, and a greater degree of deference to domestic regulatory choices.

In Chapter 8, I noted that the expansion of the non-discrimination norms, and their gradual realignment with the economic concept of a competitive distortion, was motivated in significant part by a desire to shift the centre of gravity of the jurisprudence on domestic regulation to the 'necessity' test in Article XX of the GATT. It was, after all, primarily the necessity test which permitted GATT/WTO dispute settlement bodies to assess whether or not the measure in question was optimally designed from the perspective of various kinds of technical expertise. Conversely, the more recent realignment of Articles I and III of the GATT around the concept of 'origin-based discrimination' can be understood as precisely the opposite—a move away from the necessity test as the fulcrum of interpretation and analysis, associated with a concomitant move away from technical regulatory expertise as the primary source of normative guidance concerning the legitimacy of a regulatory measure. Importantly, this has occurred at the same time as a reinterpretation of Article XX of the GATT—and it is here, probably more than in respect of Articles I and III, that the most important jurisprudential innovations have occurred, at least for the purposes of the present story.

B. 'Balancing' and proceduralization under GATT Article XX

Recall from Chapter 8 that from the 1980s onwards, the necessity test in Article XX (a), (b), and (d) of the GATT had been interpreted as requiring that WTO Members should adopt the 'least GATT inconsistent' (subsequently the 'least trade restrictive') means reasonably available to them of achieving their domestic policy objectives. This test was initially applied in a relatively strict manner, and proceeded as if the optimal means of pursuing regulatory objectives were essentially a technical question of applying lessons about ideal regulatory design from economics and other policy sciences. But, as noted above, the 1990s saw a sustained attack on this manner of applying the necessity test, as specific criticisms that it resulted in overly intrusive forms of review were combined with more a general scepticism about the neutrality and objectivity of policy knowledge produced in a rational technical mode. The result was that—at least in certain cases which seemed very clearly to involve value choices of a fundamental or even quasi-constitutional kind—WTO dispute settlement bodies could not continue to work in a rational technical mode, and began to experiment with alternative jurisprudential techniques, and to imagine a new role for themselves in resolving disputes of this kind.

Probably the most famous attempt to re-orient Article XX jurisprudence came in 2000, in the Appellate Body's decision in *Korea—Beef*. The innovation here was to modify the interpretation of the 'necessity test' so that it included a 'balancing' test of a kind very familiar to public lawyers used to proportionality analysis:

> [The] determination of whether a measure, which is not 'indispensable', may nevertheless be 'necessary' within the contemplation of Article XX(d), involves in every case a process of weighing and balancing a series of factors which prominently include the contribution made

by the compliance measure to the enforcement of the law or regulation at issue, the importance of the common interests or values protected by that law or regulation, and the accompanying impact of the law or regulation on imports or exports.[13]

The determination of whether or not a measure was 'necessary', in other words, would no longer solely be a technical question of whether it was the least trade restrictive means of achieving a legitimate regulatory objective. Rather, it would also involve a more complex 'weighing and balancing' of the trade restrictiveness of the measure against the importance of the non-trade values at stake and the measure's effectiveness in pursuing those values.

It is quite clear that this introduction of 'balancing' analysis into WTO law was a response to the legitimacy crisis described above. Self-consciously responding to scepticism of its technicalized jurisprudence, the Appellate Body here clearly proceeded from the premise that the case involved a clash of competing social interests and values. Resisting claims that WTO dispute settlement was narrowly focused on 'trade values' of economic efficiency and liberalization, it provided a test which explicitly made room for—indeed required—the consideration of the importance of 'non-trade' values as part of the standard interpretation of the necessity test. And against the claim that the application of the necessity test had been applied in a heavy-handed manner, insensitive to political realities, here was a test which held out the possibility of a much more subtle, contextual, and open-ended form of analysis, which resisted the systematic privileging of one set of values over another. Furthermore, as Neumann and Türk have noted, the Appellate Body's introduction of 'weighing and balancing' seems to have been, apart from anything else, an attempt substantively to relax the necessity test.[14] Thus, the Appellate Body went out of its way to say that the more vital or important the common interests of values that the measure is intended to protect, 'the easier it would be to accept as "necessary" a measure designed as an enforcement instrument'.[15] Similarly, the greater the contribution that a measure makes to the achievement of these common interests or values, the more easily the Appellate Body will find that it is 'necessary' for the purposes of Article XX.[16] The result is that, provided the 'non-trade' values to be protected are important, and the measure in question makes a significant contribution to their protection, then the Appellate Body is unlikely to rigorously assess the optimality of its design.

The above-quoted passage from *Korea—Beef* sparked an immediate reaction among observers of the WTO, giving rise to considerable debate about both its meaning and its normative desirability.[17] On one side, some commentators saw it as

[13] Appellate Body Report, *Korea—Measures Affecting Imports of Fresh, Chilled and Frozen Beef* (adopted 10 January 2001) WT/DS161/AB/R and WT/DS169/AB/R, para 164.

[14] J Neumann and E Türk, 'Necessity Revisited. Proportionality in World Trade Organization Law After Korea-Beef, EC-Asbestos and EC-Sardines' (2003) 37 J of World Trade 199, 210ff.

[15] *Korea—Beef (AB)* para 162.

[16] ibid para 163.

[17] M Hilf, 'Power, rules and principles. which orientation for WTO/GATT law?' (2001) 4 J of Intnl Economic L 111–30; R Howse and E Türk, 'The WTO Impact on Internal Regulations: A Case Study of the Canada—EC Asbestos Dispute' in G de Búrca and J Scott (eds), *The EU and the WTO: Legal and*

a step in the right direction. Hilf, for example, argued that the introduction of a 'sensitive balancing process' would help to ensure that all relevant interests and principles at stake would be given due weight, and none would be 'left to redundancy or inutility'.[18] Andenas and Zleptnig suggested that it would make 'the judicial process more rational, coherent, and predictable', by requiring judges to follow a structured sequence of analytical steps in their reasoning, and thereby helping to ensure that a 'structured deliberative process' would take place on questions implicating fundamental values.[19] One of the benefits of balancing analysis, they argued, is that—in principle at least—it permits all interested parties to articulate their views, and requires such views to be taken into account in the balancing process.[20]

On the other side, there were those who argued that the Appellate Body had in some sense made things worse, by opening the door to a kind of international judicial scrutiny of value choices which should rightly be the prerogative of domestic political authorities. Should the Appellate Body, it was asked, really be commenting on the relative importance of the 'non-trade' values at stake in a particular regulatory dispute, as compared to the objective of liberalizing trade? More troublingly, should it be 'weighing and balancing' these values against the trade effects of the measure, in the vein of a proportionality test *stricto sensu*?[21] There were many who saw this kind of reasoning as being beyond the legitimate competence of WTO tribunals, at least in their present state of development.[22]

In the end, subsequent clarifications from the Appellate Body took much of the energy out of this debate—and, not coincidentally, robbed the 'weighing and balancing' test of much of its jurisprudential significance. This takes a little explanation. As a number of commentators have noted in this context,[23] traditional proportionality analysis contains three elements. The first is 'effectiveness' (or 'suitability'), which involves a determination of whether a measure is capable of realizing the professed policy goal. The second is 'necessity', which requires an inquiry into whether there is an alternative measure which may achieve the policy

Constitutional Issues (Hart Publishing, Oxford 2001) 283–328; Neumann and Türk (2003) 199–233; A Desmedt, 'Proportionality in WTO law' (2001) 4 JIEL 441–80; M Andenas and S Zleptnig, 'Proportionality: WTO Law: in Comparative Perspective' (2007) 42 Texas Intl Law J 371–423; P Van den Bossche, 'Looking for Proportionality in WTO Law' (2008) 35 Legal Issues of Economic Integration 283–94.

[18] Hilf (2001) 120.

[19] Andenas and Zleptnig (2007) 378–9, 422–3.

[20] ibid 423.

[21] G Marceau and JP Trachtman, 'The Technical Barriers to Trade Agreement, the Sanitary and Phytosanitary Measures Agreement, and The General Agreement on Tariffs and Trade: A Map of the World Trade Organization Law of Domestic Regulation of Goods' (2002) 36 J of World Trade 811, 850ff.

[22] Howse and Türk (2001) 326; Neumann and Türk (2003) 199, 214–15, 232–3; Marceau and Trachtman (2002) 850–1. See also Van den Bossche (2008) 284; J Scott, 'On Kith and Kine (and Crustaceans): Trade and Environment in the EU and WTO' in JHH Weiler (ed), *The EU, The WTO and the NAFTA: Towards a Common Law of International Trade?* (OUP, Oxford 2000) 125, 162.

[23] See eg Neumann and Türk (2003) 201–5; Andenas and Zleptnig (2007) 386–9; Van den Bossche (2008) 285.

goal just as effectively but with less of an impact on other legitimate goals. The third element is proportionality *stricto sensu*, which involves an inquiry into the substantive benefits arising from the pursuit of the policy goal, as compared to the damage it causes to other goals and interests. The first two of these elements were already clearly part of the jurisprudence on Article XX of the GATT before the Appellate Body's decision in *Korea—Beef*.[24] The greatest significance of the passage cited above from *Korea—Beef*, then, was that it seemed at first glance to introduce the third element into Article XX of the GATT—that is, a substantive weighing and balancing of the relative importance of the 'trade' and 'non-trade' values at stake within regulatory disputes. In fact, on close reading, it was not at all clear that this was its effect—the 'weighing and balancing' test was, after all, introduced as part of the process of applying the necessity test, not as an additional element to it. And when, less than a year later, the Appellate Body in *EC—Asbestos* went out of its way to note that WTO Members were entirely free to choose their own 'level of protection' in respect of health risks—and, by extension, the pursuit of any other legitimate public policy goal—it seemed clear that proportionality *stricto sensu* had been ruled out.[25] Whatever it claims to be doing, in practice the Appellate Body has been extremely reluctant substantively to balance the relative importance of removing trade restrictions against other competing policy objectives. Instead, in the bulk of cases in which the necessity test is found not to have been satisfied, the basis for the decision has been the relative inefficacy of the measure in question in achieving its stated objectives, or the availability of equally efficient alternatives.[26] The necessity test, in other words, has largely remained as a 'weak' proportionality test, based on the elements of effectiveness and necessity, rather than the strong test of proportionality *stricto sensu* that seems to be implied by the Appellate Body's statement in *Korea—Beef*.

'Weighing and balancing', then, represents one attempt by the Appellate Body to incorporate new jurisprudential techniques to respond to the WTO's internal and external legitimacy crisis. But it was largely a false start, and—despite its continuing formal recitation in all cases involving Article XX—has in my view proved to have only a marginal practical impact on the interpretation and application of Article XX of the GATT, at least as far as the introduction of proportionality *stricto sensu* is concerned. But another kind of response has also developed alongside this one, which has been at least as significant. This approach rests on a distinction between the substantive preferences and value choices which are embodied in regulatory measures, and the institutions, structures, and procedures through which those choices are made. In more and more cases, panels and the Appellate Body have

[24] See Van den Bossche (2008) 286–8.

[25] *EC—Asbestos (AB)* (2001) para 168. For a similar view, see ibid 290; Neumann and Türk (2003) 227–31; DH Regan, 'The Meaning of "Necessary" in GATT Article XX and GATS Article XIV: The Myth of Cost-Benefit Balancing' (2007) 6 World Trade Rev 347–69.

[26] eg *Colombia—Ports of Entry (Panel)* (2009); *Korea—Beef (AB)* (2001); Panel Report, *China—Measures Affecting Trading Rights and Distribution Services for Certain Publications and Audiovisual Entertainment Products* (adopted 19 January 2010) WT/DS363/R. Cf Panel Report, *European Communities—Conditions for the Granting of Tariff Preferences to Developing Countries* (1December 2003) WT/DS246/R.

begun to focus on the latter, drawing attention to a lack of transparency, objectivity, procedural fairness, and even-handedness in the application of a regulatory measure—rather than its substantive rationality, in the sense of how efficiently and effectively it achieves its intended outcomes.

It is the Appellate Body's *Shrimp/Turtle* decision which best illustrates this approach. As is well known, the case concerned a US measure banning the importation of shrimp from trawling fleets based in countries which were not certified—and countries were by and large not certified if they did not require the use of turtle excluder devices (or undertake certain other defined measures). On one hand, the Appellate Body worked hard to avoid deciding the case on substantive grounds—in the sense of deciding the relative importance of trade liberalization and environmental protection where the two conflicted.[27] The United States' regulatory measure was understood in some sense as an expression of the US population's own environmental priorities and values—its own way of balancing the relative importance of trade and environmental protection—and the Appellate Body did not see its task as determining the substantive legitimacy of those values, nor as putting in place strict boundaries on the extent to which WTO Members could use trade measures to pursue them. It did not call into question the level of protection which the United States sought for turtles, nor did it balance that protection against the trade restriction caused.

Instead, it redefined its role as ensuring that the policy goal of protecting turtles was pursued through appropriate, transparent, objective, and even-handed administrative procedures. To illustrate: there were three primary bases on which the challenged measure constituted 'arbitrary and unjustifiable discrimination' under the *chapeau* of Article XX, according to the Appellate Body. One reason had to do with the failure of the US authorities to accord due process rights to exporting Members during the process of certification:

> ... with respect to neither type of certification under Section 609(b)(2) is there a transparent, predictable certification process that is followed by the competent United States government officials. The certification processes under Section 609 consist principally of administrative *ex parte* inquiry or verification by staff of the Office of Marine Conservation in the Department of State with staff of the United States National Marine Fisheries Service. With respect to both types of certification, there is no formal opportunity for an applicant country to be heard, or to respond to any arguments that may be made against it, in the course of the certification process before a decision to grant or to deny certification is made. Moreover, no formal written, reasoned decision whether of acceptance or rejection, is rendered on applications for either type of certification, whether under Section 609(b)(2)(A) and (B) or under Section 609(b)(2)(C). Countries which are granted certification are included in a list of approved applications

[27] For a similar view, see B Kingsbury, 'The Administrative Law Frontier in Global Governance' (2005) 99 Proceedings of the Annual Meeting (American Society of International Law) 143–53; Neumann and Türk (2003) 229.

published in the Federal Register; however, they are not notified specifically. Countries whose applications are denied also do not receive notice of such denial (other than by omission from the list of approved applications) or of the reasons for the denial. No procedure for review of, or appeal from, a denial of an application is provided.[28]

The certification processes, the Appellate Body concluded, 'appear to be singularly informal and casual' and result in a denial of 'basic fairness and due process' to those exporting Members whose applications for certification are rejected.[29]

Secondly, the United States had failed to engage the complaining countries in 'serious, across-the-board negotiations with the objective of concluding bilateral or multilateral agreements for the protection and conservation of sea turtles' before enforcing the prohibition against them.[30] This was particularly relevant since the US Congress itself had directed the Secretary of State to initiate negotiations on such matters, since the issue in question (the protection of migratory species) 'demands concerted and cooperative efforts on the part of many countries',[31] and since the United States had in fact negotiated and agreed one regional convention on the matter, with the result that signatories to the convention received certain significant advantages not available to all countries wishing to export to the United States. As was made clear at a later stage in the litigation, what mattered here was not the failure to conclude an agreement with the complaining countries, still less the failure to conclude an agreement in the same terms as the existing convention, but rather the failure to negotiate seriously and in good faith with all trading partners on a non-discriminatory basis, once they had done so with some.[32]

Thirdly, the US measure imposed 'a single, rigid and unbending requirement that countries . . . adopt a comprehensive regulatory program that is essentially the same as the United States' program, without inquiring into the appropriateness of that program for the conditions prevailing in the exporting countries'.[33] While it was perfectly permissible for the United States to establish a substantive standard of environmental protection for foreign exporters wishing to gain access to its markets, it was impermissible for the United States essentially to determine the *means* by which that standard would be met. It was necessary for the United States to permit a degree of flexibility or discretion as regards the means used, taking into account the conditions prevailing in the foreign country.[34]

Conceptually, then, the key move in this case was to determine the legitimacy of the US measure in question not by reference to some technically defined ideal of an optimally regulated market, nor through the application of a balancing or proportionality test, but rather by reference to the administrative ideal of good governance

[28] Appellate Body Report, *United States—Import Prohibition of Certain Shrimp and Shrimp Products* (12 October 1998) WT/DS58/AB/R, para 180, footnotes omitted.
[29] ibid para 181.
[30] ibid para 165.
[31] ibid para 168.
[32] *US—Shrimp (AB, 21.5)* (2001) paras 115–34.
[33] *US—Shrimp (AB)* (1998) para 177.
[34] ibid paras 161ff.

articulated as good process, or procedurally proper administration. What was subject to scrutiny were the procedures, structures, and institutions forming the context in which the regulatory measure was applied, not the substantive legitimacy or efficacy of its content. To some extent, the thrust of the Appellate Body's decision was to institute a degree of reflexivity on the part of WTO Members, by helping to ensure that the negative (trade) effects of their decisions on other political communities are made more visible, with a view to facilitating cooperative, other-regarding regulatory decision-making processes.

This 'procedural turn' was relatively well received by many observers of the trade regime, who saw in it a promising strategy for addressing the legitimacy deficit of the WTO in the new millennium. Proceduralization very quickly took root as one common element of many scholarly proposals to re-envision the role and purpose of the WTO in response to its legitimacy crisis. Von Bogdandy, for example, in a chapter entitled 'Legitimacy of International Economic Governance: Interpretive Approaches to WTO Law and Prospects of its Proceduralization', proposed what he called the 'co-ordinated interdependence' model as 'the most convincing [response] to the legitimacy problem' of the contemporary trade regime. Within this model, WTO law 'is an instrument to politically co-ordinate different regulatory systems', and its primary task is to 'force Members to take the economic interests of other Members into account' in their regulatory decisions, and in that sense to encourage 'other-regarding' regulatory decision-making processes.[35] The purpose of WTO law, in this view, is to rectify a flaw in domestic political processes:

> It is the nature of the domestic political process that the interests of the polity's citizens enjoy a priority over those of foreigners... Foreign interests, sometimes deeply affected through domestic decisions, do not generally have standing in domestic procedures... the Appellate Body's interpretation of WTO law can be understood as aiming to rectify this...: when a sovereign decision affects the economic interests of people in other States, their interests must be taken into account, either through a negotiated solution between the affected States, or, if impossible, through 'simulated multilateralism' in the domestic process of legislation.[36]

The Appellate Body's decision in *Shrimp/Turtle*, notes von Bogdandy, was a way of achieving precisely this result: in effect, according to this author, it encouraged Members to pursue multilateral means to address the external trade effects of domestic regulatory measures, or, if that proved impossible, to apply domestic regulatory measures in ways which meaningfully took into account the interests of other affected countries, and was in that sense other-regarding. By proceduralizing WTO obligations, he argues, the Appellate Body 'thereby avoids the extremely problematic situation of establishing substantive requirements through concretizing WTO provisions'.[37] Although von Bogdandy shies away from advocating proceduralization as a general approach, it is clear that he sees much in it to like. He contrasts

[35] A von Bogdandy, 'Legitimacy of International Economic Governance: Interpretive Approaches to WTO law and the Prospects of its Proceduralization' in S Griller (ed), *International Economic Governance and Non-economic Concerns* (Springer-Verlag, Vienna 2003) 103, 121.

[36] ibid 126.

[37] ibid 128, 132–3.

it favourably, for example, with what he calls the 'liberal model', which sees WTO law as simply an instrument to limit public interventions in economic transactions, other than those which provide the institutional underpinning of efficient markets.[38]

Howse and Nicolaïdis, furthermore, have famously proposed a model of 'global subsidiarity' as the normative foundation for a re-imagined trade regime in the aftermath of its late twentieth-century legitimacy crisis. This model, explicitly contrasted with a 'libertarian constitutional' vision similar to that described in Chapter 9, as well as with a 'European federal vision' of global constitutionalism, is based on the three basic principles of 'institutional sensitivity', 'political inclusiveness', and 'top-down empowerment'. Although they do not mention *Shrimp/Turtle* directly, the first of these principles—institutional sensitivity—seems in many respects to endorse the approach of substantive deference combined with strict procedural review adopted by the Appellate Body in that case:

> [Institutional sensitivity includes] sensitivity to the superior credentials that other institutions of governance may have in addressing the substantive value trade-offs entailed in domestic measures that the WTO dispute-settlement organs are necessarily required to review from the perspective of WTO rules on trade. This includes deference to . . . states themselves . . . At the same time, institutional sensitivity is no *mere* deference: it is consistent with strict scrutiny of national compliance with general trade-regime norms, such as nondiscrimination, and especially procedural norms, such as transparency and due process in the formulation and implementation of policies.[39]

Procedural review seems, on this view, to be a necessary response to the legitimacy deficit of the WTO—it limits the intrusiveness of WTO review, but at the same time does not reduce such review to irrelevance, nor deny the WTO any appropriate role in orienting domestic regulation.

De Búrca and Scott are somewhat more ambivalent about the particular way in which the Appellate Body constructed its procedural approach in *Shrimp/Turtle*, expressing some doubt about the ability of principles of due process to draw an adequately bright line between acceptable and unacceptable regulation, and noting the irony of the WTO itself imposing strict transparency and due process on its Members.[40] Still, they, too, note with some approval the way that the Appellate Body helped in this case to provide a degree of external accountability for WTO Members seeking to regulate in ways which detrimentally affect foreign constituencies.[41] More recently, Andenas and Zleptnig have suggested that this procedural turn on the part of the Appellate Body provides a useful combination of deference towards substantive domestic regulatory choices with close and meaningful international scrutiny of trade-restrictive regulation.[42] Others have begun to explore the

[38] ibid 128, 114–17.
[39] Howse and Nicolaïdis (2003) 87.
[40] G de Búrca and J Scott, 'The Impact of the WTO on EU Decision-making' in G de Búrca and J Scott (eds), *The EU and the WTO: Legal and Constitutional Issues* (Hart Publishing, Oxford 2001) 1, 16–29.
[41] ibid; see also Scott (2000) 133–42.
[42] Andenas and Zleptnig (2007) 411–12.

extent to which the WTO's more explicit transparency obligations may be activated and more effectively harnessed as a legitimate means of international scrutiny of domestic regulatory structures.[43] Where technical knowledge no longer seems an appropriate foundation for judgment, procedural review therefore appears to many as an appropriate basis for international oversight of domestic regulation, which retains an apparently credible distance from more substantive 'political' or 'values' questions more appropriately addressed by other (domestic) institutions.

While the Appellate Body has hardly developed its proceduralist approach to the *chapeau* of Article XX since *Shrimp/Turtle*, there are a handful of cases which have tended in a similar direction. In *US—Gasoline*—a case which preceded *Shrimp/Turtle* by two years—the Appellate Body also foreshadowed a similar approach, if in a somewhat less developed way. That case concerned the US Clean Air Act, which put in place certain requirements as to the composition and performance of gasoline sold in the United States, set by reference to certain 1990 baseline levels. The dispute concerned the way in which these baselines were set: an individual refinery baseline was set for most domestic refiners, reflecting the quality of the gasoline actually produced by them in 1990, but the baselines for most foreign refineries were set in statutory form. This worked to the detriment of a number of foreign gasoline refiners. In finding that the US measure was not in accordance with the requirements of the *chapeau* of Article XX, the Appellate Body stressed two aspects of the US government's conduct: first, its failure 'to explore . . . means, including in particular cooperation with the governments of Venezuela and Brazil [the complainants in the case], of mitigating the administrative problems relied on as justification by the United States for rejecting individual baselines for foreign refiners', and secondly, its failure to 'count the costs for foreign refiners that would result from the imposition of statutory baselines'.[44] As others have noted, this contains in embryonic form the subsequent approach adopted in *Shrimp/Turtle*—namely, an approach which is focused not on assessing the substantive appropriateness of the measure in question, but on ensuring that foreign interests are procedurally taken into account in the formulation of domestic regulations, either through direct international cooperation, or through appropriate domestic decision-making processes.

More recently, *China—Publications* concerned a US complaint against China in respect of its system for the review of the content of imported books, videos, newspapers, DVDs, journals, films, and so on, for censorship purposes. What is noteworthy about the case in the present context is that the substance of the Chinese censorship regime—its extent, and the purposes it served—were neither directly challenged by the United States, nor strictly scrutinized by the Panel or Appellate Body. Although the Chinese regime restricted a very broad range of content—including that which 'disturbs public order or destroys social stability', 'jeopardizes

[43] See eg P Ala'i, 'From the Periphery to the Center? The Evolving WTO Jurisprudence on Transparency and Good Governance' (2008) 4 JIEL 779.

[44] Appellate Body Report, *United States—Standards for Reformulated and Conventional Gasoline* (adopted 20 May 1996) WT/DS2/AB/R, at 28.

social morality', or 'jeopardizes the solidarity... of the nation'[45]—the United States accepted, for the purposes of argument, that all of these matters fell within the meaning of 'public morals' under Article XX(a) of the GATT. For its part, the Panel noted that Members 'should be given some scope to define and apply for themselves the concept of "public morals"... according to their own systems and scale of values',[46] and was content to proceed without any scrutiny of the substantive legitimacy of the Chinese censorship regime as such. Instead, all the argument in the case turned on the institutional structures through which the Chinese government implemented and applied its censorship policy—in particular, its requirement that only state-owned enterprises import and distribute the products in question, and that these enterprises conduct content review themselves. In the end, the Panel determined, and the Appellate Body agreed, that these restrictions on importation and distribution were unnecessary for the purposes of Article XX(a) of the GATT, noting in the process that an alternative means of achieving the same objective would be to separate the economic functions of importation and distribution (to be carried out by the enterprises themselves) from the regulatory function of censorship (which could be carried out by the government directly).[47] While the Appellate Body made clear that it was not requiring the Chinese government to reorganize its system in that way[48]—after all, Members have the right to choose for themselves how to bring themselves into compliance with their WTO obligations—this aspect of the decision is significant for the way that it illustrates the Appellate Body's willingness to scrutinize the structural and institutional context of sensitive domestic regulatory measures, even as it steers clear of passing judgment on their substance.

Finally, it is also worth noting the case of *Brazil—Retreaded Tyres*, which, while it does not directly illustrate the tendency towards proceduralization of review under Article XX of the GATT, does clearly illustrate the other side of the same coin—namely the relaxation of the substantive review under the necessity test, in particular through the adoption of a more relaxed standard of review, and a decreased willingness to rely on technical expertise as a basis for judgment. The case concerned a series of measures, including an import ban, which Brazil adopted to restrict the importation of retreaded tyres into its domestic market. Brazil sought to justify these measures under Article XX(b) of the GATT, on the basis that waste tyres represented a particularly significant threat to both human health and the environment in Brazil, and that its import ban on retreaded tyres was designed to reduce the number of waste tyres produced in its local market. The case is noteworthy in the present context for the lengths to which both the Panel and the Appellate Body went, to avoid second-guessing Brazil's substantive regulatory preferences, and to avoid

[45] See *China—Publications (Panel)* (2010) para 7.760.

[46] ibid para 7.759; see also Panel Report, *United States—Measures Affecting the Cross-border Supply of Gambling and Betting Services* (adopted 20 April 2005) WT/DS285/RW, paras 6.461ff.

[47] Appellate Body Report, *China—Measures Affecting Trading Rights and Distribution Services for Certain Publications and Audiovisual Entertainment Products* (adopted 19 January 2010) WT/DS363/AB/R 312ff; *China—Publications (Panel)* (2010) paras 7.887ff.

[48] *China—Publications (AB)* (2010) para 335.

interfering with their choice of regulatory instruments. Recall, for example, that the application of the necessity test under Article XX(b) requires an assessment of the contribution that the measure in question makes to the achievement of the professed public policy goal. Here, the EC argued that Brazil could not show that the import ban had been at all effective in achieving Brazil's stated regulatory objective, citing the lack of clear quantitative evidence showing such a link.[49] The Appellate Body, however, rejected the European argument: it was not necessary, in the Appellate Body's view, to show clear quantitative evidence of the extent to which the measure contributed to the reduction of waste tyres. Nor was it necessarily fatal to Brazil's case if the contribution was not 'immediately observable', or if it was impossible to clearly assess given other confounding causal factors.[50] It was enough in the circumstances to show, on the basis of rational and supportable hypotheses, that the measure was in principle 'apt to produce a material contribution' to the achievement of that objective.[51] The EC further argued that there were more effective and less trade restrictive means of achieving a reduction of the harmful effects of waste tyres—including instituting better collection and disposal techniques for waste tyres, encouraging further retreading of domestic tyres, among other measures. But, in both the Panel's and the Appellate Body's views, these alternative measures were not in fact true alternatives, but rather complementary measures, which could be adopted alongside the import ban.[52] Here, the move away from the strict standard of review characteristic of the formal-technical mode described in Chapter 8 is clear: in this case, the Appellate Body appears to have had significantly less faith in the reliability of technical claims about the most appropriate or optimal way of achieving regulatory objectives, and a consequent reluctance to join the application of the necessity test too closely to ideas of optimal regulation drawn from bodies of technical regulatory expertise.

I will offer below some of my own thoughts on this deferential and procedural turn in the jurisprudence and commentary under the GATT, but before I do, it is worth exploring briefly how similar ideas have begun to play out in another area of WTO law, namely sanitary and phytosanitary regulation.

III. Post-positivism and proceduralization under the SPS Agreement

The GATT regime began to turn its attention seriously to sanitary and phytosanitary measures as far back as the 1970s with the negotiation of the so-called Standards Code (more formally known as the Agreement on Technical Barriers to Trade) during the Tokyo Round.[53] This agreement was plurilateral rather than

[49] Appellate Body Report, *Brazil—Measures Affecting Imports of Retreaded Tyres* (adopted 17 December 2007) WT/DS332/AB/R, para 137 and surrounding.
[50] ibid para 151.
[51] ibid.
[52] ibid para 159.
[53] See above pp 250ff.

multilateral, binding only its thirty-two signatories rather than all of the GATT membership. During the 1980s, however, there was by all accounts general dissatisfaction with the operation of that agreement,[54] made worse by the emergence of a transatlantic dispute concerning hormone-treated beef (see below), which proved impossible to resolve through the procedures and norms set out in the Code. Thus, over the course of the Uruguay Round, against the backdrop of this dispute, two new agreements were negotiated in place of the Standards Code—the Uruguay Round Agreement on Technical Barriers to Trade, and the Agreement on Sanitary and Phytosanitary Measures (the SPS Agreement)—with the latter putting in place a specific set of rules for food safety and related regulation. The main innovation of the SPS Agreement, at least for present purposes, was the introduction of science-based obligations, namely, the requirement that all SPS measures be 'based on scientific principles', not 'maintained without sufficient scientific evidence', and 'based on a risk assessment, as appropriate to the circumstances, of the risks to human, animal and plant life or health'.[55] These obligations made explicit the recourse to scientific expertise as a significant arbiter of the legitimacy of food safety regulation. The SPS Agreement was therefore one of the more significant products of the Uruguay Round, both for the important new disciplines that it imposed on one particular area of domestic regulation, and for the way it exemplified the technical turn in WTO law.[56]

As a series of politically and culturally sensitive cases began to be brought during the second half of the 1990s and beyond—including most prominently *EC—Hormones* and a dispute over European regulation of GM food products—the SPS Agreement was subject to increased scrutiny and significant public criticism. To a large extent, this criticism was in the same terms as that which had been brought to bear in respect of the GATT Article XX cases. Here, it seemed, was another area of domestic regulation in which the WTO seemed to be potentially overriding the legitimate regulatory choices of democratically elected legislators, and doing so from a perspective with a distinctly 'anti-regulation bias'.[57] This concern, in other words, was about sovereignty and regulatory autonomy, and the consequences that the erosion of each would have on the democratic life of citizens of WTO Members.[58]

In the SPS context, however, these criticisms were joined by a distinct (though related) set of concerns about the proper relationship between scientific inquiry and policy-making. Although, as we shall see, the science provisions of the SPS Agreement can be understood as being compatible with a range of different views about

[54] Marceau and Trachtman (2002) 814. See also Prévost and Van den Bossche (2005)

[55] WTO, Agreement of the Application of Sanitary and Phytosanitary Measures (15 April 1994) LT/UR/A-1A/12, Arts 2.2, 5.1.

[56] See above p 251.

[57] D Winickoff, S Jasanoff, L Busch, R Grove-White, and B Wynne, 'Adjudicating the GM Food Wars: Science, Risk, and Democracy in World Trade Law' (2005) 30 Yale J of Intl L 81, 93.

[58] J Bohanes, 'Risk Regulation and WTO Law: A Procedure-Based Approach to the Precautionary Principle' (2002) 40 Columbia J of Transnational L 323, 327; VR Walker, 'Keeping the WTO from Becoming the "World Trans-science Organization": Scientific Uncertainty, Science Policy, and Factfinding in the Growth Hormones Dispute' (1998) 31 Cornell Intl LJ 251, 253.

the appropriate means of integrating scientific evidence into democratic regulatory decision-making, it is clear that their inclusion in the SPS Agreement reflected at least in part a technocratic view of this relationship, in which regulatory choices ought as far as possible to be guided by rational technical analysis and scientific evidence. This technocratic view had a strong pedigree in post-war industrial democracies, and it is no surprise that it came to be reflected in the Uruguay Round negotiations over the SPS Agreement. That said, this view had come under sustained attack domestically from at least the 1980s, largely as a result of the popularization and entrenchment of post-positivist understandings of scientific knowledge. As popular faith in the ability of science to provide a singular and singularly reliable truth about the world eroded, and as it came to be better understood that the production of scientific truth was socially and culturally contingent, new democratic challenges emerged as a counterpoint to expertise-based governance. This democratic impulse gave rise to calls, for example, for greater public participation in science-based regulatory processes, and for the integration of non-scientific perspectives and values in these decision-making procedures.

It was inevitable that these same criticisms would soon enough be brought to bear against the SPS Agreement, which—to many—seemed to reflect a somewhat naïve faith in the ability of 'sound science' to act as a neutral arbiter of regulatory legitimacy in the area of food safety and related matters. Armed with a sophisticated arsenal of post-positivist theoretical claims about the nature of the science underlying food safety regulation, a number of observers began to explore how the SPS Agreement might best be (re)interpreted or amended in the light of what was known about the nature of scientific truth, and in the light of the need for democratic, public input into formerly technicalized regulatory decision-making processes. At the level of textual interpretation and jurisprudential approach, their questions were these:

> How can a panel usefully evaluate whether the available science supports a given state's policy judgment... without interfering with cultural self-determination, when experience shows that scientific uptake is an important domain of culture and values? How can the goals of international regulatory harmonization and reducing disguised restrictions on trade be accomplished without trampling upon the value-laden choices of democratically accountable WTO member states?[59]

A range of different answers to these questions have been offered, drawing inspiration from decades of work wrestling with similar questions at the domestic level, about the appropriate means of integrating science and policy, and the appropriate role of the law in reviewing science-based regulatory decisions.

One common approach has simply been to argue for greater 'deference' on the part of WTO adjudicators to domestic regulatory choices in the SPS context, and in particular for the application of a deferential standard of review. Thus, for example, Walker suggests that, in their scrutiny of the scientific basis of a Member's SPS measures, WTO panels do not have the capacity to decide between scientifically

[59] Winickoff et al (2005) 106.

plausible alternatives, and should confine themselves to determining whether or not there is 'any reasonable scientific basis' for a Member's measure.[60] Wherever there is a good faith difference of opinion, he argues, WTO panels should find compliance with the terms of the science provisions of the SPS Agreement, provided only that the measure falls within the boundaries of what is considered reasonable within the scientific community.[61] Wirth, too, has called for some degree of deference on the part of WTO adjudicators in the light of their lack of institutional capacity adequately to evaluate scientific claims. Writing before any cases under the SPS Agreement had been decided, he proposed a number of essentially methodological criteria against which a risk assessment should be judged if it is to satisfy the disciplines contained in the SPS Agreement—including whether its assumptions are disclosed, its data are reliable and reproducible, whether its conclusions are sufficiently specific, and whether the principles underlying attempts to gather empirical data enjoy a following in the scientific community.[62]

More interesting, at least for the purposes of the present chapter, are those proposals which go beyond advocating a less intense standard of review, and instead combine substantive deference with a proceduralization of scrutiny under WTO law.[63] One of the first scholars to explore the possibilities of proceduralization was Howse, in a 1999 article responding to the democratic challenge to the SPS Agreement.[64] This challenge, he observes, suggests that the provisions of the SPS Agreement 'constrain[] the ability of democratic communities to make unfettered choices about politics that affect the fundamental welfare of their citizens' and thereby 'rob democratic communities of sovereign regulatory choices'.[65] One approach to the SPS Agreement, he acknowledges, does precisely that. To the extent that the SPS Agreement is understood as making '"science" the authority that decides whether regulations . . . are legitimate', then indeed it 'removes the ultimate power of decision from the democratic communities that the regulations purport to protect'.[66] Instead, Howse proposes an alternative vision of the object and purpose of the SPS Agreement, namely to enhance domestic democratic processes, by 'enhancing the quality of rational democratic deliberation about risk and its control'.[67] Recognizing that regulatory choices in the SPS domain involve value choices and trade-offs, the role of WTO dispute settlement, according to Howse, should be:

[60] Walker (1998) 279.

[61] ibid 280.

[62] DA Wirth, 'The Role of Science in the Uruguay Round and NAFTA Trade Disciplines' (1994) 27 Cornell Intl LJ 817, 856. Others make similar arguments: see eg C Button, *The Power to Protect: Trade, Health and Uncertainty in the WTO* (Hart Publishing, Oxford 2004) 223–4; A Herwig, 'Whither Science in WTO Dispute Settlement?' (2008) 21 Leiden J of Intl L 823, AT Guzman, 'Food Fears: Health and Safety at the WTO' (2004) 45 Virginia J of Intl L 1.

[63] For an excellent overview, see J Peel, *Science and Risk Regulation in International Law* (CUP, Cambridge 2010) ch 7.

[64] R Howse, 'Democracy, Science, and Free Trade: Risk Regulation on Trial at the World Trade Organization' (2000) 98 Michigan L Rev 2329.

[65] ibid 2329–30.

[66] ibid 2333.

[67] ibid 2330.

> ... to respect the manner in which these trade-offs are themselves made within the democratic process of each Member, provided that these trade-offs are themselves made explicitly, transparently, and in a manner consistent with democratic rationality.[68]

The core move, then, is to re-orient the international scrutiny of SPS measures away from substantive review, towards review of the processes, structures, and institutions through which regulatory choices are made, normatively grounded in a particular vision of deliberative democracy. Thus, provided only that regulatory processes accord with some vision of democratic rationality, WTO law should not interfere with the substantive outcomes of such policy process.

The SPS Agreement, Howse goes on, in fact can already be interpreted and applied fully consistently with this objective. Drawing on thinkers such as Habermas, as well as Gutmann and Thompson, Howse argues, for example, that its science provisions can and should be understood not as trumping 'citizens' intuitive judgments about which risks are acceptable and which not, but rather to help ensure that citizens' judgments result from an appropriately structured deliberative process' in which all relevant information is available.[69] This is very different, of course, from making science *determinative* of the legitimacy of SPS measures: provided public choices have been made in full awareness of all relevant facts, and according to full and complete deliberative processes, then these choices should be respected, whether or not they accord with the choices which would be made by scientists and experts.[70] Furthermore, and importantly, Howse suggests that, to the extent that they require regulators to 'attend to the voices of those [negatively] affected by the negative trade impacts of regulation, not simply shut them out of the process of determining the level of protection',[71] a number of other provisions of the SPS Agreement can be understood as enhancing democratic deliberation at the national level. Just as we saw earlier in the context of the *Shrimp/Turtle* decision, the idea here is that the purpose of WTO law is to ensure the input of foreign actors and perspectives into domestic regulatory decision-making processes, as a way of correcting flaws in the deliberative processes caused by the absence of these 'omitted voices'.[72]

Shortly afterwards, Bohanes also proposed a model for the proceduralization of review under the SPS Agreement.[73] Though his argument is also in part a response to claims that the international trade regime 'encroaches upon national sovereignty and compromises legitimate democratic choices',[74] Bohanes grounds his argument for a re-orientation of the SPS Agreement more explicitly on post-positivist thinking about the limitations of science and the socially constructed nature of risk. In part because citizens' perceptions of risk are just as significant as the 'underlying' risks themselves, and because these perceptions are based on myriad factors which are not taken into account in scientific risk assessment, Bohanes argues that 'sound science' should not be used as a benchmark for the legitimacy of SPS measures under WTO law. This conclusion propels him in a similar direction to Howse: 'democratic deliberation... should be the ultimate arbiter of risk regulation' and 'procedural

[68] ibid 2337. [69] ibid 2335. [70] ibid 2330. [71] ibid 2356.
[72] ibid. [73] Bohanes (2002). [74] ibid 327.

criteria' should be substituted for the 'current content-oriented requirements imposed on national legislation by the WTO'.[75] In other words:

> ... in exchange for a deferential standard of review of the substance of regulation, the legislative process at the origin of the measure in question would have to satisfy certain requirements—aimed at a high degree of transparency and informed decision-making ... If the requirements of informed, transparent, and comprehensive deliberation are fulfilled, however, the ultimate decision prerogative ... should rest with the legislator.[76]

This requirement of 'informed, transparent and comprehensive deliberation', according to Bohanes, may require, for example, mandatory risk assessment and cost–benefit analysis, a notice and comment period, and the involvement of all major stakeholders, as well as exceptions for emergency situations.[77]

Scott, too, sees the benefits of a procedurally-oriented approach under the SPS Agreement, though with some qualifications.[78] Noting, correctly, that the imposition of a full set of procedural standards requires the elaboration of a full underlying theory of democracy, and recognizing the variety of different conceptions of democracy at play among various WTO Members, she argues that 'no more than a "thin" conception of procedural propriety may realistically underpin adjudication in [an international] setting'.[79] Nevertheless, such a thin conception of procedural propriety, suitable for the international level, may usefully consist of procedures to ensure '"representation" of out-of-state interests, rather than [emphasis being placed] upon the communicative processes according to which these are formed, received and mediated'.[80] Writing specifically of the procedural orientation of the Appellate Body's *Shrimp/Turtle* and *EC—Hormones* decisions, she suggests that procedural considerations may 'offer a vision of dispute settlement in the WTO which is such as to nourish rather than thwart the democratic process ... [and] promise to structure decision-making in such a way as to make it more responsive to the global context and consequences of domestic decisions'.[81] In later writing, Scott also offers a further argument along similar lines, suggesting that the science provisions of the SPS Agreement may helpfully enhance the *contestability* of domestic regulation, by rendering the scientific justification of such measure 'vulnerable and contingent'—that is, subject to critical and probing scrutiny—and thereby counteracting the tendency of scientific argument to close off contestation and public deliberation.[82]

Finally,[83] Winickoff et al offer their own view of a reconstituted form of review under the SPS Agreement, drawing on the experience of administrative and judicial

[75] ibid 323.
[76] ibid 365.
[77] ibid 366.
[78] Scott (2000) 144ff; J Scott, 'European Regulation GMOs and the WTO' (2003) 9 Columbia J of European L 213.
[79] Scott (2000) 165.
[80] ibid 165–6.
[81] ibid 167.
[82] Scott (2003) 233.
[83] Other important interventions in favour of proceduralism of one stripe or another include Guzman (2004), and MJ Trebilcock and J Soloway, 'International Trade Policy and Domestic Food Safety

review of science-based regulatory decisions within the domestic US context. Like other authors noted above, their model proceeds from the observation that risk assessment is 'neither a science nor a single methodology based on sound science', but rather 'always incorporates policy and value judgments'.[84] In part as a result of this, they argue, 'public participation has an important role to play in generating reliable and conclusive risk assessments, especially in novel and contested risk situations'.[85] Adequacy of public participation, then, is the cornerstone of their vision of the judicial role under the SPS Agreement:

> ...when interpreting the SPS agreement, judges should steer away from adopting any member state's conclusions as scientific truths; they should instead act more as an administrative tribunal searching for transparency and procedural adequacy...Such an administrative role for WTO adjudicators would help preserve space for public participation at the member-state level. [Furthermore], public participation should be considered as a valid and crucial part of the risk assessment process under the SPS agreement, particularly in situations of low-certainty, low-consensus technologies.[86]

Drawing on the 'hard look' approach developed by US courts, they argue that WTO review should 'be aimed at enforcing the transparent, accountable and reasoned use of science and risk assessment, [f]ocusing on proper and legitimate procedures for the integration of science and policy'.[87] This is not the same, they note, as complete deference: the inquiry into the facts is to be searching, even if the grounds of review are narrow, and even if the court must be careful not to substitute its judgment for that of the regulator.[88]

These ideas, while very strongly present in the secondary literature in this area, have had only an uneven and partial impact on the jurisprudence under the SPS Agreement. Since 1995, there have been around forty formal complaints involving the SPS Agreement (or just over thirty, disregarding multiple complainants against the same measure). Of these, nine have resulted in decisions, though in one of those the SPS claims were not pursued, leaving only eight cases in which the SPS Agreement has been interpreted and applied.[89] Within this set of cases, it is possible to identify two quite different jurisprudential styles, characterized by two quite

Regulation: The Case for Substantial Deference by the WTO Dispute Settlement Body under the SPS Agreement' in DLM Kennedy and JD Southwick (eds), *The Political Economy of International Trade Law* (CUP, Cambridge 2002) 537.

84 Winickoff (2005) 93.

85 ibid.

86 ibid 107–8.

87 ibid 108.

88 ibid 110.

89 *Australia—Measures Affecting Importation of Salmon* WT/DS18; *Japan—Measures Affecting Agricultural Products* WT/DS76; *Japan—Measures Affecting the Importation of Apples* WT/DS245; *EC—Measures Concerning Meat and Meat Products (Hormones)* WT/DS26 and WT/DS48; *United States/Canada—Continued Suspension of Obligations in the EC—Hormones Dispute* WT/DS320 and WT/DS321; *European Communities—Measures Affecting the Approval and Marketing of Biotech Products* WT/DS291–3; *Australia—Measures Affecting the Importation of Apples from New Zealand* WT/DS367; *United States—Certain Measures Affecting Imports of Poultry from China* WT/DS392.

distinct ways of using relevant scientific expertise within the process of legal interpretation and application.[90] At one end of the spectrum there are what might be called the 'low level' cases, in which the deferential and proceduralist approaches set out above seem to have had very little if any impact. In these cases, the regulatory measure under dispute is not obviously politically sensitive, nor is it generally understood as expressive of deeply held social values and attitudes towards risk within the population of the regulating country. The decision as to the legality of the regulatory measure is therefore not understood to implicate such values, at least not in any systemic way. No doubt in part as a result of this, these decisions tend to adopt a more deferential approach to scientific expertise, in the sense that the legal question of the compatibility of a measure with WTO law seems to turn very directly on expert scientific opinion as to the justifiability or not of that measure from a scientific perspective. There is a very close intertwining of legal and scientific analysis, with no clear boundary between the two. Decisions seem to be influenced by a relatively traditional positivist view of science: differences of scientific opinion are treated in these decisions as being technical in nature, and relatively easily resolvable in close consultation with independent scientific experts. The standard of review adopted tends in practice to be somewhat stricter than in other kinds of cases, even if formally there is no difference. Scientific uncertainty is more likely to be dismissed as a legitimate basis of risk regulation on its own. Broadly speaking, the Panel in these cases tends to be more willing to adopt a particular view of appropriate scientific conclusions in the course of coming to a decision. The best examples of this jurisprudential style are the two cases brought so far against Japan (*Japan—Apples*[91] and *Japan—Varietals*[92]), as well as the Panel and compliance panel decisions in *Australia—Salmon*[93] (though perhaps less so the Appellate Body judgment in the same case), and the Panel decision in *Australia—Apples*.[94]

But there is also another jurisprudential style at work in what we might call 'high level' cases, in which the risks at issue have a high degree of political and cultural salience in the regulating country, and the underlying science is highly contested. In such cases, food safety regulations in this mode are less likely to be viewed as discrete disputes amenable to technical resolution, and more likely to be seen as expressive of underlying cultural norms and broader societal preferences regarding risk within the

[90] For a similar description of the two different impulses in the jurisprudence, see A Arcuri, 'Food Safety at the WTO After "Continued Suspension": A Paradigm Shift' in A Antoniadis, R Schutze, and E Spaventa (eds), *The European Union and Global Emergencies: A Law and Policy Analysis* (Hart Publishing, Oxford 2011) <http://papers.ssrn.com/sol3/papers.cfm?abstract_id=1633390> accessed 20 February 2011.

[91] *Japan—Measures Affecting the Importation of Apples* WT/DS245/R, Panel Report (15 July 2003), Appellate Body Report (26 November 2003), and Article 21.5 Panel Report (23 June 2005).

[92] *Japan—Measures Affecting Agricultural Products* WT/DS76/R, Panel Report (27 October 1998) and Appellate Body Report (22 February 1999).

[93] Panel Report, *Australia—Measures Affecting Importation of Salmon* (12 June 1998) WT/DS18/R; Panel Report, *Australia—Measures Affecting Importation of Salmon: Recourse to Article 21.5 by Canada* (12 June 1998) WT/DS/18/RW.

[94] Panel Report, *Australia—Measures Affecting the Importation of Apples from New Zealand* (adopted 17 December 2010) WT/DS367/R.

regulating country. In such cases, panels and the Appellate Body do not yet seem to have settled on a single, coherent approach—the overwhelming impression one receives from these cases is of a judicial body seeking to use whatever techniques and strategies are available at any particular moment to find for itself a useful and legitimate role in the review of SPS measures which avoids any impression of substantively second-guessing domestic regulators and the value choices of their constituencies. Sometimes, this might lead to something close to procedural review, but on other occasions it has led to cautious formalism and judicial minimalism.

The paradigmatic dispute of this kind is of course *EC—Hormones*, the facts and case history of which are familiar enough not to need recapitalution. As a number of commentators have noted, there are some important features of the Appellate Body's decision in *EC—Hormones* which display sensitivity to post-positivist perspectives on the nature of scientific inquiry. First, the Appellate Body rejected the Panel's use of the distinction between 'risk assessment' and 'risk management' in the interpretation of Article 5.1—where 'risk assessment' is understood as an objective scientific inquiry into risk, and 'risk management' is understood to include judgments of value as part of determining a strategy in response to that risk.[95] The Panel had used the distinction to argue that an appropriate risk assessment under Article 5.1 could not legitimately take into account 'non-scientific' factors, such as evidence relating to the potential for the abusive or illegal administration of hormones.[96] The Appellate Body disagreed, and in doing so called into question the idea that objective 'scientific' and subjective 'non-scientific' processes could so easily be separated:

> It is essential to bear in mind that the risk that is to be evaluated in a risk assessment under Article 5.1 is not only risk ascertainable in a science laboratory operating under strictly controlled conditions, but also risk in human societies as they actually exist, in other words, the actual potential for adverse effects on human health in the real world where people live and work and die.[97]

Secondly, the Appellate Body also displayed some scepticism about the limits of quantitative analysis of risk in its interpretation of the meaning of risk assessment in paragraph 4 of Annex A. It expressed considerable concern that the Panel's interpretation of that paragraph might be understood to require a quantitative assessment of risk—a result which the Appellate Body thought was wrong in principle, and contrary to the terms of the SPS Agreement.[98] Thirdly and most importantly, the Appellate Body also made clear its awareness of the contested nature of scientific inquiry in its treatment of non-mainstream scientific opinion. On this issue, the

[95] Appellate Body Report, *EC—Measures Concerning Meat and Meat Products (Hormones)* (adopted 13 February 1998) WT/DS26/AB/R and WT/DS48/AB/R, paras 181ff; see also Howse (2000) 2343–4.

[96] *EC—Hormones (Panel)* (1998) paras 8.110, 8.149.

[97] *EC—Hormones (AB)* (1998) para 187. Interestingly, a similar disagreement occurred between the Panel and the Appellate Body in the later litigation in the same case, with the same result: Appellate Body Report, *United States—Continued Suspension of Obligations in the EC—Hormones Dispute* (adopted 14 November 2008) WT/DS320/AB/R, paras 541ff.

[98] *EC—Hormones (AB)* (1998) paras 184, 186 and surrounding. See generally Scott (2000) 153.

Appellate Body emphasized that it is not a Panel's task to ensure that the measure in question conforms to 'mainstream' scientific opinion—nor even to attempt to assess the relative strengths of differing scientific evidence submitted to it. It is, the Appellate Body affirmed, perfectly permissible for a Member to base its regulatory measures on non-mainstream scientific opinion:

> Article 5.1 does not require that the risk assessment must necessarily embody only the view of a majority of the relevant scientific community... In most cases, responsible and representative governments tend to base their legislative and administrative measures on 'mainstream' scientific opinion. In other cases, equally responsible and representative governments may act in good faith on the basis of what, at a given time, may be a divergent opinion coming from qualified and respected sources. By itself, this does not necessarily signal the absence of a reasonable relationship between the SPS measure and the risk assessment, especially where the risk involved is life-threatening in character and is perceived to constitute a clear and imminent threat to public health and safety.[99]

It is hard not to read this passage as a clear rejection of the view that scientific inquiry can provide a single, certain, and secure body of objective knowledge about the world, by reference to which the legitimacy of a regulatory measure can clearly be assessed.

It is one thing to acknowledge the contested, contingent, and plural nature of scientific truth; it is quite another to re-imagine the role of WTO dispute settlement under the SPS Agreement in the light of that. Interestingly, the Appellate Body here had a chance to wholeheartedly embrace a proceduralist approach, but refused it. The Panel had determined that the requirement under Article 5.1 to base SPS measures on a risk assessment imposed a procedural obligation to ensure that a risk assessment was completed, and that its conclusions were actually taken into account.[100] But the Appellate Body disagreed, finding that Article 5.1 imposed a requirement of substantive rationality, rather than simply procedural propriety.[101]

Instead of adopting a proceduralist understanding of Article 5.1, the Appellate Body has sought to define a legitimate role for itself in part by finessing the standard of review to be adopted, as well as by trying carefully to distinguish the precise kinds of questions which ought to be asked in the process of legal interpretation from those undertaken in scientific inquiry. Thus, for example, in this case the Appellate Body began the process of defining a middle-ground approach to the standard of review, noting that a Panel must neither undertake *de novo* review of the scientific evidence, nor accord total deference to the risk assessment it reviews.[102] Furthermore, it noted, where there is a difference of opinion between scientific experts, the Panel's task is not to decide the correct view, but merely to ascertain whether the scientific evidence on which the regulating state seeks to rely comes from a 'qualified and respected source', and can rationally support the measure at issue.[103]

[99] ibid para 194.
[100] *EC—Hormones (Panel)* (1998) paras 8.113ff.
[101] *EC—Hormones (AB)* (1998) para 189.
[102] ibid para 117.
[103] ibid para 194.

These somewhat cryptic remarks were then clarified and developed somewhat in later decisions in respect of the same dispute. As is well known, the United States and Canada had imposed retaliatory sanctions after their success in the first round of WTO litigation, and a dispute arose whether the continuation of these sanctions was lawful, when the EC claimed it had brought itself into compliance with the SPS Agreement after it conducted additional risk assessments, and modified the measure in certain ways. The Panel which was formed as a result of this dispute decided that, in order to determine the legality of the continued sanctions, it had at the same time to determine whether or not the EC measure was 'based on a risk assessment' as required by Article 5.1.[104] The Panel set out the approach it would take in assessing whether the risk assessment drew appropriate conclusions from the underlying science:

> While, on some occasions, we followed the majority of experts expressing concurrent views, in some others the divergence of views were [sic] such that we could not follow that approach and decided to accept the position(s) which appeared, in our view, to be the most specific in relation to the question at issue and to be best supported by arguments and evidence. As we have told the parties and the experts during these proceedings, this Panel is not composed of scientists. The experts were also made fully aware of their role—which was *inter alia* to present scientific issues to the Panel members in a way that could be understood by them—and of the role of the Panel in the WTO dispute settlement system—which is *inter alia* one of trier of fact.[105]

The Appellate Body strongly disagreed with this approach, and in doing so set out in much starker terms the role of the Panel in the conduct of reviews under the science provisions of the SPS Agreement. The task of the Panel, the Appellate Body noted, is not to determine whether there is 'general acceptance'[106] of health risks associated with hormones, nor to determine the position which is best supported by arguments and evidence. It is not to substitute its own judgment for that of the risk assessor. Instead, the task of the Panel is the very limited one of determining 'whether th[e] risk assessment is supported by coherent reasoning and respectable scientific evidence, and is, in this sense, objectively justifiable'.[107] This does not involve balancing or arbitrating between differing scientific viewpoints. Rather it involves four core tasks: (1) identifying the specific scientific evidence on which the risk assessment is based; (2) verifying that this evidence comes from a respected and qualified source, and is legitimate science according to the standards of the relevant scientific community; (3) determining whether the risk assessor's reasoning articulated on the basis of this evidence is objective and coherent; and (4) determining whether the results of the risk assessment sufficiently warrant the specific SPS measure at issue.[108] The Panel, the Appellate Body observed, should only have used expert evidence for the

[104] eg Panel Report, *United States—Continued Suspension of Obligations in the EC—Hormones Dispute* (adopted 14 November 2008) WT/DS320/6, para 7.375 and surrounding.

[105] ibid para 7.420, footnote removed.

[106] *US—Continued Suspension (AB)* (2008) para 610.

[107] ibid para 590.

[108] ibid para 591.

purpose of answering these specific questions, not to 'test whether the experts would have done a risk assessment in the same way and would have reached the same conclusions as the risk assessor'.[109]

At least initially, it seemed to many commentators that the Appellate Body had put in place a significantly more deferential, and 'procedurally-focused' standard of review.[110] It seemed, at least, that the Appellate Body had put daylight between the *legal* question of whether or not the EC measure was 'based on a risk assessment' and the *scientific* question of whether or not the use of hormones is safe. This is crucial: if the distinction between these two forms of inquiry can be credibly and clearly articulated, then it becomes possible to make a decision on the legal question of whether the measure is 'based on a risk assessment' while at the same time remaining agnostic on the underlying scientific question as to the appropriate conclusions to draw from the relevant studies. The problem with the Panel's approach, according to the Appellate Body, was that it had in practice treated the two questions as much more closely linked, and as a result had in practice formed its own substantive view (confirmed and reinforced in consultation with independent experts) as to the appropriate conclusions to be drawn from the scientific evidence as a whole. The thrust of the Appellate Body's approach was, it seemed, to recapture a degree of autonomy for legal inquiry vis-à-vis scientific risk assessment.

That said, it is not at all clear that the Appellate Body was ultimately successful in this aim. As became clear in the subsequent *Australia—Apples* dispute, the third of the Appellate Body's four stages of inquiry—determining whether the reasoning is objective and coherent—opens the door to precisely the kind of substantive scientific scrutiny which the Appellate Body had seemed to eliminate. It is perhaps no surprise, then, that while the Appellate Body overturned the Panel's conclusion, it did *not* go on to make its own decision as to consistency, arguing that in the light of the 'numerous flaws in the Panel's analysis' and the 'highly contested nature of the facts', it was not possible for it to complete the analysis.[111] The Appellate Body was therefore ultimately able to avoid substantive review of the EC's measure through another route. There is more than a hint here of what in a different context Howse and Türk, following Sunstein, have called 'judicial minimalism',[112] or what Dunoff has labelled the 'passive virtues' of judicial decision-making.[113] The Appellate Body resolved the case—at least in a formal sense of concluding proceedings—by leaving one of the core questions undecided, and 'craft[ing] a decision . . . which resolve[d] [the] issues not through reference to high general principles but to narrow factors . . . and issues specific to the facts of the case'.[114] Although this is not exactly the proceduralism which many commentators would like

109 ibid para 592.

110 See eg MM Du, 'Standard of Review under the SPS Agreement after EC—Hormones II' (2010) 59 ICLQ 441, 442.

111 *US—Continued Suspension (AB)* (2008) para 620.

112 CR Sunstein, *One Case at a Time: Judicial Minimalism on the Supreme Court* (Harvard University Press, Cambridge, MA 1999). See Howse and Türk (2001) 306.

113 JL Dunoff, 'The Death of the Trade Regime' (1999) 10 EJIL 733, 757.

114 Howse and Türk (2001) 306.

to see, it certainly shares with the proceduralist approach a similar core desire to craft a more cautious, modest, and less intrusive judicial mode in the context of politically sensitive SPS disputes.

Another case of this kind, at least in some respects, was *EC—Biotech*, concerning a combined US, Canadian, and Argentinian complaint against various aspects of European regulation of GM foods. The key point for the purposes of the present argument is that, like *EC—Hormones*, the case was both argued and decided in ways which limited its general significance, 'bracket[ing] the key areas of disagreement between the parties' in terms of their core differences of approach to risk regulation, and studiously avoiding broad statements of principle, preferring instead to found its conclusions 'on the narrowest grounds available'.[115] For example, the complainants did not frame their case as a challenge to the European regulatory system itself—that is, they did not challenge the right of the European Union to put in place a 'prior approval' system for the control of GM foods on the European market—but rather as a complaint about the way that regulatory system was applied in practice in specific cases. In particular, they alleged that the European authorities had not in good faith applied the regulatory process they had set out for themselves, but instead established a '*de facto* moratorium' on new approvals of GM products. In the Panel report, this way of arguing the case was reflected in the emphasis the Panel placed on the procedural requirements contained in Annex C(1)(a) of the SPS Agreement, requiring 'with respect to any procedure to check and ensure the fulfilment of sanitary or phytosanitary measures' that 'such procedures are undertaken and completed without undue delay'. For a number of commentators, the Panel's choice to focus on the relatively less significant requirements of Annex C was evidence of precisely the strategy discussed above, of turning to forms of procedural scrutiny as one way of avoiding the substantive scientific question of the risk posed by GM foods.[116]

Of course, it was not possible for all aspects of the case to be decided on the procedural grounds contained in Annex C, as the Panel had to determine whether the series of EC Member State safeguard measures also challenged in the dispute were contrary to Article 5.1. Even here, however, the Panel managed to avoid directly addressing the persuasiveness of the underlying scientific arguments on which those measures were based, in part by focusing on the *form* of the risk assessments on which those measures were based. Thus, as Peel has perceptively noted, the Panel decided that the member state assessments did not constitute 'risk assessments' for the purposes of the SPS Agreement, largely 'by looking to the language used in the relevant scientific documentation', placing much more weight on the surface lan-

[115] Krisch (2010) 7–8.

[116] See Peel (2010) 254ff for a very good discussion of this point. See also generally G Goh, 'Tipping the Apple Cart: The Limits of Science and Law in the SPS Agreement after Japan-Apples' (2006) 40 J of World Trade 655; G Goh and D Morgan, 'Political Considerations and Pragmatic Outcomes in WTO Dispute Rulings' (2007) 30 University of New South Wales LJ 481.

guage of those documents, and the formalities of the conclusions that were drawn, rather than the persuasiveness of their underlying reasoning.[117]

IV. Post-neoliberalism and the re-moralization of international trade law

The picture that emerges from this chapter and the previous two is of two legal imaginations at work within the contemporary field of international trade law, corresponding to two different visions of the nature and role of the international trade regime and its legal system. On one hand, the formal-technical legal imagination associated with the neoliberal turn has come under sustained criticism, but continues to structure a great deal of legal work that goes on within the field. This is a vision in which the role of international trade law is to help to provide the institutional conditions for the emergence of a global market, largely by protecting transnational economic activity from the exercise of arbitrary public power. Arbitrariness is defined in this vision as deviation from the image of an optimally regulated free market, as rationally and technically defined by economic and other specialist bodies of knowledge. This sensibility tends to produce a form of legal work in the mould described in Chapters 8 and 9, in which the process of interpreting and applying legal concepts is closely connected to, and shaped by, the application of concepts and forms of analysis taken from bodies of technical policy expertise, in a way which sediments and naturalizes particular technical ways of knowing the world.

On the other hand, there is an emerging post-neoliberal legal imagination, which has begun to develop as a result of the WTO's legitimacy crisis of the late 1990s, and which represents the main contemporary alternative. In response to criticisms that WTO disciplines on domestic regulation constitute overreaching and trespassing into value-sensitive areas more appropriately dealt with through domestic democratic institutions, this new legal imagination is self-consciously cautious and modest in the role that it seeks to define for the trade regime. It seeks to draw new boundaries around the operation of trade law and the trade regime, so as to ensure that WTO law does not become a mechanism for the global projection and entrenchment of a single form of state–market relations, and a single vision of appropriate and legitimate regulatory intervention. Although it is much clearer what this new legal imagination rejects than what it stands for, I have suggested that the dominant alternative vision of the role of the trade regime in the post-neoliberal period is centred on an idea of deference, and more especially proceduralization: one of the primary aims is to ensure that WTO law does not unduly intrude on the substantive regulatory prerogatives of states, or in common parlance maintains the 'regulatory autonomy' of states. This idea has itself been taken up in different ways in different contexts—sometimes connoting an emphasis on basic principles of transparency, accountability, and participation; sometimes focusing on a vision of rational democratic deliberation; and sometimes centred on the promotion of 'other-regarding'

[117] Peel (2010) 252.

regulatory decision-making processes—but the core move common to them all is a re-orientation towards the institutions, structures, and processes by which regulatory decisions are made, as a means of avoiding scrutiny of the 'substance' of those decisions.

There are certain appealing aspects to this new deferential and procedural jurisprudential style: it is modest and cautious in its ambitions, and it proceeds from a profound awareness of the reality of the limited present legitimacy of the WTO among a number of public constituencies. The claim that I wish to make here, however, is that—on its own—it provides an inadequate answer to the turn of the millennium legitimacy crisis of the WTO, essentially because it does not adequately address the underlying cause of that legitimacy crisis. This requires some explanation.

First, I do not think that, in the end, the new approach can deliver on its promise of a substantively neutral—or substantively non-intrusive—form of review which guarantees regulatory 'autonomy' in any meaningful sense. For one thing, regulatory 'autonomy'—if that is understood as a national political community deciding for itself the particular state–market relations that it prefers in the absence of external constraints or influences—is itself something of an illusion in contemporary conditions. It is apparent that states' regulatory freedom is already constrained by international economic structures, and to a significant extent is subject to the logics of those structures. It is no longer possible to imagine a world in which sovereign states pursue regulatory policies and choices entirely free of the constraining and constitutive influences of the global economic structures in which they are embedded. Even in the absence of international economic law, states could not simply regulate freely without having regard to the potential reactions of foreign actors, both public and private—on which they may rely for investment, aid, and access to foreign markets for both capital and goods, and to whose coercive pressures they may in practice be subject. In a very real sense, one country's regulatory 'autonomy' is another country's external regulatory constraint. Moreover, states regulate in response to political and economic pressures which are themselves deeply shaped by the structure and operation of the global economy, and indeed of international economic law.

All this is, of course, very well understood—the simple point that I want to make here is that the deferential/proceduralist vision of WTO review radically underestimates the extent to which a state's regulatory choices are already structured, constrained, and constituted by international economic forces and international economic law, even before we consider the directly constraining impact of WTO regulatory disciplines. The point is that, even if we assume that procedural review of domestic regulation through the WTO is less 'intrusive' than substantive review in some non-trivial sense, the meaningfulness of this distinction is completely eroded once we take into account the other ways in which international economic law fundamentally structures and orientates domestic regulatory choices. The quest for a form of review which preserves a member's regulatory 'autonomy'—its freedom to decide for itself the state–market relations it wishes to adopt, free from outside influence—suddenly seems an illusory and self-deceiving goal, precisely because such autonomy is itself illusory in contemporary conditions.

But this argument can be taken further. It is also not clear to me that the kind of deferential and proceduralist jurisprudential styles currently under development in WTO law and scholarship are different in kind from forms of review which are typically thought to be more substantively 'intrusive'. This argument can be illustrated by reference to some of the cases mentioned above. Take, for example, the 'procedural' disciplines developed by the Appellate Body in the *Shrimp/Turtle* case. It turns out that it is necessary to make choices of a decidedly 'substantive' kind in order to give meaningful content to such procedural disciplines.[118] Who, for example, ought to be given consultation and participation rights in respect of environmental measures of the kind at issue in *Shrimp/Turtle*? Foreign governments? Foreign producers of shrimp? Foreign environmental groups? Other groups? And from which countries? Such choices depend on beliefs about the kinds of foreign impacts and interests which count as significant enough to require protection through procedural rights, and important enough to be balanced against the demands of domestic constituencies—beliefs not obviously different in kind from other value judgments routinely characterized as 'substantive'. How far, furthermore, should the WTO go in encouraging multilateralism and facilitating cooperation? Should it merely require some attempt at cooperative outcomes prior to unilateral solutions? Should it impose an obligation of good faith negotiation? Or should it require only non-discriminatory treatment of different trading partners?[119] If the latter, does that mean that equivalent terms have to be offered to different countries, or simply that equivalent resources must be invested in negotiations with different trading partners? Again, such questions are only resolvable by reference to 'substantive' visions of the extent to which one political community can legitimately impose costs on another in the pursuit of parochial values and goals.

Or take the more deferential approach being developed in some of the SPS disputes mentioned above, such as the Appellate Body's approach to the standard of review in *US/Canada—Continued Suspension*. There are certain situations in which review on procedural or formal grounds comes to look essentially identical to the kind of review typically characterized as substantive, even in the questions that it asks. Button makes precisely this point in the context of the review of the scientific basis of food safety regulation:

By enquiring into how a decision was reached, rather than what the decision is, procedural review promises a method of review suited to general adjudicators with no desire to second-guess the expert judgments of regulators. The temptation, though, is to stray beyond ensuring, for example, that a risk assessment was carried out to addressing *how* the risk assessment was conducted. In both cases, the adjudicator is concerned with the processes behind the regulation (not the substantive regulation itself), thereby giving the appearance that an enquiry into how a risk assessment was conducted still constitutes procedural not substantive review. It is,

[118] For the same argument in a difference context, see LH Tribe, 'The Puzzling Persistence of Process-Based Constitutional Theories' (1980) 89 Yale LJ 1063. See also P Brest, 'The Substance of Process' (1981) 42 Ohio State LJ 131.

[119] These were some of the questions at issue in Panel Report, *United States Import Prohibition of Certain Shrimp and Shrimp Products, Recourse to Article 21.5 by Malaysia* (adopted 21 November 2001) WT/DS58/RW.

however, very easy to slip from procedural review into review of the procedural aspects of substantive questions.[120]

In Button's view, once procedural review ventures into the territory of how a risk assessment was carried out, a series of new questions arise. Was the methodology appropriate? How was the data collected, and what kinds of conclusions can be drawn from the kind of data used? Were the assumptions used appropriate to the methodology? At this point, as Button notes, procedural review is essentially indistinguishable from more 'substantive' review which focuses on the correctness of the scientific conclusions drawn. Indeed, WTO law itself provides an example of precisely such slippage in the Panel decision in *Australia—Apples*, which applies the relatively deferential standard of review formulated by the Appellate Body in *EC—Hormones* and *US/Canada—Continued Suspension* as described earlier, but does so in a way which takes it into precisely the kinds of detailed methodological questions just set out.[121] Although this case was upheld on appeal, it is hard to see how the approach of the Panel in this case is meaningfully different, at least in this respect, from the approach of the Panel in *US/Canada—Continued Suspension*, which drew such strong censure from the Appellate Body.

The broader point is that deferential/procedural review cannot deliver on its promise of a 'less intrusive' form of judicial scrutiny, or even a form of review which preserves substantive regulatory autonomy for WTO Members. There is no conceivable way that WTO review can be neutral as to the substance of domestic regulation in anything but a trivial sense, and there is no way of preserving regulatory 'autonomy' where such autonomy is illusory to begin with. It is impossible to design a form of WTO review which is entirely (or even meaningfully) innocent of substantive implications—that is to say, which is neutral in respect of domestic state–market relations, which has no impact on environmental or social regulation, or which has no redistributive effects. To the extent that the proceduralization of WTO law seeks to achieve such goals, it cannot succeed.

If that is true—and this is the crucial point—then so long as it is understood as and motivated by a turn away from 'substantive' review, the proceduralization of WTO law repeats the core problem which led to the WTO's legitimacy crisis, rather than resolving it. In my view, this legitimacy crisis occurred not—or not just—because the WTO became over the course of the 1980s and 1990s more powerful and 'intrusive', and developed a far broader scope of application to 'behind the border' regulatory barriers to trade. Rather, its legitimacy was undermined because it

120 Button (2004) 152–3.

121 See generally Panel Report, *Australia—Measures Affecting the Importation of Apples from New Zealand* (adopted 17 December 2010) WT/DS367/R, at 256–410. This approach was affirmed by the Appellate Body in the same case.

came to be understood that the WTO was profoundly and substantively shaping a new global economic order—but doing so in the absence of a legitimate and legitimating purpose, and without a clear sense of responsibility for the full range of outcomes produced. It was, in other words, the separation of the exercise of public power at the international level from the pursuit of collective public purpose, and the exercise of collective moral responsibility—a separation which was sustained and legitimated by the entrenchment of what I called the 'thin' view of the role of the WTO—which led to the WTO's legitimacy crisis. Ultimately the visions of proceduralization which so far have been advanced in the WTO context continue and entrench this same institutional flaw—because their result is still to produce a form of international economic governance which profoundly affects substantive outcomes, but is deliberately blind to them. Precisely because these visions proceed from the position that a collectively produced legitimating purpose is impossible to achieve in the context of the contemporary trade regime, they seek to imagine a more modest and limited form of power which can legitimately be exercised without it. In other words, taking the absence of a legitimate collective purpose to guide the trade regime as given—as an unavoidable fact of contemporary global economic governance—it responds to the contemporary legitimacy crisis of the WTO by seeking to limit the trade regime's intrusiveness, its degree of 'intervention' into the internal democratic lives of its members. But if I am right, and the WTO is not thereby made to sit apart from 'substantive politics'—if it still profoundly affects substantive outcomes, and still has far-reaching social, distributional, and environmental effects—then the consequence is that deferentialism and proceduralism run the risk of exacerbating the legitimacy crisis of the WTO, rather than resolving it.

It follows that an important part of any adequate response to the legitimacy crisis of the WTO—indeed, perhaps the most crucial aspect—must be the reformulation of a legitimating collective purpose to ground the work of the trade regime, and as a consequence the generation of a substantive and meaningful discussion of what that purpose should be in the light of contemporary global challenges and competing normative priorities. The primary project, in other words, must be to pursue precisely the mode of governance that neoliberal thought made more difficult to achieve—the exercise of public power in international trade governance in pursuit of a collectively defined legitimating purpose, and a form of governing which does not shy away from the experience of moral responsibility for the full range of outcomes it produces—and to do so in a way which goes beyond the limited experience of collective purpose that enlivened the post-war GATT. This is precisely the kind of fundamental debate that I referred to in Chapter 5, and it is that point that I am reiterating here.

Importantly, this does not necessarily imply a rejection of the proceduralist paradigm. My point is that if the benefits of procedural review are purchased at the cost of continued inattention to collective moral responsibility for the substantive outcomes of global trade governance—as if the *real* business of governing continues to happen elsewhere, outside the trade regime—then the price is too high. If proceduralization is to be pursued as a paradigm of WTO review, then it must be informed and guided by a genuine sense of collective public purpose, and it must be accompanied by debate and discussion about the substantive norms, values, and goals which the international trade regime ought to equip itself to pursue in contemporary conditions—whether through proceduralist interventions and disciplines, or through other tools.

One obvious response to this argument must be anticipated before I conclude. If the premise of the deferential-procedural turn is correct—that such a legitimating collective public purpose is a structural impossibility in the context of contemporary global trade governance—then the argument I am making here may do little more than cast us back to the original dilemma. That is to say, it may simply lead us to re-pose the core problem of how to constitute a legitimate form of power in conditions in which the production of collective public purpose is no longer available to us.

My response is admittedly modest. It is crucial to recognize that the conditions in which a collectively defined legitimating purpose for global trade governance appears impossible are themselves socially produced—and indeed, produced in part through the work of international economic lawyers. The continued *absence* of a sense of collective purpose from global trade governance, in other words, is the result of active processes, which require continued work to sustain. There are, to sharpen the point, certain habits of thought and certain ways of understanding our professional role, which continue to be reproduced within the field and exercise a deep hold over it, and which have the effect of making the kind of discussion I would like to see *more* difficult to achieve. An obvious first step, then, would be to work to remove these imaginative roadblocks, at least as far as we contribute to their continuation. Let me conclude the book, then, by drawing attention to three ways in which the work of international economic lawyers at present makes the re-moralization of international trade law more difficult to achieve, and by suggesting some strategies by which these ideational obstacles might be eliminated. More positively, let me suggest three forms of work through which international lawyers can help to create the ideational conditions of possibility for the rejuvenation of a sense of collective public purpose in global trade governance.

First, and perhaps most importantly, it is necessary to call into question the 'thin' vision of the nature and purpose of trade law, which has in many areas of the discipline attained something of a natural and self-evident quality. In Chapter 8, I showed how the trade regime was re-imagined in theory and practice primarily as a 'marketplace'—that is, as essentially a space for the exchange of bargained concessions among states. I noted that this way of imagining the trade regime left no room for the notion of a 'collective purpose' sustaining and legitimating the work of the regime, except in the relatively trivial sense of mutually desirable negotiated outcomes. While this imagined model certainly allows us to understand some aspects of the operation of the trade regime more clearly, its entrenchment and consolidation as the dominant way of thinking and speaking about the GATT/WTO since at least the 1990s (and probably at least a decade earlier) has made it much more difficult to engage in a form of international trade politics oriented towards the discussion, definition, and pursuit of collective projects of international economic order: either such discussion appears nonsensical, since there is no room for the notion of collective purpose in the liberal imagination of the trade regime (only the specific purposes of each WTO Member); or it is short-circuited by the misleading and contestable claim that the purpose of the trade regime is self-evidently and solely the removal of barriers to international trade. The result is an impoverished discussion about what the role and purpose of the trade regime ought to be in the contemporary world.

It turns out, then, that the objectivist theoretical models of trade politics described in Chapter 6 are problematic not just because they are inadequate in an explanatory sense, as I argued in that chapter. They are also problematic because of their implicit—but still profound—*political* effects, achieved by rendering the pursuit of collective projects of international economic order more difficult to imagine or even meaningfully discuss. One useful counterweight to this tendency would be more theoretical work which re-opens space for the element of collective intentionality in international trade politics, by providing and recalling alternatives to the kinds of objectivist explanatory models of international trade politics set out in Chapter 6. Moreover, it is important in my view that existing work on the dimension of collective intentionality in the international trade regime be given far greater theoretical prominence and weight in contemporary literature on the WTO, and in the teaching of WTO law in today's classrooms. In addition, this theoretical work should be accompanied by historical work which demonstrates the contingency of contemporary understandings of the nature and purpose of international trade governance—showing the social and political contexts to which they originally responded, as well as the interests which their entrenchment presently serves. It will be clear that a number of the chapters of this book are intended as a contribution to the furthering of precisely these goals.[122] Furthermore, international lawyers need to be vigilant to avoid simply repeating the received wisdom and orthodox narratives about the purpose of the WTO and the role of law within it, since whenever we do so, we can inadvertently contribute to their naturalization. Instead, all our work must proceed from the starting point that the purpose of the trade regime is an imaginative construction rather than a social fact, that this purpose is not determined in advance but is in principle an open question, and that existing ideas about this purpose represent only one of many possible constructions, all of which are amenable to re-imagination.

Secondly, there is a need to modify the way that international economic lawyers relate to the structures of knowledge which shape our thinking, and in particular the way we use specialist technical knowledge in the interpretation, elaboration, and justification of international trade law. While, as I have shown in this chapter, there are a variety of post-positivist perspectives which have begun to have significant influence in the field, it still remains the case that the form of legal work characteristic of a technicalized legal imagination continues to have a strong hold over the

[122] See in particular Chs 2, 6, 7, and 8 above.

discipline. It remains a powerful idea that economics and other policy sciences provide a clear and determinate set of principles and techniques to guide the interpretation of international trade law, and it is not uncommon to find discussions of complex legal questions which look to economic analysis as a way of determining, for example, the most rational, efficient, or mutually beneficial way of resolving interpretive controversies. I am of course not suggesting that the use of economics and other technical bodies of knowledge is a problem in itself, and indeed it seems to me to be essential that international economic lawyers develop a greater degree of literacy and fluency in these disciplines. But one difficulty with this *way* of using economic analysis, of course, is that it tends to encourage us to address values questions in an unreconstructed technical idiom, insufficiently informed by explicit moral awareness of the value choices which are made in the process of analysis. It is a form of work which can squeeze out discussion of collective purpose, to the extent that it treats all core moral questions as determined and deducible, rather than open and contestable. The problem, in other words, is not so much the use of technical forms of knowledge, but the nature of our relationship with them. The difficulty occurs when legal processes are dominated by a particular body of technical expertise: to the extent that we treat bodies of technical knowledge as simply reflective of the way the world is, the less the structuring effects of that knowledge are visible to us, the more completely our actions and choices are governed and determined by it, and the less is our experience of moral choice and responsibility. The objective must be to create a new relationship to expert knowledge on the part of professionals in the field of international trade law, one in which our choices are not dictated by the structures of knowledge available to us, but in which we become active participants in the processes by which those structures are produced and questioned. This must not mean a rejection of specialist bodies of knowledge, but a more active, critical, and informed process of engagement with them.

In this context, what needs further emphasis in contemporary scholarship on international trade is the indeterminacy of economic and other technical bodies of knowledge which are most often used to guide our interpretive work, and as a result the incoherence of the project of using such knowledge to determine (rather than inform in a more subtle way) the content of law. Indeterminacy critique is, in my view, potentially one of the most effective—and presently under-emphasized—means of making the point that the deployment of technical knowledge is no substitute for deliberative and public moral choices. Much of this work will simply involve re-learning the lessons of three decades ago: bringing to bear the insights of prior scholarship on the use of economics as a source of normative guidance for the interpretation and evolution of law;[123] and most relevantly, re-centralizing the line of thinking I set out in Chapter 6, concerning the indeterminacy and plasticity of the concept of 'trade barrier' which structures the operation of international trade law so

[123] See generally D Kennedy, 'Law-and-Economics from the Perspective of Critical Legal Studies' in P Newman (ed), *The New Palgrave Dictionary of Economics and the Law* (Macmillan Reference Ltd, London 1998) 465–74 and the works cited therein.

deeply. I have also found it helpful to read and teach work which presents counter-intuitive notions of the meaning of 'trade distortion', and does so in a technically rigorous way. Thus, for example, while there is a tendency in contemporary trade literature to treat measures to combat climate change as potential obstacles to free trade, others have recently argued that *failure* by a particular WTO Member to take action to deal with environmental externalities may constitute an illegitimate subsidy under WTO law.[124] Whatever one's view of the substantive merit of such arguments, the point for the purposes of the present argument is that they have the salutary effect of making the plasticity and malleability of technical concepts such as 'trade distortion' abundantly clear. At the very least, then, they represent a useful intermediate step towards a freer, more informed, and above all more normatively saturated way of using technical knowledge in legal scholarship within the field of international trade.

This kind of work could usefully be accompanied by empirical work to expose the processes by which the meaning of such indeterminate concepts is sedimented and made apparently determinate in the field of international trade governance, as well as the processes and structures through which forms of technical knowledge circulate and are normalized in the field—constructing such processes as an object of study in their own right, rather than simply the taken-for-granted background from which analysis proceeds. This is precisely the kind of inquiry that I sought to model in Chapter 9. This line of inquiry will often require us to turn our attention to the 'background'[125] of trade politics—the everyday social, discursive, and documentary processes by which shared views of the world are incrementally manufactured and entrenched within the field of international trade law and governance. For international trade lawyers, this may mean looking not only at traditional formal venues of law-making and legal interpretation, but also more mundane processes at work within spaces which presently exist largely below the radar of observation and comment. WTO committees and other quasi-administrative venues within the WTO are one obvious first port of call in this respect,[126] but there will be a huge variety of other fruitful institutional and discursive spaces to explore.

At heart, the purpose of such work is to bring into visibility the structures of knowledge which define the field of international trade governance, as a precondition to understanding the ways that our choices are shaped by them. Sometimes, this process can itself lead to an experience of freedom, as interpretive choices become

[124] R Howse, *Climate Mitigation Subsidies and the WTO Legal Framework: A Policy Analysis* (International Institute for Sustainable Development, Winnipeg 2010); JE Stiglitz, 'A New Agenda for Global Warming' (2006) 3 The Economists' Voice Article 3 <http://www.bepress.com/ev/vol3/:557/art3 accessed 15 June 2011.

[125] I borrow this concept from D Kennedy, 'The Forgotten Politics of International Governance' (2001) 2 European Human Rights L Rev 117; D Kennedy, 'Challenging Expert Rule. The Politics of Global Governance' (2005) 27 Sydney L Rev 1.

[126] For an initial foray, see ATF Lang and J Scott, 'The Hidden World of WTO Governance' (2009) 20 EJIL 575. In addition, see RB Stewart and MR Sanchez Badin, 'The World Trade Organization and Global Administrative Law' (2009) Institute for International Law and Justice, New York University School of Law Working Paper <http://www.iilj.org/publications/documents/2009-7.StewartRatton-Sanchez.pdf> accessed 20 February 2011.

available to us which simply did not appear to exist beforehand. To the extent that knowledge loses its self-evidence, in other words, it loses some of its grip over our imagination. More commonly, however, making visible the structures of knowledge which shape the way we think and act leads us to a new awareness of the ways in which we are constrained. We perceive ourselves and our actions as structured and determined by the application of symbolic power, in ways which may not have been apparent before. We begin to understand our choices as in part an effect of symbolic power. This, too, is important, as it is perhaps the crucial first step towards a more nuanced understanding of our own and others' roles as agents within the terrain of symbolic contestation, and helps to instil a creative and critical relation to the structures of knowledge characteristic of the professional field in which we operate. One of the core elements of the project I am outlining, then, involves the deepening and broadening of such a creative and critical relation within the field of international economic law.

Thirdly, and finally, there is a need for more work which focuses explicitly on the subtantive outcomes of international economic law, tracing in detail the lines of causation from choices made in the global context through to their consequences on the ground. Such consequences have traditionally been rendered almost invisible as a practical matter in the context of international trade governance—particularly distributional, social, and environmental outcomes, and those which result from underlying structural forces within the global economic order. As I suggested in Chapter 5, their invisibility has been enabled in part by the pervasive sense that responsibility for such outcomes lies elsewhere—either at the domestic level, or with a different international organization with a different functional specialization. It is, in other words, a pervasive set of ideas about the limited competence and capacity of the international trade regime which has in part helped to de-link the exercise of power at the global level from a sense of collective responsibility for its social and economic outcomes. It is these ideas which constitute a mechanism by which the authority to take trade policy decisions is divorced from responsibility for some of their social consequences—and by which such a separation is made to appear normal and desirable.[127]

It has been one of the most important contributions of the global justice movement described in Chapter 3—as well as organizations and individuals inspired by similar concerns—to make such outcomes more visible in discussions around global trade governance. International law scholars should, in my view, also contribute to that project, by directing their analytical attention to the distributional and social consequences of particular legal rules and interpretative choices, focusing on those consequences which at present remain largely unacknowledged. It is not that increasing the visibility of such consequences in the domain of international trade governance will lead magically to a world in which they are taken more seriously by those with the authority to take decisions; the point, rather, is to undermine the

[127] Kinley (2009) 217 similarly rests his argument in part on the claim that responsibility must be attributed to those who 'cause' outcomes, whether or not those outcomes are usually understood to belong within an actor's domain of expertise.

power of those ideas just described, which have the effect of making such consequences appear irrelevant to decision-making at the global level, and which therefore naturalize and legitimate a mode of governance in which responsibility for some of its most significant outcomes is allocated elsewhere. Causal claims, linking decisions taken in the global context to particular social and distributional outcomes, may make this re-allocation of responsibility more difficult to sustain. The repetition of such claims in debates about global trade governance should, it is to be hoped, make such outcomes one of the reference points by which the normative legitimacy and desirability of international economic law is to be assessed.

In the end, what is needed is an inversion of the lines of argument and critique which are typically deployed in contemporary discussions of global trade governance. Too often, we begin with certain ideas about the nature and purpose of the trade regime, its mandate and domain of competence, and from that point derive a set of views about the kinds of questions it can legitimately address, and the kinds of decisions which can legitimately be made within its purview. This pattern of thought is characteristic, for example, of those who seek to defend the contemporary trade regime from those who seek to burden it with 'non-trade' issues and objectives—but, as we have seen, it is also characteristic of those voices which seek to constrain the trade regime, and limit its 'intrusion' upon domestic regulatory 'autonomy'. What is needed instead is a discussion which begins with an acknowledgement of the full range of outcomes of global trade governance, and derives from that starting point a set of ideas about the appropriate role, purpose, and competence of the international trade regime. In other words, a debate is needed which sets out with a sense of collective moral responsibility for the consequences of practices occurring within the field of global trade governance, which squarely addresses the question of what those consequences can and should legitimately be, and which, only then, on that basis, seeks to determine what role the trade regime should play in the achievement of those consequences, and how it should equip itself to do so.

Select Bibliography

Aaronson, SA, *Taking Trade to the Streets: The Lost History of Public Efforts to Shape Globalization* (University of Michigan Press, Ann Arbor, MI 2001)

—— and Zimmerman, JM, *Trade Imbalance: The Struggle to Weigh Human Rights Concerns in Trade Policymaking* (CUP, Cambridge 2008)

Abbott, F, Breining-Kaufman, C, and Cottier, T (eds), *International Trade and Human Rights: Foundations and Conceptual Issues* (University of Michigan Press, Ann Arbor, MI 2006)

Abbott, KW, 'The Trading Nation's Dilemma: The Functions of the Law of International Trade' (1985) 26 Harvard Intl LJ 501

—— 'United States—Section 337 Of The Tariff Act Of 1930' (1990) 84 AJIL 274

—— 'GATT as a Public Institution: The Uruguay Round and Beyond' (1992) 18 Brooklyn J of Intl L 31

——'The Uruguay Round and Dispute Resolution: Building a Private-Interests System of Justice' (1992) Columbia Business L Rev 111

Abram, MB, 'Human Rights and the United Nations: Past as Prologue' (1991) 4 Harvard Human Rights J 69

Adler, E, 'The Emergence of Cooperation: National Epistemic Communities and the International Evolution of the Idea of Nuclear Arms Control' (1992) 46 Intl Org 101

—— and Haas, PM, 'Conclusion: Epistemic Communities, World Order, and the Creation of a Reflective Research Program' (1992) 46 Intl Org 367

Adlung, R, 'Services Negotiations in the Doha Round: Lost in Flexibility?' (2006) 9 JIEL 865

—— and Roy, M, 'Turning Hills into Mountains? Current Commitments Under the General Agreement on Trade in Services and Prospects for Change' (2005) 39 J of World Trade 116

'Administrative and Technical Regulations: The Lesser Known Obstacles to Trade', *The OECD Observer*, No 4, June 1963

Ala'i, P, 'From the Periphery to the Center? The Evolving WTO Jurisprudence on Transparency and Good Governance' (2008) 4 JIEL 779

Alexander, K, 'The GATS and Financial Services: The Role of Regulatory Transparency' (2007) 20 Cambridge Rev of Intl Affairs 111

Alianza Social Continental, 'Final Declaration of the Summit: Peoples' Summit of the Americas' in Feinberg, R, and Rosenberg, R (eds), *Civil Society and the Summit of the Americas: The 1998 Santiago Summit* (North-South Center Press, Miami, FL 1999)

Allen, WR, 'The International Trade Philosophy of Cordell Hull, 1907–1933' (1953) 43 American Economic Rev 101

Allmand, W, 'Trading in Human Rights—The Primacy of Human Rights in International Law' (1999) *Technical Annex to the Brief to the Standing Committee on Foreign Affairs and International Trade* <http://www.dd-rd.ca/site/publications/index.php?subsection=catalogue&lang=en&id=1297>

Alston, P, *Human Rights and the Basic Needs Strategy for Development* (Human Rights and Development Working Papers, Anti-Slavery Society, London 1979)

—— 'International Trade as an Instrument of Positive Human Rights Policy' (1982) 4 HRQ 155

—— 'Making Space for New Human Rights: The Case of the Right to Development' (1988) 1 Harvard Human Rights Ybk 3
—— 'The Myopia of the Handmaidens: International Lawyers and Globalization' (1997) 3 EJIL 435
—— 'The Universal Declaration in an Era of Globalisation' in Van der Heijden et al, *Reflections on the Universal Declaration of Human Rights: A Fiftieth Anniversary Anthology* (Kluwer, The Hague, 1998)
—— 'Resisting the Merger and Acquisition of Human Rights by Trade Law: A Reply to Petersmann' (2002) 13 EJIL 815
Alvarez, JE, 'How Not to Link: Institutional Conundrums of an Expanded Trade Regime' (2001) 7 Widener L Symposium J 1
Aman, A, 'Law, Markets and Democracy: A Role for Law in the Neo-Liberal State' (2007) 51 New York Law School L Rev 801
Ancelovici, M, 'Organizing against Globalization: The Case of ATTAC in France' (2002) 30 Politics and Society 427
Andenas, M, and Zleptnig, S, 'Proportionality: WTO Law in Comparative Perspective' (2007) 42 Texas Int Law J 371
Anderson, S et al, 'Alternatives for the Americas' <http://www.web.net/comfront/alts4americas/eng/eng.html>
—— (ed), *Views from the South: The Effects of Globalization and the WTO on Third World Countries* (Food First, Oakland, CA 2000)
Arcuri, A, 'Food Safety at the WTO After "Continued Suspension": A Paradigm Shift' in Antoniadis, A, Schutze, R, and Spaventa, E (eds), *The European Union and Global Emergencies: A Law and Policy Analysis* (Hart Publishing, Oxford 2011) <http://papers.ssrn.com/sol3/papers.cfm?abstract_id=1633390>
Armbruster-Sandoval, R, 'Globalization and Transnational Labor Organizing: The Honduran Maquiladora Industry and the Kimi Campaign' (2003) 27 Social Science History 551
Arnold, PJ, 'Disciplining Domestic Regulation: The World Trade Organization and the Market for Professional Services' (2005) 30 Accounting, Organizations and Society 299
Aronson, JD, *Negotiating to Launch Negotiations: Getting Trade in Services onto the GATT Agenda* (Pew Case Studies in International Affairs: Case 125, Washington, DC 1992)
—— 'Telecom Agreement Tops Expectations' in Gary Clyde Hufbauer and Erika Wada (eds), *Unfinished Business: Telecommunications after the Uruguay Round* (Institute for International Economics, Washington, DC 1997) 17
Association for Women's Rights in Development, 'Achieving Women's Economic and Social Rights: Strategies and lessons from experience' (2006) <http://www.awid.org/eng/content/download/49095/541680/file/ESCR%20Report.pdf>
Ayres, JM, 'Political Process and Popular Protest: The Mobilization against Free Trade in Canada' (1996) 55 American J of Economics and Sociology 473
—— *Defying Conventional Wisdom: Political Movements and Popular Contention against North American Free Trade* (University of Toronto Press, Toronto 1998)
—— 'Transnational Political Processes and Contention Against the Global Economy' in Smith, J, and Johnston, H (eds), *Globalization and Resistance: Transnational Dimensions of Social Movements* (Rowman and Littlefield Publishers, Lanham, MD 2002)
——'Framing Collective Action Against Neo-Liberalism: The Case of the "Anti-Globalization" Movement' (2004) X(1) J of World-Systems Research 11

Baldwin, R, *Non-Tariff Distortions of International Trade* (George Allen & Unwin, Sydney 1970)

—— *The Multilateral Trade Negotiations: Toward Greater Liberalization?* (American Enterprise Institute for Public Policy Research, Washington, DC 1979)

—— *The Political Economy of U.S. Import Policy* (MIT Press, Cambridge, MA 1986)

—— 'U.S. Trade Policy, 1945–1988: From Foreign to Domestic Policy' in Pearson, CS, and Riedel, J (eds), *The Direction of Trade Policy: Papers in Honor of Isaiah Frank* (Basil Blackwell, Oxford 1990)

Bantjes, R, *Social Movements in a Global Context: Canadian Perspectives* (Canadian Scholars' Press, Toronto 2007)

Barnett, M, and Finnemore, M, *Rules for the World: International Organizations in Global Politics* (Cornell University Press, Ithaca, NY 2004)

Bartels, L, 'Applicable Law in WTO Dispute Settlement Proceedings' (2001) 35 J of World Trade 499

—— 'Human Rights and Democracy Clauses in the EU's International Agreements' (2005) Note Prepared for the European Parliament's Subcommittee on Human Rights <http://www.law.ed.ac.uk/file_download/publications/3_568_humanrightsanddemocracyclausesintheeusin.pdf>

—— *Human Rights Conditionality in the EU's International Agreements* (OUP, Oxford 2005)

Barton, JH, Goldstein, JL, Josling, TE, and Steinberg, RH, *The Evolution of the Trade Regime: Politics, Law, and Economics of the GATT and the WTO* (Princeton University Press, Princeton, NJ 2006)

Baxi, U, *The Future of Human Rights* (3rd edn, OUP, New Delhi 2008)

Beerman, K, 'Moving On: Chile's alternatives to NAFTA' (1996) 18 Harvard Intl Rev 64

Beetham, D, 'What Future for Social and Economic Rights?' (1995) 43 Political Studies 41

Benedek, W, De Feyter, K, and Marrella, F (eds), *Economic Globalisation and Human Rights* (CUP, Cambridge 2007)

Bernier, I, 'A UNESCO International Convention on Cultural Diversity' (2003)< http://www.diversite-culturelle.qc.ca/fileadmin/documents/pdf/update0303.pdf>

Bismuth, R, 'Financial Sector Regulation and Financial Services Liberalization at the Crossroads: The Relevance of International Financial Standards in WTO Law' (2010) 44 J of World Trade 489

Blackett, A, 'Whither Social Clause? Human Rights, Trade Theory and Treaty Interpretation' (1999) 31 Columbia Human Rights L Rev 1

Blyth, M, *Great Transformations: Economic Ideas and Institutional Change in the Twentieth Century* (CUP, New York 2002)

Bohanes, J, 'Risk Regulation and WTO Law: A Procedure-Based Approach to the Precautionary Principle' (2002) 40 Columbia J of Transnational L 323

Borgwardt, E, *A New Deal for the World: America's Vision for Human Rights* (Harvard University Press, Cambridge, MA 2005)

Bourdieu, P, 'Symbolic Power' in Denis Gleeson (ed), *Identity and Structure: Issues in the Sociology of Education* (Nafferton Books, Driffield 1977)

—— 'The Force of Law: Toward a Sociology of the Juridical Field' (1987) 38 Hastings LJ 805

In Other Words: Essays Towards a Reflexive Sociology (Adamson (trs), Polity Press, Cambridge, 1990)

—— *Language and Symbolic Power* (Raymond and Adamson (trs), Polity Press, Cambridge 1991)

—— *Practical Reason: on the Theory of Action* (Stanford University Press, Stanford, CA 1998)

Bourdieu, P, and Wacquant, LJD, *An Invitation to Reflexive Sociology* (Chicago University Press, Chicago, IL 1992)

Brecher, J, 'The Hierarchs' New World Order—and Ours' in Brecher, J, Childs, JB, and Cutler, J (eds), *Global Visions: Beyond the New World Order* (South End Press, Boston, MA 1993)

Brest, P, 'The Substance of Process' (1981) 42 Ohio State LJ 131

Broad, R (ed), *Global Backlash: Citizen Initiatives for a Just World Economy* (Rowman and Littlefield Publishers, Lanham, MA 2002)

Broadbent, JE, *The Rise and Fall of Economic and Social Rights: Thoughts on Justice and Stability in the North Atlantic Democracies* (Canadian High Commission, London 1997)

—— 'The Challenge to Economic and Social Rights: Thoughts on Citizenship in the Welfare State in the North Atlantic World' (1998) 12 Global Society 15

—— 'The Rise and Fall of Economic and Social Rights: What Next?' address to the Congress of the Canadian Federation for the Humanities and Social Sciences (May 29, 2000) <http://www.policyalternatives.ca/sites/default/files/uploads/publications/reports/docs/Rise_and_Fall_of_Economic_and_Social_Rights.pdf>

Bronson, D, and Lamarche, L, *A Human Rights Framework for Trade in the Americas* (International Centre for Human Rights and Democratic Development, Montreal 2001) <http://www.dd-rd.ca/site/_PDF/publications/globalization/frameworkFinal.pdf>

Brooks, EC, *Unravelling the Garment Industry: transnational organizing and women's work* (University of Minnesota Press, Minneapolis, MN 2007)

Broude, T, *International Governance in the World Trade Organization: Judicial Boundaries and Political Capitulation* (Cameron May, London 2004)

Brown, G, 'Stemming the Tide: Third World Network and Global Governance' (2003/04) Ybk of Intl Cooperation on Environment and Development 73

Brown, WA, *The United States and the restoration of world trade: an analysis and appraisal of the ITO charter and the General Agreement on Tariffs and Trade* (Brookings Institution, Washington, DC 1950)

Brysk, A, *The Politics of Human Rights in Argentina: Protest, Change, and Democratization* (Stanford University Press, Stanford, CA 1994)

—— (ed) *Globalization and Human Rights* (University of California Press, Berkeley, CA 2002)

Burley, AM, 'Regulating the World: Multilateralism, International Law, and the Projection of the New Deal Regulatory State' in Ruggie, JG (ed), *Multilateralism Matters: The Theory and Praxis of an Institutional Form* (Columbia University Press, New York, NY 1993)

Busch, ML, Reinhardt, E, and Shaffer, G, 'Does Legal Capacity Matter? A Survey of WTO Members' (2009) 8 World Trade Rev 559

Button, C, *The Power to Protect: Trade, Health and Uncertainty in the WTO* (Hart Publishing, Oxford 2004)

Cameron, J, and Gray, KR, 'Principles of International Law in the WTO Dispute Settlement Body' (2001) 50 ICLQ 248

Campaign for Tobacco-Free Kids, 'Public Health, International Trade and the Framework Convention on Tobacco Control' (2001) <http://www.tobaccofreekids.org/campaign/global/framework/docs/Policy.pdf>

Cassen, B, 'On the Attack (2003) 19 New Left Rev 41

Cassese, A, *Human Rights in a Changing World* (Polity Press, Cambridge 1990)

Centro de Derecho Homanos 'Miguel Agustin Pro Juarez' (Centro Pro Juarez), 'Los Derechos Humanos en los Procesos de Integracion Economica en las Americas' (Statement for the CIDH, October 2004) <http://www.choike.org/documentos/tlc_cidh_ddhh.pdf>

Charnovitz, S, 'The Supervision of Health and Biosafety Regulation by World Trade Rules' (2000) 13 Tulane Environmental L J 271

—— 'The WTO and the Rights of the Individual' (2001) 36 Intereconomics 98

—— 'Triangulating the World Trade Organization' (2002) 96 AJIL 28

—— 'Belgian Family Allowances and the challenge of origin-based discrimination' (2005) 4 World Trade Rev 7

Charvet, J, and Kaczynska-Nay, E, *The Liberal Project and Human Rights: The Theory and Practice of a New World Order* (CUP, New York, NY 2008)

Chen, Z, and Schembri, L, 'Measuring the Barriers to Trade in Services: Literature and Methodologies' in Curtis, JM, and Ciuriak, D (eds), *Trade Policy Research 2002* (Department of Foreign Affairs and International Trade, Ottawa 2002)

Chimni, BS, *International Commodity Agreements* (Croom Helm, New York, NY 1987)

Clarke, A, *The GATT, Environmental Protection and Sustainable Development* (WWF Discussion Paper, Gland, Switzerland 1991)

Clatanoff, W, 'Labor Standards in Recent U.S. Trade Agreements' (2005) 5 Richmond J of Global L and Business 109

Claude, RP, and Weston, BH (eds), *Human Rights in the World Community: Issues and Action* (3rd edn, University of Pennsylvania Press, Philadelphia, PA 2006)

Cleveland, SH, 'Human Rights Sanctions and International Trade: A Theory of Compatibility', (2002) 5 JIEL 133

Cockburn, A, St Clair, J, and Sekula, A, *Five Days that Shook the World: The Battle for Seattle and Beyond* (Verso, London 2000)

Collin, J, Lee, K, and Bissell, K, 'Global health governance? The Framework Convention on Tobacco Control' (2002) 23 Third World Q 265

Compa, LA, 'Labor Rights and Labor Standards in International Trade' (1993) 25 J of L and Policy in Intl Business 165

—— and Diamond, SF (eds), *Human Rights, Labor Rights, and International Trade* (University of Pennsylvania Press, Philadelphia, PA 2003)

Cooper, RN, 'Trade Policy is Foreign Policy' (1972) 9 Foreign Policy 18

—— 'Trade and Human Rights: A Relationship to Discover' (2002) 5 JIEL 111–32

Cottier, T, Bürgi, E, and Pauwelyn, J (eds), *Human Rights and International Trade* (OUP, Oxford 2005)

Cottrell, MP, and Trubek, DM, 'The Law of Global Space: Rethinking the Legalization of World Politics' (2010) University of Wisconsin Legal Studies Working Paper <http://wage.wisc.edu/uploads/Globalspace%20Final%20August%202,%202010.pdf>

Cowhey, PF, 'The International Telecommunications Regime: The Political Roots of Regimes for High Technology' (1990) 44 Intl Org 169

—— 'FCC Benchmarks and the Reform of the International Telecommunications Market' (1998) 11 Telecommunications Policy 911

—— and Klimenko, MM, 'The WTO Agreement and Telecommunications Policy Reforms' (2001) World Bank Policy Research Paper No 2601

—— and Aronson, JD, *Transforming Global Information and Communication Markets: The Political Economy of Innovation* (The MIT Press, Cambridge, MA 2009)

Cranston, M, *What are Human Rights?* (Bodley Head, London 1973)

Craven, M, *The International Covenant on Economic, Social and Cultural Rights: A Perspective on its Development* (Clarendon Press, New York, NY 1995)

Croome, J, *Reshaping the World Trading System: A history of the Uruguay Round* (Kluwer Law International, Dordrecht 1995)

Curtis, TB, and Vastine, JR, *The Kennedy Round and the future of American trade* (Praeger, New York, NY 1971)

Curzon, G, *Multilateral commercial diplomacy: the General Agreement on Tariffs and Trade and its impact on national commercial policies and techniques* (Michael Joseph, London 1965)

—— 'Crisis in the International Trading System' in Corbet, H, and Jackson, R (eds), *In Search of a New World Economic Order* (John Wiley and Sons, New York, NY 1974)

—— and Curzon, V, 'GATT: Trader's Club' in Cox, RW and Jacobson, HK (eds), *Anatomy of Influence: Decision Making in International Organization* (Yale University Press, New Haven, CN 1973)

—— and —— 'The Management of Trade Relations in the GATT' in Shonfield, A (ed), *International Economic Relations of the Western World, 1959–1971, Volume 1: Politics and Trade* (OUP, Oxford 1976)

Dam, KW, *The GATT: Law and International Economic Organization* (University of Chicago Press, Chicago, IL 1970)

Davis, CL, *Food Fights over Free Trade: How International Institutions Promote Agricultural Trade Liberalization* (Princeton University Press, Princeton, NJ 2003)

Davis, MC, 'The Price of Rights: Constitutionalism and East Asian Economic Development' (1998) 20 HRQ 303

de Búrca, G, and Scott, J (eds), *The EU and the WTO: Legal and Constitutional Issues* (Hart Publishing, Oxford 2001)

De Feyter, K, *Human Rights: Social Justice in the Age of the Market* (Zed Books, London 2005)

de Rivero, O, *New Economic Order and Development Law* (Pergamon Press, New York, NY 1980)

Deere, CD, and Royce, FS, *Rural Social Movements in Latin America: Organizing for Sustainable Livelihoods* (University of Florida Press, Gainesville, FL 2009)

della Porta, D, Andretta, M, Mosca, L, and Reiter, H (eds), *Globalization from Below: Transnational Activists and Protest Networks* (University of Minnesota Press, Minneapolis, MN 2006)

Desmarais, AA, *La Vía Campesina: Globalization and the Power of Peasants* (Pluto Press, London 2007)

Desmedt, A, 'Proportionality in WTO law' (2001) 4 JIEL 441

Destler, IM, *American Trade Politics* (4th edn, Institute for International Economics, Washington, DC 2005)

Devereaux, C, Lawrence, RZ, and Watkins, M (eds), *Case Studies on US Trade Negotiations: Volume 1, Making the Rules* (Peterson Institute for International Economics, Washington DC 2006)

Dezalay, Y, and Garth, BG, *The Internationalization of Palace Wars: Lawyers, Economists, and the Contest to Transform Latin American States* (University of Chicago Press, Chicago, IL 2002)

Diebold, W, *The End of the ITO*, Essays in International Finance No. 16 (International Finance Section, Department of Economics and Social Institutions, Princeton University, Princeton, NJ 1952)

Diehl, N and Kalinova, B, 'Services Barriers and their Economic Impact: Examples of Banking and Telecommunications Services in Selected Transition Economies' (2004) OECD Trade Policy Working Paper No 7

—— and Shepherd, B, 'Model Estimates of Services Barriers' (2007) OECD Trade Policy Working Paper No 51

Dillon, SA, 'A Farewell to Linkage: International Trade Law and Global Sustainability Indicators' (2002) 55 Rutgers L Rev 87

Dobson, W, and Jacquet, P, *Financial Services Liberalization in the WTO* (Institute for International Economics, Washington, DC 1998)

Dommen, C, 'Raising Human Rights Concerns in the World Trade Organization: Actors, Processes and Possible Strategies' (2002) 24 HRQ 1

——'No Sell-Out on Trade in the Human Rights Commission' (April 2003) <http://198.170.85.29/Trade-Human-Rights-Commission.htm>

—— *The WTO, international trade, and human rights* (2004) <http://www.3dthree.org/pdf_3D/WTOmainstreamingHR>

Donnelly, J, 'Human Rights and Development: Complementary or Competing Concerns?' (1984) 36 World Politics 255

—— 'In Search of the Unicorn: The Jurisprudence and Politics of the Right to Development' (1985) 15 California Western Intl L J 473

—— 'Human Rights and Western Liberalism' in An-Na'im, AA, and Deng, FM (eds), *Human Rights in Africa: Cross-Cultural Perspectives* (Brookings Institution Press, Washington, DC 1990)

—— *Universal Human Rights in Theory and Practice* (Cornell University Press, Ithaca, NY 2003)

Drake, WJ, and Nicolaïdis, K, 'Ideas, Interests, and Institutionalization: "Trade in Services" and the Uruguay Round' (1992) 46 Intl Org 37

Drezner, DW, *All Politics Is Global: Explaining International Regulatory Regimes* (Princeton University Press, Princeton, NJ 2007)

Du, MM, 'Standard of Review under the SPS Agreement after EC—Hormones II' (2010) 59 ICLQ 441

Dunoff, JL, '"Trade and": Recent Developments in Trade Policy and Scholarship—And Their Surprising Political Implications' (1997) 17 Northwestern J of Intl L and Bus 759

—— 'Rethinking International Trade' (1998) 19 University of Pennsylvania J of Intl Econ L 347

—— 'The Death of the Trade Regime' (1999) 10 EJIL 733

Eagleton-Pierce, M, *Uncovering Symbolic Power: Power Analysis, Southern Countries, and the World Trade Organization* (D Phil dissertation, University of Oxford, 2008)

Eckersley, R, 'The Big Chill: The WTO and MEAs' (2004) 4 Global Environmental Politics 24

Eckhardt, JN, 'Balancing Interests in Free Trade and Health: How the WHO's Framework Convention on Tobacco Control Can Withstand WTO Scrutiny' (2002) 12 Duke J of Comparative and Intl Law 197

Edelman, M, 'Peasant-farmer movements, third world peoples, and the Seattle protests against the World Trade Organization' (2009) 33 Dialectical Anthropology 109

'Transnational Peasant and Farmer Movements and Networks' in Anheier, H, Glasius, M, and Kaldor, M (eds), *Global Civil Society* (OUP, Oxford 2003)

Ehring, L, 'De Facto Discrimination in WTO Law: National and Most-Favored-Nation Treatment—or Equal Treatment?' (2002) 36 J of World Trade 921

Engle, K, 'View from the Margins: A Response to David Kennedy' (1994) Utah L Rev 105

—— *The Elusive Promise of Indigenous Development: Rights, Culture, Strategy* (Duke University Press, Durham, NC 2010)

Episcopal Commission for Social Affairs, 'Ethical Reflections on the Economic Crisis' in Sheridan, EF (ed), *Do Justice! The Social Teaching of the Canadian Catholic Bishops* (Jesuit Centre for Social Faith and Justice, Toronto 1987)

Espiell, HG, 'The Evolving Concept of Human Rights: Western, Socialist and Third World Approaches' in Ramcharan, BG (ed), *Human Rights: Thirty Years after the Universal Declaration* (Martinus Nijhoff, The Hague 1979)

European Commission, *GATS—The General Agreement on Trade in Services: A Guide for Business* (Office for Official Publications of The European Communities, Luxembourg 1995)

Evans, JW, *The Kennedy Round in American trade policy: the twilight of the GATT?* (Harvard University Press, Cambridge, MA 1971)

Evans, P, *Unpacking the GATT: A step by step guide to the Uruguay Round* (International Organisation of Consumers Unions, London 1994)

Evans, T, *The Politics of Human Rights: A Global Perspective* (Pluto Press, London 2001)

—— and Hancock, J, 'Doing Something Without Doing Anything: International Human Rights Law and the Challenge of Globalisation' (1998) 2 Intl J of Human Rights 1

Fabri, HR, 'Reflections on Possible Future Legal Implications of the Convention' in Obuljen, N, and Smiers, J (eds), *UNESCO's Convention on the Protection and Promotion of the Diversity of Cultural Expressions: Making it Work* (Institute for International Relations, Zagreb 2006)

Fairbrother, R, and McCorquodale, R, 'Globalization and Human Rights' (1999) 21(3) HRQ 735

Falk, G, *The Right to Food of Milk and Maize Farmers: Report of an investigative mission to Uganda* (Heidelberg, FIAN 2009) <http://www.fian.org/resources/documents/others/the-right-to-food-of-milk-and-maize-farmers/pdf>

Falkner, R, 'Regulating Biotech Trade: The Cartagena Protocol on Biosafety' (2000) 76 Intl Affairs (Royal Institute of Intl Affairs 1944) 299

Feketekuty, G, *International Trade in Services: An Overview and Blueprint for Negotiations* (AEI and Ballinger, Cambridge, MA 1988)

Findlay, C, and Warren, T (eds), *Impediments to Trade in Services: Measurement and Policy Implications* (Routledge, London 2000)

Finger, M, and Allouche, J, *Water Privatisation: Trans-national corporations and the re-regulation of the water industry* (Spon Press, London 2002)

Finlayson, JA, and Zacher, MW, 'The GATT and the Regulation of Trade Barriers: Regime Dynamics and Functions' (1981) 35 Intl Org 561

Flory, T, *Le G.A.T.T., droit international et commerce mondial* (Librairie générale de droit et de jurisprudence, Paris 1968)

FoodFirst Information Action Network, 'Agrarian Reform and the Human Right to Food in Honduras' (Report of the FIAN International and Vía Campesina Fact Finding Mission July 29—August 2, 2000) <http://www.fian.org/resources/documents/others/agrarian-reform-and-the-human-right-to-food-in-honduras>

—— La Vía Campesina, Maastricht Center of Human Rights, 'Agrarian Reform and Human Rights' (Seminar Report 15–17 April 2002) <http://www.fian.org/resources/documents/others/agrarian-reform-and-human-rights>

—— 'Right to Food of Milk and Honey Farmers: Report of an investigative mission to Zambia' (30 September 2008) <http://www.fian.org/resources/documents/others/right-to-food-of-milk-and-honey-farmers-report-of-an-invesitagtive-mission-to-zambia/pdf>

—— and La Vía Campesina, 'Declaración de Cochabamba' (International Seminar 'Agrarian Reform and Gender' 2003) <http://www.fian.org/resources/documents/others/declaration-of-cochabamba>

Footer, M, and Graber, CB, 'Trade Liberalization and Cultural Policy' (2000) 3 JIEL 115

Fox, EM, 'Globalization and Human Rights: Looking out for the Welfare of the Worst Off' (2002) 35 NYU J of Intl L and Policy 201–20

Fraser, AS, 'Becoming Human: The Origins and Development of Women's Human Rights' (1999) 21 HRQ 853

Freeman, HL, 'A Pioneer's View of Financial Services Negotiations in the GATT and in the World Trade Organization: 17 Years of Work for Something or Nothing?' (1997) 22 The Geneva Papers on Risk and Insurance 392

Friedman, E, 'Women's Human Rights: The Emergence of a Movement' in Peters, J, and Wolper, A (eds), *Women's rights, human rights: international feminist perspectives* (Routledge, New York, NY 1995)

Gabler, M, 'Norms, Institutions and Social Learning: An Explanation for Weak Policy Integration' (2010) 10 Global Environmental Politics 80

Galbraith, JK, *Economics in Perspective: A Critical History* (Houghton Mifflin, Boston, MA 1987)

Gao, H, 'Evaluating Alternative Approaches to GATS Negotiations: Sectoral, Formulae and Other Alternatives' in Sauvé, P, Panizzon, M, and Pohl, N (eds), *GATS and the Regulation of International Trade in Services* (CUP, Cambridge 2007)

—— 'Taking Justice into your Own Hand: The TBI Mechanism in China' (2010) 44 J of World Trade 633

Gardner, RN *Sterling-dollar diplomacy: Anglo-American collaboration in the reconstruction of multilateral trade* (Clarendon Press, Oxford 1956)

Gaston, GL, and Abate, RS, 'The Biosafety Protocol and the World Trade Organization: Can the Two Coexist?' (2000) 12 Pace Intl L Rev 107

Gathii, JT, 'Good Governance as a Counter-Insurgency Agenda to Oppositional and Transformative Social Projects in International Law' (1999) 5 Buffalo Human Rights L Rev 107

—— 'Re-Characterizing the Social in the Constitutionalization of the WTO: A Preliminary Analysis' (2001) 7 Widener L Symposium J 137

GATT, *International Trade, 1954* (GATT, Geneva 1955)

—— 'Resolution (Measures for the Expansion of Trade of Developing Countries as a Means of Furthering their Economic Development)' in GATT, *Basic Instruments and Selected Documents, Twelfth Supplement: Decisions, Reports etc. of the Twenty-first Session* (GATT, Geneva 1964)

—— *Trade Policies for a Better Future* (GATT, Geneva 1985)

Gayathri, PG, and Kurup, RR, 'Reconciling the Bio Safety Protocol and the WTO Regime: Problems, Perspectives and Possibilities' (2009) 1 American J of Economics and Business Administration 236

Geenan, K, Künnemann, R, and Tang, Y, *Report of the 2nd conference of the ETO-Consortium Heidelberg, September 26–27, 2008* (Heidelberg, FIAN 2008), <http://www.fian.org/resources/documents/others/report-of-the-2nd-conference-of-the-eto-consortium/pdf>

Geloso Grosso, M, 'Managing Request-Offer Negotiations under the GATS: The Case of Legal Services' (14 June 2004) OECD Trade Policy Working Paper No 2 (TD/TC/WP (2003)40/FINAL)

—— 'Managing Request-Offer Negotiations under the GATS: The Case of Environmental Services' (15 February 2005) OECD Trade Policy Working Paper No 11 (TD/TC/WP (2004)8/FINAL)

Gibney, M, and Skogly, S (eds), *Universal Human Rights and Extraterritorial Obligations* (University of Pennsylvania Press, Philadelphia, PA 2010)

Gkoutzinis, A, 'International Trade in Banking Services and the Role of the WTO: Discussing the Legal Framework and Policy Objectives of the General Agreement on Trade in Services and the Current State of Play in the Doha Round of Trade Negotiations' (2005) 39 The Intl Lawyer 877

Glendon, MA, *A World Made New: Eleanor Roosevelt and the Universal Declaration of Human Rights* (1st edn, Random House, New York, NY 2001)

—— 'The Forgotten Crucible: The Latin American Influence on the Universal Human Rights Idea' (2003) 16 Harvard Human Rights J 27

Goh, G, 'Tipping the Apple Cart: The Limits of Science and Law in the SPS Agreement after Japan-Apples' (2006) 40 J of World Trade 655

—— and Morgan, D, 'Political Considerations and Pragmatic Outcomes in WTO Dispute Rulings' (2007) 30 University of New South Wales LJ 481

Goldstein, J, 'Ideas, Institutions and American Trade Policy' (1988) Intl Org 179

—— *Ideas, Interests, and American Trade Policy* (Cornell University Press, Ithaca, NY 1993)

—— and Martin, LL, 'Legalization, Trade Liberalization, and Domestic Politics: A Cautionary Note' (2000) 54 Intl Org 603

Golt, S, *The GATT Negotiations, 1973–79: The Closing Stage and A Policy Statement by the British North American Committee—The GATT Negotiations, 1973–79: The Closing Stage* (The British-North American Committee, London 1978)

—— *Trade Issues in the Mid 1980's* (The British-North American Committee, London 1982)

Gomez, R, and Gunderson, M, 'Creation of Values and Principles: Canada's Experience with the CUSFTA and NAFTA' in Tussie, D (ed), *The Politics of Trade: The Role of Research in Trade Policy and Negotiation* (Brill Academic Publishers, Boston, MA 2009)

Goodwin, M, and Rose-Sender, K, 'Linking Corruption and Human Rights: an Unwelcome Addition to the Development Discourse' in Boersma, M, and Nelen, H (eds), *Corruption & Human Rights: Interdisciplinary Perspectives* (Intersentia, Belgium 2010)

Graber, CB, 'The New UNESCO Convention on Cultural Diversity: A Counterbalance to the WTO?' (2006) 9 JIEL 553

—— 'Substantive Rights and Obligations under the UNESCO Convention on Cultural Diversity' (NCCR Trade Working Paper 2008) <http://phase1.nccr-trade.org/images/stories/publications/Graber_maastricht_18.9.07.pdf>

Griffiths, B, *Invisible Barriers to Invisible Trade* (Macmillan, London 1975)

Grynberg, R, and Silva, S, 'Harmonization without Representation: Small States, the Basel Committee, and the WTO' (2006) 34 World Development 1123

Gupta, A, 'Peasants and Global Environmentalism' in Haenn, N and Wilk, RR (eds), *The Environment in Anthropology: A Reader in Ecology, Culture, and Sustainable Living* (New York University Press, New York, NY 2006)

Gupta, KR, *A Study of General Agreement on Tariffs and Trade* (S Chand, Delhi 1967)

Guzman, AT, 'Food Fears: Health and Safety at the WTO' (2004) 45 Virginia J of Intl L 1

Haas, PM, 'Introduction: Epistemic Communities and International Policy Coordination' (1992) 46 Intl Org 1

Habbard, AC, and Guiraud, M, *L'OMC et les droits de l'homme: une équation à résoudre: rapport de position* (FIDH, Paris 1999)

Haberler, G, Campos, R, Meade, JE, and Tinbergen, J, *Trends in International Trade: A report by a panel of experts* (GATT, Geneva 1958)

Hahn, M, 'A Clash of Cultures? The UNESCO Diversity Convention and International Trade Law' (2006) 9 JIEL 515

—— 'WTO Rules on Trade in Financial Services: A Victory of Greed over Reason?' in Grote, R, and Marauhn, T (eds), *The Regulation of International Financial Markets: Perspective for Reform* (CUP, Cambridge 2006)

Hall, PA and Taylor, RCR, 'Political Science and the Three New Institutionalisms' (1996) 44 Political Studies 936

Hansen, H, *America's Role in the World Economy* (WW Norton & Co, New York 1945)

Hansson, G, *Social clauses and international trade: an economic analysis of labour standards in trade policy* (Croom Helm, London 1983)

Hardin, A, and Holmes, L, *Services Trade and Foreign Direct Investment* (Australian Government Publication Service, Canberra 1997)

Harrison, J, *The Human Rights Impact of the World Trade Organization* (Hart Publishing, Oxford and Portland, OR 2007)

Hart, JA, *The New International Economic Order: Conflict and Cooperation in North-South Economic Relations* (Macmillan, London 1983)

Harvey, D, *A Brief History of Neoliberalism* (OUP, Oxford 2007)

Hasenclever, A, Mayer, P, and Rittberger, V, *Theories of International Regimes* (Cambridge Studies in International Relations: 55, CUP, New York 1997)

—— 'Integrating Theories of International Regimes' (2000) 26 Rev of Intl Studies 3

Helfer, LR, 'Constitutional Analogies in the International Legal System' (2003) 37 Loyola of Los Angeles L Rev 193

—— 'Regime Shifting: The TRIPs Agreement and New Dynamics of International Intellectual Property Lawmaking' (2004) 29 Yale J of Intl L 1

Henkin, L, *The Rights of Man Today* (Stevens and Sons, London 1979)

—— (ed), *The International Bill of Rights: The Covenant on Civil and Political Rights* (Columbia University Press, New York, NY 1981)

Herwig, A, 'Whither Science in WTO Dispute Settlement?' (2008) 21 Leiden J of Intl L 823

Hilf, M, 'Power, rules and principles: which orientation for WTO/GATT law?' (2001) 4 JIEL 111

Hill, H, 'From Nairobi to Beijing' in Mitchell, S, and Pradham, RD (eds), *Back to Basics from Beijing: An Australian Guide to the International Platform for Action* (Australian Council for Overseas Aid 1997)

Hill, T, 'UNCTAD and NGOs: A "Loyal Opposition"' <http://www.unsystem.org/ngls/english/factsheets/unctad_and_ngos.htm>

Hoekman, B, 'Tentative First Steps: An Assessment of the Uruguay Round Agreement on Services' (1995) World Bank Policy Research Working Paper No 1455

—— 'Assessing the General Agreement on Trade in Services' in Martin, W, and Winters, LA (eds), *The Uruguay Round and Developing Countries* (CUP, Cambridge 1996)

Horn, H, and Mavroïdis, PC, 'Economic and Legal Aspects of the Most Favoured Nation Clause' (2001) 17 European J of Political Economy 223

—— 'Still Hazy after All These Years: The Interpretation of National Treatment in the GATT/WTO Case-law on Tax Discrimination' (2004) 15 EJIL 39

Hoselitz, BF, 'Socialism, Communism and International Trade' (1949) 57 J of Political Economy 227

Howse, R, 'Democracy, Science, and Free Trade: Risk Regulation on Trial at the World Trade Organization' (2000) 98 Michigan L Rev 2329

—— 'From Politics to Technocracy—and Back Again: The Fate of the Multilateral Trading Regime' (2002) 96 AJIL 94

—— 'Montesquieu on Commerce, Conquest, War and Peace' (2006) 31 Brooklyn J Intl L 693

Howse, R, *Climate Mitigation Subsidies and the WTO Legal Framework: A Policy Analysis* (International Institute for Sustainable Development, Winnipeg 2010)

—— and Mutua, M, *Protecting Human Rights in a Global Economy: Challenges for the World Trade Organisation* (International Centre for Human Rights and Democratic Development, Montreal 2000) <https://www.dd-rd.ca/site/_PDF/publications/globalization/wto/protecting_human_rightsWTO.pdf>

—— and Nicolaïdis, K, 'Enhancing WTO Legitimacy: Constitutionalization or Global Subsidiarity?' (2003) 16 Governance 73

Hudec, RE, 'The GATT Legal System: A Diplomat's Jurisprudence' (1970) 4 J of World Trade L 615

—— *Adjudication of International Trade Disputes* (Trade Policy Research Centre, London 1978)

—— 'GATT Dispute Settlement after the Tokyo Round: An Unfinished Business' (1980) 13 Cornell Intl LJ 145

—— *The GATT Legal System and World Trade Diplomacy* (2nd edn, Butterworth Legal Publishers, Salem, NH 1990)

—— *Enforcing International Trade Law: The Evolution of the Modern GATT Legal System* (Butterworth Legal Publishers, Salem, NH 1993)

—— 'GATT/WTO Constraints on National Regulation: Requiem for an "Aim and Effects" Test' (1998) 32 Intl L 619

—— '"Like Products": The Differences in Meaning in GATT Articles I and III' in Cottier, T, and Mavroïdis, P (eds), *Regulatory Barriers and the Principle of Non-Discrimination in World Trade Law* (University of Michigan Press, Ann Arbor, MI 2000)

Human Rights Caucus, 'Statement of the Human Rights Caucus On the occasion of the Sixth Ministerial Conference of the World Trade Organization' (10 December 2005) <http://www.dd-rd.ca/site/_PDF/publications/globalization/wto/FINAL_WTO_HR_Caucus_Statement_English.pdf>

Humphrey, JP, 'The Universal Declaration of Human Rights: Its History, Impact and Juridical Character' in Ramcharan, BG (ed), *Human Rights: Thirty Years after the Universal Declaration* (Martinus Nijhoff, The Hague 1979)

—— *Human Rights and the United Nations: A Great Adventure* (Transnational Publishers, New York, NY 1984)

Humphreys, SJ, *Theatre of the Rule of Law* (CUP, Cambridge 2010)

Ikenberry, JG, 'A World Economy Restored: Expert Consensus and the Anglo-American Postwar Settlement' (1992) 46 Intl Org 289

INCHRITI, 'International NGO Committee on Human Rights in Trade and Investment: Policy Statement' (June 1998)

Indigenous Peoples' Organizations, 'Indigenous Peoples' Seattle Declaration' (NGO Position Paper 1999) <http://csdngo.igc.org/Indigenous/indig_seattle.htm>

International Centre for Human Rights and Democratic Development (Rights and Democracy), *Human Rights Impact Assessments for Foreign Investment Projects: Learning from Experiences in the Philippines, Tibet, the Democratic Republic of Congo, Argentina, and Peru* (ICHRDD, Montreal 2007) <http://www.dd-rd.ca/site/_PDF/publications/globalization/hria/full%20report_may_2007.pdf>

International Council on Human Rights Policy, 'Human Rights in the Global Economy: Report From a Colloquium' (2010) <http://www.ichrp.org/files/documents/185/210_human_rights_global_economy_colloquium_report.pdf>

International Federation for Human Rights, 'The WTO and human rights' (2001) <http://www.fidh.org/IMG/pdf/omc320a.pdf>

—— 'Understanding Global Trade & Human Rights' (Report for National Human Rights NGOs 2005) <http://www.un-ngls.org/orf/FIDH.pdf>

Iranzo, C, and Thanali Patruyo, P, 'Trade Unionism and Globalization: Thoughts from Latin America' (2002) 50 Current Sociology 57

Irwin, DA, 'The GATT in Historical Perspective' (1995) 85 American Economic Rev 323

—— Mavroïdis, PC, and Sykes, AO, *The Genesis of the GATT* (CUP, Cambridge 2008)

Ishay, MR, *The Human Rights Reader: Major Political Essays, Speeches and Documents from the Bible to the Present* (Routledge, London 1997)

—— *The History of Human Rights: From Ancient Times to the Globalization Era* (University of California Press, Berkeley, CA 2008)

Jackson, JH, *World trade and the law of GATT: a legal analysis of the General Agreement on Tariffs and Trade* (Bobbs-Merill, Indianapolis, IN 1969)

—— 'The Crumbling Institutions of the Liberal Trade System' (1978) 12 J of World Trade L 93

—— 'The Jurisprudence of International Trade: The DISC Case in GATT' (1978) 72 AJIL 747

—— 'Governmental Disputes in International Trade Relations: A Proposal in the Context of GATT' (1979) 13 J of World Trade L 1

—— 'The Birth of the GATT-MTN System: A Constitutional Appraisal' (1980) 12 L and Policy in Intl Business 21

—— *Implementing the Tokyo Round: National Constitutions and International Economic Rules* (University of Michigan Press, Ann Arbor, MI 1984)

—— 'Strengthening the International Legal Framework of the GATT MTN System: Reform Proposals for the New GATT Round' in Petersmann, E-U, and Hilf, M (eds), *The New GATT Round of Multilateral Trade Negotiations: Legal and Economic Problems* (Kluwer, Dordrecht 1988)

—— *Restructuring the GATT system* (Chatham House Papers, London 1990)

—— *The World Trading System: Law and Policy of International Economic Relations* (2nd edn, MIT Press, Cambridge, MA 1997)

—— 'The WTO "constitution" and proposed reforms: seven "mantras" revisited' (2001) 4 JIEL 67

Jarreau, JS, 'Interpreting the General Agreement on Trade in Services and the WTO Instruments Relevant to the International Trade of Financial Services' (1999) 25 North Carolina J of Intl L and Commercial Reg 1

Jessup, D, and Gordon, ME, 'Organizing in Export Processing Zones: The Bibong Experience in the Dominican Republic' in Gordon, ME, and Turner, L (eds), *Transnational Cooperation amongst Labor Unions* (Cornell University Press, Ithaca, NY 2000)

Johnston, H, and Almeida, P (eds), *Latin American Social Movements: Globalization, Democratization and Transnational Networks* (Rowman and Littlefield Publishers, Lanham, MD 2006)

Johnstone, I, 'Treaty Interpretation: The Authority of Interpretive Communities' (1990) 12 Michigan J Intl L 371

Junz, HB, 'Issues and Objectives of US Foreign Trade Policy' in *Issues and Objectives of U.S. Foreign Trade Policy* (Joint Economic Committee of Congress, Government Printing Office, Washington, DC 1967)

Juris, JS, *Networking Futures. The Movements Against Corporate Globalization* (Duke University Press, Durham, NC 2008)

Kalirajan, K, 'Restrictions on Trade in Distribution Services' (2000) Productivity Commission Staff Research Paper No 1638

Kazeki, J, 'Managing Request-Offer Negotiations under the GATS: The Case of Insurance Services' (4 November 2003) TD/TC/WP(2003)17/FINAL

Keck, ME, and Sikkink, K, *Activists Beyond Borders: Advocacy Networks in International Politics* (Cornell University Press, Ithaca, NY 1998)

Kelly, WB, Jr, 'Non-Tariff Barriers' in Balassa, BA and Kreinin, ME (eds), *Studies in International Trade Liberalization: Problems and Prospects for the Industrial Countries* (John Hopkins Press, Baltimore, MD 1967)

Kennedy, David, 'Turning to Market Democracy: A Tale of Two Architectures' (1991) 32 Harvard Intl LJ 373

—— 'The International Style in Postwar Law and Policy' (1994) 1 Utah L Rev 7

—— 'The Disciplines of International Law and Policy' (1999) 12 Leiden J of Intl L 9

—— 'The Forgotten Politics of International Governance' (2001) 2 European Human Rights L Rev 117

—— 'The Politics of the Invisible College: International Governance and the Politics of Expertise' (2001) 2 European Human Rights L Rev 463

—— 'The International Human Rights Movement: Part of the Problem?' (2002) 15 Harvard Human Rights J 101

—— *The Dark Sides of Virtue: Reassessing International Humanitarianism* (Princeton University Press, Princeton, NJ 2004)

—— 'Challenging Expert Rule: The Politics of Global Governance' (2005) 27 Sydney L Rev 1

—— 'The "Rule of Law," Political Choices, and Development Common Sense' in Trubek, DM, and Santos, A (eds), *The New Law and Economic Development: A Critical Appraisal* (CUP, Cambridge 2006)

Kennedy, Duncan, 'Three Globalizations of Law and Legal Thought: 1850–2000' in Trubek, DM, and Santos, A (eds), *The New Law and Economic Development: A Critical Appraisal* (CUP, Cambridge 2006)

Kenwood, G, and Lougheed, A, *Growth of the International Economy 1820–2000* (Routledge, London 1999)

Keohane, RO, *After Hegemony: Cooperation and Discord in the World Political Economy* (Princeton University Press, Princeton, NJ 1984)

—— and Nye, Joseph S, *Power and Interdependence: World Politics in Transition* (Little, Brown and Company, Boston, MA 1977)

—— and Nye, JS, 'The Club Model of Multilateral Cooperation and Problems of Legitimacy' in Porter, RB et al (eds), *Efficiency, Equity, and Legitimacy: The Multilateral Trading System at the Millennium* (Brookings Institution Press, Washington, DC 2001)

Key, SJ, 'Financial Services in the Uruguay Round and the WTO' (1997) Group of Thirty Occasional Paper 54

—— *The Doha Round and Financial Services Negotiations* (American Enterprise Institute Press, Washington, DC 2003)

Khagram, S, Riker, JV, and Sikkink, K (eds), *Restructuring World Politics: Transnational Social Movements, Networks and Norms* (University of Minnesota Press, Minneapolis, MN 2002)

Kimura, F, Ando, M, and Fujii, T, 'Estimating the Ad Valorem Equivalent of Barriers to Foreign Direct Investment in the Telecommunication Services Sectors in Russia' (2004) World Bank Policy Paper

Kindleberger, CP, 'The Rise of Free Trade in Western Europe' (1975) 35 J of Econ History 20

Kingsbury, B, 'The Administrative Law Frontier in Global Governance' (2005) 99 Proceedings of the Annual Meeting (American Society of International Law) 143

Kinley, D, *Civilising Globalisation: Human Rights and the Global Economy* (CUP, Cambridge 2009)

Knight, NG, 'Section 337 and the GATT: A Necessary Protection or an Unfair Trade Practice?' (1988) Georgia J of Intl and Comp L 47

Kock, K, *International trade policy and the GATT: 1947–1967* (Almqvist & Wiksell, Stockholm 1969)

Kolb, F, 'The Impact of Transnational Protest on Social Movement Organizations: Mass Media and the Making of ATTAC Germany' in della Porta, D, and Tarrow, SG (eds), *Transnational Protest and Global Activism* (Rowman and Littlefield Publishers, Oxford 2005)

Kolben, K, 'Labor Rights as Human Rights?' (2010) 50 Virginia J Intl L 449

Kono, M, and Schuknecht, L, 'Financial Services Trade, Capital Flows, and Financial Stability' (1998) WTO Staff Working Paper ERAD-98-12

Korzeniewicz, RP, and Smith, WC, *Protest and Collaboration: Transnational Civil Society Networks and the Politics of Summitry and Free Trade in the Americas* (North-South Center Press, University of Miami, FL 2001)

Koskenniemi, M, 'Constitutionalism as Mindset: Reflection on Kantian Themes About International Law and Globalization' (2007) 8 Theoretical Inquiries in L 9

Kostecki, MM, *East-West trade and the GATT System* (Macmillan for the Trade Policy Research Centre, London 1979)

Kothari, M, and Prove, P, 'The Sub-Commission and Globalization: Guest Editorial' (1998) 5 Human Rights Tribune 5

—— and Krause, T, 'Human Rights or Corporate Rights? The MAI Challenge' (1998) 5 Human Rights Tribune 17

Krisch, N, 'Pluralism in Postnational Risk Regulation: The Dispute over GMOs and Trade' (2010) 1 Transnational Legal Theory 1

Krommenacker, RJ, 'Trade Related Services and GATT' (1979) 13 J of World Trade L 510

Krueger, AO, 'Trade Policy and Economic Development: How We Learn' (1997) 87 American Econ Rev 1

Kunnemann, R, 'The Extraterritorial Scope of the International Covenant on Economic, Social and Cultural Rights' (2001) <http://www.fian.org/resources/documents/others/extraterritorial-state-obligations-international-covenant-on-economic-social-and-cultural-rights>

—— and Hausmann, U, 'Germany's extraterritorial human rights obligations' (2006) <http://www.fian.org/resources/documents/others/germanys-extraterritorial-human-rights-obligations>

Lang, ATF, 'Reflecting on Linkage: Cognitive and Institutional Change in the International Trading System' (2007) 70 MLR 523

—— and Scott, J, 'The Hidden World of WTO Governance' (2009) 20 EJIL 575

Laxer, G, 'The Defeat of the Multilateral Agreement on Investment: National Movements Confront Globalization' in Laxer, G, and Halperin, S (eds), *Global Civil Society and Its Limits* (Palgrave Macmillan, Basingstoke 2003)

Leary, VA, 'The Effect of Western Perspectives on International Human Rights' in An-Na'im, AA, and Deng, FM (eds), *Human Rights in Africa: Cross-Cultural Perspectives* (Brookings Institution Press, Washington, DC 1990)

—— 'The WTO and the Social Clause: Post Singapore' (1997) 1 EJIL 118

LeBlanc, LJ, 'Economic, Social, and Cultural Rights and the Inter American System' (1977) 19 J of Interamerican Studies and World Affairs 61

Leite, JC, *The World Social Forum: Strategies of Resistance* (Haymarket Books, Chicago, IL 2005)

Leroux, EH, 'Trade in Financial Services Under the World Trade Organization' (2002) 36 J of World Trade 413

—— 'Eleven Years of GATS Case Law: What Have We Learned?' (2007) 10 JIEL 749

Lim, AH, 'Trade and Human Rights: What's at Issue?' (2001) 35 J of World Trade 275

Lipson, C, 'The Transformation of Trade: The Sources and Effects of Regime Change' (1982) 36 Intl Org 417

Locke, J, *The Second Treatise on Civil Government* [1690] (Prometheus Books, Buffalo, NY 1986)

Long, O, *Law and Its Limitations in the GATT Multilateral Trading System* (Martinus Nijhoff, Dordrecht 1985)

Mably, P, 'Centralized Production: The Group of 33' in Tussie, D (ed), *The Politics of Trade: The Role of Research in Trade Policy and Negotiation* (Brill Academic Publishers, Boston, MA 2009)

MacDonald, L, 'Globalization and Social Movements: Comparing Women's Movements' Responses to NAFTA in Mexico, the USA and Canada' (2002) 4 Intl Feminist J of Politics 151

—— 'Gendering Transnational Social Movement Analysis: Women's Groups Contest Free Trade in the Americas' in Bandy, J, and Smith, J (eds), *Coalitions Across Borders: Transnational Protest and Neoliberal Order* (Rowman and Littlefield Publishers, Lanham, MD 2005)

Macrory, PFJ, Appleton, AE, and Plummer, MG (eds), *The World Trade Organization: Legal, Economic and Political Analysis* (Springer, New York 2005)

Malmgren, HB, 'The Border Tax Problem: Tax Harmonization in Europe and U.S. Business' (1969) XVII Canadian Tax J 34

Mander, J, and Tauli-Corpuz, V (eds), *Paradigm Wars: Indigenous Peoples' Resistance to Economic Globalization* (1st edn, Sierra Club Books, San Francisco, CA 2005)

Marceau, G, 'A Call for Coherence in International Law: Praise for prohibition against "Clinical Isolation" in WTO Dispute Settlement' (1999) 33 J of World Trade L 87

—— 'WTO Dispute Settlement and Human Rights' (2002) 13 EJIL 753

—— 'Trade and Labour' in Bethlehem, D et al (eds), *The Oxford Handbook of International Trade Law* (OUP, Oxford 2009)

—— and Trachtman, JP, 'The Technical Barriers to Trade Agreement, the Sanitary and Phytosanitary Measures Agreement, and The General Agreement on Tariffs and Trade: A Map of the World Trade Organization Law of Domestic Regulation of Goods' (2002) 36 J of World Trade 811

Marconini, M, 'The Uruguay Round Negotiations on Services' in Messerlin, PA, and Sauvant, K (eds), *The Uruguay Round: Services in the World Economy* (The World Bank, Washington, DC 1990)

Marko, M, 'An Evaluation of the Basic Telecommunications Service Agreement' (1998) Centre for Intl Econ Studies Discussion Paper No 98/09

Marouani, MA, and Munro, L, 'Assessing Barriers to Trade in Services in the MENA Region' (2009) OECD Trade Policy Working Paper No 84

Massel, MS, *Non-tariff barriers as an obstacle to world trade* (Brookings Institution, Washington, DC 1965)

Mattoo, A, 'Financial Services and the WTO: Liberalization in the Developing and Transition Economies' (16 March 1998) *African Economic Research Consortium Preliminary Draft* <http://www.aercafrica.org/documents/stnadocs/FinServMattoo.pdf>

—— 'Services in a Development Round: Three Goals and Three Proposals' (2005) 39 J of World Trade 1223
—— and Arvind Subramanian, A, 'Regulatory Autonomy and Multilateral Disciplines: The Dilemma and a Possible Resolution' (1998) 1 JIEL 303
—— and Sauvé, P (eds), *Domestic Regulation and Service Trade Liberalization* (OUP and The World Bank, Washington, DC 2003)
Mavroïdis, P, 'Das GATT als self-contained Regime' (1991) 6 Recht der International Wirtschaft 497
M'Baye, K, 'Le droit au developpement comme un droit de l'homme' (1972) 5 *Revue des Droits de L'Homme* 505
McCrudden, C, 'International economic law and the pursuit of human rights: a framework for discussion of the legality of "selective purchasing" laws under the WTO Government Procurement Agreement' (1999) 2 JIEL 3
McDorman, TL, 'International Trade Law Meets International Fisheries Law: The Canada-U.S. Salmon and Herring Dispute' (1990) 7 Intl Arbitration 107
McGuire, G, 'Australia's Restrictions on Trade in Financial Services' (1998) Staff Research Paper, Australian Productivity Commission
Mehra, M (ed), *Human Rights and Economic Globalisation: Directions for the WTO* (Global Publications Foundation, Uppsala, Sweden 1999)
Mehta, P, and Davison, A, *Trading up: The GATT agreement and developing countries* (International Organisation of Consumers Unions, London 1993)
Meyer, WH, 'Human Rights and MNC's: Theory Versus Quantitative Analysis' (1996) 18 HRQ 368
—— *Human Rights and International Political Economic in Third World Nations: Multinational Corporations, Foreign Aid, and Repression* (Praeger, Westport, CT 1998)
Mill, JS, *On Liberty* (Penguin Classics, Harmondsworth 1982)
Milner, H, 'The Political Economy of International Trade' (1999) 2 Annual Rev of Political Science 91
Mitrany, D, *A Working Peace System* (Quadrangle Books, Chicago, IL 1966)
Modak-Truran, MC, 'Section 337 and GATT in the Akzo Controversy' (1988) 9 Northwestern J of Intl L and Business 382
Montesquieu, C de, *The Spirit of Laws* [1750] (Collier Press, New York, NY 1990)
Morsink, J, 'Inherent Human Rights: The Philosophy of the Universal Declaration' (1984) 6 HRQ 309
Mourra, MH, 'Privatization of Water Management in Latin America' in Carbonneau, TE, and Mourra, MH (eds), *Latin American Investment Treaty Arbitration: The Controversies and Conflicts* (Kluwer Law International, Dordrecht 2008)
Munck, R, *Globalization and Contestation: The New Great Counter-Movement* (Routledge, New York, NY 2005)
Murray, J, 'The GATT negotiations: A statement from BEUC' (Paper presented at the 13th World Congress of the International Organization of Consumer Unions, 8 July 1991)
Mutua, MW, 'The Ideology of Human Rights' (1996) 36 Virginia J of Intl L 589
—— 'Human Rights and Powerlessness: Pathologies of Choice and Substance' (2008) 56 Buffalo L Rev 1027
Mutua, MW, 'The Transformation of Africa: A Critique of the Rights Discourse' in Gomez Isa, F, and De Feyter, K (eds), *Human Rights and Diversity: International Human Rights Law in a Global Context* (University of Deusto, Bilbao 2009)
Nader, N et al, *The Case Against 'Free Trade': GATT, NAFTA, and the Globalization of Corporate Power* (Earth Island Press, San Francisco, CA 1993)

National Farmers Union, 'The National Farmers Union: Fighting for the family farm over 30 years' (2001) <http://www.nfu.ca/nfuhistory3.pdf >

Nedelsky, J, 'Communities of Judgment and Human Rights' (2000) 1 Theoretical Enquiries in Law 245

Neeley, JS, and Ishida, H, 'Section 337 and National Treatment under GATT: A Proposal for Legislative Reform' (1989) 13 Fordham Intl LJ 276

Neumann, J, and Türk, E, 'Necessity Revisited: Proportionality in World Trade Organization Law After Korea-Beef, EC-Asbestos and EC-Sardines' (2003) 37 J of World Trade 199

Nguyen-Hong, D, 'Restrictions on Trade in Professional Services' (2000) *Productivity Commission Staff Research Paper*, AusInfo, Canberra

Nielson, J, and Taglioni, D, 'Services Trade Liberalisation: Identifying Opportunities and Gains' (2004) OECD Trade Policy Working Paper No 1 (TD/TC/WP(2003)23/FINAL and TD/TC/WP(2003)25/FINAL)

Noakes, JA, and Johnston, F, 'Frames of Protest: A Road Map to a Perspective' in Johnston, H, and Noakes, JA (eds), *Frames of Protest: Social Movements and the Framing Perspective* (Rowman and Littlefield Publishers, Lanham, MD 2005)

Nordås, HK, Pinali, E, and Geloso Grosso, M, 'Logistics and Time as a Trade Barrier' (30 May 2006) OECD Trade Policy Working Paper No 35 (TD/TC/WP(2006)3/FINAL)

O'Brien, R et al, *Contesting Global Governance: Multilateral Economic Institutions and Global Social Movements* (CUP, Cambridge 2000)

Odell, JS (ed), *Negotiating Trade: Developing Countries in the WTO and NAFTA* (CUP, Cambridge 2006)

OECD, *Quantifying the Benefits of Liberalising Trade in Services* (OECD, Paris 2003)

Office of the High Commissioner for Human Rights, 'Record of the Workshop on International Trade, Investment and Finance and Economic, Social and Cultural Rights' (6 May 2000) <http://www.unhchr.ch/tbs/doc.nsf/0/11d06750ac4e7acbc125691f002f01f0?Opendocument>

Orford, A, 'Contesting Globalization: A Feminist Perspective on the Future of Human Rights' (1998) 8 Transnational L & Contemporary Problems 171

—— and Beard, J, 'Making the State Safe for the Market: The World Bank's World Development Report 1997' (1998) 22 Melbourne University LR 195

Paasch, A, Garbers, F, and Hirsch, T (eds), *Trade Policies and Hunger: The Impact of Trade Liberalisation on the Right to Food of Rice Farming Communities in Ghana, Honduras and Indonesia* (Geneva, EAA 2007)

Pacific Economic and Cooperation Council, *Survey of Impediments to Trade and Investment in the APEC Region: A Report by the Pacific Economic Cooperation Council for APEC* (PECC, Singapore 1995)

Paine, T, *Rights of Man* [1791] (Penguin Books, Baltimore, MD 1969)

Palmeter, D, and Mavroïdis, PC, *Dispute Settlement in the World Trade Organization: Practice and Procedure* (2nd edn, CUP, Cambridge 2004)

Panourgias, LE, *Banking Regulation and World Trade Law: GATS, EU and Prudential Institution-Building* (Hart Publishing, Oxford 2006)

Pauwelyn, J, 'The Role of Public International Law in the WTO: How Far Can We Go?' (2001) 95 AJIL 535

—— *Conflict of Norms in Public International Law: How WTO Law Relates to Other Rules of International Law* (CUP, Cambridge 2004)

—— 'The Transformation of World Trade' (2005) 104 Michigan L Rev 1

—— 'Expert Advice in WTO Dispute Settlement' in Bermann, GA, and Mavroïdis, PC (eds), *Trade and Human Health and Safety* (CUP, Cambridge 2006)

Pearson, CS, 'Free Trade, Fair Trade? The Reagan Accord' in Pearson, CS, and Riedel, J (eds), *The Direction of Trade Policy: Papers in Honor of Isaiah Frank* (Basil Blackwell, Oxford 1990)

—— and Riedel, J (eds), *The Direction of Trade Policy: Papers in Honor of Isaiah Frank* (Basil Blackwell, Oxford 1990)

Peat, Marwick, Mitchell, *A Typology of Trade Barriers to International Services Industries* (EC Commission, Brussels 1986)

Peel, J, *Science and Risk Regulation in International Law* (CUP, Cambridge 2010)

Petersmann, EU, 'International and European Foreign Trade Law: GATT Dispute Settlement Proceedings Against the EEC' (1985) 22 CMLR 441

—— 'Trade Policy as a Constitutional Problem: On the "Domestic Policy Functions" of International Trade Rules' (1986) 41 Swiss Rev Intl Econ Rel 405

—— 'The WTO Constitution and Human Rights' (2000) 3 JIEL 19

—— 'Time for a United Nations "Global Compact" for Integrating Human Rights into the Law of Worldwide Organizations: Lessons from European Integration' (2002) 13 EJIL 621

Pettifor, A, 'The economic bondage of debt—and the birth of a new movement' in Amoore, L, *The Global Resistance Reader* (Routledge, New York, NY 2005)

Phillips, JC, 'Border Tax Adjustments in International Trade' (1976) 9 University of Queensland LJ 151

Physicians for a Smoke-Free Canada, 'Trade Agreements and Tobacco Use' (Submission to the WHO, 2000) <http://www.smoke-free.ca/pdf_1/pscsubmission.pdf>

Plant, R, *The Neo-Liberal State* (OUP, Oxford 2010)

Pocock, JGA, *Virtue, Commerce, and History: Essays on Political Thought and History, Chiefly in the Eighteenth Century* (CUP, Cambridge 1985)

Polanyí, K, *Origins of our time: the great transformation* (V Gollancz, London 1945)

Prebisch, R, *Towards a New Trade Policy for Development: Report by the Secretary-General of the United Nation's Conference on Trade and Development* (United Nations, New York, NY 1964)

Preeg, EH, *Traders and diplomats: an analysis of the Kennedy Round of negotiations under the General Agreement on Tariffs and Trade* (Brookings Institution, Washington, DC 1970)

—— *Traders in a Brave New World: The Uruguay Round and the Future of the International Trading System* (University of Chicago Press, Chicago, IL 1995)

Qureshi, AH, 'The Cartagena Protocol on Biosafety and the WTO—Co-Existence or Incoherence?' (2000) 49 ICLQ 835

Randel, J, *NGO Campaigning on Trade Issues: Perspectives from Europe* (Development Initiatives for Christian Aid and CIIR, London 1995)

Randhawa, PS, 'Punta del Este and After: Negotiations on Trade in Services and the Uruguay Round' (1987) 21 J of World Trade L 163

Regan, DH, 'The Meaning of "Necessary" in GATT Article XX and GATS Article XIV: The Myth of Cost-Benefit Balancing' (2007) 6 World Trade Rev 347

Reich, A, 'From Diplomacy to Law: The Juridicization of International Trade Relations' (1997) 17 Northwestern J of Intl L and Business 775

Reubens, EP (ed), *The Challenge of the New International Economic Order* (Westview Press, Boulder, CO 1981)

Reyna, RV, 'Services' in Stewart, TP (ed), *The GATT Uruguay Round: A Negotiating History* (*Vol II: Commentary*, Kluwer, The Hague 1999)

Richardson, JB, 'What Really Happened at Punta del Este: Understanding the Framework of the Uruguay Round' in Riddle, D (ed), *Toward an International Service and Information Economy* (Friedrich Ebert Foundation, Bonn 1987)

Ritchie, M, 'Cross-border Organizing' in Mander, J, and Goldsmith, E (eds), *The Case Against the Global Economy: And for a Turn Toward the Local* (Sierra Club Books, San Francisco, CA 1996)

Rivera-Torres, O, 'The Biosafety Protocol and the WTO' (2003) 26 Boston College Intl and Comparative L Rev 263

Robinson, M, 'Shaping Globalization: The Role of Human Rights' (2003) 97 Proceedings of the Annual Meeting (American Society of International Law) 1

Rodrik, D, *Has Globalization Gone Too Far?* (Institute for International Economics, Washington, DC 1997)

Roemer, R, Taylor, A, and Lariviere, J, 'Origins of the WHO Framework Convention on Tobacco Control' (2005) 95 American J of Public Health 936

Roepke, W, 'Economic Order and International Law' (1954) 86 Recueil des Cours 203

Rohlfs, JH, and Sidak, JG, 'Exporting Telecommunications Regulation: The U.S.-Japan Negotiations on Interconnection Pricing' (2002) 43 Harvard Intl LJ 317

Roll, E, *A History of Economic Thought* (5th edn, Faber, London 1992)

Roosevelt, FD, State of the Union Message on January 6, 1941, reprinted in (1941) 87 Cong Rec 44

Rootes, C, and Saunders, C, 'The Global Justice Movement in Great Britain' in della Porta, D (ed), *The Global Justice Movement: Cross-national and Transnational Perspectives* (Paradigm Publishers, Boulder, CO 2007)

Ross, RJS, 'From Anti-Sweatshop, to Global Justice, to Anti-War: Student Participation in Globalization Protests' in Podobnik, B, and Reifer, T (eds), *Transforming Globalization: Challenges and Opportunities in the Post 9/11 Era* (Brill, Boston, MA 2005)

Rosset, P, Patel, PR, and Courville, M (eds), *Promised Land: Competing Visions of Agrarian Reform* (Food First, Canada 2006)

Routledge, P, and Cumbers, A, *Global Justice Networks: Geographies of transnational solidarity* (Manchester University Press, Manchester 2009)

Rubin, SJ, 'Economic and Social Human Rights and the New International Economic Order' (1986) 1 American University J of Intl L & Policy 67

Ruggie, JG, 'International Responses to Technology' (1975) 29 Intl Org 557

—— 'International Regimes, Transactions and Change: Embedded Liberalism in the Post-war Economic Order' (1982) 36 Intl Org 379

—— 'Embedded Liberalism Revisited: Institutions and Progress in International Economic Relations' in Adler, E, and Crawford, B (eds), *Progress in Postwar International Relations* (Columbia University Press, New York, NY 1991)

Ruggiero, V, '"Attac": A Global Social Movement?' (2002) 29 Social Justice 48

Saffrin, S, 'Treaties in Collision? The Biosafety Protocol and the World Trade Organization Agreements' (2002) 96 AJIL 606

Sauvé, P, and Steinfatt, K, 'Financial Services and the WTO: What Next?' in Litan, RE, Masson, P, and Pomerleano, M (eds), *Open Doors: Foreign Participation in Financial Systems in Developing Countries* (The World Bank Group, the International Monetary Fund and the Brookings Institution Press, Washington, DC 2001)

—— 'Completing the GATS Framework: Addressing Uruguay Round Leftovers' (2002) 57 Aussenwirtschaft 301

Schattschneider, EE, *Politics, Pressures and the Tariff: A Study of Free Private Enterprise in Pressure Politics, As Shown in the 1929–1930 Revision of the Tariff* (Prentice-Hall, New York, NY 1935)

Schneiderman, D, 'Habermas, Market-Friendly Human Rights, and the Revisibility of Economic Globalization' (2004) 8 Citizenship Studies 419

Scott, C, and Macklem, P, 'Constitutional Ropes of Sand or Justiciable Guarantees? Social Rights in a New South African Constitution' (1992) 141 University of Pennsylvania L Rev 1

Scott, J, 'On Kith and Kine (and Crustaceans): Trade and Environment in the EU and WTO' in Weiler, JHH (ed), *The EU, The WTO and the NAFTA: Towards a Common Law of International Trade?* (OUP, Oxford 2000)

—— 'European Regulation GMOs and the WTO' (2003) 9 Columbia J of European L 213

Seoane, J, and Taddei, E, 'From Seattle to Porto Alegre: The Anti-Neoliberal Globalization' (2002) 50 Current Sociology 99

Shaffer, ER, Brenner, JE, and Houston, TP, 'International trade agreements: a threat to tobacco control policy' (2005) 14(Supplement 2) Tobacco Control ii19

Shaffer, GC, 'The Nexus of Law and Politics: The WTO's Committee on Trade and Environment' in Steinberg, RH (ed), *The Greening of Trade Law: International Trade Organizations and Environmental Issues* (Rowman and Littlefield Publishers, Lanham, MD 2002)

—— *Defending Interests: Public-Private Partnerships in WTO Litigation* (The Brookings Institution, Washington, DC 2003)

——, Sanchez Badin, MR, and Rosenberg, B, 'The Trials of Winning at the WTO: What Lies Behind Brazil's Success' (2008) 41 Cornell Intl LJ 383

Shelp, RK, *Beyond Industrialization: Ascendancy of the Global Service Economy* (Praeger, New York, NY 1981)

—— 'Trade in Services' (1986–7) 65 Foreign Policy 64

Shiva, V, 'The effects of the WTO on women's rights' (1995) <http://www.twnside.org.sg/title/women-ch.htm>

—— *Protect or plunder?: understanding intellectual property rights* (Zed Books, London 2001)

Sherman, LB, '"Wildly Enthusiastic" About the First Multilateral Agreement on Trade in Telecommunications Services' (1999) 51 Federal Communications LJ 61

Shue, H, *Basic Rights: Subsistence, Affluence, and U.S. Foreign Policy* (Princeton University Press, Princeton, NJ 1980)

Siegel, RL, 'Socioeconomic Rights: Past and Future' (1985) 7 HRQ 255

Sinclair, S, *GATS: how the World Trade Organization's new "services" negotiations threaten democracy* (Canadian Centre for Policy Alternatives, Ottawa 2000)

—— *The GATS Implications for Postal Services* (Canadian Centre for Policy Alternatives, Ottawa 2001)

—— and Grieshaber-Otto, G, *Facing the Facts: A Guide to the GATS debates* (Canadian Center for Policy Alternatives, Ottawa 2002)

Singh, S, 'U.N. Human Rights Commissioner Responds to the WTO' (29 August 2000) <http://www.twnside.org.sg/title/responds.htm>

Skogly, SI, and Gibney, M, 'Transnational Human Rights Obligations' (2002) 24 HRQ 781

Smith, JF, 'NAFTA and Human Rights: A Necessary Linkage' (1994) 27 UC Davies L Rev 793

Sorsa, P, 'The GATS Agreement on Financial Services: A Modest Start to Multilateral Liberalization' (1997) IMF Working Paper No 97/55

Srinivasan, TN, 'Nondiscrimination in GATT/WTO: Was there Anything to Begin with and is there Anything Left?' (2005) 4 World Trade Rev 69

Stammers, N, 'Social Movements and the Social Construction of Human Rights' (1999) 21 HRQ 980

Starr, A, *Naming the Enemy: Anti-Corporate Movements Confront Globalization* (Zed Books, London 2000)

Steinberg, RH, 'Judicial Lawmaking at the WTO: Discursive, Constitutional, and Political Constraints' (2004) 98 AJIL 247

—— 'The Hidden World of WTO Governance: A Reply to Andrew Lang and Joanne Scott' (2009) 20 EJIL 1063

Stern, RM, 'Quantifying Barriers to Trade in Services' in Hoekman, BM, English, P, and Mattoo, A (eds), *Development, Trade and the WTO: A Handbook* (The World Bank, Washington, DC 2002)

Stewart, RB, and Sanchez Badin, MR, 'The World Trade Organization and Global Administrative Law' (2009) Institute for International Law and Justice, New York University School of Law Working Paper <http://www.iilj.org/publications/documents/2009–7.StewartRatton-Sanchez.pdf>

Stewart, TP (ed), *The GATT Uruguay Round: Negotiating History (1986–1992), Vol 2: Commentary* (Kluwer Law International, The Hague 1999)

Stiglitz, JE, 'A New Agenda for Global Warming' (2006) 3 The Economists' Voice Article 3

Sunstein, CR, *One Case at a Time: Judicial Minimalism on the Supreme Court* (Harvard University Press, Cambridge, MA 1999)

Swenarchuk, M, *From Global to Local: GATS Impacts on Canadian Municipalities* (Canadian Center for Policy Alternatives, Ottawa 2002)

Szabo, I, 'Historical Foundations of Human Rights and Subsequent Developments' in Vasak, K, and Alston, P (eds), *The International Dimensions of Human Rights* (Greenwood Press, Westport, CT 1982)

Tarasofsky, R, 'The WTO Committee on Trade and Environment: Is it making a Difference?' (1999) 3 Max Planck Ybk of United Nations L 471

—— and Palmer, A, 'The WTO in crisis: lessons learned from the Doha negotiations on the environment' (2006) 82 Intl Affairs 899

Tarullo, DK, 'Logic, Myth and the International Economic Order' (1985) 26 Harvard Intl LJ 553

—— 'Beyond Normalcy in the Regulation of International Trade' (1987) 100 Harvard L Rev 546

Taylor, A, and Thomas, C (eds), *Global Trade and Global Social Issues* (Routledge Press, New York, NY 1999)

—— and Bettcher, DW, 'WHO Framework Convention on Tobacco Control: A Global "Good" for Public Health' (2000) 78 Bulletin of the World Health Organization 920

Teubner, G, 'Substantive and Reflexive Elements in Modern Law' (1983) 17 L & Society Rev 239

Tolley, H, Jr, *The U.N. Commission on Human Rights* (Westview Press, Boulder, CO 1987)

—— *The International Commission of Jurists: Global Advocates for Human Rights* (University of Pennsylvania Press, Philadelphia, PA 1994)

Trachtman, JP, 'Transcending "Trade and . . ."—an Institutional Perspective' (2002) 96 AJIL 77

'Trading Away Human Rights? The Role of the WTO' (Announcement about a Human Rights Teach-In on 30 November 1999) <http://www.hrea.org/lists/hr-education/markup/msg00062.html>

Trebilcock, MJ, and Soloway, J, 'International Trade Policy and Domestic Food Safety Regulation: The Case for Substantial Deference by the WTO Dispute Settlement Body under the SPS Agreement' in Kennedy, DLM, and Southwick, JD (eds), *The Political Economy of International Trade Law* (CUP, Cambridge 2002)

Tribe, LH, 'The Puzzling Persistence of Process-Based Constitutional Theories' (1980) 89 Yale LJ 1063

Trolliet, C, and Hegarty, J, 'Regulatory Reform and Trade Liberalization in Accountancy Services' in Mattoo, A, and Sauvé, P (eds), *Domestic Regulation and Service Trade Liberalization* (OUP and The World Bank, Washington, DC 2003)

Trubek, DM, and Santos, A (eds), *The New Law and Economic Development: A Critical Appraisal* (CUP, Cambridge 2006)

Tussie, D (ed), *The Politics of Trade: The Role of Research in Trade Policy and Negotiation* (Brill Academic Publishers, Boston, MA 2009)

Tuthill, L, 'The GATS and New Rules for Regulators' (1997) 21 Telecommunications Policy 783

UNCTAD V, *Multilateral Trade Negotiations: Evaluation and Further Recommendations Arising Therefrom* (UNCTAD, Manila 1979)

Unger, RM, *Free Trade Reimagined: The World Division of Labor and the Method of Economics* (Princeton University Press, Princeton, NJ 2010)

UN Non-Governmental Liaison Service, United Nations Conference on Trade and Development (UNCTAD) (1999) <http://www.un-ngls.org/orf/documents/publications.en/ngls.handbook/a14uncta.htm>

United States Department of the Treasury, *National Treatment Study* (Treasury Department, Washington, DC 1998)

United States Trade Representative, *2009 National Trade Estimate Report on Foreign Trade Barriers* (Office of the United States Trade Representative, Washington, DC 2009)

Uvin, P, *Human Rights and Development* (Kumarian Press, Bloomfield, CT 2004)

—— 'From the Right to Development to the Rights-based Approach: How "Human Rights" Entered Development' (2007) 17 Development in Practice 597

van den Bossche, P, 'Looking for Proportionality in WTO Law' (2008) 35 Legal Issues of Economic Integration 283

van Roozendaal, G, *Trade Unions & Global Governance: The Debate on a Social Clause* (Continuum, London 2002)

Vasak, K, 'A 30-year Struggle: The Sustained Efforts to Give Force of Law to the Universal Declaration of Human Rights' (1977) 30 UNESCO Courier 28

Verhoosel, G, *National Treatment and WTO Dispute Settlement: Adjudicating the Boundaries of Regulatory Autonomy* (Hart Publishing, Oxford 2002)

Vincent, RJ, *Human Rights and International Relations* (CUP, Cambridge 2001)

Viner, J, 'Conflicts of Principle in Drafting a Trade Charter' (1947) 25 Foreign Affairs 612

von Bogdandy, A, 'Legitimacy of International Economic Governance: Interpretive Approaches to WTO law and the Prospects of its Proceduralization' in Griller, S (ed) *International Economic Governance and Non-economic Concerns* (Springer-Verlag, Vienna 2003)

Voon, T, 'UNESCO and the WTO: A Clash of Cultures?' (2006) 55 ICLQ 635

Wacquant, LJD, 'Toward a Social Praxeology: The Structure and Logic of Bourdieu's Sociology' in Bourdieu, P, and Wacquant, LJD, *An Introduction to Reflexive Sociology* (Polity Press, Cambridge 1992)

Wade, R, 'Greening the Bank: The Struggle over the Environment 1970-1995' in Kapur, D, Lewis, JP, and Webb, R (eds), *The World Bank: Its First Half Century* (Vol 2, RR Donnelley and Sons Co, Crawfordsville, IN 1997)

Wai, R, 'Countering, Branding, Dealing: Using Economic and Social Rights in and around the International Trade Regime' (2003) 14 EJIL 35

Walker, TC, 'Two Faces of Liberalism: Kant, Paine, and the Question of Intervention' (2008) 52 Intl Studies Q 449

Walker, VR, 'Keeping the WTO from Becoming the "World Trans-science Organization": Scientific Uncertainty, Science Policy, and Factfinding in the Growth Hormones Dispute' (1998) 31 Cornell Intl LJ 251

Walton, J, 'Debt, Protest, and the State in Latin America' in Eckstein, S (ed), *Power and Popular Protest: Latin American Social Movements* (University of California Press, Los Angeles, CA 1989)

—— and Seddon, D (eds), *Free Markets & Food Riots: The Politics of Global Adjustment* (Blackwell, Oxford 1994)

Warner, M, 'Globalization and Human Rights: An Economic Model' (1999) 25 Brooklyn J of Intl L 99

Watkins, K, and Windfuhr, M, *Agriculture in the Uruguay Round: Implications for Sustainable Development in Developing Countries* (WWF Discussion Paper, Gland, Switzerland 1995)

Weiler, JHH, 'The Rule of Lawyers and the Ethos of Diplomats: Reflections on the Internal and External Legitimacy of WTO' (2001) 35 J of World Trade 191

Weinrichter, N, 'Perspectives on the changing spirit of GATT' (1999) 3 European Integration Online Papers <http://eiop.or.at/eiop/pdf/1999-010.pdf>

Weintraub, S, 'Border Tax Adjustments and the GATT' (1965) 17 Tax Executive 304

Weiss, C, 'The Many Meanings of Research Utilization' (1979) 39(5) Public Administration Review 426

Weiss, F, Denters, E, and de Waart, P (eds), *International Economic Law with a Human Face* (Kluwer Law International, The Hague 1998)

Weissbrodt, D, and Schoff, K, 'Human Rights Approach to Intellectual Property Protection; The Genesis and Application of Sub-Commission Resolution 2000/7' (2003) 5 Minnesota Intellectual Property Rev 1

Weston, BH, 'Human Rights' (1984) 6 HRQ 257

Whalley, J, 'Assessing the Benefits to Developing Countries of Liberalisation in Services Trade' (2004) 27 The World Economy 1223

WHO and WTO Secretariat, 'WTO Agreements & Public Health' (2002) <http://www.wto.org/english/res_e/booksp_e/who_wto_e.pdf>

Wilcox, C, *A Charter for World Trade* (Arno Press, New York, NY 1972)

Wilkinson, MD, 'Lobbying for Fair Trade: Northern Non-Governmental Development Organisations, the European Community and the GATT Uruguay Round' (1996) 17 Third World Q 251

Wilkinson, R, *The WTO: Crisis and the Governance of Global Trade* (1st edn, Routledge, London 2006)

—— and Hughes, S, 'International Labour Standards and World Trade: No Role for the World Trade Organisation?' (1998) 3 New Political Economy 375

Windfuhr, M, 'Compliance of Germany with its International Obligations under the International Covenant for Economic, Social and Cultural Rights (ICESCR)' (Parallel Report 2001) <http://www.fao.org/righttofood/kc/downloads/vl/docs/AH194.pdf>

Winham, GR, *International Trade and the Tokyo Round Negotiations* (Princeton University Press, Princeton, NJ 1986)

—— 'The World Trade Organization: Institution-building in the Multilateral Trade System' (1998) 21 The World Economy 349

—— 'International regime conflict in trade and environment: the Biosafety Protocol and the WTO' (2003) 2 World Trade Rev 131

—— 'An Institutional Theory of WTO Decision-Making: Why Negotiation in the WTO Resembles Law-Making in the US Congress' (2006) Munk Centre for International Studies Occasional Paper No 11

Winickoff, D, Jasanoff, S, Busch, L, Grove-White, R, and Wynne, B, 'Adjudicating the GM Food Wars: Science, Risk, and Democracy in World Trade Law' (2005) 30 Yale J of Intl L 81

Wirth, DA, 'The Role of Science in the Uruguay Round and NAFTA Trade Disciplines' (1994) 27 Cornell Intl LJ 817

Woodiwiss, A, *Human Rights* (Routledge, London 2005)

World Bank, *Governance: The World Bank's Experience* (The International Bank for Reconstruction and Development, Washington, DC 1994)

—— *Development and Human Rights: The Role of the World Bank* (The International Bank for Reconstruction and Development, Washington, DC 1998)

—— International Organisation for Migration (IOM) and OECD, *Trade and Migration: Building Bridges for Global Labour Mobility* (OECD Publishing, Paris 2004)

World Development Movement, 'States of Unrest III: Resistance to IMF and World Bank policies in poor countries' (April 2003) <http://www.wdm.org.uk/sites/default/files/statesofunrest319042003.pdf>

WTO, 'Lamy calls for mindset change to align trade and human rights' (12 January 2010) <http://www.wto.org/english/news_e/sppl_e/sppl146_e.htm>

Xu, Y and Weller, P, *The Governance of World Trade: International Civil Servants and the GATT/WTO* (Edward Elgar Publishing, Cheltenham, UK 2004)

Yoshimatsu, H, 'The Influence of Liberal Ideas on the GATT Regimes: The Case of the Tokyo Round' (1998) ICSEAD Working Paper Series Vol 98-04

Young, MA, 'The WTO's Use of Relevant Rules of International Law: An Analysis of the Biotech Case' (2007) 56 ICLQ 907

Zagel, GM, 'WTO and Human Rights: Examining Linkages and Suggesting Convergences' (International Development Law Organization Voices of Development Jurists Paper Series 2005) <http://www.worldtradelaw.net/articles/zagelhumanrights.pdf>

Zang, D, 'Divided by Common Language: "Capture" Theories in GATT/WTO and the Communicative Impasse' (2009) 32 Hastings Intl and Comparative L Rev 423

Zanini, G, and Islam, R, *World Trade Indicators 2008: Benchmarking Policy and Performance* (The World Bank, Washington, DC 2008)
Zarrilli, S, 'Managing Request-Offer Negotiations under the GATS: The Case of Energy Services' (5 November 2003) TD/TC/WP(2003)24/FINAL
Zeigler, DW, 'International trade agreements challenge tobacco and alcohol control policies' (2006) 25 Drug and Alcohol Rev 567

3D→Three, 'UN Human Rights Treaty Monitoring Bodies Review of State Implementation of International Conventions (ICESCR, ICCPR and CRC): References to Intellectual Property and Human Rights' <http://www.3dthree.org/pdf_3D/TreatyBodyIPrefs_en.pdf>

Index